Provence
& the Côte d'Azur

Avignon
& Around
p193

Haute-Provence &
the Southern Alps
p245

Nice, Monaco
& Menton
p44

Hill Towns of
the Luberon
p230

Cannes &
Around
p79

Arles & the
Camargue
p177

Marseille to
Aix-en-Provence
p141

St-Tropez
to Toulon
p109

CALGARY PUBLIC LIBRARY

JAN   2016

THIS EDITION WRITTEN AND RESEARCHED BY

Alexis Averbuck, Oliver Berry, Nicola Williams

PLAN YOUR TRIP

ON THE ROAD

PROVENÇAL CHEESES P284

LOTTIE DAVIES / LONELY PLANET ©

Contents

Welcome to Provence & the Côte d'Azur

Whether it's cruising the cliff-top roads, sunbathing on the beaches or browsing for goodies at the weekly market, Provence and the Côte d'Azur sum up the essence of France – sexy, sun-drenched and irresistibly seductive.

Lyrical Landscapes

Provence and the Côte d'Azur are made for explorers. One of the joys of travelling here is touring the back roads and soaking up the stunning variety of landscapes: fields of lavender, ancient olive groves, cliff-top roads, maquis-cloaked hills and even snow-tipped mountains. It's home to Europe's deepest canyon, oldest road and highest pass, all a dream come true for drivers – and then there's the Mediterranean itself, a bright mirror of blue reflecting back craggy cliffs, white beaches and endless skies. Take your time – getting there is half of the fun.

Artistic Legacy

It wasn't just the scenery that drew artists like Renoir, Chagall, Cézanne and Picasso here: it was the light, described by Matisse as 'soft and tender, despite its brilliance'. Whether you're gazing over a glittering sea-scape or watching a fiery sunset in the hills, a trip around this corner of France feels like stepping straight into an impressionist canvas. And with such a rich artistic legacy, it's no surprise that the region is home to a wealth of iconic art collections, not to mention studios where van Gogh, Cézanne and Renoir worked.

History Galore

Two thousand years ago, Provence was part of Roman Gaul, and the Romans left behind a fabulous legacy of monuments, structures and buildings – not to mention some of France's first vineyards. The area is littered with Roman remains, including amphitheatres in Nîmes, Arles and Orange, the magnificent Pont du Gard aqueduct and even whole towns near St-Rémy-de-Provence and Vaison-la-Romaine. Factor in a collection of prehistoric sites, medieval abbeys, elegant churches and art deco buildings, and Provence begins to feel like a living history book.

Gourmet Gastronomy

Wherever you end up in Provence, you certainly won't go hungry. Food is a central part of French life, but in Provence it becomes an all-consuming passion. Dominated by the hallowed ingredients of Mediterranean cooking – olive oil, wine, tomatoes and garlic – the region's cuisine is guaranteed to be a highlight, whether that's savouring a simple bowl of *soupe au pistou*, tasting olive oil on a farm, or indulging in a full-blown bowl of bouillabaisse on Marseille's harbourside. *Bon appetit.*

ARTUR DEBAT / GETTY IMAGES ©

Why I Love Provence & the Côte d'Azur

By Oliver Berry, Author

For me, the pleasure of Provence is its diversity. In just a single day you can have a whole holiday's worth of experiences: breakfast on the beach, a morning exploring Nice's old town, lunch at a country *auberge* (inn), an afternoon touring the hills, a vineyard visit, an early-evening shot of pastis, a game of *pétanque* and then an unforgettable sunset over the foothills of the Alps. It was the first place in France I ever visited (at the tender age of two), and I've been coming back ever since. Somehow, I can't stay away for long.

For more about our authors, see page 320

Above: Cafe terrace, Marseille (p144)

Provence & the Côte d'Azur

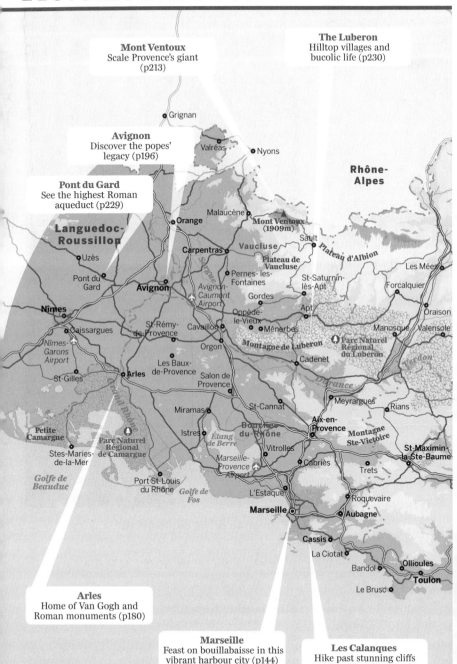

Mont Ventoux
Scale Provence's giant
(p213)

The Luberon
Hilltop villages and
bucolic life (p230)

Grignan

Avignon
Discover the popes'
legacy (p196)

Valréas

Nyons

**Rhône-
Alpes**

Pont du Gard
See the highest Roman
aqueduct (p229)

Malaucène

**Languedoc-
Roussillon**

Orange

Mont Ventoux
(1909m)

Sault

Plateau d'Albion

Uzès

Carpentras

Vaucluse

Plateau de
Vaucluse

Les Mées

Pont du
Gard

Pernes- les-
Fontaines

St-Saturnin-
lès-Apt

Forcalquier

Avignon

Avignon-
Caumont
Airport

Gordes

Apt

Oraison

Nîmes

St-Rémy-
de-Provence

Oppède-
le-Vieux

Cavaillon

Ménerbes

Manosque

Valensole

Caissargues

Orgon

Montagne de Luberon

Parc Naturel
Régional
du Luberon

Verdon

Nîmes-
Garons
Airport

Les Baux-
de-Provence

Cadenet

St-Gilles

Arles

Salon de
Provence

Durance

Miramas

St-Cannat

Meyrargues

Rians

**Petite
Camargue**

Istres

Étang
de Berre

**Bouches-
du-Rhône**

Aix-en-
Provence

Montagne
Ste-Victoire

St-Maximin-
la-Ste-Baume

Stes-Maries-
de-la-Mer

Parc Naturel
Régional
de Camargue

Vitrolles

Cabriès

Trets

**Golfe de
Beauduc**

Port St-Louis
du Rhône

Marseille-
Provence
Airport

**Golfe de
Fos**

L'Estaque

Roquevaire

Marseille

Aubagne

Cassis

La Ciotat

Ollioules

Bandol

Toulon

Le Brusc

Arles
Home of Van Gogh and
Roman monuments (p180)

Marseille
Feast on bouillabaisse in this
vibrant harbour city (p144)

Les Calanques
Hike past stunning cliffs
and secret coves (p165)

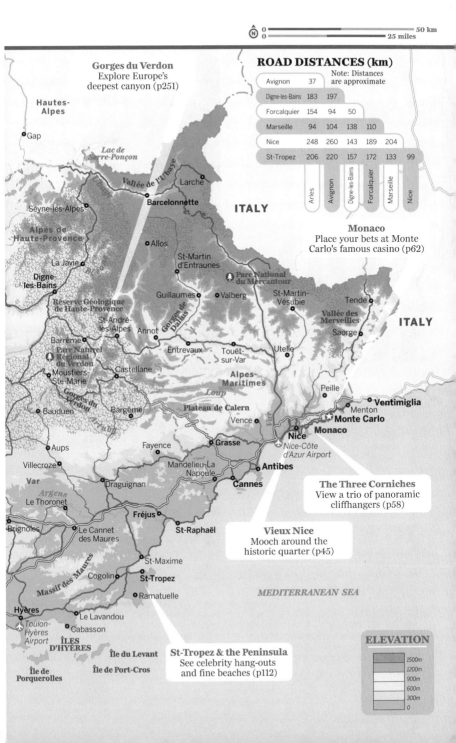

ROAD DISTANCES (km)

Note: Distances are approximate

	Arles	Avignon	Digne-les-Bains	Forcalquier	Marseille	Nice
Avignon	37					
Digne-les-Bains	183	197				
Forcalquier	154	94	50			
Marseille	94	104	138	110		
Nice	248	260	143	189	204	
St-Tropez	206	220	157	172	133	99

Gorges du Verdon
Explore Europe's deepest canyon (p251)

Monaco
Place your bets at Monte Carlo's famous casino (p62)

The Three Corniches
View a trio of panoramic cliffhangers (p58)

Vieux Nice
Mooch around the historic quarter (p45)

St-Tropez & the Peninsula
See celebrity hang-outs and fine beaches (p112)

ELEVATION

	1500m
	1200m
	900m
	600m
	300m
	0

MEDITERRANEAN SEA

Provence & the Côte d'Azur's
Top 16

Provençal Markets

1 Stalls groaning with fruit and veg, trays of cheese and *saucisson* (dry cured sausage) to sample, stallholders loudly plying their wares – markets are an essential element of Provençal life. Practically every village has at least one weekly market, packed with locals shopping and gossiping, and dozens of stalls selling everything from locally farmed produce to spices, soaps and handmade crafts. For all-round atmosphere, Cannes' Marché Forville (p87), Nice's cours Saleya (p45) and the Friday morning market (p215) in Carpentras are hard to beat.

The Luberon

2 With its hilltop villages, fields of lavender, rolling hills and laid-back lifestyle, the Luberon (p230) is the stuff of Provençal dreams. Attractions can be low-key: ambling in pretty villages, shopping at the weekly market, wine tasting and enjoying a long afternoon lunch on a panoramic terrace. They can also be energetic: the area is prime cycling territory, there are dozens of hiking trails and some unique spots to explore, such as the ochre quarries of Roussillon (p235). Right: Stone buildings, Les Grands Cléments, Villars, Luberon

TONY BURNS / GETTY IMAGES ©

BARBARA VAN ZANTEN / GETTY IMAGES ©

Vieux Nice

3 The maze of Nice's old town (p45) is the most joyous part of this exquisite city. In the morning it teems with shoppers checking out the stalls of the market on cours Saleya and the town's numerous delis. In the afternoon tourists take over, lapping up ice creams, strolling along the atmospheric, boutique-lined alleyways and admiring the superb Baroque heritage. After dark, Vieux Nice's bars, pubs and restaurants kick into life, drawing a merry crowd of all ages. Top: Crowds on cours Saleya, Vieux Nice

Pont du Gard

4 One of the most grandiose examples of Roman engineering, the triple-tiered Pont du Gard (p229) stands 50m tall and 275m across. In its day the top-tier watercourse carried an astonishing 20,000 cubic metres of water per day. The bridge's 35 arches majestically straddle the Gard River, and whether you walk across it or paddle underneath in a canoe, it is a magnificent sight. For historical context, there's a museum to visit, and there are plenty of walking trails to explore nearby.

GLENN VAN DER KNIJFF / GETTY IMAGES ©

BRUNO DE HOGUES / GETTY IMAGES ©

Gorges du Verdon

5 This massive canyon (p251), 25km long and with cliffs that tower up to 900m high, is without doubt one of Provence's natural wonders. Gouged out over millennia by the Verdon River, it's a majestic sight, and there are so many ways to enjoy it: you can hike it, you can bike it, you can cruise along the cliffs, or you can thunder down the river on a raft or kayak. It's worth seeing both from above and below to get a proper perspective on the sheer scale of the thing.

The Three Corniches

6 This stunning trio of coastal roads (p58) offers the most outstanding overview (literally!) of the Riviera. The Corniche Inférieure skirts the glittering shores, with numerous swimming opportunities. Up in the hills, the jewel in the crown of the Moyenne Corniche is the medieval village of Èze, spectacularly perched on a rocky promontory offering awe-inspiring views of the coastline. And then there is the Grande Corniche, snaking along the 500m-high cliffs, with spectacular vistas at every bend. Top right: View from Roquebrune-Cap-Martin (p73)

Marseille

7 Fresh from its stint as the European Capital of Culture in 2013, rough-and-ready Marseille (p144) is a city on the up. As one of France's most ethnically diverse cities, it's a place that crackles with life and atmosphere, and a fresh crop of flagship museums (including the fantastic MuCEM) has only added to the city's appeal. The heart of town is the beautiful Vieux Port, the old harbour, which is lined with seafood restaurants – if you want to try authentic bouillabaisse, this is the place to do it. Bottom right: Terrace, Musée des Civilisations de l'Europe et de la Méditerranée (MuCEM; p145)

Les Alpilles

8 Stretching between the Durance and Rhône rivers, this rumpled chain of hills (p222) is a favourite retreat for the rich, famous and beautiful, with celebrity-spotting potential aplenty. But it's also worth visiting for its gastronomy – the area is renowned for its top-quality olive oil, which is protected by its own Appellation d'Origine Contrôlée (AOC; a type of trademark). Local villages are also awash with stellar restaurants, especially around Les Baux-de-Provence and St-Rémy-de-Provence. Top: Les Baux-de-Provence (p225)

Les Calanques

9 The coastline around Marseille is marked by high, rocky promontories known locally as *calanques*, rising like towers from the electric-blue waters of the Mediterranean. Since 2013, this 20km stretch has been designated France's newest national park (p165), and its clifftop trails, secret coves and powder-white beaches simply cry out for exploration. Many inlets can only be reached by boat or kayak – and outside the height of summer, you might well have them all to yourself. Bottom: Calanque de Port-Miou (p166)

GERARD OSELL / GETTY IMAGES ©

A DEMOTES / GETTY IMAGES ©

Mont Ventoux

10 The defining feature of northern Provence, Mont Ventoux (p213) stands like a sentinel over the region's undulating landscape. Its reputation is mythical among cyclists, but everyone feels the pull of the *géant de Provence* (Provence's giant), be it for hiking, wildlife-watching (the mountain's biodiversity is second to none), scenic drives or panoramas. On clear days, you can see from Camargue to the Alps, and in winter, its snow-capped summit is an unforgettable sight. Top left: Skifields, Mont Ventoux

St-Tropez & the Peninsula

11 The hang-out of choice for superstars and party animals in summer – and a strangely quiet, pretty seaside town the rest of the year – St-Tropez (p112) and the surrounding peninsula have something of a split personality. Throngs of summer holidaymakers relish the brilliant clubs, fine beaches (by far the best on the coast) and great eating. Come in June or September for atmosphere minus the crowds. In winter most of St-Tropez shuts up shop, and you'll more than likely have the beaches to yourself. Top right: Harbour in St-Tropez

The Camargue

12 Pan-flat and pocked with lagoons and salt marshes, the Camargue (p186) is like a little world of its own. This massive wetland is a wonderful place to escape the hustle and bustle of the coast, whether that means horse-riding along the trails, canoeing the reed-lined channels or spotting the Camargue's famous flamingos. It's a region steeped in tradition and culture, upheld by the *gardians* (cowboys), who herd the Camargue's wild horses and hold their own festival in Arles every May. Bottom right: Greater flamingo

Palais des Papes

13 The seat of papal power for much of the 14th century, Avignon's papal palace (p196) is by far the city's best-known landmark. But there are lots more historical buildings to discover – some of them now splendid hotels. The popes didn't just build a great city, however – they also planted some fine vineyards. Châteauneuf-du-Pape is without a doubt one of the world's great reds, and going on a wine-tasting tour is part and parcel of discovering the popes' legacy.

Arles

14 Famed for its outstanding Roman architecture and for being the home of ill-fated impressionist Vincent Van Gogh, Arles (p180) is a delight: it's small, you can walk everywhere and there is something to see at every corner. There may not be any Van Gogh paintings to admire, but there are informative walking tours and art galleries in honour of the master. And then there is the food: Arles has some of the finest restaurants in the region, so don't leave without indulging in an evening of gastronomic dining. Bottom right: Cloître St-Trophime, Arles (p180)

DE AGOSTINI / C SAPPA / GETTY IMAGES ©

OSTILL / GETTY IMAGES ©

Aix-en-Provence

15 Southern sophistication is everywhere on the streets of Aix-en-Provence (p168), a graceful city with a rich artistic legacy; many impressionist and post-impressionist artists found inspiration here, most notably Paul Cézanne, whose old studio has been preserved largely unchanged since the artist's death. Elsewhere, the excellent Musée Granet (p169) houses one of the region's top art collections, with works by all the key names: Picasso, Matisse, Renoir, Gauguin and, of course, Cézanne himself. Top right: Atelier Cézanne (p169), Aix-en-Provence

Monaco

16 With its skyscrapers, casinos, boutiques and yacht-packed harbour, high-rise Monaco (p62) has been for decades the favourite playground of Europe's elite. It's not exactly beautiful – although Monte Carlo has some fine belle époque buildings, chief among them the famous casino – but it has a certain undeniable cachet. Top things to do include visiting the Musée Oceanographique and watching the daily change of the guard at 11.55am.

Need to Know

For more information, see Survival Guide (p289)

Currency
Euro (€)

Language
French

Visas
Generally not required for stays of up to 90 days (or at all for EU nationals); some nationalities will require a Schengen visa.

Money
ATMs widely available. Most hotels and restaurants take credit cards; only larger establishments accept Amex.

Mobile Phones
Local SIM cards can be used in (unlocked) European and Australian phones. Other phones must be set to roaming.

Time
Central European Time Zone (GMT/UTC +1)

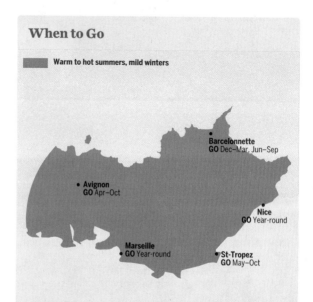

When to Go

Warm to hot summers, mild winters

Barcelonnette
GO Dec–Mar, Jun–Sep

Avignon
GO Apr–Oct

Nice
GO Year-round

Marseille
GO Year-round

St-Tropez
GO May–Oct

High Season
(Jul & Aug, Dec–Mar alpine resorts)

➡ Hotels are full, often booked months in advance and at their priciest.

➡ It is hot: 35°C is fairly common at lunch time.

➡ Alpine resorts fill up with skiers and snowboarders during the December to March ski season.

Shoulder Season
(Apr–Jun, Sep & Oct)

➡ The best time of year to travel, with good weather and no school-holiday crowds.

➡ Spring blooms and autumn colours.

➡ Prices drop in many areas compared to the peak months of July and August.

Low Season
(Nov–Mar)

➡ Very quiet, especially in rural areas and coastal resorts, where many hotels close.

➡ Attractions open shorter hours.

➡ Prices are at their lowest: 20% to 30% off summer rates.

Useful Websites

Provence–Alpes–Côte d'Azur Tourisme (www.decouverte-paca.fr) The first port of call, with a wealth of info on what to do, where to go, where to stay and much more.

Côte d'Azur Tourisme (www.cotedazur-tourisme.com) General information on the Riviera.

Visit Provence (www.visit-provence.com) Covers Marseille, Arles and the Camargue.

Tourisme Alpes Haute-Provence (www.tourism-alps-provence.com) Guide to the mountains.

Lonely Planet (www.lonelyplanet.com/france) Sights, activities, accommodation and much more.

Important Numbers

France's country code	⏶33
International dialling code	⏶00
Europe-wide emergency	⏶112
Ambulance (SAMU)	⏶15
Police	⏶17

Exchange Rates

Australia	A$1	€0.70
Canada	C$1	€0.74
Japan	¥100	€1.03
New Zealand	NZ$1	€0.66
UK	£1	€1.38
US	US$1	€0.89

For current exchange rates, see www.xe.com.

Daily Costs

Budget:
Less than €120

➡ Dorm bed: €20–€30

➡ Double room in a budget hotel: €60–€90

➡ Bistro lunch: €10–€15

➡ Bus and train tickets: €5–€10

Midrange:
€120–€220

➡ Double room in a hotel: €90–€190

➡ Set menus in restaurants: €20–€40

➡ Car hire: €25 per day

Top End:
More than €220

➡ Double room in luxury hotel: more than €190

➡ À la carte meal: €50–€100

➡ Luxury car hire: €40–50 per day

Opening Hours

Opening hours vary throughout the year. We've provided high-season opening hours; hours are shorter in low season. Most businesses close for lunch from noon to 2pm.

Banks 9am–noon and 2–5pm Monday to Friday or Tuesday to Saturday

Cafes 8am–11pm Monday to Saturday

Post offices 8.30am–5pm Monday to Friday, 8am–noon Saturday

Restaurants Lunch noon–2.30pm, dinner 7–11pm

Shops 9am–6.30pm Monday or Tuesday to Saturday

Supermarkets 8.30am–7pm Monday to Saturday, 8.30am–12.30pm Sunday

Arriving in Provence

Aéroport Nice Côte d'Azur (p297) Buses to Nice city centre every 20 minutes, to Cannes, Antibes, Monaco and Menton every 30 minutes. Budget on €25 to €30 for a taxi to Nice.

Aéroport Marseille Provence (p297) Buses to Marseille and Aix-en-Provence every 20 minutes. Direct trains to destinations including Marseille, Arles and Avignon. Allow €50 for a taxi to Marseille.

Getting Around

Public transport in France is generally good value and reasonably reliable.

Car Allows maximum freedom, especially in rural areas. Cars can be hired in most towns and cities. Driving is on the right, but automatic transmissions are rare. *Autoroutes* (motorways) are fast, but many charge tolls. Beware the *priorité à droite* rule, which means you have to give way to vehicles entering on the right.

Train France's state-owned trains are fast, efficient and great value. High-speed TGVs connect major cities; smaller towns are served by slower TER trains, sometimes supplemented by buses. Remember to time stamp your ticket before boarding.

Bus Useful for remote villages that aren't serviced by trains, but timetables revolve around school-term times; fewer services run on weekends and school holidays.

For much more on **getting around**, see p299.

PLAN YOUR TRIP NEED TO KNOW

First Time Provence & the Côte d'Azur

For more information, see Survival Guide (p289)

Checklist

➡ Check passport validity and visa requirements

➡ Book hotels, car-hire and big-name restaurants

➡ Organise travel insurance

➡ Check airline baggage restrictions and customs regulations

➡ Get a Chip and PIN credit card (magnetic strips don't work)

➡ Inform your credit-card company you're travelling abroad

What to Pack

➡ Passport and driving license

➡ Adaptor plug – France uses two-pin EU plugs

➡ Sunglasses, hat and sunscreen

➡ Towel, swimsuit and sandals for the beach

➡ Sturdy shoes for hiking and walking

➡ Corkscrew with bottle opener

➡ Smart clothes for eating out

➡ French phrasebook

➡ An adventurous appetite

Top Tips for Your Trip

➡ If you're driving, the *autoroutes* (motorways) are fast, but smaller scenic regional roads (designated D and N on highway maps) always have much better scenery.

➡ For Provençal atmosphere, you can't beat shopping at a morning market. Nearly every town and village has one at least once a week. Take your own shopping bag.

➡ Most shops, businesses and museums close for lunch (usually between noon and 2pm). Do as the locals do and head for the nearest restaurant.

➡ Don't underestimate the heat. Temperatures of 35°C are routine in summer. Schedule sightseeing for early morning or late afternoon, and spend the middle of the day somewhere shady.

What to Wear

➡ Outside Monaco, Cannes and St Tropez, fashion is pretty relaxed. Dress up rather than down for dinner (avoid jeans, shorts or trainers in upmarket establishments).

➡ Sturdy shoes are essential for walking, and a pack-down raincoat comes in handy.

➡ Topless sunbathing is routine on Côte d'Azur beaches, but it's a no-no anywhere else. Save bare chests and bikinis for the beach.

Sleeping

Advance reservations are essential in July and August. Booking online is easiest.

➡ **Chambres d'hôte** B&Bs, usually family-run and with an owner on site. They range from small farmhouses to lavish boutique hideaways; breakfast is nearly always included.

➡ **Hotels** Anything from swanky Riviera hotels to country *auberges* (inns). Unless otherwise indicated, assume breakfast is extra.

➡ **Camping** French camping grounds tend to be more like holiday parks, usually with pools, playgrounds, activities and so on. Back-to-basics camping is more common in the countryside. Wild camping (including on the beach) is illegal.

Cutting Costs

➡ **Eat cheap** Lunchtime *formules* (two courses) and *menus* (three courses) are cheaper than dinner menus. Self-catering and shopping at the market keep costs down. At restaurants, order *une carafe d'eau* (a jug of water) rather than bottled water.

➡ **Family travel** Many hotels have triple, quad and family rooms. Buy family tickets and travel passes (usually for two adults and two kids).

➡ **Free sites** Though most sights charge admission for visitors over 12, public parks, green spaces, coastline and national parks are free.

➡ **Avoid private beaches** Some beaches on the Côte d'Azur are reserved for paying guests, but there's nearly always another one nearby that's free (if crowded).

Bargaining

➡ With the exception of haggling at flea markets, bargaining is not the norm in France.

Tipping

➡ **Restaurants** If your bill says *service compris*, a 15% tip has already been added; you only need to tip more for exceptional service.

➡ **Taxis** Most people round up to the nearest euro.

➡ **Bars** For drinks at the bar, don't tip. For drinks brought to your table, tip as for a restaurant.

➡ **Hotels** A tip of €1 or €2 for the bellhop or valet is all that's required.

Language

It's a good idea to learn some useful phrases before you go; the French will appreciate the effort. Most people can speak at least a few words of English, but fluency is rare in rural areas.

 What are the opening hours?
Quelles sont les heures d'ouverture?
kel son lay zer doo-vair-tewr

French business hours are governed by a maze of regulations, so it's a good idea to check before you make plans.

 I'd like the set menu, please.
Je voudrais le menu, s'il vous plait.
zher voo-dray ler mer-new seel voo play

The best-value dining in France is the two- or three-course meal at a fixed price. Most restaurants have one on the chalkboard.

 Which wine would you recommend?
Quel vin vous conseillez?
kel vun voo kon-say-yay

Who better to ask for advice on wine than the French?

 Can I address you with 'tu'?
Est-ce que je peux vous tutoyer?
es ker zher per voo tew-twa-yay

Before you start addressing someone with the informal 'you' form, it's polite to ask permission first.

 Do you have plans for tonight/tomorrow?
Vous avez prévu quelque chose ce soir/demain?
voo za-vay pray-vew kel-ker shoz ser swar/der-mun

To arrange to meet up without sounding pushy, ask friends if they're available rather than inviting them directly.

Etiquette

➡ **Greetings** When entering or leaving a shop, it's polite to say *bonjour* and *au revoir*. When greeting friends, it's usual to give a kiss on both cheeks and ask *Comment ça va?* (How are you?)

➡ **Conversation** Use *vous* (you) when speaking to people you don't know well, or who are older than you; use *tu* (also you) with friends, family and children.

➡ **Asking for help** Say *excusez-moi* (excuse me) to attract attention; say *pardon* (sorry) to apologise.

➡ **Religious buildings** Dress modestly and be respectful when visiting.

➡ **Eating and drinking** When dining in a French home, wait for your host to start first. Always clear the plate. When you're finished, line up your fork and knife on top of your plate towards the right.

➡ **Waiters** Never, ever call waiters *garçon* – use *Monsieur* (Mr), *Mademoiselle* (Miss) or *Madame* (Mrs), or attract their attention by saying *s'il vous plaît* (please).

What's New

Direct Eurostars to the South of France

The extension of the TGV line to Marseille means there is now a direct, high-speed service all the way from London to Provence – door-to-door from Marseille St-Charles to London St Pancras now takes just 6½ hours (or you can stop off in Paris, Avignon and Aix-en-Provence along the way, should you wish). Formidable!

Promenade des Anglais World Heritage Bid

At the time of writing, the Côte d'Azur's most prestigious strip of sand was bidding for World Heritage Status, placing it on the same list of importance as other local sites such as Palais des Papes, Pont du Gard and the Roman monuments in Arles and Orange. (p45)

Plages Sans Tabac (Smoke-Free Beaches)

At long last, the powers that be in Nice and Cannes have declared several city beaches smoke-free zones – meaning the days of finding cigarette butts underfoot are happily a thing of the past.

Marseille's Museums

After several years of expensive renovations, the Musée Cantini and Musée des Beaux Arts (p150) have reopened to great fanfare, while the city's much-lauded Musée des Civilisations de l'Europe et la Méditerranée (p145) continues to draw new visitors to the city's revitalised harbourside.

Marché de la Condamine, Monaco

Monaco's fabulous new food court on place d'Armes is symptomatic of a growing trend for farm-to-table dining across the south of France. Local producers, seasonality, sustainability and low food miles are what matter most these days. (p69)

The Villa-Musée Jean-Honoré Fragonard

The risqué paintings of the Grasse-born artist Jean-Honoré Fragonard scandalised 18th-century France. The artist lived in this stately house in Grasse for a year in 1790, which is now a museum devoted to his work. It reopened in 2015 after extensive renovations. (p100)

Véloroute du Calavon

This disused railway line in the Luberon has been reinvented as a super bike path, running for a scenic 28km between Beaumettes and La Paraire. There are plans to extend the route further west and east in the coming years. (p231)

A New Home for Monaco's Luxury Shops

While millions are spent on a facelift for the prestigious Hôtel de Paris, the luxury boutiques of the Sporting d'Hiver have a new home on the lawns of the Jardins des Boulingrins, in the shape of giant ice-white 'pebbles'. The construction work is scheduled for completion in 2018.

For more recommendations and reviews, see lonelyplanet.com/provence

If You Like...

Food & Wine

Eating well, and eating often, is a cornerstone of Provençal life. From sumptuous seafood to village markets, this is a place where food matters.

Seafood Feast on bouillabaisse and *fruits de mer* at Marseille's harbourfront restaurants. (p157)

Niçois cuisine Nice's old town is awash with places to try local delicacies like *pissaladière* (Niçoise pizza), *socca* (chickpea pancakes) and classic *salade niçoise*. (p53)

Markets No matter what day it is or what village you're in, there's likely to be a market nearby, such as the famous one on Friday in Carpentras. (p215)

Pastis Provence's aniseed-flavoured aperitif comes in 90 varieties at La Maison du Pastis in Marseille. (p163)

Wine Vineyards carpet the landscape of Provence, with tasting opportunities galore – including illustrious names like Châteauneuf-du-Pape. (p205)

Muscat Unearth your favourite vintage in the cellars around Beaumes-de-Venise. (p213)

History

Provence and the Côte d'Azur are like an open book, with history unfolding in every town and village.

Ancient history Bronze Age artists left their mark carved into the walls of the Vallée des Merveilles. (p263)

Roman history Once an important province of Roman Gaul, Provence is now littered with such Roman remains as the three-tiered Pont du Gard. (p229)

Medieval abbeys Find inner peace at Provençal abbeys like the Abbaye Notre-Dame de Sénanque. (p231)

Papal Provence For a time Avignon, not Rome, was the centre of Christendom – a legacy that lives on at the Palais des Papes. (p196)

Belle époque The Riviera's golden age is commemorated at Nice's Musée Masséna. (p48)

Beaches

It's not called the coast of azure for nothing: the Mediterranean sparkles with spectacular coves and beaches.

Calanque d'En-Vau The Calanques' most photogenic cove won't disappoint: yes, the water really is that colour. (p166)

Plage de Pampelonne St-Tropez's most famous beach, unfolding over 9km. (p119)

Promenade des Anglais All right, so the beach is all pebbles, no sand – but Nice's world-famous seafront is still the place to be seen. (p45)

Plage du Layet Bare all at Cavalière's nudist beach. (p129)

Plage de Notre Dame The beach where it's easiest to escape the outside world, on the idyllic Île de Porquerolles. (p134)

Z Plage Cannes' star-studded beach is just steps from the Croisette; designer swimwear, sunglasses and cocktails are de rigueur. (p82)

Plage de la Garoupe Follow the coastal path to this super-sandy cove on Cap d'Antibes. (p91)

Getting Active

Hike, cycle, swim or sail: the region abounds with opportunities to get out and active.

Hiking Opportunities abound in Haute-Provence, especially around the Vallée de la Vésubie. (p262)

White-water rafting Brave the rapids in the majestic Gorges du Verdon. (p252)

Cycling Pedal along quiet country roads in the lovely Luberon. (p231)

Canoeing Paddle your way along the maze of channels in the Camargue. (p188)

Bungee jumping Conquer your fears with a leap from Europe's highest bungee site, the Pont de l'Artuby. (p252)

Paragliding Sail through the skies on a glorified parachute. (p252)

Mountain biking Tackle the trails around Provence's highest mountain, Mont Ventoux. (p214)

Wild Scenery

From snowy mountains to pristine wetlands, the region's national parks are awash with photogenic landscapes.

Alpha Spot wild wolves in this fascinating wildlife park, cradled amongst the mountains of the Mercantour. (p262)

Gorges du Verdon France's answer to the Grand Canyon, where vultures wheel overhead and vertigo sufferers must beware. (p251)

Colorado Provençal An other-worldly ochre landscape of rust-red valleys, pillars and hills. (p235)

Parc Naturel Régional de Camargue Spot flamingos in this fabulous coastal wetland. (p186)

Les Calanques Secluded coves and turquoise waters stud the coastline in France's newest national park. (p165)

Dramatic Drives

Driving in Provence is a nonstop thrill: spin along the cliffs, cruise the beaches or traverse high mountain roads.

Grande Corniche Follow in the footsteps of Cary Grant and Grace Kelly on this famous cliff-top coastal road. (p61)

Top: Sentier des Ocres (p235), Roussillon
Bottom: Èze (p61), Moyenne Corniche

Gorges de Daluis Take your time as you crawl along the edge of the gorges: the drops are heart-stopping. (p260)

Route des Crêtes Sweeping panoramas of the Calanques' mineral beauty unfold between Cassis and La Ciotat. (p167)

Col de Restefond de la Bonette Crawl up and over the highest road pass in Europe at 2715m. (p261)

Routes de la Lavande Cruise amongst fields of fragrant purple lavender around the Plateau de Valensole. (p250)

Festivals

No matter what the time of year, the people of Provence and the Côte d'Azur need no excuse to get out and party.

Fête du Citron Menton's madcap lemon-themed festival sees floats and parades take over the town's streets. (p76)

Carnaval de Nice Lots of towns hold carnivals, but nowhere does it with quite as much style as Nice. (p49)

Corso de la Lavande Digne-les-Bains celebrates its lavender harvest every August. (p256)

Fête des Gardians Camargue cowboys process through Arles' streets on horseback. (p183)

Chorégies d'Orange Watch opera in the stunning setting of Orange's Roman theatre. (p207)

Férias de Nîmes Nîmes' bullfighting festivals are held in June and September. (p227)

Hilltop Villages

Provence's *villages perchées* (perched villages) are a testament to the skill of medieval builders – and a sight to behold.

Èze Spellbinding views of the Med and windy pebbled lanes attract throngs of visitors and yet Èze remains magical. (p61)

Roussillon This Luberon village is famed for its distinctive red-ochre colour. (p235)

Gourdon An austere eagle's nest towering above the Gorges du Loup; the village looks magical under the snow in winter. (p98)

Ste-Agnès Europe's highest cliffhanger (780m) looms large over Menton and Italy. (p77)

Bonnieux This lovely village is one of many charming villages to be found around the Luberon. (p240)

Les Baux-de-Provence Sitting atop a limestone spur are the dramatic ruins of the old Château des Baux. (p225)

Twentieth-Century Art

Many of the 20th century's great artists came here for inspiration, and with so much bewitching scenery on show, it's not hard to see why.

Fondation Maeght One of the world's finest collections of 20th-century art in St-Paul de Vence. (p95)

Atelier Cézanne Visit the master's studio and home in Aix-en-Provence. (p169)

Musée de l'Annonciade Punching well above its weight, St-Tropez's museum has masterpieces by Signac, Braque and Picasso. (p112)

Musée d'Art Moderne et d'Art Contemporain Nice's modern-art museum pays tribute to home-grown New Realists such as Yves Klein, Niki de Saint Phalle and Arman. (p48)

Musée Granet Another must-see in Aix-en-Provence, with works that read like a who's who of modern art: Matisse, Picasso, Cézanne, Van Gogh and others. (p169)

Musée Jean Cocteau Collection Séverin Wunderman Discover the genius of Jean Cocteau, from illustrations to cinematography, at this Menton museum. (p74)

LOTTIE DAVIES / LONELY PLANET ©

Kayakers, Gorges du Verdon (p251)

Month by Month

January

Even in the depths of winter, Provence and the Côte d'Azur has its charms. The Provençal Alps are carpeted in snow, while crisp winter days flatter the Riviera. Outside of ski resorts and large cities, however, many hotels and attractions close, making travel harder.

☆ Festival International du Cirque de Monte-Carlo

The world's best circus artists compete every year for the 'Golden Clown' Award in Monte Carlo. Winners then put on a week of performances (www.monte-carlofestival.mc).

🏃 On Your Skis!

Provence and the Côte d'Azur's ski resorts are excellent: small, family friendly, dotted with trees, sunny and easily accessible by public transport (just €2 return from Nice).

🍴 Truffle Hunting

Provence's black diamond is picked from November to February (restaurants make the most of it, and so should you!), but the season culminates in January with the Messe de la Truffe in Richerenches (p210) and the Journée de la Truffe in Aups (p126).

February

February can be divine on the Riviera: the days are bright, the sky is blue and it's often mild. French school kids get two weeks off to tear down the pistes.

🎊 Carnaval de Nice

Both the decorated floats and the crowds are gigantic at this flamboyant Mardi Gras street parade (www.nicecarnaval.com) in Nice, celebrated since 1293. Don't miss the legendary flower battles.

April

April weather is much the same in Provence as it is elsewhere in Europe: full of surprises. Easter holidays can be spent on the beach as much as on the slopes. Many towns and villages hold ancestral religious celebrations strong on folklore and colour.

🎊 Féria Pascale

Held each Easter in Arles to open the bullfighting season (www.feriaarles.com), the *féria* is four days of exuberant dancing, music, concerts and bullfighting.

May

Spring may be well under way, but the sea remains cold at this time of year, and the mistral (northern wind) can be howling in Provence. May is also bank-holiday-tastic in France, with no fewer than four of them, so plan ahead for reservations.

🎊 Pèlerinage des Gitans

Roma from Europe pour into remote seaside outpost Stes-Maries-de-la-Mer to honour their patron saint on 24 and 25 May (and again in October): processions, street singing and dancing are all part of the celebrations.

☆ Monaco Grand Prix

Formula One's most anticipated race, the Monaco Grand Prix (www.acm.mc) tears around the tiny municipality in a haze of glamour, champagne, VIPs and after parties.

◎ Gardens in Bloom

Provence's gardens look lush at this time of year. Visit a flower farm (p101) or stroll in the sumptuous gardens of Villa Ephrussi de Rothschild (p60).

July

July is Provence at its most picturesque: cicadas fill the air with incessant song, lavender fields stretch in all their purple glory, it's hot, and to cool off you have a choice between pool, sea and rosé.

☆ Festival d'Avignon & Festival Off

Theatre in every guise takes to the stage at this renowned festival (www.festival-avignon.com) in Avignon; fringe Off parallels the official fest.

☆ Les Chorégies d'Orange

France's oldest festival (www.choregies.asso.fr) stages operas at the incredible Roman theatre in Orange, an unforgettable night if you can get tickets.

☆ Jazz on the Riviera

The Riviera swings to the music of two great jazz festivals: Jazz à Juan in Antibes-Juan-les-Pins (www.jazzajuan.com) and the Nice Jazz Festival (www.nicejazzfestival.fr). Book tickets well in advance.

☆ Festival d'Aix-en-Provence

A month of world-class opera, classical music and ballet is what this prestigious festival (www.festival-aix.com) offers.

August

Depending on how you look at it, this is either the worst or the best time to come to Provence. It is definitely the busiest, with every hotel fully booked, but it's also the liveliest, with events galore, night markets and an infectious party atmosphere.

☆ Fireworks by the Sea

Cannes and Monaco both hold free international fireworks festivals in July and August when pyrotechnicians from around the world compete for the 'ooohs' and 'aaahs' of the crowd.

☆ Dance the Night Away in Cannes

Cannes is *the* party spot in August. Le Palais nightclub opens for 50 nights of dancing under the stars, and two great dance-music festivals set up shop: Festival Pantiero (www.festivalpantiero.com) and Les Plages Électroniques (www.plages-electroniques.com).

October

The days may be shortening, but in the glow of the autumn sun they're a delight. You can still swim on warm days, and what's more, you're likely to have the beach to yourself.

✕ Chestnut à Gogo

Head to Collobrières in the Massif des Maures to pick, feast on and learn about chestnuts. The forest is at its loveliest for long walks too. Harvest celebrations culminate in the Fête de la Châtaigne. (p128)

☆ Transhumance

Sheep and their shepherds descend from their summer pastures and crowd the roads of Haute-Provence, from the Verdon to Col d'Allos. The same happens in reverse in June.

December

Families celebrate Christmas with midnight Mass, Provençal chants, 13 desserts (yes) and nativity scenes full of *santons* (terracotta figurines). Outside of Christmas and New Year's Eve parties, however, it is a quiet month.

Itineraries

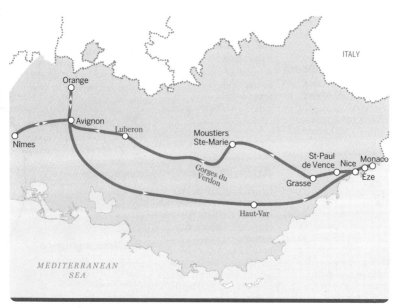

Essential Provence-Côte d'Azur

All the classics in one easy itinerary: along the coast, into the hills and back again, via gorges, villages, vineyards, Roman ruins and lavender fields.

Fly to **Nice**. On day two, mooch around Vieux Nice and amble along the Promenade des Anglais. On day three, catch a bus to stunning **Èze** to feast on views; head to **Monaco** for lunch and enjoy the rest of the day in the principality. Catch a train back to Nice. On day four, pick up a rental car and drive to the medieval wonder of **St-Paul de Vence** and its art galleries. On day five, drive to **Moustiers Ste-Marie** along the scenic N85, stopping in **Grasse** on the way for an insight into the town's perfume industry. Spend the following day in **Gorges du Verdon**.

Explore the villages of the **Luberon** on days seven and eight, and on day nine head to **Avignon**. Enjoy the city for a day, and take a day trip to **Orange** or **Nîmes** on day 11. On days 12 and 13, head to the **Haut-Var** for hilltop villages and vineyards, before returning to Nice.

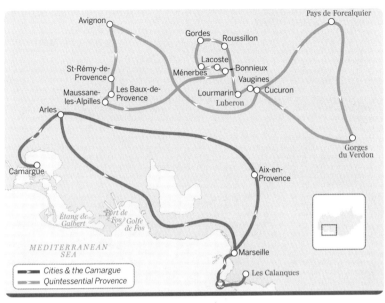

Cities & the Camargue

Quintessential Provence

Cities & the Camargue

1 WEEK

A mix of city and countryside, starting in the bustling port city of Marseille and followed by some clifftop hiking, art appreciation, Roman history and flamingo spotting. This entire itinerary can be done by public transport.

Spend your first day exploring **Marseille**: the Vieux Port, the historic Le Panier quarter and the art scene. On day two, take a boat trip to **Les Calanques** or visit Château d'If before heading up to Basilique Notre Dame de la Garde for panoramic views of the city and the sea. Go for dinner in the picturesque Vallon des Auffes. On day three, head to **Aix-en-Provence** to visit Cézanne's studio, his family house and the Bibemus quarries where he painted. Treat yourself to dinner at one of Aix' fine restaurants.

On day four, head to **Arles** and discover the places that inspired Van Gogh. Book a table for dinner at one of the city's Michelin-starred establishments. On day five, immerse yourself in the town's fine Roman heritage to learn about life in Roman times. Take a day trip to **Camargue** on day six: hire bikes if you're game, and don't forget your binoculars for birdwatching. Head back to Marseille.

Quintessential Provence

1 WEEK

This trip captures the essence of Provence, starting in bustling Avignon and ending in the mighty Gorges du Verdon, with stops at some of the area's dreamiest villages and most photogenic sights en route.

Spend day one in **Avignon**, exploring the old town and the Palais des Papes. On day two, drive down to **St-Rémy-de-Provence** in Les Alpilles. Explore Glanum and visit the asylum where Van Gogh spent the last – but most productive – year of his short life. On day three, take a day trip to **Les Baux-de-Provence**: visit the ruined castle and go olive-oil tasting around **Maussane-les-Alpilles** in the afternoon.

On day four, drive to the **Luberon** and spend the afternoon exploring a trio of lovely villages: **Bonnieux**, **Lacoste** and **Ménerbes**. On day five, visit **Gordes** and its Abbaye Notre-Dame de Sénanque and the ochre-coloured village of **Roussillon**. On day six, pack a picnic and set off to explore the gorges, forests and lavender fields around **Lourmarin**, **Vaugines** and **Cucuron**. Treat yourself to dinner at the gastronomic Auberge La Fenière. On day seven, drive back to Avignon or carry on to **Pays de Forcalquier** and the **Gorges du Verdon** for another three days.

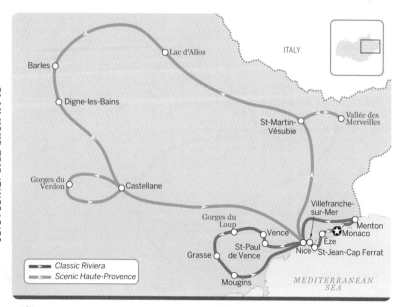

Classic Riviera
Scenic Haute-Provence

 ## Scenic Haute-Provence

 ## Classic Riviera

It's time to tear yourself away from the coast and explore the mighty, majestic Alps. Amazingly, just an hour's drive north of Nice, you'll find yourself surrounded by mountain scenery – perfect for hiking, biking and wildlife-spotting.

Start in **Nice** – enjoy a day of urban delight in Vieux Nice before hitting the road on day two. Drive to **St-Martin-Vésubie** and watch semiwild wolves in the Alpha wildlife reserve. On day three, organise a guided hike to see the amazing ancient rock art of the **Vallée des Merveilles**, then head west to explore the many hiking trails around **Lac d'Allos** on days four and five.

On day six, drive to **Digne-les-Bains**, stopping in **Barles** along the way for fossil hunting in the Réserve Géologique de Haute-Provence. Organise a lavender walk on day seven, and on day eight drive down to **Castellane**, and take a scenic tour of the **Gorges du Verdon**. Explore the canyon in a different way on day nine: go rafting, canyoning or just trekking. On day 10, drive back to Nice or carry on along the Riviera.

This tour captures all the Côte d'Azur's unmissable sights. You can do the first part by bus and train, but for the full Riviera experience a car is preferable – and a convertible would be better still.

Dedicate your first couple of days to the belle of the Côte d'Azur: **Nice**. Stroll in Vieux Nice and browse the market stalls of cours Saleya; visit Cimiez' wonderful Musée National Marc Chagall and Musée Matisse; and party till dawn in Vieux Nice's numerous bars.

On day three, take a day trip along the Corniche Inférieure, stopping at **Villefranche-sur-Mer** and **St-Jean-Cap Ferrat**. On day four, head to hilltop **Èze** for sensational views of the Med; carry on to **Monaco** for the rest of the day. Spend the following day in **Menton**.

On day six, rent a car and head for the hills: stop in **St-Paul de Vence** and **Vence**, and spend day seven motoring around the beautiful **Gorges du Loup**. On day eight, visit **Grasse**, its museums and perfumeries; leave your last day for the pretty village of **Mougins**. Drive back to Nice on day 10, continue in Haute-Provence or head west along the coast.

Plan Your Trip

Staying in Provence

Provence and the Côte d'Azur has a huge and varied range of accommodation, whether you're looking to rent your own cosy rural cottage or blow the budget on a swish Riviera pamper pad. Prices everywhere go through the roof in summer, so consider taking advantage of low-season deals.

Where to Stay

Out of anywhere in France, Provence and the Côte d'Azur has perhaps the most diverse assortment of accommodation, spanning the spectrum from super-luxury hotels with dreamy views of the coast to cosy little cottages nestled amongst vineyards and lavender fields. There's somewhere to suit all tastes and budgets – unfortunately, the region's charms are no secret, and in summer, prices skyrocket and rooms are scarce.

Hotels

Hotels in France are rated from one to five stars: one and two stars are basic, while four and five stars offer luxury services such as pools, room service and a concierges. Elevators (*ascenseurs*) are generally only found in bigger hotels. Triples and quads are widely available, and good for family travellers. Breakfast is nearly always extra, costing anything from €7 to €30 per person. Wi-fi (pronounced wee-fee) is available nearly everywhere, and generally provided for free.

Note that, in France, 'ground floor' (*rez de chaussée*) refers to the floor at street level; the 'first floor' is the floor above that.

Logis de France (www.logishotels.com) An umbrella organisation for small, independent hotels, often with a decent restaurant.

iGuide (www.iguide-hotels.com) Charming, quirky hotels and B&Bs.

Relais & Châteaux (www.relaischateaux.com) Luxury and historic hotels.

Best...

Places to Sleep
La Cascade (p98)

L'Hostellerie Jérôme (p62)

Villa Gallici (p172)

Le Cloître (p184)

Maison Valvert (p241)

Quirky Hotels
Les Cabanes d'Orion (p95)

Le 2 (p96)

Moonlight Chalet (p263)

Le Couvent (p238)

Chambre avec Vue (p240)

On a Budget
Relais International de la Jeunesse Thalassa (p69)

Château de Grasse (p98)

Hôtel Solara (p49)

Vertigo Saint-Charles (p155)

Hôtel Boquier (p197)

Chambres d'Hôte (B&Bs)

Chambres d'hôte are the French version of B&Bs. Many are on farms, wineries and historic properties, and the top places now rival hotels in terms of luxury and design. Breakfast is included in the price, and many places serve dinner (known as *table d'hôte*).

Guide de Charme (www.guidesdecharme.com) Hotels and B&Bs with bags of charm.

Fleurs de Soleil (www.fleursdesoleil.fr) Quality *chambres d'hôte*.

Bienvenue à la Ferme (www.bienvenue-a-la-ferme.com) Farmstays.

Avignon & Provence (www.avignon-et-provence.com) Hotels, B&Bs and self-catering options.

Self-Catering

Who hasn't dreamt of living in an old Provençal farmhouse or a Côte d'Azur villa with a magnificent pool? Self-catering is a great option, particularly for families or those seeking to experience 'life as a local'. Most places come with fully equipped kitchen, and many have a pool (sometimes shared with other guests).

Tourist offices generally keep lists of studios, apartments and villas to rent. Home-share sites like **Airbnb** (www.airbnb.com) have an increasing presence in Provence and the Côte d'Azur.

Gîtes de France (p296) Authentic self-catering accommodation.

Gîtes Panda (www.gites-panda.fr) Self-catering and B&Bs near nature reserves.

Sawdays (www.sawdays.co.uk) Handpicked self-catering and B&B listings.

Joie de Vivre (www.jdvholidays.com) Premium villas.

One Off Places (http://www.oneoffplaces.co.uk/destinations/Europe/France/Provence-Cote-dAzur) Quirky and unusual properties, from eco houses to windmills.

Vintage Travel (www.vintagetravel.co.uk) Villas with pools.

Camping

The French are big on camping, but they favour sites that are more like holiday parks, with swimming pool, shop, playground for the kids and (most importantly) a decent restaurant. Most cities and large towns have a *camping municipal* (municipal camping grounds) – basic, but good for cutting costs.

Most camping grounds only open between April and October. Standard rates quoted are usually for two adults with a tent and car. Electric hook-ups are available at many sites; some also have chalets or bungalows for hire. *Camping sauvage* (wild camping) is illegal.

Camping en France (www.camping.fr) Pan-France camping ground listings.

HPA Guide (http://camping.hpaguide.com) Good family-friendly camping-ground guide.

Cabanes de France (http://www.cabanes-de-france.com) Treehouses for wannabe Tarzans and Janes.

Hostels

Hostels in France vary in standard from hip to threadbare. You don't have to be young to stay in one, although rates are cheaper if you're under 26.

Sheets are provided, but sleeping bags are not allowed. In big cities, hostels are sometimes quite a long way from the city centre. Most hostels have a kitchen for guests' use.

Two other types of hostels are *gîtes d'étape* (basic lodges for hikers) and *gîtes de refuge* (high mountain huts).

The two official organisations:

Fédération Unie des Auberges de Jeunesse (www.fuaj.org)

Ligue Française pour les Auberges de la Jeunesse (www.auberges-de-jeunesse.com)

Prices

Prices vary by season:

➡ Low season (October/November to February/March)

➡ Midseason (March to May and September/October)

➡ High season (June to September)

Quoted rates don't include the daily *taxe de séjour* (tourist tax; €0.20 to €1.50).

Reservations

Out of season, many hotels and B&Bs close for a few weeks for their *congé annuel* (annual closure). From Easter onwards, things get busier, making advance booking essential. In July and August don't even contemplate the coast unless you have a reservation or are prepared to pay a fortune for the few rooms still available.

Tourist offices can invariably tell you where rooms are available; some run accommodation-reservation services.

Plan Your Trip
Eat & Drink Like a Local

Whether it's feasting on fresh-caught fish in Marseille or tucking into a rich country stew in Haute-Provence, this is one corner of France where food isn't just an important part of everyday life – it's often the main event.

Food Experiences
Meals of a Lifetime

A good tip for experiencing gourmet cuisine without breaking the bank is to book for lunch – menus are always substantially cheaper than at dinner, even at the priciest establishments.

➡ **Restaurant Pierre Reboul, Aix-en-Provence** (p173) Run by one of Provence's most renowned chefs, this address in Aix-en-Provence has two settings: a fine-dining restaurant and a more relaxed bistro.

➡ **Le Rhul, Marseille** (p160) The address to eat authentic bouillabaisse and *bourride* (fish stew).

➡ **La Colombe d'Or, St-Paul de Vence** (p95) The joy of dining at The Golden Dove isn't just the food, it's the incredible art collection, donated by artists like Picasso, Chagall and Matisse, who swapped their paintings for a slap-up meal.

➡ **Le Mas Candille, Mougins** (p104) A luxurious hotel with a lavish, Michelin-starred restaurant to match, run by young Cannes native David Chauvac.

➡ **Le Sanglier Paresseux, Caseneuve** (p240) Provençal ingredients with exciting, exotic flavours supplied by the Brazilian-born chef – and a knockout view of the Luberon hills from the terrace.

➡ **La Bastide de Moustiers, Moustiers Ste-Marie** (p255) Superstar chef Alain Ducasse's

The Year in Food
Spring (Mar–May)

Spring lambs are a traditional Easter meat across Provence; in Camargue, bull meat (stewed or cured in saucissons) is another favourite.

Summer (Jun–Aug)

Peak food season in Provence, when olives and grapes ripen, tomatoes and peppers explode with flavour, and peaches, cherries and nectarines dangle from the trees. It's a time of year made for alfresco eating – and the locals take full advantage.

Autumn (Sep–Nov)

Harvest time: this is when the year's wines and olive oils are bottled. It's also chestnut harvest in Collobrières, just in time to make marrons glacés (glazed chestnuts) for Christmas.

Winter (Dec–Feb)

Truffle season: locals head out in their droves to seek these precious wild fungi. A Christmas tradition in Provence is to serve 13 desserts; you're supposed to try them all to have luck for the coming year. In February, Menton celebrates all things citrus with its lemon festival.

COOKING COURSES

Many of the region's top chefs are more than happy to share their culinary secrets.

Le Marmiton, Avignon (p200) Top chefs host cooking classes in a 19th-century château kitchen.

L'Atelier de Cuisine Gourmande, Bormes-les-Mimosas (p133) Local chef Mireille Gedda specialises in regionally themed cooking workshops.

Les Apprentis Gourmets, Cannes (p86) A boutique kitchen serving express cooking courses, from 30 minutes to two hours.

Auberge La Fenière, Cadenet (p243) Hone your skills at this gourmet restaurant in the Luberon.

Les Bacchanales, Vence (p97) In his 1930s townhouse in Vence, chef Christophe Dufau hosts classes exploring food-and-wine pairings.

La Vigne, Villefranche-sur-Mer (p59) This lovely B&B takes a relaxed approach to learning to cook.

École de Dégustation, Châteauneuf-du-Pape (p206) Not cooking but wine tasting – an equally essential skill.

illustrious address, in a splendid setting near the Gorges du Verdon.

➡ **Le Chantecler, Nice** (p55) Le Negresco's mythical restaurant, a pink antique confection with superb service and food truly worthy of its two Michelin stars.

➡ **Sea Sens, Cannes** (p87) Even if you're not an A-lister, you'll feel like one thanks to the stellar food at this Cannes restaurant.

➡ **Chez Bruno, Lorgues** (p125) Truffles, truffles and more truffles: the black diamond finds its way into practically every dish here.

Cheap Treats

➡ **Pissaladière** The Niçois equivalent of pizza, topped with caramelised onions, olives, garlic and anchovies.

➡ **Socca** Another classic Niçois street snack, a savoury pancake made with chickpea flour.

➡ **Petits farcis** Vegetables (tomatoes, onions, courgettes, courgette flowers) filled with a stuffing of mince, cheese, breadcrumbs, egg yolk and herbs.

➡ **Tapenade** Olive dip, a common accompaniment to predinner drinks, eaten on crusty bread.

➡ **Anchoïade** Like tapenade, but made with salty anchovies and garlic.

➡ **Fromage de chèvre** Goat's cheese is the staple *fromage* of Provence – the best comes from Banon, in the Luberon.

➡ **Omelette aux truffes** Truffle tasting on the cheap – a classic omelette flavoured with fragrant black truffles.

➡ **Calissons d'Aix** Aix-en-Provence's signature cakes are sweet and irresistible.

Dare to Try

➡ **Oursin** Sea urchin is an acquired taste – eaten raw from the shell with a squeeze of lemon, it's pungent and very, very fishy.

➡ **Pieds paquets** For the adventurous diner: lambs' feet and stomachs simmered together in white wine.

➡ **Saucisson de taureau** Bull sausage is a common sight on menus around the Camargue. Trust us, it's meaty and delicious!

➡ **Saucisson de sanglier** Wild-boar sausage is cured, and it's much lower in fat than pig sausage.

➡ **Escargots** Snails are popular in rural Provence; they're very tasty doused in lashings of garlic butter, a bit like cockles or winkles.

Local Specialities

As befits a rural region, Provence's culinary specialities are rooted in *cuisine paysanne* (peasants' dishes), using unwanted fish and cheap cuts of meat to make sure that nothing is wasted.

Bouillabaisse

This pungent yellow fish stew has been brewed by Marseillais for centuries. It requires a minimum of four types of fresh fish (favourites include scorpion fish, white scorpion fish, weever, conger eel, chapon and tub gurnard) cooked in a rockfish stock with onions, tomatoes, garlic, *herbes de Provence* (a mix of thyme, rosemary, majoram, oregano and a few other herbs) and saffron (hence the colour).

The name bouillabaisse is derived from the French *bouillir* (to boil) and *baisser* (to lower, as in a flame), reflecting the cooking method required: bring it to the boil, let it bubble ferociously for 15 minutes, then reduce heat and simmer. Serve the *bouillon* (broth) first as a soup, followed by the fish flesh, in the company of a local wine, a white Cassis or dry Bandol rosé.

Authentic bouillabaisse has to be ordered a day in advance, and usually comes in a pot for two or more people to share.

Soupe de Poissons

A rich, velvety fish soup, *soupe de poissons* is made by boiling down fish, trimmings and bones into a thick broth. It's usually served with *rouille* (a spicy tomato condiment), crispy croutons and grated Gruyère cheese.

Soupe au Pistou

More stew than soup, the classic peasant dish *soupe au pistou* consists of a filling vegetable broth (beans, carrots, potatoes, courgettes, tomatoes and onions are all common ingredients), laced with lashings of olive oil, garlic and basil. Sometimes it comes with croutons, sometimes not.

Daube

A rich meaty stew, *daube* consists of beef braised in red wine, onions, celery, carrot, garlic and herbs. Like all stews, it must cook slowly for several hours; ideally, it is prepared the day before it's served.

Ratatouille

Provence is the spiritual home of the filling vegetable stew ratatouille, typically made with tomatoes, onions, courgettes, aubergines and red and green peppers, which have been cooked with aromatic *herbes de Provence*.

Brouillade de Truffes

A humble dish (scrambled eggs) with a gourmet twist (black-truffle shavings), *brouillade de truffes* allows the fungi's delicate flavour to shine through. It's a common course on truffle menus.

Stockfish (or Estocaficada)

The main ingredient of stockfish – rehydrated dried cod – puts many people off, yet well prepared (and most restaurants that serve it are pros), this Niçois dish is up there with every regional speciality.

Dried cod is soaked in running water for several days, then stewed with onions, garlic, tomatoes, peppers, potatoes and fresh herbs (fennel, thyme and parsley). Olives are added towards the end of cooking and the dish is normally served piping hot, splashed with a glug of olive oil. Nothing like it on a cold winter day!

Bourride

The fish stew *bourride* is similar to bouillabaisse but has fewer ingredients, a less prescriptive recipe, and often a slightly creamier sauce. It's customarily served with aïoli (garlic mayonnaise).

How to Eat & Drink
When to Eat

➡ The classic French breakfast is a cup of coffee and a bit of yesterday's baguette with jam; croissants and *pains au chocolats* are reserved for weekend treats but usually feature as part of a hotel breakfast alongside cheeses, yoghurts, fruit and charcuterie. Breakfast is usually served from around 7.30am to 9.30am.

L'APÉRO

L'apéro (short for *l'apéritif*, an alcoholic drink taken before dinner) is a national pastime in France, particularly in Provence and the Côte d'Azur. It's a predinner drink accompanied by snacks; a classic is a shot of pastis or a glass of chilled rosé, served with marinated olives, crusty bread and tapenade.

GRANT FAINT / GETTY IMAGES ©

Alfresco dining, Nice (p45)

➡ Lunch is often the main meal of the day; nearly everyone takes a couple of hours for lunch between noon and 2pm, often taking advantage of the *plat du jour* at a local brasserie.

➡ Although most restaurants open around 7pm, diners generally start trickling in around 8pm and often linger till 10.30pm or later.

Where to Eat

Dining *à la provençal* can mean anything from lunch in a village bistro to dining in a star-studded gastronomic temple. Irrespective of price, a *carte* (menu) or *ardoise* (blackboard) is usually hanging up outside, allowing you to check what's on offer before committing.

CUSTOMS & ETIQUETTE

➡ Forget balancing your bread on your main-course plate; crumbs on the table are fine.

➡ Using the same knife and fork for your starter and main is commonplace in many informal restaurants.

➡ *Santé* is the toast for alcoholic drinks; *bon appétit* is what you say before tucking in.

➡ The French generally end their meal with a short, sharp espresso coffee.

➡ Splitting the bill is seen as crass – except among young people.

➡ Service is generally included, so leaving a tip is optional.

Bookings are always advisable in summer, particularly if you'd like a table *en terrasse* (outside).

➡ **Auberge** Inn serving traditional country fare, often in rural areas. Some also offer rooms.

➡ **Bistro** (also spelled *bistrot*) Anything from an informal bar serving light meals to a fully fledged restaurant.

➡ **Brasserie** Very much like a cafe, except that it serves full meals (generally nonstop from 11am to 11pm) as well as drinks and coffee.

➡ **Cafe** Serves basic food (cold and toasted sandwiches), coffees and drinks.

➡ **Restaurant** Most serve lunch and dinner five or six days a week.

Menu Decoder

➡ **Plat du jour** The dish of the day, usually great value.

➡ **Formule** A two-course menu, often served only at lunch. You can usually choose either starter and main or main and dessert.

➡ **Menu** Usually two or three courses, with a more limited choice of dishes compared to the à la carte menu.

➡ **Entrées** Starters.

➡ **Plats** Main dishes, sometimes divided into *viandes* (meats) and *poissons* (fish).

➡ **Desserts** Desserts.

➡ **À la carte** Always the most expensive way to dine.

For a glossary and explanation of particular dishes, see p284.

Plan Your Trip

Outdoor Experiences

With its varied landscapes – alpine mountains and cavernous gorges, flamingo-pink wetlands, and a world-famous coastline of sparkling white sand and turquoise water – Provence has an outdoor activity to match every mood, moment and energy level.

Land

Walking

Provence is a great place to strap on your boots, especially once you escape the searing heat of the coast and head up into the mountains of Provence and the Parc National du Mercantour. The region is crossed by a number of long-distance *Grande Randonnée* (GR) trails, and a whole host of *sentiers balisés* (marked paths).

The little town of St-Martin-Vésubie in the Vallée de la Vésubie is a popular hub for hikers in the Mercantour, with regular guided walks into the remote Vallée des Merveilles, famous for its Bronze Age rock carvings. Neighbouring valleys also have hundreds of trails to explore; tourist offices stock maps, guidebooks and leaflets. This is the best region for summer walking – the altitude means that temperatures remain cooler than the coast, although snowfall makes hiking here impractical between October and March.

Further south, trails run along the clifftops and coves of the Parc National des Calanques, with glittering views of the Mediterranean accompanying every step. It's best saved for spring or autumn, as hiking in the summer heat here is more punishment than pleasure.

Between 1 July and 15 September forested areas are closed due to the high risk

The Best...

Snorkelling

Get acquainted with some of the Côte d'Azur's submarine residents at the underwater snorkelling park of Domaine du Rayol (p132).

Cycling & Mountain Biking

For an easy day ride follow the course of the Véloroute du Calavon (p231), an old railway track through the Luberon, or hurtle down tracks and trails within sight of the summit of Provence's highest mountain, Mont Ventoux (p214).

Sea-Kayaking

Paddle (p168) beneath the cliffs of the Calanques, and gain access to some of the Côte d'Azur's most beautiful – and quietest – coves.

Horse Riding

Saddle up (p187) on one of Camargue's sturdy white horses and venture out into this marshland.

Bungee Jumping

Throw yourself off Europe's highest bungee-jump site: the Pont de l'Artuby (p252), 182m above Gorges du Verdon.

Skiing

Come wintertime, snow blankets the mountains of the Mercantour, and resorts such as Allos (p259) and Valberg (p261) are packed with skiers and snowboarders.

of forest fire. Always check with the local tourist office before setting off.

Take bottled water and snacks and wear good boots (even on a hot day). Don't rely on being able to get a mobile-phone signal, especially in the mountains.

France's national map publisher, IGN, publishes the best maps for walkers, with all trails and topographical features clearly marked.

➜ **Fédération Française de Randonnée Pédestre** (FFRP, French Walking Federation; www.ffrandonnee.fr) Has the most comprehensive walking guides; some are now available as ebooks.

➜ **Guides RandOxygène** (www.randoxygene. org) Publishes three walking guides to the region, which are sold in local tourist offices; ebook versions can be downloaded from its website.

➜ **Escapado** (www.escapado.fr) Publishes downloadable routes for road cyclists, mountain bikers and walkers.

Cycling & Mountain Biking

There's no shortage of sunshine, and let's face it – you're not going to get away without tackling a few hills. The best regions for cycling tend to be away from the busy coastal roads: the quiet country roads of the Luberon, the villages of the Var and the hills of Haute-Provence are all good areas to explore.

Road bikes (*vélo de route*) and mountain bikes (*vélo tout-terrain,* VTT) can be widely hired for around €15 a day including helmet and puncture-repair kit. Children's bikes (around €12 per day) and toddler seats (around €5 per day) are also widely available. Some outlets deliver to your door.

Your first port of call for routes should, as always, be the local tourist office – it

always has a range of leaflets and guides to give away, as well as suggestions on local bike shops and rental outfits.

➜ **Véloloisir Provence** (www. veloloisirprovence.com) A superb cycling resource, detailing a range of colour-coded road- and mountain-bike routes around the Luberon, the Verdon and other areas. The website is in English and has suggestions for accommodation, guides, baggage transport and more.

➜ **Provence à Vélo** (www.provence-a-velo. fr) Another good online route resource, with suggested routes mostly covering the area north of Avignon towards Mont Ventoux.

Horse Riding

With its famous cowboys, creamy white horses and expansive sandy beaches to gallop along, the Camargue is a wonderful, windswept spot to ride. Aspiring cowboys and gals can learn the ropes on week-long *stages de monte gardiane* (Camargue cowboy courses).

Dramatically different but equally inspiring are the donkey and horse treks through lyrical chestnut and cork oak forests in the Massif des Maures, set up by the Conservatoire du Patrimoine du Freinet (p128). Donkey treks and horse rides are also offered around the Parc National du Mercantour.

Elsewhere in Provence, tourist offices have lists of stables and riding centres where you can saddle up.

➜ **Terre Equestre** (www.terre-equestre.com) Useful French-language listings site with details of horse-riding schools all over the region and further afield.

Wildlife Watching

Perhaps the easiest way to see some wildlife is to grab some flippers and a snorkel mask and go swimming – shoals of colourful fish can be spotted on practically any beach on the Côte d'Azur. For more exotic species, head for Monaco's excellent Musée Océanographique (p63).

The prime area for animal spotting is definitely the Parc National du Mercantour, where, with a bit of luck and a good pair of binoculars, you might be able to spy anything from a mouflon (big-horn sheep) to a golden eagle soaring through the skies, There's also a wild-wolf reserve to visit.

WEATHER CHECK

Whatever activity you're planning on, check the latest weather forecast at **Météo France** (www.meteofrance. com), or ask at the tourist office. Even on a sunny day in midsummer, storms, heavy rainfall and mistral winds can appear out of nowhere – so it pays to be prepared.

Ornithologists flock to see clouds of pink flamingos in the protected Camargue delta and between pink-hued salt pans on the Presqu'île de Giens near Hyères. The Gorges du Verdon is another great area thanks to its population of reintroduced griffin vultures, while seabirds can be spied in the Parc Naturel Départemental de la Grande Corniche and the Parc National des Calanques, both on the Côte d'Azur.

➡ **LPO PACA** (☑04 94 12 79 52; http:paca.lpo.fr) Organises guided birdwatching expeditions near Hyères.

Water

With such a beautiful coastline, it's no surprise there is so much to do on the water. Note that there is often a minimum age restriction for many watersports.

In summer you'll find the usual fun rides of jet skiing, waterskiing and wakeboarding (€30 to €50) at a number of beaches along the Côte d'Azur.

Kayaking & Canoeing

➡ Hiring a kayak is the best way to explore the turquoise rocky coves of the Calanques near Marseille.

➡ Canoes are ideal for paddling around the Camargue and the Pont du Gard.

Swimming, Snorkelling, Diving & Paddleboarding

You couldn't come to the coast and not get wet – whether that means a quick paddle or a proper snorkelling session.

➡ The sea is warm enough for swimming without a wetsuit between June and October.

➡ Flippers, masks and goggles are widely available from sport and dive shops along the coast.

➡ Underwater nature trails and guided snorkelling tours are available at many beaches.

➡ Local dive clubs offer courses (€300 to €500) as well as single dives (€50) to seek out the many shipwrecks that lie at the bottom of the Med.

➡ The latest craze on the Côte d'Azur is stand-up paddleboarding, which involves standing on a surfboard and steering yourself around

---

HOT-AIR BALLOONING
....

Drifting across Provence's patchwork fields in a hot-air balloon is a seductive way to take in the captivating countryside. Balloon flights last one to 1½ hours (allow three to four hours in all for getting to and from the launch pad, inflating the balloon etc) and cost from €230 per person. Flights run year-round but are subject to weather forecasts.

Operators include **Montgolfière Vol-Terre** (☑06 03 54 10 92; www.montgolfiere-luberon.com), near Roussillon, with flights in the Avignon and Luberon areas; and **Les Montgolfières du Sud** (☑04 66 37 28 02; www.sudmontgolfiere.com; 64 rue Sigalon), west of Nîmes, with balloons that fabulously float above the Pont du Gard.

---

with a long paddle. Paddleboard providers are springing up on many beaches; budget on €10 for a half-hour, €15 to €18 per hour.

Whitewater Rafting

For a white-knuckle ride, the Gorges du Verdon is famous for its foaming whitewater rapids. Dozens of operators offer trips from their main base in Castellane, along with related river activities such as floating and canyoning. Allow €35/60 for a half/full day.

Winter Sports

The few ski resorts in Haute-Provence are refreshingly low-key. Slopes are best suited to beginner and intermediate skiers and costs are lower than in the Northern Alps.

Resorts include Pra Loup (1500m to 1600m), Valberg (1600m to 1700m), Foux d'Allos (1800m) and the concrete-block Isola 2000 (2450m).

The ski season runs from December to March/April (depending on the snow conditions). As always, buying a package is the cheapest way to ski and/or snowboard. Otherwise allow €25 to €30 for a daily lift pass, and about the same again for equipment rental.

Plan Your Trip

Travel with Children

Provence and the Côte d'Azur is a wonderful place to travel with children. There's swimming and snorkelling galore, cycling through lavender fields, kayaking in the Camargue, visiting Roman ruins, walking along the Calanques and wildlife-watching in the Parc National du Mercantour, to name a few.

Best Regions for Kids

Nice, Monaco & Menton

Riviera glamour isn't just for grown-ups: skate or scooter along Nice's Promenade des Anglais; hop on a boat for a scenic cruise or a dolphin excursion; and in Monaco, watch the changing of the guard, ogle the yachts and slurp milkshakes at Stars 'n' Bars.

St-Tropez to Toulon

Buckets and spades, beachcombing, swimming, snorkelling – it's all about the beach here.

Arles & the Camargue

Quiet roads, bountiful nature, long beaches and activities galore make the Camargue one of the easiest places to visit en famille. Add evocative Roman ruins in Arles and you have the perfect holiday.

Haute-Provence & the Southern Alps

White-water activities in the Verdon, snow fun in the mountains, dinosaurs in Digne and the Vallée des Merveilles – nature is Haute-Provence's drawcard.

Provence & the Côte d'Azur for Kids

Museums & Activities

Many museums and monuments are free for kids, but rules vary – sometimes 'kids' refers to children aged under 18, sometimes to children aged under six or 12. Family tickets, covering two adults and two children, are often available.

Note that for many outdoor activities (rafting, canoeing, horse riding etc) there is often an age minimum, generally six or seven years. Check in advance to avoid disappointed faces on the day.

Food & Drink

Eating out *en famille* is commonplace, but the French will expect children to behave properly at the table – so don't let the kids run wild. Most restaurants don't open for dinner before 7.30pm, so brasseries (which serve food continuously) are often a more useful option for families.

There is usually a *menu enfant* (children's menu) – pizza, pasta and *steak haché-frites* (bunless hamburger and fries) are staples. Don't be shy about ordering a starter or half-portion as a child's meal; most restaurants will happily oblige.

Drinks can be pricey in restaurants (€5 for a soda is not unusual); save money by ordering *une carafe d'eau* (a jug of tap water) or *un sirop* (syrup; €2 at most), diluted with water. If you want a straw, ask for *une paille*.

Practical Tips

Public toilets are rare in smaller towns and villages, but automated loos are common in cities. Most visitor attractions and some service stations have dedicated loos with baby-changing facilities.

Breastfeeding is generally not a problem. Nappies, baby formula, baby food and other supplies are widely available in shops and supermarkets.

Note that children under four get free train travel, and discounted tickets are available for older kids.

Children's Highlights

Rainy Days

➡ Go Roman at Ludo, Pont du Gard (p229).

➡ Watch sharks and fish at Musée Océanographique de Monaco (p63).

➡ Test your sense of smell at Musée International de la Parfumerie (p100).

➡ Learn about the stars at Centre d'Astronomie (p250).

Wildlife Watching

➡ See wolves in the wild at Alpha (p262).

➡ Go horse-riding and flamingo-watching in the Camargue (p187).

➡ Spot fish while snorkelling in Port-Cros (p136), Domaine du Rayol (p132) or the Corniche de l'Estérel (p105).

➡ Meet goats at La Ferme des Courmettes (p99).

Outdoor Activities

➡ Clamber among rocks, caves and cliffs on the Sentier de Littoral (p93) in Cap d'Antibes.

➡ Hike one of the nature trails on the Domaine des Courmettes (p99) near Vence.

➡ Paddle a canoe under the Pont du Gard (p229).

➡ Re-live medieval battles at Château des Baux. (p225)

➡ Tackle the adventure course at **Colorado Aventures** (☑ 06 78 26 68 91; www.colorado-aventures.com; adult/child €18/14; ☺ closed Jan; 🖲).

Planning

When to Go

For swimming and sunshine, the best times are from May to September; for skiing in the mountains, the season runs from December to March.

Be careful of the heat – especially in midsummer, when the sun is fierce. It's very easy to get sunburned, even on overcast days; cover up and slap on the sunscreen.

Accommodation

Most hotels have quadruple or family rooms with extra beds for the kids. *Chambres d'hôte* (B&Bs) are a great family option; many offer dinner on the premises, which takes care of babysitting arrangements: just bring a baby monitor to wine and dine in peace.

Renting your own *gîte* (self-catering cottage) is the best idea if you don't mind staying in one place; it feels more like home, and you can cook your own meals.

Camping is popular too. Book ahead, as tent pitches and mobile homes get snapped up fast.

What to Pack

Don't panic if you forget something: you will find everything you need in French shops and supermarkets.

Babies & Toddlers

➡ A carry sling: pushchairs are a pain on cobbled lanes.

➡ A portable changing mat (changing facilities are a rarity)

➡ A screw-on seat for toddlers (restaurants don't always have high chairs)

➡ Inflatable armbands for the sea or pool

➡ Baby sunscreen and mosquito repellent

Children Aged Six to 12

➡ Entertainment for car journeys: tablets, DVD players, activity books, sketchpads (remember to pack chargers and extra plug adapters)

➡ Swimming gear, goggles, snorkel and flip-flops for the beach

➡ Binoculars for spotting wildlife

➡ Water bottle

➡ Camera and batteries

Regions at a Glance

Provence and the Côte d'Azur packs in the most incredible diversity of sights, landscapes and activities.

The coast tends to be relatively built up, with exceptions around the Camargue, the Calanques and the unspoilt Îles d'Hyères. To get away from the crowds, head inland to the sparsely populated Haute-Provence, the majestic southern Alps, the vineyards of the Var or the storybook Luberon.

Back in town, Nice is utterly delightful, its old town teeming with life and the Mediterranean lapping the shores of its promenade, whereas Marseille, France's second-biggest city, blends urban grit with culture on the rise.

And then there's Monaco, a law unto itself, with its skyscrapers, tax-haven residents, scandal-prone royal family and hedonistic fun.

Nice, Monaco & Menton

Views
Coastline
Architecture

Panoramas

The coast rises abruptly from the sea along the Riviera, reaching 800m in places, with mind-bending views along the way. Drive the Grande Corniche or visit Ste-Agnès or Èze for knock-out vistas.

Gardens

With its mild, sunny climate, the Côte d'Azur has always been a gardener's heaven. Cue the region's many exotic, botanical and themed gardens, which reach their prime in spring.

Belle Époque Legacy

The French Riviera was all the rage in the 19th century and we can thank wintering royals and high-society divas for their legacy: meringue-like buildings, operas, casinos and promenades.

p44

Cannes & Around

Art
Perfumeries
Hiking

Modern Art

Few other places have played host to so many seminal artists: Chagall, Matisse, Picasso, Renoir and Léger all spent much time here, and left plenty behind. Trail their legacy.

Grasse

From flower fields to factory, follow the making of a perfume around Grasse. The city is the world's leading perfumery hub and it has thrown its doors wide open to visitors.

Scenic Walks

From long coastal walks to ancient mule paths in the back country and breathtaking panoramas, make sure you don your boots to discover the area's most picturesque spots.

p79

St-Tropez to Toulon

Wine
Beaches
Nightlife

Vineyards

This is the home of Provence's signature rosé wines, so spare an afternoon to visit the vineyards of Côtes de Provence, Bandol or Correns' organic winemakers.

Celebrity Beaches

If 'Côte d'Azur' conjures up images of azure seas with golden sand fringed by pines and *maquis* (a type of scrubland), you've come to the right place. Take your pick from remote island beaches, nudist heavens and celebrity spots.

Clubbing

Nowhere parties quite as hard as St-Tropez in the summer. Dress to impress and bring plenty of cash to follow in the dance moves of BB, Kate Moss, Paris Hilton and more.

p109

Marseille to Aix-en-Provence

Culture
Food
Nature

Museums & Galleries

Buoyed by its tenure as European Capital of Culture in 2013, Marseille continues to buzz with artistic activity and fantastic, fascinating museums.

Eating Out

From gastronomic to traditional, all-out culinary magic to simple, straight-from-the-boat-to-your-plate fish, Marseille and Aix-en-Provence have it in shoals.

Outdoor Adventures

The rugged, mineral beauty of the Massif de la Ste-Baume and the Calanques has captivated painters and writers; follow in their footsteps with a walk, a paddle or a long drive.

p141

Arles & the Camargue

Food
Nature
History

Camarguise Cuisine

Camargue's specialities – its red rice, bull meat and seafood – are reminiscent of Spain. Try them, as well as modern French cuisine, in one of the area's mighty fine restaurants.

Birdwatching

More than 500 species of bird regularly visit the Camargue, chief among them the colourful flocks of pink flamingos. The mosquitoes seem just as abundant as the birds, so pack repellent along with your binoculars!

Roman Sites

Arles flourished under Julius Ceasar, and the town's past prosperity is still awe-inspiring: amphitheatre, theatre, necropolis and a leading mosaic-renovation centre.

p177

Avignon & Around

History
Wine
Nature

Romans & Popes

The Romans and the popes all decided to call the area home: find out why by exploring Nîmes' phenomenal Roman heritage, the Pont du Gard and Avignon's imposing Palais des Papes.

Wine Tasting

With three of Provence's most famous wines – reds Gigondas and Châteauneuf-du-Pape, and Muscat de Beaumes-de-Venise – the Avignon region is a must for wine connoisseurs.

Outdoor Activities

Ascend giant Mont Ventoux, hike the stunning Dentelles de Montmirail, paddle below Pont du Gard or along the glassy Sorgue and breathe Provence's fresh air.

p193

Hill Towns of the Luberon

Villages
Activities
History

Rural Life

Gordes, Ménerbes, Lacoste, Bonnieux: this is the Provence of your dreams. There are 101 ways to enjoy these stunning villages: stroll, cycle, attend the weekly market or stop for a long lunch.

Cycling

With its rolling hills, postcard landscapes and light traffic, the Luberon is prime cycling territory. And, happily, there is plenty of help out there to facilitate your journey, from itinerary planning to luggage-carrying services.

Religious History

Long a Protestant stronghold in a Catholic country, the Luberon is steeped in religious history, from glorious churches to peaceful abbeys.

p230

Haute-Provence & the Southern Alps

Activities
Scenery
Nature

Extreme Sports

Adrenalin junkies, Haute-Provence is for you: you can go rafting, canyoning, skydiving, bungee jumping, mountain biking, cycling, paragliding and climbing. Hiking, in comparison, will look meek, but make no mistake: trekking here is tough.

Alpine Scenery

From Europe's deepest canyons to some of its highest peaks, Haute-Provence's alpine scenery is majestic and unspoilt. Even the night sky will bowl you over with its incredible clarity.

Wildlife

The grey wolf made a much publicised comeback to the Mercantour from Italy in the 1990s, but as well as wolves you could see vultures, eagles, mountain ibexes and cute marmots.

p245

On the Road

Nice, Monaco & Menton

Best Places to Eat

➡ Olive et Artichaut (p54)

➡ Café de la Fontaine (p62)

➡ Le Mirazur (p77)

➡ Marché de la Condamine (p69)

➡ Le Beauséjour (p78)

Best Places to Stay

➡ Nice Garden Hôtel (p52)

➡ Hôtel Lemon (p76)

➡ Hôtel Victoria (p74)

➡ Hôtel Welcome (p59)

➡ L'Hostellerie Jérôme (p62)

Why Go?

There may only be 30km between Nice and Menton, but this short stretch of coastline packs a powerful punch. Nice, with its atmospheric old town, rich architectural heritage (baroque, belle époque, contemporary), raging nightlife, alfresco cafe life and culinary excellence is a natural queen of the Riviera. Road-tripping east, the Grande and Moyenne Corniches (coastal roads) mesmerise with panoramic views of the Mediterranean, while the Corniche Inférieure laces the shore with its sandy beaches, pretty fishing villages and fabulous belle époque follies. Monaco elicits mixed reactions: the world's second-smallest country is a concrete jungle with a glitzy port, its own monarchy, throngs of VIPs and high-octane casino glamour. Yet it's this very razzmatazz that enthralls, fascinates and entertains. And when you want to make a run for the hills, what better place than the Arrière-Pays Niçois, an unspoilt and tranquil hinterland of stark beauty.

Driving Distances (km)

	Beaulieu-sur-Mer	Èze	La Turbie	Menton	Monaco	Nice
Èze	5					
La Turbie	12	7				
Menton	19	19	15			
Monaco	11	10	8	10		
Nice	10	15	20	30	21	
Roquebrune-Cap-Martin	18	16	11	4	9	25

NICE

POP 343,000

With its unusual mix of real-city grit, old-world opulence, year-round sunshine and exceptional location, Nice's appeal is universal. Everyone from backpackers to romance-seeking couples and families love sitting at a cafe on cours Saleya in Vieux Nice, on a bench on the legendary Promenade des Anglais or on a smooth pebble beach for an epic sunset. Eating options are stupendous, the nightlife buzzes and the local arts scene is thriving. You could happily spend a week here and still be hungry for more.

◉ Sights

★ Vieux Nice
HISTORIC QUARTER

Nice's old town, an atmospheric mellow-hued rabbit warren, has scarcely changed since the 1700s, and getting lost in it is a highlight. Cue cours Saleya: this joyous, thriving market square hosts a well-known flower market (cours Saleya; ⊙ 6am-5.30pm Tue-Sat, to 1.30pm Sun) and a thriving food market (cours Saleya; ⊙ 6am-1.30pm Tue-Sun), a staple of local life. A flea market (cours Saleya; ⊙ 8am-5pm Mon) takes over on Monday, and the overflow from bars and restaurants seems to be a permanent fixture.

North of cours Saleya spills the rest of Vieux Nice, its dark narrow lanes crammed with delis, small food shops, boutiques and packed bars. A fish market (place St-François; ⊙ 6am-1pm Tue-Sun) fills place St-François.

Baroque aficionados will adore architectural gems Cathédrale Ste-Réparate (place Rossetti), honouring the city's patron saint; exuberant (1740) Chapelle de la Miséricorde (cours Saleya); and 17th-century Palais Lascaris (15 rue Droite; guided visit €5; ⊙ 10am-6pm Wed-Mon, guided tour 3pm Fri) FREE, a frescoed orgy of Flemish tapestries, *faïence* (tin-glazed earthenware), gloomy religious paintings and 18th-century pharmacy.

★ Promenade des Anglais
ARCHITECTURE

Palm-lined Promenade des Anglais, paid for by Nice's English colony in 1822, is a fine stage for a stroll and a flop on one of its iconic sea-blue chairs, immortalised by Niçoise sculptor Sabine Géraudie with her strikingly giant seafront sculpture La Chaise de SAB (2014). Historic highlights include the magnificent (1912) Hôtel Negresco (🖉 04 93 16 64 00; www.hotel-negresco-nice.com; 37 promenade des Anglais) and art deco (1929) Palais de la Méditerranée (🖉 04 92 14 77 30; www.lepalaisdelamediterranee.com; 13-15 promenade des Anglais; d €345; ❋ @ 🕾 ☎ ♿). In 2015 the city of Nice submitted the Promenade des Anglais as a candidate for Unesco World Heritage status.

The promenade follows the complete 4km sweep of the Baie des Anges with a cycle and skating lane. For a fantastic family outing, rent inline skates, skateboards, scooters and bikes at Roller Station (🖉 04 93 62 99 05; www.roller-station.fr; 49 quai des États-Unis; skates, boards & scooters per hour/day €5/8, bicycles €5/10; ⊙ 9am-11pm Jul & Aug, 10am-8pm Apr-Jun & Sep, 10am-6pm Oct-Mar) to whizz along the silky-smooth Prom; allow for an extra €1/2 per hour/day for protective gear (helmet and pads). You'll need some ID as a deposit. Or cruise along effortlessly on two wheels with an electric Segway from Mobilboard Nice (p48).

★ Parc du Château
GARDEN

(⊙ 9am-8pm Jun-Aug, 9am-7pm Apr, May & Sep, 10am-6pm Oct-Mar) This park, on a rocky outcrop above the old town, rewards with a cinematic panorama of Nice, the Baie des Anges and the port. Only the 16th-century Tour Bellanda remains of the 12th-century castle, razed by Louis XIV in 1706. The Cascade Donjon, an 18th-century artificial waterfall with viewing platform, and children's playground, make it popular for picnics. Hike up from the seafront or ride the free lift (Ascenseur du Château; rue des Ponchettes; ⊙ 9am-8pm Jun-Aug, 9am-7pm Apr, May & Sep, 10am-6pm Oct-Mar) FREE beneath Tour Bellanda.

Musée Matisse
ART MUSEUM

(🖉 04 93 81 08 08; www.musee-matisse-nice.org; 164 av des Arènes de Cimiez; ⊙ 10am-6pm Wed-Mon) FREE This museum, 2km north in the leafy Cimiez quarter, houses a fascinating assortment of works by Matisse, including oil paintings, drawings, sculptures, tapestries and Matisse's famous paper cut-outs. The permanent collection is displayed in a red-ochre 17th-century Genoese villa in an olive grove. Temporary exhibitions are in the futuristic basement building. Matisse is buried in the Monastère de Cimiez cemetery, across the park from the museum.

In the 1940s Matisse lived in the monumental Régina building at 71 bd de Cimiez. Originally Queen Victoria's wintering palace, it had been converted into apartments and Matisse had two that he used as studio and home (where he died in 1954).

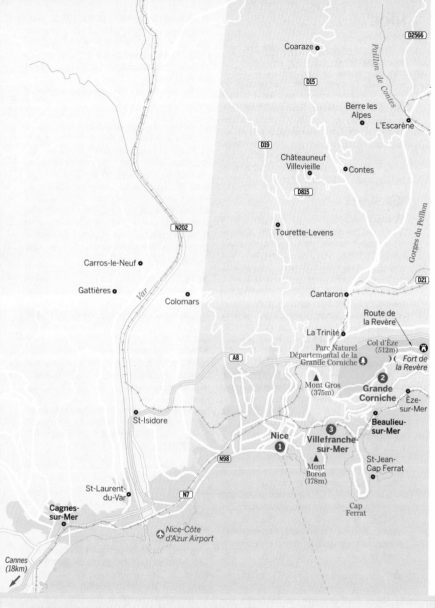

Nice, Monaco & Menton Highlights

❶ Eat well, drink well and enjoy the iconic, silky smooth Promenade des Anglais in the queen of the Riviera, **Nice** (p45).

❷ Take in huge, jaw-dropping views of the Med on a road trip along the hair-raising **Grande Corniche** (p61).

❸ Feast on the ancient charm of backstreet

Villefranche-sur-Mer (p58), where you can lunch on the local fisher's catch at Les Garçons.

❹ Hit **Monaco** (p62) to watch the changing of the

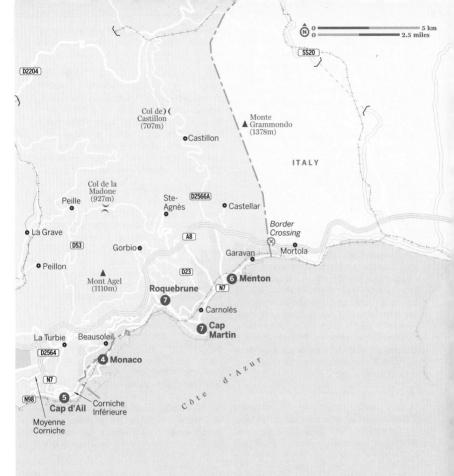

palace guard, visit the Musée Océanographique and soak up the glitz and glamour of Riviera high life in Monte Carlo.

5 Walk from **Cap d'Ail to Menton** (p78) along the shores of the brilliantly blue Mediterranean.

6 Discover Cocteau's genius in Menton's **Musée Jean Cocteau Collection Séverin Wunderman** (p74).

7 Trail architect Le Corbusier in medieval **Roquebrune** (p73) and along the beautiful shoreline of **Cap Martin** (p73).

Musée National Marc Chagall ART MUSEUM
(www.musee-chagall.fr; 4 av Dr Ménard; adult/
child €8/6; ⊘10am-6pm Wed-Mon May-Oct, to
5pm Nov-Apr) This small museum houses the
largest public collection of works by Belarusian painter Marc Chagall (1887–1985). The
main hall displays 12 huge interpretations
(1954–67) of stories from Genesis and Exodus. In an antechamber, an unusual mosaic
of Elijah in his fiery chariot, surrounded by
signs of the zodiac, is viewed through a plate-
glass window and reflected in a small pond.
From the city centre, allow about 20 minutes
to walk to the museum (signposted from av
de l'Olivetto).

★ **Musée Masséna** MUSEUM
(65 rue de France; adult/child €6/free; ⊘10am-
6pm Wed-Mon) This marvellous Italianate
neoclassical villa (1898) retraces Riviera history from the late 18th century to WWII. It's
a fascinating journey, with a roll call of monarchs, a succession of nationalities (British,
Russians, Americans), the advent of tourism,
the prominence of the carnival and more.
History is told through a mix of furniture,
vintage posters, photographs and paintings.
The city of Nice still uses the ground floor
for official occasions, so it can sometimes
close at short notice

★ **Musée d'Art Moderne
et d'Art Contemporain** ART MUSEUM
(MAMAC; www.mamac-nice.org; place Yves Klein;
⊘10am-6pm Tue-Sun) FREE European and
American avant-garde works from the
1950s to the present are the focus of this
museum. Highlights include many works
by Christo and Nice's New Realists: Niki de
Saint Phalle, César, Arman and Yves Klein.

ⓘ MONEY SAVER

The French Riviera Pass (www.
frenchrivierapass.com; 1-/2-/3-day pass
€26/38/56) covers admission to several
Nice sights: the Musée Chagall, the
Musée Matisse, MAMAC, L'OpenTour
bus, and a 30-minute Segway tour with
Mobilboard Nice. Along the coast, it
provides admission to the Musée Renoir
in Cagnes, the Musée National Fernand
Léger in Biot, the Jardin d'Èze, and the
Jardin Exotique and Musée Océanographique in Monaco. Buy it online or at
Nice tourist office (p57).

The building's rooftop also works as an exhibition space (with panoramas of Nice to
boot).

Port Lympia ARCHITECTURE
Nice's Port Lympia, with its beautiful
Venetian-coloured buildings, is often overlooked, but a stroll along its quays is lovely, as is the walk to get here: come down
through Parc du Château or follow quai
Rauba Capeu, where a massive war memorial hewn from the rock commemorates the
4000 Niçois who died in both world wars.

**Cathédrale Orthodoxe
Russe St-Nicolas** CATHEDRAL
(www.cathedrale-russe-nice.fr; av Nicolas II; ⊘9am-
noon & 2-6pm) Built between 1902 and 1912 to
provide a big enough church for the growing
Russian community, this cathedral, with its
colourful onion domes and rich, ornate interior, is the biggest Russian Orthodox church
outside Russia. The cathedral boasts dozens of intricate icons – unfortunately, there
is very little in the way of explanation for
visitors.

☞ Tours

Trans Côte d'Azur BOAT TOUR
(www.trans-cote-azur.com; quai Lunel; ⊘Apr-
Oct) Trans Côte d'Azur runs one-hour boat
cruises along the Baie des Anges and Rade
de Villefranche (adult/child €17.50/12) April
to October. Mid-June to mid-September
it sails to Île Ste-Marguerite (€39/29, one
hour), St-Tropez (€64/49, 2½ hours), Monaco (€37/28.50, 45 minutes) and Cannes
(€39/29, one hour).

L'OpenTour BUS TOUR
(www.nice.opentour.com; opposite 109 quai des
Etats-Unis; 1-/2-day pass adult €22/25, child €8)
With headphone commentary in several
languages, the open-topped bus tours (1½
hours) give you a good overview of Nice.
Hop on or off at any one of 14 stops.

Mobilboard Nice TOUR
(☏04 93 80 21 27; www.mobilboard.com/
nice-promenade; 2 rue Halévy; 30min initiation
€17, 1hr/2hr tour €30/50) For an effortless
cruise along Promenade des Anglais, hop
aboard an electric Segway. Rental includes
a 15-minute lesson on how to ride the two-
wheeled, battery-powered 'vehicle', protective helmet and audioguide. The 15km ride
to neighbouring Villefranche-sur-Mer is a
great trip (€75).

BELLET WINES

High in the hills northwest of Nice is one of France's smallest vineyards, Bellet. The tiny sun-rich appellation dates to 1941 and is highly sought after – just a dozen producers work 55 hectares of land, including Château de Bellet (☑ 04 93 37 81 57; www.chateaudebellet.com; 325 chemin de Saquier; ☺ 2-5.30pm Mon-Fri or by appointment) and nearby Domaine de Toasc (☑ 04 92 15 14 14; www.domainedetoasc.com; 213 chemin de Crémat; ☺ 2.30-5.30pm Tue-Sat), both 20 minutes north of Nice along rte de Grenoble (D6202). Both *domaines* (estates) can be visited – reserve vineyards tours and tastings in advance – and Domaine de Toasc even has a couple of self-catering properties between vines to rent.

Whites use Rolle grapes, a typical Nice variety, while reds and rosés rely on Folle Noire ('crazy black', so named because of its erratic yields) and grenache. Vines grow in terraced beds known as *restanques* and grapes are harvested by hand. Twice a year, in June and again in late November, Bellet producers hold an open-door weekend when visitors can freely wander the vineyards, talk to winemakers and taste wines from each *domaine*. Nice tourist office (p57) has details, as does www.vinsdebellet.com.

✤ Festivals & Events

Carnaval de Nice   CARNIVAL
(www.nicecarnaval.com; ☺ Feb) Held around Mardi Gras (Shrove Tuesday) since 1294. Highlights include the *batailles de fleurs* (battles of flowers), and the ceremonial burning of the carnival king on Promenade des Anglais, followed by a fireworks display.

Nice Jazz Festival   MUSIC FESTIVAL
(www.nicejazzfestival.fr; ☺ Jul) France's original jazz festival has taken on a life of its own, with fringe concerts popping up all around the venue, from Vieux Nice to Massena and the shopping streets around Rue de France.

🛏 Sleeping

Accommodation is excellent and caters to all budgets. Hotels charge substantially more during the Monaco Grand Prix. Book well in advance in summer.

Hôtel Solara   HOTEL €
(☑ 04 93 88 09 96; www.hotelsolara.com; 7 rue de France; s/d/tr/q €65/85/120/150, s/d with balcony €75/115; ☺ reception 8am-9pm; ❄ 🛜) Were it not for its fantastic location on pedestrian rue de France and the sensational terraces that half the rooms boast, we'd say the Solara was an honest-to-goodness budget-friendly choice with impeccable rooms. But with those perks (and did we mention the small fridges in each room for that evening rosé?), it is budget gold. Breakfast €8.

Hôtel Wilson   HOTEL €
(☑ 04 93 85 47 79; www.hotel-wilson-nice.com; 39 rue de l'Hôtel des Postes; s/d €55/69, with shared bathroom €47/59; 🛜) Many years of travelling, an experimental nature and exquisite taste have turned Jean-Marie's rambling 3rd-floor flat into a compelling place to stay. The 16 rooms are individual with carefully crafted decor; the cheapest share bathrooms. Unusually, guests can smoke in some rooms, so ask to see a couple if you're concerned about the smell. Breakfast €6.50.

Hôtel Belle Meunière   HOTEL, HOSTEL €
(☑ 04 93 88 66 15; 21 av Durante; dm €25-30, d/tr/q €84/99/132; 🛜 ❄) This hybrid hotel-hostel, in a 19th-century mansion by the train station, understands it's the little things in life that count: free beach mats to borrow, free parking, left-luggage service (€5 per day, available for nonguests too). Rooms are very basic and a tad tatty; if you want the only room with a balcony, ask for No 9 (a quad). Breakfast €6.

Villa Saint-Exupéry Beach Hostel   HOSTEL €
(☑ 04 93 16 13 45; www.villahostels.com; 6 rue Sacha Guitry; dm €40-50, d/tr €120/150; ❄ @ 🛜) This hostel understands what independent travellers need: facilities galore (bar, kitchen, chill-out lounge, free computers, gym, games room etc), friendly multilingual staff, tons of advice on Nice and the Riviera, and budget-friendly prices. The three- to 14-bed dorms, all with en suite bathrooms, are drab, but for the time you'll spend in them...

★ Nice Pebbles   SELF-CONTAINED €€
(☑ 04 97 20 27 30; www.nicepebbles.com; 1-/2-/3-bedroom apt from €110/190/330; ❄ 🛜) Nice Pebbles' concept is simple: offering the quality of a four-star boutique hotel in

Nice

Gare
du Sud

8

Av de l'Olivetto

R Clément Roassal

Av Mirabeau

R Vernier

R Marceau

Av Malaussena

R Trachel

Bd Raimbaldi

R Miron

Av Désambrois

R Assalit

R de L'épante

Gare Nice
Ville

Tourist
Office

R Pertinax

R de Paris

R de Belgique

Av Notre Dame

R d'Alsace-Lorraine

R E Tiranty

R de Lépante

Av Thiers

14

R Paganini

Av Maréchal Foch

R Biscarra

Cathédrale Orthodoxe
Russe St-Nicolas (450m);
Cannes (30km)

R d'Italie

Av Jean Médecin

R Lamartine

R Spitalieri

Av Georges Clemenceau

R d'Angleterre

R de Russie

63

Nice Étoile
Shopping
Mall

R Guiglia

R Berlioz

R Gounod

Av Auber

R Paul Déroulède

R Alberti

Av Durante

13

R Gustave Déloye

R Pastorelli

R Blacas

R Verdi

R Alphonse Karr

R Sacha
Guitry

R Chauvain

18

Bd Victor Hugo

R du Congrès

R Maccarani

Pass Émile Négrin

22

R du Maréchal Joffre

19

R de la Liberté

Pl
Masséna

35

20

R Masséna

17

R Dalpozzo

R Meyerbeer

R de la Buffa

16

R Paradis

Av de Verdun

R Rivoli

53

R Massenet

R Halévy

11

Jardin
Albert Ier

R St-François de Paule

2

Musée
Masséna

Av de Suède

Tourist
Office

62

33

4

10

Promenade
des Anglais

Promenade des Anglais

Q des États-Unis

Nice-Côte d'Azur
(5.5km)

Mediterranean Sea

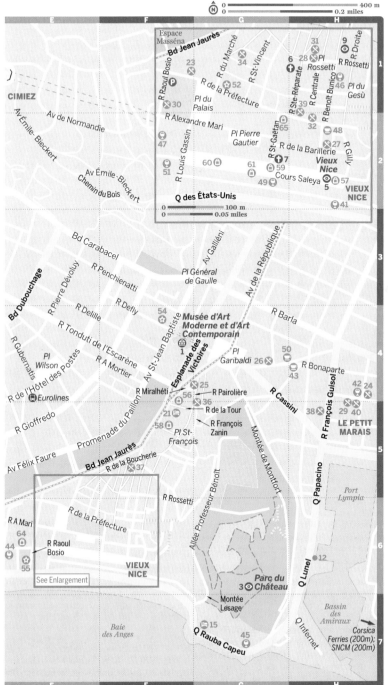

Nice

holiday flats. Apartments and villas (one to five bedrooms) are gorgeous and equipped to high standards. Guests can expect wi-fi, flat-screen TV, DVD players, fully equipped kitchens and linen bedding in most flats, and in some cases a swimming pool, balcony or terrace etc.

★ **Nice Garden Hôtel**　BOUTIQUE HOTEL €€
(☑04 93 87 35 62; www.nicegardenhotel.com; 11 rue du Congrès; s/d/tr from €75/90/138; ⊙reception 8am-9pm; ❋☏) Behind heavy iron gates hides this gem: nine beautifully appointed rooms – the work of the exquisite Marion – are a subtle blend of old and new and overlook a delightful garden with a glorious orange tree. Amazingly, all this charm

and peacefulness is just two blocks from the promenade. Breakfast €9.

Hôtel Villa Rivoli　BOUTIQUE HOTEL €€
(☑04 93 88 80 25; www.villa-rivoli.com; 10 rue de Rivoli; s/d/q from €95/175/198; ❋☏) Built in 1890, this stately villa feels like your own pied-à-terre in the heart of Nice. A marble staircase leads to spotlessly clean character-rich rooms, some with fabric-covered walls, gilt-edged mirrors and marble mantelpieces. Breakfast €12, parking €18.

Villa La Tour　BOUTIQUE HOTEL €€
(☑04 93 80 08 15; www.villa-la-tour.com; 4 rue de la Tour; d €70-172; ❋☏) This old-town favourite has 17 lovely rooms, each individually decorated to evoke a different artist – Niki

de Saint Phalle, Vaco, Klein and so forth. Riviera history buffs will appreciate the Queen Victoria room. A diminutive flower-decked roof terrace is complemented by a street terrace, ideal for watching Vieux Nice go by. Breakfast €12.50.

Hôtel Windsor BOUTIQUE HOTEL €€
(📞04 93 88 59 35; www.hotelwindsornice.com; 11 rue Dalpozzo; d €97-215; ❄@🛜🏊) High-profile artists have decorated several rooms at the Windsor with bold, sometimes unsettling designs. Traditional rooms are more soothing yet still nod to the arts with hand-painted murals. Breakfast €14, parking €13 to €19.

⭐**Hôtel La Pérouse** BOUTIQUE HOTEL €€€
(📞04 93 62 34 63; www.hotel-la-perouse.com; 11 quai Rauba Capeu; d from €330; ❄@🛜🏊) Built into the rock cliff next to Tour Bellanda, La Pérouse evokes the spirit of a genteel villa. Lower-floor rooms face a lemon-tree-shaded courtyard and pool; upper-floor rooms have magnificent sea vistas. Smart accent colours add flair to the traditional decor. Best rates are online. Breakfast €18.

Exedra DESIGN HOTEL €€€
(📞04 97 03 89 89; www.boscolohotels.com; 12 bd Victor Hugo; d from €370; ❄@🛜🏊) This historic, belle époque mansion squirrels away one of Nice's sexiest, most contemporary establishments. Everything from the furniture and fabrics to bathrooms, art works and parquetry are brilliant white with the odd hint of ivory. The icing on this dazzling five-star (white) cake is a super-chic spa and pool.

🍴 Eating

Booking is essential for weekend meals, particularly during the busy summer season. To lunch with locals, grab a pew in the midday sun on one of the many place Garibaldi cafe terraces.

⭐**Chez Pipo** NIÇOIS €
(📞04 93 55 88 82; 13 rue Bavastro; socca €2.70; ⏰11.30am-2.30pm & 5.30-11pm Tue-Sun) This bistro, with its inviting ginger-toned terrace, has cooked up some of Nice's best *socca* (savoury, chickpea-flour pancake) since 1923. For gourmets seeking something more refined than stand-up street food, Pipo is sit-down perfect.

⭐**La Rossettisserie** ROTISSERIE €
(📞04 93 76 18 80; www.larossettisserie.com; 8 rue Mascoïnat; mains €14.50-15.50; ⏰noon-2pm

DON'T MISS

ICE CREAM

Bags of spots sell it, but the best ice cream in Nice is made by *maître glacier* (master ice-cream maker) **Fenocchio** (www.fenocchio.fr; 2 place Rossetti; 1/2/3 scoops €2/3.50/5; ⏰9am-midnight Feb-Oct), in the biz since 1966. Dither too long over the 70-plus flavours of ice cream and sorbet and you'll never make it to the front of the queue. Eschew predictable favourites and indulge in a new taste sensation: black olive, thyme, rosemary, lavender, ginger chocolate, violet or typical Niçois *tourte de blette* (a sweet Swiss Chard tart made with raisins, pine kernels and parmesan cheese). Fenocchio has a **second shop** (📞04 93 62 88 80; www.fenocchio.fr; 6 rue de la Poissonerie; ⏰9am-midnight Wed-Mon).

& 7.30-10pm Mon-Sat) The Rossettisserie – a lovely play of words on rotisserie (roast house) and Rossetti (the name of the nearby square) – is a retro grocery-style space known for its succulent roast meat. Pair your choice of beef, chicken, veal or lamb with heavenly homemade mash or sautéed potatoes and ratatouille or salad. The vaulted dining room in the basement is stunning.

Déli Bo CAFE, BISTRO €
(📞04 93 56 33 04; 5 rue Bonaparte; mains €12-20; ⏰7am-8pm) Packed inside and out with knowing Niçois, this hybrid coffee shop-restaurant gets everything superbly right: a short but perfectly executed menu of chic home cuisine including several gutsy meal-sized salads, exquisite *pâtisserie* (cakes) and a relaxed urban vibe. Find it on one of Nice's most happening streets, just north of Port Lympia.

La Merenda NIÇOIS €
(www.lamerenda.net; 4 rue Raoul Bosio; mains €14-16; ⏰noon-2pm & 7-10pm Mon-Fri) Simple, solid Niçois cuisine – stockfish, calf tripe à la Niçoise with *panisse* (chunky, pan-fried sticks of chickpea-flour batter) and the like – by former Michelin-starred chef Dominique Le Stanc draws the crowds to this pocket-sized bistro where diners rub shoulders literally. The tiny open kitchen stands proud at the back of the room, and the equally small menu is chalked on the board. No credit cards.

Le Comptoir du Marché   MODERN FRENCH €
(☑04 93 13 45 01; 8 rue du Marché; mains €13-18; ⊙noon-2.30pm & 7-10.30pm Tue-Sat) With its vintage kitchen decor and great-value prices, the Comptoir does predictably well. There are five or six daily mains, scribbled on a chalkboard. The cuisine is a modern twist on traditional French recipes, with lots of offals and staples like lentil stews, confit rabbit and even *os à moelle* (bone marrow).

★**Olive et Artichaut**   PROVENÇAL €€
(☑04 89 14 97 51; www.oliveartichaut.com; 6 rue Ste-Réparate; mains €16-25; ⊙noon-2pm & 7.30-10pm Wed-Sun) Inspired by the market and his city's rich culinary roots, young Niçois chef Thomas Hubert is rapidily carving out a grand name for himself at Olive and Artichoke. The kitchen is open, the decor is contemporary design with a hip splash of vintage, and the cuisine is a magnificent reworking of local ingredients grown by small producers and farmers. Reserve or hope for a bar stool *au comptoir* (at the bar).

★**Vinivore**   BISTRO €€
(☑04 93 14 68 09; www.vinivore.fr; 10 rue Lascaris; mains €16-23; ⊙noon-2pm & 7.30-10pm Tue-Fri, 7.30-10pm Sat) The name gives it away. Carnivores with a penchant for fine *vin* (wine), this remarkable little bistro is for you. Among the 200 different wines – many organic and by small producers – are the perfect partners for chef Chun Wong's two or

three market-driven dishes chalked on the blackboad. His lunchtime *plat du jour* (dish of the day; €11.50) is always excellent value.

L'Uzine   MEDITERRANEAN €€
(☑04 93 56 42 39; 18 rue François Guisol; mains €14-20; ⊙11am-11pm Tue-Sat) This relaxed restaurant lures a young, vibrant crowd thanks to its large buzzing pavement terrace in the trendy Port Lympia area and top-quality Mediterranean cuisine. Throw live jazz on weekend evenings into the mix and the result is an address not to be missed.

Carré Llorca   BISTRO €€
(☑04 93 92 95 86; www.carrellorca.com; 3 rue de la Préfecture; mains €18-28; ⊙noon-10.30pm Mon-Sat) The menu at this contemporary bistro with urban spirit is signed off by Michelin-starred chef Jean-Michel Llorca. Neutral hues add an understated elegance to the clean-cut space, and the cuisine is Mediterranean with a generous dash of Niçois – lots of cooking *à la plancha* (grilled). The *poulpe* (octopus) served with new potatoes and Niçois sauces is delicious.

L'Escalinada   NIÇOIS €€
(☑04 93 62 11 71; 22 rue Pairolière; mains €20-25; ⊙noon-2.30pm & 7-11pm) L'Escalinada has been brilliant for grassroots Niçois cuisine for the last half-century: *petits farcis* (stuffed vegetables), homemade gnocchi with tasty *daube* (Provençal beef stew) and Marsala veal stew see tables packed jaw to jowl on a tiny pavement terrace in Vieux Nice. The complimentary aperitif is a welcome touch. No credit cards.

Le Bistrot d'Antoine   MODERN FRENCH €€
(☑04 93 85 29 57; 27 rue de la Préfecture; menus €25 & €43, mains €14-25; ⊙noon-2pm & 7-10pm Tue-Sat) What's so surprising about this super brasserie is how unfazed it is by its incredible success: it is full every night (booking essential), yet the 'bistro chic' cuisine never wavers, the staff are cool as a cucumber, the atmosphere is reliably jovial and the prices incredibly good value for the area.

Le Luna Rossa   ITALIAN €€
(☑04 93 85 55 66; 3 rue Chauvain; mains €15-30; ⊙noon-3pm & 7-11pm Tue-Fri, 7-11pm Sat; ☑) The Red Moon is like your dream Mediterranean dinner come true: fresh pasta, exquisitely cooked seafood, sun-kissed vegetables and divine meats. Wash it down with one of the excellent bottles of red or rosé from the cellar.

SNACKING À LA NIÇOISE

Essential tasting for every curious palate is the Niçois speciality *socca*, a savoury, griddle-fried pancake made from chickpea flour and olive oil, sprinkled with a liberal dose of black pepper. Also typical are *petits farcis* (stuffed vegetables), *pissaladière* (traditional onion tart topped with black olives and anchovies) and the many vegetable *beignets* (fritters).

Try them at **Chez René Socca** (2 rue Miralhéti; small plates €3-6; ⊙9am-9pm Tue-Sun, to 10.30pm Jul & Aug, closed Nov; ☑) or **Lou Pilha Leva** (☑04 93 13 99 08; 10 rue du Collet; small plates €2.80-4; ⊙9am-midnight; ☑), two dead-casual joints where a merry crowd sits around shared outdoor benches with a glass of rosé.

★ **Jan**   MODERN FRENCH €€€

(☏ 04 97 19 32 23; www.restaurantjan.com; 12 rue Lascaris; 2-/3-course lunch menu €25/32, dinner menus €52 & €72, mains €26-32; ⊘ 6.30-10pm Tue-Thu & Sat, noon-2pm & 6.30-10pm Fri) An advance reservation (which must then be confirmed by phone the day you dine) is essential at this elegant dining room, the gourmet kingdom of South African wonder-chef Jan Hendrik van der Westhuizen. Antipodean influences are light in the menu but more pronounced in the wine list. There is no à la carte menu – just a divine choice of market-sourced tasting menus.

Le Chantecler   GASTRONOMIC €€€

(☏ 04 93 16 64 00; www.hotel-negresco-nice.com; Hôtel Negresco, 37 promenade des Anglais; menus €110 & €230, mains €62-85; ⊘ dinner Wed-Sun, lunch Sun) In a sumptuous pink Regency dining room, the Negresco's twin-Michelin-starred restaurant, run by locally trained chef Jean-Denis Rieubland, is no ordinary place. Exquisite culinary creations are accompanied by the expertise of an exceptional sommelier, who will match every course with a wine or recommend a bottle for your meal.

🍷 Drinking & Nightlife

Cafe terraces on cours Saleya are lovely for an early-evening aperitif. Vieux Nice's bounty of pubs attracts a noisy, boisterous crowd. Or follow the hipsters to Le Petit Marais in the Port Lympia area, where a clutch of trendy eating and drinking addresses entice.

★ **Ark**   LOUNGE BAR

(41 quai des États-Unis; ⊘ 11am-1am) The Nice drinking scene suddenly became a whole load more glamorous with the 2015 opening of Ark, a super-chic lounge bar wedged between the sea and cours Saleya. Snag a seat on one of the drop-dead-gorgeous 2nd-floor balconies gazing out at the Med and you'll know you've hit Nice's jetsetter jackpot.

El Merkado   BAR

(www.el-merkado.com; 12 rue St-François de Paule; ⊘ 10.30am-1.30am) Footsteps from cours Saleya, this hip tapas bar struts its vintage stuff on the ground floor of a quintessential burnt-terracotta-and-green Niçois townhouse. Lounging on its pavement terrace or a sofa over after-beach drinks is the thing to do. Freshly squeezed fruit juices, artisanal mixers, a different house cocktail each day and top tapas make the place buzz.

LOCAL KNOWLEDGE

LE PETIT MARAIS

Parisians might scoff at the idea, but Le Petit Marais in Nice is nicknamed after the trendy Marais district in Paris for good reason. The Niçois *quartier* – the area of town wedged between place Garibaldi and Port Lympia – buzzes with happening eating, drinking and boutique-shopping addreses, firmly off the tourist radar but in the address book of every trendy local. Stroll the lengths of rue Bonaparte, rue Bavestro, rue Lascaris and surrounding streets to catch the city's latest hot new opening.

La Shounga   COCKTAIL BAR

(http://shounga.fr/; 12 place Guynemer; ⊘ 8.30am-12.30am; 🛜) Seriously decadent, all-day desserts, ice-cream sundaes and cocktails (€8.50) are the reason to hit the sea-facing terrace of this vibrant mojito bar. Oh, and did we mention the soft comfy armchairs, free wi-fi and 2L jugs of classic or fruit-laced mojitos (€30)? Find it on the promenade between Vieux Nice and the port.

Comptoir Central Électrique   CAFE, BAR

(www.comptoircentralelectrique.fr; 10 rue Bonaparte; ⊘ 8.30am-12.30am Mon-Sat) Potted olive trees flag the generous pavement terrace of this happening bar, one of a bunch to mushroom in the increasingly trendy Port Lympia area. Come here for wine, beer, spirits and a fabulously upcycled interior with sofas, library and eye-catching lightbulb collection evocative of the bar's former life as a lighting factory.

Little Rest'O   CAFE

(www.ateliertsade.com; 15 rue Bonaparte; ⊘ 9am-6pm Tue & Wed, to 11pm Thu-Sat) For tea in a porcelain teapot, lunch with girlfriends or a sweet aperitif, there is no more flouncy, overtly feminine address than this hybrid tearoom-gallery with art works on the walls and light bites to eat. Fresh flowers, old-fashioned glass jars of sweets and period Louis VI armchairs add bags of character to the almost theatrical decor.

BaR'Oc   WINE BAR

(10 rue Bavastro; ⊘ 7pm-12.30am) This vibrant bar is a buzzing spot for fine wine in the company of yummy tapas - parma ham and fig *tartines* (toasts), roasted chorizo or oven-baked *figatelli* (a type of salami from Corsica) – and tasting platters of cheese

and cold cuts. Two saggy scarlet sofas glam up the wooden deck out front, on which punters snuggle up in glitzy red shawls on friskier evenings.

Les Distilleries Idéales   CAFE
(www.lesdistilleriesideales.fr; 24 rue de la Préfecture; ⊙9am-12.30am) Whether you're after *un café* (a coffee) or *apéro* (predinner drink) with cheese or charcuterie platter, Les Distilleries is one atmospheric bar. Watch the world go by on the narrow street terrace or hang out inside with the 'happy hour' crowd and a good-value cocktail between 6pm and 8pm.

Ma Nolan's   PUB
(www.ma-nolans.com; 2 rue St-François de Paule; ⊙noon-2am Mon-Fri, 11am-2am Sat & Sun; 🛜) This Irish pub is big, loud and *the* pub of reference for all foreigners in town (there are plenty more like this). With live music, a pub quiz, big sport events and typical pub food (burgers, fish and chips etc), it's a pretty rowdy place. Happy hour is from 6pm to 8pm.

Le Six   GAY BAR
(www.le6.fr; 6 rue Raoul Bosio; ⊙10pm-5am Tue-Sat) Primped and pretty A-gays crowd shoulder to shoulder at Nice's compact, perennially popular gay bar. Le 6 keeps a busy event/party schedule: guest DJs, karaoke, and shower shows.

L'Abat-Jour   BAR, CLUB
(25 rue Benoît Bunico; ⊙6.30pm-2.30am Tue-Sat) With its vintage furniture, basement DJ sessions and alternative music, L'Abat-Jour is all the rage with trendies. Check its Facebook page for events.

Les Trois Diables   CLUB
(www.les3diables.com; 2 cours Saleya; ⊙5pm-2am) This stalwart of Nice's party scene ensures its longevity with a good-hearted mix of weeknight-friendly events (music quiz on Tuesday, karaoke on Wednesday) and DJs to spice up the weekend. Happy hour runs to 9pm every night.

☆ Entertainment

Nice has a strong live-music tradition, from pop rock to jazz and cabaret; many bars regularly host bands.

Le Volume   LIVE MUSIC
(www.source001.com; 6 rue Defly; ⊙11am-9pm Mon, to 12.30am Tue-Thu, to 1am Fri & Sat, 8.30pm-12.30am Sun; 🛜) This dynamic cafe, cultural centre and live-music venue is the place to tune into the current and emerging music scene. Live music and jam sessions most nights from 9pm.

Chez Wayne's   LIVE MUSIC
(www.waynes.fr; 15 rue de la Préfecture; ⊙10am-2am) Raucous watering hole Chez Wayne's is a typical English pub, with live bands every night. The pub is also sports-mad and shows every rugby, football, Aussie Rules, tennis and cricket game worth watching.

Opéra de Nice   OPERA
(www.opera-nice.org; 4-6 rue St-François de Paule) The vintage 1885 grande dame hosts operas, ballets and orchestral concerts.

Cinéma Rialto   CINEMA
(http://lerialto.cine.allocine.fr; 4 rue de Rivoli) Undubbed films, with French subtitles.

🛍 Shopping

Shops abound in Nice, ranging from the touristy boutiques of Vieux Nice to the designer temples to fashion around rue de France and the enormous **Nice Étoile** (www.nicetoile.com; av Jean Médecin) shopping mall. For vintage (fashion and objects) and contemporary art, meander the hip Petit Marais north of Port Lympia. For gourmet gifts to take home, try the following places:

Moulin à Huile d'Olive Alziari   FOOD
(www.alziari.com.fr; 14 rue St-François de Paule; ⊙8.30am-12.30pm & 2-7pm Mon-Sat) Superb olive oil, fresh from the mill on the outskirts of Nice; Alziari also produces a dizzying variety of tapenades, fresh olives and other *apéro* snacks.

Cave de la Tour   WINE
(www.cavedelatour.com; 3 rue de la Tour; ⊙7am-8pm Tue-Sat) Buy wine from *cavistes* (cellarmen) who know what they're talking about: Cave de la Tour has been run by the same family since 1947.

Pâtisserie LAC   FOOD
(www.patisseries-lac.com; cnr rues de la Préfecture & St-Gaëtan; ⊙9.30am-1pm & 2.30-7.30pm Tue-Sun) Macaroons and chocolates from chef *pâtissier* Pascal Lac.

Pâtisserie Henri Auer Confiserie   FOOD
(www.maison-auer.com; 7 rue St-François de Paule; ⊙9am-6pm Tue-Sat) Crystallised fruit, with recipes dating to 1820.

ⓘ Information

Hôpital St-Roch (☎04 92 03 33 75; www.chu-nice.fr; 5 rue Pierre Dévoluy; ⊗24hr)
Police Station (☎04 92 17 22 22; 1 av Maréchal Foch; ⊗24hr) Non-French speakers can call ☎04 92 17 20 31, where translators are on hand.
Tourist Office (☎08 92 70 74 07; www.nicetourisme.com; 5 promenade des Anglais; ⊗9am-6pm Mon-Sat) There's also a branch in front of the train station (av Thiers; ⊗8am-7pm Mon-Sat, 10am-5pm Sun).

ⓘ Getting There & Away

AIR
Nice-Côte d'Azur Airport (☎08 20 42 33 33; www.nice.aeroport.fr; ☎) France's second-largest airport has two terminals, linked by free shuttle.

BOAT
Nice is the main port for ferries to Corsica. **SNCM** (www.sncm.fr; quai du Commerce) and **Corsica Ferries** (www.corsicaferries.com; quai du Commerce) are two main companies.

BUS
There is an excellent intercity bus service from Nice; tickets cost just €1.50.
➡ Bus 100 goes to Menton (1½ hours) via the Corniche Inférieure and Monaco (40 minutes).
➡ Bus 200 goes to Cannes (1½ hours).
➡ Bus 400 goes to Vence (1¼ hours) via St-Paul de Vence (one hour).
➡ Bus 500 goes to Grasse (1½ hours).

Eurolines (www.eurolines.com; 27 rue de l'Hôtel des Postes) serves long-haul European destinations.

TRAIN

DESTINATION	FARE	DURATION	FREQUENCY
Cannes	€5.90	40 minutes	hourly
Grasse	€9.30	1¼ hours	hourly
Marseille	€35	2½ hours	hourly
Menton	€4.60	35 minutes	half-hourly
Monaco	€3.30	25 minutes	half-hourly
St-Raphaël	€11.50	1¼ hours	hourly

ⓘ Getting Around

TO/FROM THE AIRPORT
Nice-Côte d'Azur Airport is 6km west of Nice, by the sea. A taxi to Nice's centre from the rank outside the terminal costs €23 to €31 (€28 to €33 between 6pm and 7am).

WORTH A TRIP

TRAIN DES PIGNES

The narrow-gauge railway Train des Pignes (p302), chugging between the mountains and the sea, is one of Provence's most picturesque rides. The 151km track between Nice and Digne-les-Bains rises to 1000m for breathtaking views as it passes through Haute-Provence's scarcely populated backcountry.

The service runs five times a day and is ideal for a day trip inland. The beautiful medieval village of **Entrevaux** is just 1½ hours from Nice (return €20.60), perfect for a picnic and a wander through its historic centre and citadel.

NICE, MONACO & MENTON NICE

➡ Buses 98 and 99 link the airport's terminal with promenade des Anglais and Nice train station respectively (€6, 35 minutes, every 20 minutes).
➡ Bus 110 (€20, hourly) links the airport with Monaco (40 minutes) and Menton (one hour).
➡ Bus 210 goes to Cannes (€20, 50 minutes, half-hourly); bus 250 to Antibes (€10, 55 minutes, half-hourly).

BICYCLE
Vélo Bleu (☎04 93 72 06 06; www.velobleu.org) Nice's shared-bicycle service has 100-plus stations around the city – pick up wheels at one, return at another. One-day/week subscriptions costs €1/5, plus usage: free the first 30 minutes, €1 the next 30, then €2 per hour thereafter. Some stations are equipped with terminals to register directly with a credit card; otherwise you'll need a mobile phone. The handy 'Vélo Bleu' app allows you to find your nearest station, gives real-time information about the number of bikes available at each and calculates itineraries.
Holiday Bikes (www.holiday-bikes.com; 23 rue de Belgique) Rents out 50cc scooters/125cc motorcycles for €30/55.

BUS & TRAM
Buses and trams in Nice are run by **Ligne d'Azur** (www.lignesdazur.com). Tickets cost €1.50. A second tram line linking place Masséna with the airport along promenade des Anglais is planned for late 2017.

Buses are handy to get to Cimiez and the port. Night buses run from around 9pm until 2am.

The tram is great for getting across town, particularly from the train station to Vieux Nice and place Garibaldi. Trams run from 4.30am to 1.30am.

Major car-rental companies have offices at the train station. To go native, opt for two wheels.

Taxi Riviera (☑ 04 93 13 78 78; www.taxis-nice.fr)

ARRIÈRE-PAYS NIÇOIS

This quiet, little-known corner of the Côte d'Azur, 20km inland from Nice, is where Niçois come to weekend away from the urban rush. Attractions are low-key: a walk in the hills (consult www.randoxygene.org for itinerary ideas), a stroll in isolated villages, or a long lunch in a tasty *auberge* (country inn) There is a bus to Peille, but your own wheels are best.

Peillon

POP 1420

This spectacular hilltop village has long been prized by local populations for its defensive characteristics: the first houses date to the 10th century. What draws visitors from far and wide, however, is not the sleepy village but Auberge de la Madone (☑ 04 93 79 91 17; www.auberge-madone-peillon.com; 3 place Auguste Arnulf; menus from €30; ⊙ lunch & dinner Thu-Tue Feb-Oct; 🛜), where father-and-son chef-duo Christian and Thomas Millo cook up Provençal staples with a dash of modernity. Indulge in their superb cuisine in a grand dining room in winter or on a panoramic terrace in summer. And if you really cannot move after devouring Swiss chard tart with herbs, cod fillet in spice crust, Muscat pan-fried strawberries with sorbet and almond biscuit and the like, ask about one of the hotel rooms (from €98) up top.

Peille

POP 2329

Peille may not be as spectacular as Peillon, but it makes up for it with history. The village's excellent Point Info Tourisme (☑ 04 93 82 14 40; 15 rue centrale; ⊙ 10am-noon & 1-6pm Wed-Sun) offers free, tailor-made guided tours depending on how much time you have (available in English and Italian). Highlights include the medieval centre, the village museum, the church and old photographs of the village.

Then there is Peille's via ferrata (☑ 04 93 79 95 75; http://peille.free.fr/index.php; admission €3, equipment hire €16; ⊙ 9am-6pm, closed Thu afternoon low season), a daredevil mountain course equipped with ladders, fixed cables, rope bridges etc. No previous experience is required, but you must be sure-footed, reasonably fit and not scared of heights. The course takes about four hours to complete; pay admission at the tourist office or Bar l'Absinthe (☑ 04 93 79 95 75; 6 rue Félix Faure; ⊙ 8am-9pm Mon-Fri, 9am-9pm Sat & Sun, shorter hours Oct-Apr), where you can also rent equipment (€16 for helmet, harness, ropes, carabiners etc). A mountain guide costs €45 and must be booked in advance.

Bus 116 (€1.50) links Peille with La Turbie (20 minutes) and Nice (one hour) three times a day.

THE THREE CORNICHES

This trio of *corniches* (coastal roads) hugs the cliffs between Nice and Monaco, each higher than the last, with dazzling views of the Med.

Corniche Inférieure

Skimming the villa-lined waterfront between Nice and Monaco, the Corniche Inférieure, built in the 1860s, passes through the towns of Villefranche-sur-Mer, St-Jean-Cap Ferrat, Beaulieu-sur-Mer, Èze-sur-Mer and Cap d'Ail.

❶ Getting There & Around

Bus 100 (€1.50, every 15 minutes between 6am and 8pm) runs the length of the Corniche Inférieure between Nice and Menton, stopping at all the villages along the way, including Ville-franche-sur-Mer (15 minutes), Beaulieu-sur-Mer (20 minutes) and Cap d'Ail (35 minutes). Bus 81 serves Villefranche (20 minutes) and St-Jean-Cap Ferrat (30 minutes).

From Nice, trains to Ventimiglia in Italy (every 30 minutes, 5am to 11pm) stop at Ville-franche-sur-Mer (€1.20, seven minutes), Beau-lieu-sur-Mer (€1.60, 10 minutes) and Cap d'Ail (€2.80, 18 minutes).

Villefranche-sur-Mer

POP 5416

Heaped above an idyllic harbour, this picturesque village with imposing citadel overlooks the Cap Ferrat peninsula and, thanks to its deep harbour, is a prime port of call for cruise ships. The 14th-century old town, with its tiny, evocatively named streets broken by twisting staircases and glimpses of the sea, is a delight to amble (preferably broken with a long lazy lunch on the water's edge or a bijou old-town square).

◎ Sights & Activities

In the Vieille Ville (old town) don't miss eerie, arcaded rue Obscure, a historical monument a block in from the water.

La Citadelle   FORTRESS
(⌚ 04 93 76 33 27; place Emmanuel Philibert; ⌚ 10am-noon & 3-6.30pm Mon-Sat, 3-6.30pm Sun Jun-Sep, to 5.30pm Oct & Dec-May) FREE Villefranche's imposing citadel, also called Fort St-Elme and worth a visit for its impressive architecture, was built by the duke of Savoy between 1554 and 1559 to defend the gulf. Its walls today shelter the town hall, well-combed public gardens and several museum collections: the Fondation Musée Volti (⌚ 04 93 76 33 27; ⌚ 9am-noon & 2.30-7pm Mon & Wed-Sat, 2.30-7pm Sun Jul & Aug, to 6pm Mon & Wed-Sat Jun & Sep) FREE displays voluptuous bronzes by Villefranche sculptor Antoniucci Volti (1915–89); the Musée Goetz-Boumeester displays modern art in the citadel's former living quarters; and the Collection Roux comprises several hundred ceramic figurines depicting life in medieval and Renaissance times.

Chapelle St-Pierre   CHURCH
(admission €3; ⌚ 10am-noon & 3-7pm Wed-Mon Apr-Sep, 10am-noon & 2-6pm Oct-Mar, closed mid-Nov–mid-Dec) Villefranche was a favourite of Jean Cocteau (1889–1963), who sought solace here in 1924 after the death of his companion Raymond Radiguet. Several years later, Cocteau convinced locals to let him paint the neglected, 14th-century Chapelle St-Pierre, which he transformed into a mirage of mystical frescoes. Scenes from St Peter's life are interspersed with references to Cocteau's cinematic work (notably the drivers from *Orpheus*) and friends (Francine Weisweiller, whose Villa Santo Sospir in St-Jean-Cap Ferrat Cocteau also decorated; see p60).

Affrètement Maritime
Villefranchois   BOAT TOUR
(⌚ 04 93 76 65 65; www.amv-sirenes.com; Port de la Santé; ⌚ Jun-Sep) Since the creation of an international marine-mammal sanctuary between France, Monaco and Italy in 1999, a number of cetaceans frequent Riviera waters. Dolphins are common; more occasional are sperm whales and fin whales. Keep your eyes peeled during a half-day dolphin- and whale-watching expedition (adult/child €48/38). The company also organises two-hour boat trips to Monaco (adult/child €20/17).

🛏 Sleeping

La Vigne   B&B €€
(⌚ 06 18 85 75 95; www.lavigne-villefranche.com; 1387 av Léopold II; d €95-105; 🛜 🛗) The Vine is a stylish *maison d'hôte* (B&B) with a trio of simple rooms in a 1930s villa, 20 minutes on foot (1.2km) from the Vieille Ville. Living is easy and gourmet – there is no TV, just a library to browse, olive and fruit trees to seek shade between, a car called Caroline and a boat to Anaïs to explore the area with.

Picnic hampers for two (€20) and dinner (€25 to €40 per person) available on request. Cooking classes, photography workshops and French lessons too.

★ Hôtel Welcome   BOUTIQUE HOTEL €€€
(⌚ 04 93 76 27 62; www.welcomehotel.com; 3 quai Amiral Courbet; d from €235; ⌚ Jan-Oct; ❄ @ 🛜) Unusually, all 35 rooms at this burnt-orange seafront hotel have balcony and sea view. Those on the 6th floor are predictably the best, but watching the fishers pull into harbour to sell their catch is an early-morning joy from every room. Decor is faintly nautical and the hotel has a 12-man boat with skipper (and swimming towels) for guests to rent.

🍴 Eating & Drinking

Dolce Vita   CAFE €
(⌚ 04 93 01 71 31; 17 quai de l'Amiral Courbet; ⌚ 8.30am-midnight May-Sep, to 5pm Oct-Apr) Among the generous line-up of restaurant terraces along the seafront, the Sweet Life is a favourite for its hip, shabby-chic lounge-bar vibe and international bistro cuisine. Pick from comfy sofa seating by the bar or a table on the water's edge.

La Grignotière   BRASSERIE €
(3 rue Poilu; pizza €10-13, mains €14-21, menu €18; ⌚ noon-2pm & 7.30-9.30pm; 🛗) For a cheap and cheerful fill, there is no finer address along the coast than La Grignotière, known far and wide for its generous portions of grilled fish and veg, lasagne, pizza and other crowd-pleasers. Decor is old-fashioned and nothing to rave about, but the place is charming and unpretentious. It has a few tables on the pedestrian street.

★ Les Garçons   MEDITERRANEAN €€
(🖉04 93 76 62 40; 18 rue du Poilu; mains €20-26; ⏰noon-2.30pm & 7.30-10.30pm Thu-Mon) Gourmets in the know flock to this stylish address, buried in Villefranche's rabbit warren of ancient old-town backstreets. In summer tables sprawl elegantly across a bijou stone square, romantically lit by twinkling lights after dark. Cuisine is creative, local and driven by the market and local fishers' catch. Red tuna tartare with avocado is a delicious all-year staple.

La Mère Germaine   SEAFOOD €€€
(🖉04 93 01 71 39; www.meregermaine.com; 7 quai Amiral Courbet; menu €46, mains €31-51; ⏰noon-2pm & 7-10.30pm) In business since 1938, La Mère Germaine is an upmarket address for seafood, fish and more seafood, washed down with a splendid choice of wine.

ⓘ Information

Tourist Office (🖉04 93 01 73 68; www.villefranche-sur-mer.com; Port de la Santé, Jardin François Binon; ⏰10am-5pm Wed-Mon) From April to September the tourist office runs Friday-morning guided tours (€5, 1½ hours) of the citadel museums and old town. It also has information on family workshops (adult/child €5/3) held in the citadel museums.

Beaulieu-sur-Mer & St-Jean-Cap Ferrat

The seaside holiday town of Beaulieu-sur-Mer (population 3796) is well known for its well-preserved belle époque architecture. It sits at the beginning of Cap Ferrat, a wooded peninsula laden with millionaires' villas and home to the small village of St-Jean-Cap Ferrat (population 1913).

◉ Sights & Activities

★ Villa Santo Sospir   HISTORIC MANSION
(🖉04 93 76 00 16; www.villasantosospir.fr; 14 av Jean Cocteau, St-Jean-Cap Ferrat; guided tour €12; ⏰by appointment only) This villa belongs to the Weisweiller family, patrons of Jean Cocteau. In 1950 Cocteau asked Francine Weisweiller (1916–2003) if he could paint the living room. Soon the entire villa was covered in frescoes – possible to admire during 45-minute guided tours led by Eric Marteau, Francine Weisweiller's former nurse and now the villa's guardian. Weisweiller was a well-known Parisian socialite and Marteau got to know her well. His tours are therefore peppered with anecdotes about

Cocteau, Weisweiller and their peers, which means both the listening and the viewing are compelling. Book tours at least the day before.

Villa Ephrussi de Rothschild   HISTORIC MANSION
(www.villa-ephrussi.com/en; St-Jean-Cap Ferrat; adult/child €13/10; ⏰10am-6pm Mar-Oct, 2-6pm Nov-Feb) An over-the-top belle époque confection, this villa was commissioned by Baroness Béatrice Ephrussi de Rothschild in 1912. She was an avid art collector and the villa is filled with Fragonard paintings, Louis XVI furniture and Sèvres porcelain. From its balcony, nine exquisite themed gardens appear like a ship's deck. Stunning in spring, the Spanish, Japanese, Florentine, stone, cactus, rose and French gardens are delightful to stroll through – sea views are supreme and fountains 'dance' to classical music every 20 minutes.

Bus 81, which links Nice and St-Jean-Cap Ferrat, stops at the foot of the driveway leading to the villa (bus stop 'Passable').

Villa Grecque Kérylos   HISTORIC MANSION
(🖉04 93 01 01 44; www.villa-kerylos.com; Impasse Gustave Eiffel, Beaulieu-sur-Mer; adult/child €11.50/9; ⏰10am-7pm Jul & Aug, 10am-6pm Mar-Oct, 2-6pm Mon-Fri, 10am-6pm Sat & Sun Nov-Feb) This magnificent villa is a reproduction of a 1st-century Athenian villa, complete with baths, stunning mosaic floors and furniture such as dining recliners. It was designed by scholar-archaeologist Théodore Reinach in 1902, at a time when the must-have for well-to-do socialites was an eccentric house on the Côte d'Azur.

★ Cap Ferrat   WALKING
This dreamy peninsula is laced with 14km of eucalyptus-scented walking paths, all with magnificent views and wonderful coastline all the way. There are various itineraries, all easy going; tourist offices have maps.

🛏 Sleeping & Eating

Hôtel Riviera   HOTEL €€
(🖉04 93 01 04 92; www.hotel-riviera.fr; 6 rue Paul Doumer, Beaulieu-sur-Mer; d €79-130; ⏰reception 7.30am-7pm Jan-Oct; ❄🐾📶) A breath of fresh air, this tasteful two-star hotel with wrought-iron balconies and a hibiscus-laden summer patio perfect for breakfasting is hard to resist. Rooms are immaculate and comfortable, and the owners charming. Probably the best value on the coast.

Le Sloop
SEAFOOD €€

(☑04 93 01 48 63; www.restaurantsloop.com; Port de Plaisance, St-Jean-Cap Ferrat; mains €18-25; ☺noon-1.30pm & 7-9.30pm Thu-Tue) With its elegant red-and-blue nautical decor and portside terrace within grasp of the bobbing yachts, Le Sloop is a cut above the rest on this popular restaurant strip. Its seafood and shellfish are uberfresh and good value.

ℹ Information

Tourist Office (☑04 93 01 01 21; www.beaulieusurmer.fr; place Georges Clémenceau, Beaulieu-sur-Mer; ☺9am-6.30pm Mon-Sat, to 12.30pm Sun Jul & Aug, shorter hours rest of the year)

Tourist Office (☑04 93 76 08 90; www.saintjeancapferrat.fr; 5 & 59 av Denis Séméria, St-Jean-Cap Ferrat; ☺9am-4pm Mon-Fri)

Moyenne Corniche

Cut through rock in the 1920s, the Moyenne Corniche takes drivers from Nice past the Col de Villefranche (149m), Èze and Beausoleil (the French town bordering Monaco's Monte Carlo).

ℹ Getting There & Around

Bus 82 serves the Moyenne Corniche from Nice all the way to Èze (20 minutes); bus 112 carries on to Beausoleil (40 minutes, Monday to Saturday).

Èze
POP 2574

This rocky little village perched on an impossible peak is the jewel in the Riviera crown. The main attraction is the medieval village itself, with small higgledy-piggledy stone houses and winding lanes (and plenty of galleries and shops), and the mesmerising views of the coast.

You'll get the best panorama from Jardin Exotique d'Èze (☑04 93 41 10 30; adult/child €6/2.50; ☺9am-sunset), a cactus garden at the top of the village. It's also where you'll find the old castle ruins; take time to sit there or in the garden's Zen area to contemplate the stunning view: few places on earth offer such a wild panorama.

The village gets very crowded during the day; for a quieter wander, come early in the morning or late afternoon. Or even better, stay in the village. Five-star boutique Château Eza (☑04 93 41 12 24; www.chateaueza.com; rue de la Pise; d from €360; ❄🕸) has 12 sumptuous rooms and a Michelin-starred

CHEMIN DE NIETZSCHE

Walk down from the hilltop village of Èze to its coastal counterpart, Èze-sur-Mer, via the steep Chemin de Nietzsche, a 45-minute footpath named after the German philosopher Nietzsche, who started writing *Thus Spoke Zarathustra* while staying in Èze (and enjoying this path).

gastronomic restaurant, with a dreamy panoramic bar for an unforgettable aperitif.

Grande Corniche

Hitchcock was sufficiently impressed by Napoléon's cliff-hanging Grande Corniche to use it as a backdrop for his film *To Catch a Thief* (1956), starring Cary Grant and Grace Kelly. Ironically, Kelly died in 1982 after crashing her car on this very same road.

◎ Sights

Views from the spectacular Grande Corniche are mesmerising, and if you're driving, you'll probably want to stop at every bend to admire the unfolding vistas.

Fort de la Revère VIEWPOINT

Sitting 675m above the sea, the fort is the perfect place to revel in 360-degree views. An orientation table helps you get your bearings. The fort was built in 1870 to protect Nice (it served as an Allied prisoner camp during WWII). There are picnic tables under the trees for an alfresco lunch and dozens of trails in the surrounding Parc Naturel Départemental de la Grande Corniche, a protected area that stretches along the D2564 from Col d'Èze to La Turbie.

Trophée des Alpes ROMAN SITE

(☑04 93 41 20 84; http://la-turbie.monuments-nationaux.fr; 18 av Albert Ier, La Turbie; adult/child €5.50/free; ☺9.30am-1pm & 2.30-6.30pm Tue-Sun mid-May–mid-Sep, 10am-1.30pm & 2.30-5pm rest of year) This triumphal monument was built by Emperor Augustus in 6 BC to celebrate his victory over the Celto-Ligurian Alpine tribes that had fought Roman sovereignty (the names of the 45 peoples are carved on the western side of the monument). The tower teeters on the highest point of the old Roman road, with dramatic views of Monaco. Last admission is half an hour before closing time.

🛏 Sleeping & Eating

⭐ **Café de la Fontaine**   MODERN FRENCH €€
(☎ 04 93 28 52 79; 4 av Général de Gaulle, La Turbie; mains €18-25; ⊙ noon-2.30pm & 7-11pm) Those not in the know wouldn't give this inconspicuous village bistro a second glance. What they don't know is that it is Michelin-starred chef Bruno Cirino's baby – somewhere for him to go back to his culinary roots with simple yet delicious dishes reflecting *le terroir* (land) and season. Blackboard *plats* (dishes) are a perfect reflection of what's at the market.

L'Hostellerie Jérôme   GASTRONOMIC €€€
(☎ 04 92 41 51 51; www.hostelleriejerome.com; 20 rue Comte de Cessole, La Turbie; dinner menus €78 & €138; ⊙ 7-10pm daily Jul & Aug, Wed-Sun Sep, Oct & Mar-Jun) For the full wham-bam gastronomic show, reserve a table at Bruno Cirino's Michelin-starred restaurant. The Italianate chef works with local producers and fishers to create an imaginative cuisine rooted firmly in the rich *terroir* (land): warm fig tart with aniseed and pistachio sorbet, langoustine in an almond crust, roast pigeon in a black olive and Bandol wine reduction.

Five rooms (doubles €135 to €150) above ensure the perfect end to a memorably tasty evening.

ℹ Getting There & Around

Bus 116 links the town of La Turbie (population 3194) with Nice five times a day (€1.50, 35 minutes), and bus 114 goes to Monaco six times a day (€1.50, 30 minutes).

MONACO

POP 37,800 / ☎ 377

Squeezed into just 200 hectares (2.8 sq km), this confetti principality might be the world's second-smallest country (the Vatican is smaller), but what it lacks in size it makes up for in attitude. Glitzy, glam and screaming hedonism, Monaco is truly beguiling.

ℹ CENT SAVER

Save a few cents by buying a combined ticket (adult/child €19/9) covering same-day admission to both the Palais Princier de Monaco and the Musée Océanographique de Monaco; both sights sell it.

Although a sovereign state (Monaco has its own flag and national anthem), the principality's status is unusual. It is not a member of the European Union, yet it participates in the EU customs territory (meaning no border formalities crossing from France into Monaco) and uses the euro as its currency. Citizens of Monaco (Monégasques) don't pay taxes. The traditional Monégasque dialect is, broadly speaking, a mixture of French and Italian

History

Since the 13th century, Monaco's history has been that of the Grimaldi family, whose rule began in 1297. Charles VIII, king of France, recognised Monégasque independence in 1489. But during the French Revolution, France snatched Monaco back and imprisoned its royal family. Upon release, they had to sell the few possessions they still owned and the palace became a warehouse.

The Grimaldis were restored to the throne under the 1814 Treaty of Paris. But in 1848 they lost Menton and Roquebrune to France, and Monaco swiftly became Europe's poorest country. In 1860 Monégasque independence was recognised for a second time by France and a monetary agreement in 1865 sealed the deal on future cooperation between the two countries.

Rainier III (r 1949–2005), nicknamed *le prince bâtisseur* (the builder prince), expanded the size of his principality by 20% in the late 1960s by reclaiming land from the sea to create the industrial quarter of Fontvieille. In 2004 he doubled the size of the harbour with a giant floating dyke, placing Port de Monaco (Port Hercules) among the world's leading cruise-ship harbours. Upon Rainier's death, son Albert II became monarch.

◎ Sights & Activities

To explore Monaco thematically pick up 'Princess Grace' or 'Heritage Trees of Monaco' walking-tour brochures at the tourist office (p72).

⭐ **Casino de Monte Carlo**   CASINO
(www.montecarlocasinos.com; place du Casino; admission 9am-noon €10, admission from 2pm Salons Ordinaires/Salons Privées €10/20; ⊙ visits 9am-noon, gaming 2pm-2am or 4am or when last game ends) Peeping inside Monte Carlo's legendary marble-and-gold casino is a Monaco essential. The building, open to visitors every morning, is Europe's most lavish example of

belle époque architecture. Prince Charles III came up with the idea of the casino and in 1866, three years after its inauguration, the name 'Monte Carlo' – Ligurian for 'Mount Charles' in honour of the prince – was coined. To gamble or watch the poker-faced play, visit after 2pm (when a strict over-18s-only admission rule kicks in).

Slot machines, blackjack, English and European roulette, and 30/40 entertain in the main gaming room, Salle Europe, and other Salons Ordinaires. The Salons Privés, where the James Bond–esque pros play, offer European roulette, blackjack and *chemin de fer*. Trainers (sneakers) are strictly forbidden and, while not obligatory, a jacket and tie (or equivalent smart dress) is recommended in the gaming rooms for men in the evening.

★ **Musée Océanographique de Monaco** AQUARIUM
(www.oceano.mc; av St-Martin; adult/child €14/7; ⊙9.30am-8pm Jul & Aug, 10am-7pm Apr, May, Jun & Sep, to 6pm Oct-Mar) Stuck dramatically to the edge of a cliff since 1910, the world-renowned Musée Océanographique de Monaco, founded by Prince Albert I (1848–1922), is a stunner. Its centrepiece is its aquarium with a 6m-deep lagoon where sharks and marine predators are separated from colourful tropical fish by a coral reef. Upstairs, two huge colonnaded rooms retrace the history of oceanography and marine biology (and Prince Albert's contribution to the field) through photographs, old equipment, numerous specimens and interactive displays.

In all, there are around 90 tanks in the aquarium containing a dazzling 450 Mediterranean and tropical species, sustained by 250,000L of freshly pumped seawater per day. School holidays usher in free hourly light shows in the Salle de la Bileine (Skeleton Room) and feel-the-fish sessions in the kid-friendly tactile basin (45 minutes, €5); tickets for the latter are sold at the entrance.

Don't miss the sweeping views of Monaco and the Med and the cafe-clad rooftop terrace.

★ **Le Rocher** HISTORIC QUARTER
Monaco Ville, also called Le Rocher, is the only part of Monaco to have retained small, windy medieval lanes. The old town thrusts skywards on a pistol-shaped rock, its strategic location overlooking the sea, becoming the stronghold of the Grimaldi dynasty. To access Le Rocher, from place aux Armes in

LOCAL KNOWLEDGE

A SECRET BEACH

A peaceful, panoramic alternative to the sweaty busy hike with the crowds up Rampe Majeur to Le Rocher is via the Digue de Monaco (Monaco Dike) – the world's largest floating dike, 28m wide and 352m long. Scale the steps at the end of quai Antoine 1er and detour left along the dike's smooth concrete walkway to the viewpoint next to the cruise-ship terminal. The Monte Carlo panorama from here is the best there is. Backtrack to Esplanade Stefano Casiraghi and recharge batteries on the vast, designer sundeck here – ladders allow you to dip into the water. Then weave your way along the coastal path and up through the shady Jardins St-Martin to Le Rocher. En route, watch for old stone steps careering steeply down to the water and a secret shingle beach only locals know about.

the Condamine area, visitors can walk up the 16th-century red-brick Rampe Major, past the statue by Dutch artist Kees Verkade of the late Prince Rainier looking down on his beloved Monaco.

Palais Princier de Monaco PALACE
(www.palais.mc; place du Palais; adult/child €8/4; ⊙10am-6pm Apr-Oct, to 7pm Jul & Aug) Built as a fortress atop Le Rocher in the 13th century, this palace is the private residence of the Grimaldis (official residence of Prince Albert and Princess Charlene today). It is protected by the blue-helmeted, white-socked Carabiniers du Prince; changing of the guard takes place daily at 11.55am.

For a glimpse into royal life, tour the state apartments with lavish furnishings and expensive 18th- and 19th-century art typical of any aristocratic abode. Buy tickets in advance online to cut queueing time.

Cathédrale de Monaco CATHEDRAL
(4 rue Colonel Bellando de Castro; ⊙8.30am-6.45pm, closed 1st Thu of month Sep-May) FREE An adoring crowd continually shuffles past Prince Rainier's and Princess Grace's flower-adorned graves, located inside the cathedral choir of Monaco's 1875 Romanesque-Byzantine cathedral. The Monaco boys' choir, Les Petits Chanteurs de Monaco, sings Sunday Mass at 10.30am between September and June.

Monte Carlo Casino

TIMELINE

1863 Charles III inaugurates the first Casino on Plateau des Spélugues. The **atrium** ❶ is a small room with a wooden podium from which an orchestra entertains while punters purchase entrance tickets.

1864 Hôtel de Paris opens and the area becomes known as the 'Golden Square'.

1865 Construction of **Salle Europe** ❷. Cathedral-like, it is lined with onyx columns and lit by eight Bohemian crystal chandeliers weighing 150kg each.

1868 The steam train arrives in Monaco and **Café de Paris** ❸ is completed.

1878–79 Gambling moves to Hôtel de Paris while Charles Garnier is charged with building a new casino with a miniature replica of the Paris Opera House, **Salle Garnier** ❹.

1890 The advent of electricity casts a glow on architect Jules Touzet's newly added **gaming rooms** ❺ for high rollers.

1903 Inspired by female gamblers, Henri Schmit decorates **Salle Blanche** ❻ with caryatids and the painting *Les Grâces Florentines*.

1904 Smoking is banned in the gaming rooms and **Salon Rose** ❼, a new smoking room, is added.

1910 **Salle Médecin** ❽, immense and grand, hosts the high-spending Private Circle.

1966 Celebrations mark 100 years of uninterrupted gambling despite two world wars.

TOP TIPS

➡ After 2pm when gaming begins, admission is strictly for 18 years and over. Photo ID is obligatory.

➡ Don't wear trainers. A jacket for men is not obligatory (but is recommended) in the gaming rooms.

➡ In the main room, the minimum bet is €5/25 for roulette/blackjack.

➡ In the Salons Privés, the minimum bet is €15, with no maximum.

Atrium
The casino's 'lobby', so to speak, is paved in marble and lined with 28 Ionic columns, which support a balustraded gallery canopied with an engraved glass ceiling.

Hôtel de Paris

HÔTEL DE PARIS

Notice the horse's shiny leg (and testicles) on the lobby's statue of Louis XIV on horseback? Legend has it that rubbing them brings good luck in the casino.

Salon Rose
Smoking was banned in the gaming rooms following a fraud involving a croupier letting his ash fall on the floor. The Salon Rose (Pink Room; today a restaurant) was therefore opened in 1903 for smokers – the gaze of Gallelli's famous cigarillo-smoking ladies follow you around the room.

Salle Garnier
Taking eight months to build and two years to restore (2004–2006), the opera's original statuary is rehabilitated using original moulds saved by the creator's grandson. Individual air-con and heating vents are installed beneath each of the 525 seats.

Salle Europe

The oldest part of the casino, where they continue to play *trente-et-quarante* and European roulette, which have been played here since 1865. Tip: the bull's-eye windows around the room originally served as security observation points.

Café de Paris

With the arrival of Diaghilev as director of the Monte Carlo Opera in 1911, Café de Paris becomes the go-to address for artists and gamblers. It retains the same high-glamour ambience today. Tip: snag a seat on the terrace and people-watch.

Salles Touzet

This vast partitioned hall, 21m by 24m, is decorated in the most lavish style: oak, Tonkin mahogany and oriental jasper panelling are offset by vast canvases, Marseille bronzes, Italian mosaics, sculptural reliefs and stained-glass windows.

Salle Médecin

Also known as Salle Empire because of its extravagant Empire-style decor, Monégasque architect François Médecin's gaming room was originally intended for the casino's biggest gamblers. Part of it still remains hidden from prying eyes as a Super Privé room.

Salle Blanche

Today a superb bar-lounge, the Salle Blanche (White Room) opens onto an outdoor gaming terrace, a must on balmy evenings. The caryatids on the ceiling were modelled on fashionable courtesans such as La Belle Otéro, who placed her first bet here aged 18.

Jardins des Boulingrins

Place du Casino

Jardins du Casino

Terraces, gardens & walkways

Fairmont Monte Carlo

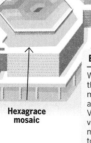

Hexagrace mosaic

BEST VIEWS

Wander behind the casino through manicured gardens and gaze across Victor Vasarely's vibrant op-art mosaic, *Hexagrace*, to views of the harbour and the sea.

Monaco

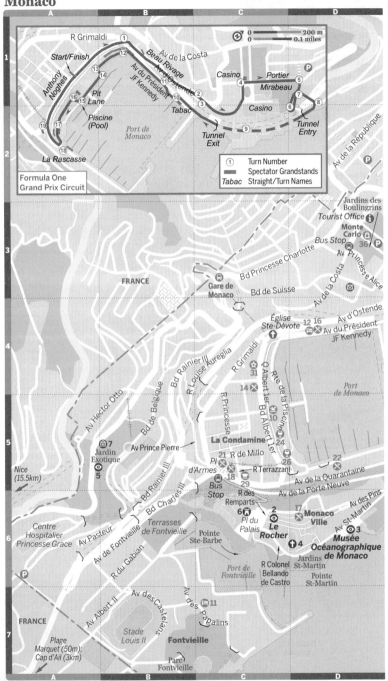

Formula One Grand Prix Circuit

R Grimaldi
Start/Finish
Beau Rivage
Av de la Costa
Anthony Noghes
Av du Président JF Kennedy
Anglo-Ostende
Casino
Portier
Mirabeau
Pit Lane
Casino
Tabac
Piscine (Pool)
Port de Monaco
Tunnel Exit
Tunnel Entry
La Rascasse

① Turn Number
Spectator Grandstands
Tabac Straight/Turn Names

Av de la République

Jardins des Boulingrins
Tourist Office
Monte Carlo
Bus Stop 36
Av Princesse Alice

Bd Princesse Charlotte

FRANCE

Gare de Monaco
Bd de Suisse
Av de la Costa

Église Ste-Dévote 12 16
Av du Président JF Kennedy

R Grimaldi
31
Bd Rainier III
R Louise Aureglia
R Princesse
14
Port de Monaco

Av Hector Otto
Bd de Belgique

Q Albert Ier
Bd Albert Ier
Rte de la Piscine
10
24
22

Jardin Exotique 7
5
Av Prince Pierre
La Condamine

Pl d'Armes 21 R de Millo
R Terrazzani
18 29

Bd Rainier III
Bd Charles III
Bus Stop
R des Remparts
Av de la Quarantaine
Av de la Porte Neuve
Av des Pins

Nice (15.5km)

6 Pl du Palais
2 Le Rocher
17 Monaco Ville
Av St-Martin

Centre Hospitalier Princesse Grace
Av Pasteur
Terrasses de Fontvieille
Pointe Ste-Barbe
4
Jardins St-Martin
3 Musée Océanographique de Monaco

R Colonel Bellando de Castro
Pointe St-Martin
Port de Fontvieille

Av de Fontvieille
R du Gabian

FRANCE

Av des Castelans
Av des Papalins
11

Plage Marquet (50m); Cap d'Ail (3km)
Av Albert II
Stade Louis II
Fontvieille
Parc Fontvieille

Monaco

◎ Top Sights
1 Casino de Monte Carlo	E3
2 Le Rocher	C6
3 Musée Océanographique de Monaco	D6

◎ Sights
4 Cathédrale de Monaco	D6
5 Jardin Exotique	A5
6 Palais Princier de Monaco	C6
7 Villa Paloma	B5
8 Villa Sauber	F1

✛ Activities, Courses & Tours
9 Digue de Monaco	E4
10 Stade Nautique Rainier III	C5

⬤ Sleeping
11 Columbus	C7
12 Hôtel Miramar	D4

✕ Eating
13 Bouchon	F2
Café Llorca	(see 32)
14 Casino	C4
15 Cosmopolitan	E2
16 La Marée	D4
17 La Montgolfière	D6
18 Marché de la Condamine	C5
19 Pierre Geronoli	F1
20 Ristorante Mozza	E2
21 Spa	C5
22 Stars 'n' Bars	D5
23 Tip Top	E3

⬤ Drinking & Nightlife
24 Brasserie de Monaco	C5
25 Café de Paris	E3
26 Joseph	C5
27 Le Teashop	E1
28 Sass Café	E2
29 Snowflake	C5
Zelo's	(see 32)

⬤ Entertainment
30 Auditorium Rainier III	E4
31 Billetterie d'Automobile Club de Monaco	C4
32 Grimaldi Forum	F2
33 Monaco Open-Air Cinema	E6
34 Opéra de Monte Carlo	E3

⬤ Shopping
35 Le Métropole	E3
36 Les Pavillons de Monte Carlo	D3

Jardin Exotique GARDEN
(www.jardin-exotique.mc; 62 bd du Jardin Exotique; adult/child €7.20/3.80; ☺9am-7pm May-Sep, to 6pm Feb-Apr & Oct, to 5pm Nov-Jan) Home to the world's largest succulent and cactus collection, from small echinocereus to 10m-tall African candelabras, the gardens tumble down the slopes of Moneghetti through a maze of paths, stairs and bridges. Views of the principality are spectacular. Admission includes the Musée d'Anthropologie, which displays prehistoric remains unearthed in Monaco, and a 35-minute guided tour of the Grotte de l'Observatoire. The prehistoric, stalactite- and stalagmite-laced cave is bizarre: it's the only cave in Europe where the temperature rises as you descend. Bus 2 links Jardin Exotique with the town centre.

Nouveau Musée National
de Monaco ART MUSEUM
(www.nmnm.mc) Monaco's national museum is split between two sumptuous villas. Seasonal contemporary-art exhibitions focus on a theme: performing arts (Serge Diaghilev, stage designs etc) at beautiful belle époque Villa Sauber (☏98 98 91 26; 17 av Princesse Grace; adult/child €6/free, Sun free; ☺11am-7pm Jun-Sep, 10am-6pm Oct-May), where a lush garden is shaded by several magnificent palms and ficus trees; and the environment (oceans, apocalypse etc) at the pearly white Villa Paloma (☏98 98 48 60; 56 bd du Jardin Exotique; adult/child €6/free, Sun free; ☺11am-7pm Jun-Sep, 10am-6pm Oct-May), built for an American in 1913.

Stade Nautique Rainier III SWIMMING
(☏93 30 64 83; quai Albert 1er; morning/afternoon/evening/full day €3.20/3.80/2.30/5.60; ☺9am-8pm Jun-Aug, to 6pm Sep–mid-Oct & May) Olympic-sized outdoor seawater pool with diving boards and a curly water slide. In winter it becomes an ice rink.

★☆ Festivals & Events

Festival International
du Cirque PERFORMING ARTS
(www.montecarlofestival.mc; ☺late Jan) Hold your breath during world-class acrobatics, or laugh out loud at the clowns.

Tennis Masters Series SPORTS
(www.montecarlotennismasters.com; ☺Apr) Fast becoming a key fixture on the professional circuit; if arriving by train alight at Monaco Country Club.

Formula One Grand Prix SPORTS
(www.formula1monaco.com; ☺late May) One of Formula One's most iconic races. Enthusiasts can walk the 3.2km circuit through town; the tourist office has maps.

THE FORMULA ONE GRAND PRIX

If there's one trophy a Formula One driver would like to have on the mantelpiece, it would have to be from the most glamorous race of the season, the Monaco Grand Prix. This race has everything. Its spectators are the most sensational: the merely wealthy survey the spectacle from Hôtel Hermitage, the really rich watch from their luxury yachts moored in the harbour, while the Grimaldis see the start and finish from the royal box at the port. Then there's the setting: the cars scream around the very centre of the city, racing uphill from the start/finish line to place du Casino, then downhill around a tight hairpin and two sharp rights to hurtle through a tunnel and run along the harbourside to a chicane and more tight corners before the start/finish.

But despite its reputation, the Monaco Grand Prix is not really one of the great races. The track is too tight and winding for modern Formula One cars, and overtaking is virtually impossible. The Brazilian triple world champion Nelson Piquet famously described racing at Monaco as like 'riding a bicycle around your living room'. Piquet clearly rides a much faster bicycle than most of us; Monaco may be the slowest race on the calendar, but the lap record is still over 160km/h, and at the fastest point on the circuit, cars reach 280km/h. Even the corner in the gloom of the tunnel is taken at 250km/h.

The 78-lap race happens on a Sunday afternoon in late May, the conclusion of several days of practice, qualifying and supporting races. Tickets (€40 to €480) are available from the Automobile Club de Monaco (www.acm.mc) online or in Monaco at its billetterie (Box Office; ☏93 15 26 24; www.formula1monaco.com; 44 rue Grimaldi; ☺9am-12.30pm & 2-5pm Mon-Fri).

by Tony Wheeler

International Fireworks Festival EVENT
(www.monaco-feuxdartifice.mc/en; ⊙ Jul & Aug) FREE A showdown of pyrotechnic expertise in the port area. The winner gets to organise the fireworks on 18 November, eve of Monaco's national holiday.

🛏 Sleeping

Accommodation in Monaco is expensive and reaches prohibitive levels during the Formula One Grand Prix when every hotel in Monaco and within a 50km radius of the principality gets booked up months in advance.

Include Monaco's country code +377 when calling hotels in Monaco from outside the principality.

Monaco

Hôtel Miramar HOTEL €€€
(☎ 93 30 86 48; www.miramar.monaco-hotel.com; 1 av du Président JF Kennedy; d €225; ✱ ❄ ⬢) This modern hotel with rooftop-terrace restaurant – think a 1950s building with 21st-century makeover – is a great option right by the port. Seven of the 11 rooms have perfect yacht-oggling balconies. Breakfast €12.

Columbus BOUTIQUE HOTEL €€€
(☎ 92 05 90 00; www.columbushotels.com; 22 av des Papalins; d from €230; ✱ @ ⬢ ⬚) Hi-tech urban chic best describes this large boutique hotel in Fontvieille. Rooms are beautifully decorated in designer greys, elegant striped fabrics and 'back to nature' bathrooms with bamboo towel racks and elegant wooden furniture. All rooms have little balconies and good views (the higher the better). The outdoor pool is only heated from May to October.

Cap d'Ail

Budget accommodation in Monaco is non-existent, but a couple of options lie within a short walk of the principality on Cap d'Ail in neighbouring France.

**Relais International de
la Jeunesse Thalassa** HOSTEL €
(☎ 04 93 78 18 58; www.clajsud.fr; 2 av Gramaglia; dm €20; ⊙ Apr-Oct) This hostel has an outstanding location right by the beach and close to the train station. Dorms are simple but well kept. The downside is a daily lock out from 10am to 5pm. Rates include sheets and breakfast, and dinner/picnics (€12/9) are available.

LOCAL KNOWLEDGE

EVERY CHEF'S DARLING

When you start to feel the heat follow locals away from the tourist crowd to the kitchen boutique of Corsican *maître glacier* **Pierre Geronoli** (38 bd d'Italie; 1/2/3 scoops €3.8/7/10.10). The master ice-cream maker, the darling of every gastronomic chef around, crafts extraordinary flavours: beetroot and raspberry, pistachio and almond, chestnut cream and honey, tomato and basil, and champagne. Buy his creations straight in a cone or tub, or as a gourmet cocktail in a super-stylish *verrine* (glass jar).

Hôtel Normandy HOTEL €
(☎ 04 93 78 77 77; www.hotelnormandy.no; 6 allée des Orangers; d €89-179; ⊙ mid-Mar–Oct; ⬢) Original modern pieces adorn the walls at this sweet hotel run by a multilingual family of artists. Rooms have charm, with simple, old-school furniture and a sea view from some. Bathrooms are dated but with the bus 100 stop (for Nice, Menton and Monaco) just 50m away and the gorgeous beach of La Mala a 20-minute walk, who can complain?

✗ Eating

★**Marché de la Condamine** MARKET €
(www.facebook.com/marche.condamine; 15 place d'Armes; ⊙ 7am-3pm Mon-Sat, to 2pm Sun) For tasty, excellent-value fare around shared tables, hit Monaco's fabulous market food court, tucked beneath the arches behind the open-air market stalls on place d'Armes. Fresh pasta (€5.50 to €9) from Maison des Pâtes, truffle cuisine from Truffle Gourmet and traditional Niçois *socca* (€2.80 per slice) from Chez Roger steal the show. Check its Facebook page for what's cooking.

Spa SUPERMARKET €
(7 place d'Armes; sandwiches €3-5, lunch menu €8; ⊙ 8am-8pm Mon-Sat, 9am-1pm Sun) Ingenious. Stock up on fruit, breads, sandwiches, pasta pots to go and other light lunch goodies at this small but thoughtfully stocked supermarket, then plop yourself down at one of its tables on the car-free market square outside and eat.

Casino SUPERMARKET €
(17 bd Albert 1er; pizza slices & sandwiches from €3.20; ⊙ 8.30am-midnight Mon-Sat, to 9pm Sun; ⬢)

It's not so much the supermarket that's worth knowing about as its excellent street-side bakery and pizzeria, which churns out freshly prepared goodies. A saviour for those keen to watch the pennies.

Tip Top   INTERNATIONAL €
(☑ 93 50 69 13; www.facebook.com/TipTopMonaco; 11 av des Spélugues; pizza €12.50-19, pasta €14.50-16, mains €14.50-21; ⊘ 9am-5am; ⛄) Closed for just four hours a day, this atmospheric bistro with a line-up of tables-for-two on the narrow pavement outside is where Monégasques gather all night long for good-value fodder and a gossip. The vibe is vintage and cuisine is hearty bistro. Check its Facebook page for the day's *plat du jour* chalked on the board.

Bouchon   FRENCH €
(☑ 97 77 08 80; www.bouchon.mc; 11 av Princesse Grace; lunch menus €18 & €20; ⊘ 7.30am-10.30pm) For a timeless taste of Paris in Monaco head to this traditional French bistro, complete with vintage zinc bar, padded leather banquet seating and ceramic tiles on the wall. The menu is equally bistro-perfect: think snails, onion soup and *steak-frites* (steak and fries), not to mention breakfast from 7.30am, oysters at 6pm and cocktails after dark.

Stars 'n' Bars   AMERICAN €€
(www.starsnbars.com; 6 quai Antoine 1er; burgers €15.50-24, mains €19.50-22; ⊘ 7.30am-midnight Mon-Fri, 9.30am-midnight Sat & Sun; ⛄) This American sports bar with TV screens and video games inside and striking terrace by the water outside is a Monaco icon. The winning Formula One racing car driven to victory by Mika Häkkinen in 1998 and 1999 hangs on one wall, and another wall displays snaps of the many stars who've hung out here. Racing memorabilia is everywhere, and burgers, ribs, sushi, steaks and salads are served all day.

Café Llorca   MODERN FRENCH €€
(☑ 99 99 29 29; www.cafellorca.mc; Grimaldi Forum, 10 av Princesse Grace; 2-course lunch menu €22, mains €16-19; ⊘ 11.30am-3pm Mon-Fri) This chic bistro on the 1st floor of the Grimaldi Forum conference centre is Michelin-starred chef Alain Llorca's gift to lunch-goers: fabulous modern French cuisine with a fusion twist at affordable prices. The two-course lunch menu including a glass of wine is a steal. In spring/summer, make a beeline for the tables (book ahead) on the terrace overlooking the sea.

Ristorante Mozza   ITALIAN €€
(☑ 97 77 03 04; www.mozza.mc; 11 rue du Portier; lunch menus €18 & €20, mains €19-38; ⊘ noon-3pm & 7-11pm Mon-Sat, 10.30am-4pm Sun; ⛄) Mozza's speciality is mozzarella – 10 varieties star in the tasty mozzarella bar here. Otherwise, it's fine traditional Italian fare, alongside unmissable culinary bastions of Italian culture such as after-work *aperitivi* (aperitifs with mouthwatering salamis, cold meats and other tasty nibbles).

Cosmopolitan   INTERNATIONAL €€
(www.cosmopolitan.mc; 7 rue du Portier; lunch menus €16, €19 & €22, mains €25-30; ⊘ 12.30-2.30pm & 7.30-11pm; ⛄) The menu at this hip restaurant features timeless classics from all corners of the world, such as fish and chips, Thai green curry, three-cheese gnocchi and veal cutlets in Béarnaise sauce, all revisited by Cosmo's talented chefs. Wash it down with one of the many wines on offer.

★ La Montgolfière   FUSION €€€
(☑ 97 98 61 59; www.lamontgolfiere.mc; 16 rue Basse; 3-/4-course menu €45/52; ⊘ noon-2pm & 7.30-9.30pm Mon-Tue & Thu-Sat) This pocket-sized restaurant is a local favourite amid the touristy jumble of Monaco's historic quarter. The Hot Air Balloon is the culinary creation of Henri and Fabienne Geraci, a couple whose time in Malaysia was clearly well spent based on Henri's outstanding fusion cuisine. In winter, he boils up *bourride* (a salted-cod stew typical of Monaco and Nice) every day.

Advance reservations essential.

La Marée   SEAFOOD €€€
(☑ 97 97 80 00; www.lamaree.mc; 7 av JF Kennedy; lunch menu Mon-Fri €35, brunch with/without wine €109/69; ⊘ noon-11pm Tue-Sun) This stunning rooftop restaurant, with chic tables gazing brazenly down on the port, is a temple to seafood. The choice of fish and shellfish is exceptional and Sunday brunch is a hot weekend date.

🍷 Drinking & Nightlife

Much of Monaco's superchic drinking goes on in its designer restaurants and the bars of luxury hotels. Stars 'n' Bars is also hot.

★ Le Teashop   TEAROOM
(place des Moulins; pot tea €4.70-7.60; ⊘ 9am-7pm Mon-Sat) This contemporary tea bar and boutique run by daughter Sharon and father Patrick woos tea lovers with 120 single-estate teas from small, family-run tea estates

in China, Japan and India. Pick your leaves, milk (soya, almond, coco) and style – in a pot, as a hot frothy latte or cool with 'bubbles' Taiwan-style (pearls of tapioca or syrup, sucked through a straw).

Organic and/or gluten-free *pâtisseries maison* (homemade cakes) provide the perfect accompaniment.

Snowflake CAFE
(☑ 97 77 24 67; www.facebook.com/SnowflakeMonaco; 3 av du Port; ⊙ 10am-1pm & 2-7pm Mon-Fri, 10am-1pm & 3-7pm Sat) This serene and stylish English bookshop, work space and cafe provides a peaceful respite from the portside tourist pandemonium. Decor is Scandinavian design, with armchairs to flop in as well as laptop-friendly desks. Check its Facebook page for creative workshops, readings and cultural happenings.

Café de Paris CAFE
(www.montecarloresort.com; place du Casino; ⊙ 7am-2am) Monaco's best-known cafe next to the casino has been in the biz since 1882 and is *the* place to people-watch. Service is brisk and occasonally snobbish, but it's the price you pay for a front-row view of Monte Carlo's razzmatazz.

Brasserie de Monaco MICROBREWERY
(www.brasseriedemonaco.com; 36 rte de la Piscine; ⊙ 4pm-1am Mon-Fri, noon-3am Sat, noon-1am Sun) Tourists and locals rub shoulders at Monaco's only microbrewery, which crafts rich organic ales and lager, and serves tasty lunch and snacking grub too. Watch out for live music and sports-event TV screenings. Happy hour 6pm to 8pm.

Zelo's LOUNGE BAR
(☑ 99 99 25 50; www.zelosworld.com; Grimaldi Forum, 10 av Princesse Grace; ⊙ 7.30pm-1am Sun-Thu, to 4am Fri & Sat) Glitzy, glam and utterly fabulous with its enormous chandeliers, intensely blue walls and ceiling fitted with hundreds of star-like lights, Zelo's is what Monaco nightlife is all about. At weekends DJs spins tunes from 11.30pm until the wee hours, while Monagèsque hipsters sip cocktails. The lounge bar has a restaurant too, with a magical summertime terrace staring out to sea.

Joseph LOUNGE BAR
(☑ 97 98 49 70; www.josephmonaco.mc; 6 rte de la Piscine; ⊙ 11am-2pm) For a generous dose of Monagesque chic, hit this designer lounge bar at the port. Tropical white sand carpets

DRESS CODE

By law it's forbidden to inline skate or walk around town bare-chested, barefoot or bikini-clad. In the evening many restaurants, bars and entertainment venues will require smart outfits (jacket and tie for men).

the floor of the stark aquarium-inspired interior, and stylish driftwood sculptures adorn the port-facing terrace. At lunchtime Joseph is more restaurant, but come dusk the piano bar, cocktails and live music kick in. Dress up to blend in.

Sass Café BAR
(☑ 93 25 52 00; www.sasscafe.com; 11 av Princesse Grace; ⊙ 7pm-3am) This popular piano bar is reminiscent of old-school cabarets with its shiny bar counter, lacquered grand piano (live jazz every night) and padded red walls.

☆ Entertainment

Monaco Open-Air Cinema CINEMA
(www.cinema2monaco.com; chemin des Pêcheurs; adult/child €11/8; ⊙ mid-Jun–Sep) Watch crowd-pleasing blockbusters, mostly in English, beneath the stars at this open-air cinema. Films start at 10pm nightly in June and July, and at 9pm in August and September. No advance reservations, so arrive when the doors open at 8.45pm (8pm August and September).

Opéra de Monte Carlo OPERA
(☑ 92 16 22 99; www.opera.mc; place du Casino) Also known as the Salle Garnier, this 1892 confection of neoclassical splendour adjoining Monte Carlo Casino was designed by Charles Garnier (who also designed the Paris opera).

Monte Carlo Philharmonic Orchestra CLASSICAL MUSIC
(www.opmc.mc) Going strong since 1856, the orchestra maintains the tradition of summer concerts in the Cour d'Honneur (Courtyard of Honour) at the Palais Princier, although tickets are like gold dust. Year-round the orchestra performs at the **Grimaldi Forum** (☑ 99 99 30 00; www.grimaldiforum.mc; 10 av Princesse Grace) and **Auditorium Rainier III** (☑ 93 10 85 00; blvd Louis II); buy tickets online or at the **Atrium du Casino** (☑ 98 06 28 28; Casino de Monte Carlo, place du Casino; ⊙ 10am-5.30pm Tue-Sat) inside Monte Carlo Casino.

DYNASTY

Monaco's longest-ruling monarch, reigning for 56 years, Rainier III (1923–2005) won the heart of the nation with his fairy-tale marriage to Grace Kelly in 1956. The legendary Philadelphia-born actress made 11 films in the 1950s, including Alfred Hitchcock's *To Catch a Thief* (1955). The movie took Kelly to Cannes and Monaco for a photo shoot, where she met Rainier. Tragically, she died in a car crash in 1982.

The soap-opera lives on with the couple's children: Prince Albert (b 1958 and monarch since 19 November 2005), Caroline and Stéphanie. Prince Albert is as well known for his sporting achievements (he's a black belt in judo and played in the national soccer team) as he is for his two illegitimate children, neither of whom are in line for the throne. Much to the joy of the nation, however, Prince Albert wed South African swimmer Charlene Wittstock – 20 years his junior – in 2011 and in December 2014 presented Monaco with a twin set of heirs, Princess Gabriella and Prince Jacques (a few seconds younger than his sister but first in line to the throne).

Les Ballets de Monte Carlo DANCE
(www.balletsdemontecarlo.com) The Monte Carlo Ballet is a word-class act. The company regularly tours internationally and performances in Monaco sell out months in advance. Buy tickets through Monaco Spectacle (www.monaco-spectacle.com).

🛍 Shopping

Monaco's streets drip with couture and designer shops; many congregate in Monte Carlo on av des Beaux Arts and av de Monte Carlo. For vaguely more mainstream (read less expensive) fashion boutiques, try Le Métropole (www.metropoleshoppingcenter.com; 17 av des Spélugues; ⊙10am-7.30pm Mon-Sat). Mid-July to mid-August, boutiques open Sunday.

Les Pavillons de Monte Carlo MALL
(allées des Boulingrins, place du Casino) No, the Tellytubbies have not moved into Monte Carlo. The five giant snow-white 'pebbles' that sprung up on the lawns of Jardins des Boulingrins in 2014 are temporary home (until 2018) to the luxury boutiques previously housed in the now-demolished Sporting d'Hiver, which is currently being rebuilt. Follow the footpath that slaloms around the striking aluminum edifices to shop at Chanel, McQueen, Sonia Rykiel, Dior et al.

ℹ Information

Centre Hospitalier Princesse Grace (Hospital; ☑ 97 98 99 00; www.chpg.mc; 1 av Pasteur)
Police Station (☑112; 3 rue Louis Notari)
Tourist Office (www.visitmonaco.com; 2a bd des Moulins; ⊙9am-7pm Mon-Sat, 11am-1pm Sun) For tourist information by the port, head to the seasonal kiosk run by the tourist office

near the cruise-ship terminal on Esplanade des Pêcheurs.

ℹ Getting There & Away

AIR

Héli-Air Monaco (☑ 92 05 00 50; www.heliair-monaco.com) runs helicopter flights between Nice and Monaco's **Héliport** (av des Ligures) several times a day (€138, seven minutes).

BUS

Bus 100 (€1.50, every 15 minutes from 6am to 9pm) goes to Nice (45 minutes) and Menton (40 minutes) along the Corniche Inférieure. Bus 110 (single/return €20/30, hourly) goes to Nice-Côte d'Azur Airport (40 minutes). Both services stop at place d'Armes and the bus stop on bd des Moulins opposite Jardins des Boulingrins. Night services run Thursday to Saturday.

CAR

Only Monaco and Alpes-Maritimes (06) registered cars can access Monaco Ville. If you decide to drive, park in one of the numerous underground car parks (first hour free, €2.40 next 20 minutes, then €1 per 20 minutes).

TRAIN

Services run about every 20 minutes east to Menton (€2.20, 15 minutes) and west to Nice (€3.30, 25 minutes). Access to the station is through pedestrian tunnels and escalators from 6 av Prince Pierre de Monaco, pont Ste-Dévote, place Ste-Dévote and bd de la Belgique. The last trains leave around 11pm.

ℹ Getting Around

BUS

Monaco's urban bus system, operated by Compagnie des Autobus de Monaco (www.cam.mc), has six lines. Line 2 links Monaco Ville to Monte Carlo and then loops back to the

Jardin Exotique. Line 4 links the train station with the tourist office, the casino and Plage du Larvotto. After 9.20pm the Bus de Nuit (9.20pm to 12.30am) follows one big loop around town; service is extended to 4am on Friday and Saturday. Tickets cost €1.50 (day ticket €5.50).

BOAT
From the dike end of quai Antoine 1er, the solar-powered Bateau Bus sails back and forth across the harbour between quai Rainier III (Monaco Ville) and quai des États-Unis (Monte Carlo). Boats sail every 20 minutes from 8am to 7.50pm; buy tickets (€2) on board.

LIFTS
A system of escalators and public lifts links the steep streets. They operate either 24 hours or 6am to midnight or 1am.

TAXI
Taxi Monaco Prestige (08 20 20 98 98; www.taximonacoprestige.com)

ROQUEBRUNE-CAP-MARTIN

POP 12,806

Beautiful Cap Martin nestles its languid shores into the sea of crystalline water between Monaco and Menton. The village of Roquebrune-Cap-Martin is actually centred on the medieval village of Roquebrune, which towers over the cape (the village and cape are linked by innumerable *very* steep steps). The amazing thing about this place is that despite Monaco's proximity, it feels a world away from the urban glitz of the principality: the coastline around Cap Martin remains relatively unspoiled and it's as if Roquebrune had left its clock on medieval time.

◉ Sights

★ Cabanon Le Corbusier   ARCHITECTURE
(06 48 72 90 53; www.capmoderne.com; promenade Le Corbusier; guided tours adult/child €15/10; guided tours only 10am & 3pm Tue-Sun Jul & Aug, 10am & 2pm Tue-Sun May, Jun & Sep–mid-Oct) The only building French architect Le Corbusier (1887–1965) ever built for himself is this rather simple – but very clever – beach hut on Cap Martin. The *cabanon*, a small beach hut that he completed in 1952, became his main holiday home until his death. The hut can be visited on excellent 2½-hour guided tours run by the Association Cap Moderne; tours depart on foot from Roquebrune-Cap-Martin train station and must be reserved in advance by phone or email.

Le Corbusier first came to Cap Martin in the 1930s to visit friend Eileen Gray, an Irish designer who had built a house here. Le Corbusier loved the area and visited often. During one of his stays, however, Le Corbusier decided to paint the interior of Gray's villa without her permission. Gray was understandably furious: Le Corbusier's paintings had ruined the perspectives of her design, and she was offended by the subject matter (kissing women; Gray was a lesbian).

No longer welcome as a guest, Le Corbusier did come back to Gray's villa in 1949, but as a tenant. It was during that stay that he met Robert Rebutato, owner of L'Étoile de Mer, the next-door cafe where he ate his meals. Friendship blossomed between the two men, and in 1951 they agreed on the construction of a beach house next door to L'Étoile de Mer so that Le Corbusier could have his own space.

The *cabanon* was designed using the Modulor, a mathematical benchmark based on the height of a man with his arms up.

Roquebrune   HISTORIC SITE
The medieval chunk of Roquebrune-Cap-Martin, Roquebrune sits 300m high on a pudding-shaped lump crowned by 10th-century Château de Roquebrune (www.roquebrune-cap-martin.com; place William Ingram, Roquebrune; adult/child €5/3; 10am-1pm & 2.30-7pm Jun-Sep, shorter hours rest of year) – an atmospheric place with simple but evocative props of life in medieval times. Of all the steep and tortuous streets leading up to the chateau, rue Moncollet, with its arcaded passages and rock-carved stairways, is the most impressive. Architect Le Corbusier is buried in the village cemetery (section J – he designed his own tombstone). Sensational sea views unfold from place des Deux Frères.

🛏 Sleeping & Eating

Fraise et Chocolat   CAFE €
(place des Deux Frères; sandwiches/panini €4/5; 8am-6pm;) Strawberry and Chocolate is a delightful cafe with an old-fashioned-deli feel on Roquebrune's main square. Stop for a drink, an ice cream or a quick bite (sandwiches and quiches) on the back terrace and swoon over the sweeping sea view.

Les Deux Frères   MODERN FRENCH €€
(04 93 28 99 00; www.lesdeuxfreres.com; place des Deux Frères; lunch/dinner menu €28/48; noon-2.30pm Wed-Sun, 7.30-10.30pm Tue-Sat;) This gourmet hotel-restaurant with

panoramic terrace is super stylish. Eight chic boutique rooms (doubles €75 to €100) – two with sweeping sea views – slumber up top, while waiters in black serve magnificent dishes (huge pieces of meat or whole fish for two, delicate fish fillets in hollandaise sauce or spinach and basil olive oil) hidden beneath silver domed platters.

★ Hôtel Victoria
DESIGN HOTEL €€€

(☑ 04 93 35 65 90; www.hotel-victoria.fr; 7 promenade du Cap Martin; d from €196; ❄ @ 🛜) Fans of Eileen Gray and Le Corbusier should make a beeline for this sensational hotel on the shores of Cap Martin. Everything from the frescoes in the stunning white-and-blue rooms to the lithographies and custom-made furniture draws from the designers' influences. All rooms are on the 1st floor and those facing the sea have balconies. Cheaper online rates.

The hotel is next to the bus 100 stop (going to Menton, Monaco and Nice) and 500m from Carnolès train station (on the Nice–Ventimille route).

ℹ Getting There & Around

BUS

Bus 100 (€1.50) goes to Monaco (20 minutes), Nice (1¼ hours) and Menton (30 minutes); it stops on av de la Côte d'Azur, which lies below Roquebrune and above Cap Martin (you'll see steps near the bus stop).

TRAIN

The Cap-Martin-Roquebrune train station is at the Cap Martin end of town; destinations include Monaco (€1.60, four minutes), Nice (€4, 30 minutes), Menton (€1.40, six minutes) and Ventimiglia (€3.70, 20 minutes); trains runs half-hourly.

WALKING

It takes 30 to 45 minutes to walk from Cap Martin to Roquebrune, depending on your fitness level (a lot less the other way around since it's downhill). You'll find several staircases linking the two parts of town.

MENTON & AROUND

A string of mountain villages peer down on Menton from the surrounding hills. The remote Parc National du Mercantour (www.mercantour.eu), a prime walking area, is just 20km away. But start your explorations on Menton's doorstep in Ste-Agnès and Gorbio.

Menton
POP 29.670

Menton used to be famous for two things: its lemons and its exceptionally sunny climate. Its belle époque glitz as the place everyone wanted to be subsequently wore off, but with the opening of the architecturally striking Musée Jean Cocteau Collection Séverin Wunderman, not to mention a sensational Michelin-starred restaurant and other fine wines and dines, Menton is enjoying something of a renaissance.

◉ Sights

The town's epicentre is the bustling, pedestrianised rue St-Michel and its ice-cream parlours and souvenir shops.

★ Musée Jean Cocteau Collection Séverin Wunderman
GALLERY

(☑ 04 89 81 52 50; www.museecocteaumenton.fr; 2 quai de Monléon; adult/child €8/free; ◉ 10am-6pm Wed-Mon) Art collector Séverin Wunderman donated some 1500 Cocteau works to Menton in 2005 on the condition that the town build a dedicated Cocteau museum. And what a museum Menton built: this futuristic, low-rise building is a wonderful space to make sense of Cocteau's eclectic work. Its collection includes drawings, ceramics, paintings and cinematographic work. Admission includes the Cocteau-designed Musée du Bastion.

Musée du Bastion
ART MUSEUM

(quai Napoléon III; combined admission with Musée Jean Cocteau adult/child €8/free; ◉ 10am-6pm Wed-Mon) Cocteau loved Menton. It was following a stroll along the seaside that he got the idea of turning a disused 1636 bastion on the seafront into a monument to his work. He restored the building himself, decorating the alcoves, outer walls, reception hall and floors with pebble mosaics. The works on display change regularly.

Salle des Mariages
ARCHITECTURE

(Registry Office; ☑ 04 92 10 50 00; place Ardoïno; adult/child €2/free; ◉ 8.30am-noon & 2-4.30pm Mon-Fri) In 1957 Jean Cocteau decorated Menton's registry office, inside the town hall. It's a distinctive space, with swirly drawings, leopard-print carpet and no windows. An audio commentary (French only) runs you through the symbolism of Cocteau's designs.

Menton

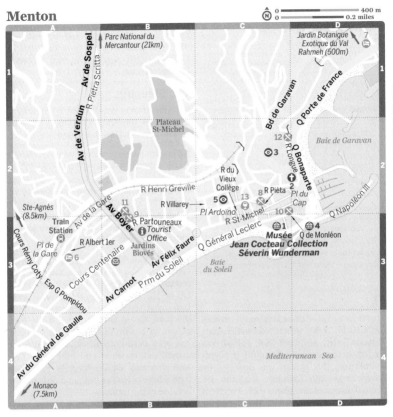

Menton

◎ Top Sights
1 Musée Jean Cocteau Collection
   Séverin Wunderman.............................C3

◎ Sights
2 Basilique St-Michel Archange...............D2
3 Cimetière du Vieux Château C2
4 Musée du Bastion...................................D3
5 Salle des Mariages.................................C2

▢ Sleeping
6 Hôtel Lemon.. A3

7 Hôtel Napoléon... D1

✕ Eating
8 Au Baiser du Mitron C2
9 Eric Kayser...B3
10 Halles Municipales.................................C2
11 Le Bistrot des Jardins............................B2
12 Le Cirke...C2

◒ Drinking & Nightlife
13 Time's..C2

Vieille Ville   HISTORIC QUARTER
Menton's old town is a cascade of pastel-coloured buildings. Meander the historic quarter all the way to the **Cimetière du Vieux Château** (montée du Souvenir; ☺ 7am-8pm May-Sep, to 6pm Oct-Apr) for great views. From place du Cap a ramp leads to southern

France's grandest baroque church, Italianate **Basilique St-Michel Archange** (place de l'Église St-Michel; ☺ 10am-noon & 4-6pm Mon-Fri Jul & Aug, 10am-noon & 3-5pm Mon-Fri Sep-Jun), whose creamy facade is flanked by a 35m-tall clock tower and 53m-tall steeple (1701–03).

WORTH A TRIP

MARKET DASH TO ITALY

Menton literally sits on the border with Italy and there is no finer reason to dash across for a dose of *la dolce vita* (the sweet life) than the all-day Friday market in Ventimiglia (Vintimille in French), the border town on the Italian side. The market sprawls over 1km along the seafront and is popular among French shoppers for its cheap fruit and veg, tasty deli counters (mozzarella-stuffed peppers, sun-dried tomatoes etc), bargain leather goods and cheap fashion. Watch out for counterfeits here; French customs take it very seriously and you risk a fine and confiscation of your goods.

Ventimiglia is at the end of the French SNCF network; there are half-hourly trains to/from Menton (€2.60, nine minutes), Monaco (€3.70, 20 minutes), Nice (€7.20, 45 minutes) and Cannes (€12.80, 1½ hours).

Jardin de la Serre de la Madone GARDEN
(☑04 93 57 73 90; www.serredelamadone.com; 74 rte de Gorbio; adult/child €8/4; ⊙10am-6pm Tue-Sun, to 5pm Dec-Mar) Beautiful if slightly unkempt, this garden was designed by American botanist Lawrence Johnston. He planted dozens of rare plants picked up from his travels around the world. Abandoned for decades, it has been mostly restored to its former glory. Guided tours (1½ hours) take place daily at 3pm. Take bus 7 to the 'Serre de la Madone' stop.

Jardin Botanique Exotique du Val Rahmeh GARDEN
(☑04 93 35 86 72; http://jardinvalrahmeh.free.fr/; av St-Jacques; adult/child €6/5.50; ⊙10am-12.30pm & 3.30-6.30pm Wed-Mon May-Aug, 10am-12.30pm & 2-5pm Wed-Mon Sep-Apr) Laid out in 1905 for Lord Radcliffe, governor of Malta, the terraces of the Val Rahmeh overflow with exotic fruit-tree collections, including the only European specimen of the Easter Island tree *Sophora toromiro*, now extinct on the island.

🎊 Festivals & Events

Fête du Citron CARNIVAL
(Lemon Festival; www.feteducitron.com; ⊙Feb) Menton's quirky two-week Fête du Citron sees sculptures and decorative floats made from tonnes of lemons weave along the seafront. Afterwards, the monumental lemon creations are dismantled and the fruit sold off at bargain prices in front of Palais de l'Europe. Each year the festival follows a different theme.

🛏 Sleeping

Accommodation gets booked up months in advance for the Fête du Citron in February (prices also soar), so plan ahead.

⭐Hôtel Lemon HOTEL €
(☑04 93 28 63 63; www.hotel-lemon.com; 10 rue Albert 1er; s/d/tr/q €59/69/85/125; 🐾) Hôtel Lemon sits in an attractive 19th-century villa with pretty garden, opposite a school. Its spacious minimalist rooms are decked out in shades of white with bright red or lemon-yellow bathrooms. Breakfast €6.50.

⭐Hôtel Napoléon BOUTIQUE HOTEL €€
(☑04 93 35 89 50; www.napoleon-menton.com; 29 porte de France; d €95-260; ❀@🐾🏊) Standing tall on the seafront, the Napoléon is Menton's most stylish option. Everything from the pool, the restaurant-bar and the back garden (a heaven of freshness in summer) has been beautifully designed. Rooms are decked out in white and blue, with Cocteau drawings on headboards. Sea-facing rooms have balconies but are a little noisier because of the traffic.

The two top-floor suites with sea views are sensational, with floor-to-ceiling windows, larger balconies and great views from the bath-tub!

🍴 Eating & Drinking

In the old town pedestrian rue du Vieux Collège is worth a meander for its tasty line-up of eateries. Rue St-Michel is littered with touristy shops selling lemon-based products, including limoncello, lemonade, lemon-infused olive oil and lemon preserve.

⭐Time's WINE BAR
(☑04 89 14 44 15; 32 rue de la République; ⊙10am-2.30pm & 4pm-midnight) With the opening of this funky wine bar-hangout, nightlife has arrived in Menton. Be it a morning coffee, a dusk cocktail with 'snacking', something for lunch from the *ardoise* (blackboard) or late-night tapas, Time's has every base covered. DJs spin deep house on Thursdays, and weekends usher in hipster-cool themed soirées and happenings.

Eric Kayser
BOULANGERIE, CAFE €

(☑ 04 93 28 25 81; www.maison-kayser.com; 1 rue Partouneaux; ☺ 7am-7pm) Fortunately for the rest of France, this Parisian baker has spread his wings to the Mediterranean, where deeply satisfying breads and pastries titillate local tastebuds. Half-baguettes filled with different sandwich fillings, generously topped focaccia slices and *pain citron* (lemon bread) ensure the perfect picnic. Eat in or take away. Find a smaller branch in Menton's indoor Halles Municipales (quai de Monléon; ☺ 7.15am-1pm), a food market by the seafront.

Le Bistrot des Jardins
PROVENÇAL €€

(☑ 04 93 28 28 09; www.lebistrotdesjardins.com; 14 av Boyer; 2-/3-course menu €22/30, mains €19-38; ☺ noon-2pm & 7.30-9.30pm Tue-Sat, noon-2pm Sun) Advance reservations are inevitably required at this delightful patio garden restaurant with lilac tableclothed tables languishing alfresco between flowering magnolias and aromatic pots of thyme, sage and other Provençal herbs. The traditional, market-inspired cuisine is equally attractive – the springtime green asparagus served with preserved purple artichoke and parmesan is worth a trip in itself.

Le Cirke
SEAFOOD €€

(☑ 04 89 74 20 54; www.restaurantlecirke.com; 1 square Victoria; lunch menus €26 & €29, dinner menus €30 & €45, mains €18-35; ☺ noon-1.30pm & 7.15-9.30pm Wed-Mon) From paella to bouillabaisse (fish stew), grilled fish to fried calamari, this smart Italian-run restaurant is the place to turn to for delicious seafood. The wine list is a mix of Italian and French wines, and the service is as sunny as Menton itself.

★ Le Mirazur
GASTRONOMIC €€€

(☑ 04 92 41 86 86; www.mirazur.fr; 30 av Aristide Briand; lunch menu €47, dinner menus €85 & €140; ☺ 12.15-2pm & 7.30-10pm Wed-Sun Mar-Dec) Design, cuisine and sea view (the full sweep of the Med above Menton town below) are all spectacular at this 1930s villa with a twinset of Michelin stars. This is the culinary kingdom of daring Argentinian chef Mauro Colagreco, who flavours dishes not with heavy sauces, but with herbs and flowers from Le Mirazur's dazzling flower garden, herb and citrus orchard and vegetable patch.

Find it 3km northeast of Menton off the coastal D6007 to Italy. Cooking classes too.

🛈 Information

Tourist Office (☑ 04 92 41 76 76; www.tourisme-menton.fr; 8 av Boyer; ☺ 9am-12.30pm & 2-6pm Mon-Sat)

🛈 Getting There & Away

Bus 100 (€1.50, every 15 minutes) goes to Nice (1½ hours) via Monaco (40 minutes) and the Corniche Inférieure. Bus 110 links Menton with Nice–Côte d'Azur Airport (single/return €20/30, one hour, hourly).

There are regular train services (half-hourly) to Ventimiglia in Italy (€2.60, nine minutes), Monaco (€2.20, 11 minutes) and Nice (€4.60, 35 minutes).

Ste-Agnès & Gorbio

Ste-Agnès' claim to fame – Europe's highest seaside village – is not for nothing: sitting snug on a rocky outcrop at 780m, the village (population 1223) looks spectacular and

---

LOCAL KNOWLEDGE

THE BAKER'S KISS

A Kiss from the Baker, or Au Baiser du Mitron (www.aubaiserdumitron.com; 8 rue Piéta; ☺ 8am-7pm Tue-Sat, to 2pm Sun) as it is otherwise known, is no ordinary *boulangerie* (bakery). Its shelves are a veritable showcase of breads from the Côte d'Azur, inland Provence and places elsewhere in the world that innovative baker Kevin Le Meur has travelled to. Loaves of ink-black bread made with vegetal charcoal, quinoa and chickpea flour sit neatly on wooden shelves next to plump rounds of bacon-topped *fougasses* (a flat bread stuffed with olives, pancetta or anchovies), Niçois *grisses*, lavender-flavoured buns and fruit breads laced with nuts, figs, apricots and cranberries. *Les Montagnards* (mountain breads) – shaped in *boules* (big balls), *couronnes* (crowns) and *baguettines* (mini bageuttes) – come from an old family recipe and are made to last. Whatever the loaf – Russian *borodinsky*, Swedish *limpa* or Italian ciabatta – everything is baked in Kevin Le Meur's traditional *four à bois* (wood bread oven) from 1906 using 100% natural ingredients and no preservatives. Then, of course, there is his signature *tarte au citron* de Menton (Menton lemon tart)...

WALKING FROM CAP D'AIL TO MENTON

With the exception of in Monaco, you can walk the 13km between Cap d'Ail and Menton without passing a car. The Sentier du Littoral follows the rugged coastline from the hedonistic Plage Mala (a tiny gravel cove where a couple of restaurants double as private beach and cocktail bars) in Cap d'Ail to Plage Marquet in the Fontvieille neighbourhood of Monaco. The path then picks up at the other end of Monaco, in Larvotto, from where you can walk to Menton along the beaches and wooded shores of Cap Martin, including the beautiful Plage Buse.

The walk is easy going, but visitors should note that the stretch of coast between Monaco and Cap d'Ail is inaccessible in bad weather. The path is well signposted and you can easily walk small sections or make a day trip out of it, including beach stops and lunch in Monaco. If you don't fancy walking through Monaco you can catch bus 6 from Larvotto to Fontvieille.

commands dramatic views of the area. For the most breathtaking panorama, climb the 200 or so steps to the rubbly 12th-century château ruins with their intriguing flower beds, based on allegorical gardens found in medieval French poetry.

The drawbridged entrance to huge subterranean Fort Ste-Agnès (www.sainteagnes. fr; Ste-Agnès; adult/child €5/2; ☺10.30am-noon & 3-7pm Tue-Sun Jun-Sep, 2.30-5.30pm Sat & Sun Oct-May) sits at the top of the village. This 2500-sq-metre defence was built between 1932 and 1938 as part of the 240km-long Maginot line, a series of fortifications intended to give France time to mobilise its army if attacked. The fort is in good condition: it was maintained throughout the Cold War as a nuclear-fallout shelter and the army only moved out in 1990. Interestingly, it is thanks to this active military history that the village of Ste-Agnès is so picturesque today: all new

developments were prohibited in the village during the army's presence, a measure that the village has since maintained.

A well-signposted path leads to neighbouring Gorbio, another drop-dead-gorgeous Provençal hilltop village. Just 2km as the crow flies from Ste-Agnès, it is much more convoluted to get there by car, so walking is a good option. Allow one hour on the way down, and 1¼ hours back up, particularly if you've had lunch at the exquisite Le Beauséjour (☑04 93 41 46 15; 14 place de la République, Gorbio; lunch/dinner menu €29/44, mains €17-25; ☺noon-2.30pm Thu-Tue Apr-Oct, 7.15-9.30pm Jul-Sep). The stuff of Provençal lunch dreams, 'Beautiful Stay' serves up local fare in a buttermilk house overlooking the village square. Inside, the dining room, which looks like it's straight out of a glossy design magazine, proffers panoramic views of the tumbling vale. No credit cards.

Cannes & Around

Best Places to Eat

➜ L'Atelier Jean-Luc Pelé (p92)

➜ Bobo Bistro (p86)

➜ Le Sot l'y Laisse (p104)

➜ Auberge de Courmes (p98)

➜ Bistrot Gourmand Clovis (p99)

Best Modern Art

➜ Musée Picasso (p89)

➜ Musée Renoir (p97)

➜ Chapelle du Rosaire (p96)

➜ Fondation Maeght (p95)

➜ Bastion St-Jaume (p91)

Why Go?

There are few places in the world where you can go from showbiz glitz and opulent luxury to remote rural life within 45 minutes. This is one of them. Glamorous Cannes sets camera flashes popping at its film festival in May, when stars pose in tuxes and full-length gowns on the red carpet of La Croisette – you could fine dine alongside the famous and drink till dawn in the seaside town's designer bars. A 'take two' scenario could find you fleeing the congested city to walk along peaceful trails and wander farmers' flower-filled fields by day and dine decadently by night.

Equally compelling is the region's art heritage: Matisse, Picasso and Renoir all stopped here for inspiration, and the works they left behind are superb. Then there's the Massif de l'Estérel, with its rugged, flaming, red-rock beauty and top-rated walks.

Driving Distances (km)

	Antibes	Biot	Cannes	Grasse	Mougins	St-Raphaël
Biot	7					
Cannes	13	16				
Grasse	28	16	21			
Mougins	14	13	6	11		
St-Raphaël	53	50	37	55	38	
Vence	20	15	31	26	25	68

Cannes & Around Highlights

1 Revel in exceptional 20th-century art at **Fondation Maeght** (p95) and play *pétanque* (similar to lawn bowls) in hilltop stunner St-Paul de Vence.

2 Trail Picasso at the **Musée Picasso** (p89) in Antibes and Vallauris' **Musée National Picasso 'La Guerre et la Paix'** (p94).

3 Lap up sun-drenched views of the Med, the Alps and billionaires' mansions along the **Cap d'Antibes coastal path** (p93).

4 Retrace three millennia of perfume making and visit a flower farm in **Grasse** (p100).

5 Flee the crowds with a hairpin-turn- and gourmet-lunch-laced road trip through the dramatic **Gorges du Loup** (p98).

6 Lose yourself in the vibrant colour palette of the **Corniche de l'Estérel** (p105), flaming scarlet at sunset.

7 Mingle with yachties in upmarket **Antibes** (p89) at the town's morning Marché Provençal, in its five-star farm-to-table eateries and – by night – at the dramatic foot of *Nomade*.

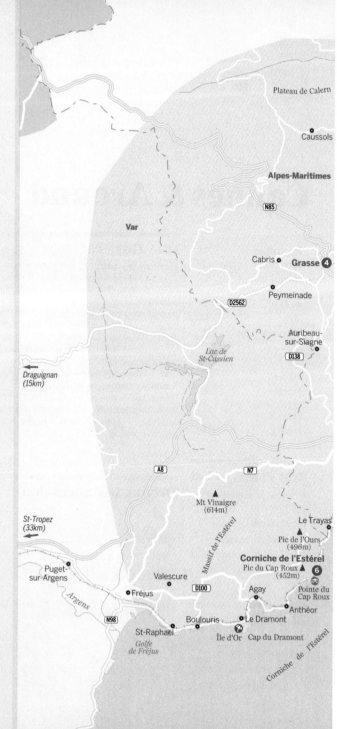

CANNES TO BIOT

Cannes

POP 74,626

As you walk among the couture shops and palaces of La Croisette, the wealth and glamour of it all cannot fail to impress: admiring Ferraris and Porsches cruising by and celebrity spotting on the glitzy sunlounger-striped beaches and liner-sized yachts moored at the port are hot Cannes pastimes.

For those not seduced by Cannes' hedonistic air, there's enough natural beauty to make a trip worthwhile: the harbour, the bay, the clutch of islands off the coast and the old quarter, Le Suquet, all spring into life on a sunny day.

◎ Sights

★ **La Croisette** ARCHITECTURE

The multistarred hotels and couture shops lining the iconic bd de la Croisette (aka La Croisette) may be the preserve of the rich and famous, but anyone can enjoy strolling the palm-shaded promenade – a favourite pastime among Cannois at night, when it twinkles with bright lights. Views of the Bay of Cannes and nearby Estérel mountains are beautiful, and seafront hotel palaces dazzle in all their stunning art deco glory.

Legendary addresses include the **Martinez** and the **Carlton InterContinental**, with twin cupolas modelled on the breasts of the courtesan La Belle Otéro, infamous for her string of lovers – Tsar Nicholas II and Britain's King Edward VII among them.

Palais des Festivals
et des Congrès LANDMARK

(Festival & Congress Palace; 1 bd de la Croisette; guided tour adult/child €4/free) Posing for a selfie on the 22 steps leading up to the main entrance to this concrete bunker – unlikely host to the world's most glamorous film festival – at the western end of La Croisette is a Cannes essential. Afterwards, wander along the **Allée des Étoiles du Cinéma**, a footpath of 46 celebrity hand imprints in the pavement – pick up the start of it with the hands of Meryl Streep in front of the tourist office.

The only way to enter the festival building and walk into the auditorium, tread the stage and learn about cinema's most glamorous event is with a Palais des Festivals guided tour organised by the Cannes tourist office (p88). Tours can only be booked in person at the tourist office; check dates on its website.

Vieux Port & Le Suquet HISTORIC QUARTER

On the western side of the Palais des Festivals lies the real Cannes. The yachts that frame the **Vieux Port** (Old Port) don't seem to impress the local men playing *pétanque* on **Sq Lord Brougham**. Follow rue St-Antoine and snake your way up **Le Suquet**, Cannes' oldest *quartier,* for great views of the bay.

🏃 Activities

Cannes is blessed with sandy beaches, although much of the bd de la Croisette stretch is taken up by private beaches, leaving just a small strip of free sand near the Palais des Festivals for the bathing hoi polloi.

Plage du Midi SWIMMING

(bd Jean Hibert) **FREE** West of Vieux Port.

Plage de la Bocca SWIMMING

FREE West of Vieux Port.

Plage Vegaluna SWIMMING

(☑ 04 93 43 67 05; www.vegaluna.com; La Croisette; sun-loungers €15-25; ⊙ 9.30am-7pm; 🛜 👪) Family-friendly private beach.

Z Plage SWIMMING

(☑ 04 93 90 12 34; La Croisette; ⊙ 9.30am-6pm May-Sep) Expect to pay €36/32/42 for the blue loungers on the front row/other rows/pier of the super-stylish Z Plage, the beach of Hôtel Martinez. Booking ahead is advised.

☞ Tours

Trans Côte d'Azur BOAT TOUR

(☑ 04 92 98 71 30; www.trans-cote-azur.com; quai Max Laubeuf) June to September, this boat company sails to St-Tropez (adult/child return €48/38) and Monaco (€52/38). Shorter, two-hour cruises (€27/17) take in the dramatic contrasts of the Estérel's red cliffs, green forests and intense azure waters.

✮✮ Festivals & Events

Cannes lives for music in the summer, so come prepared to party hard.

Festival de Cannes FILM FESTIVAL

(www.festival-cannes.com; ⊙ May) You won't get in, but it's fun because you see all the celebs walking around.

Festival d'Art Pyrotechnique FIREWORKS

(www.festival-pyrotechnique-cannes.com; ⊙ Jul-Aug) Around 200,000 people cram onto La Croi-

CANNES & AROUND CANNES

STARRING AT CANNES

For 12 days in May, all eyes turn to Cannes, centre of the cinematic universe, where 33,000 producers, distributors, directors, publicists, stars and hangers-on descend to buy, sell or promote more than 2000 films. As the premier film event of the year, the Festival de Cannes attracts around 4000 journalists from all over the world.

At the centre of the whirlwind is the colossal, 60,000-sq-metre Palais des Festivals, where the official selections are screened. The palace opened in 1982, replacing the original Palais des Festival – since demolished. The inaugural festival was scheduled for 1 September 1939, as a response to Mussolini's Fascist-propaganda film festival in Venice, but Hitler's invasion of Poland brought the festival to an abrupt end. It restarted in 1946 – and the rest is history.

Over the years the festival split into 'in competition' and 'out of competition' sections. The goal of 'in competition' films is the prestigious Palme d'Or, awarded by the jury and its president to the film that best 'serves the evolution of cinematic art'. Notable winners include Francis Ford Coppola's *Apocalypse Now* (1979), Quentin Tarantino's cult *Pulp Fiction* (1994) and American activist Michael Moore's anti-Bush-administration polemic *Fahrenheit 9/11* (2004). More recent winners include *La Classe* (2008), a film by Laurent Cantet about teaching in tough Parisian suburbs; *Winter Sleep* (2014) by Turkish director Nuri Bilge Ceylan; and *Dheepan* (2015) by French director Jacques Audiard, which tells the tale of how a former Tamil Tiger from Sri Lanka gains asylum in France.

The vast majority of films are 'out of competition'. Behind the scenes the Marché du Film (www.marchedufilm.com) sees nearly $1 billion worth of business negotiated in distribution deals. And it's this hard-core commerce, combined with all the televised Tinseltown glitz, that gives the film festival its special magic.

Tickets to the film festival are off limits to average Joes. What you can get are free tickets to selected individual films, usually after their first screening. Invitations must be picked up on the day at Espace Cannes Cinéphiles (La Malmaison, 47 La Croisette; ⊙9am-5.30pm during festival) and are limited.

sette every summer to admire the outstanding fireworks display over the Bay of Cannes. Magical. Held on six nights from July to August.

Les Plages Électroniques   MUSIC FESTIVAL
(www.plages-electroniques.com; 1-day pass €16-21, 2-/3-day pass €31.10/41.10; ⊙ Jul-Aug) DJs spin on the sand at the Plage du Palais des Festivals during this relaxed festival. Held July to August, once a week for five or six weeks.

Festival Pantiero   MUSIC FESTIVAL
(www.festivalpantiero.com; tickets €25-30; ⊙early Aug) Electronic-music and indie-rock festival on the terrace of the Palais des Festivals; very cool.

🛏 Sleeping

Cannes is a key conference centre and hotels fill up with every event, so try to plan ahead if you want to stay in the city. Search and book accommodation online through the tourist office with Cannes Hôtel Réservation (www.cannes-hotel-reservation.fr); for self-catering apartments, try Riviera Pebbles (www.rivierapebbles.com).

Hôtel Alnea   HOTEL €
(☎04 93 68 77 77; www.hotel-alnea.com; 20 rue Jean de Riouffe; s/d/tr €76/88/99; 🕸🛜) At this breath of fresh air in a town of stars, Noémi and Cédric have put their heart and soul into things, offering bright, colourful two-star rooms, original paintings and numerous little details such as the afternoon coffee break, the honesty bar and loans of the bike or *boules* (to play *pétanque*). Breakfast €8.50.

Hôtel de Provence   HOTEL €€
(☎04 93 38 44 35; www.hotel-de-provence.com; 9 rue Molière; s €118-139, d €161-189; 🕸🛜) This traditional Provençal townhouse with buttermilk walls and lavender-blue shutters disguises a minimalist-chic interior. Almost every room sports a balcony, climaxing with a 7th-floor suite with stunning rooftop terrace. The Provence also has self-catering studios for three to six people in the neighbourhood. Breakfast €9.80.

Hôtel Le Mistral   BOUTIQUE HOTEL €€
(☎04 93 39 91 46; www.mistral-hotel.com; 13 rue des Belges; d €95-135; 🕸🛜) This 10-room hotel wins the *palme d'or* for best value in town:

Cannes

0 — 200 m
0 — 0.1 miles

Villa Garbo (500m)

Bd de la République

Hôtel Le Canberra (50m)

Bd d'Alsace

R Marceau

Pl Gambetta

R Chabaud

R d'Antibes

R Tesseire

R des Allies

R Florian

R Molière

Hôtel de Provence (30m)

R du Batéguier

R Commandant André

R du Dr Gérard Monod

R des Frères Pradignac

La Croisette

Plage Vegaluna (200m); Z Plage (500m)

R Jean Jaurès

R H Vagliano

R Hoche

R Macé

R des États-Unis

R des Serbes

Baie de Cannes

Cannes Train Station

R 24 Août

R Maréchal Foch

R des Belges

R Notre Dame

Esplanade Georges Pompidou

R Buttura

R d'Antibes

R Bivouac Napoléon

Sq Mérimée

Bd de la Croisette

Tourist Office

Jetée Albert Édouard

R Venizélos

Hôtel Montaigne (450m)

Pl du 18 Juin

R Jean de Riouffe

Pl Général de Gaulle

R Maréchal Joffre

R Rouguière

Prm de la Pantiero

Vieux Port

R Émile Négrin

Sq Lord Brougham

R Louis Blanc

R du Marché Forville

R du Dr Gazagnaire

R Meynadier

R Félix Faure

Pl Bernard Cornut Gentille

Bus Station

Q St-Pierre

Q Max Laubeuf

Boats to Îles de Lérins (30m); Trans Côte d'Azur (30m); Compagnie Planaria (50m); Riviera Lines (50m)

Av des Anciens Combattants d'Afrique du Nord

Bd Victor Tuby

R Forville

R du Suquet

R St-Antoine

R Louis Perissol

R du Pré

R de la Castre

Le Suquet

R Georges Clemenceau

R du Port

Sq du Général Leclerc

Plage de la Bocca (200m)

Bd Jean Hibert

R des Suisses

R des Orangers

R St-Dizier

Cannes

two-star rooms are small but decked out in flattering red and plum tones, bathrooms feature lovely designer fittings, there are sea views from the top floor, and the hotel is just 50m from La Croisette. Breakfast €9.

Colette BOUTIQUE HOTEL €€
(☑ 04 93 39 01 17; www.hotelcolette.com; 5 place de la Gare; d €125-330; ❄@🛜) With the much-awaited renovation of the now suitably swank train station complete, four-star boutique Colette opposite the station looks right at home. Bright, contemporary furnishings give the space a youthful air, and cheaper last-minute rates are good value (for Cannes). Breakfast €15.

Hôtel Splendid HOTEL €€
(☑ 04 97 06 22 22; www.splendid-hotel-cannes.com; 4-6 rue Félix Faure; d from €154; ❄@) This sparkling white ship of an 1871 palace enchants with beautifully decorated rooms, vintage furniture, an old-world feel with creature comforts, a fabulous location and stunning views. A handful of rooms equipped with kitchenettes are ideal for longer stays and families.

Hôtel 7e Art BOUTIQUE HOTEL €€
(☑ 04 93 68 66 66; www.7arthotel.com; 23 rue du Maréchal Joffre; s/d from €91/114; ❄🛜) Hôtel 7e Art puts boutique style within reach of budgeters. The owners got the basics right: great beds, sparkling-clean baths, snappy design and excellent soundproofing (fortu-

nate, given that the hotel sits on the corner of a very large, very busy, very noisy road). Perks like iPod docks in every room far exceed what you'd expect at this price. Breakfast €9.50.

Hôtel Montaigne BOUTIQUE HOTEL €€
(☑ 04 97 06 03 40; www.hotel-montaigne.eu; 4 rue Montaigne; d from €169; ❄@🛜♨🚹) The Montaigne is bright, vivacious and contemporary with fresh, minimalist decor and soothing beige and burgundy hues. It has a spa with jet pool, *hammam* (Turkish steambath) and plenty of tantalising self-pampering packages to pick from. Families are well catered for with communicating rooms and kitchenettes.

Villa Garbo BOUTIQUE HOTEL €€€
(☑ 04 93 46 66 00; www.villagarbo-cannes.com; 62 bd d'Alsace; d from €400; ❄@🛜🚹) For outstanding style and service, check into Villa Garbo. Its spacious suites, all equipped with kitchenettes, are decked out in grey/fuchsia or chocolate/orange and finished to the highest standards (Egyptian-cotton sheets, iPod docking stations, king-size beds, open bar every night etc). The biggest downside of this excellent establishment is its location at a very busy junction.

Hôtel Le Canberra BOUTIQUE HOTEL €€€
(☑ 04 97 06 95 00; www.hotel-cannes-canberra.com; 120 rue d'Antibes; d from €169; ❄@🛜♨) This boutique stunner, just a couple of blocks back from La Croisette, is the epitome of

DON'T MISS

COOK YOUR OWN LUNCH

Part restaurant, part cooking school is probably the best way to describe **Les Apprentis Gourmets** (📞 04 93 38 78 76; www.lesapprentisgourmets.fr; 6 rue Teisseire), a boutique kitchen in the heart of Cannes. Cooking classes (€32 to €74) last one to two hours and focus on themes, or meals to take away at the end of the class. Best up is the express lunch (€17, 30 minutes), during which you cook one *plat* (main course), to be gobbled up afterwards around a shared table with your fellow cooks on the mezzanine above the kitchen. The school also hosts cooking classes for children aged six to 12 years (€32).

Cannes glamour: designer grey rooms with splashes of candy pink, sexy black-marble bathrooms with coloured lighting, heated pool (April to October) in a bamboo-filled garden, intimate atmosphere (there are just 35 rooms) and impeccable service. Rooms overlooking rue d'Antibes are cheapest.

🍴 Eating

Most private beaches have restaurants, particularly delightful on warm sunny days, although you pay for the privilege of eating *les pieds dans l'eau* (by the sea). Expect to pay around €25 to €30 for a main of grilled fish or meat, or a gourmet salad.

★**PhilCat**   SANDWICHES €
(Promenade de la Pantiéro; sandwiches & salads €3.50-6; ⊙ 7am-7pm; 📞) Phillipe and Catherine's prefab cabin on the waterfront is one of Cannes' finest lunch dates. Join locals on its sea-view terrace for giant salads, panini and the best *pan bagna* (a gargantuan bun filled with tuna, onion, red pepper, lettuce and tomato, and dripping in olive oil; €5) on the Riviera. The 'super' version (€5.30) throws anchovies into the mix.

La Boulangerie par Jean-Luc Pelé   BOULANGERIE €
(www.jeanlucpele.com; 3 rue du 24 août; lunch menus €6-9.50; ⊙ 7.30am-7.30pm Mon-Sat) This swanky artisanal bakery by Cannois chocolatier and *pâtissier* Jean-Luc Pelé casts a whole new spin on eating cheap in Cannes. Creative salads, sandwiches, wraps and bagels – to eat in or out – burst with local flavours and provide the perfect prelude to the utterly sensational cakes and desserts Pelé is best known for.

Gourmets note: macarons, unusually, come in sweet and savoury flavours. Foie gras and fig, anyone?

★**Bobo Bistro**   MEDITERRANEAN €
(📞 04 93 99 97 33; 21 rue du Commandant André; pizza €12-16, mains €15-20; ⊙ lunch & dinner Mon-Sat, dinner Sun) Predictably, it's a 'bobo' (bourgeois bohemian) crowd that gathers at this achingly cool bistro in Cannes' fashionable Carré d'Or (Golden Square). Decor is stylishly retro, with attention-grabbing *objets d'art* like a tableau of dozens of spindles of coloured yarn. Cuisine is local, seasonal and invariably organic: artichoke salad, tuna carpaccio with passionfruit, roasted cod with mash *fait masion* (homemade).

La Casa di Nonna   ITALIAN €
(📞 04 97 06 33 51; 41 rue Hoche; mains €10-15; ⊙ 8.30am-7pm) Flowers on the tables, fresh floral decor, Italian food just like an Italian *nonna* makes and delicious homemade cakes make this hybrid restaurant-tearoom a real hit in Cannes. Be it breakfast, midmorning coffee, lunch or early-evening drinks, Grandma's House is gourmet gold.

New York, New York   BRASSERIE €
(📞 04 93 06 78 27; www.nynycannes.com; 1 allée de la Liberté; pizza €12-18, mains €15-32; ⊙ 8am-2am; 📶📞) This trendy grill house scores top billing for its vast, people-watching pavement terrace beneath the glittering white facade of Hôtel Splendid. Its huge burgers, tender steaks, wood-fired pizzas and industrial-chic decor are equally popular with Cannes' hip crowd. Food is served throughout the day.

Aux Bons Enfants   FRENCH €€
(www.aux-bons-enfants.com; 80 rue Meynadier; menus €29, mains €16; ⊙ noon-2pm & 7-10pm Tue-Sat) A people's-choice place since 1935, this informal restaurant cooks up regional dishes such as *aïoli garni* (garlic and saffron mayonnaise served with fish and vegetables), *daube* (a Provençal beef stew) and *rascasse meunière* (pan-fried rockfish), all in a convivial atmosphere. No credit cards or reservations.

Petit Paris   BRASSERIE €€
(www.le-petitparis.fr; 13 rue des Belges; mains €22-36; ⊙ 8am-midnight; 📞📱) Little Paris smacks of the French capital city with its quintessential Parisian-brasserie decor. Like any

brasserie worth its French fries, it serves food all day as well as sterling breakfasts to suit all suits – pick from Parisian, English, American or Scandinavian – from 8am.

Sea Sens
FUSION €€€

(🖉04 63 36 05 06; www.five-hotel-cannes.com; 1 rue Notre Dame; lunch menus €29 & €39, dinner menus €65-115, mains €23-68; ⏱7.30-11pm Tue-Sat; 🛜) Perched on the 5th floor of the Five Seas Hotel, this single-Michelin-starred restaurant blends French gastronomy and Asian elegance with panoramic views of Le Suquet and Cannes' rooftops. Pastry chef Jerôme De Oliveira's champion desserts are the sweet highlight. Lunch here is excellent value.

Mantel
MODERN EUROPEAN €€€

(🖉04 93 39 13 10; www.restaurantmantel.com; 22 rue St-Antoine; menus €35-60, mains €34-45; ⏱noon-2pm Fri-Mon, 7.30-10pm Thu-Tue) Discover why Noël Mantel is the hotshot of the Cannois gastronomic scene at his refined old-town restaurant. Service is stellar and the seasonal cuisine divine: try the wonderfully tender glazed veal shank in balsamic vinegar or the original poached octopus *bourride*-style.

L'Affable
MODERN FRENCH €€€

(🖉04 93 68 02 09; www.restaurant-laffable.fr; 5 rue Lafontaine; lunch/dinner menus €28/44, mains €26-43; ⏱noon-2.30pm & 7-10.30pm Mon-Fri, 7-10.30pm Sat) Modern French cuisine is showcased at L'Affable. Everything from the ingredients and the cooking to the presentation is done to perfection, whether it be the roasted veal with its vegetable medley, the seared sea bream with white butter and asparagus or the house speciality, the Grand Marnier soufflé, which arrives practically ballooning at your table. Bookings essential.

🍷 Drinking & Nightlife

Bars around the Carré d'Or (Golden Square) – the area bordered by rue Commandant André, rue des Frères Pradignac, rue du Batéguier and rue du Dr Gérard Monod – tend to be young, trendy and nightlife busy. For a more sophisticated atmosphere, try the beach or top hotel bars. Pick up the free monthly *Le Mois à Cannes* at the tourist office for full event listings.

Going out in Cannes is taken very seriously: dress to impress if you'd like to get into the most sought-after clubs and events.

Armani Caffè
CAFE

(🖉04 93 99 44 05; 42 bd de la Croisette; ⏱8.30am-8pm) The alfresco cafe of Italian fashion-design house Armani is predictably chic, stylish and full of panache. Sit beneath taupe parasols in a prettily manicured garden and enjoy the comings and goings of La Croisette over a chilled glass of prosecco (€10). Salads, pasta and panini too.

Sun 7 Bar
COCKTAIL BAR

(www.sun7cannes.com; 5 rue du Dr Gérard Monod; ⏱5pm-5am; 🛜) An unpretentious, happening

CANNES & AROUND CANNES

LOCAL KNOWLEDGE

TASTEFUL SHOPPING

When it comes to shopping with taste, forget Chanel, Gucci and the gaggle of other designer fashion houses strutting their desirable stuff down Cannes' catwalk-like streets.

The insider scoop is **Fromagerie Ceneri** (🖉04 93 39 63 68; www.fromagerie-ceneri. com; 22 rue Meynadier; ⏱10am-6pm Mon, 8am-7.30pm Tue-Sat, 8.30am-12.30pm Sun) – the only place in Cannes to shop for cheese and dairy products. With cowbells strung from the wooden ceiling and a stunning array of cheeses, this master *fromager-affineur* (cheesemonger and ripener), in business since 1968, is a rare and precious breed on the Riviera. Its selection of *chèvre* (goat's cheese) from Provence is second to none, as is its cheeseboard from elsewhere in France.

For local folklore, hit **Marché Forville** (rue du Marché Forville; ⏱7am-1pm Tue-Sun, 8am-6pm Mon), Cannes' busy food market, a couple of blocks back from the port. It dates to 1934 and remains one of the region's key markets. On Monday the fresh fruit, veg, fish and meat stalls are replaced by an all-day *brocante* (flea market).

Simultaneously indulge your inner fashionista and your inner foodie with a pair of chocolate stiletto heels from **JP Paci** (www.chocolaterie-paci.fr; 28 rue Hoche; ⏱9.30am-7pm Mon-Sat). Artisan chocolatier Jean-Patrice also crafts perfectly formed rounds of Camembert cheese, ravioli squares, red roses, tool boxes and flowerpots out of chocolate – all to sweet realist perfection.

place, Sun 7 attracts a pretty young crowd keen to knock back a few drinks and shake their stuff at the weekend. It's more laid-back on week nights. Find the week's events chalked on the blackboard outside.

JW Grill   LOUNGE BAR

(☑ 04 92 99 70 92; 50 bd de la Croisette; ⊙ 11am-11pm) This dazzling white lounge bar and grill with designer sofas facing out to sea is possibly the most beautiful on the Croisette. Come dusk, indulge in a €16 glass of Champagne and revel in the chic five-star location. There's food too (mains €28 to €46). Find the grill on the ground floor of the JW Marriott hotel.

Le Bâoli   CLUB

(☑ 04 93 43 03 43; www.lebaoli.com; Port Pierre Canto, bd de la Croisette; ⊙ 8pm-6am Thu-Sat) This is Cannes' coolest, trendiest and most selective night spot – so selective, in fact, that your entire posse might not get in unless you're dressed to the nines. It's part club, part restaurant, so one way to ensure you'll get in is to book a table and make a night of it. Located at the eastern end of La Croisette.

Les Marches   CLUB

(☑ 04 93 39 77 21; www.lesmarches-club.com; Palais des Festivals, 1 bd de la Croisette; ⊙ 8pm-6am May-Sep, 11.30pm-6am Fri & Sat Oct-Apr) Few hobnobbing spots in Cannes are as sweet as the rooftop terrace of this chic club in Palais des Festivals.

Gotha Club   CLUB

(☑ 04 93 45 11 11; Casino Palm Beach; place Franklin Roosvelt; cover €25-50; ⊙ until midnight May, until dawn Jul & Aug) Only open in May during the film festival and again in July and August, this club is a hot ticket in DJ land. Bringing together some of most happening names in music with a spectacular setting at the seafaring end of La Croisette, Gotha is a glitzy VIP favourite. Door policy is tight: no guys without girls and only fabulous-looking people.

☆ Entertainment

Cinéma Les Arcades   CINEMA

(http://arcadescannes.cine.allocine.fr; 77 rue Félix Faure; tickets €9.50) Catch a movie in English.

❶ Information

Tourist Office (☑ 04 92 99 84 22; www.cannes-destination.fr; 1 bd de la Croisette; ⊙ 9am-8pm Jun-Aug, 10am-7pm Sep-May)

❶ Getting There & Around

BUS

Transport Alpes-Maritimes (TAM) runs express services to Nice (bus 200, €1.50, 1½ hours, every 15 minutes), Nice-Côte d'Azur Airport (bus 210, €20, 50 minutes, half-hourly), Mougins (bus 600, €1.50, 20 minutes, every 20 minutes) and Grasse (bus 600, €1.50, 45 minutes).

City bus **Navette City Palm** (www.palmbus.fr; €1.50) follows a loop that takes in the **bus station** (place Cornut Gentille), La Croisette, rue d'Antibes and the train station. It has no set stops; just flag it down as it passes.

BICYCLE

Mistral Location (☑ 04 93 39 33 60; www.mistral-location.com; 4 rue Georges Clémenceau) Rents out bicycles/scooters/cars from €18/30/74 per day.

CAR

Find all the big car-hire companies at the train station.

Street parking is limited to two hours in the centre. Car parks such as **Parking Croisette** (Port Canto, 1 bd de la Croisette), **Parking Forville-Suquet** (7 rue Pastour) or the train station's **Parking Gare SNCF** (1 rue Jean Jaurès) have no restriction but charge a fee (first hour free, then €2.70 per hour).

TRAIN

Cannes' gleaming white train station is well connected with other towns along the coast.
Nice €5.90, 40 minutes, every 15 minutes
Antibes €3, 12 minutes, at least twice hourly
Monaco €9.60, one hour, at least twice hourly
St-Raphaël €7.40, 30 minutes, every 20 minutes
Marseille €31.30, two hours, half-hourly

Îles de Lérins

The two islands making up Lérins – Île Ste-Marguerite and Île St-Honorat – lie within a 20-minute boat ride of Cannes. Tiny and traffic free, they're oases of peace and tranquillity, a world away from the hustle and bustle of the Riviera.

Camping is forbidden, and there are no hotels and only a couple of eating options, so bring a picnic and a good supply of drinking water.

Boats for the islands leave Cannes from quai des Îles, at the end of quai Laubeuf on the western side of the harbour. **Riviera Lines** (☑ 04 92 98 71 31; www.riviera-lines.com; quai Laubeuf) runs ferries to Île Ste-Marguerite (adult/child €13.50/9 return), while **Com-**

pagnie Planaria (www.cannes-ilesdelerins.com; quai Laubeuf) operates boats to Île St-Honorat (adult/child €16.50/8 return).

In St-Raphaël, Les Bateaux de St-Raphaël (p106) also runs excursions to Île Ste-Marguerite (adult/child €22/12 return).

Île Ste-Marguerite

Covered in sweet-smelling eucalyptus and pine, Ste-Marguerite makes a wonderful day trip from Cannes. Its shores are a succession of castaway beaches ideal for picnics, and there are numerous walking trails.

The island served as a strategic defence post for centuries. Fort Royal (☑ 04 93 38 55 26; adult/child €6/3; ⊙ 10.30am-1.15pm & 2.15-5.45pm Tue-Sun), built in the 17th century by Richelieu and later fortified by Vauban, today houses the Musée de la Mer, with exhibits on the island's Graeco-Roman history, artefacts from the numerous shipwrecks littering the shores and a small aquarium focusing on Mediterranean fauna and flora.

You can also visit the cells of the former state prison, where the most famous inmate was the Man in the Iron Mask, and walk around the compound, which boasts grand views of the coast.

Île St-Honorat

Forested St-Honorat was once the site of a powerful monastery founded in the 5th century. Now it's home to 25 Cistercian monks who own the island but welcome visitors. At 1.5km by 400m, St-Honorat is the smallest (and most southerly) of the two Lérins islands.

The Monastère Fortifié, guarding the island's southern shores, is all that remains of the original monastery. Built in 1073 to protect the monks from pirate attacks, its entrance stood 4m above ground level and was accessible only by ladder (later replaced by the stone staircase evident today). The elegant arches of the vaulted prayer cloister on the 1st floor date from the 15th century, and there's a magnificent panorama of the coast from the donjon terrace.

In front of the donjon is the walled, 19th-century Abbaye Notre Dame de Lérins, built around a medieval cloister. In the souvenir shop you can buy the 50%-alcohol Lérina, a ruby-red, lemon-yellow or pea-green liqueur concocted from 44 different herbs. The monks also produce wine from their small vineyard.

THE MAN IN THE IRON MASK

The Man in the Iron Mask was imprisoned by Louis XIV (r 1661–1715) in the fortress on Île Ste-Marguerite from around 1687 until 1698, when he was transferred to the Bastille in Paris. Only the king knew the identity of the man behind the mask, prompting a rich pageant of myth and legend to be woven around the ill-fated inmate.

More than 60 suggested identities have been showered on the masked prisoner, among them the Duke of Monmouth (actually beheaded under James II), the Comte de Vermandois (son of Louis XIV, said to have died from smallpox in 1683) and the king's brother (a twin or an illegitimate older brother). Some theorists claim the Man in the Iron Mask was actually a woman.

Antibes-Juan-les-Pins

POP 76,580

With its boat-bedecked port, 16th-century ramparts and narrow cobblestone streets festooned with flowers, lovely Antibes is the quintessential Mediterranean town. Picasso, Max Ernst and Nicolas de Staël were captivated by Antibes, as was a restless Graham Greene (1904–91), who settled here with his lover, Yvonne Cloetta, from 1966 until the year before his death.

Greater Antibes embraces Cap d'Antibes, an exclusive green cape studded with luxurious mansions (p93), and the modern beach resort of Juan-les-Pins. The latter is known for its 2km-long sandy beach and its nightlife, a legacy of the sizzling 1920s when Americans swung into town with their jazz music and oh-so-brief swimsuits.

⊙ Sights & Activities

For a quick cool-down between sights, take a refreshing dash through the artsy fountains on place du Général de Gaulle.

Musée Picasso   MUSEUM
(www.antibes-juanlespins.com; Château Grimaldi, 4 rue des Cordiers; adult/concession €6/3; ⊙ 10am-noon & 2-6pm Tue-Sun, to 8pm Wed & Fri Jul & Aug) Picasso himself said: 'If you want to see the Picassos from Antibes, you have to see them in Antibes'. The 14th-century Château Grimaldi was Picasso's studio from July to

Antibes

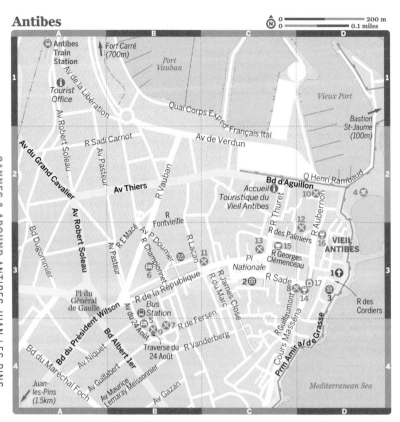

Antibes

December 1946 and now houses an excellent collection of his works and fascinating photos of him. The sheer variety – lithographs, paintings, drawings and ceramics – shows how versatile and curious an artist Picasso was. The museum also has a room dedicated to Nicolas de Staël, another painter who adopted Antibes as home.

★**Bastion St-Jaume**   MONUMENT

(quai Henri Rambaud; ⊙10am-11pm Jun-Aug, to 6pm Sep-May) **FREE** Stroll along the rampart walkway, *Promenade des Arts*, to the harbour, where luxury yachts jostle for the limelight with *Nomade* (2010), an 8m-tall sculpture of a man looking out to sea. The work of Catalan artist Jaume Plensa, the mirage-like piece is built from thousands of white letters and is lit at night – a magnificent sight. It squats on the terrace of the Bastion St-Jaume, the site of a Roman temple, a 17th-century fortified tower and, until 1985, a shipyard.

Vieil Antibes   HISTORIC QUARTER

Old Antibes is a quaint mix of boutiques and restaurants planted charmingly on ancient squares and alleyways within sturdy city walls. The *Cathédrale d'Antibes* (rue de la Paroisse), built on the site of an ancient Greek temple, has an ochre neoclassical facade; its tall, square Romanesque bell tower dates from the 12th century. The Marché Provençal (p92) is the place to be in the mornings, and views from the sea walls of urban Nice (spot the airport runway) and snowy alpine peaks beyond are superb.

Fort Carré   MONUMENT

(rte du Bord de Mer; guided tour only adult/child €3/free; ⊙10am-6pm Tue-Sun Jul & Aug, to 4.30pm Tue-Sun Sep-Jun) The impregnable 16th-century Fort Carré, enlarged by Vauban in the 17th century, dominates the approach to Antibes from Nice. It served as a border defence post until 1860, when Nice, until then in Italian hands, became French. Tours depart half-hourly; some guides speak English.

Musée Peynet et du Dessin Humoristique   MUSEUM

(place Nationale; adult/concession €3/1.50; ⊙10am-noon & 2-6pm Tue-Sun) More than 300 humorous pictures, cartoons and costumes by Antibes-born cartoonist Raymond Peynet, as well as brilliant temporary exhibitions.

Plage de la Gravette   SWIMMING

(quai Henri Rambaud) Right in the centre of Antibes, you'll find Plage de la Gravette, a small patch of sand by the *remparts* (ramparts).

Plage de la Salis   SWIMMING

This beach, with unbeatable views of old Antibes and the Alps, is 20 minutes from Antibes.

Pointe Bacon   SNORKELLING, SWIMMING

The stretch of coast between Plage de la Salis and Cap d'Antibes, especially the section around Pointe Bacon, is fringed with rocky coves, where snorkellers frolic in clear waters.

Plage de la Garoupe   SWIMMING

This stretch of Cap d'Antibes was first raked clear of seaweed in 1922 by Cole Porter and American artist Gerald Murphy to create a sandy beach. Its golden sand is shared today by a small public beach overlooked by the excellent-value terrace of *Le Rocher* (☎04 93 67 51 36; 925 chemin de la Garoupe, Plage de la Garoupe; mains €17-22) and the private *Plage Keller* (with white-tablecloth dining, and sun loungers on a jetty).

★☆ **Festivals & Events**

July is *the* party month in Antibes and Juan-les-Pins. The headline event is Juan's jazz festival, but a number of fringe music festivals are also picking up.

Jazz à Juan   MUSIC

(www.jazzajuan.com; ⊙mid-july) This major festival, celebrated in mid-July in Juan-les-Pins, has been running for more than 50 years. Every jazz great has performed here, and the festival continues to attract big music names.

🛏 **Sleeping**

Relais International de la Jeunesse   HOSTEL €

(☎04 93 61 34 40; www.clajsud.fr; 272 bd de la Garoupe; dm €20; ⊙Apr-Oct; 🛋🖘) With sea views the envy of neighbouring millionaires, this basic-but-friendly hostel is particularly popular with 'yachties' looking for their next job in Antibes' port. Rates include sheets and breakfast. Daily lock-out 11am to 5pm.

★**Hôtel La Place**   HOTEL €€

(☎04 97 21 03 11; www.la-place-hotel.com; 1 av du 24 août; d €155-175; 🖳@🖘) It's rare to find contemporary chic next to a city bus station, but The Place does it awfully well. Its 14 rooms are spacious, stylish and dressed in soothing taupe and aubergine or aniseed green. Three have bijou balconies, and breakfast (€13) is served in the airy lounge. No lift.

Hôtel La Jabotte   B&B €€

(☎04 93 61 45 89; www.jabotte.com; 13 av Max Maurey; d €120-170; 🖳@🖘) A hotel with a *chambre d'hôte* (B&B) feel, La Jabotte is 50m

CANNES & AROUND ANTIBES-JUAN-LES-PINS

from the sea. Ten Provençal rooms look out onto an exquisite patio where breakfast is served on warm days. From Vieil Antibes it's a 1.5km walk (20 minutes) towards Plage de la Salis along coastal blvd James Wyllie.

Le Relais du Postillon — HOTEL €€
(☑04 93 34 20 77; www.relaisdupostillon.com; 8 rue Championnet; d €83-149; ⊙reception 7.30am-11pm; ❊☎) Housed in a 17th-century coach house, great-value Postillon is a charmer with its modern rooms, boutique decor and ground-floor cafe-bar with winter fireplace and summer terrace. Breakfast €9.

✗ Eating

Irish and Brit-style pubs and bars serving English breakfasts and American burgers line bd Aguillon. By the water on quai des Pêcheurs fishers sell their morning's catch from 9am to 12.30pm. For picnic goodies, hit Antibes' Fromagerie l'Etable (1 rue Sade; ⊙8am-1pm & 4-7pm Tue-Sat, 8am-1pm Sun) for cheese and deli products, and dazzling morning market Marché Provençal (cours Masséna; ⊙7am-1pm Tue-Sun Sep-Jun, daily Jul & Aug) for everything else.

★ L'Atelier Jean-Luc Pelé — SANDWICHES €
(☑04 92 95 78 21; 27 rue de la République; ⊙9am-7.30pm Mon-Sat, to 7pm Sun) Normandy-born, Cannes-adopted pastry chef Jean-Luc Pelé knows how to please. His creatively filled bagels and wraps (€5), salads and quiches (€9.50 with drink and dessert) to take away form the perfect gourmet picnic. Equally delicious are Pelé's nut and olive breads, jumbo macarons, cakes and chocolate (did we mention the chocolate fountain on one wall?).

La Ferme au Foie Gras — DELI €
(www.vente-foie-gras.net; 35 rue Aubernon; sandwiches €4-7; ⊙8am-7pm Tue-Sun) Now, this is our idea of what a good sandwich should be like: filled with smoked duck breast, onion chutney or fig jam, truffle cheese and fresh salad. And many people seem to think the same: a queue snakes down from the tiny counter of The Foie Gras Farm every lunchtime.

La Badiane — FUSION €
(☑04 93 34 45 41; 3 traverse du 24 août; lunch menus €17-18.50, mains €13-15; ⊙lunch Mon-Fri) Salmon tartare (raw and marinated), fresh pesto lasagne and scrumptious quiches are among the seasonal dishes cooked up with passion and care at this trendy lunch address. Find it on a pedestrian street – one of the finest

in Antibes for lunchtime dining – behind the bus station.

Big Moustache — BURGERS €
(☑04 93 34 31 20; 30 rue Fourmillière; burgers €15; ⊙8.30am-5pm Tue-Sat) Artisanal bread, homemade sauces, veg 'fresh from the earth' and the pick of epicurean cheeses go into the gourmet burgers at Big Moustache. There are generally four or five meaty choices and two veggie burgers chalked on the *ardoise* (blackboard) each day, always with plenty of rocket, spinach leaves and other freshly picked seasonal goodies. Kids *menu* €6.

★ Nacionale — INTERNATIONAL €€
(☑04 93 61 77 30; www.restaurant-nacional-antibes.com; 61 place Nationale; tapas €9-26, mains €19-29; ⊙noon-2pm & 7-10pm Tue-Sat, noon-2pm Sun) 'Beef & Wine' is the strapline of this contemporary wine-bar-styled space, popular for its gourmet burgers with foie gras, beefy steaks in pepper or port sauce and other grilled meats. The in-crowd adores it for aperitifs and tapas. Don't be put off by its location in busy place Nationale: it has a beautiful walled patio garden secreted away out back.

Le Broc en Bouche — MODERN FRENCH €€
(☑04 93 34 75 60; 8 rue des Palmiers; mains €22-28; ⊙noon-2pm & 7-10pm Thu-Mon) No two chairs, tables or lights are the same at this lovely bistro. Every item has been lovingly sourced from antique shops and car-boot sales, giving the place a sophisticated but cosy vintage feel. The charming Flo and Fred have put the same level of care and imagination into their cuisine, artfully preparing Provençal and modern French fare.

🍷 Drinking & Nightlife

Pedestrian bd d'Aguillon heaves with merry Anglophones falling out of the busy 'English' and 'Irish' pubs.

★ Balade en Provence — ABSINTHE BAR
(25 cours Masséna; ⊙6pm-2am) Flirt with the green fairy at Balade en Provence, complete with original 1860 zinc bar, a few round tables and all the accessories (four-tapped water fountain, sugar cubes etc).

Drinkers Club — BAR
(12 rue Aubernon; ⊙4.30pm-2.30am Mon-Fri, from 1pm Sat & Sun; ☎) The in-crowd flops off the beach (or yacht they're crewing on) and onto the pavement terrace of this buzzing lounge bar for early-evening cocktails, wine and bruschetta (€10). This is also the hot spot to

CAP D'ANTIBES: A WALK AROUND BILLIONAIRES BAY

You feel like a shrunken Alice in Wonderland on this select peninsula: larger-than-life villas and parasol pine trees loom high above you at every turn, and the frenzied sound of cicadas provides an unearthly soundtrack in summer. A walk around 'Billionaires Bay' – naturally majestic and packed with millionaires' mansions – is a Riviera highlight.

The easiest way to access the lush green cape is aboard bus 2 from Antibes bus station to the 'Phare' bus stop. From here, cross the road and follow in pilgrims' footsteps along ave Malespine (bear left where the road forks) and route du Phare uphill to Chapelle de la Garoupe. The tiny chapel (closed for renovation at the time of writing), filled with poignant offerings from fishing families, crowns the highest point of Cap d'Antibes. Sweeping views of the coastline, from St-Tropez to Italy, mesmerise. The neighbouring Phare de la Garoupe, a square brick lighthouse with scarlet beacon, can't be visited.

Panorama celebrated, walk back downhill to bd du Cap and pick up chemin de la Garoupe. A 10-minute walk past high-walled properties and towering pines brings you down to the bright-turquoise, crystal-clear water of the pretty, relentlessly popular Plage de la Garoupe. At the far end of the sandy beach, pick up the signposted Sentier Littoral (coastal footpath) that ducks and dives along the shoreline to Eilenroc (1¼ hours, 3.2km) on the cape's southern tip. The path is partly paved, very rocky in places and riddled with steep steps and the occasional scary drop (wear decent shoes). It provides a superb lookout on the rugged coastline and is memorable for its many tiny sundecks and picnic spots, considerately crafted into the stone. Weave your way around the cape, past solitary fishers tucked into the rocks and knowing locals lunching with the five-star view, until you reach the start of chemin des Douaniers, an inland-bound footpath wedged between the high stone walls of Villa Eilenroc and neighbouring Château de la Croë. Famously home to the Duke of Windsor and Wallis Simpson in the late 1930s, the pearly white Victorian-style chateau was originally built for an English aristocrat in 1927 and renovated most recently by its current owner, Russian billionaire Roman Abramovic.

Duck through the doorway at the foot of chemin des Douaniers and continue for another 800m along the signposted footpath to Villa Eilenroc (☑04 93 67 74 33; av Mrs Beaumont, Cap d'Antibes; adult/child €2/free; ⊙2-5.30pm Wed & 1st & 3rd Sat of month). The villa, designed in 1867 by Charles Garnier for a Dutchman who reversed the name of his wife, Cornélie, to come up with the villa's name, has clearly seen better days – its scantily furnished interior lacks its history's glamour. But a stroll around the 11-hectare park with rosery, olive grove and aromatic garden goes some way towards evoking the beauty of the villa's belle époque heyday. On the shore below the villa, Plage de Galets is a bijou pebble cove well worth a dip and/or sun-kissed siesta. From Eilenroc, it is a five-minute walk along av Mrs Beaumont to the 'Fontaine' bus stop on bd JF Kennedy.

The southwestern tip of Cap d'Antibes, also linked by bus 2 from Antibes, is graced with the legendary Hôtel du Cap Eden Roc. Dating from 1870, it hit the big time just after WWI when a literary salon held here one summer (previous guests had come for the winter season only) was attended by Hemingway, Picasso et al. The icing on the cake was the immortalisation of the hotel (as the thinly disguised Hôtel des Étrangers) by F Scott Fitzgerald in his novel *Tender Is the Night* (1934).

In the centre of Cap d'Antibes, the serene Jardin Botanique de la Villa Thuret (☑04 97 21 25 00; www6.sophia.inra.fr/jardin_thuret; 90 chemin Raymond; ⊙8am-6pm Mon-Fri Jun-Sep, 8.30am-5.30pm Mon-Fri Oct-May) FREE is a 3.5-hectare botanical garden created in 1856 and showcasing 2500 species. It provides the perfect opportunity to study the sun-rich cape's lush and invariably exotic flora up close.

catch sports matches screened on TV, DJs and live music.

Brasserie Le Clémenceau — CAFE
(24 rue Georges Clémenceau; ⊙7.30am-8pm) For breakfast or *un café* (a coffee) in the morning sun, this local-loved cafe with pavement terrace arranged around an age-old stone fountain hits the spot every time. Fruit milkshakes, smoothies and a down-to-earth lunch *menu* (€13.50) keep it busy all day.

VALLAURIS

Picasso (1881–1973) discovered ceramics in the small potters' village of Vallauris in 1947. Attracted by its artistic vibe, he settled in the village between 1948 and 1955, during which time he produced some 4000 ceramics. He also completed his last great political composition, the *Chapelle La Guerre et La Paix* (War and Peace Chapel), a collection of dramatic murals painted on plywood panels and tacked to the walls of a disused 12th-century chapel, now the Musée National Picasso 'La Guerre et la Paix' (☑04 93 64 71 83; www.musee-picasso-vallauris.fr; place de la Libération; adult/child €4/free; ☉10am-7pm Jul & Aug, 10am-12.15pm & 2-5pm Wed-Mon Sep-Jun).

Picasso left Vallauris another gift: a dour bronze figure clutching a sheep, *L'Homme au Mouton*, now on place Paul Isnard (adjoining place de la Libération). But his biggest legacy was the revival of the ceramics industry in Vallauris, an activity that might have died out had it not been for the 'Picasso effect'.

La Siesta Club
CLUB

(☑04 93 33 31 31; 2000 rte du Bord de Mer; admission €20; ☉7pm-5am Thu-Sat mid-Jun–early Sep) This legendary establishment is famous up and down the coast for its summer beachside nightclub and all-night dancing under the stars. Find La Siesta 6km north of Vieil Antibes on the D6098.

❶ Information

Tourist Office (☑04 22 10 60 10; www. antibesjuanlespins.com; 42 av Robert Soleau; ☉9am-7pm Mon-Sat Jul & Aug, 9am-12.30pm & 1.30-6pm Mon-Fri, 9am-noon & 2-6pm Sat, 9am-1pm Sun Sep-May) By Antibes train station; excellent source of tourist information and guided walking tours of Old Antibes and 'Painters on the French Riviera' (adult/child €7/3.50).

Accueil Touristique du Vieil Antibes (☑04 93 34 65 65; 32 bd d'Aguillon; ☉10am-noon & 1-6pm Mon-Sat Jul & Aug, to 5pm Tue-Sat Sep-Jun) Old-town info point, steps from the water.

❶ Getting There & Away

BUS

The Nice–Cannes service (www.envibus.fr; bus 200, €1.50) stops by the tourist office. Local bus services (€1) for Opio, Vence and St-Paul de Vence leave from the **bus station** (☑04 89 87 72 01; place Guynemer; ☉ticket office 9am-12.30pm & 2-5pm Mon-Sat).

CAR

Vieil Antibes is mostly pedestrianised; park outside the centre and walk. There are several car parks along the port on av de Verdun.

TRAIN

Antibes' train station is on the main line between Nice (€3.70, 30 minutes, five hourly) and Cannes (€3, 10 minutes, five hourly).

Biot
POP 9750

This 15th-century hilltop village was once an important pottery-manufacturing centre specialising in earthenware oil and wine containers. Metal containers brought an end to this, but Biot is still active in handicraft production, especially glassmaking. The dynamic tourist office (☑04 93 65 78 00; www.biot.fr; 46 rue St-Sébastien; ☉9am-noon & 2-6pm Mon-Fri, 2-6pm Sat & Sun) has various itineraries to discover this arts heritage (downloadable as the *Visit Biot* app).

The village was also the one-time headquarters (1209–1387) of the Knights Templar, then the Knights of Malta: the picturesque place des Arcades, dating from the 13th and 14th centuries, is a reminder of this illustrious past.

At the foot of the village, the Verrerie de Biot (www.verreriebiot.com; chemin des Combes; ☉9.30am-6pm Mon-Sat, 10.30am-1.30pm & 2.30-6.30pm Sun) FREE produces bubbled glass by rolling molten glass into baking soda; bubbles from the chemical reaction are then trapped by a second layer of glass. Watch skilled glass-blowers at work and browse the adjacent art galleries and shop.

The Musée National Fernand Léger (www.musee-fernandleger.fr; chemin du Val de Pome; adult/child €5.50/free; ☉10am-6pm Tue-Sun May-Oct, to 5pm Nov-Apr), 1.5km south, presents Fernand Léger's work and life: his brush with cubism, his ongoing interest in architecture, society and cinema, and the influence of his stays in America. Bus 10 between Antibes and Biot stops near the museum (at stop Musée Fernand Léger).

THE ARRIÈRE-PAYS

The 'coast' in Côte d'Azur is what many people come to see, but the *arrière-pays* (hinterland) has a charm of its own. Less crowded and incredibly varied, it has something for everyone, from keen walkers to culture vultures and foodies.

St-Paul de Vence

POP 3600

Once upon a time, St-Paul de Vence was a small medieval village atop a hill looking out to sea. Then came the likes of Chagall and Picasso in the postwar years, followed by showbiz stars such as Yves Montand and Roger Moore, and St-Paul shot to fame. The village is now home to dozens of art galleries as well as the exceptional Fondation Maeght.

The village's tiny cobbled lanes get overwhelmingly crowded in high season – come early or late to beat the rush.

◎ Sights & Activities

The Village　　　　　　　　　　HISTORIC QUARTER

Strolling the narrow streets is how most visitors pass time in St-Paul. The village has been beautifully preserved and the panoramas from the ramparts are stunning. The main artery, rue Grande, is lined with art galleries. The highest point in the village is occupied by the Église Collégiale; the adjoining Chapelle des Pénitents Blancs was redecorated by Belgian artist Folon.

Many more artists lived in or passed through St-Paul de Vence, among them Soutine, Léger, Cocteau, Matisse and Chagall. The latter is buried with his wife, Vava, in the cemetery at the village's southern end (immediately to the right as you enter). The dynamic tourist office runs a series of informative, themed guided tours (1½ hours, adult/child €5/free).

Across from the entrance to the fortified village, the pétanque pitch, where many a star has had a spin, is the hub of village life. The tourist office rents out balls (€2) and organises one-hour pétanque lessons (€5 per person, reserve in advance).

Fondation Maeght　　　　　　　　　　MUSEUM

(www.fondation-maeght.com; 623 chemin des Gardettes; adult/child €15/10; ⊙10am-7pm Jul-Sep, to 6pm Oct-Jun) Created in 1964 by Aimé and Marguerite Maeght, this fabulous museum has one of Europe's largest collections of 20th-century art. Works are exhibited on a rotating basis; along with the excellent temporary exhibitions, this means you rarely see the same piece twice. The museum is 500m downhill from the village, in a building designed by Josep Lluís Sert. Itself a masterpiece, it integrates a Giacometti courtyard, Miró sculptures across terraced gardens, coloured-glass windows by Braque and mosaics by Chagall and Tal-Coat.

🛏 Sleeping & Eating

Les Vergers de Saint-Paul　　BOUTIQUE HOTEL €€

(☑04 93 32 94 24; www.vergersdesaintpaul.com; 940 rte de la Colle; d/tr €160/190; ✴🅿🛜🌊) This elegant hotel has something of a belle époque feel about it, with the art deco stripy fabrics, parquet floors, resplendent white facade and wrought-iron balconies. There is a splendid pool too, with assorted loungers. If you can, snag a room in the main building rather than those in the annexe. Breakfast €14.

★ Les Cabanes d'Orion　　　　　B&B €€€

(☑06 75 45 18 64; www.orionbb.com; Impasse des Peupliers, 2436 chemin du Malvan; d from €260; 🛜🌊🅿) Dragonflies flit above water lilies in the emerald-green swimming pool (filtered naturally), while guests slumber amid a chorus of frogs and cicadas in luxurious cedar-wood treehouses perched in the trees at this enchanting, ecofriendly B&B. Children are well catered for with mini-*cabanes* (cabins) in two of the treehouses. There is a minimum three-night stay from April to October.

In winter Orion offers special cocooning packages, with sauna sessions and gourmet baskets complete with organic hot meals and champagne for a cosy night in.

La Colombe d'Or　　　　　　　　　　HOTEL €€€

(☑04 93 32 80 02; www.la-colombe-dor.com; place de Gaulle; d €250-430, mains €19-55; ⊙restaurant noon-2.30pm & 7.30-10.30pm late Dec-Oct; 🛜🌊) This world-famous inn could double as the Fondation Maeght's annexe: The Golden Dove was the party HQ of dozens of 20th-century artists (Chagall, Braque, Matisse, Picasso etc) who paid for their meals in kind, resulting in an extraordinary private art collection. Rooms are strung with unique pieces, as are the dining room and garden.

Hotel guests get access to the lovely pool, crowned by a Calder mobile.

★ Le Tilleul　　　　　　　　MODERN FRENCH €€

(☑04 93 32 80 36; www.restaurant-letilleul.com; place du Tilleul; lunch menus €25 & €29, mains €18-25; ⊙8.30am-10.30pm; 🅿) Considering its location on the *remparts*, it could have easily plumbed the depths of a typical tourist trap; instead, divine and beautifully presented dishes grace your table at Le Tilleul and the all-French wine list includes a generous selection of options by the glass. Sit under the shade of a big lime-blossom tree. Breakfast and afternoon tea too.

❶ Getting There & Around

St-Paul is served by Lignes d'Azur (www.lignesdazur.com) bus 400 running between Nice (€1.50, one hour, at least hourly) and Vence (€1.50, 15 minutes). The town is closed to traffic, but there are several car parks (€2.70 per hour) surrounding the village.

Vence

POP 19,180

Despite its well-preserved medieval centre, visitors often skip Vieux Vence altogether to head straight to Matisse's otherworldly Chapelle du Rosaire. Yet Vence deserves more than a flying visit. It's worth spending a little time here, if only to appreciate its comparatively quiet medieval streets and enjoy some of its gastronomic talent. A fruit-and-veg market fills place du Jardin several mornings a week, with antiques on Wednesday.

◉ Sights

★ Chapelle du Rosaire   ARCHITECTURE

(Rosary Chapel; 📞04 93 58 03 26; 466 av Henri Matisse; adult/child €6/3; ⏱2-5.30pm Mon, Wed & Sat, 10-11.30am & 2-5.30pm Tue & Thu mid-Dec–mid-Nov) An ailing Henri Matisse moved to Vence in 1943, to be cared for by his former nurse and model, Monique Bourgeois, who'd since become a Dominican nun. She persuaded him to design this extraordinary chapel for her community. The artist designed everything from the decor to the altar and the priest vestments. From the road, you can see the blue-and-white ceramic roof tiles, wrought-iron cross and bell tower. Inside, light floods through the glorious blue, green and yellow stained-glass windows.

The colours respectively symbolise water/the sky, plants/life, the sun/God's presence; the back windows display Matisse's famous seaweed motif, those on the side a stylised, geometric leaf-like shape.

A line image of the Virgin Mary and child is painted on white ceramic tiles on the northern interior wall. The western wall is dominated by the bolder Chemin de Croix (Stations of the Cross). St Dominic overlooks the altar. Matisse also designed the chapel's stone altar, candlesticks and cross. The beautiful priests' vestments are displayed in an adjoining hall.

Vieux Vence   HISTORIC QUARTER

Much of the historical centre dates back to the 13th century. The Romanesque cathedral on the eastern side of the square was built in the 11th century on the site of an old Roman temple. It contains Chagall's mosaic of Moses (1979), appropriately watching over the baptismal font.

The daring Fondation Émile Hugues (www.museedevence.com; 2 place du Frêne; adult/child €8/free; ⏱11am-6pm Tue-Sun), with its wonderful 20th-century art exhibitions, inside imposing Château de Villeneuve, is a nice contrast to Vence's historic quarter.

🛏 Sleeping

★ Le 2   B&B €€

(📞04 93 24 42 58; www.le2avence.fr; 2 rue des Portiques; d incl breakfast €105-165; ❄🕸) This 'bed & bistro', as it's tagged itself, is a welcome addition to staid Vence. Nicolas and his family have turned this medieval town house into a hip new establishment offering four very modern rooms and a pocket-sized cellar featuring local musicians one night a week. Value and atmosphere guaranteed.

★ La Maison du Frêne   B&B €€€

(📞04 93 24 37 83; www.lamaisondufrene.com; 1 place du Frêne; d €185; ⏱Feb-Dec; ❄🕸) This arty guesthouse is quite astonishing. Yes, that Niki de Saint Phalle is an original. And yes, the César too. It's an essential sleepover for true art lovers, if only to enjoy the superb rooms with their classic or contemporary looks and original works. Owners and avid art collectors Thierry and Guy are a mine of information on the local art scene.

🍴 Eating

L'en Champs Thé   CAFE €

(📞09 83 31 77 33; www.lenchampsthe.fr; 1 place du Peyra; mains €10-15; ⏱8.30am-5pm Tue-Sat, to 3pm Sun) A play on the French word *'enchanté'* (meaning 'delighted, pleased'), L'en Champs Thé is a sparky family-run tearoom and organic *épicerie* (grocery) with summer terrace on a car-free old-town square. Cuisine is seasonal, sun-inspired and *fait maison*

A CULTURED TRIO

Sprawling seaside towns like Villeneuve-Loubet, Cagnes-sur-Mer and Le Cannet lack charm and can overwhelm, but a trio of cultural highlights justify the detour. Le Domaine des Collettes, today the evocative **Musée Renoir** (www.cagnes-tourisme.com; chemin des Colettes, Cagnes-sur-Mer; adult/child €6/free; ⊙10am-1pm & 2-6pm Jun-Sep, 10am-noon & 2-5pm Oct-Mar, to 6pm Apr & May), was home and studio to an arthritis-crippled Pierre-Auguste Renoir (1841–1919), who lived here with his wife and three sons from 1907 until his death. Works of his on display include *Les Grandes Baigneuses* (The Women Bathers; 1892), a reworking of the 1887 original, and rooms are dotted with photographs and personal possessions. The magnificent olive and citrus groves are as much an attraction as the museum itself. Many visitors set up their own easel to paint.

Equally wonderful is **Musée Escoffier de l'Art Culinaire** (Escoffier Museum of Culinary Arts; fondation-escoffier.org; 3 rue Auguste Escoffier, Villeneuve-Loubet; adult/child €5/free; ⊙10am-noon & 2-7pm Wed & Sat, 2-7pm Sun-Tue, Thu & Fri Jul & Aug, 2-6pm Sep, Oct & Dec-Jun), which retraces the history of modern gastronomy. Escoffier (1846–1935), inventor of the *pêche Melba* and dried potato among other things, was France's first great chef and a celebrity amongst Europe's well heeled.

The third in the cultured trio is Le Cannet's **Musée Bonnard** (☑04 93 94 06 06; www.museebonnard.fr; 16 bd Sadi Carnot, Le Cannet; adult/concession €5/3.50; ⊙10am-8pm Fri-Sun, Tue & Wed, to 9pm Thu Jul & Aug, to 6pm Tue-Sun Sep-Jun), at home in a restored belle époque villa with a striking contemporary extension. Instantly recognisable by their intense colour, the works of neo-Impressionist painter Pierre Bonnard (1867–1947) form the backbone of the museum's permanent collection. Bonnard arrived in Le Cannet fresh from Paris in 1910 and lived in a seafront villa with his wife, Martha, until his death. It was in Le Cannet that Bonnard painted his best works, including several landscapes of St-Tropez, Antibes and other Riviera resorts.

(homemade) – as Richard, the apron-clad '*fée maison*' (house fairy) will proudly tell you as he dashes between tables.

Le Michel Ange MEDITERRANEAN €
(☑04 93 58 32 56; 1 place Godeau; 2-/3-course menus €17/22, mains €14; ⊙noon-2.30pm & 6.30-9.30pm Tue-Sat, noon-2.30pm Sun) With tables beneath a leafy tree on a fountain-clad square behind the cathedral, this casual eatery gets top billing among locals. Kid-clad families swarm here at weekends for its car-free outdoor space and easy, excellent-value cuisine that embraces everything from pizza to stockfish. Reservations recommended. Check its Facebook page for weekly *menus*.

Restaurant La Litote MODERN FRENCH €€
(☑04 93 24 27 82; http://lalitote.fr; 5 rue de l'Évêché; 2-/3-course menus €25/30, mains €18; ⊙noon-2.30pm & 7-10pm Tue-Sat) Chef Stéphane Furlan delights diners with a regularly changing *menu* featuring seasonal delights like garlicky *escargots à la Niçoise* (snails) with anchovies and local mesclun, or stuffed squid with vegetables in parsley sauce. Summer dining is alfresco on a tree-shaded square; winter is in the stone-walled dining room with open fire.

Les Bacchanales GASTRONOMIC €€€
(☑04 93 24 19 19; www.lesbacchanales.com; 247 av de Provence; 2-/3-/5-course lunch menus €32/40/60, 4-/5-/7-course dinner menus €65/75/95; ⊙12.30-2pm & 7.30-10pm Thu-Mon) At home in a 1930s town house, chef Christophe Dufau combines his culinary art (creative and seasonal, with every dish paired with the perfect wine) with fine art (daring original works on the walls). Feast on fish with artichokes and liquorice followed by fresh Gorges de Loup goat's cheese.

Should your tastebuds be totally besotted, you can enrol in a cooking class.

ℹ Information

Tourist Office (☑04 93 58 06 38; www.ville-vence.fr; 8 place du Grand Jardin; ⊙9am-7pm Mon-Sat, 10am-6pm Sun Jul & Aug, 9am-6pm Mon-Sat Sep, Oct & Mar-Jun, 9am-5pm Mon-Sat Nov-Mar) The tourist office has several good leaflets on self-guided tours in and around Vence.

ℹ Getting There & Around

Lignes d'Azur (www.lignesdazur.com) bus 400 to and from Nice (€1.50, 1¼ hours, at least hourly) stops on place du Grand Jardin. Medieval Vence is pedestrian; park on place du Grand Jardin or in the streets leading to the historical centre.

Around Vence

The Pays Vençois is an enticing mix of fertile land, rocky heights and quirky attractions. A car is essential to get around.

Les Gorges du Loup

A combination of perilously perched villages, sheer cliffs, waterfalls, densely wooded slopes and gushing rivers, the Gorges du Loup is a scenic, unspoiled part of the world, known for spectacular drives and walking trails.

The highlight of the western side of the gorges (the D3) is the fortified village of Gourdon (elevation 760m, population 421), teetering on a rock edge to peer down on a magnificent coastal panorama that sweeps 80km from Nice to Théoule-sur-Mer. Views from the elegant landscaped gardens of 12th- to 17th-century Château de Gourdon (☑ 04 93 09 68 02; www.chateau-gourdon. com; Gourdon; adult/reduced €7/5; ☺ gardens by appointment only Apr-Sep) or panoramic place Victoria at the top of the souvenir-shop-riddled village are second to none. Or ditch the seasonal tourist crowd for paragliding school Ascendance (☑ 06 13 50 44 64, 06 61 42 08 64; www.ascendance06.com; Auberge de Gourdon, rte de Caussol, Gourdon) and its unforgettable 15-/30-minute maiden flights in tandem (€80/110), one-day discovery courses (€140) and piloting lessons.

On the eastern side, off the D2210, the isolated hamlet of Courmes is reached by a single, winding lane. Further south is the hamlet of Le Pont du Loup. Standing over the Loup River, under what's left of the old railway bridge (bombed during WWII), this is where villagers from Gourdon came to cultivate flowers and fruit trees. They would arrive on foot, along the chemin du Paradis, a mule track very popular with walkers today. Count on 80 minutes from Gourdon to Le Pont du Loup, 90 minutes to Le Bar-sur-Loup.

Testament to this fertile past is sweet factory Confiserie Florian (☑ 04 93 59 32 91; www.confiserieflorian.com; chemin de la Confiserie, Le Pont du Loup; ☺ 8am-noon & 2-5.30pm Mon-Fri, 9am-6.30pm Sat & Sun), where jams, candied fruits and crystallised violets, roses and verveine leaves have been cooked up in a 19th-century flour mill since 1921. Free 20-minute tours show you how clementines and other fruits are candied by being simmered in syrup for three minutes every second day over a 45-day period; visit weekdays to see the kitchens in action. Tours end in the boutique, where you can taste and buy. Or nip up the hill to Florian's neighbouring La Boutique du Chocolat (16 chemin de la Confiserie, Le Pont du Loup) for a refreshing cone of rose-petal, jasmine or violet ice cream or poppy sorbet (one/two scoops €2/3.50).

Further down from Le Pont du Loup, on the D2210, hilltop Le Bar-sur-Loup (population 2990) pops onto the horizon. Bitter-orange trees are cultivated in terraces around the beautifully intact medieval village.

🛏 Sleeping & Eating

⭐ La Cascade   B&B €

(☑ 04 93 09 65 85; www.gitedelacascade.com; 635 chemin de la Cascade, Courmes; d/tr/q €75/100/140; ❄ 🖨 ♻ 🐾) 'The Waterfall' is a rural idyll. An old sheepfold, it sits snug in 4 hectares of land, with forest, ponds, swimming pool, *pétanque* pitch and majestic views of the Gorges du Loup. In summer it feels like the edge of the world, while winter is about cosying up by the fire. Dinner (€25 for three courses, including drinks) is another highlight.

Château de Grasse   HOTEL €

(☑ 04 93 42 06 29; www.chateaudegrasse. com; 6 place Francis Paulet, Le Bar-sur-Loup; d/q €100/120; 🖨 🐾) Perched right at the top of the village, it's hard to imagine that Le Bar-sur-Loup's majestic 13th-century castle once lay in ruins. It's now an appealing hotel with irresistible wooden-deck terrace out front and German owner Heinrich at the helm. Six huge rooms ooze 'country-chic' elegance, with soft-toned fabrics and sweeping valley views. Simple/buffet breakfast €6/12.

⭐ Auberge de Courmes   MODERN FRENCH €€

(☑ 04 93 77 64 70; www.aubergedecourmes. com; 3 rue des Platanes, Courmes; menu €24, Sun lunch €27; ☺ noon-2pm Wed-Mon Sep-Jun, noon-2pm Thu-Mon Jul & Aug, evening by reservation only, closed Jan & Feb; 🖨 🐾) In the hamlet of Courmes, at the foot of mountains 10km north of Le Pont du Loup, this flowery inn is gorgeous for a long, lazy lunch alfresco. Talented young chef Richard Auray cooks up two starters and two mains using seasonal produce from the Nice market. Sunday lunch is hot with locals, so book before making the windy trek here.

The *auberge* (country inn) has five small, simple rooms (doubles including breakfast/half board €65/110); there are no TVs in the rooms and wi-fi is hit-and-miss, but who needs either when deer roam the village at night and fireflies put on a show (in June)?

L'École des Filles   MODERN FRENCH €€
(☑ 04 93 09 40 20; www.restaurantecoledesfilles.fr; 380 av Amiral de Grasse, Le Bar-sur-Loup; lunch formule €24, 2-/3-/4-course menus €35/39/45; ⊙ noon-2pm & 7-9pm Tue, Wed, Fri & Sat, 7-9pm Thu, noon-2pm Sun) As the name suggests, this is the village's former girls' school and what makes it so special is that it has retained the charm of an old village school: in winter, meals are served in the 'classrooms', with their stone walls and patchwork of colourful cushions and crockery; in summer, the old playground becomes a lively terrace. The creative menu changes weekly.

Tourrettes-sur-Loup

POP 4082

Dubbed the 'city of violets' after its signature flower, Tourrettes is a postcard-perfect, 15th-century hilltop village. Walking around the town won't take you more than half an hour or so; other attractions are in the surrounding area.

◎ Sights & Activities

There are some great walks to do around the town, many with panoramic views. The **tourist office** (☑ 04 93 24 18 93; www.tourrettessurloup.com; 2 place de la Libération; ⊙ 8.30am-1pm & 2-6pm Mon-Fri, 9am-1pm & 2-6pm Sat) on Tourrettes' central square has plenty of itinerary information.

La Ferme des Courmettes   FARM
(☑ 04 93 59 31 93; www.chevredescourmettes.com; rte des Courmettes; ⊙ 9am-12.30pm & 4-6pm Mar-Dec) ✔ An organic goat's-cheese producer, this farm welcomes visitors. To see its 70 goats being milked, arrive sharp at 8am. Farm tours (one hour, €63 for up to 10 people, available in English) include tastings of the cheese – divine and incredibly diverse in taste. Find the farm 4.4km along the perilously steep and hairpin-laced rte des Courmettes, signposted off the D2210 to Tourrettes.

Bastide aux Violettes   FARM, MUSEUM
(☑ 04 93 59 06 97; Quartier de la Ferrage; ⊙ 10am-noon & 2-5.45pm Tue-Sat, 2-6pm Sun Jul & Aug, 10am-noon & 2-5.45pm Tue-Sat Sep-Jun) **FREE** To find out more about Tourrettes' famous violet, head to the Bastide aux Violettes, 10 minutes' walk from the centre of town. This modern space takes you through the history of the flower, its uses and cultivation (you can see fields).

Domaine des Courmettes   WALKING
(☑ 04 92 11 02 32; www.courmettes.com; rte des Courmettes; ⊙ 8am-8pm Mar-Dec) ✔ **FREE** This nature reserve on the lofty Plateau des Courmettes protects millennia-old holly oaks and rare birds. There are three circular *sentiers de randonée* (walking trails) to follow, ranging from an easy 1.2km to a steep 5.5km hike uphill to the top of the **Pïc des Courmettes** (1280m). Grab a map and pick up trailheads at the visitor centre.

The visitor centre occupies a beautiful 19th-century farmhouse that offers accommodation (dorms €35, breakfast €7.50)

🛏 Sleeping & Eating

⭐ **Le Mas des Cigales**   B&B €€
(☑ 04 93 59 25 73; www.lemasdescigales.com; 1673 rte des Quenières; d €135; ❋ 🛜 🛝) With its pretty Provençal *mas* (farmhouse), tumbling garden, picture-perfect pool, sweeping views and feast of a breakfast, it's likely you'll never want to leave this five-room *chambre d'hôte*, run with care and passion by Belgian couple Stefaan and Véronique. Active types will adore the tennis courts, *pétanque* pitch and bicycles. Dinner (€30 to €35) is cooked up twice a week.

⭐ **Bistrot Gourmand Clovis**   MODERN FRENCH €€
(☑ 04 93 58 87 04; www.clovisgourmand.fr; 21 Grand Rue; 2-/3-/4-course menus €38/45/52; ⊙ 12.30-2pm & 7.30-10pm Wed-Sun; ☑) This achingly cool bistro in the cobbled heart of Tourrettes is a stunner – for its stylish contemporary decor and its creative cuisine, honoured with a Michelin star. Chef Julien Bousseau works with only the best seasonal produce from the region and the results are superb. The wine list stays very much in Provence and is equally appealing. Bookings essential.

Col de Vence

The northbound D2 from Vence leads to photogenic **Coursegoules**, a hilltop village with 11th-century castle ruins and fortifications, via Col de Vence (963m), a mountain pass offering good views of the *baous* (rocky promontories) typical of this region. The landscape across these lofty plateaus is very arid, a far cry from the orchards and lush valleys around the Loup River. Various walking trails criss-cross the area.

Grasse

POP 52,212

It is the abundance of water in the hills that helped turn Grasse into a perfume centre. Tanners, who needed reliable water supplies to clean their hides, first settled here in the Middle Ages. With the advent of perfumed gloves in the 1500s, the art of perfumery took shape. Glove makers split from the tanners and set up lucrative perfumeries. New irrigation techniques allowed flower growing to boom, sealing Grasse's reputation as the world fragrance capital.

Today, Grasse is still surrounded by jasmine, centifolia-rose, mimosa, orange-blossom and violet fields, but the industry, which counts some 30 perfumeries, is rather discreet, with only a handful offering tours of their facilities.

◉ Sights & Activities

Attractions in Grasse focus on its celebrated perfume industry, a refreshing change from traditional sights and activities.

★ **Musée International de la Parfumerie** MUSEUM
(MIP; www.museesdegrasse.com; 2 bd du Jeu de Ballon; adult/child €4/free; ◎10am-7pm Wed-Mon Apr-Sep, 10.30am-5.30pm Wed-Mon Oct-Mar; ♿) This whiz-bang museum is a work of art: housed in an 18th-century mansion, daringly enlarged with a modern glass structure, it retraces three millennia of perfume history through beautifully presented artefacts, bottles, videos, vintage posters, olfactive stations and explanatory panels. The museum offers interesting insights into how the industry developed in Grasse. Kids are well catered for with dedicated multimedia stations, a fragrant garden, a film testing sense of smell, and the reproduction of a 19th-century perfume shop.

Guided **tours** of the museum (in English and French) take place at 3pm on Saturday and Sunday September to June, and at 11am and 3pm daily in July and August.

Villa-Musée Fragonard ART MUSEUM
(23 bd Fragonard; ◎10am-7pm May-Sep, 10.30am-5.30pm Wed-Mon Oct-Apr) FREE His paintings shocked and titillated 18th-century France with their licentious love scenes. See why inside this wonderful villa where controversial Grasse-born artist Jean-Honoré Fragonard (1732–1806) stayed for a year in 1790 with his cousin, perfume merchant Alexandre Maubert (1743–1827). The exquisitely renovated, sumptuous villa is strung with paintings (originals and copies) by Fragonard and his descendants: the stunning *trompe l'œil* fresco in the stairwell by his son, who would have been 13 at the time, is a highlight.

Musée d'Art et d'Histoire de Provence HISTORY MUSEUM
(☎04 93 36 80 20; 2 rue Mirabeau; ◎10am-7pm Wed-Mon May-Sep, 11am-6pm Oct-Apr) FREE This local-history museum, at home since 1921 in an aristocratic *hôtel particulier* (mansion), is a wonderful evocation of life in the 18th century. Rooms are laid out pretty much as they were when the marquise of Clapiers-Cabris lived here – he loathed his mother, who lived opposite, so much that he had a gorgon's head carved over his door to leer through her windows. Don't miss the ground-floor kitchen, decorative art collection and gardens with beautiful springtime wisteria.

Before entering the museum, pause for a moment to admire, lower down the street, the beautiful (if now abandoned), eclectic facade of what was **Hugues-Aîné Perfumery** in the 19th century; look for the pigeons fluttering in and out of the boarded-up bay window and balcony.

Musée Jean-Honoré Fragonard ART MUSEUM
(www.fragonard.com; 14 rue Jean Ossola; ◎10am-6.30pm) FREE On Grasse's main pedestrian street, this small museum displays 10 major works by Grassois painter Jean-Honoré Fragonard, beautifully exhibited in an 18th-century town house – admire the splendid ceiling fresco on the ground floor. Paintings by Marguerite Gérard (1761–1837), Fragonard's sister-in-law and protégé, and Jean-Baptiste Mallet (1759–1835), another Grasse native, fill two other small rooms on the 1st floor.

Usine Historique & Musée du Parfum - Fragonard MUSEUM
(☎04 93 36 44 65; www.fragonard.com; 20 bd Fragonard; ◎9am-7pm Jul & Aug, 9am-12.30pm & 2-6.30pm Sep-Jun) FREE At the entrance to the old town, next to the Jardin des Plantes, is this ochre-coloured mansion where the Fragonard perfumery began in 1926 – perfumers were at work here as early as 1782. Visits take in the original equipment used

Grasse

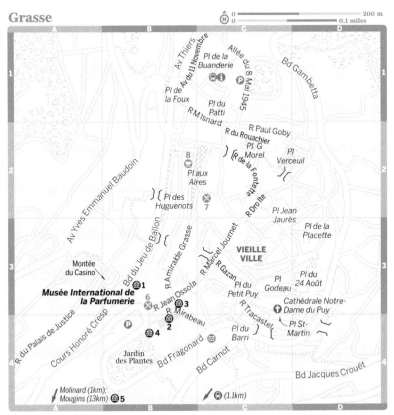

for extraction and distilling, include a small Musée du Parfum (Perfume Museum) on the 1st floor, and end in the shop where you can buy Fragonard scents.

The perfumer has several other boutiques in the old town specialising in women's fashion, kids' wear and homewares.

Domaine de Manon   FARM
(⏰ 06 12 18 02 69; www.le-domaine-de-manon. com; 36 chemin du Servan, Plascassier; adult/child €6/free) 🌿 Curious noses can enjoy a (literal) field trip to this wonderful flower farm. Centifolia rose and jasmine have been cultivated here for three generations, and Carole Biancalana, the current producer, will take you on a tour of her fields and explain how the flowers are grown and processed. Domaine's production is sold exclusively to *haute couture* label Dior.

Tours only take place during flowering on Tuesday at 10am early May to early June for roses, and on Tuesday at 9am from August

Grasse

◉ Top Sights
1 Musée International de la
    Parfumerie B3

◉ Sights
2 Musée d'Art et d'Histoire de
    Provence B4
3 Musée Jean-Honoré Fragonard B3
4 Usine Historique & Musée du
    Parfum - Fragonard B4
5 Villa-Musée Fragonard B4

◉ Eating
6 Café des Musées....................................B3
7 Restaurant Lou Candeloun C2

◉ Drinking & Nightlife
8 Les Comptoirs NamasThé..................B2

to mid-October for jasmine; ring ahead to double-check, since exact times vary from year to year, depending on flowering.

DON'T MISS

CREATE YOUR OWN SCENT

It can take months for a *nez* (nose or perfumer who, after 10 years' training, can identify up to 3000 smells) to create a perfume. And you'll understand why the instant you plant yourself in front of a nose's organ – a line-up of miniature ginger-glass bottles containing 127 'notes' ranging from green amber, sandalwood, vanilla, hyacinth, lily of the valley to civet (unpleasant animal smell, apparently extracted from the secretion of a cat's gland), rose petals (sickly sweet) and woody complex. The fact that many bottles contain not one but several essences pre-mixed only adds to the olfactory bewilderment. The number of combinations is dizzying.

Perfume workshops won't turn you into a perfumer overnight, but the olfactory education they offer is fascinating – and great fun for adults and kids alike. Molinard runs a 90-minute Atelier des Parfums (€69) in its out-of-town Grasse factory, where you can create your own perfume. The *nez* will quiz you on scents you like and dislike, explain the structure of a perfume (base, heart and head notes) and guide you through the subtle blends of your creation. 'Graduates' leave with a 130mL bottle of their perfume. The less adventurous can opt for the 30-minute Bar des Fragrances (€30), which involves creating your own 30mL bottle of perfume from a smaller, less overwhelming choice of essences.

Galimard offers similar workshops (€45) at its Studio des Fragrances. Sessions last 1½ to two hours, and participants leave with a 100mL bottle of their own bespoke *eau de parfum*. Fragonard's 2½-hour Ateliers Apprenti Parfumeur (perfumer apprentice workshops; €65 including 100mL eau de toilette) take place in town at its Usine Historique (p100).

The *domaine* is located 7km southeast of the centre of Grasse, in the small village of Plascassier (officially part of Grasse). Head in the direction of Valbonne along the D4 as you leave Grasse, and then follow signs for 'Vieux Village' when you get to Plascassier. The *domaine* will be on your left, opposite a hair salon.

☞ Tours

Perfumery Tours　　　　　　　　　　　TOUR
Three well-known perfumeries run free guided tours of their modern, out-of-town facilities: **Molinard** (☑ 04 93 36 01 62; www.molinard.com; 60 bd Victor Hugo; ⏱ 9.30am-6.30pm), 1km out of town with a sumptuous showroom – it has a boutique in town on place aux Aires); **Galimard** (☑ 04 93 09 20 00; www.galimard.com; 73 rte de Cannes; ⏱ 9am-12.30pm & 2-6pm); 3km from Grasse centre on the southbound N85; and **Fragonard** (La Fabrique des Fleurs; ☑ 04 93 77 94 30; www.fragonard.com; Les 4 Chemins, rte de Cannes; ⏱ 9am-6pm Feb-Oct, 9am-12.30pm & 2-6pm Nov-Jan).

Tours take visitors through every stage of perfume production, from extraction and distillation to the work of the 'nose'. Tours leave every 15 to 30 minutes and are available in a number of languages. Visits end in the factory shops, where you can buy fragrances (much cheaper than couture perfumes, where some 60% of what you pay is packaging).

🍴 Sleeping & Eating

There is a dire lack of decent accommodation in Grasse, so you'll have to get out of the city for a good night's sleep. Cafe and restaurant terraces frame car-free place aux Aires, the elongated main square in old-town Grasse. For superb coffee and chocolate, **Les Comptoirs NamasThé** (27 place aux Aires) tucked in the arcades, hits the spot every time. Look for the sign 'Torréfacteur de Cafés'.

Café des Musées　　　　MODERN FRENCH €
(1 rue Jean Ossola; lunch menus €12 & €16, mains €10-23; ⏱ 9am-6pm) This stylish cafe is the perfect stop for lunch (creative salads, carefully crafted daily specials, soup or pasta of the day) or a gourmet coffee break (pastry with coffee or tea €7.50), ice cream or crêpes between sights.

**Restaurant Lou
Candeloun**　　　　　　　MODERN FRENCH €€
(☑ 04 93 60 04 49; www.loucandeloun.eresto.net; 5 rue des Fabreries; lunch menu €15, dinner menus €29 & €40, mains €25; ⏱ 12.30-2.30pm Mon, 12.30-2.30pm & 7.30-10pm Tue-Sat) Tucked down a dark, unassuming alleyway, this is Grasse's

most gourmet choice. Chef Alexis Mayroux changes his menu daily to match the mood of local market stalls – his themed *menus autour d'un produit* (menus around a product), such as springtime artichokes or asparagus, are a treat. Dining is inside, beneath elegant old-stone vaults.

Le Mas du Naoc   B&B €€
(☑ 04 93 60 63 13; www.lemasdunaoc.com; 580 chemin du Migranié, Cabris; d/tr €160/230; 🖥🌊) This vine-covered 18th-century *chambre d'hôte* 4km southwest of Grasse slumbers in the shade of century-old olive, jasmine, fig and orange trees. Soft natural hues dress Sandra and Jérôme Maingret's four lovely rooms, and the coastal panorama from the pool is inspirational. Find the *mas* signposted off the D4 to Cabris. No children under seven; minimum two-night stay April to October.

ⓘ Information

Tourist Office (☑ 04 93 36 66 66; www.grasse.fr; place de la Buanderie; ⊙ 9am-6pm Mon-Fri, from 10am Tue, 9am-1pm & 2-6pm Sat; 🖥) The tourist office, at Grasse bus station, provides maps and information on the town.

ⓘ Getting There & Around

BUS

Bus 600 goes to Cannes (50 minutes, every 20 minutes) via Mouans-Sartoux (25 minutes) and Mougins (30 minutes). Bus 500 goes to Nice (1½ hours, hourly). All buses leave from the **bus station** (place de la Buanderie); fares are €1.50.

CAR

Grasse's one-way street system is maddening and often congested, so park as soon as you can and walk. If arriving from Nice, park at Parking Notre Dame des Fleurs. If arriving from Cannes, park at Parking Honoré Cresp. Allow €1.70 per hour.

TRAIN

The station is downhill from the centre; shuttle buses (€1.50) to 'Centre Ville' depart from in front of the train station. There are regular rail services to Nice (€9.30, 1¼ hours, hourly) via Cannes (€4.40, 30 minutes).

Mougins

POP 18,200

Pinprick Vieux Mougins looks almost too perfect to be real. Picasso discovered the medieval village in 1935 with lover Dora Marr and lived here with his final love, Jacqueline Roque, from 1961 until his death. Mougins

has since become something of an elite location, with prestigious hotel-restaurants, the country's most sought-after international school and Sophia Antipolis (France's Silicon Valley) nearby.

⊙ Sights

⭐ **Musée d'Art Classique de Mougins**   ART MUSEUM
(www.mouginsmusee.com; 32 rue Commandeur; adult/child €12/5; ⊙ 10am-6pm) The brainchild of compulsive art collector and British entrepreneur Christian Levett, this outstanding museum contains 600 works spanning 5000 years. The collection aims to show how ancient civilisations inspired neoclassical, modern and contemporary art, thus the collection is organised by civilisations – Rome, Greece and Egypt – with antiquities juxtaposed with seminal modern works. The top floor is dedicated to armoury, with excellent interactive displays bringing to life the helmets, spears and shields.

Musée de la Photographie André Villers   PHOTOGRAPHY MUSEUM
(Porte Sarrazine; ⊙ 10am-noon & 2-6pm Tue-Fri, 11am-7pm Sat & Sun) FREE The small but perfectly formed Musée de la Photographie has some fascinating black-and-white photos of Picasso, snapped by celebrated photographers such as André Villers and Jacques Henri Lartigue. It also hosts regular exhibitions on anything from fashion to war photography.

⭐ **Les Jardins du MIP**   GARDEN
(www.museesdegrasse.com; 979 chemin des Gourettes, Mouans-Sartoux; adult/child €3/free; ⊙ 10am-6pm Tue-Sun Apr-Oct) 🌿 These gardens – part of Grasse's Musée International de la Parfumerie (p100) – showcase plants used in perfumery. Half the garden is displayed as fields to show how local flowers such as rose, jasmine and lavender are grown commercially. The other half is organised by olfactive families (woody, floral, ambered etc), which visitors can pick, rub

ⓘ COMBINED TICKET

If you're planning on visiting both the Musée International de la Parfumerie and Les Jardins du MIP in Mougins, you can buy a combined ticket for €5, which includes a bus ticket between Grasse and the gardens (bus 20 or 21).

LUNCH & ART IN MOUANS-SARTOUX

If you're motoring from Cannes or Mougins to Grasse, little Mouans-Sartoux (population 10,490) is worth a pit stop for an oustanding lunch and an extraordinary afternoon of art.

Beneath quintessential Provence plane trees on the central old-town square, Le Sot l'y Laisse (☑ 04 93 75 54 50; place Suzanne de Villeneuve; menu €29, mains €14-18.50; ⊙ noon-2pm & 8-10pm Wed-Sun) enchants with whitewashed walls and sea-blue beams inside, parasol-shaded tables out. Order the catch of the day with *citrons confits* (preserved lemons) and seasonal vegetables in a Noilly Prat emulsion, brave the pan-fried duck hearts, or go for the restaurant's fabulous signature dish: *fricassée de Sot l'y Laisse* (a type of chicken stew that includes the *sot l'y laisse* – literally, the 'fool leaves it there', which refers to the 'oyster' of meat hidden on the back of poultry). End on a sweet high with apricot shortbread tart and pistachio ice cream.

Afterwards, meander across the leafy square into the 16th-century stone gate of Château de Mouans, historic host to contemporary-art centre Espace de l'Art Concret (www.espacedelartconcret.fr; place Suzanne de Villeneuve; adult/child €7/free; ⊙ 11am-7pm Jul & Aug, 1-6pm Wed-Sun Sep-Jun). Admire changing contemporary-art installations in the chateau, the pretty gardens and the purpose-built Donation Albers-Honegger extension – a lime-green concrete block ferociously clashing with its historic surroundings. All the old familiars (Eduardo Chillida, Yves Klein, Andy Warhol, César, Philippe Starck) are here, along with lesser-known practitioners and temporary exhibitions. Art lovers with kids: don't miss the 'treasure' trail of concrete slabs emblazoned with different words to find in the woods.

and smell their way around. The gardens are about 3km northwest of historic Mougins, towards Mouans-Sartoux. Take bus 20 or 21 from Grasse bus station.

🛏 Sleeping & Eating

Mougins' fountain-clad central square, place du Commandmant Lamy, and surrounding car-free streets are lined with restaurant pavement terraces cooking up ample dining options with quaint old-town views.

Les Rosées   B&B €€€
(☑ 04 92 92 29 64; www.lesrosees.com; 238 chemin de Font Neuve; d €245-318; 🛜 ♨) 🏊 This chic and authentic, 400-year-old stone manor house with five romantic suites, pool, sauna, jacuzzi and century-old olive trees is a haven of tranquillity. The decor mixes modern and vintage – the owners have their own interior-design venture – and breakfast is a copious organic affair. Find it 1.4km north of Mougins.

Le Mas Candille   GASTRONOMIC €€€
(☑ 04 92 28 43 43; www.lemascandille.com; bd Clément Rebuffel; lunch menu €49, dinner menus €95 & €135; ⊙ 12.30-2.30pm & 7.30-10pm Wed-Sun May-Sep) Mougins' most luxurious, five-star hotel, spa and restaurant has it all. Rooms are heavenly, the spa is bliss, and in the hotel restaurant (open to nonguests)

young Cannes-born chef David Chauvac cooks Michelin-starred Provençal cuisine inspired by humble childhood visits to Cannes' gourmet Marché Forville with his mother.

Spectacular views of Grasse and the Alps from the sumptuous dining room and summer terrace are the icing on the cake.

🍷 Drinking & Nightlife

La Cave de Mougins   WINE BAR
(www.lacavedemougins.com; 50 av Charles Mallet; ⊙ 11am-11pm Tue-Sat) The cellar of this wine bar is worth the detour, not just for its hundreds of vintages but also for its stunning vaulted ceiling, events-packed calendar (tastings, meet-the-winemakers evenings, little concerts etc) and atmospheric terrace. By day nibble pâté and cheese platters with a glass of wine.

ℹ Information

Tourist Office (☑ 04 92 92 14 00; www. mougins-tourisme.com; 39 place des Patriotes; ⊙ 9.30am-6pm or 7pm Mon-Sat, 10am-2pm Sun Jul & Aug, 9.30am-6pm Mon-Sat Jun & Sep, 9am-5pm Mon-Fri, 9.30am-5pm Sat Oct-May)

ℹ Getting There & Around

Bus 600 (€1.50, every 20 minutes) between Cannes and Grasse stops in Mougins and Mouans-Sartoux.

MASSIF DE L'ESTÉREL

Corniche de l'Estérel

A walk or drive along the winding Corniche de l'Estérel (also called the Corniche d'Or, 'Golden Coast'; the N98), opened by the Touring Club de France in 1903, is an attraction in its own right. Views are spectacular and small summer resorts and dreamy inlets (perfect for swimming), all accessible by bus or train, dot its 30km length. The most dramatic stretch is between Anthéor and Théoule-sur-Mer, where the tortuous, narrow N98 skirts through sparsely built areas.

🏃 Activities

With its lush green Mediterranean forests, intensely red peaks and sterling sea views, the Estérel is a walker's paradise. Local tourist offices have leaflets detailing the most popular walks, including Pic de l'Ours (496m) and Pic du Cap Roux (452m). Buy IGN's Carte de Randonnée (1:25,000) No 3544ET *Fréjus, Saint-Raphaël & Corniche de l'Estérel* for more serious walks.

Those preferring a more informed hike can sign up for a three-hour guided walk with a forest ranger from the Office National des Forêts (National Forestry Office) or nature guide at St-Raphaël tourist office (p106). Access to the range is prohibited on windy or particularly hot days because of fire risks; check with the tourist office before setting off.

With its 36km of coastline, the corniche has more than 30 beaches running the gamut of possibilities: sandy, pebbly, nudist, cove-like, you name it. But wherever you go, the sea remains that crystal-clear turquoise and deep blue, an irresistible invitation to swim.

The Estérel is also a leading dive centre, with numerous WWII shipwrecks and pristine waters. Much of the coast is protected, meaning its fauna and flora are among the best around.

Sentier du Littoral   WALKING
Running 11km between Port Santa Lucia (the track starts behind the naval works) and Agay, this coastal path (yellow markers) takes in some of the area's most scenic spots. It takes roughly 4½ hours to complete, but from May to October you could make a day of it by stopping at some of the idyllic beaches scattered along the way.

You can choose to walk smaller sections; the most scenic is around Cap du Dramont, crowned by a signal station, which you can do as a loop from Plage du Débarquement. This long, sandy beach is where the US 36th Infantry Division landed on 15 August 1944 as part of Operation Dragoon (Provence landing). The large memorial park has a car park easily accessible from the N98.

Plage d'Agay   SWIMMING
One of the best beaches along the Corniche de l'Estérel for activities (beach volleyball, kids' clubs, water sports etc).

Plage Beaurivage.   SWIMMING
One of the best beaches along the Corniche de l'Estérel for activities (beach volleyball, kids' clubs, water sports etc).

Rade d'Agay   SWIMMING
For a scenic swim off a sandy beach, the beaches along this stretch of the Corniche de l'Estérel are perfect.

**Anthéor–Le
Trayas Coast**   SNORKELLING, SWIMMING
The section of the Corniche de l'Estérel between Anthéor and Le Trayas is famed for its jewel-like *calanques* (tiny coves) and brilliant snorkelling. The landscape here is much more rugged, with many coves only accessible by boat.

Centre de Plongée Île d'Or   DIVING
(📞04 94 82 73 67; www.dive.fr; 986 bd 36ème Division du Texas, Agay) Multilingual, CMAS-accredited diving club offering individual dives as well as courses.

Euro Plongée   DIVING, SNORKELLING
(📞04 94 19 03 26; www.europlongee.fr; Port de Boulouris) A reputable, family-friendly dive club with CMAS accreditation. Offers individual dives and courses, as well as great two-hour snorkelling tours (€30), which are fantastic for families – kids will love spotting starfish, sea anemones, urchins and other colourful Mediterranean residents.

🛏 Sleeping & Eating

Villa Matuzia   PROVENÇAL €€
(📞04 94 82 79 95; www.matuzia.com; 15 bd Ste Guitte, Agay; mains €21-30, lunch menu €22, dinner menus €43 & €65; ⊙lunch & dinner Wed-Sun, closed Sun evening Oct-May; ❄️ 🛜) The tastiest place to dine in the Estérel is this Provençal house 200m from the sea. It serves elaborate Mediterranean cuisine (fabulous catch of

the day) and the setting is charming: a cosy dining room in winter and a lush summer terrace. Its two bedrooms (doubles including breakfast €75), each with a little patio, are the best value on the entire coast.

❶ Getting There & Around

BUS

Bus 8 runs between St-Raphaël and Agay, stopping at Le Dramont on the way; three services a day go all the way to Le Trayas. Tickets cost €1.10.

CAR

The corniche gets very busy in summer: if you need to go somewhere, as opposed to enjoy a scenic drive, take the inland N7 or the A8 motorway.

TRAIN

Mandelieu-La Napoule, Le Trayas, Agay, Le Dramont and Boulouris all have stations on the St Raphaël–Nice line, but only a handful of services each day stop there.

St-Raphaël

POP 34,716

St-Raphaël is a good base for exploring the Estérel rather than a destination in itself. The very dynamic **tourist office** (✆04 94 19 52 52; www.saint-raphael.com; 99 quai Albert 1er; ⊙9am-7pm Jul & Aug, 9am-12.30pm & 2-6.30pm Mon-Sat Sep-Jun) can help you book activities in the region.

A great way to discover the coast is to board **Les Bateaux de St-Raphaël** (www.bateauxsaintraphael.com; quai Nomy; ⊙May-Sep) for a scenic cruise along the Corniche de l'Estérel (adult/child €16/10) to St-Tropez (adult/child €25/15, crossing time one hour) and Île Ste-Marguerite (adult/child €22/12).

The pick of accommodation in town is seasonal **L'Hirondelle Blanche** (✆04 94 11 84 03; www.hirondelle-blanche.fr; 533 av des Chèvrefeuilles; d €89-169; ⊙May–mid-Oct), an elegant early-20th-century villa with six romantic rooms run with panache by avuncular artist George. 'The White Swallow' is full of charm, with paintings and books everywhere. For dinner, try **Les Charavins** (✆04 94 95 03 76; 36 rue Charabois; mains €18-26; ⊙dinner Thu-Tue, lunch Thu, Fri, Mon & Tue), a wine bar with French fare like frogs' legs, onion soup and steaks, or gastronomic **Elly's** (✆04 94 83 63 39; www.elly-s.com; 54 rue de la Liberté; lunch menus Tue-Fri €24, dinner menus €35-70, mains €32; ⊙noon-1.30pm & 7-9.30pm Tue-Sat), where

works of modern art serve as a striking backdrop to modern French cuisine.

There are regular trains from St-Raphaël to Nice (€15, 1¼ hours, half-hourly), Cannes (€10.20, 30 minutes, half-hourly) and Marseille (€27.30, 1½ hours, hourly). Bus 4 goes to Fréjus' old town (€1.10) from St-Raphaël bus station.

Fréjus

POP 53,298

Settled by Massiliots (Greek colonists from Marseille) and colonised by Julius Caesar around 49 BC as Forum Julii, Fréjus is a quiet place. The appealing old town is a maze of pastel buildings, shady plazas and winding alleys, climaxing with extraordinary medieval paintings in an episcopal complex wedged between a trio of market squares.

◎ Sights

Fréjus' Roman ruins are not brilliantly preserved, but their abundance bears witness to the importance of Forum Julii at the time, with its strategic location on Via Aurelia and its port.

★**Cloître de la Cathédrale de Fréjus**   CATHEDRAL
(http://cathedrale-frejus.monuments-nationaux.fr; 58 rue de Fleury; adult/child €5.50/free; ⊙10am-12.30pm & 1.45-6.30pm Jun-Sep, 10am-1pm & 2-5pm Tue-Sat Oct-May) Fréjus' star sight is its 11th- and 12th-century **cathedral**, one of the region's first Gothic buildings. Its **cloister** features rare 14th- and 15th-century painted wooden ceiling panels depicting angels, devils, hunters, acrobats and monsters in vivid comic-book fashion. The meaning and origin of these are unknown. Only 500 of the original 1200 frames survive. Afterwards, peek at the octagonal 5th-century **baptistery**, which incorporates eight Roman columns; it is one of the oldest Christian buildings in France and is exceptionally well preserved.

Musée Archéologique   ARCHAEOLOGY MUSEUM
(place Calvini; adult/child €2/free; ⊙9.30am-12.30pm & 2-6pm Tue-Sun Apr-Sep, 9.30am-noon & 2-4.30pm Tue & Thu-Sat Oct-Mar) The small but fascinating Musée Archéologique features treasures unearthed in and around Fréjus, from everyday objects to rare finds such as a double-faced marble statue of Hermes, a head of Jupiter and a stunning 3rd-century mosaic depicting a leopard.

Fréjus

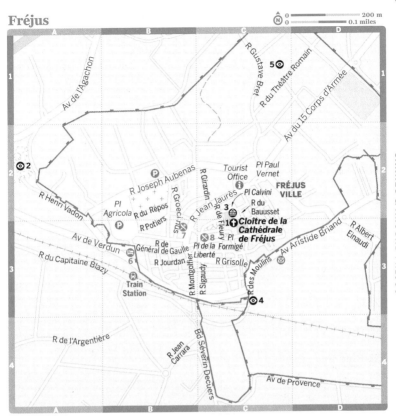

Porte d'Orée
ROMAN SITES

(rue des Moulins; ☉9.30am-12.30pm & 2-6pm Tue-Sun Apr-Sep, 9.30am-noon & 2-4.30pm Tue-Sat Oct-Mar) At the southeastern edge of the old city is the 3rd-century Porte d'Orée, the only remaining arcade of monumental Roman thermal baths.

Théâtre Romain
ROMAN SITES

(Roman Theatre; rue du Théâtre Romain; adult/child €2/free; ☉9.30am-12.30pm & 2-6pm Tue-Sun Apr-Sep, 9.30am-noon & 2-4.30pm Tue-Sat Oct-Mar) North of the old town are the ruins of a Théâtre Romain. Part of the stage and the theatre's outer walls are all that remain.

Les Arènes
ROMAN SITES

(Amphitheatre; ☎04 94 51 34 31; rue Henri Vadon; adult/child €2/free; ☉9.30am-12.30pm & 2-6pm Tue-Sun Apr-Sep, 9.30am-noon & 2-4.30pm Tue-Sat Oct-Mar) West of the old town, past the ancient **Porte des Gaules**, is the mostly rebuilt 1st- and 2nd-century Les Arènes.

It was one of Gaul's largest amphitheatres (seating 10,000 spectators). The site has been damaged by archaeological digs, but a comprehensive renovation program hopes to breathe new life into it.

ⓘ CENT SAVER

A seven-day **Fréjus Pass** (€4.60) covers admission to the Roman amphitheatre and theatre, archaeological museum and Cocteau's chapel. To visit the cathedral cloister and baptistry as well, buy a seven-day **Fréjus Pass Intégral** (€6.60). Participating sights, except the cathedral, sell passes.

Chapelle Cocteau ART MUSEUM

(Chapelle Notre Dame de Jérusalem; ☑ 04 94 53 27 06; rte de Cannes; adult/child €2/free; ☺ 9.30am-12.30pm & 2-6pm Tue-Sun Apr-Sep, 9.30am-noon & 2-4.30pm Tue-Sat Oct-Mar) This was one of the last pieces of work embarked upon by Jean Cocteau (1889–1963), best known for the fishers' chapel he decorated in Villefranche-sur-Mer. Cocteau began work on Chapelle Notre Dame in Fréjus in 1961, but it remained incomplete until the artist's legal heir, Édouard Dermit, finished his former companion's work in 1988. The chapel is about 5km northeast of the old city, in the quarter of La Tour de Mare (served by bus 13), on the N7 towards Cannes.

🛏 Sleeping

Auberge de Jeunesse Fréjus-St-Raphaël HOSTEL €

(☑ 04 94 53 18 75; www.fuaj.org; chemin du Counillier; dm €19.78; ☺ Mar-Oct; ☎) A rambling, pretty basic HI-affiliated hostel set in 10 hectares of pine trees, where you can also pitch your tent. Take bus 7 from St-Raphaël or Fréjus train stations to stop Les Chênes, then cross the roundabout and take chemin du Counillier on your left (600m). Daily lockout between noon and 5.30pm; rates include breakfast and sheets.

Hôtel L'Aréna HOTEL €€

(☑ 04 94 17 09 40; www.hotel-frejus-arena.com; 145 rue du Général de Gaulle; d/tr €154/204; ❄☎☎⚒) With its sienna-coloured walls and lush garden, L'Aréna is a very pleasant option. The Provençal decor is starting to age, but the rooms remain comfortable. Those in the Jasmine annexe are more spacious, but there is no lift in that building.

The duplexes are ideal for families (with two single beds on a mezzanine). Breakfast €17.

🍴 Eating

Swoon over seasonal fruit, veg and other culinary goodies at the twice-weekly market that fills almost every street in the old town on Wednesday and Saturday mornings.

★**Mon Fromager** DELI €

(☑ 04 94 40 67 99; www.mon-fromager.fr; 38 rue Sieyès; plat du jour €13.90, 5-cheese platter €10.90; ☺ shop 9am-7pm Tue-Sat, lunch noon-2pm Tue-Sat; ☑) Enterprising cheesemonger Philippe Daujam not only sells cheese – he also cooks it up into tasty lunches in his deli-style restaurant with tables (faux cow-skin table mats included) arranged in front of the cheese counter and on the street outside. Locals flock here for the excellent-value *plat du jour* (dish of the day) and can't-go-wrong cheese platters with salad.

Maison de la Tarte BOULANGERIE €

(33 rue Jean Jaurès; tarts & sandwiches from €2.80; ☺ 7am-7pm Mon-Sat Aug-Jun; ☑) If you're planning a picnic, stop at this mouth-watering bakery. Tarts of every kind (lemon meringue, pear and chocolate, raspberry and almond etc), sold by the slice, fill the front window and back shelves. Sandwiches and quiches are equally good.

ⓘ Information

Tourist Office (☑ 04 94 51 83 83; www.frejus.fr; 249 rue Jean Jaurès; ☺ 9.30am-7pm Jul & Aug, 9.30am-12.30pm & 2-6.30pm Mon-Sat Jun & Sep, 9am-noon & 2-6pm Mon-Sat Oct-May)

ⓘ Getting There & Away

BUS

Bus 4 links Fréjus with St-Raphaël (€1.10).

CAR

Parking du Clos de la Tour, on the edge of the old town, is free.

TRAIN

From Fréjus' small train station there are hourly services to/from Cannes (€7.90, 40 minutes), St-Raphaël (€1.40, three minutes) and Nice (€12, 70 minutes).

St-Tropez to Toulon

Why Go?

Sizzling St-Tropez lives up to its reputation as a mythical fishing port with magnificent sex appeal. While away the days strolling the village and people-watching in the place des Lices, or sipping a cappuccino alongside the yacht-lined quay. Then head out to explore the peninsula's soul-stirring coastal paths, chichi beach clubs and vine-knitted capes. When you're ready to move out of the limelight, you'll be enveloped by nature in the Massif des Maures, where thick chestnut groves harbour small villages and surprising vistas. The main trio of islands in the Îles d'Hyères offers a splendid, quiet coastal escape. Inland, in the Haut-Var, meander stone villages, each with its own character and history, and meet the laid-back people who maintain an unpretentious but enviable way of life. Oh, and allow plenty of time to dine well.

Best Places to Eat

➡ Chez Bruno (p125)

➡ Le Clos des Vignes (p127)

➡ La Pescalune (p125)

➡ Domaine de la Maurette (p123)

➡ La Vague d'Or (p116)

Best Places to Stay

➡ Le Mas du Langoustier (p135)

➡ Hôtel des Deux Rocs (p125)

➡ Hôtel Byblos (p116)

➡ Hôtel de la Tour (p139)

➡ Château de Valmer (p121)

Driving Distances (km)

	Bandol	Collobrieres	Draguignan	Hyères	St-Tropez
Collobrieres	72				
Draguignan	103	56			
Hyères	39	30	82		
St-Tropez	97	30	52	50	
Toulon	20	38	83	18	68

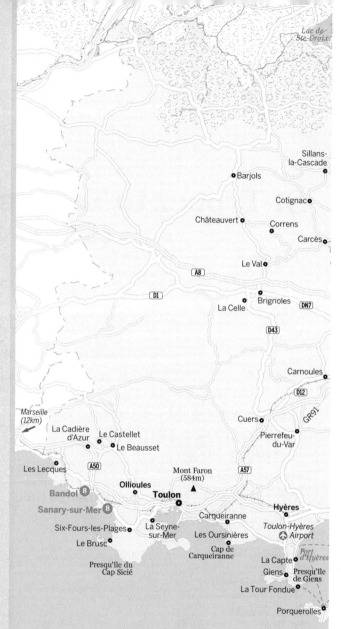

St-Tropez to Toulon Highlights

1 Frolic with celebrities in **St-Tropez** (p112) during high season, and soak up the golden light in winter.

2 Find your way through the Massif des Maures to serene **Monastère de la Verne** (p128).

3 Roam the tranquil back roads of the **Haut-Var** (p122) and its tiny hilltop villages.

4 Take a dramatic cape-to-cape walk around the **St-Tropez peninsula** (p113).

5 Spend the day wandering (or snorkelling) at the lush Mediterranean garden of the **Domaine du Rayol** (p132).

6 Enjoy the island paradise of **Île de Porquerolles** (p133).

7 Go nuts on sweet chestnuts in **Collobrières** (p128).

8 Promenade on the quay at **Sanary-sur-Mer** (p139) and taste **Bandol** (p140) wines.

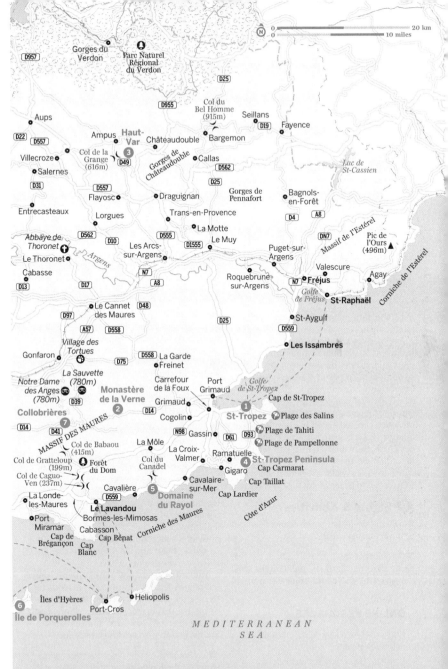

PRESQU'ÎLE DE ST-TROPEZ

Jutting out into the sea, between the Golfe de St-Tropez and the Baie de Cavalaire, is the St-Tropez peninsula. From swanky St-Tropez on the northern coast, fine-sand beaches of buttercream yellow and gold – easily the loveliest on the Côte d'Azur – ring the peninsula. Inland, the flower-dressed hilltop villages of Gassin and Ramatuelle charm the socks off millions.

St-Tropez

POP 4903

Pouting sexpot Brigitte Bardot came to St-Tropez in the '50s to star in *Et Dieu Créa la Femme* (And God Created Woman; 1956) and overnight transformed the peaceful fishing village into a sizzling jet-set favourite. Tropeziens have thrived on their sexy image ever since: at the Vieux Port, yachts like spaceships jostle for millionaire moorings, and infinitely more tourists jostle to admire them.

Yet there is a serene side to this village trampled by 60,000 summertime inhabitants and visitors on any given day. Out of season the St-Tropez of mesmerising quaint beauty and 'sardine scales glistening like pearls on the cobblestones' that charmed Guy de Maupassant (1850–93) comes to life. Meander cobbled lanes in the old fishing quarter of La Ponche, sip pastis at a place des Lices cafe, watch old men play *pétanque* (a variant on the game of bowls) beneath plane trees, or walk in solitary splendour from beach to beach along the coastal path.

☉ Sights & Activities

For St-Tropez' fabled beach scene, head out to the Peninsula (p119).

★ **Vieux Port**   PORT

Yachts line the harbour and visitors stroll the quays at the picturesque old port. In front of the sable-coloured town houses, the **Bailli de Suffren statue** (quai Suffren), cast from a 19th-century cannon, peers out to sea. The bailiff (1729–88) was a sailor who fought with a Tropezien crew against Britain and Prussia during the Seven Years' War. As much of an institution as the bailiff is portside cafe Sénéquier (p117).

Duck beneath the archway, next to the tourist office, to uncover St-Tropez' daily morning **fish market**, on place aux Herbes.

★ **Place des Lices**   SQUARE

St-Tropez' legendary and very charming central square is studded with plane trees, cafes and *pétanque* players. Simply sitting on a cafe terrace watching the world go by or jostling with the crowds at its extravaganza of a twice-weekly **market** (place des Lices; ☉ 8am-1pm Tue & Sat), jam-packed with everything from fruit and veg to antique mirrors and sandals, is an integral part of the St-Tropez experience.

Artists and intellectuals have met for decades in St-Tropez' famous Café des Arts, now simply called **Le Café** (www.lecafe.fr; place des Lices; lunch/dinner menus €18/32; ☉ 8am-11pm), not to be confused with the newer, green-canopied Café des Arts on the corner of the square. Aspiring *pétanque* players can borrow a set of boules from the bar. Locals tend to hang on the other side of the square.

★ **Musée de l'Annonciade**   ART MUSEUM

(place Grammont; adult/child €6/free; ☉ 10am-1am & 2-6pm Wed-Mon) In a gracefully converted 16th-century chapel, this small but famous museum showcases an impressive collection of modern art infused with that legendary Côte d'Azur light. Pointillist Paul Signac bought a house in St-Tropez in 1892 and introduced other artists to the area. The museum's collection includes his *St-Tropez, Le Quai* (1899) and *St-Tropez, Coucher de Soleil au Bois de Pins* (1896).

Vuillard, Bonnard and Maurice Denis (the self-named 'Nabis' group) have a room to themselves. The Fauvist collection includes works by Derain and Matisse, who spent the summer of 1904 here. Cubists George Braque and Picasso are also represented.

★ **La Ponche**   HISTORIC QUARTER

Shrug off the hustle of the port in St-Tropez' historic fishing quarter, La Ponche, northeast of the Vieux Port. From the southern end of quai Frédéric Mistral, place Garrezio sprawls

---

ONLINE RESOURCES

Visit Var (www.visitvar.fr) Information on the Var region.

Vins de Provence (www.vinsde-provence.com) Wine.

Maisons d'Hôtes du Var (www.mhv-provence.com) Stylish B&Bs.

east from 10th-century **Tour Suffren** to place de l'Hôtel de Ville. From here, rue Guichard leads southeast to sweet-chiming **Église de St-Tropez** (place de l'Ormeau), a St-Trop landmark built in 1785 in Italian Baroque style. Inside is a bust of St Torpes, honoured during Les Bravades in May.

Follow rue du Portail Neuf south to **Chapelle de la Miséricorde** (rue de la Miséricorde), built in 1645 with a pretty bell tower and colourful tiled dome.

★ **Citadelle de St-Tropez**　　MUSEUM
(☎04 94 54 84 14; admission €3; ⊙10am-6.30pm Apr-Sep, 10am-12.30pm & 1.30-5.30pm Oct-Mar) Built in 1602 to defend the coast against Spain, the citadel dominates the hillside overlooking St-Tropez to the east. The views are fantastic. Its dungeons are home to the excellent **Musée de l'Histoire Maritime**, an all-interactive museum inaugurated in July 2013 retracing the history of humans at sea, from fishing, trading, exploration, travel and the navy.

Sentier du Littoral　　WALKING
A spectacular coastal path wends past rocky outcrops and hidden bays 35km south from St-Tropez, around the peninsula to the beach at Cavalaire-sur-Mer. In St-Tropez the yellow-flagged path starts at **La Ponche**, immediately east of Tour du Portalet, and curves around Port des Pêcheurs, past St-Tropez' citadel. It then leads past the walled **Cimitière Marin** (Marine Cemetery), **Plage des Graniers** and beyond.

The tourist office has maps with distances and walking times (eg to Plage des Salins: 8.5km, 2½ hours).

☞ **Tours**

Les Bateaux Verts　　BOAT TOUR
(☎04 94 49 29 39; www.bateauxverts.com; quai Jean Jaurès) Les Bateaux Verts offers trips around Baie des Cannebiers (dubbed 'Bay of Stars' after the celebrity villas dotting its coast) April to September (adult/child €10.50/6), as well as seasonal boats to Cannes (€37.80/24.40) and Porquerolles (€42.30/27.80), and shuttle boats to Marines de Cogolin, Port Grimaud, Ste-Maxime and Les Issambres.

★★ **Festivals & Events**

Les Bravades　　RELIGIOUS FESTIVAL
Since 1558 Tropeziens have turned out in traditional costume to watch an ear-splitting army of 140 musket-firing *bravadeurs* pa-

HEADLESS HERO

A grisly legend provided St-Tropez with its name in AD 68. After beheading a Roman officer named Torpes for becoming a Christian, the emperor Nero packed the decapitated body into a small boat, along with a dog and a rooster, who were to devour his remains. Miraculously, the body came ashore in St-Tropez un-nibbled, and the village adopted the headless Torpes as its saint.

rade with a bust of St Torpes. Les Bravades (Provençal for 'bravery') is held 16 to 18 May.

Les Bravades des Espagnols　　CARNIVAL
Blazing guns and colourful processions on 15 June celebrate victory over the 21 Spanish galleons that attacked in 1637.

🛏 **Sleeping**

St-Tropez is no shoestring destination, but campgrounds sit southeast along Plage de Pampelonne. Most hotels close occasionally in winter; the tourist office lists what's open and has a list of B&Bs. If you're driving, double-check the parking arrangements.

★ **Hôtel Lou Cagnard**　　HOTEL €€
(☎04 94 97 04 24; www.hotel-lou-cagnard.com; 18 av Paul Roussel; d €81-171; ⊙Mar-Oct; ❄🐾) Book well ahead for this great-value courtyard charmer, shaded by lemon and fig trees, and owned by schooled hoteliers. The pretty Provençal house has a jasmine-scented garden strung with fairy lights. Bright, beautifully clean rooms are decorated with painted furniture. Five have ground-floor garden terraces. The cheapest rooms have private washbasin and stand-up bathtub but share a toilet; most have air-con.

Hôtel Le Colombier　　HOTEL €€
(☎04 94 97 05 31; http://lecolombierhotel.free. fr; impasse des Conquettes; d/tr from €105/235; ⊙mid-Apr–mid-Nov; ❄🐾) An immaculately clean converted house, five minutes' walk from place des Lices, the Colombier's fresh, summery decor is feminine and uncluttered, with bedrooms in shades of white, and vintage furniture.

Hôtel Les Palmiers　　HOTEL €€
(☎04 94 97 01 61; www.hotel-les-palmiers.com; 26 bd Vasserot; d €140-275; ❄🐾) In an old villa opposite place des Lices, Les Palmiers

St-Tropez

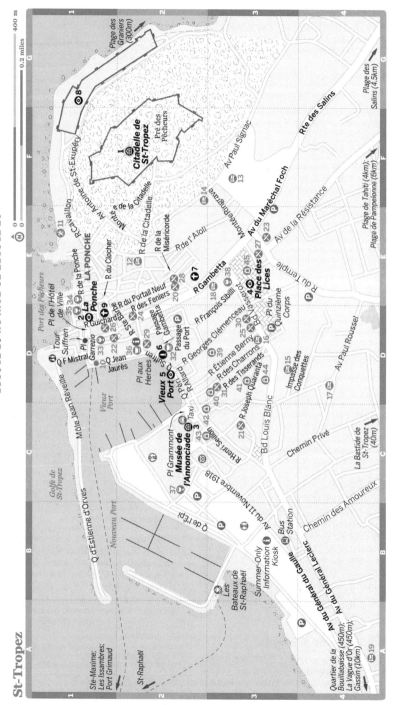

400 m
0.2 miles

Plage des
Graniers
(300m)

Plage des
Salins (4.5km)

Rte des Salins

Plage de Tahiti (4km);
Plage de Pampelonne (6km)

Citadelle de
St-Tropez

Pré des
Pêcheurs

Av Paul Signac

Av de la Résistance

Av du Maréchal Foch

Montée de la Citadelle

Av Antoine de St-Exupéry

R Cavaillon

R Ste-Anne

R de la Ponche

LA PONCHE

La Ponche

R du Clocher

R de la Citadelle

R de la
Miséricorde

R de l'Aïoli

Montée Ringrave

R du Temple

Port des Pêcheurs

Pl de l'Hôtel
de Ville

Tour
Suffren

Garrezio

Q F Mistral

Pl des
Herbes

R Guichard

R du Portail Neuf

R des Feniers

R des Féniers

Passage Gambetta

R Gambetta

Place des
Lices

Pl du
Quinzième
Corps

R François Sibilli

R Georges Clémenceau

R Étienne Berny

R des Charrons

R des Tisserands

R Joseph Quaranta

Bd Louis Blanc

Bd d'Aumale

Impasse des
Conquettes

Av Paul Roussel

Chemin Privé

La Bastide de
St-Tropez
(40m)

Vieux
Port

Pl Jean
Jaurès

Q Jean
Jaurès

Passage
du Port

Q Péri

Q Allard

R Henri Seillon

Taxi

Pl Grammont

Musée de
l'Annonciade

Av du 11 Novembre 1918

Q de l'Épi

Bus
Station

Summer-Only
Information
Kiosk

Chemin des Amoureux

Av du Général du Gaulle

Av du Général Leclerc

Quartier de la
Bouillabaisse (450m);
La Vague d'Or (450m);
Gassin (10km)

Golfe de
St-Tropez

Nouveau Port

Môle Jean Réveille

Q d'Esthenne d'Orves

Vieux
Port

Les
Bateaux de
St-Raphaël

Ste-Maxime;
Les Issambres;
Port Grimaud

St-Raphaël

St-Tropez

has simple, bright rooms around a stylish courtyard. Choose one in the main building rather than the annexe.

Pastis DESIGN HOTEL €€€
(☏04 98 12 56 50; www.pastis-st-tropez.com; 61 av du Général Leclerc; d from €375; ❄❀☀) This stunning town house–turned-hotel is the brainchild of an English couple besotted with Provence and passionate about modern art. You'll die for the pop-art-inspired interior, and long for a swim in the emerald-green pool. Every room is beautiful, although those overlooking av Leclerc are noisy.

Hôtel Ermitage BOUTIQUE HOTEL €€€
(☏04 94 81 08 10; www.ermitagehotel.fr; av Paul Signac; r €180-850; ❄❀) Kate Moss and Lenny Kravitz favour St-Trop's latest rocker crash pad, which draws inspiration from St-Tropez from the '50s to the '70s: disco meets midcentury modern. Rooms are decorated in bold, glossy colours – the smallest have the shower in the room itself. There are knockout views over town from the bar terrace.

B Lodge Hôtel HOTEL €€€
(☏04 94 97 58 72; www.hotel-b-lodge.com; 23 rue de l'Aïoli; d from €170; ☉Dec-Oct; ❄❀) Behind the traditional building exterior hide some very modern rooms indeed, with minimalist decor, dark soft furnishings and feature stone walls. The cheapest rooms don't have air-con, which, at this price, feels rather stingy. But those with balconies and Citadelle views are fabulous. Prices drop significantly in winter.

✖ Eating

Prices are high: the glamour dust sprinkled on fish and chips doesn't come cheap! Many restaurants close in winter. Reservations are essential in high season.

Don't leave town without sampling *tarte Tropézienne,* an orange-blossom-flavoured double sponge cake filled with thick cream, created by a Polish baker and christened by Brigitte Bardot in the 1950s.

Quai Jean Jaurès is lined with mediocre restaurants with great portside views. Cheaper eats cluster near Quai de l'Épi and the new port.

GLITZY LIVING

In addition to Pastis and Hôtel Ermitage, St-Tropez is home to other celebrity-studded hangs, with prices to match.

Hôtel Byblos (☑04 94 56 68 00; www.byblos.com; av Paul Signac; r/ste from €340/875; ⊙mid-Apr–Sep; @ 🛜 ⌨) Hôtel Byblos remains a perennial favourite among Hollywood A-listers, who come for the exclusive atmosphere, smack in the centre of St-Tropez. Renowned Alain Ducasse restaurant Rivea and Byblos' Les Caves du Roy club scene round out the fun.

Pan Deï Palais (☑04 94 17 71 71; www.pandei.com; 52 rue Gambetta; d from €690) This elegant town house with a lush central courtyard is decked out along luxe Indian themes. Swan about like a rajah.

La Bastide de Saint-Tropez (☑04 94 55 82 55; www.bastidesaint-tropez.com; rte des Carles; r/apt from €550/1120; ⊙Feb-Dec; ❋ 🛜 ⌨) Staying at La Bastide de Saint-Tropez, on the edge of the town, is like living in your own sprawling country villa.

La Vague d'Or (☑04 94 55 91 00; www.residencepinede.com; Résidence de la Pinède, Plage de la Bouillabaisse; menus from €275; ⊙7.30-10pm mid-Apr–mid-Oct) Wonder-chef Arnaud Donckele has established a gastronomic temple with three Michelin stars at the Résidence de la Pinède: expect Mediterranean ingredients and flavours, with a one-of-a-kind twist.

Le Bistrot à la Truffe (☑04 94 43 95 18; www.bistrot-la-truffe.com; 2 rue de l'Eglise; menus from €69; ⊙11.30am-10pm Apr-Sep) Bruno Clément, arguably France's most famous truffle chef – who has an elaborate restaurant north in Lorgues – has opened Le Bistrot à la Truffe to dish up extravagant truffle-dosed creations.

★**La Tarte Tropézienne** CAFE, BOULANGERIE €
(www.latartetropezienne.fr; place des Lices; mains €13-15; ⊙6.30am-7.30pm, lunch noon-3pm) This cafe-bakery is the creator of the eponymous cake, and therefore the best place to buy St-Tropez' delicacy. But to start, choose from delicious daily specials, salads and sandwiches, which you can enjoy in the bistro inside or on the little terrace outside.

Several branches dot St-Tropez, and you'll see them around the Côte d'Azur – perfect for catering to your sweet tooth.

Le Gorille CAFE €
(☑04 94 97 03 93; www.legorille.com; 1 quai Suffren; sandwiches/mains €7/17; ⊙7am-7pm Thu-Tue Apr-Oct) This portside hang-out gets its name from its previous owner – the short, muscular and apparently very hairy Henri Guérin! Stop here for breakfast or a postclubbing *croque-monsieur* (grilled cheese and ham sandwich, sometimes topped with béchamel) and fries.

La Ramade BISTRO €
(☑04 94 81 58 67; 3 rue du Temple; menus €16; ⊙noon-2pm & 7-10.30pm Feb–mid-Nov) Simple, unpretentious and a bargain: a rarity in St-Tropez. Dine heartily by the hearth in winter or on the terrace in summer, just a block from place des Lices.

★**Le Sporting** BRASSERIE €€
(place des Lices; mains €16-30; ⊙8am-1am) There's a bit of everything on the menu at always-packed Le Sporting, but the speciality is the hamburger topped with foie gras and morel cream sauce. The Brittany-born owner also serves perfect buckwheat crêpes, honest lunch deals (€13), and a simple salad and *croque-monsieur*.

La Table du Marché BISTRO €€
(☑04 94 97 01 25; www.christophe-leroy.com; 11 rue des Commerçants; lunch/dinner menus €21/32; ⊙noon-2pm & 7-10pm Apr-Oct; ☑) This comfortable bistro by St-Tropez' savviest chef, Christophe Leroy, is a success story. The lobster gratin and truffle- and celery-stuffed ravioli are unforgettable, and vegetarians are properly catered for. On the ground floor of the renovated historic town house, a *salon de thé* (tearoom) offers tasty pastries and treats all day long.

Le G' BISTRO €€
(☑07 86 31 11 22; 67 rue du Portail Neuf; lunch/dinner menus €16/35; ⊙noon-2pm & 7.30-11pm Tue-Sun) Casual and tiny, Le G' is tucked into the old town of St-Tropez as the lanes climb toward the citadel. The busy chef works in a small open-plan kitchen, so come prepared

to wait, but the generous portions, delicious daily menus and cheerful service make it a super deal. For sun-worshippers, a few tables spill onto the pavement.

Chez les Garçons MODERN FRENCH €€
(04 94 49 42 67; www.chezlesgarcons.com; 11/13 rue du Cépoun; menus €32; 9-11pm Thu-Sun Mar, Apr & Oct, daily May-Sep) Super-friendly staff serve delicate specialities like a perfectly poached egg with foie gras, all under the watchful eyes of Marilyn, Brigitte and Audrey (art on the wall). There's a lively gay bar next door.

Au Caprice des Deux TRADITIONAL FRENCH €€€
(04 94 97 76 78; www.aucapricedesdeux.com; 40 rue du Portail Neuf; mains €25-36; 7.30-10.30pm nightly Jul & Aug, Wed-Mon Apr-Jun & Sep, Thu-Sat Oct-Mar) This traditional *maison de village* (old stone terraced house) with coffee-coloured wooden shutters is a fancy-night-out favourite with locals. Its intimate interior is as traditional as its French cuisine: think beef filet with truffles or duck.

Salama MOROCCAN €€€
(04 94 97 59 62; http://formastec.free.fr/salama; 1 rue des Tisserands; mains €22-35; 7-11pm Apr-Oct) Lounge on cushioned exotic furnishings, wash down heavenly scented couscous and *tajines* with fresh mint tea, and finish with a lime sherbet.

Auberge des Maures PROVENÇAL €€€
(04 94 97 01 50; www.aubergedesmaures.fr; 4 rue du Docteur Boutin; mains €35-45; 7.30-10pm Apr-Oct) The town's oldest restaurant remains the locals' choice for always-good, copious portions of earthy Provençal cooking, like *daube* (braised beef stew) or tapenade-stuffed lamb shoulder. Book a table (essential) on the leafy courtyard.

Drinking & Nightlife

Dress to kill. And bring more money than you think you'll need. Many places close in winter, but in summer it's party central seven days a week.

To tap into the local gay scene, hit Chez les Garçons or L'Esquinade.

Sénéquier CAFE
(www.senequier.com; quai Jean Jaurès; 8am-1am year-round) Sartre wrote parts of *Les Chemins de la Liberté* (Roads to Freedom) at this portside cafe – in business since 1887 – that's popular with boaties, bikers and tourists. Look

for the terrace crammed with pillar-boxred tables and director's chairs. Be warned, however, that a mere coffee costs €8...

Les Caves du Roy CLUB
(www.lescavesduroy.com; Hôtel Byblos, av Paul Signac; 7pm-5am Fri & Sat Apr-Oct, nightly Jul & Aug) This star-studded bar at the infamous Hôtel Byblos remains the perennial champion of nightclubs in St-Tropez, if not the whole Riviera. Dress to impress if you hope to get in and mingle with starlets and racecar drivers.

Bar du Port CAFE, BAR
(www.barduport.com; quai Suffren; 7am-3am year-round) Young, happening harbourside bar for beautiful people, with chichi decor in shades of white and silver.

Bar at l'Ermitage BAR
(www.ermitagehotel.fr; Hôtel Ermitage, av Paul Signac; 5pm-midnight Apr-Oct) Escape the crowds at the laid-back Ermitage, kitted out in distressed '50s-modern furniture, with enchanting views of the rooftops of old St-Tropez and the sea.

L'Esquinade CLUB
(2 rue du Four; midnight-7am daily Jun-Sep, Thu-Sat only Oct-May) Where the party winds up when you want to dance until dawn. Open year-round and the Tropéziens' top choice, it's also distinctly gay-friendly.

White 1921 BAR
(www.white1921.com; place des Lices; 8pm-late mid-May–Sep) One of the newest entries on the St-Tropez scene, White 1921 is owned by Louis Vuitton. It's a chic alfresco champagne lounge in a renovated all-white town house on the place des Lices. Can't make it home? Stay over in one of the swanky rooms (from €345).

Café de Paris CAFE
(www.cafedeparis.fr; 15 quai Suffren; 8am-2am year-round) The terrace is *the* place to sport your new strappy sandals at afternoon aperitifs; service is the friendliest along the port.

Le Petit Bar BAR
(2 rue Sibille; 7pm-late) This tiny, bright and central lounge slings cocktails year-round.

VIP Room CLUB
(04 94 97 14 70; www.viproom.fr; av du 11 Novembre 1918; Apr-Aug) New York loft–style club at the Nouveau Port; around for aeons and still lures in the occasional VIP.

ST-TROPEZ BEACH CLUBS

St-Tropez' seaside scene is defined by its restaurants and clubs (which blanket the sand), and they're all wildly different. Mattresses (€15 to €20) and parking (€5 to €6) are extra. Most open May to September (call ahead); all are marked on the tourist-office map. Book lunch (well ahead) at any of the following.

Aqua Club (☑ 04 94 79 84 35; www.aqua-club-plage.fr; rte de l'Épi, Plage de Pampelonne; mains €22-29; ☺ Feb-Oct) A friendly mixed gay and straight crowd, the most diverse by far on Pampelonne, settles in here for relaxed drinks or steaks. Has a longer opening season than most.

La Plage des Jumeaux (☑ 04 94 58 21 80; www.plagedesjumeaux.com; rte de l'Épi, Plage de Pampelonne; mains €25-40; ☺ noon-3pm; ☑ ⊕) The top pick of St-Tropez' beach restaurants, Jumeaux serves beautiful seafood (including fabulous whole fish, ideal to share) and sun-busting salads on its dreamy white-and-turquoise-striped beach. Families are well catered for, with playground equipment, beach toys and a kids menu.

Moorea Plage (☑ 04 94 97 18 17; www.mooreaplage.fr; rte des Plages, Plage de Tahiti; mains €23-44) Ideal for conversation and backgammon, this relatively laid-back club and restaurant is tops for steak.

Pearl Beach (☑ 04 98 12 70 70; www.thepearlbeach.com; quartier de la Bouillabaisse; mains €23-35; ☺ mid-Feb–Dec) Pearl Beach is on the way into town on rte de St-Tropez, and offers family-friendly beachside dining.

Club 55 (☑ 04 94 55 55 55; www.leclub55.fr; 43 bd Patch, Plage de Pampelonne; ☺ 10am-late Apr-Sep) The longest-running beach club dates to the 1950s and was originally the crew canteen during the filming of *And God Created Woman*. Now it caters to celebs who do *not* want to be seen. The food is – remarkably – nothing special.

Nikki Beach (☑ 04 94 79 82 04; www.nikkibeach.com/sttropez; rte de l'Épi, Plage de Pampelonne; ☺ 10am-midnight Apr-Sep) Favoured by dance-on-the-bar celebs who want to be seen. The deafening scene ends at midnight.

Le Pigeonnier   CLUB
(☑ 04 94 97 84 26; 13 rue de la Ponche; ☺ May-Aug) The least flash, with a *tenue intelligemment négligée* (trendy casual) dress code.

🔒 Shopping

St-Tropez is loaded with couture boutiques, gourmet food shops and art galleries.

Le Dépôt   CLOTHING
(www.ledepot-saint-tropez.com; 6 bd Louis Blanc; ☺ 10am-noon & 2-6.30pm Tue-Sat) A chic boutique of designer clothes and accessories, mostly secondhand and vintage.

De l'Une à l'Autre   CLOTHING
(6 rue Joseph Quaranta; ☺ 10am-12.30pm & 2.30-6.30pm Mon-Sat) Preloved designer labels at affordable prices.

Atelier Rondini   SHOES
(www.rondini.fr; 16 rue Georges Clémenceau; ☺ 9.30am-6.30pm Tue-Sat, 10.30am-1.30pm & 3.30-6.30pm Sun) Colette brought a pair of sandals from Greece to Atelier Rondini (open since 1927) to be replicated. It's still making the iconic sandals for about €135.

K Jacques   SHOES
(☑ 04 94 97 41 50; www.kjacques.com; 39bis rue Allard; ☺ 10am-1pm & 3-7pm Mon-Sat, 10.30am-1pm & 3.30-7pm Sun) Handcrafting sandals (€145 to €220) since 1933 for such clients as Picasso and Brigitte Bardot. There's another branch (16 rue Seillon) nearby.

Benoît Gourmet & Co   FOOD, WINE
(☑ 04 94 97 73 78; 6 rue des Charrons; ☺ 10am-noon & 2-5pm Mon-Sat) Everything gourmet (caviar, Champagne and foie gras included).

ℹ️ Information

The English-language brochure *Out and About* is available in local tourist offices, or check www.golfe-saint-tropez-information.com.
Pôle de Santé (☑ 04 98 12 53 08; www.ch-saint-tropez.fr; D559, Gassin) Nearest hospital, 11km from St-Tropez.
Police Station (☑ 04 94 12 70 00; rue François Sibilli)

Tourist Office (☑08 92 68 48 28; www.sainttropeztourisme.com; quai Jean Jaurès; ☺9.30am-1.30pm & 3-7.30pm Jul & Aug, 9.30am-12.30pm & 2-7pm Apr-Jun & Sep-Oct, to 6pm Mon-Sat Nov-Mar) Occasional walking tours April to October. Has a kiosk in Parking du Port in July and August.

ℹ Getting There & Around

BOAT

Services are reduced or cut in winter; check online.

Les Bateaux Verts (p113) runs shuttle boats connecting St-Tropez with Ste-Maxime (one way/return €7.50/13.50, 15 minutes), Les Issambres (€8.50/15, 25 minutes), Marines de Cogolin (€6.70/12, 15 minutes) and Port Grimaud (€6.70/12, 20 minutes).

Les Bateaux de St-Raphaël (☑04 94 95 17 46; www.bateauxsaintraphael.com) connects St-Tropez (Nouveau Port) and St-Raphaël (adult/child €15/10, one hour) mid-April to October. The train station in St-Raphaël is 200m from the dock.

Sea taxi (☑06 12 40 28 05; www.taxi-boat-saint-tropez.com) boat taxis can be booked for anywhere around St-Tropez.

BUS

VarLib (☑04 94 24 60 00; www.varlib.fr) tickets cost €3 from the St-Tropez **bus station** (☑04 94 56 25 74; av du Général de Gaulle) for anywhere within the Var *département*, including Ramatuelle (35 minutes), St-Raphaël (1¼ hours to three hours, depending on traffic) via Grimaud and Port Grimaud, and Fréjus (one hour). Buses to Toulon (two hours, seven daily, fewer in summer) stop at Le Lavandou (one hour) and Hyères (1½ hours).

Buses serve Toulon-Hyères Airport (1½ to two hours), but some require a transfer.

TAXI

Taxi (☑04 94 97 05 27) A taxi rank is at Vieux Port in front of the Musée de l'Annonciade.

BICYCLE & SCOOTER

Rolling Bikes (☑04 94 97 09 39; www.rolling-bikes.com; 14 av du Général Leclerc; per day bikes/scooters/motorcycles from €17/46/120, plus deposit) Do as the locals do and opt for two wheels.

The Peninsula

South of St-Tropez unfurl manicured vineyards and quiet, narrow lanes dotted with châteaux, solitary stone *bastides* (country houses) and private villas. The Sentier du Littoral (p113) snakes along the entire coastline, including several dramatic capes. The golden sands of France's chicest beach, Plage de Pampelonne, line the peninsula's eastern side, where you'll find St-Tropez' storied beach-club scene.

The yield of regional **vineyards** – Côtes de Provence wine – can be tasted at châteaux along the D61 and the D93 and around the peninsula. Tourist offices have lists, or check www.routedesvinsdeprovence.com and **Les Maîtres Vignerons de la Presqu'île de St-Tropez** (☑04 94 56 40 17; www.vignerons-saint-tropez.com; D98, La Foux; ☺8.30am-7pm Mon-Sat), where you can also shop. **Mas de Pampelonne** (☑04 94 97 75 86; Chemin des Moulins; ☺10am-1pm & 3-6pm Mon-Tue & Thu-Sat mid-Apr–Oct, reduced hours rest of the year) is known for its crisp rosé.

Plage de Pampelonne & Around

◉ Sights & Activities

★ **Plage de Pampelonne**   BEACH
The 5km-long, celebrity-studded Plage de Pampelonne sports a line-up of exclusive beach restaurants and clubs in summer. Find public access (and parking for €5.50) near Moorea Plage; otherwise, join the crowds at one of the beach clubs. The northern edge of the beach begins 4km southeast of St-Tropez with **Plage de Tahiti**.

Plage des Salins   BEACH
(rte des Salins) Just east of St-Tropez, Plage des Salins is a long, wide sandy beach at the southern foot of Cap des Salins.

ℹ GETTING TO ST-TROPEZ

During high season, those in the know avoid horrendous four-hour traffic bottlenecks on the one road into St-Tropez (or €40 parking, which is hard to find) by parking in Port Grimaud or Ste-Maxime and taking a Les Bateaux Verts shuttle boat (p113).

By train, the most convenient station is in St-Raphäel, which is served by Les Bateaux de St-Raphaël boats in high season, or a slower bus. Taxis from the train station cost €100 to €130.

Note that there is no luggage storage at the train station or any public place in the Var.

ST-TROPEZ TO TOULON THE PENINSULA

BEST BEACHES

➡ Plage de Pampelonne (p119) – this divine 9km stretch of golden sand is St-Tropez' most legendary, complete with a clutch of fabulous addresses.

➡ Plage du Layet, Cavalière – nudist beach with legendary shabby-chic beach restaurant, Chez Jo (p132).

➡ Port-Cros and Porquerolles – two islands with ample unspoilt golden sand to romp on.

➡ Plage d'Hyères – a favourite for its fabulous restaurant, with tables over the water.

At the northern end of the beach, on a rock jutting out to sea, is the **tomb** of Émile Olivier (1825–1913), who served as first minister to Napoleon III until his exile in 1870. It looks out towards **La Tête de Chien** (Dog's Head), named after the legendary dog who declined to eat St Torpes' remains.

Sémaphore de Camarat   LIGHTHOUSE
(⊙ guided tour only Jun-Sep) FREE Pampelonne stretches for 9km from **Cap du Pinet** to **Cap Camarat**, a rocky cape dominated by France's second-tallest lighthouse (110m), operational since 1861, electrified in 1946 and automated from 1977. Scale it for giddy views of St-Tropez and the peninsula. Book tours at Ramatuelle's tourist office.

Pointe du Capon   WALKING
This beautiful cape, 1km south of Plage des Salins, is criss-crossed with walking trails.

🛏 Sleeping

La Vigneraie 1860   CAMPGROUND €
(☑ 04 94 97 17 03; www.la-vigneraie-1860.fr; chemin des Moulins; per site/adult €12.50/10; ⊙ reception 8am-noon & 5-8pm) This simple caravan and camping ground just off of Plage de Pampelonne offers one of the few ways to live on the cheap and still get a chance to hang out in one of the most exclusive locales in the region. Surrounded by vineyards, it has basic showers and apartments (from €90). Cash only.

Ramatuelle

High on a hill, this labyrinthine walled village with a tree-studded central square got its name from 'Rahmatu'llah', meaning 'Divine Gift' – a legacy of the 10th-century Saracen occupation. Jazz and theatre fill the tourist-packed streets during August's **Festival de Ramatuelle** (www.festivalderamatuelle. com) and **Jazz Fest** (www.jazzfestivalramatuelle. com), and it's a wonderfully scenic stroll.

If you follow the road (rte des Moulins de Paillas) up over the hilltop the 2.5km toward Gassin, you'll take in grand views and historic **windmills**.

🛏 Sleeping

Ferme Ladouceur   B&B €€
(☑ 04 94 79 24 95; www.fermeladouceur.com; D61, quartier Les Roullière; d incl breakfast €125-140; ⊙ Apr-Sep) Have breakfast beneath a fig tree at this lovely *chambre d'hôte* in a 19th-century *bastide*. The rustic restaurant (*menu* including wine €45) is open to anyone who fancies an evening taste of good old-fashioned farm cuisine. Find it north of Ramatuelle, signposted off the D61 to St-Tropez.

Auberge de l'Oumède   B&B €€€
(☑ 04 94 44 11 11; www.aubergedeloumede.com; Chemin de l'Oumède; d from €200; ⊙ May-Sep; ❉ 🛜 🐾) This isolated *bastide* down a single-lane track, 3.5km west of Ramatuelle, is indeed a rare treat. It has seven impeccable rooms and a pool – handy should you really not want to leave.

✕ Eating & Drinking

As in St-Tropez, reservations on the peninsula are essential.

Chez Camille   SEAFOOD €€€
(☑ 04 98 12 68 98; www.chezcamille.fr; rte de Bonne Terrasse, Pampelonne-Ramatuelle; menus €44-79; ⊙ 12.30-2pm & 8-9.30pm Wed-Mon Apr-Sep) Deep terracotta walls hide this blue-and-white-tiled fishing cottage dating from 1913. Now into its fourth generation, the beachside restaurant cooks up just one thing over a wood-fuelled grill: fish. From the D93 follow signs for Bonne Terrasse; it's 6km east of Ramatuelle, just south of Plage de Pampelonne.

Café de l'Ormeau   CAFE
(☑ 04 94 79 20 20; place de l'Ormeau; ⊙ 7am-7pm Apr-Oct, reduced hours rest of year) Lovely vine-covered cafe terrace for coffee or light meals (mains €15 to €18).

ℹ Information

Ramatuelle Tourist Office (☑ 04 98 12 64 00; www.ramatuelle-tourisme.com; place de l'Ormeau; ⊙9am-1.30pm & 2-7pm Mon-Fri, 9.30am-1.30pm & 3.30-6.30pm Sat & Sun Jul & Aug, shorter hours rest of year) Stocks local maps and vineyard info.

Gassin

In medieval Gassin, 11km southwest of St-Tropez atop a rocky promontory, narrow streets wend up to the village church (1558). The village's most compelling feature is the 360-degree view of the peninsula, St-Tropez bay and the Maures forests.

🛏 Sleeping & Eating

Hôtel Bellovisto   PENSION €
(☑ 04 94 56 17 30; www.bellovisto.eu; place des Barrys; d/tr from €70/110; ⊙ Apr-Sep; ❋ 🛜) A large part of the charm of this hilltop hotel is the cafe-clad square with panoramic view on which it resides. The hotel itself is dead simple: local bar on the ground floor displaying *pétanque* club trophies, a fine restaurant (mains €28) and nine rooms up top.

Au Vieux Gassin   PROVENÇAL €€
(☑ 04 94 56 14 26; www.auvieuxgassin-restaurant. com; place des Barrys; menu €32; ⊙ 11.30am-2pm & 6.30-9.30pm Mar-Oct) This popular eatery gets packed with locals on weekends, digging into regional specialities, and tables spill onto the grand terrace in summer.

Gigaro & Cap Lardier

On the southeastern coast of the Presqu'île de St-Tropez, **Cap Taillat** is guarded by the Conservatoire du Littoral and shelters some of France's rarest plant species as well as a population of Hermann tortoises. **Cap Lardier**, the peninsula's southernmost cape, is protected by the Parc National de Port-Cros (p135).

Seaside hamlet **Gigaro** harbours a sandy beach, some lovely eating and sleeping options, and a water-sports school. From the far end of the beach, a board maps the Sentier du Littoral (p113) that works its way around the coast to **Cap Lardier** (4.7km, 1½ hours) and past Cap Taillat to L'Escalet (9km, 2¾ hours). From Gigaro, the narrow but drop-dead-gorgeous D93 winds inland over the **Col de Collebasse** (129m) to Ramatuelle – a good ride for mountain bikers. **L'Escalet**, accessible by a 2.5km road signposted off the D93, is a pretty little rocky cove.

🛏 Sleeping & Eating

Le Refuge   PENSION €€
(☑ 04 94 79 67 38, 06 17 95 65 38; www.lerefuge-cotedazur.fr; plage de Gigaro, Gigaro; r/studios incl breakfast €80/110; ⊙ Apr-Sep; 🛜) This rustic seaside house sits back off the sand. Ten humble rooms and five studios with kitchenette provide simple accommodation and open onto private little tabled terraces. Proprietors cook up tasty grills at the restaurant of the same name at the start of the coastal path. Wi-fi downstairs.

⭐**Château de Valmer**   HOTEL €€€
(☑ 04 94 55 15 15; www.chateauvalmer.com; 81 blvd de Gigaro; d from €332, treehouses €505; ⊙ May-Sep; ❋ @ 🛜 ☒) This fabulous 19th-century wine-producer's mansion is for nature bods with a penchant for luxury. Sleep above vines in a *cabane perchée* (treehouse), stroll scented vegetable and herb gardens and play hide-and-seek around century-old palm and olive trees. Located between La Croix-Valmer and Gigaro.

Les 3 Îles   B&B €€€
(☑ 04 94 49 03 73; www.3iles.com; 1779 blvd du Littoral, Quartier du Vergeron; d/ste incl breakfast €245/315; ⊙ mid-Mar–mid-Oct; ❋ 🛜 ☒) The same seductive view of the sea and those

MARKET DAYS NEAR ST-TROPEZ

Monday Bormes-les-Mimosas, Port Grimaud.

Tuesday Bandol, Callas, Cotignac, Fayence, Hyères, Lorgues, St-Tropez.

Wednesday Bormes-les-Mimosas, La Garde Freinet, Salernes, Sanary-sur-Mer, Tourtour.

Thursday Aups (truffles November to March), Bargemon, Callas, Collobrières (July and August), Fayence, Grimaud, Hyères, Port Grimaud, Ramatuelle.

Friday Entrecasteaux, La Motte, Port Grimaud.

Saturday Carcès, Claviers, Cogolin, Draguignan, Fayence, Hyères, St-Tropez, Tourtour.

Sunday Ampus, Cavalière (all-day flea market), Collobrières, Gassin (April to October), La Garde Freinet, Port Grimaud, Ramatuelle, Salernes, Vidauban.

golden Îles d'Hyères glistening on the horizon awaits you in each of the five carefully thought-out rooms and infinity pool. Tropézienne Catherine and husband Jean-Paul are the creative energy behind this faultless, oh-so-chic *maison d'hôte*. Located between La Croix-Valmer and Gigaro.

Couleurs Jardin   SEAFOOD **€€**
(✆ 04 94 79 59 12; www.restaurantcouleursjardin.com; Plage de Gigaro, Gigaro; mains €25-35; ⊙ noon-2.30pm & 7-10pm Apr-Sep) Eclectic and hip, this imaginative beachside space is *the* place to dine and/or drink. Loll on cushioned seating beneath the trees or pick a table on the terrace with nothing between you and the deep blue sea. Cuisine is fish and market fuelled.

Golfe de St-Tropez

Port Grimaud sits on the edge of the Golfe de St-Tropez. A mosquito-filled swamp in the 1960s, this modern pleasure port is now barricaded from the busy N98 by high walls. Its yacht-laden waterways comprise 12km of quays, but the town is best used as an access point for shuttle boats (p113) to St-Tropez or to catch **Le Petit Train de Grimaud** (✆ 06 62 07 65 09; www.petit-train-de-grimaud.com; adult/child return €7/4; ⊙ Apr-Sep), which makes a circuit from the port to the historic inland village, Grimaud (five to seven daily, 50 minutes).

Grimaud

This medieval postcard-perfect hilltop village sits 3km inland from the Golfe de St-Tropez. It's crowned with the dramatic shell of **Château du Grimaud**, built in the 11th century, fortified in the 15th century, destroyed during the Wars of Religion (1562–98), rebuilt in the 17th century, and wrecked again during the French Revolution. Magical evening concerts are held on the stage within the ruins during the music festival, **Les Grimaldines**, in July and August.

For a bite to eat, stop in to **Fleur de Sel** (✆ 04 94 43 21 54; 4 place du Cros; lunch menu from €17, mains €20-40; ⊙ noon-2.30pm & 7-9pm Tue-Sat Mar-Nov) for excellent local fare in the midst of the historic village.

Grimaud's **tourist office** (✆ 04 94 55 43 83; www.grimaud-provence.com; 1 bd des Aliziers; ⊙ 9am-12.30pm & 2-6pm Mon-Sat Sep-Jun, daily Jul & Aug), at the foot of the village on the

D558, has information on walks, some with a guide.

South of Grimaud, along the St-Tropez-bound D61, visit **Caves des Vignerons de Grimaud** (✆ 04 94 43 20 14; 36 av des Oliviers, D61, Grimaud; ⊙ 9am-noon & 2-5pm Tue-Sat), a cooperative where you can stock up on Vin de Pays du Var for little more than €2.50 a litre.

HAUT-VAR

The northern half of the Var *département* (north of the A8 autoroute), known as the Northern or Upper Var, is vastly different from its coastal counterpart. Peaceful hilltop villages drowse beneath the midday sun, and are within easy reach of the wild Gorges du Verdon. Skip Draguignan, the hard-nosed main town where the French army maintains its largest military base, and head for the hills: lush vineyards, earthy black truffles and a bounty of gastronomic delights. The best way to get around: your own wheels.

❶ Information

Most villages have their own websites and excellent tourist offices. Check www.visitvar.fr for details on the whole region. The Haut-Var is divided into sections served by their own tourist boards and governments. Going from Draguignan counterclockwise:

➡ Dracénie (www.tourisme-dracenie.com)

➡ Haut Var-Verdon (www.haut-var.com)

➡ Provence Verte (www.provenceverte.fr)

➡ Coeur du Var (www.coeurduvar.com)

For area winemakers, visit www.vinsde-provence.com. Le Var Campsites booklets are available at tourist offices, while **Gîtes de France** (www.gites-de-france-var.fr) has country rentals.

Le Pass Sites Var is a free pass with discounts on admission to 28 abbeys, chapels, gardens and museums in the Var. Get the online coupon for the sights you are interested in at www.visitvar.fr.

East of Draguignan

The hills and villages to the east and south of Draguignan fall into the terrain of the Dracénie region. As you depart the city sprawl nearest the autoroute, you'll emerge into a picturesque spread of vineyards and hilltop villages.

Les Arcs-sur-Argens & La Motte

The extended urban development around Les Arcs and La Motte is nothing special, but the nearby area (such as the stretch along the D25) is rich in vineyards and wine-tasting opportunities. There are some great restaurants, and the medieval quarter of Les Arcs is a fun stroll. St Roseline was born there in 1263 in the 12th-century château where she later performed the 'miracle of roses': turning bread into roses.

◎ Sights & Activities

★**Chapelle de Ste-Roseline**   CHURCH
(☑ 04 94 73 37 30; chemin de Ste-Roseline, D91, Les Arcs-sur-Argens; ⊗ 2.30-6pm Tue-Sun Feb-Dec) **FREE** A 1975 mosaic by Marc Chagall illuminates this 13th-century Romanesque chapel, 4.5km east of Les Arcs-sur-Argens on the road to La Motte. The church contains the corpse of St Roseline (1263–1329), who was born at the château in Les Arcs and became a Carthusian nun and the mother superior here. She experienced visions during her lifetime and was said to be able to curtail demons. Concerts are held in the chapel in July and August.

★**Maison des Vins Côtes
de Provence**   WINERY
(☑ 04 94 99 50 20; www.caveaucp.fr; N7, Les Arcs-sur-Argens; ⊗ 10am-6pm Mon-Sat, to 5pm Sun) This bacchanalian House of Wines, 2.5km southwest of Les Arcs-sur-Argens on the N7, is a one-stop shop to taste, learn about and buy (at producers' prices) Côtes de Provence wines. Each week 16 of the 800 wines from 250 wine estates are selected for tasting. Knowledgeable multilingual staff advise you on the dream dish to eat with each wine.

Château Ste-Roseline   WINERY
(☑ 04 94 99 50 30; www.sainte-roseline.com; D91, Les Arcs-sur-Argens; ⊗ 9am-12.30pm & 2-6.30pm Mon-Fri, 10am-noon & 2-6pm Sat & Sun) Sample and buy a prestigious *cru classé* (top vintage) wine, produced here since the 14th century. The château adjoins the Chapelle de Ste-Roseline.

⊨ Sleeping & Eating

Le Mas du Péré   B&B **€€**
(☑ 04 94 84 33 52; www.lemasdupere.com; 280 chemin du Péré, La Motte; d incl breakfast from €94, studios per week from €535; ❋ @ ⛟ ⚲) Signposted from the centre of La Motte village, this is a convenient spot from which to go wine tasting in the region. Perfectly clean, well-appointed rooms in muted tones look out on the pool. Some have dappled terraces, and studios have kitchenettes.

★**Logis du Guetteur**   TRADITIONAL FRENCH **€€**
(☑ 04 94 99 51 10; www.logisduguetteur.com; place du Château, Les Arcs-sur-Argens; menus from €35; ⊗ noon-2pm & 7.15-9.30pm daily Feb-Dec; ❋ ⚲) This super restaurant perches on the tippety top of Les Arcs in a 12th-century château. In winter dine in the renovated *cave* (wine seller) beneath oil paintings of white peacocks and cornucopia, and in summer out on the terrace with views all around. Food is impeccable, service attentive and the ambience one of a kind. Stay over in simple rooms (€130 to €185).

★**Domaine de la Maurette**   BISTRO **€€**
(☑ 04 94 45 92 82; www.vins-maurette.fr; rte de Callas, D25, La Motte; lunch menus €13, 3-course menus from €26; ⊗ noon-2pm daily, 7.30-9.30pm Tue-Sun) For an authentic Provençal feast, head east out of La Motte along the D47 to this rustic wine estate on the intersection of the D47 and D25. Taste and buy wine, and eat on a vine-covered terrace in a roadside inn with attached winery, where the atmosphere of chattering people enjoying wholesome, homemade food is nothing short of electric.

Callas

From the central village square in Callas (population 1400) you get a stunning panorama of the red-rock **Massif de l'Estérel**. The village lanes wind up the hill in a warren of bends. At the southern foot of Callas is **Moulin de Callas** (☑ 04 94 39 03 20; www.moulindecallas.com; Quartier les Ferrages, D25, Callas; ⊗ 10am-noon & 3-7pm Mon-Sat Jun-Sep, reduced hours rest of year), where Nicole and Serge's family have cultivated olives to make oil since 1928. Learn about olive oil (tours are by appointment) and buy it in the on-site shop, as well as a broad selection of other Provençal goods. **Callas Tourist Office** (☑ 04 94 39 06 77; callastourisme@dracenie.com; place du 18 Juin 1940) has info on the region.

Bargemon

The medieval village of Bargemon (population 1100) juts onto a promontory, from

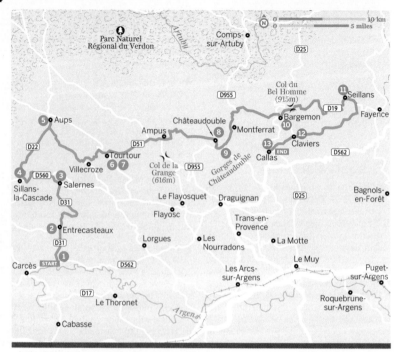

Driving Tour
Haut-Var Hilltop Villages

START DOMAINE DE ROUCAS
END CALLAS
LENGTH 95KM; ONE DAY

To find sleepy, unspoilt villages teetering on hilltops, from the D562, pick up the northbound D31 towards Entrecasteaux and Salernes. You'll wind past pretty vineyards with dry-stone walls, olive trees and vivid burnt-orange soil. After 1.5km pop into **1 Domaine de Roucas** for wine tasting. Continuing 4km, hilltop **2 Entrecasteaux**, its giant 17th-century château featuring formal gardens, perches dramatically along the river.

Bear right along the D31 towards Salernes and Aups, then drive another wiggly 6km to **3 Salernes**, where handmade terracotta tiles called *terres cuites* (literally 'baked earth') have been manufactured since the 18th century. The tourist office has a list of workshops to visit.

In Salernes pick up the westbound D2560 and subsequent D560 to **4 Sillans-la-Cascade**, on the banks of the River Bresque, a gem of a fortified village with a waterfall. Then it's 9km north along the D22 to **5 Aups**

and another 10km southeast past olive groves and lavender gardens to the typical 'eagle nest' gold-stone village of **6 Tourtour**. Buy olive oil in the village and, in mid-December, watch olives being pressed in its 17th-century **7 moulin à huile**; the tourist office runs guided tours of the mill.

Six kilometres further east along the D51 you'll encounter Ampus, then continue east 9km to **8 Châteaudouble**, an astonishing village clinging to a cliff of the **9 Gorges de Châteaudouble**.

Just 7km east of here is **10 Bargemon**, a village with a maze of medieval streets and ramparts to stroll and an excellent bistro, La Pescalune, in which to dine.

11 Seillans, a scenic 12km drive east, is an irresistibly pretty, typical Provençal village with cobbled lanes coiling to its crown, and a village inn, Hôtel des Deux Rocs, that only the stone-hearted will be able to resist.

If you have any gas left in your proverbial tank, you can circle back south (Fayence is best seen from a distance) to **12 Claviers** and **13 Callas**, yet more picturesque villages.

which you have excellent views across the valley to Claviers. Market day is Thursday.

Don't miss La Pescalune (☑06 29 94 66 64; www.la-pescalune.fr; 13 rue de la Résistance; mains €15-25; ⊙noon-2pm Thu & Sun, 7-9.30pm Tue-Sun), an intimate bistro alongside the church where popular chef Virginie Martinetti creates seasonal, market-fresh cuisine with a twist.

For those who fancy a day cycling, the tourist office (☑04 94 47 81 73; www.ot-bargemon.fr; av Pasteur; ⊙9.15am-12.15pm & 2.15-6pm Mon-Fri) rents bikes.

Seillans

Adjoining the Seillans tourist office is a gallery (www.seillans.fr; adult/child €3/free; ⊙2.30-5.30pm Mon-Sat) of work by Dorothea Tanning and Max Ernst, who lived here in the 1960s and '70s.

Hôtel des Deux Rocs (☑04 94 76 87 32; www.hoteldeuxrocs.com; 1 place Font d'Amont; d €75-130; ⊙noon-2pm Wed-Sun, 7-9.30pm Tue-Sun Feb-Dec), a boutique hotel with fig-flower Fragonard soap in the bathrooms, a fine collection of B&W family photos and a gourmet restaurant (mains €17 to €20), wins the prize hands down for most atmospheric village inn. Scipion, knight of the Flotte d'Agout, lived here in the 17th century. Today, the soulful *bastide* is home to the Malzacs, who run this 13-room hotel with extraordinary panache. Summer dining is alfresco around a fountain.

West of Draguignan

The quaint villages and rolling hills west of Draguignan ascend north toward the Gorges du Verdon (p251), a worthwhile visit in its own right. The region encompasses the area known as Provence Verte and some of the Coeur du Var, and is renowned for its wine and truffles, so expect excellent meals and markets.

Lorgues & Around

Bustling Lorgues (population 9340), 13km west of Draguignan, is fountain filled and crowned by a beautiful church. The tourist office has maps of walks, and a list of the numerous village hotels. The large weekly market fills the centre of town Tuesday mornings.

⊙ Sights

★ **Abbaye de Thoronet**   HISTORIC SITE
(☑04 94 60 43 90; http://thoronet.monuments-nationaux.fr; Le Thoronet; adult/child €7.50/free; ⊙10am-6.30pm Mon-Sat, 10am-noon & 2-6.30pm Sun Apr-Sep, reduced hours Oct-May) The simplest in a trio of great Cistercian abbeys (the other two are Silvacane and Notre-Dame de Sénanque), uninhabited Abbaye de Thoronet, 12km southwest of Lorgues, was built between 1160 and 1190. It's remarkable for its ultra-austere architecture: pure proportions, perfectly dressed stone and the subtle fall of light and shadow are where its beauty lies.

Domaine de l'Abbaye   WINERY
(☑04 94 73 87 36; rte de Carcès, D84, Le Thoronet; ⊙9am-noon & 1-6pm Mon-Sat, by appointment Sun) Excellent wines are produced in vineyards originally cultivated by monks in the 12th century.

🍽 Sleeping & Eating

★ **Chez Bruno**   GASTRONOMIC €€€
(☑04 94 85 93 93; www.restaurantbruno.com; rte des Arcs, D10; menus €73-160; ⊙12.30-2.30pm & 7.30-9.30pm daily mid-Jun–mid-Sep, closed Mon & dinner Sun mid-Sep–mid-Jun) France's most famous truffle restaurant can be found in a country house 2.5km southeast of Lorgues. In his Michelin-starred restaurant, chef Bruno Clément cooks almost exclusively with those knobbly, pungent delicacies, getting through an incredible 1000kg of the world's most expensive foodstuff every year. Unable to move after your black-diamond feast? Stay in one of the lovely rooms (€160 to €320).

ℹ Information

Lorgues Tourist Office (☑04 94 73 92 37; www.lorgues-tourisme.fr; 12 rue du 8 Mai; ⊙9am-12.15pm & 2.30-6pm Mon-Sat, plus 9am-12.15pm Sun Jul & Aug) Near the southern entrance to town; has maps of walks and a list of hotels.

Tourtour

Tourtour (population 536) is a beautiful amber-stoned village with a churchyard stretching across a promontory offering panoramic views. It makes a handy place to break your journey, stroll the cobbled lanes filled with galleries and shops, or indulge your truffle fancy. **Market days** are Wednesday and Saturday mornings.

🛏 Sleeping & Eating

Restaurants congregate on the shady place des Ormeaux on the upper edge of town.

Maison de la Treille
B&B €€

(🖉 04 89 53 02 37; www.tourtour.fr; rue Grande 22; d incl breakfast €100; ☺ Mar-Nov; 🛜) The hefty brass knocker piercing the olive-green front door, the lush bush of lavender outside and the covered breakfast terrace on the top floor immediately catch the eye at this charming *maison d'hôte* in one of the Northern Var's most beautiful hilltop villages.

L'Alechou
BISTRO €

(🖉 04 94 70 54 76; 16 rue Grande; mains €9-15; ☺ lunch & dinner daily) On the cuter-than-cute main street, overwhelmingly friendly L'Alechou is a perfect spot for lunch between flowerpots.

Les Chênes Verts
GASTRONOMIC €€€

(🖉 04 94 70 55 06; rte de Villecroze, D51; menus €60-160; ☺ noon-1.45pm & 7.30-9pm Thu-Mon Aug-May) It might seem odd that this walled property shuts in June and July. But there is good reason. 'The Green Oaks' is famed for its luxurious truffle cuisine: winter food! The stiff waiters and eclectic decor are hardly wowing, but the cuisine is irreproachable, hence it's earned one Michelin star.

ℹ Information

Tourist Office (🖉 04 94 70 59 47; www.tourisme-tourtour.com; montée de St-Dénis; ☺ 10am-12.30pm & 3-6.30pm Jun-Aug, reduced hours rest of the year) Stocked with accommodation and activity listings.

Aups

Amber-hued Aups (population 2170) is a gateway to the Gorges du Verdon to the north, but from November to late February those alien-looking nuggets of black fungus, *Tuber melanosporum*, take top billing. They can be viewed (and bought, if you have the coin) at the Thursday-morning **truffle market** on Aups' central plane tree–studded square. Truffle hunts and pig-snouting demonstrations lure a crowd on the fourth Sunday in January during Aups' **Journée de la Truffe** (Day of the Truffle).

The **tourist office** (🖉 04 94 84 00 69; www.aups-tourisme.com; place Frédéric Mistral; ☺ 9am-

12.15pm & 2.30-5.30pm Mon-Sat Sep-Jun, to 7pm Mon-Sat & 9am-12.30pm Sun Jul & Aug), on the central square, has information on other gastronomic festivities and a list of local truffle hunters.

Entrecasteaux

Entrecasteaux (population 1100), with its giant 17th-century **château**, old stone houses sun-baked every shade of gold, and fountain-clad square, perches dramatically over a river. Grab a coffee at the green-canopied **Bar Central** (🖉 04 94 04 43 53; ☺ 8am-10pm) – you won't get more local than this – which overlooks the château's manicured gardens. The village is known for its honey. Pick some up at local producers like **Les Ruchers d'Entrecasteaux** (🖉 06 87 43 88 94; Chemin des Plantades, St-Antonin du Var), just southeast of town. Surrounding wineries include the yellow-stone farmhouse at **Domaine de Roucas** (🖉 04 94 04 48 14; rte de Carcès, D31; ☺ 9am-6pm), which welcomes tasters.

Cotignac

Parts of the tiny stone village of Cotignac (population 2000) are dramatically built into tuffa cliff faces. The River Cassole carves its heart, and villagers stroll the tree-lined promenade of cours Gambetta. The Tuesday-morning **market** is lively, and the tourist office has maps of walks to the village's chapels and fountains. **Les Vignerons de Cotignac** (🖉 04 94 04 60 04; http://vignerons.cotignac-info.com; 1 rue Arnoux Borghino; ☺ 9am-12.30pm & 2.30-7pm Mon-Sat Jul & Aug, reduced hours rest of year), on the upper edge of the village, is the spot to buy the local rosé.

🛏 Sleeping

Hostellerie de Cotignac
HOTEL €€

(🖉 04 94 04 27 04; www.hostellerie-decotignac.fr; 2 cours Gambetta; d from €100; ❄🛜) This well-run hotel is perfectly situated in the center of Cotignac and offers impeccably maintained modern rooms with luxe bathrooms, and an in-house restaurant. Step out your door onto the central square, which fills with the weekly market or coffee-sipping locals.

Mas de l'Olivette
B&B €€

(🖉 04 94 80 28 73; www.masdelolivette.com; rte d'Entrecasteaux, D50; d €100, studios per week €800; ❄🛜) The lovely Jean-Claude and Yannick welcome you so warmly to their tiny

B&B that it feels like home. The two impeccable, beautifully appointed guest rooms can adjoin for families. The spotless free-standing studio has kitchen and terrace. Views stretch through the olive groves, and bathrooms are kitted out with L'Occitane products.

✖ Eating

★ **Le Clos des Vignes** TRADITIONAL FRENCH €€
(☑ 04 94 04 72 19; www.restaurant-le-clos-des-vignes.fr; rte de Monfort, D22; lunch/dinner menus from €18/24; ☺ noon-2pm & 7.30-9.30pm Tue-Sun) Seek out this farmhouse for the home-cooked cuisine (by husband Jean-Luc) and the warm welcome (by wife Dany). Dining is on the terrace, which is enclosed in winter, and the rhythm is slow and easy: French country life at its finest. Look for the signed dedication by Brad and Angelina, who are patrons and neighbours.

La Table des Coquelicots TRADITIONAL FRENCH €€
(☑ 04 94 69 46 07; 10 cours Gambetta; lunch/dinner menus €14/27; ☺ noon-2.30pm & 7.30-9.30pm daily, closed Tue dinner & Wed Sep-May) Choose between the elegant, muted-tone dining room or the terrace under the plane trees for people-watching. Open year-round, La Table offers classic food and enormous profiteroles.

ℹ Information

Tourist Office (☑ 04 94 04 61 87; http://ot-cotignac.provenceverte.fr; Pont de la Cassole, 475 rte de Carcès; ☺ 9am-12.30pm & 2-7pm Mon-Sat, 9am-1pm Sun Jul & Aug, reduced hours rest of year) Near the bridge at the southern end of the village.

Correns

In 1997 the mayor of Correns (population 889), on the banks of the River Argens, decided to make the village's 200 hectares of AOC Côtes de Provence vineyards organic. Local farmers have also since turned organic to produce honey, chicken, eggs, olive oil and goat cheese.

The most prestigious vineyard, **Château de Miraval** (www.miraval-provence.com), was a monastery in the 13th century, then legendary Miraval recording studio, where Pink Floyd recorded part of *The Wall* in 1979. It shut its doors to passers-by when Brad Pitt, Angelina Jolie and kids moved into the dreamy gold-stone property on the vast 400-hectare estate in 2008, but it still makes wine. The couple wed at Miraval in 2014.

✚ Activities

★ **Vallon Sourn** OUTDOOR ACTIVITIES
(D45, west of Correns) The wonderfully cool Vallon Sourn, where the green waters of the Argens flow peacefully, is perfect for walking, cycling and even summertime bathing. A scenic drive/ride from Correns village will get you there: head north on the D45 towards Châteauvert.

Vignerons de Correns WINERY
(☑ 04 94 59 59 46; www.vigneronsdecorrens.fr; chemin de l'Église, Correns; ☺ 2.30-7pm Mon-Fri, 9.30am-12.30pm & 2.30-7pm Sat) Taste and buy Château de Miraval and other big Correns wine names such as Domaine de la Grande Pallière at wine cooperative and shop Vignerons de Correns. Also has branches in Le Val and Aups.

Les Caves du Commandeur WINERY
(☑ 04 94 59 54 46; 18 rue des Moulins, D22, Montfort-sur-Argens; ☺ 9am-12.30pm & 2.30-6.30pm Mon-Sat) This *domaine* of AOC Côtes de Provence and IGP Var wines has a giant, modern facility dedicated to tasting in Montfort-sur-Argens, 6km east of Correns.

⌂ Sleeping & Eating

Auberge de Correns TRADITIONAL FRENCH €€
(☑ 04 94 59 53 52; www.aubergedecorrens.fr; 34 place du Général de Gaulle; mains €11-18; ☺ noon-1.45pm & 7-8.45pm Thu-Mon, daily Jul & Aug) Lunch well, and predominantly organically, at Auberge de Correns, where the cuisine is innovative and market driven, the wine list features local varieties and mains are as sizeable as the five elegant guest rooms (doubles €85).

ℹ Information

Correns Tourist Office (☑ 04 94 37 21 31; www.correns.fr; 2 rue Cabassonne; ☺ 9am-12.30pm & 2-6pm Mon-Thu Jul & Aug, Tue-Sat rest of year) Has lists of estates for tasting and buying wine.

La Celle

Forge your way through the urban sprawl of Brignoles to reach the recently restored 12th-century Romanesque **Ancienne Abbaye de la Celle** (☑ 04 94 59 19 05; ☺ by tour only 11am, 2.30pm, 3.30pm & 4.30pm Tue-Sat) **FREE**. For a special treat, dine or stay at fabled **Hostellerie de l'Abbaye de la Celle** (☑ 04 98 05 14 14; www.abbaye-celle.com; 19 place du Général de Gaulle; lunch/dinner menus from

ST-TROPEZ TO TOULON WEST OF DRAGUIGNAN

€38/70; ⊘ lunch & dinner daily, closed Tue & Wed winter). Superstar chef Alain Ducasse is the creative energy behind this refined four-star restaurant-hotel. Afterwards try one of the 88 local vintages at **La Maison des Vins des Coteaux Varois en Provence** (✐ 04 94 69 33 18; Abbaye de La Celle; ⊘ 10am-noon & 2-6pm Mon-Sat).

MASSIF DES MAURES

Shrouded by a forest of pine, chestnut and cork oak trees, the Massif des Maures arcs inland between Hyères and Fréjus. Roamed by wild boars, its near-black vegetation gives rise to its name, derived from the Provençal word *mauro* (dark pine wood). Traditional industries (chestnut harvests, cork, pipe-making) are their lifeblood.

La Garde Freinet

Conservatoire du
Patrimoine du Freinet   WALKING, COURSE
(✐ 04 94 43 08 57; www.conservatoiredufreinet. org; Chapelle St-Jean, place de la Mairie; ⊘ 9am-12.30pm & 2.30-5.30pm Mon-Sat) Local traditions unfold in the village of La Garde Freinet (topped by the 13th-century **ruins of Fort Freinet**) at this environment-driven set-up that hosts exhibitions (flora, fauna, cork harvesting) and organises themed discovery walks (adult/child €9/4.50) and workshops (free to €90; for example, art in nature, drystone walls, honey making, forest photography).

Village des Tortues

Village des Tortues   WILDLIFE RESERVE
(✐ 04 94 78 26 41; www.villagetortues.com; Gonfaron; adult/child €12/8; ⊘ 9am-7pm Mar-Nov, to 6pm Dec-Feb) About 20km north of Collobrières, this sanctuary protects one of France's most endangered species, the Hermann tortoise (*Testudo hermanni*). Once common along the Mediterranean coast, it is today found only in the Massif des Maures and on Corsica. In summer the best time to see the tortoises is in the morning and late afternoon. Watch them hatch from mid-May to the end of June. A great palaeontology trail has vicious-looking models of the tortoise's ancestors lurking among the bushes.

The site has a well-documented trail from the clinic, where wounded tortoises are treated, to egg hatcheries and nurseries, where young tortoises (a delicacy for magpies, rats, foxes and wild boars) spend the first three of their 60 to 100 years.

Collobrières & Around

Hidden in the forest, the leafy village of Collobrières (population 1950) is *the* place to taste chestnuts. Across the 11th-century bridge, the tourist office can help you participate in the October chestnut harvest, celebrated with the **Fête de la Châtaigne**, or join a guided forest walk.

◉ Sights & Activities

★**Monastère de la Verne**   MONASTERY
(✐ 04 94 43 45 51; http://la.verne.free.fr; off D14; adult/child €6/3; ⊘ 11am-6pm Wed-Mon Jun-Aug, to 5pm Wed-Mon Feb-May & Sep-Dec) Majestic, 12th- to 13th-century Monastère de la Verne perches unbelievably on the hip of a mountain deep in the forest, but with a view to the sea. The Carthusian monastery was founded in 1170, possibly on the site of a temple to the goddess Laverna, protector of the bandits who hid in the Maures. The Huguenots destroyed most of the original charterhouse in 1577. Since 1982 the solitary complex has been home to 24 nuns of the Sisters of Bethlehem.

The monastery's restoration has been a labour of love. A 20-minute video details the work. Highlights include the austere Romanesque church, the prior's cell, complete with a small formal garden and workshop, the bakery and the olive mill. The shop (closed Sunday) is full of excellent artisanal food, soaps, art and crafts made by the nuns. Walking trails lead from the monastery into its forested surroundings.

From Collobrières, follow rte de Grimaud (D14) east for 6km, then turn right (south) on to the D214 and drive another 6km to the monastery; park at the lot and walk the final section, which is unpaved.

Forest Walks   WALKING
The Collobrières tourist office gives hiking directions to the **Châtaignier de Madame**, the biggest chestnut tree in Provence, with a mighty 10.4m circumference; and the two biggest **menhirs** (each over 3m) in the Var region, now heritage-listed monuments, which were raised between 3000 BC and 2000 BC. Three **shorter walking trails** are mapped on the noticeboard outside.

🛏 Sleeping

The tourist office lists local *gîtes* (cottages) and B&Bs online.

Hôtel Les Maures   HOTEL €
(☑ 04 94 48 07 10; www.hoteldesmaures.fr; 19 blvd Lazare Carnot, Collobrières; d €40; ❄ 🛜) This no-frills central hotel is basic but clean, and has a popular brasserie.

Hôtel Notre Dame   HOTEL €€
(☑ 04 94 48 07 13; www.hotel-notre-dame.eu; 15 av de la Libération, Collobrières; d from €98; ❄ 🛜 ☒) The town's most high-end option has rooms decorated around rich colour schemes.

🍴 Eating

Les Olivades   BISTRO €
(place de la Libération, Collobrières; menus from €13.50; ⊘ noon-2pm daily, plus 7-9pm Jun-Aug) This refreshingly down-to-earth little bistro sits on the main square and dishes up simple, inexpensive local fare.

★ La Petite Fontaine   TRADITIONAL FRENCH €€
(☑ 04 94 48 00 12; place de la République, Collobrières; 3-/5-course menus €27/33; ⊘ noon-2.30pm & 7-10pm Tue-Sun Apr-Sep, noon-2.30pm Tue-Sat, 7-10pm Fri & Sat Oct-Mar) Locals throng from miles around to sit at a tree-shaded table and feast on seasonal forest mushrooms and chestnuts at one of southern France's most charming, relaxed village inns. The walls inside are exposed stone, and the fruit tarts for dessert...out of this world. Reservations essential. No credit cards.

We dare you to try the *broussain*: leftover cheeses mixed with Marc de Provence liqueur, olive oil and garlic – pungent!

Ferme de Peïgros   REGIONAL CUISINE €€
(☑ 04 94 48 03 83; http://fermedepeigros.pagesperso-orange.fr; Col de Babaou; menus €22; ⊘ noon-2pm daily, plus 7-9.30pm Jul & Aug) Treat your taste buds to wild boar or farm-made chestnut ice cream and grand massif views at this goat farm 1.8km along a gravel track from the top of the Col de Babaou (8km from Collobrières). No credit cards.

🔒 Shopping

Confiserie Azuréenne   FOOD
(☑ 04 94 48 07 20; www.confiserieazureenne.com; ⊘ 9.30am-12.30pm & 1.30-6.15pm) This local producer of chestnut products has a well-stocked shop of *marrons glacés* (candied chestnuts), chestnut ice cream, *crème de marrons* (chestnut cream), chestnut liqueur

DON'T MISS

WONDERFUL ROADWAYS

The D14 runs through Collobrières, the largest town in the massif and chestnut capital of the universe, and is graced with superb panoramas. It's particularly popular with cyclists. Similarly dramatic, the D39 from Collobrières soars north to **Notre Dame des Anges** (780m) before plunging down to Gonfaron. Running parallel to the D14, the N98 skims through vineyards and cork oak plantations from St-Tropez to Bormes-les-Mimosas.

From La Môle – where you can find a delicious meal at **Auberge de la Môle** (☑ 04 94 49 57 01; place de l'Église, La Môle; lunch/dinner menus €23/55; ⊘ noon-2pm & 7-9pm Tue-Sat, noon-2pm Sun) – the breathtakingly narrow **Col du Canadel** (D27) dives dramatically to the coast, dishing up unbeatable views of the Massif des Maures, coastline and offshore islands.

etc, and a small free museum showing how chestnuts are processed.

ℹ Information

Tourist Office (☑ 04 94 48 08 00; www.collobrieres-tourisme.com; bd Charles Caminat; ⊘ 9am-12.30pm & 2-5.30pm Tue-Sun, closed Sun & Mon Sep-Jun) Has maps for local walks.

CORNICHE DES MAURES

The Corniche des Maures (D559) unwinds beautifully southwest from La Croix-Valmer to Le Lavandou along a shoreline trimmed with sandy beaches ideal for swimming, sunbathing and windsurfing.

The coastal D559 is served by VarLib buses (www.varlib.fr) running between St-Tropez and Toulon.

Rayol-Canadel-sur-Mer to Le Lavandou

Tiny **Plage du Rayol** and **Plage de l'Escale** are particularly enchanting beaches: they're backed by pine trees and have a restaurant on the sand. As the D559 hugs the coast going west, you'll reach **Plage du Layet**, the beautiful beach at **Cavalière** (not to be confused with Cavalaire-sur-Mer).

1

FREDERIC PACOREL / GETTY IMAGES ©

2

4

QUAI DES PECHEURS

P. EOCHE / GETTY IMAGES ©

1. Diving (p37)
Dive into the azure waters to see colourful Mediterranean marine life, including pale-purple jellyfish, but don't get too close!

2. Île de Port-Cros (p136)
France's smallest national park, Parc National de Port-Cros, was created in 1963 to protect the 7-sq-km island. The port, pictured above, offers accommodation and bistros from April to October.

3. Calanque d'En-Vau (p166)
The Calanques' most photogenic cove won't disappoint. With its pebbly beach and emerald water encased by cliffs, it's a beautiful spot to swim or kayak.

4. Île de Porquerolles (p133)
Despite the large influx of day trippers, beautiful Porquerolles is wholly unspoilt.

DAVID C TOMLINSON / GETTY IMAGES ©

ROUTE DES CRÊTES

For breathtaking views of the islands, follow Route des Crêtes as it winds its way through maquis-covered hills some 400m above the sea. From Bormes-les-Mimosas, follow the D41 uphill (direction Collobrières) past the Chapelle St-François and, 1.5km north of the village centre, turn immediately right after the sign for Col de Caguo-Ven (237m).

Relais du Vieux Sauvaire (☑04 94 05 84 22; rte des Crêtes; mains €17-32; ☺noon-2.30pm & 7-9.30pm Jun-Sep; ⚓) is the hidden gem of these hills. With 180-degree views you could only dream of, this restaurant and pool (most people come for lunch and then stay all afternoon) is one of a kind. The food is as sunny as the views: pizzas, melon and Parma ham, or whole sea bass in salt crust.

Past the restaurant, Route des Crêtes joins the final leg of the panoramic Col du Canadel road. On the *col* (mountain pass), turn left to plunge into the heart of the forested Massif des Maures or right to the sea and the coastal Corniche des Maures (D559).

Once a fishing village, Le Lavandou is now an overbuilt family-oriented beach resort with a small but intact old town and 12km of golden sand. The faux castle on the seafront is the **tourist office** (☑04 94 00 40 50; www.ot-lelavandou.fr; quai Gabriel Péri; ☺9am-noon & 2.30-6pm Mon-Sat). Opposite, boats sail to the Îles des Hyères.

○ Sights

★ Domaine du Rayol
GARDEN

(☑04 98 04 44 00; www.domainedurayol.org; av des Belges, Rayol-Canadel-sur-Mer; adult/child €10.50/7.50; ☺9.30am-7.30pm Jul & Aug, to 6.30pm Apr-Jun, Sep & Oct, to 5.30pm Nov-Mar) This stunning, lush garden, with plants from all Mediterranean climates the world round, is wonderful for a stroll or a themed nature walk. The dense flora cascade down the hillside from a villa to the sea, and while the flowers are at their best in April and May, it's always worth a visit. In summer, at the estate's gem of a beach, you can snorkel around underwater flora and fauna with an experienced guide; bookings are essential.

Also reserve ahead for open-air musical concerts or in-depth workshops. The estate's Café des Jardiniers serves light organic lunches and refreshing hibiscus-peach infusions.

⌂ Sleeping & Eating

Le Relais des Maures
INN €€

(☑04 94 05 61 27; www.lerelaisdesmaures.fr; av Charles Koeklin, Rayol-Canadel-sur-Mer; r €105) This inn, tucked just off the southern side of the D559, has homey guest rooms, some with sea views, and an excellent restaurant (menus from €32) that is worth a stop in its own right for its seasonally changing menus of locally sourced produce.

Chez Jo
SEAFOOD €€

(☑04 94 05 85 06; Plage du Layet, Cavalière; mains €20-30; ☺noon-2pm May-Sep) Buzzing with barefoot, overly bronzed, sarong-clad beach lovers with unexpected piercings and a fondness for nude bathing, this beach restaurant grills everything up straight from the sea. It's bare bones and without a sign in sight to tell you it's here; dining is around a few tables on the sand or on a wooden deck above the water. No credit cards.

Bormes-les-Mimosas

POP 7845 / ELEV 180M

This 12th-century village is spectacularly flowered with mimosas in winter, deep-fuchsia bougainvilleas in summer. Its tourist office takes bookings for botanical walks (€9) and hikes (€7) with a forest warden in the nearby **Forêt du Dom**.

Old cobbled streets are lined with artists galleries and boutiques selling traditional Provençal products.

⌂ Sleeping & Eating

★ Hôtel Bellevue
HOTEL €

(☑04 94 71 15 15; www.bellevuebormes.com; place Gambetta; d/q from €65/90; ☺Jan-Sep; ✳☏♿) Utterly charming, this sweet hotel has sensational views, spotless, pretty rooms and friendly service. Two rooms are wheelchair accessible. There's a restaurant too.

Hostellerie du Cigalou
HOTEL €€€

(☑04 94 41 51 27; www.hostellerieducigalou.com; place Gambetta; d €189-245; ✳☏⚓) A plush hotel with fantastic views and a dreamy pool.

Eating

⭐ **La Rastègue** GASTRONOMIC €€
(☎04 94 15 19 41; www.larastegue.com; 48 bd du Levant; menus €35-49; ⏰7-9pm Tue-Sat, noon-1.45pm Thu & Sun Apr-Nov) Jérôme Masson rules over the kitchen, his wife, Patricia, over the dining room, and they sure do excel. They've earned a Michelin star with their ever-changing menu of superb Provençal fare, inviting dining room and sea-view terrace. The open kitchen allows you to see the chef at work.

⭐ **L'Atelier de Cuisine Gourmande** PROVENÇAL €€
(☎04 94 71 27 80; 4 place Gambetta; mains €18-20; ⏰by reservation noon-2pm Sep-Jun) Mireille Gedda offers the most authentic of local cuisine, with flavours from the *terroir* (land). Her husband serves. She also runs classes.

ℹ Information

Tourist Office (☎04 94 01 38 38; www.bormeslesmimosas.com; 1 place Gambetta; ⏰9am-12.30pm & 2.30-6pm daily Apr-Sep, Mon-Sat Oct-Mar; ☎) Organises local walks.

ÎLES D'HYÈRES & ÎLES DU FUN

Legend says gods turned swimming princesses into the Îles d'Hyères – and they *are* magical. Their mica-rich rock, which glitters and gleams in the sunlight, gives them their other name, the Îles d'Or (Islands of Gold). Avoid July and August, though, when they are overrun.

Porquerolles, at 7km long and 3km wide, is the largest; Île de Port-Cros, in the middle, is a national park; and its eastern sister, Île du Levant, is both an army camp and a nudist colony. Wild camping and cars are forbidden throughout the archipelago.

Dubbed the Îles du Fun, Bendor and Embiez, west of the Îles d'Hyères off Toulon's shores, are more sub-Disney than the stuff of myth.

Islanders refer to the rest of France as the 'continent'.

ℹ Getting There & Away

ÎLES DE PORQUEROLLES, DE PORT-CROS & DU LEVANT
⇒ Îles de Porquerolles and de Port-Cros: Mainland ports are La Tour Fondue, Port d'Hyères

and Le Lavandou. June to September boats also go to/from Toulon, St-Tropez, Port Miramar, La Croix-Valmer and Cavalaire-sur-Mer.
⇒ Île du Levant: Ten minutes by boat from Port-Cros. Frequent boats sail year-round from Le Lavandou and Port d'Hyères, and in July and August from Port Miramar, La Croix-Valmer and Cavalaire-sur-Mer.

Transport Littoral Varois (☎04 94 58 21 81; www.tlv-tvm.com) Year-round boats link La Tour Fondue with Île de Porquerolles (return €19.50, 20 minutes), and Port d'Hyères with Île de Port-Cros (return €28.10, one hour) and Île du Levant (return €28.10, 90 minutes); going to two islands costs €31.50.

Vedettes Îles d'Or et Le Corsaire (☎04 94 71 01 02; www.vedettesilesdor.fr; 15 quai Gabriel Péri) From Le Lavandou, Cavalaire-sur-Mer and La Croix Valmer, seasonal boats run to/from Île du Levant (return €28 to €33, 35 to 55 minutes), Île de Port-Cros (€28 to €33, 35 to 55 minutes) and Île de Porquerolles (€30 to €41, 50 minutes). La Croisière Bleue tours (all three islands €54) and thrice-weekly summer-only boats to St-Tropez (€43 to €54, two hours) require reservations. November to May, boats only connect Le Lavandou, Levant and Port-Cros.

ÎLE DE BENDOR
Boats (adult/child return €12/9, 10 minutes) sail year-round from Bandol. See www.bendor.com.

ÎLES DES EMBIEZ
Boats (adult/child return €14/9, 15 minutes) sail year-round from Le Brusc, 5km south of Sanary-sur-Mer. See www.les-embiez.com.

Île de Porquerolles

POP 250

Despite the huge influx of day trippers (up to 6000 a day in July and August), beautiful Porquerolles is wholly unspoilt: two-thirds of its sandy white beaches, pine woods, maquis and eucalyptus are protected by the Parc National de Port-Cros, and a wide variety of indigenous and tropical flora thrive, including Requien's larkspur, which grows nowhere else in the world. April and May are the best months to spot some of the 114 bird species. Pottering along the island's rough unpaved trails on foot or by bicycle, breaking with a picnic lunch on the beach and a dip in crystal-clear turquoise water is heavenly.

Avoid July and August, when the risk of fire closes the interior of the island and makes some trails inaccessible. In general, smoking is forbidden outside the village.

⊙ Sights

Porquerolles' vineyards cover a square kilometre of the western part of the island, and are tended by three wine producers. Each offers *dégustation* (tasting) sessions of their predominantly rosé wines.

Place d'Armes   SQUARE
A tree-shaded *pétanque* pitch dominates central place d'Armes. Music concerts fill Église Ste-Anne on its southern side in summer. Day in, day out, this hub of Porquerollais life buzzes with outdoor cafes and ice-cream stands and cyclists pedalling to and fro. Once the last of the day-tripper boats has sailed, a Zen lull falls across the square.

Fort Ste-Agathe   FORT
(☑ 04 94 58 07 24; www.portcrosparcnational.fr; adult/child €4/2; ☺ by guided tour only Apr–mid-Sep) This 16th-century fortification contains historical and natural-history exhibits, and its tower has lovely island views. Much of the building dates from between 1812 and 1814, when Napoléon had it rebuilt after the British destroyed it in 1793. From place d'Armes, walk uphill along chemin Ste-Agathe (between Villa Ste-Anne and Auberge des Glycines) to reach the fort. Admission is only with timed, guided national-park tours. Tours of nearby windmill Moulin du Bonheur cost €2.

Jardin Emanuel Lopez & Conservatoire Botanique National Méditerranéen   GARDEN
(☑ 04 94 58 07 24; chemin du Phare; ☺ 9.30am-12.30pm & 2-6pm Apr-Oct) FREE This wonderful ornamental garden is planted with palm varieties, cypress, vanilla and grenadier trees, cactus and bamboo, sweetly scented jasmine and every herb known to grow under the Provençal sun. It's also home to the Parc National de Port-Cros Maison du Parc.

Domaine Perzinsky   WINERY
(☑ 04 94 58 34 32; www.perzinsky.com; chemin de la Pépinière; ☺ 10am-noon & 3-6pm mid-Apr–Sep)

TRUE LOVE
Three toasters and a towel set just weren't enough. In 1911, newly married Mrs Fournier received the perfect wedding present from hubby François: the island of Porquerolles! Their descendants still own a big piece of the island, including Le Mas du Langoustier.

Framed by a fabulous formation of parasol pines, Domaine Perzinsky is an easy stop en route to Plage d'Argent and, unusually, requires no advance reservation for tastings.

Domaine de la Courtade   WINERY
(☑ 04 94 58 31 44; www.lacourtade.com; ☺ by appointment year-round) Domaine de la Courtade offers tastings of its predominantly rosé wines.

Domaine de l'Île   WINERY
(☑ 04 98 04 62 30; www.domainedelile.com; ☺ by appointment Mon-Fri year-round) This producer, focusing on rosé, offers tastings.

🏃 Activities

Porquerolles' northern coast is laced with beautiful sandy beaches. Cliffs line the island's more dangerous southern coast, where swimming and diving are restricted to Calanque du Brégançonnet to the east and Calanque de l'Oustau de Diou to the west. Get maps at the tourist office.

The map sold at the tourist office has four cycling itineraries, 6.5km to 13.8km long. More detail is included in a cyclo-guide (€6) in French, available at the Parc National de Port-Cros Maison du Parc. Bike-hire outfits line the port and place d'Armes.

Plage de la Courtade   SWIMMING
This beautiful sandy beach is a mere 800m walk east from the port (follow the track uphill behind the tourist office).

Plage de Notre Dame   SWIMMING
Porquerolles' largest and most beautiful beach, Plage de Notre Dame, is about 3.5km east of the port (follow the track uphill behind the tourist office).

Plage d'Argent   SWIMMING
West of the village, Plage d'Argent, a good 2km along a potholed track past vineyards, is popular with families because of its summer beachside cafe-restaurant, lifeguards and toilets.

Plage du Langoustier   SWIMMING
Secluded Plage du Langoustier is located at a former lobster farm 4.5km from the village on the northern shores of the Presqu'île du Langoustier.

Locamarine 75   BOATING, KAYAKING
(☑ 06 08 34 74 17, 04 94 58 35 84; www.locamarine75.com; Porquerolles; speedboat rental from €95; ☺ 9am-7pm) Speedboat-rental outlet

at the port; also has kayaks (double kayak half-/full-day rentals €35/45).

Base Nautique KAYAKING
(☑06 60 52 37 06; www.ileo-porquerolles.fr; 1/3/6hr kayak rental €20/35/45) On Plage de la Courtade; has kayaks, windsurfers, catamarans and scuba diving.

🛏 Sleeping & Eating

Accommodation is pricey and limited and it gets booked months in advance. The tourist office has details on self-catering apartments/villas and three B&Bs. Prices plummet in the low season. Most hotels also have restaurants.

An admirable picnic of juicy cherries, fresh goat's-milk cheese etc can be bought from the stands on place d'Armes and the two small grocery stores (they close for two hours just after noon).

⭐ **L'Oustaou** PENSION €€
(☑04 94 58 30 13; www.oustaou.com; place d'Armes; d from €150; ☺Apr-Oct; ⊛🔊) Super-clean rooms with modern decor either face the village square or have marvellous port views. It's lovely for couples, with a hint of romance. Downstairs, tuck into modern French standards or burgers (mains €16 to €26).

Villa Ste-Anne INN €€
(☑04 94 04 63 00; www.sainteanne.com; place d'Armes; s/d per person incl half-board from €150/175; ☺Apr–mid-Sep; ⊛) The main draw of this typical Porquerollais inn on the square is its terracotta-tiled restaurant terrace that overlooks the *pétanque* pitch. Borrow a set of boules should you fancy a spin. Indulge in an aperitif and *petit friture* (tiny deep-fried fish dipped in spicy *rouille*, a saffron-garlic mayonnaise).

⭐ **Le Mas du Langoustier** HOTEL €€€
(☑04 94 58 30 09; www.langoustier.com; d per person incl half-board from €150; ☺May-Sep; ⊛🔊⛵️🛥) The 'to die for' choice: guests have been known to drop in by helicopter at this exceptional hotel with a glamorous history (dating to 1931), vineyards and stunning views from its seaside perch. Everything, from its rooms to its Michelin-star restaurant is impeccable. Some apartments for families.

Auberge des Glycines PENSION €€€
(☑04 94 58 30 36; www.auberge-glycines.com; 22 place d'Armes; d incl breakfast from €170; ☺year-round; ⊛🔊🛥) This inn overlooking the village square ranks as highly in the dining stakes as it does in sleeping. Decor is tra-

ditional (note the cicada collection hanging on the wall in reception) and dining is Porquerollaise – in other words, shoals of fish. Three-course *menus* are €38.

Les Mèdes HOTEL €€€
(☑04 94 12 41 24; www.hotel-les-medes.fr; 2 rue de la Douane; d from €130, 4-person apt from €225; ☺Jan-Oct; ⊛@🔊🛥) This hotel-residence mixes traditional hotel rooms with self-catering apartments. The icing on the cake: a terraced garden with fountain pool and sun loungers.

L'Escale BRASSERIE €
(☑04 94 58 30 18; 2 rue de la Ferme; menus from €13; ☺noon-2pm daily year-round, plus 7-9.30pm May-Aug) Tuck into good, homemade seafood and meat dishes on a broad terrace overlooking the port.

ℹ Information

Tourist Office (☑04 94 58 33 76; www.porquerolles.com; ☺9am-6.15pm Mon-Sat, to 1pm Sun Jul & Aug, reduced hours rest of year) Brochures and maps, one marked with cycling and walking paths (€3).

Parc National de Port-Cros Maison du Parc (☑04 94 58 07 24; www.portcrosparcnational.fr; Jardin Emanuel Lopez; ☺9.30am-12.30pm & 2-6pm Apr-Oct) National-park office with maps, information and guided tours.

ℹ Getting Around

BICYCLE

Rent at the port or place d'Armes.

Le Cycle Porquerollais (☑04 94 58 30 32; www.cycle-porquerollais.com; 1 rue de la Ferme; half-/full-day from €15/12; ☺year-round) Le Cycle Porquerollais rents bikes and sits just alongside the place d'Armes.

TAXI

Bateaux-Taxi Le Pélican (☑06 09 52 31 19; www.bateaux-taxi.com) This boat taxi can circle Porquerolles or go to the mainland.

Luggage Taxi (☑06 81 67 77 12; ☺mid-Feb–Dec) Hire a cart and driver to move your luggage around the carless island of Porquerolles.

SLEEPING ON THE SEA

To sleep aboard a sailboat, contact **Bateaudhote.fr** (☑06 82 15 93 76; www.bateaudhote.fr; cabins per night from €150) or **Via Skipper** (☑06 26 93 49 47; www.viaskipper.com; per day from €600).

Île de Port-Cros

France's smallest national park, **Parc National de Port-Cros**, was created in 1963 to protect the 7-sq-km island of Port-Cros and a 13-sq-km zone of water around it.

Until the end of the 19th century, the islanders' vineyards and olive groves ensured their self-sufficiency. Today, high-season tourism is their sustenance. Bring picnic supplies and drinking water; the few port bistros open April to October, but there's nothing elsewhere but beauty.

◉ Sights & Activities

Walkers (and birdwatchers) must remain on 30km of marked trails. Fishing, fires, camping, dogs, motorised vehicles and bicycles are not allowed, nor is smoking outside the village.

Fort de l'Estissac   FORT
(www.portcrosparcnational.fr; ⊙ 10.30am-12.30pm & 2-5pm May-Oct) FREE Climb the tower of this imposing 16th-century fort, which hosts summer exhibitions.

Sentier des Plantes   WALKING
The 15th-century **Fort du Moulin** is the starting point for the Sentier des Plantes (Botanical Trail; 4km, 1½ to two hours), a lovely aromatic trail that wends its way past wild lavender and rosemary to **Plage de la Palud** (30 minutes), a beautiful beach on the island's northern shore.

Sentier Sous-Marin   SNORKELLING
(Underwater Trail; ☑ 04 94 01 40 70; Plage de la Palud; ⊙ mid-Jun–mid-Sep) FREE This 35-minute underwater circuit is marked by buoys with explanatory panels – the bay is home to 500 algae species and 180 types of fish. The Maison du Parc at the port sells an underwater leaflet (€5). Rent equipment from portside outfit **Sun Plongée** (☑ 06 80 32 14 16, 04 94 05 90 16; www.sun-plongee.com; ⊙ mid-Mar–mid-Nov). And check to see if there are jellyfish before diving in!

Circuit de Port-Man   WALKING
From Plage de la Palud, the Circuit de Port-Man (four hours) follows the coastline to secluded Plage de Port-Man on the island's far-northeastern tip before looping back inland.

Sentier des Crêtes   WALKING
The demanding Sentier des Crêtes (7.5km; three hours) explores the southwestern corner of the island and climaxes atop Mont Vinaigre (194m).

🛏 Sleeping & Eating

Accommodation requires booking months in advance, and is limited to the small port area.

Hostellerie Provençale   PENSION €€
(☑ 04 94 05 90 43; www.hostellerie-provencale.com; d per person incl half-board from €149; ⊙ Apr–mid-Nov; ❄ 🛜 🏊) Run by the island's oldest and largest family since 1921, this bustling portside *hostellerie* (inn) sports five bright rooms facing the water; the best have a balcony. The eye-catching cocktail bar and restaurant sit on the waterfront with canary-yellow sun umbrellas.

Hôtel Le Manoir de Port-Cros   PENSION €€€
(☑ 04 94 05 90 52; www.hotel-lemanoirportcros.com; d per person incl half-board from €170; ⊙ Apr-Oct; ❄ 🏊) This enchanting 23-room manor with white turreted facade 300m from Port-Cros' port is the exclusive option. Find it nestled in a sweet-smelling eucalyptus grove with outdoor pool, upmarket restaurant and the elegant air of bygone island life.

La Trinquette   BISTRO €€
(☑ 04 94 05 93 75; www.restaurant-trinquette-port-cros.fr; menus €22-28; ⊙ 8am-midnight Apr-Oct) Dine at the edge of the soft harbour sand on steaks, seafood or pasta before heading out on walks across the island.

ℹ️ Information

Maison du Parc (☑ 04 94 01 40 70; www.portcrosparcnational.fr) Walking, diving and snorkelling information, plus an island map marked with the island's four main trails, and guides (in French) to underwater fauna and flora. Located at the port; opening hours coincide with boat arrivals.

Île du Levant

Île du Levant, an 8km strip of an island, has a split personality. Ninety per cent of it is a closed military camp, and the remaining pocket of **Héliopolis** (www.iledulevant.com.fr), on the island's south-western edge, is a nudist colony.

The post office, cafes and hotels are clustered around the central square, place du Village, 1km uphill from the port along rte de l'Ayguade. There is no ATM. From place du Village a nature trail leads east into the **Domaine des Arbousiers**, a nature reservation in the eastern part of the colony sheltering rare island plants. The tourist office has information on guided tours.

Baring all is not obligatory except on beaches, like sandy Plage Les Grottes, east of Port de l'Ayguade. From the port, walk in the direction of Plage de Sable Levant along Sentier Georges Rousseau, a rocky coastal path. Signs reading 'Nudisme Intégral Obligatoire' mark the moment you have to strip.

Boats dock at Port de l'Ayguade near the tourist-information hut (☑ 04 94 05 93 52; www.iledulevant.com.fr; ☺ Easter–mid-Sep).

TOULON & AROUND

Relatively unspoilt coastline turns increasingly urban as you head west to Toulon. A final pocket of blue and green surrounds La Londe-les-Maures (population 9300), midway between Le Lavandou and Hyères. Explore its olive groves, vineyards and flower gardens on guided walks organised by the tourist office (☑ 04 94 01 53 10; www.ot-lalondelesmaures.fr; ☺ 9am-6pm Mon-Sat, to 1pm Sun) or hire a bike and wine taste by pedal power.

Hyères & Presqu'île de Giens

POP 56.600

With its statuesque palm trees, casino, medieval Vieille Ville (Old Town) on a hillside north of its new town, and its zippy bustle, Hyères retains some of the charm that made it the Côte d'Azur's first resort. The city's other grand asset is the Presqu'île de Giens (Giens Peninsula). The tourist office runs superb tours of both.

◉ Sights & Activities

★ Vieille Ville   HISTORIC QUARTER
On the western side of place Georges Clemenceau, 13th-century Porte Massillon (look for the clock) is the entrance to Hyères' Old Town. West along cobbled rue Massillon is beautiful arcaded rue des Porches, with its polished flagstones and collection of boutiques.

The rambling hillside grove of Parc St-Bernard abuts the striking Villa Noailles. Back downhill, Parc Castel Ste-Claire, a 17th-century convent converted into a private residence, was home to American writer Edith Wharton from 1927.

WORTH A TRIP

CAP DE CARQUEIRANNE

Immediately west of Hyères, Cap de Carqueiranne is a partly forested stretch of headland, criss-crossed by tiny lanes. The coastal path that edges its way from the town of Carqueiranne is a scenic means of exploring the pretty cape. Reserve ahead at L'Oursinado (☑ 04 94 21 77 06; www.oursinado.com; chemin du Pas des Gardéens; menus €58; ☺ noon-1.30pm & 7-9.30pm Tue-Sun Jul & Aug, Thu-Mon & lunch Tue mid-Feb–Jun & Sep–mid-Nov; 🐾), hidden on a cliff above the tiny port of Les Oursinières. Sit on its tree-framed terrace, gaze down at pounding waves and feast on Toulonnais bouillabaisse (order 48 hours in advance), the local version of the legendary Marseille fish stew.

Today Castel Ste-Claire houses the headquarters of the Parc National de Port-Cros (www.portcrosparcnational.fr).

Villa Noailles   LANDMARK
(☑ 04 98 08 01 98; www.villanoailles-hyeres.com; ☺ 2-7pm Wed-Thu & Sat-Mon, 4-10pm Fri Jul-Sep, reduced hours rest of year) FREE A cubist maze of concrete and glass, the villa was designed by Robert Mallet-Stevens in 1923 as a winter residence for devoted lover of modern art Vicomte Charles de Noailles. It hosts exhibitions.

★ Presqu'île de Giens   OUTDOOR ACTIVITIES
This beach-fringed peninsula briefly became an island in 1811 after huge storms. It is a launch pad for day trips to the Îles d'Hyères and a walker's and spotter's paradise: the protected wetland area harbours amazing birdlife, including pink flamingos, herons, egrets, teals and cormorants. A beautiful Sentier du Littoral (Coastal Path) loops the peninsula.

La Capte   BIRDWATCHING
Pink flamingos add a splash of colour to the otherwise barren landscape of La Capte, two narrow sand bars supporting the Salins des Presquiers salt pans and a lake 4km south of Hyères' centre. A 1½-hour (12.5km) cycling itinerary loops the salt pans, and the Hyères tourist office runs guided bird-discovery nature walks (adult/child €5/free).

The western sand-bar road dubbed the rte du Sel (Salt Rd) is particularly spectacular. It's accessible only in summer.

Sleeping

Aged hotels in the Old Town are beat by great-value ones on Presqu'île de Giens.

Hôtel Le Méditerranée
HOTEL €€

(☑ 04 94 00 52 70; www.hotel-lemediterranee.com; 8 av de la Méditerranée, Hyères Beach Rd; s & d from €78, tr/q from €96/109; ⊙ Feb-Nov; ❄ 🔊 🅿) This friendly hotel abutting Hyères' horse-racing track is a one-minute walk to the Plage d'Hyères. Bathrooms are modern, rooms are painted in typical Provençal colours and the best has a balcony.

Hôtel Bor
BOUTIQUE HOTEL €€€

(☑ 04 94 58 02 73; www.hotel-bor.com; 3 allée Émile Gérard, Hyères Beach; d from €150; ⊙ Mar-Oct; ❄ @ 🔊 🅿) This sleek hotel on the sand screams design. Palm trees and potted plants speckle its wood-decking terrace, and sun loungers beg to be used on its pebble beach. Rooms are in muted natural colours.

✕ Eating

Joy
PROVENÇAL €€

(☑ 04 94 20 84 98; www.restaurant-joy.com; 24 rue de Limans, Hyères; lunch/dinner menus from €23/45; ⊙ noon-1.30pm & 7-9.30pm Tue-Sat, noon-1.30pm Sun) This contemporary restaurant in an intimate bistro setting is a culinary joy. Fresh, seasonal menus change constantly and could include anything from seafood-stuffed ravioli to cinnamon-spiced foie gras.

Le Marais
BEACH RESTAURANT €€

(☑ 09 54 12 72 09; www.lemaraisplage.fr; 1366 blvd de la Marine, D42, Presqu'île de Giens; mains €15-30; ⊙ 11am-2am Apr-Oct) Smack on the soft sands of Presqu'île de Giens, this popular beach restaurant cooks up pasta, pizza and fresh fish in a mod building, near the airport, with sailboats tacking offshore.

❶ Information

Tourist Office (☑ 04 94 01 84 50; www.hyeres-tourisme.com; Rotonde du Park Hôtel, av de Belgique, Hyères; ⊙ 9am-6pm Mon-Fri, to 4pm Sat, plus Sun Jul & Aug) Fabulous guided walks.

❶ Getting There & Around

AIR

Toulon-Hyères Airport (TLN; ☑ 08 25 01 83 87; www.toulon-hyeres.aeroport.fr; 🔊) Three kilometres south of Hyères, 25km east of Toulon, this airport serves six European cities, some seasonally. Daily flights to Paris Orly (Air France). Le Réseau Mistral bus 102 serves the Toulon train and bus stations (40 minutes) via Hyères centre (10 minutes), which is also served by bus 63; tickets are €1.40. St-Tropez is served by VarLib (p119; tickets €3).

BOAT

Transport Littoral Varois (p133) runs services to Îles d'Hyères.

BUS

From the **bus station** (www.reseaumistral.com; place du Maréchal Joffre, Hyères), bus 67 goes to the train station (five minutes), Port d'Hyères (15 minutes) and La Tour Fondue (35 minutes). All fares €1.40.

TAXI

Taxis Radio Hyèrois (☑ 04 94 00 60 00; www.taxis-hyeres.com)

TRAIN

From **Hyères' train station** (place de l'Europe), local trains chug to/from Toulon (€5 to €8, 30 to 45 minutes). The Marseille–Hyères line (€15 to €25, two hours, four daily) stops in Cassis, La Ciotat, Bandol, Ollioules-Sanary and Toulon, and usually requires a transfer.

Toulon

POP 167,200

Rough-round-the-edges Toulon just doesn't fit in with the glittering Côte d'Azur. Built around a *rade* (a sheltered bay lined with quays), France's second-largest naval port has a certain rough charm, and isn't quite as terrible as it once was, though most visitors just pass through.

◉ Sights & Activities

Musée de la Marine
MARITIME MUSEUM

(☑ 04 94 02 02 01; place Monsenergue; adult/child €5/free; ⊙ 10am-6pm Wed-Mon) A good, modern seafaring museum with exhibits, models and paintings illustrating Toulon's rich naval history.

Mont Faron
MOUNTAIN

North of the city, Mont Faron (584m) towers over Toulon, and the views are, as you would expect, epic. Near the summit, Mémorial du Débarquement de Provence (☑ 04 94 88 08 09; Mont Faron; adult/child €4/free; ⊙ 10am-noon & 2-4.30pm Tue-Sun) commemorates the Allied landings of Operation Dragoon, which took place along the coast here in August 1944. There are pleasant walks in the surrounding forest. To get here, catch a ride on the Téléphérique du Mont Faron (☑ 04 94 92 68

25; www.telepherique-faron.com; return adult/child €7/5; ☉10am-6pm) cable car.

Les Bateliers de la Rade
BOAT TOUR

(☑04 94 46 24 65; www.lesbateliersdelarade.com; quai de la Sinse; adult/child €10/6; ☉May-Sep) From the port you can take a guided boat tour around the *rade*, with a commentary on the local events of WWII (the commentary is in French, but there are leaflets in English).

🍴 Sleeping & Eating

Chicag' Hostel
HOSTEL €

(☑04 89 66 52 66; www.chicaghosteltoulon.com; 3 rue des Bonnetières; dm from €25; 🤶) 🗡 This hostel is an antidote to Toulon's poor press: the brainchild of Clara and Bjorg, two young Toulonnais passionate about their city. It is a charming place with three eight-bed dorms and a common room/kitchen that doubles as a cafe. Every bit of furniture has been re-cycled or upcycled by the team, giving it a wonderfully quirky feel.

Hôtel Little Palace
HOTEL €

(☑04 94 92 26 62; www.hotel-littlepalace.com; 6-8 rue Berthelot; s/d/tr €55/65/75; ❄@🤶) The over-the-top Italian-inspired decor lacks au-thenticity and the lighting leaves something to be desired, but Little Palace is well run and friendly. No lift.

Le Chantilly
BRASSERIE €€

(place Puget; mains €15-28; ☉7am-11pm) Going strong since 1907, Le Chantilly will sort you out for food, whatever the time of day.

ℹ️ Information

Tourist Office (☑04 94 18 53 00; www.toulontourisme.com; 12 place Louis Blanc; ☉9am-6pm Mon-Sat) Maps and walking-tour brochures.

ℹ️ Getting There & Away

AIR
Toulon-Hyères Airport is nearby.

BOAT
Corsica Ferries (www.corsica-ferries.fr; Port de Commerce, 2 av de l'Infanterie-de-Marine) Ferries run to Corsica and Sardinia.
Bateliers de la Côte d'Azur (☑04 94 05 21 14; www.bateliersdelacotedazur.com; quai Cron-stadt) In summer go to the Îles d'Hyères.

BUS
VarLib (www.varlib.fr) buses (€3) operate from the **bus station** (☑04 94 24 60 00; bd de Tessé), next to the train station. Buses to St-

Tropez (six daily) go via Hyères (35 minutes) and Le Lavandou (one hour).

The tourist office sells a one-day pass (per person €6) that includes unlimited travel on local **Le Réseau Mistral** (☑04 94 03 87 00; www.reseaumistral.com) buses and commuter boats, and a return ticket for the Mont Faron Téléphérique.

TRAIN
Frequent connections include Marseille (€12, 50 minutes), St-Raphaël (€17, 50 minutes), Cannes (€22, 1¼ hours) and Nice (€27, 1¾ hours).

TOWARDS MARSEILLE

Sanary-sur-Mer

Pretty as a picture, seaside Sanary-sur-Mer is a stroller's dream. Watch the fishers unload their catch on the quay, or admire the tradi-tional fishing boats from one of the seafront cafes. Wednesday's colourful market draws crowds from miles around. Shops line inte-rior streets. Novelist Aldous Huxley (1894–1963) called Sanary home in the early 1930s.

🚩 Tours

Découverte du Vivant
BOAT TOUR

(☑06 10 57 17 11; www.decouverteduvivant.fr; adult/child €78/55; ☉Sun Jun-Oct) Observe various dolphin species from aboard a boat with naturalist photographers on a day out-ing. Pack a picnic.

Croix du Sud V
BOAT TOUR

(☑06 09 87 47 97; www.croixdusud5.com; quai Charles de Gaulle) From mid-April to Septem-ber, boat tours serve the *calanques* (rocky inlets) east of Marseille (adult/child from €26/16) and Île de Porquerolles (€40/23).

🍴 Sleeping & Eating

★ Hôtel de la Tour
HOTEL €€

(☑04 94 74 10 10; www.sanary-hoteldelatour.com; 24 quai Charles de Gaulle; d incl breakfast €90-130; ❄🤶) Some of the excellent, large rooms in this renovated Victorian-era hotel have awesome portside views. The charming de-cor is clean and inviting, and the restaurant with harbourside terrace offers delicious Provençal meals and elegant service.

L'Esplanade
SEAFOOD €€

(☑04 94 74 08 56; www.restaurant-esplanade.fr; Parking de l'Esplanade; lunch/dinner menus from

€23/37; ⊙noon-2.30pm & 7.30-10.30pm Tue-Sun May-Sep, shorter hours rest of year) Dine in portside elegance on the catch of the day.

Le Bard'ô
MEDITERRANEAN €€

(☑04 94 88 42 56; www.le-bardo.com; Plage de Portissol; lunch/dinner menus €17/34; ⊙noon-2pm & 7-10.30pm Apr-Oct) Just south of Sanary, on Portissol beach, this seafront club is perfect for everything from leisurely coffees and delicious meals to late-night DJs and live music. The lunch menu is a bargain but available in limited quantities, so arrive early.

🛈 Information

Tourist Office (☑04 94 74 01 04; www. sanarysurmer.com; 1 quai du Levant; ⊙9am-1pm & 2-5pm Mon-Sat)

Bandol & Around

The built-up town of Bandol, a favourite among French holidaymakers, lends its name to the area's excellent wines. The *appellation* comprises eight neighbouring communities, including Le Castellet, Ollioules, Évenos and Sanary-sur-Mer.

🏃 Activities

★ Maison des Vins
WINE TASTING

(Oenothèque des Vins du Bandol; ☑04 94 29 45 03; www.maisondesvins-bandol.com; place Lucien Artaud, Bandol; ⊙10am-1pm & 3-6.30pm Mon-Sat, 10am-1pm Sun) Bandol's 49 vineyards carefully manage their prized production of red, rosé and white. Pascal Perier, the manager at the Maison des Vins, is a living Bandol encyclopaedia. He provides tastings, keeps

a well-supplied shop and can direct you to surrounding vineyards (most require an appointment).

Sentier du Littoral
WALKING

This yellow-marked coastal trail runs 12km (allow 3½ to four hours) from Bandol's port to La Madrague in St-Cyr-les-Lecques, with the beautiful Calanque de Port d'Alon roughly halfway.

🛏 Sleeping & Eating

Golf Hôtel
HOTEL €€

(☑04 94 29 45 83; www.golfhotel.fr; 10 promenade de la Corniche; d/q from €80/120; ⊙Jan-Nov; ❄🔇📶) A prime address for beachside sleeping; some of the rooms have terraces facing the sea.

Key Largo
HOTEL €€

(☑04 94 29 46 93; www.hotel-key-largo.com; 19 corniche Bonaparte; d €80-120; ❄📶) On the point between the port and Renécros beach, the Key Largo has simply furnished rooms; the most expensive have views of the bay.

L'Ardoise
BISTRO €€

(☑04 94 32 28 58; 25 rue du Dr Marçon; lunch menu €16, dinner menus €27-41; ⊙noon-2pm & 7.30-10.30pm Wed-Sun) The gourmet address in Bandol, L'Ardoise serves Mediterranean cuisine inspired by the seasons and faraway climes in a very bistro dining room.

L'Espérance
BISTRO €€

(☑04 94 05 85 29; 21 rue du Dr Marçon; lunch/dinner menus from €25/30; ⊙noon-1.30pm Wed-Thu, Sat & Sun, 7-9pm Tue-Sun) Reserve ahead to get a spot in this tiny Provençal restaurant run ably by a husband-and-wife team.

Marseille to Aix-en-Provence

Best Places to Eat

➡ Petit Pierre Reboul (p173)

➡ La Table de Ventabren (p176)

➡ Le Café des Épices (p160)

➡ Le Petit Verdot (p173)

➡ Le Rhul (p160)

➡ La Cantinetta (p160)

Best Places to Stay

➡ Villa Gallici (p172)

➡ Intercontinental Marseille – Hôtel Dieu (p157)

➡ L'Épicerie (p172)

➡ Casa Honoré (p157)

Why Go?

Radiating from the boat-lined Vieux Port, Marseille's irresistible magnetism draws you into its vibrant, polyglot heart. The city has undergone a facelift in recent years and now boasts world-class museums in showpiece buildings, myriad galleries and top-notch performing arts. It also retains earthy, bustling markets and districts spiced with Middle Eastern flavour, as well as fantastic restaurants. Allow yourself at least 48 hours to take in Marseille's compelling sights, its azure coast, and the dramatic Les Calanques – rocky inlets gashed by the seas of the ice age, resulting in the spectacular coastline that snakes southeast to Cassis. Heading north from Marseille, the landscape softens to the green and purple hues of the Pays d'Aix (Aix Country) that Cézanne loved so much, with charming, bourgeois Aix-en-Provence at its centre.

Driving Distances (km)

	Aix-en-Provence	Cassis	Marignane (Airport)	Marseille
Cassis	49			
Marignane (Airport)	34	56		
Marseille	34	23	26	
Salon de Provence	34	72	34	30

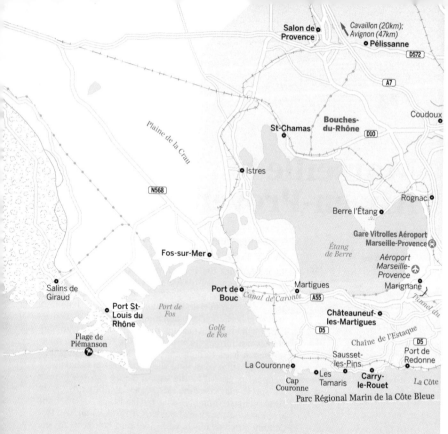

Marseille to Aix-en-Provence Highlights

1 Peruse the explosion of new galleries and museums in **Marseille** (p145), like MuCEM.

2 Stroll Marseille's **Vieux Port** (p144) before settling into a sunny cafe for people-watching.

3 Dip into the rocky coves of **Calanque de Sormiou** (p166) and **Calanque de Morgiou** (p166) for gorgeous walks and lunch with sea views.

4 Restaurant-hop around mod bistros in **Marseille** (p157) or sup *bouillabaisse*

St-Canadet

St-Cannat
N7

Domaine de
la Brillane

Manosque
(30km)

D96

Rians

0 ———— 10 km
0 ———— 5 miles

Chaîne de la Trévaresse

Couteron
D13A

A51

D13

D543

D96

D10

Vauvenargues

Montagne
7 Ste-Victoire

Ventabren

D10

Aix-en-
Provence
6

Le Tholonet

D17

Aqueduc de
Roquefavour 1

A8

Beaurecueil

St-Antonin-sur-Bayon

D46

Châteauneuf-
le-Rouge

Les
Milles

D7

D6

A8

D96

Vitrolles

A51

A52

Gardanne

Trets

A7

D9

Cabriès

D8

St-Maximin La
Ste-Baume (9km)

N560

A55

A55

A7

Chaîne de l'Étoile

D908

Nans-les-Pins

L'Estaque

Rove

Calanque
de Niolon

Bleue

Rade de
Marseille

D4

Auriol

Roquevaire

D45A

Col de l'Espigoulier
(728m)

D2

La St-Baume

Massif de
la Ste-Baume

Aubagne

Gémenos

GR98

Marseille
1 2 4

A50

Îles du
Frioul 8

Île
Ratonneau

8
Île d'If

Plage du
Prado

Parc
Borély

Île Pomègues

La Pointe-Rouge

D559

Mont Puget (564m)

Cassis
5

Massif des Calanques

Les Goudes

GR98

Morgiou

Calanque
de Morgiou

Cap Croisette

Callelongue

Sormiou

3

3

Cap Canaille
(399m)

La Ciotat

Les Lecques

Île de Jarre

Calanque
de Sormiou

Cap Morgiou

Route des
Crêtes

La Madrague

Toulon
(16km)

Île Calseraigne

Baie de Cassis

Cap de
l'Aigle

Île
Verte

A50

Île
de Riou

Calanque d'En-Vau
Calanque de Port-Pin
Calanque de Port-Miou

Port
d'Alon

Bandol

Ferries to Corsica,
Sardinia, Tunisia
& Algeria

at classic coastal restaurants
like **Le Rhul** (p160).

5 Drive the high-drama
Route des Crêtes (Road of
Crests) before wine tasting at
Cassis (p167).

6 Revel in elegant
architecture and fine arts in
Aix-en-Provence (p168).

7 Climb **Montagne Ste-
Victoire** (p175), one of
Cézanne's inspirations.

8 Follow in the footsteps
of the Count of Monte Cristo
at **Château d'If** (p154), or
picnic at neighbouring **Îles du
Friou** (p154).

MARSEILLE

POP 858,902

Marseille is a rich, pulsing port city bubbling over with history, cutting-edge creative spaces and hip multicultural urbanites. Since Greek settlers came ashore around 600 BC, waves of immigrants have made Marseille (now France's second-largest city) their home.

The city is looking fabulous after its tenure as the European Capital of Culture in 2013. Its maritime heritage thrives at the vibrant Vieux Port (Old Port), or you can explore the ancient Le Panier neighbourhood, set on a hill above the water; the République quarter, with its swanky boutiques and Haussmannian buildings; and the stunning contemporary architecture of the Joliette area around Marseille's famous striped Cathédrale de la Major. Along the coast, seaside roads and cycling tracks veer around sun-scorched coves and sandy beaches.

History

Around 600 BC, Greek mariners founded Massilia, a trading post, at what is now Marseille's Vieux Port. In the 1st century BC, the city lost out by backing Pompey the Great rather than Julius Caesar: Caesar's forces captured Massilia in 49 BC and directed Roman trade elsewhere.

Marseille became part of France in the 1480s, but its citizens embraced the Revolution, sending 500 volunteers to defend Paris in 1792. Heading north, they sang a rousing march, ever after dubbed 'La Marseillaise' –

now the national anthem. Trade with North Africa escalated after France occupied Algeria in 1830 and the Suez Canal opened in 1869. After the world wars, a steady flow of migration from North Africa began and with it the rapid expansion of Marseille's periphery.

◉ Sights

Marseille is divided into 16 *arrondissements* (districts). Sights concentrate around the Vieux Port and Le Panier districts. Dynamic dockland redevelopment is transforming La Joliette to the north.

The city's main thoroughfare, La Canebière stretches east from Vieux Port towards the train station. Various morning markets fill earthy cours Julien, an elongated square with palm trees: fresh flowers on Wednesday and Saturday, antique books alternate Saturdays, and stamps or antique books on Sunday.

The tourist office has a brochure detailing a walking tour of Marseille's museums.

★ **Vieux Port**   HISTORIC QUARTER
(Map p152; Ⓜ Vieux Port) Ships have docked for more than 26 centuries at the city's birthplace, the colourful Old Port. The main commercial docks were transferred to the Joliette area north of here in the 1840s, but the old port remains a thriving harbour for fishing boats, pleasure yachts and tourists. Guarding the harbour are Fort St-Nicolas (Map p152; ⊘ 8am-7.45pm May-Aug, shorter hours rest of year; Ⓜ Vieux Port) FREE on the south side and, across the water, Fort St-Jean (p145), founded in the 13th century by the

---

MARSEILLE IN...

Two Days

Start at the **Vieux Port** with breakfast at **La Caravelle** (p162) and a waterside stroll to the cutting-edge **MuCEM** and **Villa Méditerranée**. Lunch at **La Passarelle** (p160), then hike up to the **Basilique Notre Dame de la Garde** (p151) or explore **Le Panier**, not missing the **Centre de la Vieille Charité** (p150). Dine at nearby, excellent **Le Café des Épices** (p160).

On day two, take in magnificent turquoise waters at **Les Calanques** (p165), or catch a boat to revel in Monte Cristo intrigues at **Château d'If** (p154). Reward your exploration with bouillabaisse in postcard-pretty **Vallon des Auffes** (p151).

Four Days

Make art and architecture the centre of the third day, taking in the **Musée des Beaux Arts** (p150) and other galleries. In the evening, visit artsy cours Julien for an aperitif, before dinner at **La Cantinetta** (p160). On the fourth day, take your own picnic and sail to the **Îles du Frioul** (p154) to lounge in a natural paradise of birdlife and pebble beach and in the evening soak up Marseille's ebullient nightlife, or spend the day exploring **Aix-en-Provence** (p168).

Knights Hospitaller of St John of Jerusalem, and home to MuCEM, the state-of-the-art museum.

The **cross-port ferry** (Map p152; ☉10am-1.15pm & 2-7pm; Ⓜ Vieux Port) in front of the town hall is a fun way to get out on the water, however briefly.

The port's southern quay is dotted with theatres and bars, and restaurants and cafes buzz until the wee hours a block east on **place Thiars** and **cours Honoré d'Estienne d'Orves**.

Nearby **Abbaye St-Victor** (Map p152; 3 rue de l'Abbaye; ☉9am-7pm; Ⓜ Vieux Port) `FREE` is the birthplace of Christianity in Marseille, built on a 3rd-century-BC Greek necropolis. **Musée du Santon** (Map p152; ☎04 91 13 61 36; www.santonsmarcelcarbonel.com; 49 rue Neuve Ste-Catherine; ☉10am-12.30pm & 2-6.30pm; Ⓜ Vieux Port) `FREE` with its boutique and neighbouring **Atelier du Santon** (Map p152; 47 rue Neuve Ste-Catherine; Ⓜ Vieux Port) are home to handcrafted tiny kiln-fired figures or *santons* (from *santoùn* in Provençal, meaning 'little saint'). The custom of creating a nativity scene with figurines dates from the Avignon papacy of John XII (1319–34).

Perched at the peninsula's edge, the **Jardin du Pharo** (Map p148; Ⓜ Vieux Port) `FREE` is a perfect picnic spot and ideal for watching sunsets.

★ **Le Panier**   HISTORIC QUARTER
(Map p152; Ⓜ Vieux Port) From the Vieux Port, hike north up to this fantastic history-woven quarter, which is fabulous for a wander with its artsy ambience, cool hidden squares and sun-baked cafes. In Greek Massilia it was the site of the *agora* (marketplace), hence its name, which means 'the basket'. During WWII the quarter was dynamited and afterwards rebuilt. Today it's a mishmash of lanes hiding artisan shops, *ateliers* (workshops) and terraced houses strung with drying washing.

Its centerpiece is Centre de la Vieille Charité (p150), and nearby Cathédrale de la Major (p150) stands guard between the old and new ports.

★ **Musée des Civilisations de l'Europe et de la Méditerranée**   MUSEUM
(MuCEM, Museum of European & Mediterranean Civilisations; Map p148; ☎04 84 35 13 13; www.mucem.org; 7 Promenade Robert Laffont; J4 adult/child €5/free, plus temporary exhibitions €8/free, 1st Sun of month free; ☉10am-8pm Wed-Mon Jul & Aug, 11am-7pm Wed-Mon Sep, Oct, May & Jun,

DON'T MISS

ART GALLERIES & MUSEUMS

Marseille's galleries and museums have flourished in recent years. In addition to the many makeovers of local institutions like La Friche La Belle de Mai (p151), the Musée des Beaux Arts (p150) and the Musée Cantini (p150), spectacular new facilities have been built for MuCEM and the **Fonds Régional d'Art Contemporain** (FRAC; ☎04 91 91 27 55; www.fracpaca.org; 20 bd de Dunkerque; adult/child €5/free; ☉noon-7pm Tue-Sat; Ⓜ Joliette). The outstanding arts organisation **Marseille Expos** (www.marseilleexpos.com) distributes an excellent map of hot galleries and sponsors the festival **Printemps de l'Art Contemporain** each May. Its website lists what's on.

11am-6pm Wed-Mon Nov-Apr; ⚐; Ⓜ Vieux Port, Joliette) The icon of modern Marseille, this stunning museum explores the history, culture and civilisation of the Mediterranean region through anthropological exhibits, rotating art exhibitions and film. The collection sits in a bold, contemporary building, J4, designed by Algerian-born, Marseille-educated architect Rudy Ricciotti. It is linked by a vertigo-inducing **footbridge** to the 13th-century **Fort St-Jean** (Map p152; Ⓜ Vieux Port) `FREE`, from which there are stupendous views of the Vieux Port and the Mediterranean. The fort grounds and their gardens are free to explore.

The history of the fort is explained in the **Salle du Corps de Garde** (guardhouse room). For a unique perspective, walk the path that twists its way between the glass wall of the J4 building and its outer lace shell. Free first Sunday of the month.

★ **Villa Méditerranée**   MUSEUM
(Map p152; www.villa-mediterranee.org; bd du Littoral, esplanade du J4; ☉noon-6pm Tue-Fri, 10am-6pm Sat & Sun; ⚐; Ⓜ Vieux Port, Joliette) `FREE` This eye-catching white structure next to MuCEM is no ordinary 'villa'. Designed by architect Stefano Boeri in 2013, the sleek white edifice sports a spectacular cantilever overhanging an ornamental pool. Inside, a viewing gallery with glass-panelled floor (look down if you dare!), and two or three temporary multimedia exhibitions evoke aspects of the Mediterranean, be they sea life, history or transport.

Vieux Port

AN ITINERARY

Start with an early morning coffee on the balcony at La Caravelle, with views of the boats bobbing in the harbor and Basilique Notre Dame de la Garde across the way. Mosey down the quay to the sparkling **MuCEM** ❶ and its cantilevered neighbour **Villa Méditerranée** ❷ for a morning of art and culture. You'll enter through Fort St-Jean, and wind through roof-top gardens to reach the state-of-the-art museums. Alternatively, take in green-and-white striped **Cathédrale de la Major** ❸ then explore the apricot-coloured alleys of **Le Panier** ❹, browsing the exhibits at the **Centre de la Vieille Charité** ❺, and shopping in the neighbourhood's tiny boutiques.

In the afternoon, hop on the free cross-port ferry to the harbour's south side and take a **boat trip** ❻ to Château d'If, made famous by the Dumas novel *The Count of Monte Cristo*. Or stroll under Norman Foster's mirrored pavilion, then wander into the **Abbaye St-Victor** ❼, to see the bones of martyrs enshrined in gold. As evening nears, you can catch the sunset from the stone benches in the **Jardin du Pharo** ❽. Then as the warm southern night sets in, join the throngs on cours Honoré d'Estienne d'Orves, where you can drink pastis and people-watch beneath a giant statue of a lion devouring a man – the **Milo de Croton** ❾.

Cathédrale de la Major
The striped facade of Marseille's cathedral is made from local Cassis stone and green Florentine marble. Its grand north staircase leads from Le Panier to La Joliette quarter

Villa Méditerranée ❷

MuCEM ❶

Palais & Jardin du Pharo

Musée des Civilisations de l'Europe et de la Méditerranée (MuCEM)
Explore the icon of modern Marseille, this stunning museum designed by Rudy Ricciotti and linked by vertigo-inducing footbridge to 13th-century Fort St-Jean. You'll get stupendous views of the Vieux Port and the Mediterranean.

IMAGE SUPPLIED BY MUCEM/LISA RICCIOTTI ©

Centre de la Vieille Charité

Before the 18th century, beggar hunters rounded up the poor for imprisonment. The Vieille Charité almshouse, which opened in 1749, improved their lot by acting as a workhouse. It's now an exhibition space and only the barred windows recall its original use.

Le Panier

The site of the Greek town of Massilia, Le Panier woos walkers with its sloping streets. Grand Rue follows the ancient road and opens out into place de Lenche, the location of the Greek market. It is still the place to shop for artisanal products.

GARDEL BERTRAND/GETTY IMAGES ©

Frioul If Express

Catch the Frioul If Express to Château d'If, France's equivalent to Alcatraz. Prisoners were housed according to class: the poorest at the bottom in windowless dungeons, the wealthiest in paid-for private cells, with windows and a fireplace.

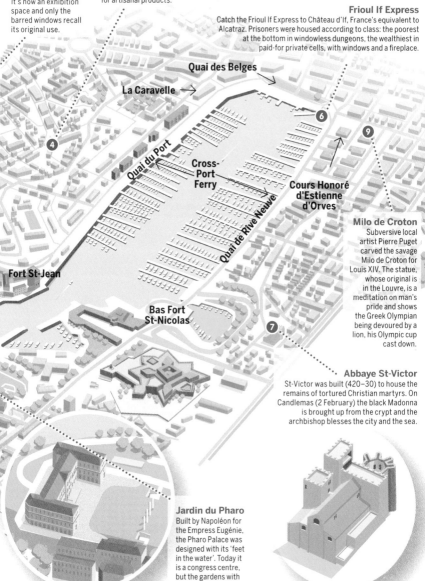

Quai des Belges

La Caravelle →

4

Quai du Port

Cross-Port Ferry

Quai de Rive Neuve

6

9

Cours Honoré d'Estienne d'Orves

Milo de Croton

Subversive local artist Pierre Puget carved the savage Milo de Croton for Louis XIV. The statue, whose original is in the Louvre, is a meditation on man's pride and shows the Greek Olympian being devoured by a lion, his Olympic cup cast down.

Fort St-Jean

Bas Fort St-Nicolas

7

Abbaye St-Victor

St-Victor was built (420–30) to house the remains of tortured Christian martyrs. On Candlemas (2 February) the black Madonna is brought up from the crypt and the archbishop blesses the city and the sea.

Jardin du Pharo

Built by Napoléon for the Empress Eugénie, the Pharo Palace was designed with its 'feet in the water'. Today it is a congress centre, but the gardens with their magnificent view are open all day.

Marseille

Fonds Régiona d'Art
Contemporain (150m)

25

Joliette

4

Pl de la
Joliette

18

Bd de
Dunkerque

Joliette

Bassin de
la Grande
Joliette

Gare Maritime
(Ferry Terminal 1-Arenc)

**Gare
Maritime**

Gare Maritime
(Ferry Terminal 2)

SNCM

Passenger-Ferry
Terminal

Q de la Joliette

R de Mazenod

Av Robert Schuman

R de l'Evêché

Nouvelle
Cathédrale
de la Major

**LE
PANIER**

Pl des
Moulins

Pl de
Lenche

Mediterranean
Sea

Bd du Littoral

R St-Laurent

Corsica

Calanques

Avant-Port
de la
Joliette

**Musée des Civilisations
de l'Europe et de
la Méditerranée** 2

Fort
St-
Jean

Tunnel St-Laurent

Îles du Frioul;
Château d'If

Palais
du Pharo

3 15

Jardin
du Pharo

Bas
Fort St-
Nicolas

Bd Charles Livon

R des Catalans

Av Pasteur

R Sainte

See Central Marseille Map (p152)

5 20

8

Av de la Corse

Pl du 4
Septembre

Av de la Corse

John F Kennedy

R Cap Dessemond

R Charras

R Sauveur

Bd Tellène

Corniche Président

19

17 6

Vallon
des
Auffes

13

R Guidicelli

R du Vallon

R des Auffes

R d'Endoume

Bd Marius Thomas

Le Rhul (450m);
Villa Monticelli (2.2km);
Prado beaches & Parc Borély
(5.25km); Les Calanques (12km)

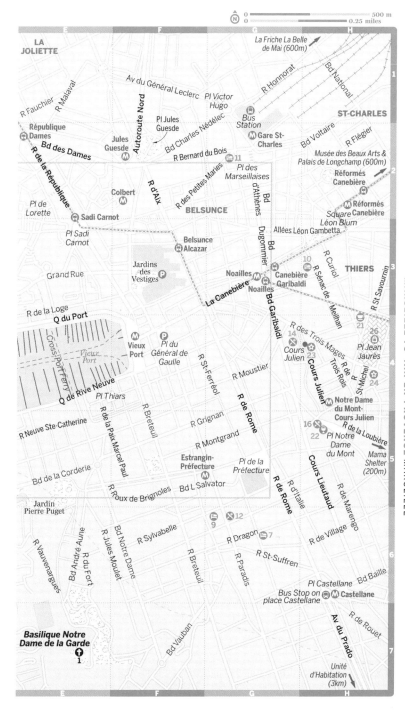

Marseille

★**Centre de la Vieille Charité** MUSEUM
(Map p152; http://vieille-charite-marseille.com; 2 rue de la Charité; ⊙10am-6pm Tue-Sun; Ⓜ Joliette) FREE In the heart of the Le Panier quarter is the Centre de la Vieille Charité, built as a charity shelter for the town's poor by local architect and sculptor Pierre Puget (1620–94). The beautiful complex, with stunning arched sienna-stone courtyard, houses rotating exhibitions and two small museums: the Musée d'Archéologie Méditerranéenne (Museum of Mediterranean Archeology; Map p152; ☑04 91 14 58 59; http://musee-archeologie-mediterraneenne. marseille.fr; adult/child €5/free; ⊙10am-6pm Tue-Sun; Ⓜ Joliette) and the Musée d'Arts Africains, Océaniens et Améridiens (Museum of African, Oceanic & American Indian Art; Map p152; ☑04 91 14 58 38; http://maaoa.marseille.fr; ⊙10am-6pm Tue-Sun; Ⓜ Joliette), as well as a relaxing cafe.

★**Cathédrale de Marseille**
Notre Dame de Major CATHEDRAL
(Map p152; ⊙10am-6.30pm Tue-Sun; Ⓜ Joliette) FREE Standing guard between the old and new ports is the striking 19th-century Cathédrale de la Major. Its Byzantine-style striped facade is made of local Cassis stone and green Florentine marble. It has a newly renovated grand staircase on the north side, which makes an impressive gateway to La Joliette.

La Joliette HISTORIC QUARTER
(Ⓜ Joliette, 🚊 Joliette) North of Le Panier along the waterfront, the old maritime neighbour-

hood of La Jolliette has been reborn. Ferries still depart for ports around the Med, but the long sweep of 19th-century commercial facades along Quai de la Joliette have been given an impressive scrub.

Les Docks (Map p148; 10 place de la Joliette; Ⓜ Joliette, 🚊 Joliette) is a historic complex that has been redeveloped and includes shops and galleries akin to London's Docklands.

Nearby, Les Terraces du Port (Map p148; 9 quai de Lazaret; ⊙10am-8pm; Ⓜ Joliette, 🚊 Joliette) is a vast new shopping mall filled with upscale international chains. It has a huge public terrace on level 2 with fab views of the port and coast.

★**Musée Cantini** ART MUSEUM
(Map p152; ☑04 91 54 77 75; http://musee-cantini. marseille.fr; 19 rue Grignan; adult/child €5/free; ⊙10am-6pm Tue-Sun; Ⓜ Estrangin-Préfecture) Behind grand gates inside a 17th-century *hôtel particulier* (mansion), the recently renovated Musée Cantini has superbly curated art exhibitions, and excellent permanent collections of 17th- and 18th-century Provençal art, including André Derain's *Pinède, Cassis* (1907) and Raoul Dufy's *Paysage de l'Estaque* (1908). Expect the best of contemporary and modern art, brilliantly hung.

★**Musée des Beaux Arts** ART MUSEUM, PALACE
(☑04 91 14 59 30; http://musee-des-beaux-arts. marseille.fr; 7 rue Édouard Stephan; adult/child €5/free; ⊙10am-6pm Tue-Sun; 🚼; Ⓜ Cinq Avenues-Longchamp, 🚊 Longchamp) Spectac-

ularly set in the colonnaded Palais de Longchamp, Marseille's oldest museum is a treasure trove of Italian and Provençal painting and sculpture from the 17th to 21st centuries. The palace's shaded park is one of the centre's few green spaces, and is popular with local families. The spectacular fountains were constructed in the 1860s, in part to disguise a water tower at the terminus of an aqueduct from the River Durance.

Musée d'Histoire de Marseille   MUSEUM
(Map p152; ☑ 04 91 55 36 00; http://musee-histoire.marseille.fr; 2 rue Henri-Barbusse; adult/child €5/free; ☉ 10am-6pm Tue-Sun; Ⓜ Vieux Port) In a completely renovated, 15,000-sq-metre modern space within the Centre Bourse shopping mall, this museum offers fascinating insight into Marseille's long history. Highlights include the remains of a 3rd-century-AD merchant vessel, discovered in the Vieux Port in 1974. To preserve the soaked and decaying wood, it was freeze-dried where it now sits behind glass.

★**Basilique Notre Dame de la Garde**   CHURCH
(Montée de la Bonne Mère; Map p148; www.notredamedelagarde.com; rue Fort du Sanctuaire; ☉ 7am-8pm Apr-Sep, to 7pm Oct-Mar; ☐ 60) **FREE** This opulent 19th-century Romano-Byzantine basilica occupies Marseille's highest point, La Garde (162m). Built between 1853 and 1864, it is ornamented with coloured marble, murals depicting the safe passage of sailing vessels and superb mosaics. The hilltop gives 360-degree panoramas of the city. The church's bell tower is crowned by a 9.7m-tall gilded statue of the Virgin Mary on a 12m-high pedestal. It's a 1km walk from the Vieux Port, or take bus 60 or the tourist train.

La Friche La Belle de Mai   CULTURAL CENTRE
(☑ 04 95 04 95 04; www.lafriche.org; 41 rue Jobin; ☐ 49, stop Jobin) This former sugar-refining plant and subsequent tobacco factory is now a vibrant arts centre with a theatre, artists' workshops, cinema studios, multimedia displays, skateboard ramps, electro/world-music parties et al – check its program online.

L'Unité d'Habitation   ARCHITECTURE
(La Cité Radieuse; ☑ 04 91 16 78 00; www.marseille-citeradieuse.org; 280 bd Michelet; ☉ 9am-6pm; ☐ 83, 21, stop Le Corbusier) **FREE** Visionary international-style architect Le Corbusier redefined urban living in 1952 with the completion of his vertical 337-apartment 'garden city', also known as La Cité Radieuse (The Radiant City). Today mostly private apartments, it also houses a hotel, Hôtel Le Corbusier, the high-end restaurant Le Ventre de l'Architecte and a rooftop terrace. Architecture buffs can book guided tours (adult/child €10/5) that include a model apartment; contact the tourist office.

Along the Coast

Mesmerising views of another Marseille unfold along corniche Président John F Kennedy, the coastal road that cruises south to small, beach-volleyball-busy Plage des Catalans (Map p148; 3 rue des Catalans; ☉ 8.30am-6.30pm; ☐ 83) and fishing cove Vallon des Auffes (Map p148; ☐ 83), crammed with boats.

Further south, the vast Prado beaches, are marked by Jules Cantini's 1903 marble replica of Michelangelo's *David*. The beaches, all gold sand, were created from backfill from the excavations for Marseille's metro. They have a world-renowned skate park. Nearby lies expansive Parc Borély.

Promenade Georges Pompidou continues south to Cap Croisette, from where the beautiful *calanques* (rocky inlets) can be reached on foot.

To head down the coast, take bus 83 from the Vieux Port. At av du Prado switch to bus 19 to continue further. La Navette Maritime Vieux Port–Pointe Rouge (☑ 04 91 91 92 10; www.rtm.fr; €5, good for 90min on all public transport; ☉ hourly late Apr-Sep) runs boats between Vieux Port and La Pointe-Rouge, just to the south of the Prado beaches; the City Pass does not cover the ticket.

Parc Borély   PARK, GALLERY
(av du Parc Borély; ☐ 19, 83, stop Parc Borély) Parc Borély encompasses a lake, botanical garden and the just-renovated 18th-century Château Borély, hosting art exhibitions.

ⓘ **CITY PASS**

Marseille City Pass (24-/48-/72-hour €24/31/39) The Marseille City Pass covers admission to city museums, public transport, a guided city tour, a Château d'If boat trip and more, plus other discounts. It's not necessary for children under 12, as for them many attractions are greatly reduced or free. Buy it online at www.resamarseille.com or at the tourist office.

Central Marseille

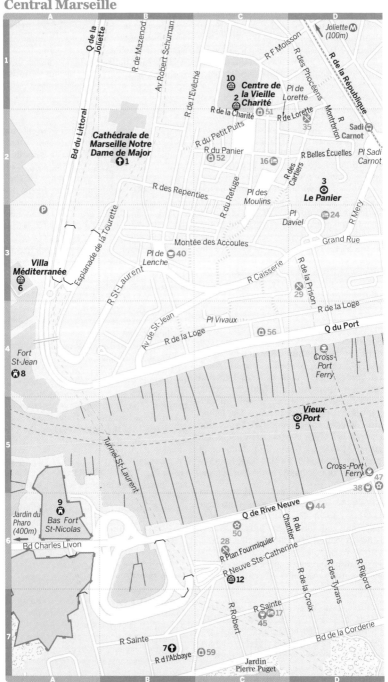

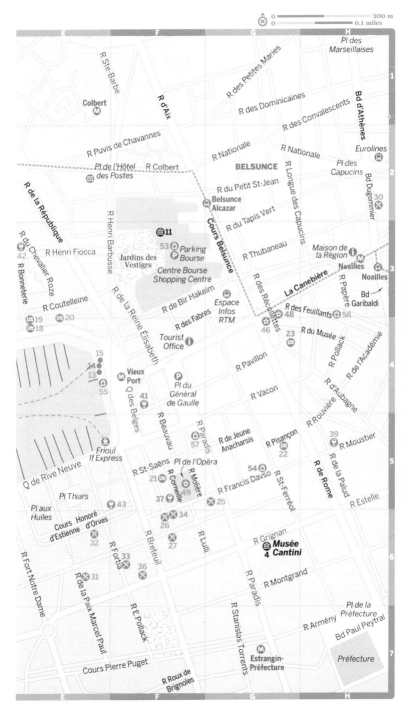

Central Marseille

Musée d'Art Contemporain   ART MUSEUM
(Museum of Contemporary Art, MAC; ☑ 04 91 25 01 07; http://mac.marseille.fr; 69 av de Haïfa; adult/child €5/free; ☉10am-6pm Tue-Sun; ☐23, 45, stop Haïfa-Marie-Louise) Creations of Marseille-born sculptor César Baldaccini (1921–98) jostle for space with works by Christo, Nice new realists Ben and Klein, and Andy Warhol. From the Prado metro stop, take bus 23 or 45 to the Haïfa-Marie-Louise stop.

★ **Château d'If**   ISLAND, CASTLE
(www.if.monuments-nationaux.fr; adult/child €5.50/free; ☉9.30am-6.10pm mid-May–mid-Sep, shorter hours rest of year) Immortalised in Alexandre Dumas' classic 1844 novel *Le Comte de Monte Cristo* (The Count of Monte Cristo), the

16th-century fortress-turned-prison Château d'If sits on the tiny Île d'If, 3.5km west of the Vieux Port. Political prisoners were incarcerated here, along with hundreds of Protestants, the Revolutionary hero Mirabeau and the Communards of 1871.

Frioul If Express (Map p152; www.frioul-if-express.com; 1 quai des Belges) boats leave for Château d'If (€10.50 return, 20 minutes, around nine daily) from the Vieux Port.

Îles du Frioul   ISLANDS
A few hundred metres west of Île d'If are the Îles du Frioul, the barren, dyke-linked, white-limestone islands of Ratonneau and Pomègues. Seabirds and rare plants thrive on these tiny islands, which are each about

2.5km long, totalling 200 hectares. Ratonneau has three beaches. Frioul If Express boats to Château d'If also serve the Îles du Frioul (one/two islands €10.50/15.60 return, 35 minutes, around 20 daily).

☞ Tours

L'Open Tour   BUS TOUR
(☏04 91 91 05 82; www.marseille.opentour.com; adult/child €19/8) Travel between key sights and museums aboard a hop-on, hop-off open-top bus. Tickets at the tourist office or on board.

Guided Tour   WALKING TOUR
(www.resamarseille.com; tours €9; ☺May-Aug; Ⓜ Vieux Port) From the tourist office.

Marseille Provence Greeters   WALKING TOUR
(www.marseilleprovencegreeters.com) Free walking tours led by locals; website registration required a week in advance.

Tourist Train   TOURIST TRAIN
(Map p152; ☏04 91 25 24 69; www.petit-train-marseille.com; 174 quai du Port; ☺10am-12.30pm & 2-6pm; Ⓜ Vieux Port) Electric trams with two circular routes: to Notre Dame basilica (year-round; adult/child €8/4) and Le Panier (April to mid-November; adult/child €7/3). Tours last 65 minutes and depart every 30 minutes, less frequently in winter.

Croisières Marseille Calanques   BOAT TOUR
(Map p152; ☏04 91 33 36 79; www.croisieres-mar-seille-calanques.com; Vieux Port; Ⓜ Vieux Port) Runs two-hour return trips from the Vieux Port taking in six *calanques* (family/adult/child €74/23/18); three-hour return trips past 12 *calanques* to Cassis (family/adult/child €92/29/22); and 1½-hour trips around the Baie de Marseille (€10), including Château d'If (add €5.50).

Icard Maritime   BOAT TOUR
(Map p152; www.visite-des-calanques.com; quai des Belges; Ⓜ Vieux Port) Runs trips to the *calanques* and the coastal islands, including one option that stops for a swim (four hours, €32).

♛♝ Festivals & Events

Carnaval de Marseille   CARNIVAL
(☺Mar or Apr) Marseille's version of Carnival, with mad costumes and decorated floats.

Festival de Marseille   PERFORMING ARTS
(www.festivaldemarseille.com; ☺Jun-Jul) Three weeks of international dance, theatre, music and art.

Five Continents Jazz Festival   MUSIC FESTIVAL
(www.festival-jazz-cinq-continents.com; ☺Jul) Acid jazz, funk and folk music.

Foire aux Santonniers   CHRISTMAS
(☺Dec) Since 1803 traditional *santon* makers have flocked to Marseille for this fair.

🛏 Sleeping

There are modest hotels close to the train station, but the good local-transit system means that it's easy to reach the hotels scattered around the Vieux Port. There's also a hotel in Le Corbusier's L'Unité d'Habitation (p151).

★Hôtel Hermès   DESIGN HOTEL €
(Map p152; ☏04 96 11 63 63; www.hotelmarseille.com; 2 rue Bonneterie; s €64, d €85-102; ❉ ☎; Ⓜ Vieux Port) Nothing to do with the Paris design house, this excellent-value hotel has a rooftop terrace with panoramic Vieux Port views. Grab breakfast (€9) on a tray in the bright breakfast room and ride the lift to the 5th floor to eat à la rooftop. Contemporary rooms have white walls and a splash of lime green or red to complement their Scandinavian-like design.

Vertigo Saint-Charles   HOSTEL €
(Map p148; ☏04 91 91 07 11; www.hotelvertigo.fr; 42 rue des Petites Maries; dm from €25; @ ☎; Ⓜ Gare St-Charles) This snappy boutique hostel kisses dodgy bunks and hospital-like decor goodbye. Here it's 'hello' to vintage posters, designer chrome kitchen, groovy communal spaces and polite multilingual staff. Double rooms are particularly good; some have a private terrace. No curfew (or lift, alas). A second, all-dorm facility is closer to the Vieux Port.

Hôtel Relax   HOTEL €
(Map p152; ☏04 91 33 15 87; www.hotelrelax.fr; 4 rue Corneille; r €60-70; ❉ ☎; Ⓜ Vieux Port) Overlooking Marseille's Opera House, this simple, family-run, 20-room hotel lacks good noise insulation and space, but given the location, cleanliness and extras like fridges and hairdryers, it's a bargain. No lift.

Hôtel Sylvabelle   HOSTEL €
(Map p148; ☏04 91 37 75 83; www.hotel-sylvabelle-marseille.com; 63 rue Sylvabelle; dm €23, r from €60; ☎; Ⓜ Estrangin-Préfecture) The Hôtel Sylvabelle is clean and fresh, and has managed to retain very attractive prices. Six of the 20 rooms share toilets on the landing, the rest are en suite. The furnishings are

MARSEILLE TO AIX-EN-PROVENCE MARSEILLE

simple; service can be perfunctory. The dorms can get noisy. There's no lift.

★ Hôtel Edmond Rostand DESIGN HOTEL €€

(Map p148; ☑ 04 91 37 74 95; www.hoteledmondrostand.com; 31 rue Dragon; d €90-115, tr €127-141; ❄@🌐; Ⓜ Estrangin-Préfecture) Ignore the grubby outside shutters of this excellent-value Logis de France hotel in the Quartier des Antiquaires. Inside, decor is a hip mix of contemporary design and vintage, with a great sofa area for lounging and 16 rooms dressed in crisp white and soothing natural hues. Some rooms overlook a tiny private garden, others the Basilique Notre Dame de la Garde.

★ Hôtel St-Louis HOTEL €€

(Map p152; ☑ 04 91 54 02 74; www.hotel-st-louis.com; 2 rue des Récollettes; r €90-140; ❄🌐; Ⓜ Noailles, 🚃 Canebière Garibaldi) The vintage-1800s facade draws the eye. Inside, thoughtfully remodelled rooms (some with little balconies), good mattresses, wooden furniture, a central location and an elevator (starting on the 1st floor) ensure comfort. Service is extremely helpful and services such as laundry are a bargain.

★ Au Vieux Panier B&B €€

(Map p152; ☑ 04 91 91 23 72; www.auvieuxpanier.com; 13 rue du Panier; d €100-140; Ⓜ Vieux Port) The height of Le Panier shabby chic, this super-stylish *maison d'hôte* woos art lovers with original works of art. Each year artists are invited to redecorate, meaning its six rooms change annually. Staircases and corridors are like an art gallery, and a drop-dead gorgeous rooftop terrace peeks across terracotta tiles to the sea on the horizon.

Decoh SELF-CONTAINED €€

(Map p148; ☑ 04 91 37 74 95; www.decoh.fr; 31-33 rue Dragon; apt & studios €125-180; ❄@🌐) The creative, vintage-loving team at the Edmond Rostand hotel are behind this appealing, hotel-serviced self-catering accommodation on rue Paradis, rue Dragon and rue Albert. Studios sleep two people and apartments four; the super-stylish antique furniture recalls eras from the 1950s to the 1970s. Stay a night, a week or a month. Cook for yourself, or breakfast at the Hôtel Edmond Rostand.

Le Ryad BOUTIQUE HOTEL €€

(Map p148; ☑ 04 91 47 74 54; www.hoteldemarseille.fr; 16 rue Sénac de Meilhan; s €80-125, d €95-140; 🌐🛗; Ⓜ Noailles, 🚃 Canebière Garibaldi) With high ceilings, arched alcoves, warm colours and minimalist decor, super-stylish Le Ryad draws sumptuous influence from Morocco. Beautiful bathrooms, garden-view rooms and great service compensate for the sometimes sketchy neighbourhood. Despite the four-storey walk up, it's worth booking the top-floor room for its tiny rooftop terrace. Breakfast €12.

Hôtel La Résidence du Vieux Port DESIGN HOTEL €€

(Map p152; ☑ 04 91 91 91 22; www.hotel-residence-marseille.com; 18 quai du Port; d €125-200, ste €185-204; ❄@🌐; Ⓜ Vieux Port) Marseille's top-view hotel is *The Jetsons* meets Mondrian, with swoop-backed furniture and bold primary colours. Every room looks sharp, and more expensive portside rooms have balconies with knockout views of the old port and Notre Dame. The ultimate is the 8th-floor Suite Ciel (Sky Suite).

Mama Shelter DESIGN HOTEL €€

(☑ 01 43 48 48 48; www.mamashelter.com; 64 rue de la Loubière; d €69-149; ❄🌐🛗; Ⓜ Notre Dame du Mont-Cours Julien) Sleeping in Marseille doesn't get much funkier than this. With design by Philippe Starck, nifty extras like Kiehl's bathroom products, and free in-room movies, this is the affordable-chic kid on the block.

★ Hôtel Le Richelieu HOTEL €€

(Map p148; ☑ 04 91 31 01 92; www.lerichelieu-marseille.com; 52 corniche Président John F Kennedy; d €90-120; ❄@🌐; 🚌 83) An eternal favourite for its beach-house vibe and fabulous sea views, this coastal choice near Plage des Catalans is excellent value. Rooms are oddly shaped, but the owners keep them looking fresh, and the best even face the Med. Breakfast (€14) on the terrace is a morning treat of which you'll never tire.

Hotel Bellevue HOTEL €€

(Map p152; ☑ 04 96 17 05 40; www.hotelbellevue-marseille.com; 34 quai du Port; d €90-170; ❄@🌐; Ⓜ Vieux Port) Rooms at this old-fashioned ho-

---

ⓘ ONLINE RESOURCES

Marseille Tourisme (www.marseille-tourisme.com)

Marseille City Website (www.marseille.fr)

Visit Provence (www.visitprovence.com) Bouches du Rhône département; great itineraries.

tel are tastefully decorated with midbudget simplicity, but their portside views are million-dollar. Breakfast (€10) on the pocket-sized balcony of its cafe-bar La Caravelle (p162) – Marseille's coolest portside spot – is a Marseille highlight.

Hôtel Saint-Ferréol
HOTEL €€

(Map p152; ☑ 04 91 33 12 21; www.hotelsaintferreol.com; 19 rue Pisançon; d €99-140; ❖ @ ⸫; M Vieux Port) Service is exceptional at this traditional three-star hotel, tucked down an alley off one of Marseille's main shopping streets. Rooms are individually decorated, many inspired by artists like Van Gogh and Cézanne, with spotless bathrooms, powerful air-con and quality double glazing that ensures perfect peace. Breakfast €10.50.

Villa Monticelli
B&B €€

(☑ 04 91 22 15 20; www.villamonticelli.com; 96 rue du Commandant Rolland; r €110-120; ❖ ⸫; ⸫ 83, 19, stop Prado St-Giniez, M Rond-Point du Prado) Colette and Jean are passionate about their city, and the five exquisite *chambre d'hôte* rooms in their stunning villa are worth the slightly outer-city location. Breakfast is a delight of homemade local specialities served on the panoramic-view terrace.

★Intercontinental Marseille – Hôtel Dieu
HOTEL €€€

(Map p152; ☑ 04 13 42 42 42; www.marseille.intercontinental.com; 1 place Daviel; r €230-600; ❖ @ ⸫ ⸫; M Colbert, ⸫ Sadi Carnot) Landmark is an understatement. Based on an 18th-century hospital, the Hôtel-Dieu, the Intercontinental has a commanding position in Le Panier, overlooking the Vieux Port. This grand U-shaped stone building features tall arched windows framed by local golden-hued stone and masonry. The 172 rooms and 22 suites are posh; 72 rooms have views of the port, while 33 have private terraces.

The history of the hotel goes back as far as the 12th century, when a much earlier hospital was built on the site. Its eventual replacement, the Hôtel-Dieu, took over 100 years to build and was opened by Napoléon III in 1866. It finally closed in 1993.

Casa Honoré
B&B €€€

(Map p152; ☑ 04 96 11 01 62; www.casahonore.com; 123 rue Sainte; d €150-200; ❖ ⸫ ⸫; M Vieux Port) Los Angeles meets Marseille at this four-room *maison d'hôte*, built around a central courtyard with a lap pool shaded by banana trees. The fashion-forward style reflects the owner's love for contemporary interior design, using disparate elements like black wicker and the occasional cow skull, which come together in one sexy package.

✗ Eating

Vieux Port and the surrounding pedestrian streets teem with cafe terraces, but choose carefully. For world cuisine, try cours Julien and nearby rue des Trois Mages. For pizza, roast chickens, and Middle Eastern food under €10, nose around the streets surrounding Marché des Capucins (p164).

★Pizzaria Chez Étienne
REGIONAL CUISINE €

(Map p152; 43 rue de Lorette; pizza €13-15, mains €15-20; ☉ noon-2.15pm & 8-11pm Mon-Sat; M Colbert) This old Marseillais haunt has the best pizza in town, as well as succulent *pavé de boeuf* (beef steak) and scrumptious *supions frits* (pan-fried squid with garlic and parsley). Since it's a convivial meeting point for the entire neighbourhood, pop in beforehand to reserve a table (there's no phone). No credit cards.

La Part des Anges
BISTRO €

(Map p152; ☑ 04 91 33 55 70; http://lapartdesanges.com; 33 rue Sainte; mains €18-22; ☉ 9am-2am Mon-Sat, 9am-1pm & 6pm-2am Sun; M Vieux Port) No address buzzes with Marseille's hip, buoyant crowd more than this fabulous all-rounder wine bar, named after the alcohol that evaporates through a barrel during wine or whisky fermentation: the angels' share. Take your pick of dozens of wines by the glass and be sure to tell the bartender if you want to eat (tables can't be reserved in advance).

Le Comptoir Dugommier
CAFE €

(Map p152; ☑ 04 91 62 21 21; www.comptoirdugommier.fr; 14 bd Dugommier; ☉ 7am-5pm Mon-Sat, occasional evenings; ⸫; M Noailles, ⸫ Canebière Garibaldi) A handy pit stop by the train station, this old-timer cafe with tin moulding, wooden floors and vintage signs makes an atmospheric escape from the busy street outside. The clientele is completely mixed, and there's free wi-fi and classic French fare.

La Casertane
ITALIAN, DELI €

(Map p152; ☑ 04 91 54 98 51; 71 rue Francis Davso; mains €10-15; ☉ 9am-7.30pm Tue-Sat; M Vieux Port) Lunch on a mind-boggling array of Italian deli meats and salads, or choose from daily specials, often involving homemade pastas, at this delightful deli a couple of blocks from the Vieux Port. Convivial staff and the bustling flow of customers make for lively meals.

MARSEILLE TO AIX-EN-PROVENCE MARSEILLE

Lavender Trail

Pilgrims come from all over to follow the Routes de la Lavande (www.routes-lavande.com), tracking Provence's aromatic purple bloom. In flower from June to August, it usually hits peak splendour in late July. Cruise the fields, visit mountainside distilleries or scoop up all things lavender at abundant local markets.

Sault

1 The slopes of Mont Ventoux (p215), north of Lagarde d'Apt, make for prime high-altitude lavender. Aim to visit during the Fête de la Lavande (www.saultenprovence .com), usually on 15 August.

Plateau de Valensole

2 For sheer heady expansiveness, you can't beat the Plateau de Valensole's carpets of lavender, stretching, dreamlike, as far as the eye can see. Cruise across it on the D6 or D8 east of Manosque, and the A51.

Abbaye Notre-Dame de Sénanque

3 Follow the winding D177 north of Gordes to this idyllic 12th-century Cistercian abbey (p231), tucked between hills and surrounded by brilliant fields of lavender. Resident monks tend the crops and stock their shop with monk-made goodies.

Forcalquier

4 Folks come from throughout the region for the booming Monday-morning market in Forcalquier (p248). An embarrassment of riches, the market has vendors selling lavender everything, plus mountain honey, creamy cheeses and handmade sausages.

Château du Bois

5 Provence is dotted with distilleries, but if you make it to tiny Lagarde d'Apt (p000) you're in for a treat: 80 hectares of Lavande des Alpes de Haute Provence, 'true lavender' (*Lavandula angustifolia*).

1. Rows of lavender, Sault (p215); 2. Beehives in lavender fields, Plateau de Valensole; 3. Lavender for sale

1€
le
Bouquet
de
Lavandin

Sylvain Depuichaffray CAFE, BOULANGERIE €
(Map p152; 04 91 33 09 75; www.sylvaindepu-ichaffray.fr; 66 rue Grignan; quiche €3, salads €6; 7.30am-4pm Mon, to 7pm Tue-Sat; Vieux Port) Perfect for a light lunch of quiche or salad followed by a sweet treat.

★**Le Café des Épices** MODERN FRENCH €€
(Map p152; 04 91 91 22 69; www.cafedesepices.com; 4 rue du Lacydon; lunch/dinner menus from €25/45; noon-3pm & 6-11pm Tue-Fri, noon-3pm Sat; ; Vieux Port) One of Marseille's best chefs, Arnaud de Grammont, infuses his cooking with a panoply of flavours: squid-ink spaghetti with sesame and perfectly cooked scallops, or coriander- and citrus-spiced potatoes topped by the catch of the day. Presentation is impeccable, the decor playful, and the colourful outdoor terrace between giant potted olive trees nothing short of superb.

★**La Cantinetta** ITALIAN €€
(Map p148; 04 91 48 10 48; 24 cours Julien; mains €16-20; noon-2pm & 7.30-10.30pm Mon-Sat; Notre Dame du Mont-Cours Julien) The top table at cours Julien serves perfectly al dente housemade pasta, paper-thin prosciutto, marinated vegetables, *bresaola* (air-dried

beef) and risotto. Tables in the convivial dining room are cheek by jowl, and everyone seems to know each other. Or escape to the sun-dappled, tiled patio garden. If you're lucky, gregarious chef-owner Pierre-Antoine Denis will regale you with the day's specials. Reservations essential.

★**Café Populaire** BISTRO €€
(Map p148; 04 91 02 53 96; http://cafepopulaire.com; 110 rue Paradis; tapas €6-16, mains €17-22; noon-2.30pm & 8-11pm Tue-Sat; Estrangin-Préfecture) Vintage furniture, old books on the shelves and a fine collection of glass soda bottles lend a retro air to this trendy, 1950s-styled *jazz comptoir* (counter) – a restaurant despite its name. The crowd is chic, and smiling chefs in the open kitchen mesmerise with daily specials like king prawns *à la plancha* (grilled) or beetroot and coriander salad.

La Passarelle PROVENÇAL €€
(Map p152; 04 91 33 03 27; www.restaurantlapassarelle.fr; 52 rue Plan Fourmiguier; mains €18-22; noon-2.30pm & 8-10.30pm May-Oct, reduced hours rest of year; Vieux Port) Retro tables and chairs sit on a decking terrace beneath a shady sail, plump in the middle of the leafy-

DON'T MISS

BOUILLABAISSE

Originally cooked by fishermen from the scraps of their catch, bouillabaisse is Marseille's signature dish. True bouillabaisse includes at least four kinds of fish, and sometimes shellfish. Don't trust tourist traps that promise cheap bouillabaisse; the real deal costs at least €50 per person. It's served in two parts: the broth (*soupe de poisson*), rich with tomato, saffron and fennel; and the cooked fish, deboned tableside and presented on a platter. On the side are croutons, *rouille* (a bread-thickened garlic-chilli mayonnaise) and grated cheese, usually gruyère. Spread *rouille* on the crouton, top with cheese, and float it in the soup. Be prepared for a huge meal and tons of garlic.

Le Rhul (04 91 52 01 77; www.lerhul.fr; 269 corniche Président John F Kennedy; bouillabaisse €53; noon-2pm & 5-9pm; 83) This long-standing classic has atmosphere (however kitschy): it's a 1940s seaside hotel with Mediterranean views. This is one of the most reliably consistent spots for authentic bouillabaisse, but go the classic one better and get the *bourride* (minimum two people), a hard-to-find variation brimming with garlic in white sauce.

L'Epuisette (Map p148; 04 91 52 17 82; www.l-epuisette.com; Vallon des Auffes; bouillabaisse €90; noon-1.30pm & 7.30-9.30pm Tue-Sat; 83) This swanky restaurant has a Michelin star and knockout water-level views from an elegantly austere dining room. Sup on some of Marseille's top bouillabaisse, which comes as part of a four-course menu.

Restaurant Michel (Chez Michel; Map p148; 04 91 52 30 63; www.restaurant-michel-13.fr; 6 rue des Catalans; bouillabaisse €65; 6-9.30pm; 83) This deceptively shabby-looking restaurant opposite Plage des Catalans has been the culinary pride and joy of the Michel family since 1946. Contrary to appearances, it serves some of Marseille's most authentic bouillabaisse and *bourride* (both €65 per person).

green *potager* (vegetable garden) where much of the kitchen's produce is grown. Philippe and Patricia's menu is predominantly organic, with other products strictly local, and cuisine is charmingly simple – the catch of day with vegetables, beef with polenta...

Le Grain de Sel   MODERN FRENCH €€

(Map p152; ☑ 04 91 54 47 30; 39 rue de la Paix Marcel Paul; 2-/3-course menus €22/26, mains €18-25; ☺ noon-2pm, noon-1.30pm Tue-Thu, noon-1.30pm & 8-9.30pm Fri & Sat; Ⓜ Vieux Port) The Salt Grain is always packed, generally with gourmet locals who love their food. The menu at the slender bistro is short but reads like a poem with its descriptions of inventive dishes such as cherry gazpacho with yellow tomatoes, pistacho and *brousse* (a type of cheese) as starter, or apricot clafoutis with almond-milk ice cream and rosemary mousse for dessert.

Le Goût des Choses   BISTRO €€

(Map p148; ☑ 04 91 48 70 62; http://legoutdeschoses.fr; 4 place Notre Dame du Mont; lunch/dinner menus from €16/27; ☺ noon-1.45pm & 7.30-10pm Wed-Sun) Think standard French fare with a slight Middle Eastern twist at this convivial bistro just off cours Julien. Book ahead, as locals pack the place for the good-value, delicious cuisine.

Malthazar   PROVENÇAL €€

(Map p152; ☑ 04 91 33 42 46; 19 rue Fortia; 2-/3-course lunch menus €19/22, dinner menu €32; ☺ noon-2pm & 8-11pm daily; Ⓜ Vieux Port) The cuisine is Provençal, seasonal and creative. But what really woos at this trendy club-like address with its very long bar is the *patio à ciel* – a stunning patio garden with slide-back glass ceiling, a great mix of textures and an attention-grabbing black chandelier strung from one of three hefty wooden beams. Dress sharp.

Les Arcenaulx   TRADITIONAL FRENCH €€

(Map p152; ☑ 04 91 59 80 30; www.les-arcenaulx.com; 27 cours Honoré d'Estienne d'Orves; lunch/dinner menus from €25/39, mains €23-30; ☺ noon-2pm & 8-11pm Mon-Sat; Ⓜ Vieux Port) Dine in grandiose style in this cavernous former Louis XIV warehouse with antiquarian-and-contemporary bookshop or visit the neighbouring *salon de thé* (tearoom) for savoury tarts, cakes and ice cream.

Le Môlé Passédat   MODERN FRENCH €€€

(Map p148; www.passedat.fr; 1 esplanade du J4, MuCEM; La Table lunch/dinner menus from €52/73,

LOCAL KNOWLEDGE

THE PERFECT SUNSET

Le Chalet du Pharo (Map p148; ☑ 04 91 52 80 11; www.le-chalet-du-pharo.com; Jardin du Pharo, 58 bd Charles Livon; mains €16-30; ☺ noon-3pm daily, 7.30-9.30pm Mon-Sat; Ⓜ Vieux Port) Only Marseillais and those in the know are privy to this little chalet with a very big view, secreted in the Jardin du Pharo. Its hillside terrace, shaded by pines and parasols, stares across the water at Fort St-Jean, MuCEM and the Villa Méditerranée beyond. Grilled fish and meat dominate the menu. Reservations via its website are essential. No credit cards.

La Cuisine 2/3-course menus €22/35; ☺ La Table 12.30-3pm & 7.30-10.30pm Mon & Wed-Sat, 12.30-3pm Sun, La Cuisine 12.30-3pm Wed-Mon) Few kitchens are so stunningly located as this. On the top floor of Marseille's iconic museum, MuCEM, Michelin-starred chef Gérald Passédat cooks up exquisite French fare alongside big blue views of the Mediterranean and Marseillais coastline. La Table is the gastronomic restaurant; La Cuisine, with self-service dining around shared tables (no sea view), is the cheaper choice. Reserve both online.

There are also cooking courses (€85 to €135).

Self-Catering

Pain de l'Opéra   BOULANGERIE €

(Map p152; 61 rue Francis Davso; ☺ 7am-8pm; Ⓜ Vieux Port) Some of the best pastries near the Vieux Port; also has savoury options.

Boulangerie Aixoise   BOULANGERIE €

(Map p152; ☑ 04 91 33 93 85; 45 rue Francis Davso; ☺ 6.30am-8pm Mon-Sat; Ⓜ Vieux Port) Lines form out the door and onto the red-chaired terrace in front.

✖ Along the Coast

Chez Jeannot   INTERNATIONAL €€

(Map p148; ☑ 04 91 52 11 28; www.pizzeriachezjeannot.com; 129 rue du Vallon des Auffes; mains €13-22; ☺ noon-2pm & 7.30-10pm Tue-Sat, noon-2pm Sun; ☐ 83) With a magical setting overlooking the story-book Vallon des Auffes harbour, this affable joint has fresh salads, pasta and shellfish, plus piping-hot pizzas. Fish is so-so.

GAY VENUES

Website http://marseille.actu-gay.eu covers Marseillais gay life – a small scene that is in constant flux and only really converges on weekends, but the city is generally gay friendly.

Caffè Noir (Map p152; http://cargo-spa.com/caffe-noir; 3 rue Moustier; ⊗2pm-late; Ⓜ Vieux Port) Caffè Noir, with its severe black facade and black pavement terrace staggering down the street in three steps, more than lives up to its name. Inside and out, a young, mixed, hard-drinking crowd gathers. Has a neighbouring sauna.

L'Endroit (Map p152; ☎04 91 33 97 25; 8 rue Bailli de Suffren; ⊗7pm-6am Tue-Sat; Ⓜ Vieux Port) Dive through the tiny door to the Vieux Port's only gay bar. Theme nights include karaoke.

Le Trash (☎04 91 25 52 16; www.trash-bar.com; 28 rue du Berceau; ⊗9pm-2am Wed-Mon; Ⓜ Baille) Le Trash bills itself as Marseille's cruising bar, for good reason. Occasional cover charge (€10).

Péron SEAFOOD €€€
(Map p148; ☎04 91 52 15 22; www.restaurant-peron. com; 56 corniche Président John F Kennedy; menus from €69; ⊗noon-2pm & 8-10.15pm; 🚌83) This designer place set out over the sea is one of the premier addresses in Marseille for a no-holds-barred gastronomic seafood extravaganza. Stunning views unfold over the Med and on your plate, with highlights including lobster risotto and always-fresh fish.

 Drinking & Nightlife

In the best tradition of Mediterranean cities, Marseille embraces the cafe-lounger lifestyle. Near the Vieux Port, head to place Thiars and cours Honoré d'Estienne d'Orves for cafes that bask in the sun by day and buzz into the night. Cours Julien is a fine place on a sunny day to watch people come and go at the many characterful shops, cafes and restaurants in one of Marseille's most interesting neighbourhoods. Up in Le Panier, place de Lenche and rue des Pistoles are ideal places to while away an afternoon while soaking up the area's boho charms.

La Caravelle BAR
(Map p152; 34 quai du Port; ⊗7am-2am; Ⓜ Vieux Port) Look up or miss this standout upstairs hideaway, styled with rich wood and leather, a zinc bar and yellowing murals. If it's sunny, snag a coveted spot on the portside terrace. On Friday there's live jazz from 9pm to midnight.

Le Montmarte CAFE
(Map p152; ☎04 91 56 03 24; 4 pl de Lenche; mains from €6; ⊗9am-11pm; Ⓜ Vieux Port, Joliette) Place de Lenche is a lovely small square in Le Panier with glimpses of the Vieux Port.

Among several cafes here, this one captures the neighbourhood vibe and is a fine place to hang out with a drink on a lazy afternoon.

Bar de la Marine BAR
(Map p152; ☎04 91 54 95 42; 15 quai de Rive Neuve; ⊗7am-1am; Ⓜ Vieux Port) Though it is often erroneously thought that Marcel Pagnol filmed the card-party scenes in *Marius* at this Marseille institution, it did figure in the film *Love, Actually*. Come for a drink, not the food, and a lounge on this simple bar's waterside pavement along the Vieux Port, and don't leave without peeking at the original vintage interior.

Au Petit Nice CAFE, BAR
(Map p148; ☎04 91 48 43 04; 28 place Jean Jaurès; ⊗10am-2am Tue-Sat; Ⓜ Notre Dame du Mont-Cours Julien) Cheap and cheerful: €2 beers in a happening courtyard cafe with a youthful crowd. (This is *not* the hotel of the same name.)

Dame Noir BAR
(Map p148; http://ladamenoir.fr; 30 place Notre Dame du Mont; ⊗7pm-2am Wed-Sat; Ⓜ Notre Dame du Mont-Cours Julien) Hip cats spill onto the pavement from this bar. No sign; look for the red lights by the door. DJs spin Thursday to Saturday at its dance party, Le Dancing at Trolleybus.

Trolleybus CLUB
(Map p152; ☎04 91 54 30 45; www.letrolley.com; 24 quai de Rive Neuve; ⊗midnight-6am Thu-Sat; Ⓜ Vieux Port) Shake it to techno, funk and indie in between games of *pétanque* (a variant on the game of bowls) at this mythical Marseillais club with four *salles* (rooms) beneath 17th-century stone vaults at the Vieux

MARSEILLE TO AIX-EN-PROVENCE MARSEILLE

Port. The club has been around for aeons but never fails to pull in the crowds.

U.Percut
CLUB

(Map p152; www.u-percut.fr; 127 rue Sainte; ⊙7pm-2am Tue-Sat; ⋒Vieux Port) One of the most recent additions to Marseille's cool night scene, U.Percut is popular for its eclectic live music and early-evening tapas.

Polikarpov
BAR

(Map p152; 24 cours Honoré d'Estienne d'Orves; ⊙8am-1.30am; ⋒Vieux Port) Scarcely shut, this alfresco bar with buzzing pavement terrace just a couple of blocks from the Vieux Port markets itself as 'Massilia vodkabar'. Yes, vodka is its mainstay, but there's no obligation.

Les Buvards
WINE BAR

(Map p152; ⊋04 91 90 69 98; 34 Grand Rue; ⊙noon-2.30pm & 6pm-midnight Mon-Sat; ⋒Vieux Port, ⋒Sadi Carnot) Marseille's finest selection of natural wines, by small regional producers in the main, is what tempts at this lovely wine bar. Pair your chosen glass with a charcuterie (cold meat) or cheese platter for aperitif perfection.

Au Son des Guitares
CLUB

(Map p152; 18 rue Corneille; ⊙11.30pm-4am Thu-Sun; ⋒Vieux Port) Popular with Corsican locals, this small club next to the opera has limited dancing, lots of drinking (though drinks are overpriced) and, occasionally, a Corsican singer. Look sharp to get in.

☆ Entertainment

Cultural events are covered in *L'Hebdo* (€1.20), available around town, or www.marseillebynight.com and www.journalventilo. fr (all in French). Tickets are sold at *billetteries* (ticket counters) at Espace Culture (Map p152; ⊋04 96 11 04 60; http://espaceculture. net; 42 La Canebière; ⊙10am-6.45pm Mon-Sat; ⋒Vieux Port) and the tourist office (p164). Cultural centre La Friche La Belle de Mai (p151) hosts theatre, cinema and music.

Espace Julien
LIVE MUSIC

(Map p148; ⊋04 91 24 34 10; www.espace-julien. com; 39 cours Julien; ⋒Notre Dame du Mont-Cours Julien) Rock, *opérock*, alternative theatre, reggae, hip hop, Afro groove and other cutting-edge entertainment all appear on the bill; the website lists gigs.

L'Intermédiaire
LIVE MUSIC

(Map p148; ⊋06 87 87 88 21; www.lintermediaire. fr; 63 place Jean Jaurès; ⊙9pm-2am Wed-Sun;

⋒Notre Dame du Mont-Cours Julien) This grungy venue with graffitied walls is one of the best for DJs and live bands (usually techno or alternative).

Dock des Suds
LIVE MUSIC

(⊋04 91 99 00 00; www.dock-des-suds.org; 12 rue Urbain V; ⊙closed Aug; ⋒National, ⋒Arenc le Silo) Eclectic live music in a large venue in the La Joliette neighbourhood north of the Vieux Port.

Le Pelle Mêle
JAZZ

(Map p152; ⊋04 91 54 85 26; 8 place aux Huiles; ⊙5.30pm-2am Tue-Sat; ⋒Vieux Port) Jive to jazz or fill the busy pavement terrace. Live bands every evening (except Tuesday) at 7.30pm, but drinks are pricey.

Opéra Municipal de Marseille
OPERA

(Map p152; ⊋04 91 55 11 10; http://opera.marseille.fr; 2 rue Molière; ⋒Vieux Port) Season runs September to June.

Théâtre National de Marseille
THEATRE

(La Criée; Map p152; ⊋04 91 54 70 54; www.theatrelacriee.com; 30 quai de Rive Neuve; ⋒Vieux Port) Dance and drama, sometimes in English.

Olympique de Marseille
FOOTBALL

(www.om.net) Marseille's cherished football team plays at Nouveau Stade Vélodrome (www.lenouveaustadevelodrome.com; 3 bd Michelet; ⋒Rond-Point du Prado). Buy tickets at OM's Boutique Officielle (Map p152; ⊋04 91 33 20 01; 44 La Canebière; ⊙10am-7pm Mon-Sat; ⋒Noailles, ⋒Canebière Garibaldi) for as little as €25.

🛍 Shopping

For chic shopping and large chains, stroll west of the Vieux Port to the 6th *arrondissement*, especially pedestrianised rue St-Ferréol. Major chains fill Centre Bourse (Map p152; www.centre-bourse.com; 17 cours Belsunce; ⊙10am-7.30pm Mon-Sat) and line rue de la République.

La Maison du Pastis
DRINK

(Map p152; www.lamaisondupastis.com; 108 quai du Port; ⊙10am-5pm Mon-Sat; ⋒Vieux Port) Sample over 90 varieties of the region's speciality, pastis (an aniseed-flavoured aperitif), or try absinthe.

Atelier 1 par 1
FASHION

(Map p152; 49 rue du Panier; ⋒Vieux Port, Joliette) Creations by a collective of local fashion designers fill this tiny shop, and its neighbour opposite, in Le Panier.

Marché Saint Victor   MARKET
(Map p152; http://marchesaintvictor.fr; 33 rue d'Endoume; ⊙8am-2pm Tue-Sun, plus 6-8pm Tue & Wed, 6-10.30pm Thu-Sat; Ⓜ Vieux Port) This modern covered market offers several outfits selling excellent cheeses, rotisserie meats and other fresh goodies. A Spanish deli serves up *pintxos* (Basque tapas) too.

72% Pétanque   BEAUTY
(Map p152; ☑ 04 91 91 14 57; www.philippechailloux.com; 10 rue du Petit Puits; ⊙10.30am-6.30pm; Ⓜ Vieux Port, Joliette) Brilliantly coloured soaps with scents such as chocolate.

Librairie de la Bourse   BOOKS
(Map p152; ☑ 04 91 33 63 06; 8 rue Paradis; ⊙9am-12.30pm & 2-5pm Tue-Sat; Ⓜ Vieux Port) Maps and Lonely Planet guides.

Compagnie de Provence   BEAUTY
(Map p152; www.compagniedeprovence.com; 18 rue Francis Davso; ⊙10am-7pm Mon-Sat; Ⓜ Vieux Port) For super-stylish liquid and bar soap, au naturel or scented with olive oil, fig or a wilder Provençal fragrance, hit this iconic *savon de Marseille* boutique. Funky washbags, travel kits and other accessories also.

❶ Information

EMERGENCY

Hôpital de la Timone (☑ 04 91 38 60 00; 264 rue St-Pierre; Ⓜ La Timone) Located 1km southeast of place Jean Jaurès.

Police (☑ 17, 04 88 77 58 00; 66-68 La Canebière; ⊙24hr; Ⓜ Noailles)

AROMATIC MARKETS

Marché Place Jean Jaurès (Map p148; place Jean Jaurès; ⊙8am-1pm Thu & Sat; Ⓜ Noailles) Fresh food, clothing, cheap gadgets and more on a large square. On Wednesday it's flowers.

Marché des Capucins (Map p152; place des Capucins; ⊙8am-7pm Mon-Sat; Ⓜ Noailles, ⒼCanebière Garibaldi) Fruit, veg, fish and dried goods.

Marché de la Joliette (Map p148; place de la Joliette; ⊙8am-2pm Mon, Wed & Fri; Ⓜ Joliette) Food and nonfood items. On Monday there are also flowers.

Fresh Fish Market (Map p152; quai des Belges; ⊙8am-1pm; Ⓜ Vieux Port) Small and touristy fixture at the Vieux Port.

TOURIST INFORMATION

Tourist Office (Map p152; ☑ 04 91 13 89 00; www.marseille-tourisme.com; 11 La Canebière; ⊙9am-7pm Mon-Sat, 10am-5pm Sun; Ⓜ Vieux Port) Marseille's useful tourist office has plenty of information on everything, including guided tours on foot or by bus, electric tourist train or boat.

Maison de la Région (Map p152; www.region-paca.fr; 61 La Canebière; ⊙11am-6pm Mon-Sat; Ⓜ Noailles) Info on Provence and the Côte d'Azur.

❶ Getting There & Away

For transport information, see www.lepilote.com.

AIR

Aéroport Marseille-Provence (MRS; ☑ 04 42 14 14 14; www.marseille.aeroport.fr) Located 25km northwest of Marseille in Marignane; it is also called Aéroport Marseille-Marignane.

BOAT

Passenger-Ferry Terminal (Map p148; www.marseille-port.fr; Ⓜ Joliette) Located 250m south of place de la Joliette.

SNCM (Map p148; ☑ 08 91 70 18 01; www.sncm.fr; 61 bd des Dames; Ⓜ Joliette) Regular ferries from Nice and Marseille to Corsica and Sardinia, plus long-distance routes to Algeria and Tunisia.

BUS

Bus Station (Map p148; www.lepilote.com; 3 rue Honnorat; Ⓜ Gare St-Charles) On the northern side of the train station. Buy tickets here or from the driver. Services to some destinations, including Cassis, use the stop on place Castellane (Map p148; Ⓜ Castellane), south of the centre.

Eurolines (Map p152; www.eurolines.com; 3 allées Léon Gambetta; Ⓜ Noailles) International services.

CAR

Most major car-rental firms have offices in or close to the train station.

TRAIN

Eurostar (www.eurostar.com) Services operate one to five times weekly between Marseille and London (from €240, 6½ hours) via Avignon and Lyon.

Gare St-Charles (⊙ticket office 5.15am-10pm daily; Ⓜ Gare St-Charles SNCF) Regular and TGV trains serve the station, which is a junction for both metro lines. The **left-luggage office** (items stored from €5.50; ⊙8.15am-9pm daily) is next to platform A.

Avignon €20.50, 35 minutes

MASSIF DE LA STE-BAUME

From Marseille head towards Gémenos, then take the eastbound D2 towards 'Vallée St-Pons & La Ste-Baume'. The going gets verdantly dramatic, the road snaking uphill through the scrubby terrain of the Parc Départemental de St-Pons. After 8km, the sea pops onto the horizon, then the road climbs to Col de l'Espigoulier (728m), a mountain pass with coastline views. The winding descent is dominated by the mountain ridge Massif de la Ste-Baume.

At the D45A/D2 junction, continue on the D2 to La Ste-Baume (8km), from where a 40-minute forest trail leads to the Grotte de Ste-Madeleine FREE (950m), a mountain cave where Mary Magdalene is said to have spent the last years of her life. Its entrance offers a breathtaking panorama of Montagne Ste-Victoire, Mont Ventoux and the Alps.

Finally, take the D80 northeast via Nans-les-Pins, then turn right on the N560 (about 20km all up) to reach the pastel-hued town of St-Maximin La Ste-Baume. Its fabulous Gothic Ste-Madeleine basilica was built in 1295 as the home of what are claimed to be the relics of Mary Magdalene, discovered in a crypt on the site around 1279. Afterwards lunch on Provençal specialities in the adjacent convent, now the sumptuous Hôtel Le Couvent Royal (04 94 86 55 66; www.couvent-royal.fr; place Jean Salusse, St-Maximin La Ste-Baume; lunch/dinner menus from €17/39, d from €80).

Nice €37, 2½ hours
Paris Gare de Lyon From €60, three hours on TGV

Getting Around

TO/FROM THE AIRPORT

From the airport's 'Vitrolles Aéroport Marseille-Provence' train station, linked to the airport terminal by a free shuttle, there are direct services to several cities, including Arles and Avignon.

Navette Marseille (www.navettemarseilleaeroport.com; adult/child €8.20/4.10; 4.30am-11.30pm) Links the airport and Gare St-Charles every 15 to 20 minutes.

BOAT

Boats run across the Vieux Port (p145), to offshore islands Frioul and If (p154), and to Pointe Rouge (p151). Tours (p155) go to the *calanques*.

CAR

Marseille is challenging for drivers. Central car parks include **Parking Bourse** (rue Reine Elisabeth; 24hr; Vieux Port) and **Parking de Gaulle** (22 place du Général de Gaulle; 24hr; Vieux Port) off La Canebière. Expect to pay at least €2 per hour, €30 per 24 hours).

PUBLIC TRANSPORT

Marseille has two metro lines (Métro 1 and Métro 2), two tram lines (yellow and green) and an extensive bus network. Bus, metro or tram tickets (per hour/day €1.60/5.20) are available from machines in the metro, at tram stops and on buses. Most buses start in front of the **Espace Infos RTM** (Map p152; 04 91 91 92 10;

www.rtm.fr; 6 rue des Fabres; 8.30am-6pm Mon-Fri, 8.30am-noon & 1-4.30pm Sat; Vieux Port), where you can obtain information and tickets.

The metro runs from 5am to 10.30pm Monday to Thursday, and until 12.30am Friday to Sunday. Trams run 5am to 1am daily.

TAXI

Taxi Radio Marseille (04 91 02 20 20; www.taximarseille.com)

AROUND MARSEILLE

Cradling Marseille's built-up metro area are spectacular stretches of coast hiding crystal-line coves, charming towns and celebrated vineyards.

Les Calanques

Marseille abuts the wild and spectacular Parc National des Calanques (www.calanques-parcnational.fr), a 20km stretch of high, rocky promontories, rising from brilliant-turquoise Mediterranean waters. The sheer cliffs are occasionally interrupted by small idyllic beaches, some impossible to reach without a kayak. The Marseillais cherish the Calanques, and come to soak up sun or take a long hike. The promontories have been protected since 1975 and shelter an extraordinary wealth of flora and fauna: 900 plant species, Bonelli's eagle, and Europe's largest

MARSEILLE TO AIX-EN-PROVENCE LES CALANQUES

lizard (the 60cm eyed lizard) and longest snake (the 2m Montpellier snake).

From October to June the best way to see the Calanques (including the 500 sq km of the rugged inland Massif des Calanques) is to hike the many maquis-lined trails. Marseille's tourist office leads guided walks (no kids under eight) and has information about trail and road closures. It also has an excellent hiking map of the various *calanques*, as does Cassis' tourist office, and their websites.

In July and August trails close due to fire danger: take a boat tour from Marseille (p155) or Cassis, though they don't stop to let you swim. Otherwise, drive or take public transport, though roads are rough, parking scarce and the going slow. The roads into each *calanque* are often closed to drivers, unless they have a reservation at one of the *calanque* restaurants. You must instead park at a public lot then walk the rest of the way in.

Sea kayaking from Marseille or Cassis is wondrous. Raskas Kayak (☑04 91 73 27 16; www.raskas-kayak.com; Marseille; half-/full-day tour €35/65) organises sea-kayaking tours and tourist offices have details of many more guides.

For access to the *calanques* closest to Marseille, drive or take bus 19 down the coast to its terminus at La Madrague, then switch to bus 20 to Callelongue, a small *calanque* with restaurants (note that the road to Callelongue is open to cars weekdays only mid-April to May and closed entirely June to September). From there you can walk to Calanque de la Mounine and Calanque de Marseilleveyre along spectacular trails over the clifftops.

Calanque de Sugiton is also easy to access without a car. Take bus 21 from av du Prado, at Castellane, towards Luminy and get off at the last stop. From there follow the path (about a 45-minute walk).

⊙ Sights

Calanque de Sormiou INLET

The largest *calanque* hit headlines in 1991 when diver Henri Cosquer from Cassis swam through a 150m-long passage 36m underwater into a cave to find its interior adorned with wall paintings dating from around 20,000 BC. Now named Grotte Cosquer, the cave is a protected historical monument and closed to the public. Many more are believed to exist.

Take bus 23 from Marseilles' Rond-Point du Prado metro to La Cayolle stop, from where it is a 3km walk.

Two seasonal restaurants with fabulous views serve lunch (and require reservations). Le Château (☑04 91 25 08 69; http://lechateausormiou.fr; Calanque de Sormiou; mains €20-25; ⊙noon-2.30pm & 7.30-9.30pm Apr-Sep) has the best food but does not take credit cards; Le Lunch (☑04 91 25 05 37; www.restaurant-lunch.com; Calanque de Sormiou; mains €16-28; ⊙noon-2.30pm & 8-10pm late Mar–mid-Oct) (which also serves dinner) has the better view. Diners with reservations are allowed to drive into the *calanque*; otherwise, mid-April to May the road's open to cars weekdays only and closed entirely June to September.

Calanque de Morgiou INLET

Windswept Cap Morgiou separates Sormiou from Morgiou, with a pretty little port bobbing with fishing boats, and sheer rock faces from which climbers dangle. An evening spent at its one (seasonal) restaurant, Nautic Bar (☑04 91 40 06 37; Calanque de Morgiou; mains €18-27; ⊙noon-2.30pm & 7.30-9.30pm May-Oct, closed Sun evening & Mon Apr), is dreamy. No credit cards.

Morgiou beach is a one-hour walk from the car park. The hair-raisingly steep, narrow road (3.5km) is open to motorists weekdays only mid-April to May, closed entirely June to September (motorists with a Nautic Bar reservation are always allowed through).

En-Vau, Port-Pin & Port-Miou INLET

East of Calanque de Morgiou, the stone-sculptured coast brings you to three remote *calanques*: En-Vau, Port-Pin and Port-Miou. Calanque d'En-Vau has a pebbly beach and emerald waters encased by cliffs. Its entrance is guarded by the Doigt de Dieu (God's Finger), a giant rock pinnacle. A *steep* three-hour marked trail leads from the car park (closed July to mid-September) on the Col de la Gardiole to En-Vau. The slippery and sheer descents into En-Vau are for the truly hardcore only.

Approaching En-Vau from the east, it is a solid 1½-hour walk on the GR98 from Calanque de Port-Miou, immediately west of Cassis. En route you pass the neighbouring Calanque de Port-Pin, a 30-minute walk from Port-Miou.

Cassis' tourist office (p168) distributes free maps of the walking trails.

Cassis

POP 7663

Nestled at the foot of a dramatic rocky outcrop crowned by a 14th-century château (now a hotel open only to guests), this little fishing port is all charm, hence the enormous crowds that pile into its Vieux Port with its bustling restaurants, play on its shingle beaches, visit its terraced vineyards and sip fabled white Cassis wine.

The town's name comes from its Roman title Carsicis Portus, meaning 'crowned port', so christened for the rock Couronne de Charlemagne (Crown of Charlemagne), which is visible from far out at sea.

🏃 Activities

The tourist office has information on rock climbing, deep-sea diving, sea kayaking and walking (including a one-hour trail to Port-Pin).

Twelve estates producing the Cassis appellation wines ribbon the hillsides; the tourist office has a list of suggested itineraries and estates you can visit to taste and buy; most require advance reservation. It also offers guided tours (€25 per person) twice per week, on electric bicycles.

Les Bateliers Cassidains CRUISE
(☑ 06 86 55 86 70; www.cassis-calanques.com) Boats travel to Les Calanques year-round from Quai St-Pierre; buy tickets at the portside kiosk. A 45-minute trip to three *calanques* (Port-Miou, Port-Pin and En-Vau) costs €16/9.50 per adult/child; a 65-minute trip covering these plus Oule and Devenson is €19/13. No credit cards.

🛏 Sleeping

Le Clos des Arômes HOTEL €
(☑ 04 42 01 71 84; www.leclosdesaromes.fr; 10 rue Abbé Paul Mouton; s/d from €49/69; ❄ 🛜) A short climb uphill from the portside madness, this charming garden hotel is a bit worn, but spotless. Dining at dusk in the courtyard is a peaceful affair. No lift.

Cassis Hostel HOSTEL €
(☑ 09 54 37 99 82; www.cassishostel.com; 4 av du Picouveau, Les Heures Claires; dm/d incl breakfast €30/85; 🛜 🏊) On the hill above town, this place is simple but has a kitchen, a beautiful terrace and a pool.

LOCAL KNOWLEDGE

TOP VIEWS

Europe's highest maritime cliff, the hollow limestone **Cap Canaille** (399m), towers above the southeastern side of the **Baie de Cassis** (Cassis Bay). From the top, captivating views unfold across Cassis and **Mont Puget** (564m), the highest peak in the Massif des Calanques.

Offering equally heart-stopping panoramas, the **Route des Crêtes** (Road of Crests, D141; closed during high winds) wiggles 16km along the clifftops from Cassis to La Ciotat.

Hôtel Cassitel HOTEL €€
(☑ 04 42 01 83 44; www.cassitel.com; place Clémenceau; d €99-109; ❄ 🛜) Smack on the harbourfront section of the village, this simple hotel has that key attribute: a wonderful location. Rooms are simple, but many have harbour views.

🍴 Eating & Drinking

La Poissonnerie SEAFOOD €
(☑ 04 42 01 71 56; 5 quai JJ Barthélemy; menu du pêcheur €20; ⊙ lunch Tue-Sun, dinner Tue-Sat Feb-Dec) Run by two brothers (one fishes, one cooks), this locals' favourite offers everything from a humble plate of sardines with a glass of white wine (€13.90) to grilled fish, or bouillabaisse (€40). No credit cards.

Fleurs de Thym BISTRO €€
(☑ 04 42 01 23 03; www.fleursdethym.com; 5 rue Lamartine; 3-course menu €26; ⊙ 7.30-10.30pm) Provençal specialities with an emphasis on seafood. The tiny, quaint dining room spills onto a flower-filled terrace.

La Villa Madie GASTRONOMIC €€€
(☑ 04 96 18 00 00; www.lavillamadie.com; av de Revestel-anse de Corton; winter/summer menus from €75/95, mains €52-72; ⊙ noon-1.15pm & 7-9.15pm Tue-Sun, closed Tue Oct-May) This two-Michelin-star gastronomic temple beautifully prepares the freshest seafood in inventive, exquisitely presented combinations alongside sparkling sea views. Two accompanying bistros offer scaled-down but equally delicious options.

Le Chai Cassidain WINE BAR
(☑ 04 42 01 99 80; www.le-chai-cassidain.com; 7 rue Séverin Icard; ⊙ 9.30am-1pm & 3-10pm daily,

closed Mon Nov-Mar) Local wines by the glass and often free tastings.

ℹ Information

Tourist Office (☑ 08 92 39 01 03; www.ot-cassis.com; quai des Moulins; ⊙ 9am-7pm Mon-Sat, 9.30am-12.30pm & 3-6pm Sun Jul & Aug, shorter hours rest of year; ⊛) Calanque maps, guided tours of the village and vineyards.

ℹ Getting There & Away

Buses go from Cassis to Marseille (five daily); schedules are at www.lepilote.com. Buses stop at rond-point du Pressoir, a five-minute walk along av du Professeur René Leriche and rue de l'Arène to the port.

Cassis train station (av de la Gare), 3.5km east of the centre, is on the Marseille–Hyères line. Buses 2, 3 and 4 run to the town centre.

If you drive during high season when town parking is scarce, park in the large lot at the entrance of town and take the free *navette* (shuttle) down to the harbour.

Côte Bleue

The Côte Bleue clambers from Marseille's western edge, past gritty fishing villages, to Cap Couronne. Marine-life-rich waters around the sandy cape are protected by the **Parc Régional Marin de la Côte Bleue.**

The Blue Coast has a precious trove of **calanques**, which compete with the famous ones between Marseille and Cassis. At **Calanque de Niolon**, 12km west of L'Estaque, rocky spurs ensnare the perilously perched village of Niolon, which has a handful of cafes and the lovely **Auberge du Mérou** (☑ 04 91 46 98 69; www.aubergedumerou.fr; 3-course menu €27-38; ⊙ noon-2pm & 7.30-10pm Jun-Sep, closed Sun & Mon evening Oct-May), with a seaview terrace.

From the tiny waterside Port du Redonne, a single-track road climbs over to Les Figuières (1km), the Petit Méjean (1.7km) and the Grand Méjean (1.8km). In Grand Méjean you can pick up a stunning 2.1km-long coastal trail to Calanque de l'Érevine.

Overbuilt **L'Estaque** (www.estaque.com) once lured artists from the impressionist, Fauvist and cubist movements. A trail follows in the footsteps of Renoir, Cézanne, Dufy and Braque around the port and shabby old town. On the water's edge buy *chichi frégi* (sugar-coated doughnuts) and *panisses* (chickpea-flour cakes) to munch.

PAYS D'AIX

Picturesque Pays d'Aix (Aix Country), within which oh-so-elegant Aix-en-Provence is ensconced, sits 25km or so north of Marseille.

Aix-en-Provence

POP 145,273

A pocket of left-bank Parisian chic deep in Provence, Aix (pronounced like the letter X) is all class: its leafy boulevards and public squares are lined with 17th- and 18th-century mansions, punctuated by gurgling moss-covered fountains. Haughty stone lions guard its grandest avenue, cafe-laced cours Mirabeau, where fashionable Aixois pose on polished pavement terraces sipping espresso. While Aix is a student hub, its upscale appeal makes it pricier than other Provençal towns.

History

Aix marks the spot where Roman forces enslaved the inhabitants of the Ligurian Celtic stronghold of Entremont, 3km north. In 123 BC the military camp was named Aquae Sextiae (Waters of Sextius) for the thermal springs that still flow today. In the 12th century the counts of Provence proclaimed Aix their capital, which it remained until the Revolution, when it was supplanted by Marseille. The city became a centre of culture under arts patron King René (1409–80): painter Paul Cézanne and novelist Émile Zola are its most famous sons.

◉ Sights & Activities

Art, culture and architecture abound in Aix. Of special note are the town's many fountains. Some, like the 1860 **Fontaine de la Rotonde** (pl du Général de Gaulle), are quite grand. Others, such as the 1819 **Fontaine du Roi René** (cours Mirabeau) and the 1734 **Fontaine d'Eau Chaude** (cours Mirabeau) have simpler charms (the former features the king holding a bunch of grapes, while the latter has warm – 18°C – water from a spring).

★ **Vieil Aix**　　　　　　　HISTORIC QUARTER
The mostly pedestrianised old city of Aix is a stroller's and window-shopper's paradise of narrow boutique-lined lanes and hidden squares filled with cafes or markets.

★ **Cours Mirabeau**　　　　HISTORIC QUARTER
No avenue better epitomises Provence's most graceful city than this fountain-studded

CÉZANNE SIGHTS

The life of local lad Paul Cézanne (1839–1906) is treasured in Aix. To see where he ate, drank, studied and painted, follow the **Circuit de Cézanne** (Cézanne Trail), marked by bronze plaques embedded in the footpath. The essential English-language guide to the plaques and other artist-related sites, *In the Steps of Cézanne*, is free at the tourist office (p175).

Atelier Cézanne (☑04 42 21 06 53; www.atelier-cezanne.com; 9 av Paul Cézanne; adult/child €5.50/free; ⏰10am-6pm Jul & Aug, reduced hours rest of year) Cézanne's last studio, 1.5km north of the tourist office on a hilltop, was painstakingly preserved (and recreated: not all the tools and still-life models strewn around the room were his) as it was at the time of his death. Though the studio is inspiring, none of his works hang there. Take bus 1 or 20 to the Atelier Cézanne stop or walk from there.

Terrain des Peintres The Terrain des Peintres is a wonderful terraced garden perfect for a picnic, from where Cézanne, among others, painted the Montagne Ste-Victoire. The view of the jagged mountain is inspirational. The gardens are opposite 62 av Paul Cézanne. You'll find it a 10-minute walk uphill from the Atelier Cézanne stop (bus 1 or 20).

Bastide du Jas de Bouffan (☑04 42 16 11 61; www.cezanne-en-provence.com; adult/child €6/free; ⏰guided tours from 10.30am daily Jun-Sep, Tue, Thu & Sat May & Oct, Wed & Sat Nov-Mar; ☐6, stop Corsy) In 1859 Cézanne's father bought Le Jas de Bouffan, a country manor west of Aix' centre where Cézanne painted furiously in the decades that followed, producing 36 oils and 17 watercolours depicting the house, farm, chestnut alley, green park and so forth. Visits are by guided tour only and should be reserved in advance at the tourist office. Take bus 6 from La Rotonde (av Victor Hugo) to the Corsy stop or walk the 20 minutes from town.

Carrières de Bibemus (Bibémus Quarries; ☑04 42 16 11 61; www.cezanne-en-provence. com; 3090 chemin de Bibémus; adult/child €6/free; ⏰tours from 9.45am daily Jun-Sep, from 10.30am Mon, Wed, Fri & Sun Apr-May & Oct, from 3pm Wed & Sat Nov-Mar) In 1895 Cézanne rented a *cabanon* (cabin) at Les Carrières de Bibemus, on the edge of town, where he painted prolifically. Atmospheric one-hour tours of the ochre quarry take visitors on foot through the dramatic burnt-orange rocks Cézanne captured so vividly on canvas. Book tours in advance at the tourist office, wear sturdy shoes and avoid wearing white.

street, sprinkled with Renaissance *hôtels particuliers* and crowned with a summertime roof of leafy plane trees. Named after the revolutionary hero Comte de Mirabeau, it was laid out in the 1640s. Cézanne and Zola hung out at Les Deux Garçons (p174), one of a clutch of busy pavement cafes.

Among the most impressive *hôtels particuliers* is **Hôtel d'Espargnet** (1647) at No 38, now home to the university's economics department. Photography and contemporary art get an airing inside **Hôtel de Castillon**, now the **Galerie d'Art du Conseil Général des Bouches du Rhône** (☑04 13 31 50 70; www.culture-13.fr; 21bis cours Mirabeau; ⏰10.30am-1pm & 2-7pm Mon-Sat) `FREE`.

★**Quartier Mazarin**   HISTORIC QUARTER
South of cours Mirabeau, Quartier Mazarin was laid out in the 17th century, and is home to some of Aix' finest buildings. **Place des Quatre Dauphins** is particularly

enchanting and has a fountain (1667) with water-spouting dolphins.

★**Musée Granet**   MUSEUM
(www.museegranet-aixenprovence.fr; place St-Jean de Malte; adult/child €5/free; ⏰11am-7pm Tue-Sun) Housed in a 17th-century priory of the Knights of Malta, this exceptional museum is named after the Provençal painter François Marius Granet (1775–1849), who donated a large number of works. Its collection includes 16th- to 20th-century Italian, Flemish and French works. Modern art reads like a who's who: Picasso, Léger, Matisse, Monet, Klee, Van Gogh and Giacometti, among others, as well as the museum's pride and joy: nine Cézanne works. Excellent temporary exhibitions.

Cathédrale St-Sauveur   CHURCH
(rue de la Roque; ⏰8am-noon & 2-6pm) Built between 1285 and 1350 in a potpourri of

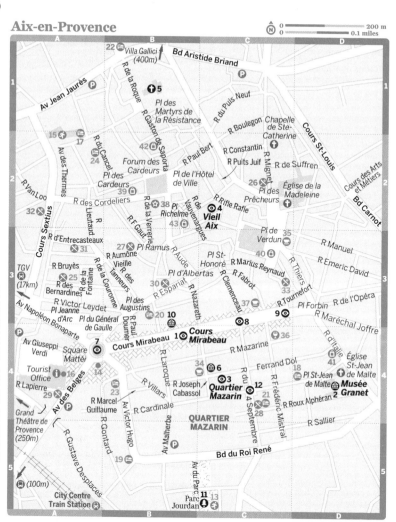

MARSEILLE TO AIX-EN-PROVENCE AIX-EN-PROVENCE

styles, this cathedral includes a Romanesque 12th-century nave in its southern aisle, chapels from the 14th and 15th centuries, and a 5th-century sarcophagus in the apse. More recent additions include the 18th-century gilt baroque organ. Acoustics make Sunday-afternoon Gregorian chants unforgettable.

Caumont Centre d'Art   MUSEUM
(☑04 42 20 70 01; www.caumont-centredart. com; 3 rue Joseph Cabassol; adult/child €11/8.50; ⊙10am-7pm May-Sep, to 6pm Oct-Apr) Built over a period of 30 years beginning in 1715, the elegant Hôtel de Caumont was one of the

finest residences during the heyday of the Quartier Mazarin. Now you can get a taste of this classic elegance thanks to years of restorations that were finished in 2015. There are grand galleries with rotating exhibits of high-end art; admission includes a tour of the opulent interior.

Fondation Victor Vasarely   GALLERY
(☑04 42 20 01 09; www.fondationvasarely.fr; 1 av Marcel Pagnol; adult/child €9/4; ⊙10am-1pm & 2-6pm Tue-Sun; ⊛; ☐4, 6, stop Vasarely) This gallery, 4km west of the city, was designed by Hungarian optical-art innovator Victor

Aix-en-Provence

Vasarely (1906–97). A masterpiece, its 16 interconnecting six-walled galleries were purpose built to display and reflect the patterning of the artist's 44 acid-trip-ready, floor-to-ceiling geometric artworks.

Parc Jourdan PARK
South of Aix' centre is the peaceful Parc Jourdan, home to the town's **Boulodrome Municipal**, where locals gather beneath plane trees to play *pétanque*.

Thermes Sextius SPA
(☎04 42 23 81 82; www.thermes-sextius.com; 55 av des Thermes; day pass from €99) These modern thermal spas are built on the site of Roman Aquae Sextiae's springs, the excavated remains of which are displayed beneath glass in the lobby.

⚲ Tours

Tourist Office Tours WALKING TOUR
(300 av Giuseppe Verdi; adult/child €9/5) The tourist office runs a regular schedule of guided walking tours in English, covering Cézanne and the old town. Most start on particular days of the week at 10am.

Mini-Tram TOUR
(☎04 42 01 09 98; www.cpts.fr; adult/child €7/3; ⊙10am-4pm late Mar–mid-Nov) Departs from place du Général de Gaulle in front of the Apple Store and winds through the Quartier Mazarin, along cours Mirabeau and around Vieil Aix. Multilingual.

★☆ Festivals & Events

★ **Festival**
d'Aix-en-Provence PERFORMING ARTS
(☎04 34 08 02 17; www.festival-aix.com; ⊙Jul) World-renowned month-long festival of classical music, opera, ballet and buskers.

🛏 Sleeping

Hôtel les Quatre Dauphins BOUTIQUE HOTEL €
(☎04 42 38 16 39; www.lesquatredauphins.fr; 54 rue Roux Alphéran; s €62-72, d €72-87; ❈ 🖝) This sweet 13-room hotel slumbers in a former private mansion in one of the loveliest parts of town. Rooms are fresh and clean, with excellent modern bathrooms. Those with sloping, beamed ceilings in the attic are quaint but not for those who cannot pack light – the terracotta-tiled staircase is not suitcase friendly.

ⓘ AIX DISCOUNTS

The **Cézanne Passport** (per person €12) covers the artist's three main sights: the Atelier Cézanne, Bastide du Jas de Bouffan and Carrières de Bibemus. Buy it at the tourist office or the first two listed Cézanne sights. The **Aix-Aix Region Pass** (per person €2) includes discounts on local museums and tourist office-run walking tours.

Hôtel Cardinal
HOTEL €

(☏ 04 42 38 32 30; www.hotel-cardinal-aix.com; 24 rue Cardinale; s/d €68/78; 🖥) Slightly rumpled rooms are quaintly furnished with antiques and tasselled curtains. There are also six gigantic suites in the annexe up the street, each with a kitchenette and dining room – ideal for longer stays.

Hôtel Paul
HOTEL €

(☏ 04 42 23 23 89; www.aix-en-provence.com/hotelpaul/; 10 av Pasteur; s/d/tr from €55/65/77; 🖥) On the edge of Vieil Aix, this bright, 24-room bargain has a quiet garden and a TV lounge. Fans in summer. Free motorcycle and bike parking. No credit cards.

★ L'Épicerie
B&B €

(☏ 06 08 85 38 68; www.unechambreenville.eu; 12 rue du Cancel; d €100-130; 🖥🍴) This intimate B&B is the fabulous creation of born-and-bred Aixois lad Luc. His breakfast room recreates a 1950s grocery store, and the flowery garden out the back is perfect for excellent evening dining and weekend brunch (book ahead for both). Breakfast is a veritable feast. Two rooms accommodate families of four.

Hôtel des Augustins
HOTEL €€

(☏ 04 42 27 28 59; www.hotel-augustins.com; 3 rue de la Masse; d €109-249; 🌡🖥) A heartbeat from the hub of Aixois life, this 15th-century convent building with magnificent stone-vaulted lobby and sweeping staircase has volumes of history: Martin Luther stayed here after his excommunication from Rome. Filled with hand-painted furniture, the largest, most luxurious rooms have spa baths; two rooms have private terraces beneath the filigreed bell tower.

Hôtel Saint-Christophe
HOTEL €€

(☏ 04 42 26 01 24; www.hotel-saintchristophe.com; 2 av Victor Hugo; r €108-178; 🌡🖥🍴) The Saint-Christophe is a proper hotel, with a big lobby and a central location. Rooms nod to art deco in their styling, and have the standard midbudget amenities, including good bathrooms; some have terraces, some can sleep four. Parking (€14) by reservation.

★ Villa Gallici
HISTORIC HOTEL €€€

(☏ 04 42 23 29 23; www.villagallici.com; 18 av de la Violette; r €235-700; 🌡🖥🏊) Your palatial estate just north of town, this 200-year-old villa has a beautiful pool and garden area. The buildings are decorated in a traditional and opulent manner; rooms brim with luxuries and yes, that lavender you smell grows naturally outside your window. It's a relaxed 500m walk to the centre.

Hôtel Cézanne
BOUTIQUE HOTEL €€€

(☏ 04 42 91 11 11; www.hotelaix.com; 40 av Victor Hugo; r €150-280; 🌡@🖥) Purple flags fly proud outside Aix' swishest hotel, a contemporary study in clean lines, with sharp-edged built-in desks, top-end fabrics and design-driven decor. In any other city its location next to the train station would be deemed a flaw. Reserve ahead for free parking.

Hôtel Aquabella
HOTEL €€€

(☏ 04 42 99 15 00; www.aquabella.fr; 3 rue des Étuves; d/tr €210/230) Should wallowing like a Roman in Aix-en-Provence's thermal waters tickle your fancy, check into this three-star hotel adjoining the Thermes Sextius spa. Rates include spa access and there is really nothing more delightful after a hard day boutique shopping than a lounge in the eucalypt-scented *hammam* (Turkish steambath) followed by a dip in the pool, with a view of Roman ruins.

✗ Eating

Aix excels at Provençal cuisine, and restaurant terraces spill out across dozens of charm-heavy old-town squares, many pierced by an ancient stone fountain: place des Trois Ormeaux, place des Augustins, place Ramus and vast Forum des Cardeurs are particular favourites.

★ Maison Nosh
CAFE €

(☏ 06 52 86 22 39; www.maison-nosh.com; 42-44 cours Sextius; mains from €5; ⊙10am-6pm Mon-Sat) Bright and welcoming, this bakery-cafe dishes up tasty casual fare with a dash of wit. Coffee drinks and juices are served throughout the day along with beautiful baked goods. From 11am, the kitchen serves hot and simple meals such as the best hot dog you'll ever have (it comes on a wooden platter), as well as sandwiches and salads.

★ **Jacquou Le Croquant** PROVENÇAL €

(☎ 04 42 27 37 19; www.jacquoulecroquant.com; 2 rue de l'Aumône Vielle; plat du jour €11, menus from €14; ☺ noon-3pm & 7-11pm) This veteran address, around since 1985, stands out on dozens of counts: buzzy jovial atmosphere, flowery patio garden, funky interior, early-evening opening, family friendly, hearty homecooking, a menu covering all price ranges, and so forth. Cuisine from south-western France is its speciality, meaning lots of duck, but the vast menu covers all bases.

★ **Farinoman Fou** BOULANGERIE €

(www.farinomanfou.fr; 3 rue Mignet; ☺ 7am-7pm Tue-Sat) Tucked just off place des Prêcheurs is this truly phenomenal bakery, with a constant queue outside its door. The crunchy, different-flavoured breads baked by artisan *boulanger* Benoît Fradette are reason enough to sell up and move to Aix. The bakery has no shop as such; customers jostle for space in bread ovens and dough-mixing tubs.

La Tarte Tropézienne PATISSERIE, CAFE €

(av des Belges; sandwich/salad menu €7/8, mains €12-14) A handy stop en route to/from the bus and train stations, this modern patisserie-cafe is known for its sugar-encrusted *tarte Tropézienne* (cream-filled cake from St-Tropez), displayed in cabinets like jewels beneath glass. Grab a wedge (€2.90) to take out or eat in – on red director chairs on a decking terrace. Excellent-value gourmet sandwiches and salads.

Charlotte BISTRO €

(☎ 04 42 26 77 56; 32 rue des Bernardines; 2-/3-course menus €16.50/20; ☺ 12.30-2pm & 8-10.30pm Tue-Sat; ☂) It's all very cosy at Charlotte, where everyone knows everyone. French classics like veal escalope and beef steak are mainstays, and there is always a vegetarian dish and a couple of imaginative *plats du jour*. In summer everything moves into the garden.

★ **Petit Pierre Reboul** BISTRO €€

(Petit II R; ☎ 04 82 75 72 81; www.bistrotpetitpierre.com; 11 Petite Rue St-Jean; 2-course menus €19-34, 3-course menus €27-39; ☺ noon-2.30pm & 7.30-10.30pm Mon-Sat) This brightly coloured address, hidden down a back alley, is the bistro arm of Pierre Reboul's gastronomic restaurant next door. The vibe is contemporary design (think acid-bright fabrics and lampshades made from pencils), and the menu throws in the odd adventurous dish alongside stalwarts like burgers, Caesar salad, grilled meats, and mussels and fries.

★ **Le Petit Verdot** FRENCH €€

(☎ 04 42 27 30 12; www.lepetitverdot.fr; 7 rue d'Entrecasteaux; mains €15-25; ☺ 7pm-midnight Mon-Sat) Delicious menus are designed around what's in season, and paired with excellent wines. Meats are often braised all day; vegetables are tender, stewed in delicious broths. Save room for an incandescent dessert. Lively dining occurs around tabletops made of wine crates (expect to talk to your neighbour), and the gregarious owner speaks multiple languages.

Le Formal MODERN FRENCH €€

(☎ 04 42 27 08 31; www.restaurant-leformal.com; 32 rue Espariat; lunch menu from €26, 3/7-course dinner menus €42/49; ☺ noon-2pm Tue-Fri, 7.30-10pm Tue-Sat) Chef Jean-Luc Le Formal is well established in France's foodie circles with his first-class establishment. Impeccably mannered staff serve delicious and inventive meals in the vaulted-cellar dining rooms. Reserve ahead for the superb seven-course truffle menu (€79).

Jardin Mazarin FRENCH €€

(☎ 04 42 58 11 42; www.jardinmazarin.com; 15 rue du 4 Septembre; menu €34, mains €15-20; ☺ noon-2.30pm & 8-10.30pm Tue-Sat) Something of a hidden address, this elegant restaurant serenades the ravishing *hôtel particulier* in which it languishes. Two salons sit beneath splendid beamed ceilings, but the real gem is outside: a luxuriant green garden with a fountain and a line-up of tables beneath a wicker shade. Peace, perfect peace, far from the madding crowd.

★ **Restaurant Pierre Reboul** GASTRONOMIC €€€

(☎ 04 82 75 72 60; www.restaurant-pierre-reboul.com; 11 Petite Rue St-Jean; menus €54-151; ☺ noon-2pm & 7.30-10pm Tue-Sat) Aix' newest

SWEET TREAT

Aix' sweetest treat since King René's wedding banquet in 1473 is the marzipan-like local speciality, *calisson d'Aix*, a small, diamond-shaped, chewy delicacy made on a wafer base with ground almonds and fruit syrup, and glazed with icing sugar. Traditional *calissonniers* still make them, including **Roy René** (www.calisson.com; 13 rue Gaston de Saporta; ☺ 9.30am-1pm & 2-6.30pm Mon-Sat, 9am-4pm Sun), which has a tiny museum, and a factory on the edge of town that is open for tours (€5).

DON'T MISS

MARKETS

➡ At the daily **food market** (place Richelme; ⊙7am-noon), trestle tables groan each morning under the weight of marinated olives, goat's cheese, garlic, lavender, honey, peaches, melons, cherries and a bounty of other sun-kissed fruit, veg and seasonal food. Plane trees provide ample shade on the atmospheric T-shaped square, endowed with a couple of corner cafes where Aixois catch up on the gossip over *un café* (a coffee) once their shopping is done.

➡ Flower markets fill place des Prêcheurs (Sunday morning) and place de l'Hôtel de Ville (Tuesday, Thursday and Saturday mornings).

➡ The **flea market** (place de Verdun; ⊙Tue, Thu & Sat mornings) has quirky vintage items.

culinary star invents playful, gorgeous creations. With a minimalist sensibility in the relaxed dining room and on the exquisitely presented plates, Reboul crafts new juxtapositions using fresh but timeless ingredients. Think perfectly seared duck with a savoury, unexpectedly Asian-influenced broth, sea foam and tender pasta. The lunch special includes mineral water, coffee and a glass of wine.

His bistro next door, Petit Pierre Reboul (p173), is excellent too.

🍷 Drinking & Nightlife

The scene is fun but fickle. For nightlife, hit the drinking dens on rue de la Verrerie and place Richelme. Open-air cafes crowd the city's squares, especially Forum des Cardeurs, place de Verdun and place de l'Hôtel de Ville (our favourite, for its more intimate scale and shady trees).

★ Book in Bar   CAFE
(www.bookinbar.com; 4 rue Cabassol; ⊙9am-7pm Mon-Sat) There is no more literary spot to partake in *un café* than this particularly fine English bookshop with cafe. Look out for occasional book readings, jazz evenings etc.

La Mado   CAFE
(Chez Madeleine; ☑04 42 38 28 02; www.lamado-aix.com; 4 place des Prêcheurs; ⊙7am-2am) This smart daytime cafe, with steel-grey parasols

and box-hedged terrace on a busy square, is unbeatable for coffee and fashionable-people watching; its food, lunch or dinner (lunch/dinner menus €18/32), is equally excellent. The Mado has been around for years, so the old guard dine while the hipsters shine.

Les Deux Garçons   CAFE
(53 cours Mirabeau; ⊙7am-2am) Cézanne and Zola once lingered in this classic brasserie-cafe. Food is classic French, but the spot is better as a drinks place. Ignore the slow service and gaze across the small lane to the former shop where Cézanne's father once sold hats.

Le Mistral   CLUB
(www.mistralclub.fr; 3 rue Frédéric Mistral; ⊙midnight-6am Tue & Sat, nightly during student holidays) If anyone's awake past midnight, chances are they'll wind up at this happening basement club, with three bars and a dance floor. DJs spin house, R&B, techno and rap.

☆ Entertainment

The city has a clutch of good cinemas (www.lescinemasaixois.com).

Scat Club de Jazz   LIVE MUSIC
(☑04 42 23 00 23; http://scatclub.free.fr/scatnet; 11 rue de la Verrerie; ⊙11pm-late Tue-Sat) For a late-night hang-out, descend into this literal hole for jazz, rock, blues or whatever band is booked.

Grand Théâtre de Provence PERFORMING ARTS
(☑04 42 91 69 70; www.legrandtheatre.net; 380 av Max Juvénal) State-of-the-art theatre presenting music and opera.

Shopping

Aix' most chic clothing shops fan out from pedestrian rue Marius Reynaud.

La Chambre aux Confitures   FOOD
(www.lachambreauxconfitures.com; 16bis rue d'Italie; ⊙10am-1pm & 3-7pm Mon-Fri, 10am-7.30pm Sat, 10am-1pm Sun) Do as locals do: ask to taste a jam, chutney or jelly in this outstanding boutique bursting with exotic, unexpected flavours. Best-seller jams include clementine and calisson or apricot and lavender.

Cave du Félibrige   WINE
(☑04 42 96 90 62; www.aix-en-provence.com/cave-felibrige; 8 rue des Cordeliers; ⊙10am-7pm Mon-Sat) A truly splendid array of wines.

ℹ Information

Tourist Office (☑ 04 42 16 11 61; www.aixen-provencetourism.com; 300 av Giuseppe Verdi; ⊘ 8.30am-7pm Mon-Sat, 10am-1pm & 2-6pm Sun, to 8pm Mon-Sat Jun-Sep; ☏) Touch screens add a high-tech air to the usual collection of brochures. Sells tickets for guided tours and cultural events. Helpful staff.

ℹ Getting There & Away

Consult www.lepilote.com for all transport information, www.info-ler.fr for some regional buses and www.navetteaixmarseille.com for shuttle buses to/from Marseille.

BUS

Aix' **bus station** (☑ 08 91 02 40 25, 04 42 91 26 80; place Marius Bastard) is a 10-minute walk southwest from La Rotonde. Sunday service is limited. Services:

Aéroport Marseille Provence €8.20 on bus 40, 40 minutes, every 30 minutes

Arles €10.50, 1½ hours, seven daily

Avignon €17.40, 1¼ hours, six daily

Marseille €5.70, 25 minutes, every 10 minutes

Toulon €13.90, one hour, seven daily

TRAIN

The **city-centre train station** (av Victor Hugo), at the southern end of av Victor Hugo, serves Marseille (€8, 45 minutes).

Aix' TGV station, 15km from the centre and accessible from the bus station (bus 40, €4.10, 15 minutes, every 15 minutes), is a stop on the Paris–Marseille line. The Eurostar that connects London, Lyon, Avignon and Marseille does not stop at Aix' TGV station. To go to London you must change at Lille or Paris.

ℹ Getting Around

Aix en Bus (www.aixenbus.fr; €1) runs local buses; La Rotonde is the main hub. The tourist office has schedules. Minibus 2 links the city-centre train station with La Rotonde.

Taxi Mirabeau (☑ 04 42 21 61 61)

Around Aix-en-Provence

Mountains immortalised in oil and watercolour by Cézanne, wineries and some fabulous lunches are just a short drive from Aix.

⊙ Sights & Activities

★**Montagne Ste-Victoire**   MOUNTAIN
East of Aix towers Cézanne's favourite haunt, the magnificent silvery ridge of Montagne Ste-Victoire, its dry slopes carpeted in *garrigue* (scented scrub), lush pine forests, burnt-orange soil and Coteaux d'Aix-en-Provence vineyards. Many hike the mountain's north side, but the south side, though steeper, is quite beautiful.

If you take the D17 along the south side, pick up info on hiking and biking at the **Maison de Ste-Victoire** (☑ 04 13 31 94 70; www.grandsitesaintevictoire.com; Chemin départemental 17; ⊘ 10am-6pm Mon-Fri, 10.15am-7pm Sat & Sun) in St-Antonin-sur-Bayon. The mountain is closed July and August due to the threat of forest fire (though roads remain open). Driving the loop around Ste-Victoire is gorgeous, or catch bus 110 (www.lepilote.com) from La Rotonde in Aix to Payloubier/St-Antonin-sur-Bayon.

★**Château de Vauvenargues**   CHÂTEAU
(☑ 04 42 26 48 82; 4 rue René Nicol) On the northern side of Montagne Ste-Victoire, the D10 passes **Vauvenargues**, home to 14th-century Château de Vauvenargues, where Picasso is buried. The red-brick castle, bought by the artist in 1958 and his home between 1959 and 1961, still belongs to the Picassos. It opened its doors to visitors in 2009 to raise money for its restoration. It is again closed to the public, but views of it from the evocative village, with Ste-Victoire in the background, are spectacular.

FRENCH CONCENTRATION CAMP

Camp des Milles (☑ 04 42 39 17 11; www.campdesmilles.org; 40 chemin de la Badesse, Les Milles; adult/child €9.50/7.50; ⊘ 10am-7pm, ticket office closes 6pm) Eight kilometres southwest of Aix, this tile factory in Les Milles manufactured 30,000 tonnes of bricks and tiles per year from 1882 until 31 August 1939, when it was turned into a WWII concentration camp. Unnervingly intact, the camp has been preserved as a memorial. Modern exhibits and historical documents illustrate how 10,000 prisoners from 38 countries were held here. Poignant paintings and prose inscribed on the walls by prisoners remain untouched, as does one of the wagons used to transport 2000 prisoners by rail from Les Milles to Auschwitz.

Among the artists and intellectuals interned at Camp des Milles was surrealist painter Max Ernst (1891–1976). Several exhibits are free.

SALON DE PROVENCE

Delve into old-town Salon, fortified in the 12th century, from **place Crousillat**, the prettiest square. From 1547 until his death in 1566, the philosopher Nostradamus lived at **Maison de Nostradamus** (☏ 04 90 56 64 31; 11 rue Nostradamus; adult/child €5/3.15; ⏰ 9am-noon & 2-6pm Mon-Fri, 2-6pm Sat & Sun). Scrolls of Nostradamus' prophecies line the walls, while often-macabre wax figures recreate key scenes from his life. His remains lie behind a plaque inside the Gothic 14th-century **Collégiale St-Laurent** (place St-Laurent).

From the turn of the 20th century until the 1950s, soap was a buoyant business thanks to Salon's abundance of olive oil and the palm and copra oils arriving from the French colonies. **Savonnerie Marius Fabre** (☏ 04 90 53 82 75; www.marius-fabre.fr; 148 av Paul Borret; ⏰ 9.30am-12.30pm & 2-7pm Mon-Sat Apr-Sep, reduced hours rest of year, call for tour times) FREE, run by three generations dating from 1900, paints a vivid portrait of the industry with its small museum. **Savonnerie Rampal-Latour** (☏ 04 90 56 07 28; www.rampal-latour.com; 71 rue Félix Pyat; tours free; ⏰ shop 9am-noon & 2-6pm Mon-Fri, call for tour times) FREE sells soap at factory prices in its beautiful 1907 boutique. Both offer factory tours.

Aqueduc de Roquefavour　　HISTORIC SITE
Take the D64 13km west of Aix to stroll through the trees beneath the Aqueduc de Roquefavour, the world's largest stone aqueduct, built in 1861 to transport water from the River Durance to Marseille. Afterwards lunch at Hôtel-Restaurant Arquier.

Domaine de la Brillane　　WINERY
(☏ 04 42 54 21 44; www.labrillane.com; 195 rte de Couteron; ⏰ 10am-1pm Sat & by appointment) Make an appointment at this organic estate to taste esteemed reds and rosés. Find the brilliant ochre-coloured château surrounded by vineyards 7km north of Aix-en-Provence, signposted 1km off the northbound D13 from Aix to St-Canadet.

🛏 Sleeping & Eating

Hôtel-Restaurant
Arquier　　TRADITIONAL FRENCH €€
(☏ 04 42 24 20 45; www.arquier-restaurant-hotel.com; 2980 rte du Petit-Moulin; r €60-70, weekday/ weekend menus from €15.50/25; ⏰ restaurant noon-2pm; 🕾) This roadside inn with tables along the river gets packed with Aixois enjoying the enormous weekday lunch buffet. Terrace tables proffer a prime view of the Aqueduc de Roquefavour. Stay in simple, comfortable rooms overlooking restful greenery.

⭐ **La Table de Ventabren**　MODERN FRENCH €€€
(☏ 04 42 28 79 33; www.latabledeventabren.com; 1 rue Cézanne; lunch menu Wed-Sat €40, multicourse menus €65-92; ⏰ noon-1.15pm Wed-Sun, 7.45-9.15pm Tue-Sun May-Sep, reduced hours rest of year) Reason enough to visit medieval Ventabren, a hilltop village 16km west of Aix-en-Provence, is this Michelin-starred restaurant with canvas-canopied terrace, magical on summer evenings. Inside find exposed stone and design-led details. Chef Dan Bessoudo creates inventive French dishes and out-of-this-world desserts. Afterwards, hike to the ruined Château de la Reine Jeanne for panoramic views.

Arles & the Camargue

Best Places to Eat

➡ L'Atelier (p185)

➡ Le Gibolin (p185)

➡ Le Mazet du Vaccarès (p189)

➡ La Telline (p189)

➡ La Cabane aux Coquillages (p190)

Best Places to Stay

➡ Le Cloître (p184)

➡ L'Hôtel Particulier (p184)

➡ Hôtel de l'Amphithéâtre (p183)

➡ Lodge Sainte Hélène (p190)

➡ Le Mas de Peint (p188)

Why Go?

Forget all about time in this hauntingly beautiful part of Provence roamed by black bulls, white horses and pink flamingos. This is slow-go Provence, a timeless wetland chequered with silver salt pans, waterlogged rice paddies and movie-style cowboys. Birds provide the most action on this 780-sq-km delta wedged between the Petit Rhône and Grand Rhône. Grab your binoculars, squat in a shack between bulrushes and know, as another flamingo flits across the setting sun, that these magnificent waters, steeped in legend and lore, have a soul of their own.

The main town of the region, diminutive Arles, is a show-stopper. Wander the narrow golden-hued streets that inspired Van Gogh and find the town's lovely restored Roman amphitheatre, top-notch art and history museums, and world-class restaurants. It'll be hard to tear yourself away.

Driving Distances (km)

	Salin de Giraud	Le Sambuc	Stes-Maries-de-la-Mer	La Capelière	Aigues-Mortes
Le Sambuc	15				
Stes-Maries-de-la-Mer	61	59			
La Capelière	22	13	41		
Aigues-Mortes	70	62	33	56	
Arles	38	31	37	21	51

Arles & the Camargue Highlights

❶ Discover Roman **Arles** (p180), trail Van Gogh and enjoy some of Provence's finest restaurants.

❷ Watch rose-pink flamingos at the wondrous **Parc Ornithologique du Pont de Gau** (p186).

❸ Spot local flora and fauna from the trails around **La Capelière** (p187) and **Salin de Badon**.

❹ Pick a fine restaurant to try near **Le Sambuc** (p189).

❺ Gallop like the wind on a horse trek at **Domaine de la Palissade** (p187).

❻ Bike along the edge of the world to a 19th-century lighthouse on the **Digue à la Mer** (p187).

❼ Birdwatch on the **Étang de Vaccarès** (p186) then dine with lighthouse keepers at legendary **Le Mazet du Vaccarès** (p189).

❽ Follow in the footsteps of pilgrims to **Stes-Maries-de-la-Mer** (p189) and its hallowed church.

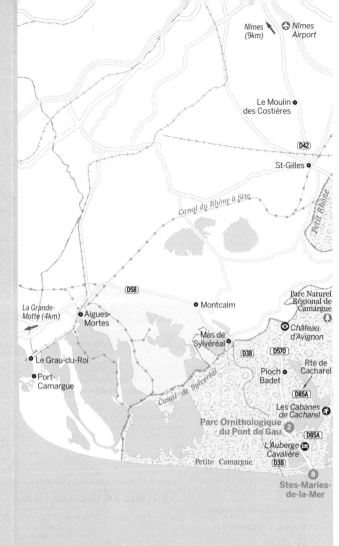

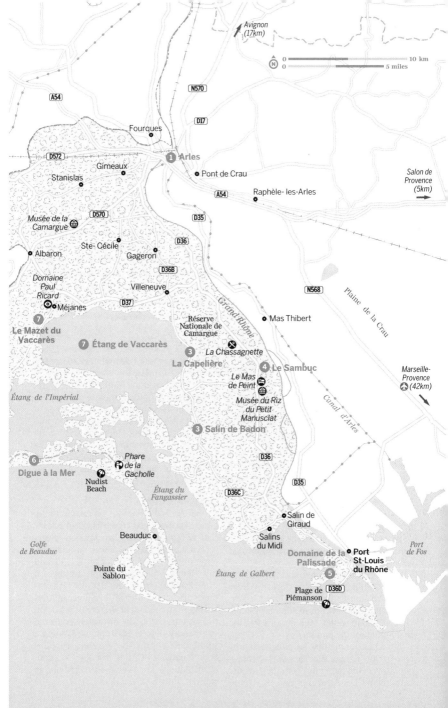

Arles

POP 53,575

Roman treasures, sultry stone squares and a festive atmosphere that crescendos during bullfights makes Arles a seductive stepping stone into the Camargue. And if its colourful sun-baked houses evoke a sense of déjà vu, it's because you've seen them already on a Van Gogh canvas.

Long before the Dutch artist captured starry nights over the Rhône, the Romans had been won over by the charms of the Greek colony Arelate. In 49 BC Arles' prosperity and political standing rose meteorically when it backed a winner in Julius Caesar. After Caesar plundered Marseille, which had supported his rival Pompey the Great, Arles eclipsed Marseille as the region's major port. Soon its citizens were living the high life with gladiator fights and chariot races in magnificent open-air theatres. Still impressively intact, the 12,000-seat theatre and 20,000-seat amphitheatre now stage events including Arles' famous *férias*, with their controversial lethal bullfights, less bloody *courses Camarguaises* and three-day street parties.

Arles' Saturday market is one of the best in Europe.

◉ Sights & Activities

Arles' Roman sights are fantastic, not to be missed. Though Van Gogh lived here and painted 200-odd canvases in Arles, there are no Van Gogh pieces here today; and Van Gogh's little 'yellow house' on place Lamartine, which he painted in 1888, was destroyed during WWII. Nevertheless, there are several ways to pay homage to the master, and the Fondation Vincent van Gogh brings in a work each season.

By 2018, Arles is slated to be graced with a cultural centre designed by world-renowned architect Frank Gehry.

Unless otherwise noted, the last entry to sights is 30 minutes prior to closing. Winter hours are shorter than those listed below; places that close at 7pm in summer usually close at 5pm in winter. Museums are free the first Sunday of the month.

Buy a pass for multiple sights at the tourist office or any Roman site: Passeport Avantage (€16) covers the museums, both theatres, the baths, crypt, Les Alyscamps and the Cloître

St-Trophime; the Passeport Liberté (€12) gives you the choice of six sights total, including two museums.

The **Museon Arlaten** (www.museonarlaten. fr) is closed for renovations until 2018.

★ **Les Arènes**   ROMAN SITE
(Amphithéâtre; adult/child incl Théâtre Antique €9/free; ⊙ 9am-8pm Jul & Aug, to 7pm May-Jun & Sep, shorter hours rest of the year) Slaves, criminals and wild animals (including giraffes) met their dramatic demise before jubilant 20,000-strong crowds during Roman gladiatorial displays at Les Arènes, built around the early 2nd century AD. During the early medieval Arab invasions the arch-laced circular structure – 136m long, 107m wide and 21m tall – was topped with four defensive towers. By the 1820s, when the amphitheatre was returned to its original use, 212 houses and two churches had to be razed on the site.

Buy tickets for bullfights, *courses Camarguaises*, theatre and concerts at the ticket office next to the entrance.

★ **Théâtre Antique**   ROMAN SITE
(☑ 04 90 96 93 30; bd des Lices; adult/child €5.50/ free, adult/child joint ticket with Les Arènes €9/ free; ⊙ 9am-7pm May-Sep, shorter hours rest of the year) Still used for summertime concerts and plays, this outdoor theatre dates to the end of the 1st century BC. For hundreds of years it was a source of construction materials, with workers chipping away at the 102m-diameter structure (the column on the right-hand side near the entrance indicates the height of the original arcade). Enter on rue de la Calade.

★ **Église & Cloître**
St-Trophime   CHURCH, CLOISTER
(place de la République; church free, cloister adult/ child €5.50/free; ⊙ 9am-7pm May-Sep, shorter hours rest of the year) Arles was an archbishopric from the 4th century until 1790, and this Romanesque-style church was once a cathedral. Built in the late 11th and 12th centuries, it's named after St Trophime, an Arles bishop from the 2nd or 3rd century AD. On the western portal, the intricately sculpted tympanum depicts St Trophime holding a spiral staff. Inside, the treasury contains bone fragments of Arles' bishops. Occasional exhibitions are hosted in neighbouring cloister, Cloître St-Trophime.

Arles

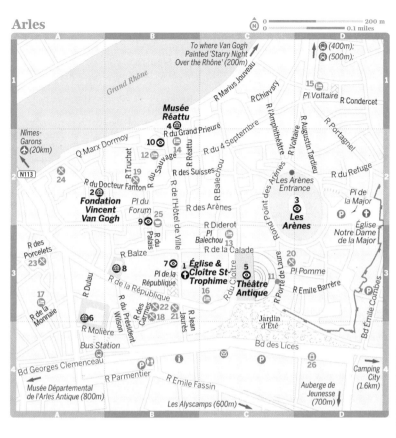

Arles

VINCENT

It's easy to forget that Vincent van Gogh was only 37 when he died, as he appears much older in some of his self-portraits. Born in 1853, the Dutch painter arrived in Arles in 1888 after living in Paris with his younger brother Theo, an art dealer who financially supported Vincent from his own modest income. In Paris he had become acquainted with seminal artists Edgar Degas, Camille Pissarro, Henri de Toulouse-Lautrec and Paul Gauguin.

Revelling in Arles' intense light and bright colours, Van Gogh painted with a burning fervour, unfazed by howling mistrals. During a mistral he would kneel on his canvases and paint horizontally, or lash his easel to iron stakes driven deep into the ground. He sent paintings to Theo for him to try to sell, and dreamed of founding an artists' colony here, but only Gauguin followed up his invitation. Their differing artistic approaches (Gauguin believed in painting from imagination, Van Gogh in painting what he saw) and their artistic temperaments came to a head with the argument in December 1888 that led to Van Gogh lopping off part of his own ear.

In May 1889 Van Gogh voluntarily entered an asylum, Monastère St-Paul de Mausole (p222) in St-Rémy-de-Provence. During his one year, one week, and one day's confinement he painted 150-odd canvases, including masterpieces like *Starry Night* (not to be confused with *Starry Night over the Rhône*, painted in Arles).

In February 1890 his 1888 Arles-painted work *The Red Vines* was bought by Anne Boch, sister of his friend Eugene Boch, for 400 francs (around €50 today) – the only painting he sold in his lifetime. It now hangs in the Pushkin State Museum of Fine Arts.

On 16 May 1890 Van Gogh moved to Auvers-sur-Oise, just outside Paris, to be closer to Theo. But on 27 July that year he shot himself and died two days later with Theo at his side. Theo subsequently had a breakdown, was committed and died, aged 33, just six months after Vincent. Less than a decade later, Van Gogh's talent started to achieve recognition, with major museums acquiring his work.

★ Fondation Vincent Van Gogh
ART MUSEUM

(☎ 04 90 49 94 04; www.fondation-vincentvangogh-arles.org; 35ter rue du Docteur Fanton; adult/child €9/4; ⊗ 11am-7pm Tue-Sun Apr–mid-Sep, to 6pm mid-Sep–Mar) This Van Gogh–themed gallery is a must-see, as much for its contemporary architecture and design, as for the art it showcases. It has no permanent collection; rather, it hosts one or two excellent exhibitions a year, always with a Van Gogh theme and always including at least one Van Gogh masterpiece. Architectural highlights include the rooftop terrace and the coloured-glass bookshop ceiling.

★ Musée Réattu
ART MUSEUM

(☎ 04 90 49 37 58; www.museereattu.arles.fr; 10 rue du Grand Prieuré; adult/child €9/free; ⊗ 10am-6pm Tue-Sun, to 5pm Dec-Feb) This splendid modern-art museum is housed in the exquisitely renovated 15th-century Grand Priory of the Knights of Malta. Among its collections are works by 18th- and 19th-century Provençal artists and two paintings and 57 sketches by Picasso. It hosts wonderfully curated cutting-edge exhibitions.

Place du Forum
ROMAN SITE

(adult/child €4.50/free; ⊗ cryptoportiques 9am-7pm Jul & Aug, shorter hours rest of the year) Just as social, political and religious life revolved around the forum in Roman Arles, so this busy plane-tree-shaded square buzzes with cafe life today. Underneath it lie the underground galleries of **Cryptoportiques** – the forum's subterranean foundations and buried arcades (89m long and 59m wide). These were carved out – the plaza was lower in Roman times – in the 1st century BC. Access is from the **Hôtel de Ville** (Town Hall; place de la République).

Thermes de Constantin
ROMAN SITE

(rue du Grand Prieuré; adult/child €4/free; ⊗ 9am-7pm Jul & Aug, shorter hours rest of the year) Partly preserved Roman baths that were built for Emperor Constantin's private use in the 4th century.

Espace Van Gogh
GALLERY

(☎ 04 90 49 39 39; place Félix Rey) The former hospital where Van Gogh had his ear stitched and was later locked up – not to be confused with the asylum Monastère St-Paul de Mausole (p222) – hosts the occasional exhibition. Other times, its small courtyard garden is worth a peek.

Musée Départemental Arles Antique MUSEUM
(☎04 13 31 51 03; www.arles-antique.cg13.fr; av de la Première Division Française Libre; adult/child €8/5; ⊙10am-6pm Wed-Mon) This striking, state-of-the-art cobalt-blue museum perches on the edge of what used to be the Roman chariot-racing track (circus), 1.5km southwest of the tourist office. The rich collection of pagan and Christian art includes stunning mosaics and an entire wing dedicated to archaeological treasures highlighting Arles' commercial and maritime past.

Les Alyscamps CEMETERY
(av des Alyscamps; adult/child €4/free; ⊙9am-7pm May-Sep, shorter hours rest of the year) Van Gogh and Gauguin both painted this necropolis, founded by the Romans 1km southwest of the centre.

Walking Tours WALKING TOUR
Mapped out in a tourist-office brochure (€1 or download it free online at www.arlestourisme.com, or with an app), evocative walking circuits of the city take in scenes painted by Van Gogh, and Roman or medieval sights.

Festivals & Events

Féria d'Arles BULLFIGHTING
(Féria de Pâques; www.feriaarles.com; ⊙Easter) Festival heralding the start of bullfighting season, with bullfighting in Les Arènes most Sundays in May and June.

Fête des Gardians CULTURAL FESTIVAL
(⊙1 May) Mounted Camargue cowboys parade and hold games during this festival.

Fêtes d'Arles PERFORMING ARTS
(www.festivarles.com; ⊙2 weeks starting around late Jun) Dance, theatre, music and poetry.

L'Abrivado des Bernacles BULL PARADE, EVENT
(www.feriaarles.com; ⊙1st Mon in Jul) Camargue *gardians* (cowboys) shepherd bulls for 15km from paddock to Les Arènes for the season's most prestigious *course Camarguaise,* the **Cocarde d'Or**. Hundreds of aficionados on bike, scooter, foot and horseback follow the *gardians.*

Féria du Riz BULLFIGHTING
(www.feriaarles.com; ⊙Sep) Bullfights during this week-long festival mark the start of the rice harvest.

Sleeping

Arles has reasonably priced, excellent year-round accommodation, which only really fills up during *férias*. Hotels' private parking tends to be pricey.

★ **Hôtel de l'Amphithéâtre** HISTORIC HOTEL €
(☎04 90 96 10 30; www.hotelamphitheatre.fr; 5-7 rue Diderot; s/d/tr/q €61/79/129/139; ❄@🛜👪) Crimson, chocolate, terracotta and other rich, earthy colours dress the exquisite 17th-century stone structure of this stylish hotel, with narrow staircases, a roaring fire and alfresco courtyard breakfasts. The romantic suite has a dreamy lilac-walled terrace overlooking rooftops. Breakfast €8.50.

Le Belvédère Hôtel BOUTIQUE HOTEL €
(☎04 90 91 45 94; www.hotellebelvedere-arles.com; 5 place Voltaire; s €65, d €70-95; ❄🛜) This sleek 17-room hotel is one of the best Arlésian pads. Red-glass chandeliers (and friendly staff) adorn the lobby breakfast area and the super-clean rooms and bathrooms are fitted out in stylish red, chocolate brown and grey. Breakfast €7.50.

Hôtel du Musée BOUTIQUE HOTEL €
(☎04 90 93 88 88; www.hoteldumusee.com; 11 rue du Grand Prieuré; s/d/q from €65/75/120; ⊙mid-Mar–Oct; ❄🛜) In a fine 17th- to 18th-century building, this impeccable hotel has comfortable rooms, a checkerboard-tiled breakfast room and a sugar-sweet patio garden brimming with pretty blossoms. Breakfast €8.50, parking €10.

ADVANCE PLANNING

Mosquitoes Bring insect repellent. Mosquitoes are savage here.

Driving the Camargue Carry water and binoculars. Gas up before leaving town.

Arles féria (bullfighting festival) tickets They're snapped up fast.

Gîte at Salin de Badon Bare-bones but nature rich, this prime real estate fills quickly.

High-end restaurants Reserve in advance.

Bicycle rental Companies in Stes-Maries-de-la-Mer deliver bikes to your door for free; book ahead.

Auberge de Jeunesse
HOSTEL €

(☏ 04 90 96 18 25; www.fuaj.org; 20 av Maréchal Foch; dm incl breakfast & sheets €21; ⊙ mid-Feb–mid-Dec, reception closed 10am-5pm) This sunlit place, made up of eight-bed dorms, is 10 minutes' walk from the centre. Its bar closes at 11pm, just like its gates (except during *férias*).

Camping City
CAMPGROUND €

(☏ 04 90 93 08 86; www.camping-city.com; 67 rte de Crau; sites €20; ⊙ Apr-Sep) Southeast 1.5km on the road to Marseille, Camping City is the closest campground to Arles. Bike hire and laundry facilities are available and there are supermarkets nearby. To get here, take bus 2 to the Hermite stop.

★ Le Cloître
DESIGN HOTEL €€

(☏ 04 88 09 10 00; www.hotel-cloitre.com; 18 rue du Cloître; s/d €100/117-165; @ 🛜) Unbeatable value, the Cloister – 12th-century neighbour to the Cloître Ste-Trophime – is the perfect fusion of historic charm and contemporary design. Its 19 rooms across two floors offer high ceilings, bold colours and a funky mix of patterns and textures. Breakfast (€13), served in the wonderfully airy and 1950s-styled breakfast room, is a particularly stylish affair. No elevator. Free bikes.

There is no lovelier way to end the day than with an *apéro* (aperitif) on the chic rooftop terrace, privy to wonderful views of the sculpted stone facade of the Ste-Trophime cloister.

Hôtel Arlatan
HISTORIC HOTEL €€

(☏ 04 90 93 56 66; www.hotel-arlatan.fr; 26 rue du Sauvage; s/d from €75/95; ⊙ mid-Mar–mid-Nov; ❄ @ 🛜 ☲) The heated swimming pool, pretty garden and plush rooms decorated with antique furniture are just some of the things going for this hotel. Add to that a setting steeped in history, with Roman foundations visible through a glass floor in the lobby and 15th-century paintings on the ceiling of one lounge.

★ L'Hôtel Particulier
BOUTIQUE HOTEL €€€

(☏ 04 90 52 51 40; www.hotel-particulier.com; 4 rue de la Monnaie; d/ste from €309/429; ⊙ Easter-Oct) This exclusive boutique hotel with restaurant, spa and *hammam* (Turkish steambath) oozes chic charm. From the big black door with heavy knocker to the crisp white linens and minimalist decor, everything about this 18th-century private mansion enchants.

✕ Eating

Arles and its environs are foodie heaven. Reserve ahead; hours are reduced in winter.

L'Entrevue
MOROCCAN €

(☏ 04 90 93 37 28; www.lentrevue-restaurant.com; place Nina Berberova; mains €15-19; ⊙ noon-2pm & 7.30-10.30pm; 🖵) Excellent, heaping terracotta *tians* (bowls) of organic *tajines* and couscous are briskly served quayside at this colourful address, just around the corner from the Fondation Vincent van Gogh.

A BULLISH AFFAIR

The *course Camarguaise* is a local Camargue variation of the bullfight, but one in which the bulls aren't harmed. It sees amateur *razeteurs* (from the word 'shave'), wearing skin-tight white shirts and trousers, get as close as they dare to the *taureau* (bull) to try to snatch rosettes and ribbons tied to the bull's horns, using a *crochet* (a razor-sharp comb) held between their fingers. Their leaps over the arena's barrier as the bull charges make spectators' hearts lurch.

Bulls are bred on a *manade* (bull farm) by *manadiers*, who are helped in their daily chores by *gardians* (Camargue cattle-herding cowboys). These mounted herdsmen parade through Arles during the Fête des Gardians (p183) in May.

Many *manades* also breed the creamy white *cheval de Camargue* (Camargue horse) and some welcome visitors; ask at tourist offices in Arles (p185) and Stes-Maries-de-la-Mer (p192).

A calendar of *courses Camarguaises* is online at the **Fédération Française de la Course Camarguaise** (French Federation of Camargue Bullfights; ☏ 04 66 26 05 35; www.ffcc.info), with many occurring at the arena in Stes-Maries-de-la-Mer. *Recortadores* (a type of bull-baiting with lots of bull-jumping) also happens during the bullfighting season (Easter to September).

Au Jardin du Calendal
CAFE €

(☏04 90 96 11 89; www.lecalendal.com; 5 rue Porte de Laure; mains €14-18; ⊙8am-8.30pm; ☏) The leafy courtyard garden at Le Calendal hotel, right by Les Arènes, is perfect for grabbing breakfast, lunching on gourmet salads, or sampling evening snacks.

Comptoir du Sud
CAFE €

(☏04 90 96 22 17; 2 rue Jean Jaurès; sandwiches €4.50-6; ⊙9am-5pm Tue-Fri) Gourmet sandwiches, wraps and bagels (tasty chutneys, succulent meats) and little salads are served at this *épicerie fine* (gourmet grocery). Take away or eat in on bar stools and end with a sweet wedge of homemade *clafoutis* (cherry pie) for dessert.

★ Le Gibolin
BISTRO €€

(☏04 88 65 43 14; 13 rue des Porcelets; menus €27-32, glass wine €4.50-5.50; ⊙12.15-2pm & 8-10pm Tue-Sat Sep-Jul) Sup on peerless home cooking (think cod with fennel confit and crushed potatoes, and *pot au feu* – beef stew), while the friendly patroness bustles between dark wood tables sharing her knowledge and passion for natural wines at Arles' most beloved natural-wine bar. Pairings are naturally *magnifique*. No credit cards.

Au Brin de Thym
BISTRO €€

(☏04 90 97 85 18; brindethym@gmail.com; 22 rue du Docteur Fanton; menus from €25; ⊙noon-2pm & 7-9pm daily Apr-Sep, Thu-Mon Oct-Mar) This effortless bistro in a renovated townhouse offers Arles' best relaxed fine dining. The menu is short, with creative dishes based on seasonal ingredients, without being fussy and the atmosphere is inviting with lively music and happy diners.

★ L'Atelier
GASTRONOMIC €€€

(☏04 90 91 07 69; www.rabanel.com; 7 rue des Carmes; lunch/dinner menus from €65/125; ⊙sittings begin noon-1pm & 8-9pm Wed-Sun) Consider this not a meal, but an artistic experience (with two shiny Michelin stars no less). Every one of the seven or 13 edible works of art is a wondrous composition of flavours, colours and textures courtesy of charismatic chef Jean-Luc Rabanel. Many products are sourced from the chef's organic veggie patch and wine pairings are an adventure in themselves. Half-day cooking classes with/ without lunch are €200/145.

Next door, Rabanel's À Côté (☏04 90 47 61 13; www.bistro-acote.com; 21 rue des Carmes; menus €29; ⊙noon-1.30pm & 7.30-9pm daily) offers delicious bistro fare.

DON'T MISS

ARLES' SATURDAY MARKET

Plan to be in Arles for the whopping Saturday morning market (bd Georges Clemenceau & bd des Lices; ⊙Sat). Camargue salt, goats' cheese and *saucisson d'Arles* (bull-meat sausage) scent the air. Stalls line both sides of the street and visitors and locals alike browse, sample and buy everything from lavender honey and the region's freshest seasonal produce to baby chicks. The scene shifts to bd Émile Combes on Wednesday morning. Stock up for a picnic, or reserve ahead for a late lunch at one of the outstanding local restaurants.

🍷 Drinking & Entertainment

The place du Forum (p182) makes for great cafe sitting. Café van Gogh (11 place du Forum), otherwise called Café de la Nuit, was depicted in Van Gogh's *Café Terrace at Night* (1888). Painted starry-yellow to recreate the painting's feel, it's always packed with tourists.

Roma bands such as Los Reyes and the Gypsy Kings (from Arles no less, discovered while busking in St-Tropez) have performed on the city's streets. Catch Roma bands performing during Stes-Maries-de-la-Mer pilgrimages. Otherwise watch a sangria-fuelled dinner show at La Guinguette du Patio de Camargue (☏06 59 62 18 73; www.la-guinguette-patio-camargue.com; 49 Chemin de Barriol; ⊙meals nightly, occasional performances). The tourist office has lists of what's on.

❶ Information

Tourist Office (☏04 90 18 41 20; www.arlestourisme.com; esplanade Charles de Gaulle, Blvd des Lices; ⊙9am-6.45pm Apr-Sep, to 4.45pm Mon-Fri & 12.45pm Sun Oct-Mar; ☏) Sell maps, cycling itineraries and sightseeing passes; several smartphone apps.

❶ Getting There & Around

BUS

There are services to Aix-en-Provence (€10, 1¾ hours), Stes-Maries-de-la-Mer (€2.50, one hour; www.tout-envia.com) and Nîmes (€1.50, one hour; www.edgard-transport.fr) from the **central bus station** (☏08 10 00 08 16; www.lepilote.com; 24 bd Georges Clemenceau).

Envia (☑ 08 10 00 08 18; www.tout-envia.
com; 24 bd Georges Clemenceau; tickets
€0.80; ☺7am-6.30pm Mon-Fri, 7.30am-noon
& 2-5.30pm Sat) Local buses run 6.30am to
7.30pm Monday to Saturday, and 9.30am to
5.30pm Sunday. Free minibuses circle most of
the old city every 25 minutes from 7.10am to
7.15pm Monday to Saturday.

BICYCLE

Europbike (☑ 06 38 14 49 50; www.europbike-
provence.net; per day adult €10-18, child €8,
electric e-bike €35; ☺8am-6pm) Rents bikes
and runs tours.

TAXI

Arles Taxi Radio (☑ 04 90 96 90 03)

TRAIN

The **train station** (av Paulin Talabot) has services to Nîmes (€9 to €16, 30 to 60 minutes),
Marseille (€16, one hour) and Avignon (€8,
20 minutes). The closest TGV stations are in
Avignon and Nîmes.

Camargue Countryside

Just south of Arles, Provence's rolling
landscapes yield to the flat, marshy wilds
of the Camargue, famous for teeming
birdlife – roughly 500 species. Allow ample
time to birdwatch: grey herons, little egrets,

ARLES & THE CAMARGUE CAMARGUE COUNTRYSIDE

PINK FLAMINGOS

Each year in the Camargue some 10,000
pink or greater flamingo (*Phoenicop-
terus ruber*) couples nest on the Étang
du Fangassier. This 4000-sq-metre
artificial island, constructed in 1970 as a
flamingo-breeding colony, is one of the
rare spots in Europe that guarantees the
flamingo protection from predators.

This well-dressed bird stands between 1.5m and 2m tall and has an
average wing span of 1.9m. When the
flamingo feels threatened, its loud hiss
is similar to the warning sound made
by a goose. Flamingo courtship starts
in January, with mating taking place
from March to May. Come the end of
August or early September, thousands
take flight to Spain, Tunisia and Senegal,
where they winter in warmer climes
before returning to the Camargue in
February. Some 6000 to 7000 flamingos, however, remain in the Rhône delta
year-round.

---

shelducks, avocets, oystercatchers and
yellow-legged gulls are among the species to
spot. King of all is the pink flamingo, which
enjoys the mild winters of these expansive
wetlands.

Equally famous are the Camargue's small
white horses; their mellow disposition
makes horseback riding the ideal way to
explore the region's patchwork of salt pans
and rice fields, and meadows dotted with
grazing bulls. Bring binoculars and mosquito repellent.

Enclosed by the Petit Rhône and Grand
Rhône rivers, most of the Camargue wetlands fall within the 850-sq-km **Parc Naturel
Régional de Camargue** (www.parc-camargue.
fr), established in 1970 to preserve the area's
fragile ecosystems while sustaining local agriculture. Get information at the Musée de la
Camargue.

On the periphery, the 600-sq-km lagoon
Étang de Vaccarès and nearby peninsulas
and islands form the **Réserve Nationale
de Camargue** (www.reserve-camargue.org), a
nature reserve founded in 1927, with an information centre at La Capelière.

The Camargue's two largest towns are the
seaside pilgrim's outpost Stes-Maries-de-la-
Mer and, to the northwest, the walled town
of Aigues-Mortes.

☉ Sights

Musée de la Camargue   MUSEUM
(Musée Camarguais; ☑04 90 97 10 82; www.
parc-camargue.fr; D570, Mas du Pont de Rousty;
adult/child €5/free, 1st Sun of month free; ☺9am-
12.30pm & 1-6pm Wed-Mon Apr-Oct, 10am-12.30pm
& 1-5pm Nov-Mar) Inside a 19th-century sheep
shed 10km southwest of Arles, this museum
evokes traditional local life: exhibitions cover history, ecosystems, farming techniques,
flora and fauna. *L'Oeuvre Horizons* by Japanese artist Tadashi Kawamata – aka a wood-
en observatory shaped like a boat – provides
a bird's-eye view of the agricultural estate,
crossed by a 3.5km walking trail. The headquarters of the Parc Naturel Régional de
Camargue are also based here.

★**Parc Ornithologique
du Pont de Gau**   NATURE PARK
(☑04 90 97 82 62; www.parcornithologique.
com; D570, Pont du Gau; adult/child €7.50/5;
☺9am-sunset Apr-Sep, from 10am Oct-Mar) Pink
flamingos pirouette overhead and stalk the
watery landscape at this bird park, home to
every bird species known to set foot in the

Camargue. Watch them from the 7km of beautiful trails that meander through the site. Find the park on the D570 in Pont du Gau, 4km north of Stes-Maries-de-la-Mer.

★ **Digue à la Mer** DIKE

`FREE` This 2.5m-high dike was built in the 19th century to cut the delta off from the sea. A 20km-long walking and cycling track runs along its length linking Stes-Maries with the solar-powered Phare de la Gacholle (1882), a lighthouse automated in the 1960s. Footpaths cut down to lovely sandy beaches, and views of pink flamingos strutting across the marshy planes are second to none. Walking on the fragile sand dunes is forbidden.

★ **La Capelière** NATURE PARK

(☑ 04 90 97 00 97; www.reserve-camargue.org; La Capelière; permits adult/child €3/1.50; ☺ 9am-1pm & 2-6pm daily Apr-Sep, 9am-1pm & 2-5pm Wed-Mon Oct-Mar; 🖐) ◆ This information centre for the Réserve Nationale de Camargue sells permits for the observatories and 4.5km of nature trails at wild Salin de Badon, former royal salt pans 7km south. True birders must not miss a night in its gîte (dorms €12), a cottage with 20 beds over seven rooms, kitchen, toilet and solar electricity. BYO food, drinking water, bedding and mosquito spray. At La Capelière's 1.5km-long Sentier des Rainettes (Tree-Frog Trail) discover flora and fauna native to freshwater marshes.

★ **Domaine de la Palissade** NATURE PARK

(☑ 04 42 86 81 28; www.palissade.fr; rte de la Mer; adult/child €3/free; ☺ 9am-6pm mid-Jun–mid-Sep, to 5pm mid-Sep–mid-Nov & Mar–mid-Jun, 9am-5pm Wed-Sun mid-Nov–Feb) This remote nature centre, 12km south of Salin de Giraud, organises fantastic forays through marshland, scrubby glasswort, flowering sea lavender (August) and lagoons, on foot and horseback; call ahead to book horse treks (€18 per hour). Before hitting the scrub, rent binoculars (€2) and grab a free map of the estate's three marked walking trails (1km to 8km) from the office.

Château d'Avignon CASTLE

(☑ 04 13 31 94 54; www.chateaudavignon.fr; rte d'Arles, D570; adult/child €4/free; ☺ 9.45am-12.30pm & 1.30-5.30pm Wed-Sun Apr-Oct, Thu & Fri by appointment only Nov-Mar) The park surrounding this 18th-century château is free to wander. The castle itself was owned by Lou-

BEST TREKS & SAFARIS

Cabanes de Cacharel

Camargue Découverte

Kayak Vert Camargue (p188)

La Maison du Guide

Le Mas de Peint (p188)

is Prat-Noilly, a Marseillais merchant, who used it as a hunting lodge.

🏃 Activities

Horse Riding

La Maison du Guide OUTDOORS

(☑ 04 66 73 52 30; www.maisonduguide.camargue.fr) Discovery weekends by naturalist Jean-Marie Espuche embrace birdwatching, cycling, horse riding and sunrise nature walks.

Cabanes de Cacharel HORSE RIDING

(☑ 06 11 57 74 75, 04 90 97 84 10; www.cabanes-decacharel.com; rte de Cacharel, D85A; 1/2/3hr horse trek €20/30/40) Farms along rte d'Arles (D570) offer *promenades à cheval* (horseback riding) astride white Camargue horses, but a more authentic experience can be had at these stables, just north of Stes-Maries-de-la-Mer along the parallel rte de Cacharel (D85A). Horse-and-carriage rides too (one hour, €15).

Camargue Découverte ADVENTURE TOUR

(☑ 06 85 35 10 04; www.camargue-decouverte.com; 24 rue Porte de Laure) Delve into the delta by 4WD jeep on safari-style half-day trips, which can be combined with horseback rambles.

Boating & Water Sports

Tiki III BOATING

(☑ 04 90 97 81 68; www.tiki3.fr; ☺ mid-Mar–mid-Nov) *Le Tiki III* is a paddleboat moored at the mouth of the Petit Rhône, 1.5km west of Stes-Maries-de-la-Mer next to Camping Le Clos du Rhône.

Absolut Kiteboarding WATER SPORTS

(☑ 06 88 15 10 93; www.absolutkiteboarding.fr; 36 rte d'Arles, Salin de Giraud; group/private lesson €130/300) Ride the waves and the wind with this recommended kitesurfing school, headed by Patrick. March to November you're on the water, December to February on dry ground. The school runs a shop and rents gear (€70). Find it at the northern entrance to Salin de Giraud, on the D36.

AIGUES-MORTES

Actually located over the border from Provence in the Gard *département*, the pictur-esque town of Aigues-Mortes sits 28km northwest of Stes-Maries-de-la-Mer at the western extremity of the Camargue. Set in flat marshland and encircled by high stone walls, the town was established in the mid-13th century by Louis IX to give the French crown a Mediterranean port under its direct control. Cobbled streets inside the walls are lined with restaurants, cafes and bars, giving it a festive atmosphere and making it a charming spot from which to explore the Camargue.

Scaling the ramparts rewards you with sweeping views. Head to the top of the tower, **Tour de Constance** (www.tourdeconstance.com; adult/child €7.50/free; ☉10am-7pm May-Aug, to 5.30pm Sep-Apr); the 1.6km wall-top walk takes about one hour.

L'Hermitage de St-Antoine (☑06 03 04 34 05; www.hermitagesa.com; 9 bd Intérieur Nord; r incl breakfast €88; ❄), inside the walled town, has four artfully appointed rooms, one with a small private terrace. **Hôtel L'Escale** (☑04 66 53 71 14; http://hotel.escale.free. fr; 3 av Tour de Constance; d €40-68, q €75-85; 🛜📶) caters fantastically to budget travellers.

The **tourist office** (☑04 66 53 73 00; www.ot-aiguesmortes.fr; place St-Louis; ☉9am-6pm) is inside the walled city.

Kayak Vert Camargue
CANOEING
(☑04 66 73 57 17; www.kayakvert-camargue.fr; Mas de Sylvéréal; kayak 1hr/day €10/32; ☉7am-7pm Mar-Oct) For canoeing and kayaking on the Petit Rhône, contact Kayak Vert Camargue, 14km north of Stes-Maries-de-la-Mer off the D38.

🐎 Courses

Manade Salierène
COURSE
(☑04 66 86 45 57; www.manadesalierene.com; D37, Mas de Capellane) Get a taste of cowboy life with a one-week *stage de monte gardiane* (Camargue cowboy course). Initiation/perfection courses (adult/child €750/665) include accommodation and meals with the *manadier's* (bull breeder's) family.

🛏 Sleeping

Ranch-style motel accommodation lines the D570 heading into Stes-Maries-de-la-Mer. The tourist offices list self-catering *cabanes de gardian* (traditional whitewashed cowboy cottages) and farmstays.

★ Mas de Calabrun
HOTEL €€
(☑04 90 97 82 21; www.mas-de-calabrun.fr; rte de Cacharel, D85A; d/roulotte €129/169; ☉mid-Feb–mid-Nov; @🛜📶) From the striking equestrian sculpture in its front courtyard to the swish pool, stylish restaurant terrace and fabulous views of open Camargue country-side, this hotel thoroughly deserves its three stars. The icing on the cake, however, is its trio of *chic roulottes* (old-fashioned 'gypsy'

wagons), which promise the perfect romantic getaway. Breakfast buffet €15.

★ Cacharel Hotel
HOTEL €€
(☑04 90 97 95 44; www.hotel-cacharel.com; rte de Cacharel, D85A; s/d/tr/q €132/144/156/178, horse riding per hour €32; ☉year-round; @🛜📶📶) This isolated farmstead, 400m down an unpaved track off the D85A just north of Stes-Maries-de-la-Mer, perfectly balances modern-day comforts with rural authenticity. Photographic portraits of the bull herder who created the hotel in 1947 (son Florian runs the three-star hotel with much love today) give the vintage dining room soul. Rooms sit snug in whitewashed cottages, some overlooking the water.

Swings in the paddock, horse riding with a *gardian* (cowboy), boules to play *pétanque* and bags of open space make it a perfect family choice.

★ Le Mas de Peint
BOUTIQUE HOTEL €€€
(☑04 90 97 20 62; www.masdepeint.com; Le Sambuc; d from €270, lunch/dinner menus from €41/59; ☉mid-Mar–mid-Nov; ❄🛜📶) So chic and gentrified it almost feels out of place in the Camargue, this upmarket *mas* (farm-house) – part of the luxurious Châteaux & Hôtels Collection – is right out of design mag *Côte Sud*. The good news: nonguests are welcome in its gourmet restaurant and swish, poolside canteen.

The operators also run flamenco, bull-herding and birdwatching weekends.

Eating

The Camargue countryside, especially around Le Sambuc and Villeneuve, harbours top eateries, from simple roadside dining or family inns to Michelin-starred gastrotemples.

Estrambord CAMARGUAIS €
(☏04 90 97 20 10; www.lestrambord.fr; Le Sambuc; 3-course menu €16-20; ☺noon-2pm Sun-Fri) A roadside diner, Camargue-style. Feast on local specialities from seafood to bull.

★La Telline CAMARGUAIS €€
(☏04 90 97 01 75; www.restaurantlatelline.fr; rte de Gageron, Villeneuve; mains €24-35; ☺noon-1.15pm & 7.30-9pm Fri-Mon) A true local favourite, this isolated cottage restaurant with sage-green wooden shutters could not be simpler or more authentic. Summer dining is in a small and peaceful flower-filled garden, and the no-frills menu features a straightforward choice of *tellines* (edible molluscs), salad or terrine as starter followed by grilled fish or meat, or a beef or bull steak. No credit cards.

★Le Mazet du Vaccarès CAMARGUAIS, SEAFOOD €€
(Chez Hélène et Néné; ☏04 90 97 10 79; www.mazet-du-vaccares.fr; south of Méjanes; 3-course menu €35; ☺10am-11pm Fri-Sun, closed mid-Aug–mid-Sep & mid-Dec–mid-Jan) Gorging on fish in this legendary lakeside cabin is a feast for the eyes and belly. Memorabilia from Hélène and Néné's days as lighthouse keepers in Beauduc fill the restaurant with soul. The jovial couple cook up one fixed *menu* built from the catch of local fishers. From Domaine Paul Ricard, it is signposted 2.5km drive south along potholed gravel.

Chez Bob CARMARGUAIS €€
(☏04 90 97 00 29; http://restaurantbob.fr; Mas Petite Antonelle, rte du Sambuc, Villeneuve; menu €45; ☺noon-2pm & 7.30-9pm Wed-Sun) This house restaurant is an iconic address adored by Arlésians. Feast on grilled bull chops, duck breasts and lamb beneath trees or inside between walls plastered in photos, posters and other memorabilia collected over the years by Jean-Guy, alias 'Bob'. Find his pad 20km south of Arles in Villeneuve, 800m after the crossroads on the D37 towards Salin. Reserve online.

La Chassagnette GASTRONOMIC €€€
(☏04 90 97 26 96; www.chassagnette.fr; rte du Sambuc; mains €37-39; ☺noon-1.30pm & 7-9.30pm Thu-Mon Mar-Jun, Sep & Oct, daily Jul & Aug, reduced hours Nov-Mar) Inhaling the scent of sun-ripened tomatoes is one of many pleasures at this 19th-century sheepfold – the ultimate top-euro Camargue dine. Alain Ducasse prodigy Armand Arnal cooks up a 100% organic menu, grows much of it himself and woos guests with a mosquito-protected outside terrace. Look for the fork and trowel sign, 12km southeast of Arles on the southbound D36, just north of Le Sambuc.

Stes-Maries-de-la-Mer

POP 2400

This remote seaside outpost has a rough-and-tumble holidaymaker feel, with white-washed buildings crowding dusty streets. During its Roma pilgrimages, street-cooked pans of paella fuel chaotic crowds of carnivalesque guitarists, dancers and mounted cowboys. Tickets for bullfights and *courses Camarguaises* are sold at the seafront village arena.

⊙ Sights & Activities

Stes-Maries-de-la-Mer is fringed by 30km of fine-sand beaches, easily reached by bicycle. Nudist beaches surround the Gacholle lighthouse off the Digue à la Mer (p187).

★Église des Stes-Maries CHURCH
(www.sanctuaire-des-saintesmaries.fr; place Jean XXIII; ☺rooftop 10am-noon & 2-5pm Mon-Sat, 2-5pm Sun) This 12th- to 15th-century church, with its dark, hushed, candle-wax-scented atmosphere, draws legions of pilgrim Roma to venerate the statue of Sara, their revered patron saint, during the Pèlerinage des Gitans. The relics of Sara and those of Marie-Salomé and Marie-Jacobé, all found in the crypt by King René in 1448, are enshrined in a wooden chest, stashed in the stone wall above the choir. Don't miss the panorama from the rooftop terrace (€2.50).

BEST NATURE TRAILS

Digue à la Mer (p187)

La Capelière & Salin de Badon (p187)

Parc Ornithologique du Pont de Gau (p186)

Musée de la Camargue (p186)

Domaine de la Palissade (p187)

Boating

Les Quatre Maries
BOATING

(🖉04 90 97 70 10; www.bateaux-4maries.camargue.fr; 36 av Théodore Aubanel; 1½hr adult/child €12/6; ⊘mid-Mar–Oct) Powerboat company offering trips through the marshy Camargue.

Le Camargue
BOATING

(🖉06 17 95 81 96; http://bateau-camargue.com; 5 rue des Launes; 1½hr adult/child €12/6; ⊘mid-Mar–Oct) Explore the Camargue marshlands via this powerboat company, with a kiosk on Av Théodore Aubanel.

Cycling

Bicycles are ideal on the Camargue's flat terrain. East of Stes-Maries-de-la-Mer, seafront paths like Digue à la Mer (p187) are reserved for walkers and cyclists. The following both deliver bikes for free to hotels.

Le Vélo Saintois
CYCLING

(🖉04 90 97 74 56; www.levelosaintois.camargue.fr; 19 rue de la République; per day adult/child €15/13.50, tandem €30; ⊘9am-7pm Mar-Nov), with an English-language list of cycling routes, rents bikes of all sizes.

Le Vélociste
CYCLING

(🖉04 90 97 83 26; www.levelociste.fr; place Mireille, Stes; per day adult/child €15/13.50; ⊘9am-7pm Mar-Nov) rents and organises cycling-horseback (€36) or cycling-canoeing (€30) packages.

🛏 Sleeping

Hôtel Méditerranée
HOTEL €

(🖉04 90 97 82 09; www.hotel-mediterranee.camargue.fr; 4 av Frédéric Mistral; d/tr/q from €48/75/85; ⊘mid-Mar–mid-Nov; 🐾) This whitewashed cottage hotel, festooned with an abundance of flowerpots steps from the sea, is truly a steal. Its 14 rooms – three with their own little terrace garden – are spotlessly clean, and breakfast (€7) is served in summer on a pretty vine-covered patio garden – equally festooned with strawberry plants, geraniums and other potted flowers. Bike rental €15 per day.

Camping Le Clos du Rhône
CAMPGROUND €

(🖉04 90 97 85 99; www.camping-leclos.fr; rte d'Aigues Mortes; tent, car & 2 adults €26.50; ⊘Apr-Oct; @🛜🌊🏊) Right by the beach, this large and well-equipped campground sports the whole range of accomodation options: tent pitches, wooden chalets, self-catering cottages. The pool with two-lane water slide and a beachside spa with jacuzzi and *hammam* make it a real family favourite.

★Lodge Sainte Hélène
BOUTIQUE HOTEL €€€

(🖉04 90 97 83 29; www.lodge-saintehelene.com; chemin Bas des Launes; d €150-190; 🅿@🛜🌊) These designer-chic, pearly-white terraced cottages strung along a lake edge are prime real estate for birdwatchers and romance seekers. The mood is exclusive, remote and so quiet you can practically hear flamingo wings flapping overhead. Each room comes with a birdwatchers' guide and binoculars, and dynamic owner Benoît Noel is a font of local knowledge. Breakfast €15.

🍴 Eating

★La Cabane aux Coquillages
SEAFOOD €

(🖉06 10 30 33 49; www.degustationcoquillageslessaintesmariesdelamer.com; 16 av Van Gogh; shellfish €6.50-12.50; ⊘noon-3pm & 5-11pm Apr-Nov) The shellfish-and-*apéro* branch of neighbouring Ô Pica Pica, this bright blue 'shack' with crates of crustaceans piled high

---

THE STORY OF THE MARYS & GITAN PILGRIMAGES

Catholicism first reached European shores in what's now tiny Stes-Maries-de-la-Mer. The stories say that Stes Marie-Salomé and Marie-Jacobé (and some say Mary Magdalene) fled the Holy Land in a little boat and were caught in a storm, drifting at sea until washing ashore here.

Provençal and Catholic lore diverge at this point: Catholicism relates that Sara, patron saint of the *gitans* (Roma Gitano people, also known as gypsies), travelled with the two Marys on the boat. Provençal legend says Sara was already here and was the first person to recognise their holiness. In 1448 skeletal remains said to belong to Sara and the two Marys were found in a crypt in Stes-Maries-de-la-Mer.

Gitans continue to make pilgrimages, **Pèlerinage des Gitans**, here on 24 and 25 May (often staying for up to three weeks), dancing and playing music in the streets, and parading a statue of Sara through town. The Sunday in October closest to the 22nd sees a second pilgrimage dedicated to the two Stes Maries; *courses Camarguaises* are also held at this time.

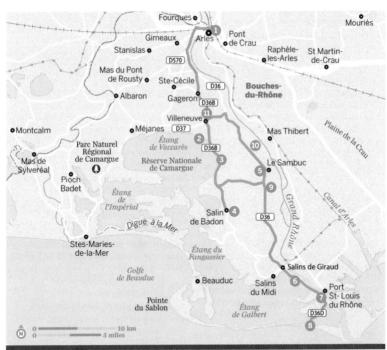

Driving Tour
The Wild Southeast

START ARLES
END VILLENEUVE
LENGTH 85KM; ONE DAY

For a jaunt to the edge of the world, drive south from ① **Arles** along the D570 (direction Stes-Maries-de-la-Mer). After 2.8km, turn left onto the D36 (direction Le Sambuc and Salin de Giraud) and within seconds you're in the Parc Naturel Régional de Camargue. Four kilometres on, turn right onto the D36B (direction Gageron) and at the crossroads continue straight.

Soon after, the D36B dramatically skims the eastern shores of the ② **Étang de Vaccarès** (p186). The wetland is at its most savage here and much of the area is off limits, making the nature trails and wildlife observatories at ③ **La Capelière** (p187) particularly precious. Play voyeur as little egrets and grey herons frolic in the marshes, and buy a permit for the nature trails at ④ **Salin de Badon** (7km south).

Cut back to ⑤ **Le Sambuc** for lunch at La Chassagnette (p189), Estrambord (p189)

or Le Mas de Peint (p188), which also offers horse-riding and jeep tours by appointment.

South along the D36C skip through Salin de Giraud, an unexceptional village that grew up around Europe's largest *salins* (salt pans), producing 800,000 tonnes per year. Take in the windswept panorama of the pans, salt mountains and diggers 2km south of the village at the ⑥ **point de vue** (viewpoint) along the D36D.

The unforgettable final 12km leg of this southbound journey passes pink flamingos wading through water on your way to ⑦ **Domaine de la Palissade** (p187), a nature centre with walks and horse treks.

The road terminates at ⑧ **Plage de Piémanson** 3.7km south, where campervans park overnight on the sand.

On the return to Arles along the D36, you can swing into the tiny ⑨ **Musée du Riz du Petit Manusclat** and ⑩ **Domaine de Beaujeu**, to learn about and buy local produce. Then dine well at ⑪ **La Telline** (p189) in Villeneuve.

DINING SUR LA PLAGE

Lunch *sur la plage* (on the beach) never fails to seduce and Stes-Maries-de-la-Mer lives up to the promise with two hip and dandy beach restaurants, both open May to September.

Heading east towards the Digue à la Mer on sandy Plage Est is **La Playa** (☑ 06 29 48 82 01; www.laplaya-en-camargue.fr; Plage Est; mains €17-20; ☺ 8am-midnight May-Sep; ☎), a chic choice, with a particularly vibrant *apéro* (predinner drink) and after-dark scene, shoals of fresh fish cooked up *à la plancha* (grilled), and a great daytime buzz revolving around tasty lunches, free wi-fi and super-comfy sunloungers on the sand.

In the opposite direction, on equally sandy Plage Ouest, is **Calypso – Lou Santen** (☑ 07 71 03 43 46; av Riquette Aubanel, Plage Ouest; fish & shellfish platters €12-16, mains €19.50-23; ☺ 10am-7pm May-Sep, to 11pm Sat Jul & Aug), shaded by a typical reed pergola with a picture-postcard view of the sea. Feast on good-value, finger-licking bowls of *moules* (mussels) at tables on an elevated wooden-decking terrace, then rent a sunlounger (€12) for a sand-side siesta.

inside and a gaggle of sea-blue chairs outside is pure gold. Wash down half a dozen oysters (€6.50), locally harvested *tellines* (€8.50) or your choice of *fritures* (deep-fried and battered baby prawns, baby squid or anchovies, €12.50) with a glass of chilled white, and enter nirvana.

★ **Ô Pica Pica** SEAFOOD €€
(☑ 06 10 30 33 49; www.degustationcoquillages-lessaintesmariesdelamer.com; 16 av Van Gogh; mains €17-22; ☺ noon-3pm & 7-11pm Mar-Nov) Fish and shellfish do not come fresher than this. Watch them get gutted, filleted and grilled in the 'open' glass-walled kitchen, then devour your meal on the sea-facing pavement terrace or out back in the typically Mediter-

ranean white-walled garden. Simplicity is king here: plastic glasses, fish and shellfish platters; no coffee and no credit cards.

❶ Information

Tourist Office (☑ 04 90 97 82 55; www.saintesmaries.com; 5 av Van Gogh; ☺ 9am-7pm) Guided walking tours (€7) depart 2pm Tuesday and Friday.

❶ Getting There & Around

Le Vélo Saintois (p190) and Le Vélociste (p190) hire bicycles. Seasonal buses to/from Arles (www.lepilote.com; €2.90, one hour, eight daily) use the bus shelter at the northern entrance to town on av d'Arles (the continuation of rte d'Arles and the D570).

Avignon & Around

Best Places to Eat

➡ L'Oustau de Baumanière
(p225)

➡ Le Verger des Papes (p206)

➡ Le Moulin à Huile (p211)

➡ Le Vivier (p219)

➡ 83.Vernet (p201)

➡ Christian Etienne (p201)

Best Places
to Stay

➡ Hôtel La Mirande (p200)

➡ Sous les Figuiers (p223)

➡ La Prévôté (p219)

➡ Mas de l'Amarine (p224)

Why Go?

Encircled by crenellated ramparts dating back 800 years, Avignon lords above the mighty Rhône. Its 14th-century hilltop palace – the former seat of popes – defines the skyline and begs for exploration, while the narrow streets and leafy squares fanning out beneath it invite wandering.

Rolling countryside unfurls outside Avignon, dotted with ancient villages and vineyards that produce some of France's best wines. Sample renowned vintages in Châteauneuf-du-Pape or in the saw-toothed Dentelles de Montmirail. Discover incredibly preserved Roman ruins in Orange, Nîmes and St-Rémy-de-Provence, and explore medieval streets in Vaison-la-Romaine and Les Baux-de-Provence.

The glass-green River Sorgue – ready-made for canoeing – connects picturesque towns like L'Isle-sur-la-Sorgue, celebrated for antiques shopping, and Fontaine-de-Vaucluse, the river's mysterious source. Hikers and bikers flock to windswept Mont Ventoux, Provence's highest peak, rising from purple lavender fields that perfume the summer breeze.

Driving Distances (km)

	Nîmes	Carpentras	Vaison-la-Romaine	Orange	St-Rémy-de-Provence
Carpentras	67				
Vaison-la-Romaine	80	24			
Orange	53	22	28		
St-Rémy-de-Provence	41	45	70	48	
Avignon	42	25	46	27	20

Avignon & Around Highlights

1 Explore palaces, bridges and ancient streets in **Avignon** (p196).

2 Sample France's great wines in **Châteauneuf-du-Pape** (p205).

3 Revive Rome at the **Théâtre Antique** (p207) in Orange.

4 Climb to hilltop, medieval **Vaison-la-Romaine** (p209).

5 Paddle beneath the famous **Pont du Gard** (p229).

6 Village-hop through the **Dentelles de Montmirail** (p211).

7 Ascend Provence's mightiest peak, **Mont Ventoux** (p213).

8 Antique-shop and explore canals in **L'Isle-sur-la-Sorgue** (p218).

9 Spot royalty, explore Roman ruins and make a pilgrimage to Van Gogh's last home in **St-Rémy-de-Provence** (p222).

10 Joust with gladiatorial ghosts at the spectacular arena in **Nîmes** (p226).

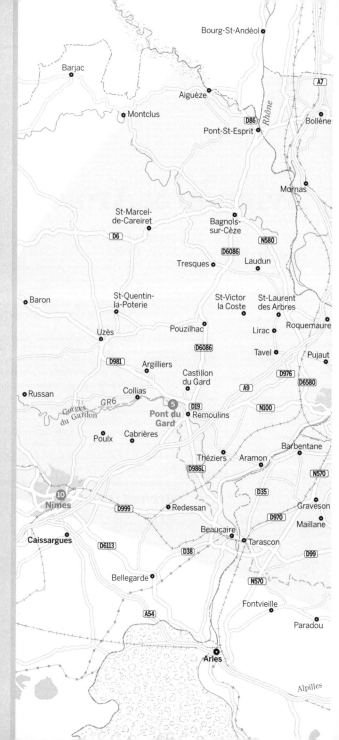

AVIGNON

POP 91,250

Graceful Avignon's turn as the seat of papal power bestowed on the city a treasury of magnificent art and architecture, none grander than the massive medieval fortress and papal palace, Palais des Papes. Ringed by incredibly preserved 800-year-old stone ramparts, Avignon is now a lively student city, its ancient cobbled streets lined with inviting boutiques and its leafy squares overflowing with cafe tables. In July thousands come for the renowned performing-arts festival.

History

Avignon first gained its ramparts – and reputation for arts and culture – during the 14th century, when Pope Clement V fled political turmoil in Rome. From 1309 to 1377, seven French-born popes invested huge sums in the papal palace and offered asylum to Jews and political dissidents. Pope Gregory XI left Avignon in 1376, but his death two years later led to the Great Schism (1378–1417), during which rival popes (up to three at one time) resided at Rome and Avignon, denouncing and excommunicating one another. Even after the matter was settled and an impartial pope, Martin V, established himself in Rome, Avignon remained under papal rule. Avignon and Comtat Venaissin (now the Vaucluse *département*) were ruled by papal legates until 1791.

◉ Sights & Activities

Ticket offices for sights close 30 to 60 minutes before overall closing time.

★ **Palais des Papes**   PALACE
(Papal Palace; www.palais-des-papes.com; place du Palais; adult/child €11/9, with Pont St-Bénezet €13.50/10.50; ⊙9am-8pm Jul, to 8.30pm Aug,

---

ⓘ AVIGNON PASS

An excellent-value discount card, Avignon Passion yields cheaper admission to big-hitter museums and monuments in Avignon and Villeneuve-lès-Avignon. The first site visited is full price, but each subsequent site is discounted. The pass is free, is valid 15 days, covers a couple of tours too, and is available at the tourist office (p203) and at museums.

---

shorter hours Sep-Jun) Palais des Papes, a Unesco World Heritage Site, is the world's largest Gothic palace. Built when Pope Clement V abandoned Rome in 1309, it was the papal seat for 70-odd years. The immense scale testifies to the papacy's wealth; the 3m-thick walls, portcullises and watchtowers show their insecurity.

It takes imagination to picture the former luxury of these bare, cavernous stone halls, but multimedia audioguides (€2) assist. Highlights include 14th-century chapel frescoes by Matteo Giovannetti, and the Chambre du Cerf with medieval hunting scenes.

Ask at the ticket desk about **guided tours**.

★ **Place du Palais**   SQUARE
A golden statue of the Virgin Mary (weighing 4.5 tonnes) stands on the dome of Romanesque **Cathédrale Notre Dame des Doms** (built 1671–72), outstretched arms protecting the city. Next to the cathedral, the hilltop **Rocher des Doms** gardens provide knockout views of the Rhône, Mont Ventoux and Les Alpilles; there's also a **playground**. Opposite the palace, the much-photographed building dripping with carvings of fruit and heraldic beasts is the 17th-century former mint, **Hôtel des Monnaies**.

★ **Pont St-Bénezet**   BRIDGE
(bd du Rhône; adult/child 24hr ticket €5/4, with Palais des Papes €13.50/10.50; ⊙9am-8pm Jul, to 8.30pm Aug, shorter hours Sep-Jun) Legend says Pastor Bénezet had three saintly visions urging him to build a bridge across the Rhône. Completed in 1185, the 900m-long bridge with 20 arches linked Avignon with Villeneuve-lès-Avignon. It was rebuilt several times before all but four of its spans were washed away in the 1600s.

If you don't want to pay to visit the bridge, admire it free from Rocher des Doms park or Pont Édouard Daladier or on Île de la Barthelasse's chemin des Berges.

Don't be surprised if you spot someone dancing: in France, the bridge is known as Pont d'Avignon after the nursery rhyme: 'Sur le pont d'Avignon/L'on y danse, l'on y danse...' (On Avignon Bridge, all are dancing...)

★ **Musée Calvet**   MUSEUM
(☑04 90 86 33 84; www.musee-calvet.org; 65 rue Joseph Vernet; adult/child €6/3; ⊙10am-1pm & 2-6pm Wed-Mon) Elegant Hôtel de Villeneuve-Martignan (built 1741–54) provides a fitting backdrop for Avignon's fine-arts museum, with 16th- to 20th-century oil paintings,

compelling prehistoric pieces, 15th-century wrought iron, and the elongated landscapes of Avignonnais artist Joseph Vernet.

★ **Musée du Petit Palais** MUSEUM
(www.petit-palais.org; place du Palais; adult/child €6/free; ⊙10am-1pm & 2-6pm Wed-Mon) The archbishops' palace during the 14th and 15th centuries now houses outstanding collections of primitive, pre-Rennaissance, 13th- to 16th-century Italian religious paintings by artists including Botticelli, Carpaccio and Giovanni di Paolo – the most famous is Botticelli's *La Vierge et l'Enfant* (1470).

★ **Collection Lambert** GALLERY
(www.collectionlambert.com; 5 rue Violette; adult/child €10/8; ⊙11am-6pm Tue-Sun Sep-May, to 7pm daily Jul & Aug) Reopened in summer 2015 after significant renovation and expansion, Avignon's contemporary-arts museum focuses on works from the 1960s to the present. Work spans from minimalist and conceptual to video and photography – in stark contrast to the classic 18th-century mansion housing it.

Musée Angladon MUSEUM
(www.angladon.com; 5 rue Laboureur; adult/child €6.50/4.50; ⊙1-6pm Tue-Sun mid-Mar–Nov, closed Mon & Tue mid-Nov–mid-Mar; 🛜) Tiny Musée Angladon harbours impressionist treasures, including *Railway Wagons*, the only Van Gogh in Provence (look closely and notice the 'earth' isn't paint but bare canvas). Also displayed is a handful of early Picasso sketches and artworks by Cézanne, Sisley, Manet and Degas; upstairs are antiques and 17th-century paintings.

Le Carré du Palais WINE TASTING
(☑04 90 27 24 00; www.carredupalaisavignon.com; 1 place du Palais) The historic Hôtel Calvet de la Palun building in central Avignon has been renovated into a wine centre promoting and serving Côtes du Rhône and Vallée du Rhône appellations. Stop in to get a taste of the local vintages.

☞ Tours

The tourist office (p203) leads year-round themed, guided walks (from €15) in English and French, and has good self-guided-tour maps, also online.

Les Grands Bateaux de Provence BOAT TOUR
(☑04 90 85 62 25; www.mireio.net; allées de l'Oulle; boat tours incl meal adult/child from €40/28) Runs day-long boat tours to Arles,

ℹ️ **SLEEPING: AVIGNON AREA**

For stays in July during the Festival d'Avignon, reserve by January (if not earlier); expect minimum-stay requirements and premium rates. Ask if there's parking. Orange and Carpentras, both 30 minutes away, are dull by comparison but make less expensive bases.

Châteauneuf-du-Pape and Tarascon. Dinner cruises draw older crowds with dancing and live entertainment.

Avignon Wine Tour TOUR
(☑06 28 05 33 84; www.avignon-wine-tour.com; per person €80-100) Visit the region's vineyards with a knowledgeable guide, leaving you free to enjoy the wine.

★☆ Festivals & Events

★ **Festival d'Avignon** PERFORMING ARTS
(www.festival-avignon.com; ⊙Jul) The three-week annual Festival d'Avignon is one of the world's great performing-arts festivals. Over 40 international works of dance and drama play to 100,000-plus spectators at venues around town. Tickets don't go on sale until springtime, but hotels sell out by February.

Festival Off PERFORMING ARTS
(www.avignonleoff.com; ⊙Jul) The Festival d'Avignon is paralleled by a simultaneous fringe event, Festival Off, with eclectic (and cheaper) experimental programming. La Carte Off (€16) gives a 30% discount.

🛏 Sleeping

★ **Hôtel Boquier** HOTEL €
(☑04 90 82 34 43; www.hotel-boquier.com; 6 rue du Portail Boquier; s & d/tr/q from €65/86/99; ❄🛜♿) It sits on a rather shabby side street, but the owners' infectious enthusiasm and the colourful rooms at this small hotel compensate; try for themed rooms Morocco or Lavender. Excellent value. Breakfast €9.

Hôtel Mignon HOTEL €
(☑04 90 82 17 30; www.hotel-mignon.com; 12 rue Joseph Vernet; s €40-60, d €65-77, tr €80-99, q €105; ❄@🛜♿) Bathrooms might be tiny and the stairs steep and narrow, but Hôtel Mignon (literally 'Cute Hotel') remains excellent value. Its 16 rooms are clean and comfortable, and the hotel sits on Avignon's smartest shopping street. Breakfast €7.

Avignon

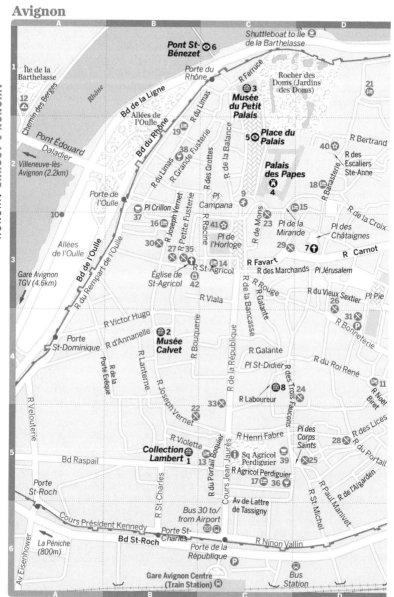

Hôtel Splendid

HOTEL €

(☑ 04 90 86 14 46; www.avignon-splendid-hotel. com; 17 rue Agricol Perdiguier; s €54-76, d €76-100, tr €110; ❄ ⓢ) ✈ Splendidly set on a side street off cafe-clad place des Corps Saints, Hôtel Splendid is one of several hotels on the same street and is a great budget base for exploring Avignon – by day and night. Breakfast €9.

La Péniche

HOUSEBOAT €

(☑ 04 90 25 40 61, 06 62 37 25 17; www.chambre-peniche.fr; chemin île Piot, Île de la Barthelasse; houseboats €80-95; ❄ ⓢ ⓦ) Rock to sleep

Orange (33km); Parking des Italiens (300m);

Camping & Auberge Bagatelle CAMPGROUND €
(☑ 04 90 86 30 39; www.campingbagatelle.com; Île de la Barthelasse; dm incl breakfast from €21, sites for tent, car & 2 people €25; ☺ reception 8am-9pm; @) Shaded and just 20 minutes' walk from the city centre on an adjacent small island in the Rhône. It also has basic two- to eight-bed dorms.

★ **Le Limas** B&B €€
(☑ 04 90 14 67 19; www.le-limas-avignon.com; 51 rue du Limas; s/d/tr from €130/150/250; ﹡@ 🗟) This chic B&B in an 18th-century town house, like something out of *Vogue Living*, is everything designers strive for when mixing old and new: state-of-the-art kitchen and minimalist white decor complementing antique fireplaces and 18th-century spiral stairs. Breakfast on the sun-drenched terrace is divine, darling.

Lumani B&B €€
(☑ 04 90 82 94 11; www.avignon-lumani.com; 37 rue du Rempart St-Lazare; d/ste from €110/160; ﹡🗟) Art fills this fabulous *maison d'hôte*, a wealth of inspiration for painters. Rooms include two suites and there's a fountained garden.

Hôtel de l'Horloge HOTEL €€
(☑ 04 90 16 42 00; www.hotels-ocre-azur.com; place de l'Horloge; d €125-200; ﹡🗟) Most rooms at this super-central 19th-century stone-walled hotel (with elevator) are straightforward (comfortable, all mod cons), but five terrace rooms have the edge with knockout views – room 505 overlooks the Palais des Papes.

Villa de Margot B&B €€
(☑ 04 90 82 62 34; http://demargot.fr; 24 rue des Trois Colombes; d €110-190; ﹡🗟) A charming, quiet old-city address, this 19th-century private home, converted into an elegant guesthouse, has a walled garden and rooftop views. Rooms are styled like their names: 'Oriental', 'Royal', 'Art Deco' and 'Romantic'.

Autour du Petit Paradis APARTMENT €€
(☑ 04 90 81 00 42; www.autourdupetitparadis.com; 5 rue Noël Biret; apt nightly €120-200, weekly from €665; ﹡@ 🗟👪) Live like a local in a 17th-century stone house converted into a small apartment-hotel. Scrupulously maintained, each has a kitchenette, ideal for travellers who like style but want to cook their own local cuisine.

La Banasterie B&B €€
(☑ 06 87 72 96 36; www.labanasterie.com; 11 rue de la Banasterie; r €100-145; ﹡@ 🗟) Earthy tones warm up the cosy rooms in this town house

aboard Avignon's most unique *chambre d'hôte* (B&B). Moored across the river, a 10-minute walk on Île de la Barthelasse, this four-room barge-houseboat gleams and has a small self-catering kitchen. Extras include a wading pool and free bikes.

Avignon

turned B&B tucked behind the Palais des Papes. There's no elevator, but the husband-and-wife team who run the place offer heaps of local knowledge and a home away from home.

★ Hôtel La Mirande   HOTEL €€€

(☏ 04 90 14 20 20; www.la-mirande.fr; 4 place de la Mirande; d from €450; ❄@🛜) Avignon's top hotel occupies a converted 16th-century palace, with dramatic interiors decked in oriental rugs, gold-threaded tapestries, marble staircases and over-the-top Gallic style. Low-end rooms are small but still conjure the feeling of staying overnight in someone's private château. Its restaurant, **Le Marmiton** (4 place de la Mirande; mains from €35, chef's table €86), is a slow and glittering affair and also offers cooking classes (from €90).

Le Marmiton has a twice-weekly chef's table (reservations essential); afternoon tea is served (albeit slowly) in the lobby or garden.

Eating

Place de l'Horloge is crammed with touristy restaurants that don't offer the best cuisine or value in town. Delve instead into the pedestrian old town where ample pretty squares tempt: place des Châtaignes and place de la Principle are two particularly beautiful restaurant-clad squares.

Restaurants open seven days during the summer festival season, when reservations become essential.

Local treat *papaline d'Avignon* is a pink chocolate ball filled with potent Mont Ventoux herbal liqueur.

L'Epice and Love   FRENCH €

(☏ 04 90 82 45 96; 30 rue des Lices; mains €11-12; ⊙ 7-10pm Mon-Sat) Tables are cheek by jowl at this tiny bohemian restaurant – our favorite for budget dining – with nothing fancy, just straightforward bistro fare, stews, roasts and other reliably good, home-style French dishes. Cash only.

Ginette et Marcel   CAFE €

(☏ 04 90 85 58 70; 27 place des Corps Saints; tartines €4-7; ⊙ 11am-11pm Wed-Mon; 🍴) Set on one of Avignon's most happening plane-tree-shaded squares, this vintage cafe styled like a 1950s grocery is a charming spot to hang out and people-watch over a *tartine* (open-face sandwich), tart, salad or other light dish – equally tasty for lunch or an early-evening *apéro* (predinner drink). Kids adore Ginette's cherry- and violet-flavoured cordials and Marcel's glass jars of old-fashioned sweets.

★ 83.Vernet
MODERN FRENCH €€

(☑ 04 90 85 99 04; www.83vernet.com; 83 rue Joseph Vernet; menus lunch €19.50, dinner €24-30; ⊙ noon-3pm & 7pm-1am Mon-Sat) Forget flowery French descriptions. The menu is straightforward and to the point at this strikingly contemporary address, magnificently at home in the 18th-century cloistered courtyard of a medieval college. Expect pan-seared scallops, squid *à la plancha* (grilled) and beef steak in pepper sauce, and watch for weekend events that transform the lounge-style restaurant into the town's hippest dance floor.

★ Restaurant L'Essentiel
FRENCH €€

(☑ 04 90 85 87 12; www.restaurantlessentiel.com; 2 rue Petite Fusterie; lunch menu €15, dinner menus €31-45; ⊙ noon-2pm & 7-9.45pm Tue-Sat) Snug in an elegant, caramel-stone *hôtel particulier* (private mansion), The Essential is one of the finest places to eat in town – inside or in the wonderful courtyard garden. Begin with zucchini flowers poached in a crayfish and truffle sauce, then continue with rabbit stuffed with candied eggplant, perhaps.

Numéro 75
MODERN FRENCH €€

(☑ 04 90 27 16 00; www.numero75.com; 75 rue Guillaume Puy; 2-/3-course menus from €30/37; ⊙ noon-2pm & 7.30-9.35pm Mon-Sat) The chic dining room, in the former mansion of absinthe inventor Jules Pernod, is a fitting backdrop to the stylised Mediterranean cooking. Menus change nightly and include just a handful of mains, but brevity guarantees freshness. Starter/main-course-sized *salades goumandes* (€9/18), served only at lunchtime, are good value. On balmy nights, reserve a table in the elegant courtyard garden.

La Cuisine du Dimanche
PROVENÇAL €€

(☑ 04 90 82 99 10; www.lacuisinedudimanche. com; 31 rue de la Bonneterie; lunch menu €17, mains €18-25; ⊙ noon-1.30pm & 8-9.45pm Jun-Sep, Wed-Sun Nov-Mar) Spitfire chef Marie shops every morning at Les Halles to find the freshest ingredients for her earthy flavour-packed cooking. The menu changes daily, although staples include scallops and simple roast chicken with pan gravy. The narrow stone-walled dining room mixes contemporary resin chairs with antique crystal goblets to reflect the chef's eclecticism. Evening dining is only à la carte.

L'Épicerie
BISTRO €€

(☑ 04 90 82 74 22; www.restaurantlepicerie.fr; 10 place St-Pierre; menus lunch/dinner from €16/23; ⊙ noon-2.30pm & 8-10pm) Racing-green tables, chairs and parasols flag this popular bistro on a gorgeous cobblestone square. The Grocery makes its own foie gras, served with a Muscat-fired onion chutney, and mains reflect the market. Excite *apéro* tastebuds with an *assiette de l'épicerie* (€19), a mixed platter of Provençal produce: tomato *crème brûlée*, melon wedges, stuffed veg, olive cake, tapenade and so on.

Fou de Fafa
BISTRO €€

(☑ 04 32 76 35 13; 17 rue des Trois Faucons; 2-/3-course menu €25/31; ⊙ 6.30-11pm Wed-Sun; ⊙) A typical French bistro, Fou de Fafa's strength lies in simplicity – fresh ingredients, bright flavours, convivial surroundings (and a notably early opening time handy for families with young children). Dining is between soft golden-stone walls and the chef gives a fresh spin to classics. *Magret de canard* (duck breast) in a strawberry and balsamic reduction, anyone?

★ Christian Etienne
PROVENÇAL €€€

(☑ 04 90 86 16 50; www.christian-etienne.fr; 10 rue de Mons; lunch/dinner menus from €35/75; ⊙ noon-2pm & 7.30-10pm Tue-Sat) One of Avignon's top tables, this much-vaunted restaurant occupies a 12th-century palace with a leafy outdoor terrace, adjacent to Palais des Papes. Interiors feel slightly dated, but the refined Provençal cuisine remains exceptional, and the restaurant has earned a Michelin star.

Les 5 Sens
GASTRONOMIC €€€

(☑ 04 90 85 26 51; www.restaurantles5sens.com; 18 rue Joseph Vernet; menus lunch €16-22, dinner €40-59; ⊙ noon-1.30pm & 7.45-11.30pm Tue-Sat) Chef Thierry Baucher, one of France's *meilleurs ouvriers* (top chefs), reveals his southwestern origins in specialities such as *cassoulet* (rich bean, pork and duck stew) and foie gras but skews contemporary-Mediterranean in gastronomic dishes such as butternut-squash ravioli with escargots. Surroundings are sleek; service is impeccable.

Self-Catering

Les Halles
MARKET €

(www.avignon-leshalles.com; place Pie; ⊙ 6am-1.30pm Tue-Fri, to 2pm Sat & Sun) Over 40 food stalls showcase seasonal Provençal ingredients. Cooking demonstrations are held at 11am Saturday. Outside on place Pie, admire Patrick Blanc's marvellous vegetal wall.

LOCAL KNOWLEDGE

EDGY EATING

Canal-side **rue des Teinturiers** (literally 'street of dyers') is a picturesque pedestrian street known for its alternative vibe in Avignon's old dyer's district. A hive of industrial activity until the 19th century, the street today is renowned for its bohemian bistros, cafes and gallery-workshops. Stone 'benches' in the shade of ancient plane trees make the perfect perch to ponder the irresistible trickle of the River Sorgue, safeguarded since the 16th century by **Chapelle des Pénitents Gris**. Those in the know dine at **L'Ubu** (04 90 80 01 01; 13 rue des Teinturiers; starters/mains €7.50/16.50; ⊙ noon-2.30pm & 7-10.30pm), with a tiny, daily-changing menu chalked on the blackboard.

La Tropézienne PATISSERIE €
(04 90 86 24 72; 22 rue St-Agricol; ⊙ 8.30am-7.30pm Mon-Fri, to 2pm Sat) St-Tropez' famous cream-and-cake *tarte Tropézienne,* plus other treats.

Monoprix SUPERMARKET €
(24 rue de la République; ⊙ 8am-9pm Mon-Sat) Catch-all supermarket in the centre of Avignon.

🍷 Drinking & Nightlife

Chic yet laid-back Avignon is awash with gorgeous, tree-shaded pedestrian squares buzzing with cafe life. Favourite options, loaded with pavement terraces and drinking opportunities, include place Crillon (full-frontal view of medieval Avignon's crenellated city walls), place Pie (green views of Les Halles' vegetal facade), place de l'Horloge (hard-core tourist zone with kids' carousel) and Place des Corps Saints (more laid-back).

★ Balthazar BISTRO, BAR
(04 88 07 36 09; www.bistrotbalthazar.com; 74 place des Corps Saints; ⊙ 8.30-1am Mon-Sat) With its deep-red canopy and black seating, Balthazar makes a bold statement. It's hip for casual lunch and dinner dining, but it's at its most rocking for early-evening aperitifs and after-dark drinks. When the munchies hit, French classics like *pot au feu* (beef stew) and braised pork cheek are on offer alongside tasty homemade burgers and other funkier fare (*menus* from €24).

★ La Manutention BAR, CAFE
(4 rue des Escaliers Ste-Anne; ⊙ noon-midnight) No address better reflects Avignon's artsy soul than this bistro-bar at cultural centre La Manutention. Its leafy terrace basks in the shade of Palais des Papes' stone walls and, inside, giant conservatory-style windows open onto the funky decor of pocket-size bar Utopia. Grilled *tartines* (€4.50) and light *assiettes* (mixed platters) make ideal companions to pre- or posttheatre drinks; there's a cinema too.

L'Esclave GAY
(04 90 85 14 91; 12 rue du Limas; ⊙ 11.30pm-7am Tue-Sun) Avignon's inner-city gay bar rocks well into the wee hours, pulling a clientele that is not always that quiet, based on dozens of neighbour-considerate 'be quiet' signs plastered outside.

Cafe la Scène CAFE
(04 90 86 14 70; 19 place Crillon; ⊙ 9am-1am) On pretty place Crillon, La Scène's outdoor tables are good for drinks and small bites; inside there's a dance floor and cabaret.

Milk Shop CAFE
(09 82 54 16 82; www.milkshop.fr; 26 place des Corps Saints; bagels €5-7, shakes €4.50; ⊙ 7.45am-7pm Mon-Fri, 9.30am-7pm Sat; 🛜) Keen to mingle with Avignon students? Make a beeline for this *salon au lait* ('milk bar') where super-thick ice-cream shakes are slurped through extra-wide straws. Bagels, cupcakes and other American snacks create a deliberate US vibe, while comfy armchairs and wi-fi encourage hanging out.

★ Entertainment

Avignon is one of the premier cities for theatre in France; tickets for concerts and events are sold at the tourist office *billetterie* (box office).

Opéra Théâtre d'Avignon PERFORMING ARTS
(04 90 82 81 40; www.operagrandavignon.fr; place de l'Horloge; ⊙ box office 11am-6pm Tue-Sat) Built 1847, Avignon's main classical venue presents operas, plays, chamber music and ballet from October to June.

AJMI JAZZ, LIVE MUSIC
(Association pour le Jazz & la Musique Improvisée; 04 90 86 08 61; www.jazzalajmi.com; 4 rue des Escaliers Ste-Anne, La Manutention) Inside La Manutention arts centre, AJMI showcases improvisational jazz at its intimate 2nd-floor (no elevator) black-box theatre.

Shopping

Find high-end antique shops along the rue du Limas, mainstream shopping on rue de la République, and boutiques on its side streets, such as rue St-Agricol.

Oliviers & Co BEAUTY, FOOD
(04 90 86 18 41; www.oliviers-co.com; 19 rue St-Agricol; ⊙2-7pm Mon, 10am-7pm Tue-Sat) Fine olive oil and olive-oil-based products such as soap, creams and biscuits.

❶ Information

Police Station (✆04 32 40 55 55; 14 bd St-Roch)

Centre Hospitalier Avignon (✆04 32 75 33 33; www.ch-avignon.fr; 305 rue Raoul Follereau) Marked on maps as Hôpital Sud, 2.5km south of the central train station; take bus 2, 6, 14.

Tourist Office (✆04 32 74 32 74; www. avignon-tourisme.com; 41 cours Jean Jaurès; ⊙9am-6pm Mon-Fri, to 6pm Sat, 10am-noon Sun Apr-Oct, shorter hours rest of year) Offers guided walking tours and information on other tours and activities, including boat trips on the Rhône and wine-tasting trips to nearby vineyards. Smartphone apps too.

Tourist Office Annexe (Avignon TGV station; ⊙Jun-Aug) During summer, Avignon has an information booth at the TGV station.

❶ Getting There & Away

AIR

Aéroport Avignon-Provence (AVN; ✆04 90 81 51 51; www.avignon.aeroport.fr; Caumont) In Caumont, 8km southeast of Avignon. Direct flights to London, Birmingham and Southampton in the UK.

BUS

The **bus station** (bd St-Roch; ⊙information window 8am-7pm Mon-Fri, to 1pm Sat) is next to the central railway station. Tickets are sold on board. For schedules, see www.lepilote.com, www.info-ler.fr and www.vaucluse.fr. Long-haul companies **Linebus** (✆04 90 85 30 48; www. linebus.com) and **Eurolines** (✆04 90 85 27 60; www.eurolines.com) have offices at the far end of bus platforms and serve places like Barcelona.

Aix-en-Provence €45, 1¼ hours
Arles €6, 1½ hours
Carpentras €2, 45 minutes
Nîmes €1.50, 1¼ hours
Orange €2, 45 minutes

CAR

Find car-hire agencies at both train stations (reserve ahead, especially in July). Narrow, one-way streets and impossible parking make driving within the ramparts difficult: park outside the walls. The city has 900 free spaces at Parking de L'Ile Piot, and 1150 at Parking des Italiens, both under surveillance and served by the free TCRA shuttle bus. On directional signs at intersections, 'P' in yellow means pay lots; 'P' in green, free lots. Pay **Parking Gare Centre** (✆04 90 80 74 40; bd St-Roch; ⊙24hr) is next to the central train station.

TRAIN

Avignon has two train stations: **Gare Avignon Centre** (42 bd St-Roch), on the southern edge of the walled town, and **Gare Avignon TGV** (Courtine), 4km southwest in Courtine. Local shuttle trains link the two every 20 minutes (€1.60, five minutes, 6am to 11pm). Or, from the TGV station, get into Avignon on LER bus 18 or 22, or TCRA bus 10. LER bus 18 serves Arles too. There is no luggage storage.

Some TGVs to/from Paris (€90 to €130, 3½ hours) stop at Gare Avignon Centre, but TGVs to/from Marseille (€26, 35 minutes) and Nice (€45 to €60, 3¼ hours) only use Gare Avignon TGV. **Eurostar** (www.eurostar.com) services operate one to five times weekly between Avignon TGV and London (from €180, 5¾ hours) en route to/from Marseille.

Gare Avignon Centre is served by regular-speed TER trains.

Arles €8, 20 minutes
Marseille €24, 1¼ to two hours
Marseille airport (Vitrolles station) €18, one to 1½ hours
Nîmes €11, 30 minutes
Orange €6.50, 22 minutes

❶ Getting Around

TO/FROM THE AIRPORT

From the airport TCRA bus 30 (www.tcra.fr; €1.30, 25 minutes, Monday to Saturday) goes to the post office and LER bus 22 (www.info-ler.fr; €1.50) goes to the Avignon bus station and TGV station. Taxis cost about €35.

BICYCLE & MOTORCYCLE

Vélopop (✆08 10 45 64 56; www.velopop.fr) Shared-bicycle service, with 17 stations around town. The first half-hour is free; each additional half-hour is €1. Membership per day/week is €1/5.

Provence Bike (✆04 90 27 92 61; www. provence-bike.com; 7 av St-Ruf; bicycles per day/week from €12/65, scooters €25/150; ⊙9am-6.30pm Mon-Sat, plus 10am-1pm Sun Jul) Rents city bikes, mountain bikes, scooters and motorcycles.

BOAT

Shuttleboat to Île de la Barthelasse (Navette Fluviale) The free shuttleboat from near the base of Pont Saint Bénezet (p196) to Île de la Barthelasse runs mid-February through December.

BUS

TCRA (Transports en Commun de la Région d'Avignon; ☑ 04 32 74 18 32; www.tcra.fr) Buses run from 7am till about 8pm. The main transfer points are Poste (main post office) and place Pie. For Villeneuve-lès-Avignon, take bus 5. Tickets (€1.30) are sold on board.

TAXI

Taxi-Radio Avignon (☑ 04 90 82 20 20)

AROUND AVIGNON

Villeneuve-lès-Avignon

POP 12,872

Across the Rhône from Avignon, compact Villeneuve-lès-Avignon has monuments to rival Avignon's but none of the crowds. Meander the cloisters of a medieval monastery, take in hilltop views from Fort St-André and lose yourself in spectacular gardens at Abbaye St-André – reason enough to visit.

⊙ Sights

The Avignon Passion discount pass is valid here.

★ Abbaye et Jardins de l'Abbaye
MONASTERY, GARDEN
(☑ 04 90 25 55 95; www.abbayesaintandre.fr; rue Montée du Fort, Fort St-André; adult/child abbey €13/free, garden €6/free; ⊙ 10am-6pm Tue-Sun May-Sep, 10am-1pm & 2-5pm Tue-Sun Mar & Oct, to 6pm Apr) The resplendent vaulted halls of this 10th-century abbey, within Fort St-André, can only be visited by guided tour. The stunning terrace gardens, however – built atop the abbey vaults and classed among France's top 100 gardens – can be roamed without a guide. Pathways meander among fragrant roses, iris-studded olive groves, wisteria-covered pergolas and the ruins of three ancient churches. The views of Avignon and the Rhône are spectacular.

Fort St-André
FORT
(☑ 04 90 25 45 35; rue Montée du Fort; adult/child €5.50/free; ⊙ 10am-6pm Jun-Sep, 10am-1pm & 2-5pm Oct-May) King Philip the Fair (aka Philippe le Bel) wasn't messing around when he built defensive 14th-century Fort St-André on the then-border between France and the Holy Roman Empire: the walls are 2m thick! Today you can walk a small section of the ramparts and admire 360-degree views from the **Tour des Masques** (Wizards' Tower) and **Tours Jumelles** (Twin Towers).

Chartreuse du Val de Bénédiction
MONASTERY
(☑ 04 90 15 24 24; www.chartreuse.org; 58 rue de la République; adult/child €8/free; ⊙ 9.30am-6.30pm May-Sep, to 5pm Oct-Mar) Shaded from summer's heat, the three cloisters, 24 cells, church, chapels and nook-and-cranny gardens of the Chartreuse du Val de Bénédiction make up France's biggest Carthusian monastery, founded in 1352 by Pope Innocent VI, who was buried here 10 years later in an elaborate mausoleum.

Tour Philippe-le-Bel
LANDMARK
(☑ 04 32 70 08 57; Montée de la Tour; adult/child €2.60/free; ⊙ 10am-12.30pm & 2-6pm Tue-Sun May-Oct, 2-5pm Feb-Apr) King Philip commissioned the Tour Philippe-le-Bel, 500m outside Villeneuve, to control traffic over Pont St-Bénézet to and from Avignon. The steep steps spiraling to the top reward climbers with stunning river views.

Musée Pierre de Luxembourg
MUSEUM
(☑ 04 90 27 49 66; 3 rue de la République; adult/child €3.60/free; ⊙ 10am-12.30pm & 2-6pm Tue-Sun May-Oct, 2-5pm Nov-Apr) Inside a 17th-century mansion, this museum's masterwork is Enguerrand Quarton's *The Crowning of the Virgin* (1453), in which angels wrest souls from purgatory. Rounding out the collection are 16th- to 18th-century paintings.

🛏 Sleeping & Eating

Find cafes and food shops around place Jean Jaurès, near Musée Pierre de Luxembourg. The tourist office has information on lodging, including several top-end inns.

YMCA-UCJG
HOSTEL €
(☑ 04 90 25 46 20; www.ymca-avignon.com; 7bis chemin de la Justice; dm €53, without bathroom €38; ⊙ reception 8.30am-6pm, closed Nov-Dec; ☎ 🛋) This spotless hostel just outside Villeneuve-lès-Avignon, and a 15-minute walk from Avignon, has some private rooms plus a swimming pool with panoramic views. Sheets are included, but towels cost €2. There is wheelchair access. Take TCRA bus 4 to the Monteau stop.

★ Carré Cardinal
B&B €€

(☏ 04 90 22 00 00; 57 rue de la République; d/tr/ste from €85/110/120; ❉ 🛜) Pretty rooms in this renovated historic building across from the Chartreuse du Val de Bénédiction are kitted out with creamy linens, flat-screen TVs and modern bathrooms. Two let onto the internal courtyard; one is a two-storey suite.

Les Jardins de la Livrée
B&B €€

(☏ 04 86 81 00 21; www.la-livree.fr; 4bis rue du Camp de Bataille; r incl breakfast €88-120; ⊘ closed Jan–mid-Mar & late Oct–mid-Dec; ❉ 🛜 ▣) High-walled gardens and a lovely pool make this town-centre, four-room *chambre d'hôte* feel far removed. Free parking.

🛈 Information

Tourist Office (☏ 04 90 25 61 33; www.tourisme-villeneuvelezavignon.fr; 1 place Charles David; ⊘ 9.30am-12.30pm & 2-6pm Mon-Fri, to 1pm Sat, plus Sun Jul & Aug) Guided English-language tours in July and August.

🛈 Getting There & Away

TCRA (p204) bus 5 links Villeneuve-lès-Avignon with Avignon (it's only 2km, but dull walking).

NORTH OF AVIGNON

Châteauneuf-du-Pape's world-renowned vineyards extend north of Avignon to Orange, a small city famous for excellently preserved Roman antiquities. Just east, Vaison-la-Romaine is also rich in ancient treasures, its narrow medieval streets an adventure to explore. Just beyond lie the compact, saw-toothed Dentelles de Montmirail mountains, with small villages known for great wines. Lording over all is windswept Mont Ventoux, Provence's mighty mountain, a magnet for bicyclists and recognised the world over as a feature of the Tour de France.

Châteauneuf-du-Pape

POP 2210

Carpets of vineyards unfurl around tiny, medieval Châteauneuf-du-Pape, epicentre of one of the world's great wine-growing regions. Only a small ruin remains of the château, once the summer residence of Avignon's popes, dismantled for stone after the Revolution, and ultimately bombed by Germany in WWII. Now it belongs to picnickers and day hikers, who ascend the hill for

DON'T MISS

BEST REGIONAL MARKETS

To appreciate Provence's seasonal bounty, visit its markets (www.marches-provence.com); most run from 8am to noon. In Nîmes, the covered food market operates daily; Avignon's Les Halles (p201) operates Tuesday to Sunday.

Monday Bédoin, Fontvieille.

Tuesday Tarascon, Vaison-la-Romaine.

Wednesday Malaucène, Sault, St-Rémy-de-Provence, Valréas.

Thursday Beaucaire, L'Isle-sur-la-Sorgue (small), Maillane, Maussane-les-Alpilles, Orange, Villeneuve-lès-Avignon.

Friday Carpentras, Châteauneuf-du-Pape.

Saturday Pernes-les-Fontaines, Richerenches, St-Rémy-de-Provence, Villeneuve-lès-Avignon.

Sunday L'Isle-sur-la-Sorgue (large).

360-degree panoramas of the Rhône Valley. It's an ideal half-day trip for wine tasting and lunch before continuing to Orange.

⊙ Sights & Activities

The tourist office has material (also online) detailing which wineries allow visits, their tasting fees and whether they offer English-language tours. Some require appointments.

A car is easiest, but a tourist-office brochure illustrates a 16km **walking circuit** or you could hire a bicycle.

Château Mont-Redon
WINERY

(☏ 04 90 83 72 75; www.chateaumontredon.com; rte d'Orange, D88; ⊘ 9am-7pm Apr-Sep, reduced hours rest of year; ❉) Three kilometres from Châteauneuf-du-Pape, Mont-Redon is gorgeously placed amid sweeping vineyards. Large, and easy for drop-ins, it can attract weekend crowds for its respectable wines, including an excellent, mineral-y white. Tastings free.

Domaine de la Solitude
WINERY

(☏ 04 90 83 71 45; www.domaine-solitude.com; rte de Bédarides, D192; ⊘ 10am-6pm Mon-Fri, by appointment Sat & Sun) Two kilometres east of the village, appreciate Châteauneuf-du-Pape from this family-run estate, cultivated for 600 years by descendants of Pope Urban

VIII. Call ahead to receive a warm welcome, in English, as you discover elegant, rounded wines, with supple, never-harsh tannins. Tastings (free) include visits to the barrel cellar.

Caves du Verger des Papes WINERY
(☏ 04 90 83 58 08; www.caveduverger.com; 4 montée du Château; ☉10am-7pm Tue-Sat, to 4pm Sun Jul & Aug, reduced hours rest of year) `FREE` Beneath the town's namesake château, these small, magnificent wine caves date back 2000 years. The bar carries 80 of the town's 250 labels. English is spoken.

École de Dégustation COURSE
(Tasting School; ☏ 04 90 83 56 15; www.oenologie-mouriesse.com; 2 rue des Papes; 2hr class €40) To appreciate the region's stellar wine, book a two-hour wine-tasting class.

🛏 Sleeping & Eating

★ **Le Mas Julien** B&B €€
(☏ 04 90 34 99 49; www.mas-julien.com; 704 chemin de St Jean, Orange; d incl breakfast €105-135, studios from €135; ❈ 🛜 ☒) A 17th-century stone farmhouse surrounded by vineyards, Le Mas Julien's four rooms blend contemporary and Provençal style, and there's a studio apartment with kitchen that sleeps three. After a day exploring, nothing beats sprawling by the big pool, glass in hand. Between Orange and Châteauneuf-du-Pape, it's an ideal base for an extended stay.

★ **Le Verger des Papes** TRADITIONAL FRENCH €€
(☏ 04 90 83 50 40; www.vergerdespapes.com; 4 rue du Château; lunch/dinner menus €20/31; ☉noon-2pm & 7-9pm Wed-Sat, noon-2pm Sun & Tue) Perched beneath the Châteauneuf-du-Pape château, The Popes' Orchard has drop-dead vistas of the Rhône from its stone terrace – ideal for a lingering lunch or romantic dinner (arrive before sunset). Specialities include rack of lamb for two, plus *entrecôte* of beef, served with macaroni-and-cheese spiked with *cèpes* (a type of mushroom). Park at the château and walk down. Reservations essential.

La Mère Germaine TRADITIONAL FRENCH €€
(☏ 04 90 22 78 34; www.lameregermaine.fr; place de la Fontaine; lunch/dinner menus from €24/39; ☉noon-2pm & 7-9pm mid-Mar–Oct, closed Wed Nov–mid-Mar; ❈ 🛜) Open since 1922, La Mère Germaine is the classic village *auberge* (inn), with a fine restaurant, good for a date, featuring vineyard views. Solicitous service includes local wines by the glass, paired well with classic cooking, such as foie gras and duck breast. Some of the simple, elegant rooms (doubles including breakfast €95) with modern bathrooms also have views.

🛍 Shopping

Chocolaterie Bernard Castelain FOOD
(☏ 04 90 83 54 71; www.vin-chocolat-castelain.com; 1745 rte de Sorgues; ☉9am-noon & 2-7pm Mon-Sat) The specialities at this artisan chocolatier include *picholines* (dark-chocolate-covered roasted almonds that look like Provençal olives) and *Palets des Papes* (Châteauneuf-du-Pape liqueur-infused truffles).

ⓘ Information

Tourist Office (☏ 04 90 83 71 08; www.pays-provence.fr; place du Portail; ☉9.30am-6pm Mon-Sat, closed lunch & Wed Oct-May)

ⓘ Getting There & Away

If you are driving from Avignon (18km, 30 minutes) take D907 north to D17. From Orange (10km, 15 minutes) take D68 south.

CHÂTEAUNEUF-DU-PAPE WINES: A PRIMER

Thank geology for these luscious wines: when glaciers receded, they left a thick layer of *galets* scattered atop the red-clay soil; these large pebbles trap the Provençal sun, releasing heat after sunset, helping grapes ripen with steady warmth.

The Romans first planted vines here 2000 years ago, but wine-growing took off after Pope John XXII built a castle in 1317, planting vineyards to provide the court with wine. From this papally endorsed beginning, wine production flourished.

Most Châteauneuf-du-Pape is red; only 6% is white (rosé is forbidden). Strict regulations – which formed the basis for the *Appellation d'Origine Contrôlée* (AOC) system – govern production. Reds come from 13 grape varieties – grenache is the biggie – and should age five years minimum. The full-bodied whites drink well young (except for all-roussanne varieties) and make an excellent, mineral-y aperitif that's hard to find elsewhere (but taste before buying; some may lack acidity).

TransVaucluse (www.vaucluse.fr) operates a limited bus service to/from Orange (€1.50, 30 minutes, two or three services Monday to Saturday) and Avignon (€2, one hour, one or two services Monday to Saturday), but same-day round trips are impossible. Buses stop at the intersection of av Louis Pasteur and rue de la Nouvelle Poste.

Orange

POP 29,645

Considering the exceptional beauty of its Roman theatre and monumental archway – both Unesco World Heritage Sites – ultraconservative Orange is surprisingly untouristy, and eerily quiet in winter. Accommodation is good value for the region, but it's nearly impossible to find dinner Sunday or Monday nights.

History

The House of Orange, the princely dynasty that had ruled Orange since the 12th century, made its mark on the history of the Netherlands through a 16th-century marriage with the German House of Nassau, and then English history through William of Orange. Orange was ceded to France in 1713 by the Treaty of Utrecht. To this day, many members of the royal house of the Netherlands are known as the princes and princesses of Orange-Nassau.

Sights

★**Théâtre Antique**   ROMAN SITES
(www.theatre-antique.com; rue Madeleine Roch; adult/child €9.50/7.50; ⊙9am-7pm Jun-Aug, to 6pm Apr, May & Sep, 9.30am-5.30pm Mar & Oct, 9.30am-4.30pm rest of year; 🛜) Orange's Roman theatre is among France's most impressive Roman sites. Its size and age are awe-inspiring: designed for 10,000 spectators, it's believed to have been built during Augustus Caesar's rule (27 BC to AD 14). The 103m-wide, 37m-high stage wall is one of three in the world still standing in entirety (others are in Syria and Turkey) – minus a few mosaics, plus a new roof. Admission includes audioguide (and excellent free smartphone app) and access to Musée d'Art et d'Histoire.

Come for epic theatrical spectaculars, including the fabulous **Chorégies d'Orange** (www.choregies.asso.fr), an international opera festival in July and August – balmy nights in this millennia-old venue are magical.

ⓘ ROMAN PASS

....

Roman Pass (adult/child €18/13.50)
The Roman Pass is a joint ticket that allows access to Orange's Roman theatre and museum, plus the amphitheatre in Nîmes. It's valid for seven days, and you can buy it at any of the venues.

Musée d'Art et d'Histoire   MUSEUM
(www.theatre-antique.com; rue Madeleine Roch; adult/child €5.50/4.50; ⊙9.15am-7pm Jun-Aug, to 6pm Apr, May & Sep, shorter hours rest of year) This small museum – there's free admission with a Théâtre Antique ticket – displays various unassuming treasures, including portions of the Roman survey registers (precursors to the tax department) and friezes that once formed part of the Roman theatre's scenery.

★**Colline St-Eutrope**   GARDEN
For bird's-eye views of the theatre – and phenomenal vistas of Mont Ventoux and the Dentelles de Montmirail – follow montée Philbert de Chalons or montée Lambert up Colline St-Eutrope (St Eutrope Hill; elevation 97m), once the Romans' lookout point. En route, pass ruins of a 12th-century **château**, once the residence of the princes of Orange.

Arc de Triomphe   ROMAN SITES
Orange's 1st-century-AD monumental arch, the Arc de Triomphe – 19m high and wide, and 8m thick – stands on the Via Agrippa. Restored in 2009, its brilliant reliefs commemorate 49 BC Roman victories with carvings of chained, naked Gauls.

Sleeping

Hôtel Saint Jean   HOTEL €
(📞04 90 51 15 16; www.hotelsaint-jean.com; 1 cours Pourtoules; s/d/tr/q €70/85/100/120; ❄🛜) Simple, spiffy hotel, near the theatre, with comfortable proportions and colourful Provençal fabrics. Free bike storage, double-pane windows and flat-screen TVs add value. Parking €6.

Hôtel l'Herbier d'Orange   HOTEL €
(📞04 90 34 09 23; www.lherbierdorange.com; 8 place aux Herbes; s/d/q from €59/64/88; ❄@🛜♿) Friendly, enthusiastic owners keep this small, basic hotel looking spick and span, with double-pane windows and gleaming bathrooms. Find it sitting prettily on a small square shaded by tall plane trees. Parking €4.50.

Orange

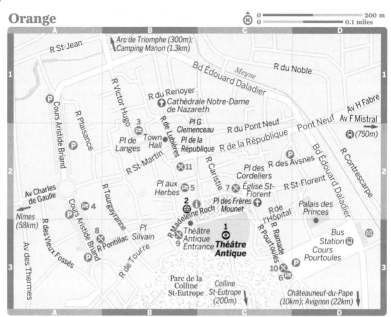

Orange

Camping Manon   CAMPGROUND €

(📞 04 32 81 94 96; www.camping-manon.com; 1321 rue Alexis Carrel, Quartier Le Jonquier; sites for cyclist/car €20/25.50; ☺ Apr-Sep; @🛜❄🀄) This good campground has been recently overhauled and has pool, hot tub, tennis, laundry and a minimart.

Hôtel Arène Külm   HOTEL €€

(📞 04 90 11 40 40; www.hotel-arene.fr; place de Langes; d/ste from €125/205; 🌬@🛜❄🀄) It might be part of the generic Best Western chain, but the Arène is beautifully positioned in the old town and retains some individuality. Kids love the two heated pools (one indoors, one out); parents appreciate the family-size rooms.

Hôtel Le Glacier   HOTEL €€

(📞 04 90 34 02 01; www.le-glacier.com; 46 cours Aristide Briand; d €58-195; 🌬@🛜) All 28 rooms are individually decorated and impeccably maintained by the charming owners, who pay attention to details. There's easy parking in front of the hotel, and bike rental. Breakfast €10.

🍴 Eating

It's worth wandering away from the line-up of cafe terraces opposite the Théâtre Antique on place des Frères Mounet to delve into the pedestrian squares of Orange's softly hued old town. Market stalls spill across streets in the town centre every Thursday.

À la Maison
BISTRO €

(☑04 90 60 98 83; 4 place des Cordeliers; 2-/3-course menu lunch €12.50/15, dinner €25/32; ☺noon-2pm & 7-10pm Mon-Sat) There's no lovelier spot on a warm night than the leafy courtyard, wrapped around an old stone fountain and a trio of plane trees, at this simple bistro across from the walls of the Théâtre Antique. Its name, 'At Home', is a perfect reflection of the reception you'll get.

Les Artistes
BISTRO, CAFE €

(place de la République; 1-/2-/3-course menu €11/13.50/15.50; ☺8-2am) A hybrid drinking/dining address with a chic contemporary interior and a vast pavement terrace on a pedestrian old-town square, The Artists buzzes from dawn to dark. Happy hour (5pm to 8pm) is great value, as are its meal-sized salads and other brasserie fare.

Le Parvis
PROVENÇAL €€

(☑04 90 34 82 00; www.restaurant-le-parvis-orange.com; 55 cours Pourtoules; 2-/3-course menu lunch €23/29, dinner €36/46; ☺noon-1.45pm & 7.30-9.15pm Tue-Sat) Nobody speaks above a whisper at Orange's top table, where chef Jean-Michel Bérengier has cooked up superb Provençal food for the past 25 years.

La Grotte d'Auguste
TRADITIONAL FRENCH €€

(☑04 90 60 22 54; www.restaurant-orange.fr; Théâtre Antique, rue Madeleine Roch; lunch/dinner menu from €16/21; ☺noon-2pm & 7-10pm Tue-Sat) Location is key at Auguste's Grotto, tucked beneath Orange's Roman theatre. Summer dining overlooks the ruins of a 2nd-century Hemicycle temple. Cuisine is traditional French, with lots of meat cuts and gourmet treats like black truffles.

Au Petit Patio
TRADITIONAL FRENCH €€

(☑04 90 29 69 27; 58 cours Aristide Briand; lunch/dinner menus from €18/26; ☺noon-1.30pm Mon-Sat, 7-9.15pm Mon-Wed, Fri & Sat) Au Petit Patio is a popular spot for a lingering lunch (*menus* include wine and coffee) or an indulgent dinner (foie gras is homemade) with excellent service and a charming outdoor terrace.

❶ Information

Tourist Office (☑04 90 34 70 88; www.otorange.fr; place des Frères Mounet; ☺9am-6.30pm Mon-Sat, 9am-1pm & 2-6.30pm Sun, closed Sun Oct-Mar) Brochures and hotel bookings.

❶ Getting There & Around

BUS

Buses operated by **TransVaucluse** (www.vaucluse.fr) serve Avignon (€2, 45 minutes) and Vaison-la-Romaine (€2, 45 minutes) from the **bus station** (☑04 90 34 15 59; 201 cours Pourtoules).

TRAIN

Orange's **train station** (av Frédéric Mistral) is 1.5km east of the town centre.

Avignon €6.50, 22 minutes
Lyon €35, 2¼ hours
Marseille €25, 1¾ hours
Marseille airport (Vitrolles station) €22, 1½ hours

BICYCLE

Sport Aventure (☑04 90 34 75 08; 1 place de la République; half-day/day/week €12/18/69) is a central bike shop; delivers within 20km radius.

Vaison-la-Romaine
POP 6275

Tucked between seven hills, in a dramatic setting, Vaison-la-Romaine has long been a traditional exchange centre, and it still has a thriving Tuesday market. The village's rich Roman legacy is obvious – 20th-century buildings rise alongside France's largest archaeological site. A Roman bridge crosses the River Ouvèze, dividing the contemporary town's pedestrianised centre and the spectacular walled, cobbled-street hilltop Cité Médiévale – one of Provence's most magical ancient villages – where the counts of Toulouse built their 12th-century castle. Vaison is a good base for jaunts into the Dentelles or Mont Ventoux, but tourists throng here in summer: reserve ahead.

◉ Sights & Activities

★ Gallo-Roman Ruins
ROMAN SITES

(☑04 90 36 50 48; www.provenceromaine.com; adult/child incl all ancient sites, museum & cathedral €8/4; ☺9.30am-6.30pm Jun-Sep, 9.30am-6pm Apr & May, 10am-noon & 2-5.30pm Oct-Mar) The ruined remains of Vasio Vocontiorum, the Roman city that flourished here between the 6th and 2nd centuries BC, fill two central Vaison sites. Two neighbourhoods of this once opulent city, **Puymin** and **La Villasse**, lie on either side of the tourist office and av du Général de Gaulle. Admission includes entry to the 12th-century Romanesque cloister at **Cathédrale Notre-Dame de Nazareth** (cloister only €1.50; ☺10am-12.30pm

& 2-6pm Mar-Dec), a five-minute walk west of La Villasse and a soothing refuge from the summer heat.

In **Puymin**, see houses of the nobility, mosaics, workers' quarters, a temple and the still-functioning, 6000-seat **Théâtre Antique** (c AD 20). To make sense of the remains (and collect your audioguide, €3), head for the **Musée Archéologique Gallo-Roman**, which revives Vaison's Roman past with incredible swag – superb mosaics, carved masks and statues that include a 3rd-century silver bust and marble renderings of Hadrian and wife Sabina.

The Romans shopped at the colonnaded boutiques and bathed at **La Villasse**, where you'll find **Maison au Dauphin**, which has splendid marble-lined fish ponds.

★ **Cité Médiévale**   HISTORIC SITE
Cross the **Pont Romain** (Roman bridge) in the footsteps of frightened medieval peasants, who clambered to the walled city during valley conflicts. Steep cobblestone alleyways wend beneath stone ramparts and a 14th-century **bell tower**, past romantic fountains and mansions with incredibly carved doorways. Continue uphill to the 12th-century **château** and be rewarded with eagle's-eye vistas.

Cycling Routes   CYCLING
(www.escapado.fr) Vaison's position is ideal for village-hopping. The tourist office stocks excellent brochures detailing multiple cycling circuits, rated by difficulty, from 26km to 91km.

★★ Festivals & Events

Festival de Vaison-la-Romaine DANCE FESTIVAL
(www.vaison-danses.com; ⊘ Jul) Three-week-long festival held at the Roman Théâtre Antique. Book by April.

Choralies   MUSIC FESTIVAL
(www.choralies.fr; ⊘ Aug) Europe's largest choral festival is held every three years. Upcoming festivals will be held in 2016 and 2019.

Festival des Chœurs Lauréats MUSIC FESTIVAL
(www.festivaldeschoeurslaureats.com; ⊘ late Jul) The best choirs in Europe.

🛏 Sleeping

★ **Hôtel Burrhus**   HOTEL €
(☑ 04 90 36 00 11; www.burrhus.com; 1 place de Montfort; d €64-97, apt €140; ❈ 🛜) On Vaison's vibrant central square, this blue-shuttered hotel is quaint and old from the outside and brilliantly contemporary inside, with

---

BLACK DIAMONDS

Provence's cloak-and-dagger truffle trade is operated from the back of cars, with payment exclusively in cash. Little-known **Richerenches**, 23km northwest of Vaison-la-Romaine, a deceptively wealthy village with a medieval Templar fortress, hosts France's largest wholesale truffle market. It's lovely to visit year round, but especially so on Saturday mornings during truffle season (mid-November to mid-March), when the main street fills with furtive *rabassaïres* (truffle hunters), selling to *courtiers* (brokers) representing dealers in Paris, Germany, Italy and beyond. So covert are the transactions you'll likely never see a truffle change hands at this wholesale market. Head to av de la Rabasse for the retail stalls.

Black truffles (*Tuber melanosporum*) cost up to €1000 per kilogram *wholesale*, up to €4000 retail. Although *trufficulteurs* (truffle growers) try tricks like injecting spores into oak roots, humankind has so far been unable to increase crops of this quasi-mystical fungus. Only nature can dictate if it will be a good or bad year – weather is the major determinant of yield.

Richerenches villagers celebrate an annual **Truffle Mass** in the village church, when parishioners place truffles instead of cash into the collection plate. Then they're auctioned to support the church. The Mass falls on the Sunday nearest 17 January, feast day of St Antoine, patron saint of truffle harvesters. Contact Richerenches' **tourist office** (☑ 04 90 28 05 34; www.richerenches.fr; place Hugues de Bourbouton; ⊘ 10am-1.30pm & 2-6pm Mon-Sat) for details.

If you want to unearth truffles yourself, **Dominique and Eric Jaumard** (☑ 04 90 66 82 21; www.truffes-ventoux.com; La Quinsonne, 634 chemin du Traversier, Monteux; ⊘ Oct–mid-Mar) arrange seasonal hunts and year-round walks on their truffle-rich land, 7km southwest of Carpentras, in Monteux. Or buy truffles fresh, in season, at weekly regional markets, including Vaison-la-Romaine (Tuesday) and Carpentras (Friday).

original artworks and sculptures strung in its enchanting maze of vintage corridors and staircases. Don't miss the giant Roman-inspired terracotta pot, 1.8m tall, suspended between rooftops above the sofa-clad interior patio. No lift. Breakfast €9.

L'École Buissonière   B&B €
(☑04 90 28 95 19; www.buissonniere-provence.com; D75, Buisson; s/d/tr/q incl breakfast from €52/65/82/99; 🐾) Five minutes north of Vaison, in the countryside between Buisson and Villedieu, hosts Monique and John have transformed their stone farmhouse into a tastefully decorated three-bedroom B&B, big on comfort. Breakfast features home-made jam, and there's an outdoor summer kitchen.

Camping du Théâtre Romain   CAMPGROUND €
(☑04 90 28 78 66; www.camping-theatre.com; chemin de Brusquet; sites per 2 people with tent & car €25.40; ☉mid-Mar–mid-Nov; 🐾▨) Opposite the Théâtre Antique. Very sunny, and there's a pool.

L'Évêché   B&B €€
(☑04 90 36 13 46; http://eveche.free.fr; rue de l'Évêché; s/d/tr from €85/95/120) With groaning bookshelves, vaulted ceilings, higgledy-piggledy staircase, intimate salons and exquisite art, this five-room *chambre d'hôte*, in the medieval city, is fabulously atmospheric. Knowledgeable owners Jean-Loup and Aude also lend bikes.

Hostellerie Le Beffroi   HISTORIC HOTEL €€
(☑04 90 36 04 71; www.le-beffroi.com; rue de l'Évêché; d €100-160, tr €190; ☉Apr-Jan; 🐾) Within the medieval city's walls, this *hostellerie* (inn), dating from 1554, fills two buildings (the 'newer' one was built in 1690). A fairy-tale hideaway, its rough-hewn stone-and-wood-beamed rooms are small but romantic, and its restaurant opens onto a rose-and-herb garden with swings for the kids.

✕ Eating

★ Bistro du'O   BISTRO €€
(☑04 90 41 72 90; www.bistroduo.fr; rue du Château; lunch/dinner menus from €19/31; ☉noon-2pm & 7.30-10pm Tue-Sat) No address seduces more than this thoroughly modern gastro-bistro squirrelled away in a 13th-century vaulted cellar in the medieval city. Dynamic couple Gaëlle (front of house) and Philippe (chef) have been the creative duo behind the address since summer 2013, and local seasonal produce is their muse.

Fussy eaters, note that the choice of dishes is short – but superb: a perfect reflection of what's at the market that day.

Le Bateleur   PROVENÇAL €€
(☑04 90 36 28 04; www.le-bateleur.com; 1 place Théodore Aubanel; lunch/dinner menus from €24/32; ☉noon-2pm Tue-Fri & Sat, 7.30-9.30pm Tue-Sat) The best seats at this simple Provençal dining room overlook the river, but you'll need no distractions from the artfully presented quality regional cooking.

★ Le Moulin à Huile   GASTRONOMIC €€€
(☑04 90 36 20 67; www.moulin-huile.com; quai Maréchal Foch, rte de Malaucène; lunch/dinner menus from €39/59; ☉noon-2pm & 7.30-10pm Tue-Sat, noon-2pm Sun mid-Apr–Nov) Michelin-starred chef Robert Bardot showcases gastronomic prowess in a former olive-oil mill with baby-blue wooden shutters by the river. Lunch on a simple truffle omelette (€55). In summer dine outside in the peachy garden, steps from the river (go for the upper terrace rather than the lower one with plastic chairs).

You can also make a night of it in one of three handsome guest rooms (€140 to €160, open year-round).

ⓘ Information

Tourist Office (☑04 90 36 02 11; www.vaison-ventoux-tourisme.com; place du Chanoine Sautel; ☉9.30am-noon & 2-5.45pm Mon-Sat year-round, plus 9.30am-noon Sun mid-Mar–mid-Oct) Helps book rooms.

ⓘ Getting There & Away

BUS

TransVaucluse/Autocars Lieutaud (www.cars-lieutaud.fr) buses serve Orange (€2, 45 minutes) and Avignon (€4, via Orange, two hours). **Cars Comtadins** (☑04 90 67 20 25; www.sudest-mobilites.fr) buses serve Carpentras (€2, 45 minutes) and Malaucène (€1, 30 minutes). For schedules, see www.vaucluse.fr. The bus stop is on av des Choralies, 400m east of the tourist office.

Dentelles de Montmirail

The Dentelles' 8km-long limestone ridge rises abruptly from peaceful vineyard-covered plains about 20km north of Carpentras. The rocky spires take their name from the *dentelles* (lace) they resemble. Forty kilometres of footpaths wind through the Mediterranean scrub – look for buzzards, eagles and fluorescent-green lizards. Climbers favour the southern face. Around the ridge, find wonderful, tiny villages famous for wine.

❶ Getting There & Away

TransVaucluse (www.vaucluse.fr) line 4 connects Orange and Vaison-la-Romaine, via Séguret and Sablet. Line 11 connects Carpentras and Vaison, via Le Barroux. LaCoVe (☑ 04 84 99 50 10, 08 00 88 15 23; www.transcove.com; tickets €2) buses operate Monday to Saturday on the Carpentras–Beaumes-de-Venise–Gigondas route, but you must phone the day before for pick-up.

Gigondas

POP 548 / ELEV 282M

Wine cellars and cafes surround the sun-dappled central square of Gigondas, famous for prestigious red wine. Wine-tasting here provides an excellent counterpoint to Châteauneuf-du-Pape: both use the same grapes, but the soil is different. In town, Caveau de Gigondas (☑ 04 90 65 82 29; www.caveaudugigondas.com; place Gabrielle Andéol; ◷ 10am-noon & 2-6.30pm) represents 100 small producers and offers free tastings – most bottles cost just €12 to €17. The tourist office (☑ 04 90 65 85 46; www.gigondas-dm.fr; rue du Portail, Gigondas; ◷ 9am-12.30pm & 2.30-6.30pm Mon-Sat, 10am-1pm Sun Jul & Aug, shorter hours rest of the year) has a complete list of wineries.

Above the central square, along the Cheminement de Sculptures, enigmatic outdoor sculptures line narrow pathways, leading ever upward to castle ruins, campanile, church and cemetery with stunning vistas.

Séguret & Around

POP 884 / ELEV 250M

Medieval Séguret clings to a hillside above undulating vineyards. Narrow, cobbled streets, lined with flowering vines, wend past a 15th-century fountain, a 12th-century church, and uphill to castle ruins (park below the village and walk). Séguret makes a good base for cyclists and hikers, and lovers of quiet countryside.

🛏 Sleeping & Eating

La Bastide Bleue INN €

(☑ 04 90 46 83 43; www.bastidebleue.com; rte de Sablet; s/d/tr/q incl breakfast €60/79/105/131; ❷ ⊠ ❖) Good for families, with several quad rooms, this cozy 18th-century inn is simply decorated in classic Provençal style; some

rooms have exposed wooden beams. Outside there's a vineyard-view pool. The rustic restaurant (menus €22 to €26) serves good regional cooking (reserve).

Domaine de Cabasse INN €€

(☑ 04 90 46 91 12; www.cabasse.fr; rte de Sablet; d €140-180; ◷ Apr-Oct; ❈ ❷ ⊠ ❖) A wine-producing estate 800m south of Séguret, Domaine de Cabasse has 12 sunlit rooms, a pretty terrace restaurant, pool, tennis, and wines galore from its barrel-lined cellar. Meals include veggies from the garden: consider half-board (€47 per person, in addition to lodging costs).

Les Genêts TRADITIONAL FRENCH €€

(☑ 04 90 46 84 33; D977, Sablet; menus lunch/dinner from €15/28; ◷ noon-2pm Tue-Sun & 7.30-9pm Tue-Sat) Weekday classic-French lunch menus at this roadhouse restaurant 3km south of Séguret are great value – €14.50 with wine – and everything is fresh. Book a table on the vineyard-view terrace.

Suzette

POP 127 / ELEV 425M

Tiny Suzette sits high in the hills between Malaucène and Beaumes-de-Venise, with incredible views that provide perspective on the landscape and make the winding drive worthwhile. Get your bearings at the village-centre table d'orientation (orientation plaque).

🛏 Sleeping & Eating

★ Ferme le Dégoutaud B&B €

(☑ 04 90 62 99 29; www.degoutaud.fr; rte de Malaucène; s/d/tr/q incl breakfast €65/75/85/95; cottages per week from €560; ❷ ⊠) ⦸ This 16th-century working farm, 2.5km northeast of Suzette, has simple, spotless rooms of stone and wood, and self-catering cottages surrounded by spectacular countryside. The farm produces olive oil, honey, jam and organic apricot and cherry juice – sample them at breakfast. Outside there's a summer kitchen and an infinity pool with knockout views. Tops for nature lovers.

Les Coquelicots PROVENÇAL €

(☑ 04 90 65 06 94; www.restaurant-les-coquelicots.com; mains €14-20; ◷ noon-2pm & 7-8.30pm Thu-Tue Jun-Aug, reduced hours rest of year) High on a hill, surrounded by vineyards, Les Coquelicots makes a perfect lunchtime destination when day-tripping the Dentelles, and showcases the flavours of Provence with dishes like lamb with anchovy butter and salt-cod aïoli. Book the terrace for incredible views.

Le Barroux

POP 710 / ELEVATION 325M

Charming wee Le Barroux clings to a hillside beneath medieval Château du Barroux and makes for a good sightseeing stop and lunch break.

⊙ Sights

Château du Barroux   CHÂTEAU

(☑ 04 90 62 35 21; www.chateau-du-barroux.com; adult/child €5/free; ⊙ 10am-7pm Jul-Sep, 2-6pm Oct, 10am-7pm Sat & Sun Apr & May, 2.30-7pm Jun) Built in the 12th century to protect Le Barroux from Saracen invaders, Château du Barroux is one of Provence's few castles. Its fortunes rose and fell, but its last indignity was in WWII, when retreating Germans set it ablaze – it burned for 10 days. Only ghosts remain, but it's great fun to explore, especially for kids unaccustomed to such architectural drama.

Abbaye Ste-Madeleine   CHURCH

(☑ 04 90 62 56 31; www.barroux.org) Two kilometres north of Le Barroux along thread-narrow lanes, this abbey hears Gregorian chants sung by Benedictine monks at 9.30am daily (10am Sunday and holidays). The Romanesque-style monastery, built in the 1980s, is surrounded by lavender. Its shop carries delicious monk-made almond cake. Hats, miniskirts, bare shoulders and mobile phones are forbidden.

🍽 Sleeping & Eating

Les Géraniums   TRADITIONAL FRENCH €€

(☑ 04 90 62 41 08; www.hotel-lesgeraniums.com; place de la Croix; lunch/dinner menus from €18/30; ⊙ 12.15-2pm & 7.15-9pm Jun-Oct) For a lazy lunch (and a parking spot), book a terrace table at Les Géraniums, an old-fashioned country *auberge* with stunning valley views. Upstairs are simply furnished, good-value rooms (doubles €90 to €100).

Beaumes-de-Venise

POP 2425 / ELEV 126M

Snugly sheltered from mistral winds, Beaumes-de-Venise is famous for its *or blanc* (white gold) – sweet muscat wines, best drunk young and cold (perfect with Cavaillon melons). Attend tastings at local co-operative **Balma Vénitia** (☑ 04 90 12 41 00;

www.beaumes-de-venise.com; 228 rte de Carpentras; ⊙ 9am-12.30pm & 2-7pm Apr-Sep, reduced hours Oct-Mar). The excellent **tourist office** (☑ 04 90 62 94 39; www.ot-beaumesdevenise.fr; 122 place du Marché; ⊙ 9.15am-12.15pm & 2-6pm Mon-Sat, also 10am-1pm Sun mid-Jul–mid-Aug) has English-language brochures of wineries.

Taste Beaumes' olive oil at **Moulin à Huile de la Balméenne** (☑ 04 90 62 93 77; www.labalmeenne.fr; 82 av Jules Ferry; ⊙ 9am-noon & 2-6.30pm Mon-Sat year-round, also 2-6.30pm Sun Easter-Aug), open since 1867. For gifts, consider organic soap and bath products from **Savonnerie des Dentelles** (☑ 04 90 37 61 80; www.savonnerie-des-dentelles.com; rte de Sarrians, 42 ZA La Barcillonne; ⊙ 9am-noon & 2.30-6pm Mon-Fri) 🍃, 1.6km southwest of Beaumes-de-Venise.

Sprawling 19th-century gardens, vineyards and olive groves surround **Château Juvenal manor** (☑ 04 90 62 31 76; www.chateau-juvenal-provence.com; 120 chemin du Long-Serre, St-Hippolyte-le-Graveyron; d from €150; ❋ 🤖 ⛵), with four upmarket rooms, billiards, spa, hot tub and fabulous pool. On Tuesday and Friday evenings there's an excellent *table d'hôte* (set menu at a fixed price; €45 with wine; 48-hour advance reservations required). It's 5km west of Beaumes-de-Venise.

Mont Ventoux

Visible for miles around, Mont Ventoux (1912m), nicknamed *le géant de Provence* (Provence's giant), stands like a sentinel over northern Provence. From its summit, accessible by road between May and October (the white glimmering stuff you see in summer is *lauzes*, broken white stones, not snow), vistas extend to the Alps and, on a clear day, the Camargue.

Because of the mountain's dimensions, every European climate type is present on

> ### ℹ LAVENDER VERSUS LAVANDIN
>
> When shopping for lavender, it's worth knowing that the most sought-after product is fine lavender (in French, *lavande fine*; in Latin, *Lavandula angustifolia*, *L. vera*, *L. officinalis*), not spike lavender (*L. latifolia*) or the hybrid lavandin (*L. hybrida*). The latter are high in camphor and are used in detergents and paint solvents, not perfume.

its slopes, from Mediterranean on its lower southern reaches to Arctic on its exposed northern ridge. As you ascend the relentless gradients (which regularly feature in the Tour de France), temperatures can plummet by 20°C, and there's twice as much precipitation as on the plains below. The relentless mistral wind blows 130 days a year, sometimes at a speed of 250km/h. Bring warm clothes and rain gear, even in summer. You can ascend by road year-round, but you cannot traverse the summit from 15 November to 15 April.

This climatic patchwork is reflected in the mountain's diverse fauna and flora, now actively protected by Unesco Biosphere Reserve status. Some species live nowhere else, including the snake eagle and several other birds as well as butterflies.

Three principal gateways – Bédoin, Malaucène and Sault – provide services in summer, but they're far apart. In addition to their tourist offices, find information at **Destination Ventoux** (www.destination-ventoux.com) and **Provence Cycling** (www.provence-cycling. com).

 Activities

Walking

The GR4 crosses the Dentelles de Montmirail before scaling Mont Ventoux's northern face, where it meets the GR9. Both traverse the ridge. The GR4 branches eastwards to Gorges du Verdon; the GR9 crosses the Vaucluse Mountains to the Luberon. The essential map for the area is *3140ET Mont Ventoux*,

---

<blockquote>**WORTH A TRIP**

RIVER GORGES DU TOULOURENC

On hot days you can't beat this easy, family-friendly walk beneath Mont Ventoux's wild, northern face. Wear shorts and water shoes, and hike upstream, splashing in calf-deep water, and explore a spectacular, ever-narrowing limestone canyon. By bike, take the tiny road from Malaucène to the hamlet of Veaux (road signs say 'hameau de Veaux', maps say 'Veaux'); by car, the road via Entrechaux is less winding. Park at the blue bridge over the water. Two hours upstream, there's a Roman bridge – a good turnaround point. Carry food and water.</blockquote>

---

by **IGN** (www.ign.fr). Bédoin's tourist office stocks maps and brochures detailing walks for all levels.

In July and August tourist offices in Bédoin and Malaucène facilitate night-time expeditions up the mountain to see sunrise (participants must be over 15 years old).

Cycling

Tourist offices distribute *Les Itinéraires Ventoux,* a free map detailing 11 itineraries – graded easy to difficult – and highlighting artisanal farms en route. For more cycling trails, see www.lemontventoux.net. Most cycle-hire outfits also offer electric bikes.

Station Ventoux Sud Bike Park　CYCLING
(☑ 04 90 61 84 55; www.facebook.com/Ventoux-BikePark; Chalet Reynard; half-/full day €10/14; ☺10am-5pm Sat & Sun, weekday hours variable) Near the Mont Ventoux summit, at Chalet Reynard, mountain bikers ascend via rope tow (minimum age 10 years), then descend ramps and jumps down three trails (5km in total). In winter it's possible to mountain bike on snow. Bring bike, helmet and gloves or rent all gear at Chalet Reynard. Call to check opening times, which are highly weather dependent.

Bédoin Location　CYCLING
(☑ 04 90 65 94 53; www.bedoin-location.fr; 20 rte de Malaucène, Bédoin; per half-/full day from €15/20; ☺9am-7pm Mar-Nov) Opposite the tourist office in Bédoin, this sports shop rents and repairs mountain and road bikes and delivers to the summit of Mont Ventoux.

La Route du Ventoux　CYCLING
(☑ 04 90 67 07 40; www.larouteduventoux.com; rte du Ventoux, Bédoin; road bikes/mountain bikes/ tandems per day from €35/25/50; ☺8am-7pm Mon-Sat May-Aug, 9am-6pm Mar, Apr & Oct, plus 8am-12.30pm Sun Jul) Rents bicycles of many types in Bédoin.

Ventoux Bikes　CYCLING
(☑ 04 90 62 58 19; www.ventoux-bikes.fr; 1 av de Verdun, Malaucène; road bikes per day from €40; ☺9am-7pm Mon-Sat Apr-Nov) Malaucène's hub for road-bike rental and sale, offering multiple calibres, plus gear.

Albion Cycles　CYCLING
(☑ 04 90 64 09 32; www.albioncycles.com; rte de St-Trinit, Sault; mountain-/road-bike rental per day €26/36; ☺9am-12.30pm & 3-6.30pm Tue-Sat Mar-Nov) Sault's bicycle-rental and -sale outlet, including electric-assistance bikes.

Skiing

Access **Chalet Reynard** (www.chalet-reynard. fr) from Bédoin or Sault, not Malaucène, to sled or ski Mont Ventoux's south summit. Traverse the isolated back side, via the D974 from Malaucène, to reach tiny north-facing ski area Mont Serein. It's fun for a few turns, but nothing serious. Snow melts by April.

Bédoin

POP 3279 / ELEV 295M

On Mont Ventoux's southwestern flanks, peppy Bédoin is the most upbeat of the gateways, chock-a-block with cafes and shops. Its geographic position diminishes the mistral, which contributes to its popularity with cyclists. In July and August the **tourist office** (☑04 90 65 63 95; www.bedoin. org; Espace Marie-Louis Gravier, 1 rte de Malaucène; ⊙9.30am-12.30pm & 2-6pm Mon-Sat, 9.30am-12.30pm Sun mid-Jun–Aug, reduced hours rest of year), an excellent information source on all regional activities, guides walks into the forest. **Market day** is Monday.

Malaucène

POP 2746 / ELEV 377M

Despite deceptively lovely plane-tree-lined streets, Malaucène can feel a bit drab, except in summer, when hikers and bikers arrive. Its blessing is geographical: on the saddle between Mont Ventoux and the Dentelles, it's well positioned for mountain sorties. Pope Clement V had a second home here in the 14th century: his legacy remains in the Gothic-Romanesque **Église St-Michel & St-Pierre**, constructed in 1309 on the site of an ancient temple. The **tourist office** (☑04 90 65 22 59; http://villagemalaucene.free.fr; place de la Mairie; ⊙9.15am-12.15pm & 2.30-5.30pm Mon-Fri, 9am-noon Sat) stocks information on Mont Ventoux but (surprisingly) not the Dentelles, and keeps erratic hours.

Sault

POP 1285 / ELEV 800M

At the eastern end of the Mont Ventoux massif, drowsily charming Sault has incredible summertime vistas over lavender fields. Visit **André Boyer** (☑04 90 64 00 23; www.nougat-boyer.fr; place de l'Europe) for honey-and-almond nougat, family made since 1887. Sault's **tourist office** (☑04 90 64 01 21; www.saultenprovence.com; av de la Promenade; ⊙9.30am-12.30pm & 1.30-6.30pm Mon-Sat Jun-Aug, reduced hours rest of year), a

GORGES DE LA NESQUE

Abutting the Forêt de Venasque (and connected via walking trail GR91), the sheer-walled, 20km-long Gorges de la Nesque is protected as a Unesco Biosphere Reserve. Other than driving or hiking, a novel means of exploring this spectacular limestone canyon (or nearby Mont Ventoux) is alongside a donkey from **Les Ânes des Abeilles** (☑04 90 64 01 52; http://abeilles.ane-et-rando. com; rte de la Gabelle, Col des Abeilles; day/weekend from €50/95). Beasts carry up to 40kg (ie small children or bags).

good resource for Mont Ventoux and Gorges de la Nesque, has lists of artisanal lavender producers such as **GAEC Champelle** (☑04 90 64 01 50; www.gaec-champelle.fr; rte de Ventoux) 🖉, a roadside farmstand northwest of town whose products include a great gift for cooks: *herbes de Provence*–infused *fleur de sel* (gourmet salt).

Carpentras & Around

POP 29.562

Try to visit Carpentras on a Friday morning, when the streets spill over with more than **350 stalls** laden with bread, honey, cheese, olives, fruit and a rainbow of *berlingots*, Carpentras' striped, pillow-shaped hard-boiled sweets. During winter the pungent truffle market murmurs with hushed-tone transactions. The truffle season is kicked off by Carpentras' biggest fair, held during the **Fête de St-Siffrein** on 27 November, when more than 1000 stalls spread across town.

Markets aside, this slightly rundown agricultural town has but a handful of historic sights. A Greek trading centre and later a Gallo-Roman city, it became papal territory in 1229, and was also shaped by a strong Jewish presence, as Jews who had been expelled from French crown territory took refuge here.

⊙ Sights

★**Synagogue de Carpentras**   SYNAGOGUE
(☑04 90 63 39 97; place Juiverie; ⊙10am-noon & 3-4.30pm Mon-Thu, 10-11.30am & 3-3.30pm Fri) Carpentras' remarkable synagogue dates to 1367 and is the oldest still in use in France.

Carpentras

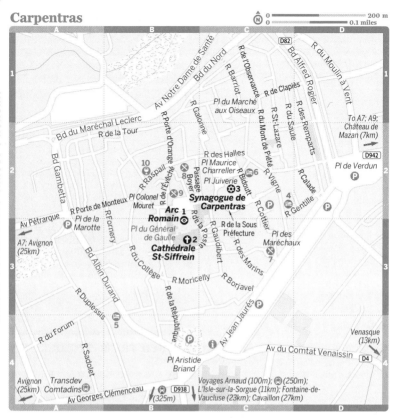

Carpentras

Although Jews were initially welcomed into papal territory, by the 17th century they had to live in ghettos in Avignon, Carpentras, Cavaillon and L'Isle-sur-la-Sorgue: the synagogue is deliberately inconspicuous. The wood-panelled prayer hall was rebuilt in 18th-century Baroque style; downstairs are bread-baking ovens, used until 1904. For access, ring the doorbell on the half-hour.

Alternatively, join the excellent 1½-hour **guided tour** (adult/child €5/3.50) organised by the tourist office every Tuesday at 10.30am from April to September.

★ **Cathédrale St-Siffrein** CATHEDRAL
(place St-Siffrein; ⊙ 8am-noon & 2-6pm Mon-Sat) Carpentras' cathedral was built between 1405 and 1519 in meridional Gothic style but is crowned by a distinctive contemporary bell tower. Its **Trésor d'Art Sacré** (Treasury of Religious Art) holds precious 14th- to 19th-century religious relics that you can only see during the Fête de St-Siffrein and on guided walks with the tourist office.

★ Arc Romain
ROMAN SITES

Hidden behind Cathédrale St-Siffrein, the Arc Romain was built under Augustus in the 1st century AD and is decorated with worn carvings of enslaved Gauls.

🛏 Sleeping

Le Malaga
HOTEL €

(☑ 04 90 60 57 96, 06 16 59 85 59; www.hotel-malaga-carpentras.fr; 37 place Maurice-Charretier; s/d/q €40/45/67; 🖭🚹) Given the price and city-centre location, the eight no-frills rooms are good value, if a bit threadbare, noisy and lacking in air-con. Downstairs there's a brasserie.

Hôtel du Fiacre
HOTEL €€

(☑ 04 90 63 03 15; www.hotel-du-fiacre.com; 153 rue Vigne; s €70-150, d €80-150; ⊙ reception 8am-9pm; 🖭) The faded grandeur of this 18th-century mansion with ochre facade is charming – from marble staircase to canopied beds. Outside there's a lovely sunny courtyard. Good service and value. Breakfast €10.

Hotel le Comtadin
HOTEL €€

(☑ 04 90 67 75 00; www.le-comtadin.com; 65 bd Albin Durand; d €80-110; ❄🖭) Formerly a private mansion, now a fresh-looking mid-range hotel under the Best Western banner, Le Comtadin's best rooms face an interior courtyard; less expensive rooms face the street. Breakfast €13.

Château de Mazan
HOTEL €€€

(☑ 04 90 69 62 61; www.chateaudemazan.com; place Napoléon, Mazan; d €160-300, ste €300-440; ⊙ Mar-Dec; ❄@🖭) This magnificent 18th-century mansion, 7km east of Carpentras in the village of Mazan, belonged to the Marquis de Sade. Today it houses 30 regal rooms. Its refined *haute-cuisine* restaurant, l'Ingénue (mains lunch/dinner from €15/25), merits a special trip.

🍴 Eating & Drinking

★ La Maison Jouvaud
PATISSERIE €

(40 rue de l'Évêché; boxes of sweets from €10; ⊙ 10am-7pm Mon, 8am-7pm Tue-Fri, 9am-7pm Sat & Sun) No address is sweeter than Jouvard, a vintage-styled cake shop, tearoom and homeware boutique festooned at every turn with delectable cakes, chocolates, sugared almonds, candied fruits and the feistiest mountain of homemade meringues imaginable waiting to seduce on the bar. The drinks menu includes *chocolat à l'ancienne* (hot

chocolate), milk with honey, and a beautiful selection of Mariage Frères teas.

Chez Serge
PROVENÇAL €€

(☑ 04 90 63 21 24; www.chez-serge.com; 90 rue Cottier; lunch/dinner menus from €17/27; ⊙ noon-2pm & 7.30-10pm Jun-Sep, noon-1.30pm & 7.30-9.30pm Oct-May; 🖭🚹) Perhaps the hottest address in town, this savvy little courtyard restaurant plays at 'shabby chic' with its distressed wood and granite, Panton chairs and contemporary finishings. Serge's Place is the spot to sample Provence's black truffles, honoured with their own menu and simple *plats* (dishes) like truffle omelette, truffle-laced pasta and truffle risotto.

La Galusha
PROVENÇAL €€

(☑ 04 90 60 75 00, 06 62 79 25 42; www.galusha.fr; 30 place de l'Horloge; lunch/dinner menus from €14.50/24; ⊙ noon-1.30pm & 7.30-9.30pm Tue-Sun) Venetian glass ceiling lamps and whimsical Arcimboldo paintings lend a warm glow to the romantic interior of this upmarket dining room, tucked on the ground floor of a 15th-century building with enchanting flower-filled patio out the back. In the kitchen Nîmes-born chef Stéphan Laurent cooks up modern Provençal cuisine, catering to lighter lunchtime appetites with giant salads (€14.50).

Angel'Art Galerie
COCKTAIL BAR

(☑ 06 10 13 41 94; www.facebook.com/AngelArt-Galerie; 59 rue Raspail; ⊙ 6pm-1am Mon, 9am-1am Tue-Sat) This hybrid art gallery–cocktail lounge is one of the hippest spaces in town – alongside its equally trendy neighbours, with whom it shares brightly coloured sunshade sails, strung from one side of the tiny pedestrian street to the other.

ℹ Information

Tourist Office (☑ 04 90 63 00 78; www.carpentras-ventoux.com; 97 place du 25 Août 1944; ⊙ 9am-1pm & 2-7pm Mon-Sat, 9.30am-1pm Sun, shorter hours rest of year) Excellent website, guided tours in English (adult/child €5/3.50), helpful staff and an adjoining boutique of local culinary products like *berlingots*, honey and AOC Ventoux wine.

ℹ Getting There & Around

TRAIN

Local trains connect Carpentras' **train station** (av de la Gare) to Avignon Centre station (30 minutes, hourly) and Avignon TGV station (38 minutes).

BUS

The **bus station** (place Terradou) is 150m south-west of the tourist office, which has schedules, as does **TransVaucluse** (www.vaucluse.fr). Services are operated by **Transdev Comtadins** (☑04 90 67 20 25; www.sudest-mobilites. fr; 192 av Georges Clémenceau) and **Voyages Arnaud** (☑04 90 63 01 82; www.voyages-ar-naud-carpentras.com; 8 av Victor-Hugo).

Avignon €2, 40 minutes
Cavaillon €2, 45 minutes
L'Isle-sur-la-Sorgue €2, 35 minutes
Orange €2, 55 minutes
Vaison-la-Romaine €2, 45 minutes, via **Ma-laucène** €2, 35 minutes

CAR

Free parking is northeast of the tourist office, along av Jean Jaurès.

EAST OF AVIGNON

The small towns between Avignon and the Luberon are defined by water. Pernes-les-Fontaines' aesthetic derives from scores of fountains, some dating to the 15th century; L'Isle-sur-la-Sorgue, famous for antiques trading, is bisected by the glassy River Sorgue; and Fontaine-de-Vaucluse is home to the river's source.

Pernes-les-Fontaines

POP 10,711

Once the capital of the Comtat Venaissin, Pernes-les-Fontaines is now a sleepy village of ancient buildings. It's known for its 40 fountains that splash and gurgle in shady squares and narrow cobbled streets. Among those not to missed: **Fontaine du Cormoran** (pont Notre-Dame, 1761), **Fontaine Reboul** (place Reboul, 15th century) and **Fontaine du Gigot** (rue Victor-Hugo, 1757).

◉ Sights

Maison du Costume Comtadin　　MUSEUM
(☑04 90 61 31 04; www.costumescomtadin.com; rue de la République; ⊙10am-12.30pm & 3-6.30pm Wed-Mon Jul–mid-Sep, reduced hours rest of year) **FREE** A 19th-century Provençal costume museum.

Maison Fléchier　　MUSEUM
(☑04 90 61 31 04; pl Fléchier) **FREE** This cultural museum displays local crafts in a historic building.

🛏 Sleeping & Eating

Mas La Bonoty　　PROVENÇAL €€
(☑04 90 61 61 09; www.bonoty.com; chemin de la Bonoty; lunch/dinner menus from €19/32; ⊙12.15-1.30pm & 7.30-9.15pm; 🛜🅿) It's worth getting lost to find this 18th-century farmhouse-hotel, which has earned its reputation as a laudable Provençal restaurant. *Menus* feature hearty fare – thyme-roasted duckling, foie gras and rack of lamb – served on linen-dressed tables in an atmospheric stone-walled dining room. Attractive, simple rooms (doubles including breakfast €90 to €100) are available with half-board.

☞ Tours

Town & Fountain Walk　　WALKING TOUR
A free walking-tour map from the tourist office details strolls through quaint streets past such historic sights as the Maison du Costume Comtadin, Maison Fléchier and a fortified 11th-century church. Follow a rough path to the top of the medieval clock tower (*tour de l'horloge*) for panoramic views.

ⓘ Information

Tourist Office (☑04 90 61 31 04; www. tourisme-pernes.fr; place Gabriel Moutte; ⊙9am-1pm & 2-6.30pm Mon-Fri, to 5pm Sat, 9.30am-12:30pm Sun Jul & Aug, reduced hours rest of year)

L'Isle-sur-la-Sorgue

POP 19,395

A moat of flowing water encircles the ancient and prosperous town of L'Isle-sur-la-Sorgue, 7km west of Fontaine. This 'Venice of Provence' is home to several antiques villages, housing 300 dealers between them. Sunday is the big market day, with antique vendors participating as well, while Thursday offers a smaller market through the village streets.

L'Isle dates to the 12th century, when fishermen built huts on stilts above what was then a marsh. By the 18th century, canals lined with 70 giant wheels powered silk factories and paper mills.

◉ Sights

Old Town　　HISTORIC SITE
The exceptional historic centre is contained within canals dotted by creaking water-wheels – the one by the tiny park at ave des Quatre Otages is particularly photogenic.

The former **Jewish quarter** exists in name only: the ghetto's synagogue was destroyed in 1856. The ancient **fishermen's quarter**, a tangle of narrow passageways, dead-ends in L'Isle's eastern corner and retains a town-within-a-town feeling.

A tourist-office brochure details the attractions, and there's a smartphone app.

Collégiale Notre Dame des Anges   CHURCH
(Our Lady of Angels; place de la Liberté; ⊙10am-noon & 3-6pm daily Jul-Sep, Tue-Sat Oct-Jun) The stately exterior of the Collégiale Notre Dame des Anges, in L'Isle's historic centre, shows no sign of the Baroque theatrics inside: 122 gold angels ushering forward the Virgin Mary, and a magnificent 1648-built organ, on the left as you face the altar (the pipes on the right are mute, there purely for visual symmetry).

Campredon Centre d'Art   MUSEUM
(☑04 90 38 17 41; http://islesurlasorgue.fr/campredon.html; 20 rue du Docteur Tallet; adult/child €7/free; ⊙10am-12.30pm & 2-5.30pm Tue-Sat) Rotating contemporary-art exhibitions fill this 18th-century mansion.

Partage des Eaux   PARK
A country lane runs riverside from the old town 2km east towards the serene *partage des eaux* (parting of the waters), where the Sorgue splits into the channels that surround the town. It's a perfect spot for idling on grassy banks, skipping stones and watching birds. Waterside cafes sell ice cream.

🛌 Sleeping

Hotel Nevons   HOTEL €
(☑04 90 20 72 00; www.hotel-les-nevons.com; 205 chemin des Nevons; d €70-120, tr €120-140, q €140-160; ❄@🔊🏊💨) This modern, generic hotel (with elevator) near the town parking lot could be anywhere, but its rooms are good value and have gleaming bathrooms. The rooftop pool has knockout views. The family suite (€150 to €180) sleeps five.

★La Prévôté   B&B €€€
(☑04 90 38 57 29; www.la-prevote.fr; 4bis rue Jean-Jacques Rousseau; d incl breakfast €150-225; ⊙closed late Feb–mid-Mar & mid-Nov–early Dec; 🔊) Straddling a creek running *through* the house, this former 17th-century convent has been converted into a *très* sexy *chambre d'hôte*, its dreamy rooms decked out in luxe style: locally loomed high-thread-count linens, silk draperies and antiques reuphol-

DON'T MISS

PADDLING THE SORGUE

There is no more enchanting means of meandering from Fontaine-de-Vaucluse 8km downstream to neighbouring L'Isle-sur-la-Sorgue (or it can be done in reverse) than in a canoe or kayak. Take guided or self-guided two-hour trips (adult/child €17/11) from late April to October with **Canoë Évasion** (☑04 90 38 26 22; www.canoe-evasion.net; rte de Fontaine de Vaucluse (D24), Fontaine de Vaucluse) or **Kayak Vert** (☑04 90 20 35 44; www.canoe-france.com; Quartier la Baume, Fontaine de Vaucluse).

Life jackets are provided, but children must be able to swim 25m. Afterwards you're returned by minibus to your car.

stered in contemporary fabrics. It also has an excellent gastronomic restaurant (p220).

🍴 Eating

Au Chineur   BISTRO €€
(☑04 90 38 33 54; 2 esplanade Robert-Vasse; lunch menus from €13, mains €15-20; ⊙7am-midnight) Antique bric-a-brac hangs from the rafters at this quayside bistro with excellent people-watching. Expect simple classics and good-value lunches; between mealtimes, find cheese-and-charcuterie plates, tarts and nibbles.

La Villa   MODERN FRENCH €€
(☑04 90 38 24 50; www.lavillarestaurant.fr; 682 av Jean Monnet; mains €15-22; ⊙7.30-9.15pm Wed-Sun & noon-2pm Sun) Los Angeles meets Provence at La Villa, 1.7km north of the centre, where tables line a portico surrounding a swimming pool. Everyone dresses sharp, filling the concrete-and-velvet, rustic-chic interior. Up-tempo lounge beats set a lively mood. Reserve.

★Le Vivier   GASTRONOMIC €€€
(☑04 90 38 52 80; www.levivier-restaurant.com; 800 cours Fernande Peyre; weekday menus from €26, weekend dinner menus €53-75; ⊙noon-1.30pm Tue-Thu & Sun, 7.30-10pm Tue-Sat) One kilometre northeast of the centre, swanky Michelin-starred 'Fishpond' is renowned for its imaginative, contemporary cooking. Prime local ingredients appear in dishes served riverside on the terrace or in the dining room. Reservations essential.

La Prévôté GASTRONOMIC €€€

(☑ 04 90 38 57 29; www.la-prevote.fr; 4bis rue Jean-Jacques Rousseau; menus lunch €23, dinner €41-75; ☉ noon-1.30pm & 7.30-9.30pm Thu-Mon) La Prévôté's excellent gastronomic restaurant is run by chef Jean-Marie Alloin, who concocts dishes like foie gras ravioli, and pear sorbet with thyme-and-rosemary chocolates – *délicieux*!

🛍 Shopping

Antiques Villages ANTIQUES

(☉ noon-6pm Fri, 10am-6pm Sat-Mon) If your manor house needs that perfect Louis XV chandelier, look no further. The former mills and factories along L'Isle-sur-la-Sorgue's main road contain seven fascinating-to-explore antiques villages with 300-plus high-end stalls. For bargains, it's better to come mid-August or Easter for the **antiques fairs.**

La Manufacture ARTS, FASHION

(http://manufactureisle.canalblog.com; 21 impasse de l'Hôtel de Palerme; ☉ 10am-7pm Tue-Sun) A collective showcasing the work of 25-odd local artists and artisans, La Manufacture is a one-stop shop for funky furniture, original jewellery, designer clothing, dogs crafted from rubber wellington boots and so on. Find it at the end of an alley off L'Isle's main pedestrian street, rue de la République.

ℹ Information

Tourist Office (☑ 04 90 38 04 78; www.oti-delasorgue.fr; place de la Liberté; ☉ 9am-12.30pm & 2.30-6pm Mon-Sat, 9.30am-1pm Sun) In the centre of the old town.

ℹ Getting There & Around

BICYCLE

David Bollack (☑ 06 38 14 49 50; veloservices.jimbo.com; 3 rue du Docteur Tallet; per day from €15; ☉ 9am-1pm & 2-7pm) Reservations are essential for weekend rentals from this old-town bike shop; also delivers to Fontaine-de-Vaucluse.

Luberon Biking (☑ 04 90 90 14 62; www.luberon-biking.fr; 10 av de la Gare; per day adult/child €22/12) Wide range of bicycle rentals and delivery available. Reserve on weekends.

BUS

Voyages Raoux (www.voyages-raoux.fr) buses serve Avignon (€2, 40 minutes) and Fontaine-de-Vaucluse (€1.50, 15 minutes). Voyages Arnaud buses (p218) serve Carpentras (€2, 30 minutes) and Cavaillon (€1.50, 30 minutes), via L'Isle-sur-la-Sorgue.

CAR

Free parking lines the canals, but spaces are rare on weekends.

TRAIN

L'Isle-sur-la-Sorgue Fontaine-de-Vaucluse Train Station (av Julien Guigue, L'Isle-sur-la-Sorgue) is on the train line between Marseille (€17, 1½ hours), Cavaillon (€3, 10 minutes) and Avignon (€5, 30 minutes). Eight per day continue to Avignon TGV station (€6, 40 minutes).

Fontaine-de-Vaucluse

POP 661

France's most powerful spring surges from beneath the pretty village of Fontaine-de-Vaucluse, at the end of a U-shaped valley beneath limestone cliffs. The rain that falls within 1200 sq km gushes out here as the River Sorgue. The miraculous appearance of this crystal-clear flood draws 1.5 million tourists each year – aim to arrive early in the morning before the trickle of visitors becomes a deluge; avoid it Sundays in summer.

Stroll beyond the village's tourist distractions and you quickly sense the peace and beauty that inspired Italian poet Petrarch (1304–74), who wrote his most famous works here – sonnets to his unrequited love, Laura.

◉ Sights & Activities

★ **La Fontaine** SPRING

At the foot of craggy cliffs, an easy 1km walk from the village, the River Sorgue surges from the earth's depths. The spring is most dazzling after heavy rain, when water glows azure blue, welling up at an incredible 90 cu metres per second. Jacques Cousteau was among those who attempted to plumb the spring's depths, before an unmanned submarine touched base (315m down) in 1985.

Musée d'Histoire Jean Garcin: 1939–1945 MUSEUM

(☑ 04 90 20 24 00; www.vaucluse.fr; chemin de la Fontaine; adult/child €3.50/free; ☉ 10am-6pm Wed-Mon Apr-Oct & Jan-Feb, Sat & Sun Mar, Nov & Dec) Excellent examination of life in occupied France during WWII.

🛏 Sleeping & Eating

Hôtel du Poète HISTORIC HOTEL €€

(☑ 04 90 20 34 05; www.hoteldupoete.com; d €98-240; ☉ Mar-Nov; ❄ 🐾 ❄) Drift to sleep to the sound of rushing water at this elegant small hotel, inside a restored mill on the river's banks. By day, lie poolside in the sun-dappled shade among the park-like grounds. Breakfast €17.

Pétrarque et Laure   BRASSERIE €€
(☑04 90 20 31 48; place Colonne; lunch/dinner menus from €14/19; ☺noon-3pm & 7-10pm) Fontaine-de-Vaucluse's restaurants tend toward the *touristique;* this one is no exception, but it manages to serve reasonably priced, good-quality food (try the local trout) on a wonderful tree-shaded terrace beside the river.

ℹ Information

Tourist Office (☑04 90 20 32 22; www.oti-delasorgue.fr; Résidence Jean Garcin; ☺10am-1pm & 2.30-6.30pm May-Sep, reduced hours rest of year) By the bridge, mid-village.

ℹ Getting There & Away

BICYCLE
A tourist-office brochure details three easy back-roads biking routes. Bike shops in L'Isle-sur-la-Sorgue deliver to Fontaine.

BUS
Voyages Raoux buses serve Avignon (€2, one hour) and L'Îsle-sur-la-Sorgue (€1.50, 15 minutes).

CAR
The narrow road to Gordes (14km, 20 minutes) from Fontaine-de-Vaucluse makes a scenic, less-travelled alternative to reach the Luberon. Parking in town costs €4.

Pays de Venasque

The seldom-visited, beautiful Venasque Country is perfect for a road trip: a rolling landscape of oak woodlands, dotted with villages atop rocky promontories and hundreds of *bories* (domed stone huts from the Bronze Age). The region is famous for its early-summer ruby-red cherries.

The **Forêt de Venasque**, criss-crossed by walking trails (including long-distance GR91), lies east of Venasque. Cross the Col de Murs mountain pass (627m) to pretty little **Murs**, and see the remains of **Le Mur de la Peste** (the Plague Wall), built in 1720 in a vain attempt to stop the plague from entering papal territory. You could also walk into the Luberon from here, calling at Gordes and the Abbaye Notre-Dame de Sénanque (p231). IGN's map *Balades en forêts du*

THE LEGEND OF ST VÉRAN

Il était une fois – once upon a time – Fontaine-de-Vaucluse was plagued by a vile half-dragon, half-serpent called the Couloubre. Enter St Véran, who slayed the beast and saved the town. A statue outside the village's 11th-century Romanesque church, **Église St-Véran**, commemorates the slaying. Follow the legend up the cliff to the 13th-century **ruins of a castle** built to protect the saint's tomb – views are as incredible as the tale.

Ventoux de Venasque et St-Lambert (€9) outlines several family-friendly walks.

Venasque

POP 1184 / ELEV 320M
Tiny Venasque teeters on a rocky spur, its twisting streets and ancient buildings weathered by howling winds. So picturesque are the village and its views that everyone is forever reaching for their cameras.

◉ Sights

Romanesque Church   CHURCH
(Église Notre-Dame; ☺9.15am-5pm) The church contains the pride of the Pays de Venasque: an unusual late-Gothic *Crucifixion* painting (1498).

★Baptistry   CHURCH
(☑04 90 66 62 01; place de l'Église; adult/child €3/free; ☺9.15am-noon & 1-6.30pm, 9.15am-5pm winter) Tucked behind the Romanesque church, this baptistry was built in the 6th century on the site of a Roman temple.

🛏 Sleeping & Eating

Les Remparts   PROVENÇAL €€
(☑04 90 66 02 79; www.hotellesremparts.com; 36 rue Haute; lunch/dinner menus from €22/27; ☺noon-1.30pm & 7.30-9.30pm daily Apr-Oct; 🛜☑🐾) Built into the city's ramparts, this aptly named restaurant-hotel serves good traditional Provençal cooking, copious lunchtime salads and – *quelle surprise* – a dedicated vegetarian *menu*. The terrace has stunning valley views: sit outside. There's yummy cherry juice if you're driving. Upstairs are eight spiffy, great-value rooms (singles/doubles/triples/quads including breakfast €55/65/85/100).

❶ Information

Venasque Tourist Office (☑ 04 90 66 11 66; www.tourisme-venasque.com; Grand Rue; ☺ 10am-noon & 2-6pm Mon-Sat Apr-Oct) Stocks excellent hiking information.

LES ALPILLES

This silvery chain of low, jagged mountains strung between the Rivers Durance and Rhône delineates a *très* chic side of Provence, notably around upmarket St-Rémy-de-Provence, known for fine restaurants and summertime celebrity-spotting. The entire region is full of gastronomic delights – AOC olive oil, vineyards and Michelin-starred restaurants. History comes to life at magnificent ruined castles and at one of Provence's best Roman sites, the ancient city of Glanum.

St-Rémy-de-Provence

POP 10,826

See-and-be-seen St-Rémy has an unfair share of gourmet shops and restaurants – in the spirit of the town's most famous son, prophecy-maker Nostradamus, we predict you'll need to let your belt out a notch. Come summer, the jet set wanders the peripheral boulevard and congregates at place de la République, leaving the quaint historic center strangely deserted. The low season is quiet.

❍ Sights

★ Site Archéologique de Glanum   ROMAN SITES

(☑ 04 90 92 23 79; www.glanum.monuments-nationaux.fr; rte des Baux-de-Provence; adult/child €7.50/free, parking €2.70; ☺ 9.30am-6.30pm Apr-Sep, 10am-5pm Oct-Mar, closed Mon Sep-Mar) Spectacular archaeological site Glanum dates to the 3rd century BC. Walking the main street towards the sacred spring around which Glanum grew, you pass the fascinating remains of a once-thriving city, complete with baths, forum, marketplace, temples and houses. Two ancient Roman

---

❶ ST-RÉMY DISCOUNT PASS

Pick up the free **Carte St-Rémy** at the first sight you visit, get it stamped, then benefit from reduced admission at St-Rémy's other sights.

---

monuments – a triumphal arch (AD 20) and mausoleum (30 to 20 BC) – mark the entrance, 2km south of St-Rémy.

★ Monastère St-Paul de Mausole   HISTORIC SITE

(☑ 04 90 92 77 00; www.saintpauldemausole.fr; adult/child €4.70/free; ☺ 9.30am-6.30pm Apr-Sep, 10.15am-4.30pm Oct-Mar, closed Jan-March) Van Gogh admitted himself to Monastère St-Paul de Mausole in 1889. The peaceful asylum's security led to his most productive period – he completed 150-plus drawings and some 150 paintings here, including his famous *Irises*. A reconstruction of his room is open to visitors, as are a Romanesque **cloister** and **gardens** growing flowers that feature in his work. From the monastery entrance, a **walking trail** is marked by colour panels, showing where the artist set up his easel.

St-Paul remains a psychiatric institution: an exhibition room sells artwork created by patients.

Musée Estrine   MUSEUM

(☑ 04 90 92 34 72; www.musee-estrine.fr; 8 rue Lucien Estrine; adult/child €7/free; ☺ 10am-6pm Tue-Sun mid-Jun–mid-Sep, reduced hours rest of year, closed Dec-Feb) Twentieth-century modern art and rotating contemporary-art exhibitions fill a beautiful 18th-century *hôtel particulier* (mansion).

Musée des Alpilles   MUSEUM

(☑ 04 90 92 68 24; www.mairie-saintremydeprovence.fr; 1 place Favier; adult/child €4.50/free; ☺ 10am-6pm Tue-Sun May-Sep, 1-5.30pm Tue-Sat Oct-Apr) An engaging little museum chronicling the area's rich heritage, with fossils and crafts, bull-fighting exhibits, Augustin Gonfond's painstaking illuminations, and contemporary engravings.

★ Festivals & Events

Route des Artistes   ART FESTIVAL

(artistes13210.canalblog.com) Professional artists sell work in the streets one Sunday each month, May to October.

Féria de St-Rémy   CULTURAL FESTIVAL

(www.mairie-saintremydeprovence.fr; ☺ mid-Aug) Bull-running, festivities and fireworks.

Fête Votive de St-Rémy   RELIGIOUS FESTIVAL

(www.mairie-saintremydeprovence.fr) Six-day celebration of St-Rémy's patron saint, held in late September, with bullfights and parades.

🛏 Sleeping

Hôtel Canto Cigalo
HOTEL €

(☎04 90 92 14 28; www.cantocigalo.com; 8 chemin Canto Cigalo; d €75-98; ✱⊛@🖰🏊) This excellent-value 20-room hotel with apricot facade and blue wooden shutters is a 10-minute stroll south of town. Simple and spotless, its frilly-feminine rooms are decorated in dusty rose, with wicker and white-wood furniture. Unusually, guests have the choice of a gluten-/lactose-free breakfast (€10.50) as well as regular *petit-déj* (€9) with homemade bread and jam. South-facing rooms have air-con.

★ Sous les Figuiers
BOUTIQUE HOTEL €€

(☎04 32 60 15 40; www.hotelsouslesfiguiers.com; 3 av Gabriel St-René Taillandier; d €98-122; tr €188; ✱⊛@🖰🛋) A five-minute walk from town, this country-chic house hotel has 14 art-filled rooms facing a leafy garden – lovely for unwinding after a day's explorations. The owner is a painter (who runs half-day classes costing €85 per person) and has exquisite taste, marrying design details like velvet and distressed wood, Moroccan textiles, and rich colour palettes. Breakfast €13.50.

La Maison du Village
BOUTIQUE HOTEL €€€

(☎04 32 60 68 20; www.lamaisonduvillage.com; 10 rue du 8 Mai 1945; d €176-220; ✱⊛🖰) This hotel is St-Rémy all over – exclusive, eclectically stylish and appealing to all the senses. Gorgeous rooms, smack in the centre, come in a number of configurations, and there's a Diptyque fragrance and candle shop.

🍴 Eating

Les Filles du Pâtissier
CAFE €

(☎06 50 61 07 17; 3 place Favier; mains €15-20; ⊙10am-10pm, closed Wed Apr-Oct) Particularly perfect on sultry summer nights, this upbeat, colourful cafe has vintage tables filling one corner of a delightful car-free square in the old town. Its daily-changing menu features market-driven salads and tarts, and come dusk it morphs into a wine bar with charcuterie plates and occasional live music. Don't miss the homemade *citronnade* (lemonade) and melon-fizz soda.

Café de la Place
CAFE €

(☎04 90 92 02 13; www.cafedelaplace-stremy. fr; place de la République; mains €14-25; ⊙7am-12.30am) St-Rémy's no-frills, casual hang-out for locals abuts the place de la République car park but is always packed, serving fresh local dishes, wine and coffee.

LOCAL KNOWLEDGE

FÊTE DE LA TRANSHUMANCE

Every spring throughout parts of southern France, an incredible migration, largely on foot, takes place as thousands of sheep are led from the coast to the mountains to summer on alpine pastures. The journey takes about six days, and sheep, goats and donkeys block many tertiary routes to the Alps, leading to the amusement or annoyance of many a tourist.

In St-Rémy-de-Provence on Pentacost Monday this tradition is honoured as shepherds kitted out in traditional dress lead about 6000 sheep through St-Rémy's streets on their way to the mountains, and market-day festivities fill the town.

Michel Marshall
PATISSERIE €

(☎04 90 95 03 54; 2 place Joseph Hilaire; pastries €5-7; ⊙9am-6pm Mon-Sat) St-Remy's most refined patisserie is elegant for afternoon tea.

La Cuisine des Anges
BISTRO €€

(☎04 90 92 17 66; www.angesetfees-stremy.com; 4 rue du 8 Mai 1945; menus €28, mains €18-21; ⊙noon-2.30pm & 7.30-11pm Mon, Wed, Sat & Sun, 7.30-11pm Thu & Fri; ✱🖰) Packed with locals and tourists, this casual *maison d'hôte* has been around for an age and just doesn't lose its edge. Light Provençal dishes are derived from organic local ingredients and served in the interior patio or wooden-floored dining room with textured paintings and zinc-topped tables. Upstairs is cute B&B Le Sommeil des Fées (d €63 to €84), with five rooms.

★ Maison Drouot
MODERN FRENCH €€€

(☎04 90 15 47 42; http://maisondrouot.blogspot. fr; 150 rte de Maillane, D5; menus lunch €23-49, dinner €45-65; ⊙12.30-2.30pm & 7.30-11pm Wed-Sun) There are few lunch addresses as charming. Snug in a 19th-century oil mill with a terrace basking in the shade of a fig tree and a vine-covered pergola, this restaurant is pure style. Contemporary Provençal cuisine – made strictly from local products (listed in the menu) – is served with a creative twist in a thoroughly modern interior.

Find the mill-restaurant five minutes out of town, opposite supermarket Intermarché on the D5 towards Maillane.

WORTH A TRIP

SWEET RETREAT

Mas de l'Amarine (☏04 90 94 47 82; www.mas-amarine.com; Ancienne voie Aurélia; d €190-270, 2-/3-course lunch menus €29/35, dinner mains €36) A sweet retreat to eat and sleep, Mas de l'Amarine is five minutes' drive east of town. Contemporary artwork fills this fashion-forward *auberge* (country inn), a romantic old *mas* (farmhouse) and 1950s artists retreat with drystone walls, great fireplaces and funky Fatboy beanbags by the pool. Many ingredients cooked in the restaurant, open to nonguests, come fresh from the magnificent gardens.

Reservations, well in advance, are essential.

🛍 Shopping

St-Rémy's packed with boutiques and shops. Hours are reduced in winter, and some close.

★ **Joël Durand** CHOCOLATE
(☏04 90 92 38 25; www.chocolat-durand.com; 3 bd Victor Hugo; ☉9.30am-12.30pm & 2.30-7.30pm) Among France's top chocolatiers, Provençal herbs and plants – lavender, rosemary, violet and thyme – are used with unexpected flavours, like Earl Grey.

Le Petit Duc FOOD
(☏04 90 92 08 31; www.petit-duc.com; 7 bd Victor Hugo; ☉10am-7pm) Biscuits made using ancient Roman, Renaissance, alpine and Arlésien recipes.

La Cave aux Fromages CHEESE
(☏04 90 92 32 45; 1 place Joseph Hilaire; ☉10am-7pm, reduced hours Oct-Apr) Thrilling cheese shop with a 12th-century ripening cellar and cheese and charcuterie plates.

Espace Anikado FASHION, ARTS
(☏04 90 94 53 22; http://anikado.canalblog.com; 1 bd Marceau; ☉10.30am-6.30pm) There is no finer shop for vibrant local art, craft and design than Espace Anikado. Eye-catching, colourful and oozing creativity, the hybrid boutique-gallery showcases fashion, jewellery, shoes, furniture and more by local designers. It also hosts Provençal art exhibits.

Moulin à Huile du Calanquet FOOD
(☏04 32 60 09 50; www.moulinducalanquet.fr; Vieux Chemin d'Arles; ☉9am-noon & 2-6.30pm Mon-Sat, plus Sun Apr-Oct) Brother-and-sister-run olive-oil mill located 4.5km southwest of St-Rémy, with tastings and homemade tapenade, fruit juice and jam.

ⓘ Information

Websites www.alpilles.com and www.alpilles.fr list information on the region.

Tourist Office (☏04 90 92 05 22; www.saintremy-de-provence.com; place Jean Jaurès; ☉9.15am-12.30pm & 2-6.30pm Mon-Sat, 10am-12.30pm Sun mid-Apr–mid-Oct, shorter hours rest of year) Helpful, with transport schedules, walking maps of town and Van Gogh sites, and summertime guided tours (book ahead).

ⓘ Getting There & Around

BICYCLE

Rentals and free delivery within a 20km radius of St-Rémy from **Telecycles** (☏04 90 92 83 15; www.telecycles-location.com; per day €20) and **Vélo-Passion** (☏04 90 92 49 43; www.velopassion.fr; per day €15-20). Or add a zip to your pedal power with a battery-assisted electric bike from **Sun e-Bike** (☏04 32 62 08 39; www.sun-e-bike.com; 16 bd Marceau; per day €36; ☉9am-6.30pm Apr-Sep, shorter hours rest of year).

BUS

Allô Cartreize (☏08 10 00 13 26; www.lepilote.com) buses depart place de la République for Avignon (€3.60, one hour), Les Baux-de-Provence (€2.40, 15 minutes, weekends June and September, daily July and August), Arles (€2.40, 45 minutes, Monday to Saturday) and Cavaillon (€1.70, 30 minutes).

CAR

St-Rémy gets packed in summer; there's parking by the tourist office (parking Jean-Jaurès) and north of the periphery (parking Général-de-Gaulle).

Around St-Rémy-de-Provence

Vineyards and olive groves line valleys below craggy peaks, covered in fragrant Mediterranean scrub. Rugged castles, ancient olive-oil mills, a troglodyte monastery and unusual attractions dot the countryside.

Jardin de l'Alchimiste

Jardin de l'Alchimiste GARDEN
(Alchemist's Garden; ☏04 90 90 67 67; www.jardin-alchimiste.com; Mas de la Brune, Eygalières; adult/child €8/3; ☉10am-6pm daily May, 10am-6pm

Sat & Sun Jun-Sep) Eleven kilometres east of St-Rémy, in Eygalières, fascinating Jardin de l'Alchimiste – inspired by the nearby 16th-century house of an alchemist – is planted in arcane medieval patterns and filled with blossoming trees and herbs reputed to hold mystical properties. It's a magical destination for a Sunday-afternoon drive.

Les Baux-de-Provence

POP 392

Clinging precariously to an ancient limestone *baou* (Provençal for 'rocky spur'), this fortified hilltop village is one of the most visited in France (best as a day trip). It's easy to understand why: narrow cobbled streets wend car-free past ancient houses, up to a splendid ruined castle.

◎ Sights

Château des Baux CASTLE, RUIN
(☑04 90 54 55 56; www.chateau-baux-provence.com; adult/child Apr-Sep €10/8, Oct-Mar €8/6; ⊙9am-8.15pm Jul & Aug, to 7.15pm Apr-Jun & Sep, reduced hours rest of year) Crowning the village of Les Baux, these dramatic maze-like ruins date to the 10th century. The clifftop castle was largely destroyed in 1633, during the reign of Louis XIII, and is a thrilling place to explore – particularly for rambunctious kids. Climb crumbling towers for incredible views, descend into disused dungeons, and flex your knightly prowess with giant medieval weapons dotting the open-air site. Medieval-themed entertainment and hands-on action – shows, duels, catapult demonstrations and so on – abound in summer.

Carrières de Lumières LIGHT SHOW
(☑04 90 54 55 56; www.carrieres-lumieres.com; rte de Maillane; adult/child €10.50/8.50;

⊙9.30am-7.30pm Apr-Sep, 10am-6pm Oct-Dec & Mar) A high-end sound-and-light show, Carrières de Lumières is an odd, strangely thrilling attraction. In the chilly halls of a former limestone quarry, gigantic projections illuminate the rough cave walls and floor, accompanied by oration and swelling music. Programs change annually and there are joint tickets with the Château des Baux. Dress warmly.

🛏 Sleeping & Eating

The tourist office has information on the few accommodation options in town; restaurants tend toward the touristy.

★ **L'Oustau de Baumanière** GASTRONOMIC €€€
(☑04 90 54 33 07; www.oustaudebaumaniere.com; lunch/dinner menus from €90/160, mains €60-100; 🅿@🛜🐾) A legendary table beneath vaults, L'Oustau serves rarefied cuisine, with many ingredients plucked from the organic garden. Upstairs are five-star hotel rooms (doubles from €200). Head chef and owner Jean-André Charial also hosts Saturday-morning cooking classes (€170 including lunch) and innovative *table d'hôte* sessions (€160), during which guests watch the chef work and share a kitchen lunch with him.

Wine aficionados will adore the half-day wine-discovery workshops (€190), during which you delve into L'Oustau's amazing cellars packed with 60,000-odd bottles and taste the best vintages from the region, accompanied by lunch.

❶ Information

Tourist Office (☑04 90 54 34 39; www.lesbaux-deprovence.com; Maison du Roy; ⊙9.30am-5pm Mon-Fri, 10am-5.30pm Sat & Sun)

OLIVE-OIL MILLS

The Alpilles' southern edge contains some of Provence's best-known *moulins d'huile* (oil mills), where four types of olive, freshly harvested from November to January, are pummelled and pressed into silken AOC Vallée des Baux-de-Provence oil.

In Maussane-les-Alpilles, the cooperative **Moulin Jean-Marie Cornille** (☑04 90 54 32 37; www.moulin-cornille.com; rue Charloun Rieu, Maussane-les-Alpilles; ⊙9.30am-6.30pm Mon-Sat, 11am-6pm Sun) sells direct to the public, though its 200,000L sell out by mid-August. You can tour the mill at 11am on Tuesday and Thursday June to September.

At Mouriès, 6km southeast of Maussane, pop in for tastes of exceptional oils milled at **Moulin Coopératif** (☑04 90 47 53 86; www.moulincoop.com; Quartier du Mas Neuf, Mouriès; ⊙9am-noon & 2-6pm Mon-Sat). The village celebrates a **Fête des Olives Vertes** (Green Olive Festival) in mid-September, and the arrival of the year's new oil with the **Fête des Huiles Nouvelles** in early December.

WORTH A TRIP

TARASCON

Château de Tarascon (☑04 90 91 01 93; www.tarascon.fr; adult/child €7/free; ⊘ 9.30am-6.30pm Jun-Sep, to 5.30pm Oct-May, last entry 45min before close) The mighty walls of the 15th-century Château de Tarascon rise straight out of the Rhône, in the relaxed village of Tarascon. A beauty of a castle, the imposing fortress was built by Louis II to defend Provence's frontier. Today it's a great destination for a half-day trip. Cross the mossy inner courtyard and explore the dainty chapel, ancient pharmacy and carved grotesques as you make your way to the crenellated rooftop for stunning river views.

After losing battles and suffering a lengthy imprisonment, Louis' son King René (1409–80) turned away from politics and towards the arts, writing poetry, decorating the castle in rich Renaissance style, organising courtly tournaments and instigating the **Fêtes de la Tarasque**, an Easter parade to celebrate St Martha's taming of Tarasque, a monstrous lion-headed, tortoise-shelled, fish-bellied beast that legend says once lurked in the river. This colourful festival still takes place today.

❶ Getting There & Around

BUS

Allô Cartreize (p224) has services to St-Rémy-de-Provence (€2.40, 15 minutes) and Arles (€2.40, 30 minutes) on weekends from May to September and daily in July and August.

CAR

Driving is easiest, but parking is hellish. Find metered spaces (€5 per day) far down the hill at the village's edge; there's free parking outside Carrières de Lumières. Good luck.

Nîmes & Around

Nîmes

POP 144,092

Though not technically Provence, Nîmes' incredible Roman monuments and zippy atmosphere merit a day trip to Languedoc. The old town is filled with good shopping, cafes and bars. It's also an important transportation hub for the Camargue.

The Pont du Gard aqueduct, 23km northeast, once supplied the Roman city with water.

◉ Sights

★**Les Arènes**   ROMAN SITES
(www.arenes-nimes.com; place des Arènes; adult/child €9.50/free; ⊘9am-8pm Jul & Aug, shorter hours rest of year) Nîmes' twin-tiered amphitheatre is the best preserved in France. Built around 100 BC, the arena would have seated 24,000 spectators and staged gladiatorial contests and public executions, and it still provides an impressive venue for gigs, events and summer bullfights. An audioguide provides context as you explore the arena, seating areas, stairwells and corridors (rather marvellously known to Romans as *vomitories*), and afterwards you can view replicas of gladiatorial armour and original bullfighters' costumes in the museum.

★**Maison Carrée**   ROMAN SITES
(place de la Maison Carrée; adult/child €5.80/free; ⊘10am-8pm Jul & Aug, shorter hours rest of year) Constructed in gleaming limestone around AD 5, this temple was built to honour Emperor Augustus' two adopted sons. Despite the name, the Maison Carrée (Square House) is actually rectangular – to the Romans, 'square' simply meant a building with right angles. The building is beautifully preserved, complete with stately columns and triumphal steps. There's no need to go inside unless you are interested in the relatively cheesy 22-minute 3D film.

★**Carré d'Art**   MUSEUM
(www.carreartmusee.com; place de la Maison Carrée; permanent collection free, exhibitions adult/child €5/3.70; ⊘10am-6pm Tue-Sun) The striking glass-and-steel building facing the Maison Carrée was designed by British architect Sir Norman Foster. Inside is the **municipal library** and the **Musée d'Art Contemporain**, with permanent and temporary exhibitions covering art from the 1960s onwards. The rooftop restaurant makes a lovely spot for lunch.

Jardins de la Fontaine   ROMAN SITES
(Tour Magne adult/child €3.40/free; ⊘Tour Magne 9.30am-6.30pm) The elegant Jardins de la Fontaine conceal several Roman remains, most notably the 30m-high **Tour Magne**, raised around 15 BC. Built as a display of imperial power, it's the largest of a chain

Nîmes

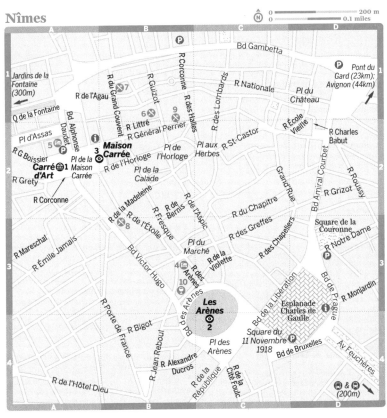

Nîmes

of towers that once punctuated the city's 7km-long Roman ramparts. At the top of its 140 steps, there's an orientation table to help you interpret the panoramic views over Nîmes.

Elsewhere around the gardens are the Source de la Fontaine – once the site of a spring, temple and baths – and the crumbling Temple de Diane, located in the gardens' northwestern corner.

🎉 Festivals & Events

Féria de Pentecôte
& Féria des Vendanges   BULLFIGHTING

Nîmes becomes more Spanish than French during its two *férias* (bullfighting festivals): the five-day Féria de Pentecôte (Whitsuntide Festival) in May or June, and the three-day Féria des Vendanges on the third weekend in September. Each is marked by daily *corridas* (bullfights).

🛏 Sleeping & Eating

Place aux Herbes and place du Marché buzz with cafes. **Les Halles** (rues Guizot, Général Perrier & des Halles; ⊙ 6.30am-1pm) is Nîmes' vast covered market.

★ Hôtel de l'Amphithéâtre   HOTEL €€
(☑ 04 66 67 28 51; www.hoteldelamphitheatre. com; 4 rue des Arènes; s/d/f €72/92/130) Down a narrow backstreet leading away from Les Arènes, this tall town house ticks all the boxes: smart rooms with shabby-chic furniture and balconies overlooking place du Marché; a sleek palette of greys, whites and taupes; and a great buffet breakfast. It's run by an expat Cornishman and his French wife.

Royal Hôtel   HOTEL €€
(☑ 04 66 58 28 27; www.royalhotel-nimes.com; 3 bd Alphonse Daudet; d €102-122, f €184; ❋ 🛜) This upmarket hotel offers grace and style. Bedrooms have a choice of street views or an outlook over the grand place d'Assas. They're split into standard and superior, all with modern-meets-heritage decor; it's worth bumping up a level for extra space and air-con. The downstairs restaurant, La Boduegita, offers solid Med dining.

🍴 Eating & Drinking

La Petite Fadette   CAFE €
(☑ 04 66 67 53 05; 34 rue du Grand Couvent; menus €9.50-14.50; ⊙ 8am-7pm) Salads and crispy *tartines* (open toasted sandwiches) are the order of the day at this homely cafe, with a cute rococo interior lined with vintage photos, and outside tables on a small courtyard on the rue du Grand Couvent. The food isn't fancy, but portions are huge: try the smoked salmon or the cured ham and goat's cheese.

★ Le Cerf à Moustache   BISTRO €€
(☑ 09 81 83 44 33; 38 bd Victor Hugo; mains €14-35; ⊙ 11.45am-2pm & 7-11pm Tue-Sat) Despite its weird name, the Deer with the Moustache has quickly established itself as one of Nîmes' top bistros, with quirky decor (including reclaimed furniture and a wall full of old-book doodles), matched by chef Julien

---

ℹ ROMAN SIGHT COMBO TICKET
···
Pass Nîmes (adult/child €11.70/free) Save on Nîmes' three major Roman sites with a combination ticket, good for three days.

Salem's creative take on the classics. Go basic with burgers and risotto, or upmarket with crusted lamb and chunky steaks.

Au Plaisir des Halles   TRADITIONAL FRENCH €€
(☑ 04 66 36 01 02; 4 rue Littré; menus €25-60; ⊙ noon-2pm & 7.30-10pm Tue-Sat) Unfussy market-fresh dining is the order of the day here, served with an excellent choice of Languedoc wines. It's in a quiet spot, just along from the covered market.

Grand Café de la Bourse et du Commerce   BAR
(bd des Arènes; ⊙ 8am-midnight) Step back in time to a more elegant era at this opulent 19th-century cafe opposite Les Arènes, gleaming with chandeliers and mirrors.

ℹ Information

Tourist Office (☑ 04 66 58 38 00; www.ot-nimes.fr; 6 rue Auguste; ⊙ 8.30am-8pm Mon-Fri, 9am-7pm Sat, 10am-6pm Sun Jul & Aug, shorter hours rest of year; 🛜) Also an annexe (⊙ 10am-6pm Mon-Sat Apr-Sep, to 5pm Mon-Fri Oct-Mar) on esplanade Charles de Gaulle.

ℹ Getting There & Around

AIR

Aéroport de Nîmes Alès Camargue Cévennes (FNI; ☑ 04 66 70 49 49; www.nimes-aeroport. fr) Nîmes' airport, 10km southeast of the city on the A54, is served only by Ryanair, which flies to/from London Luton, Liverpool, Brussels and Fez.

An **airport bus** (€5.50, 30 minutes) to/from the train station connects with all flights.

BUS

The **bus station** (☑ 04 66 38 59 43; rue Ste-Félicité) is next to the train station. Local buses are run by **Edgard** (www.edgard-transport.fr; tickets €1.50). To get to Pont du Gard take line B21 (40 minutes, hourly Monday to Saturday, two on Sunday).

CAR

Nîmes' narrow streets and one-ways render driving confusing. Find (pricey) pay lots by Arènes, Jardins de la Fontaine and Maison Carrée.

TRAIN

TGVs run hourly to/from Paris' Gare de Lyon (€35 to €110, three hours) from Nîmes' **train station** (bd Talabot).

Local destinations, with at least hourly departures, include the following:

Arles €9, 30 minutes

Avignon Centre €10 to €15, 30 minutes

Montpellier €10, 30 minutes

Pont du Gard

The Romans didn't do anything on a small scale, and this awe-inspiring aqueduct is no exception. At 50m, it's the world's highest Roman monument. Walk across for a birds-eye view over the river or, better yet, canoe under the bridge.

⊙ Sights & Activities

★ **Pont du Gard**   ROMAN SITES
(☑ 04 66 37 50 99; www.pontdugard.fr; car & up to 5 passengers/up to 5 cyclists or walkers €18/€15, after 8pm €10; ⊙ visitor centre & museum 9am-8pm Jul & Aug, shorter hours rest of year) Southern France has some fine Roman sites, but nothing can top Unesco World Heritage–listed Pont du Gard, 21km northeast of Nîmes. This fabulous three-tiered aqueduct was once part of a 50km-long system of channels built around 19 BC to transport water from Uzès to Nîmes. The scale is huge: 48.8m high, 275m long and graced with 35 precision-built arches; the bridge was sturdy enough to carry up to 20,000 cu metres of water per day.

Each block was carved by hand and transported from nearby quarries – no mean feat, considering the largest blocks weigh over 5 tonnes. Amazingly, the height of the bridge descends by just 2.5cm across its length, providing just enough gradient to keep the water flowing – an amazing demonstration of the precision of Roman engineering. The Musée de la Romanité provides background on the bridge's construction, and the Ludo play area helps kids to learn in a fun, hands-on way.

You can walk across the tiers for panoramic views over the River Gard, but the best perspective on the bridge is from downstream, along the 1.4km Mémoires de Garrigue walking trail. Early evening is a good time to visit, as admission is cheaper and the bridge is stunningly illuminated after dark.

DON'T MISS

SUMMER LIGHT

Consider an evening return and see Pont du Gard spectacularly illuminated every night mid-May to mid-September, sunset to midnight. The first two weekends in June, a jaw-dropping display of pyrotechnics and fireworks showcase the span, starting around 10pm.

There are large car parks on both banks of the river, a 400m walk from the bridge.

Canoeing on the River Gard   CANOEING
Arrive at the Pont du Gard in style by paddling 8km (about two hours) downriver from Collias, 4km west of the D981. Kayak Vert (☑ 04 66 22 80 76; www.kayakvert.com; from Collias adult/child €22/11, from Russan €41/20) and Canoë Le Tourbillon (☑ 04 66 22 85 54; www.canoe-le-tourbillon.com; from Collias adult/child €22/11, from Russan €35/22), both based near the village bridge, rent out kayaks and canoes from March/April to October.

Depending on the season and the height of the river, you can make a longer journey by being dropped at Pont St Nicholas (19km, four to five hours) or Russan (32km, six to seven hours); the latter includes a memorable trip through the Gorges du Gardon.

❶ Getting There & Away

BUS

Buses stop on D981, 1km north of the visitor centre. In summer some buses travel to Pont du Gard parking. **Edgard** (www.edgard-transport.fr) bus B21 operates daily to/from Nîmes, bus A15 from Avignon.

CAR

Pont du Gard is 21km northeast of Nîmes and 26km west of Avignon. From autoroute A9, take exit 23 at Remoulins, towards Uzès. Park on *rive gauche* for the museum and services.

Hill Towns of the Luberon

Best Places to Eat

➡ Le Sanglier Paresseux (p240)

➡ La Closerie (p244)

➡ La Table de Pablo (p237)

➡ Auberge La Fenière (p243)

➡ Le Mas Tourteron (p234)

Best Places to Stay

➡ Maison Valvert (p241)

➡ La Bastide du Bois Bréant (p242)

➡ La Bouquière (p241)

➡ Le Couvent (p238)

➡ Les Balcons de Luberon (p234)

Why Go?

Named after the mountain range running east–west between Cavaillon and Manosque, the Luberon is a Provençal patchwork of hilltop villages, vineyards, ancient abbeys and kilometre after kilometre of fragrant lavender fields. It's a rural, traditional region that still makes time for the good things in life – particularly fine food and even finer wine. Nearly every village hosts its own weekly market, packed with stalls selling local specialities, especially olive oil, honey and lavender.

Covering some 600 sq km, the Luberon massif itself is divided into three areas: the craggy Petit Luberon in the west, the higher Grand Luberon mountains and the smaller hills of the Luberon Oriental in the east. They're all worth exploring, but whatever you do, don't rush – part of the fun of exploring here is getting lost on the back lanes, stopping for lunch at a quiet village cafe, and taking as much time as you possibly can to soak up the scenery.

Driving Distances (km)

	Apt	Bonnieux	Cavaillon	Gordes	Lacoste
Bonnieux	10				
Cavaillon	35	25			
Gordes	21	19	17		
Lacoste	15	5	21	23	
Roussillon	13	10	28	9	14

VAUCLUSE MOUNTAINS

Some of Provence's quintessential sights – impossibly pretty villages, beehive-shaped *bories* (primitive dry-limestone dwellings), lavender fields and a stunning Cistercian abbey – lie just a few kilometres apart on the rugged northern side of the Luberon.

Make reservations as far ahead as possible for lunch and dinner, lest you go hungry. Every table fills in high season.

❶ Getting Around

The Luberon, an hour from Avignon, is just 60km in length. Having a car makes travel much easier, as bus services are limited, but parking in some small villages can be a nightmare in summer.

The D900 bisects the valley from east to west. Secondary roads are slow and winding; watch out for roadside gullies.

BICYCLE

Don't be put off by the hills – the Luberon is a fantastic destination for cyclists. Several bike routes criss-cross the countryside, including Les Ocres à Vélo, a 51km route that takes in the ochre villages of Apt, Gargas, Rustrel, Roussillon and Villars, and the **Véloroute du Calavon** (www.af3v.org/-Fiche-VVV-.html?voie=107), a purpose-built bike path that follows the route of a disused railway line for 28km between Beaumettes in the west (near Coustellet), via Apt, to La Paraire in the west (near St-Martin-de-Castillon). Plans are underway to extend the trail all the way from Cavaillon to the foothills of the Alps, but it'll be a while before it's completed.

For longer trips, **Le Luberon à Vélo** (☑ 04 90 76 48 05; www.leluberonavelo.com; 203 rue Oscar Roulet, Robion) is a 236km itinerary that takes in pretty much the whole Luberon. Tourist offices stock detailed route leaflets and can provide info on rental, luggage transport, accommodation and so on.

Several companies offer e-bikes, which incorporate an electric motor. They're not scooters – you still have to pedal – but the motor helps on the ascents.

Luberon Biking (☑ 04 90 90 14 62; http://www.luberon-biking.fr; Velleron; per day from €22, per week €120) Delivers bikes straight to your door throughout the Luberon area, and also runs guided bike tours.

Luberon Cycles (☑ 04 86 69 19 00; 86 quai Général-Leclerc; per half-day/day from €12/16; ☺9am-noon & 2-6pm Mon-Sat) Bike hire and general cycling supplies and services in Apt.

Sun-e-Bike (☑ Bonnieux 04 90 74 09 96, St-Rémy-de-Provence 04 32 62 08 39; www.location-velo-provence.com; per day €36) Rents electric bikes. The rental offices are in Bonnieux and St-Rémy-de-Provence, but you can recharge your battery at various other locations around the Luberon valley.

Bachelas Cycles (☑ 04 92 75 12 47; www.bachelas-cycles.com; 5 blvd de la République; per day/week from €19/€81; ☺9am-12.30pm & 2-7pm Mon-Wed, Fri & Sat) Bike hire (standard and e-bike) in Forcalquier and Manosque (☑ 04 92 72 15 84; www.bachelas-cycles.com; 24 bd de la Plaine; ☺8.30am-12.30pm & 2-8pm Mon-Sat).

BUS

Most villages in the Luberon have a limited bus service that revolves around school term times. The main hub is Apt, which has buses to local villages, and a regular bus link to Cavaillon and Avignon. The **Trans Vaucluse** (www.vaucluse.fr) website has downloadable timetables.

The fare to all destinations is calculated by how far you travel; local destinations cost €1.50, further destinations a flat-rate €2.

TRAIN

The nearest train station is on the western side of the valley in Cavaillon, which is served by regular regional trains from Avignon. From Cavaillon, several buses a day run east to Apt.

Gordes & Around

Like a giant wedding cake rising over the Rivers Sorgue and Calavon, the tiered village of Gordes juts spectacularly out of the white-rock face of the Vaucluse plateau. Gordes is high on many tourists' must-see lists (notably celebrity Parisians): summer brings a cavalcade of buses, and car parks (€3) are choked. Arrive early or late, or expect to be crammed onto narrow footpaths, dodging tourists and buses. Come sunset, the village glows gold – an eye-popping sight.

◉ Sights & Activities

★ Abbaye Notre-Dame
de Sénanque   CHURCH
(☑ 04 90 72 05 72; www.abbayedesenanque.com; adult/child €7/3; ☺9.45-11am Mon-Sat, tours by reservation) Situated 4km northwest of Gordes off the D177, this supremely peaceful spot provides one of the classic postcard images of this part of Provence: a graceful Cistercian abbey surrounded by swathes of purple lavender. The best displays are usually in July and August, but you certainly won't be on your own when you visit.

Founded in 1148, the abbey is still home to a small monastic community, so it's only possible to visit the cloistered interior by

Hill Towns of the Luberon Highlights

1 Smell the lavender around **Abbaye Notre-Dame de Sénanque** (p231).

2 Escape the heat in the peaceful **Forêt des Cèdres** (p240).

3 Shop for ingredients at the Saturday-morning market in **Apt** (p237).

4 Hike through the crimson moonscapes of the **Colorado Provençal** (p235).

5 Admire the view from the hilltop church in **Bonnieux** (p240).

6 Explore the abandoned streets of **Oppède-le-Vieux** (p243).

7 Visit ancient dwellings at the **Village des Bories** (p234).

8 Follow in Peter Mayle's footsteps in **Ménerbes** (p242).

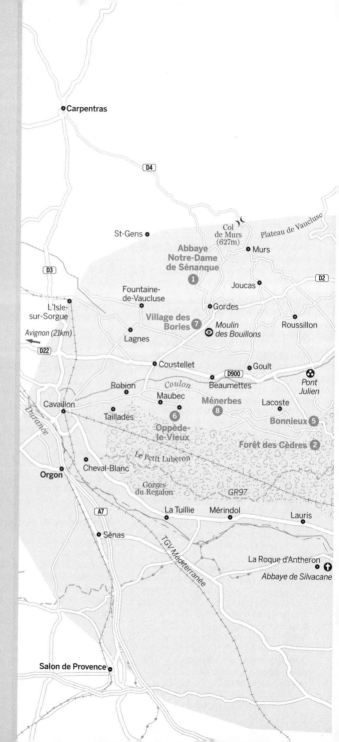

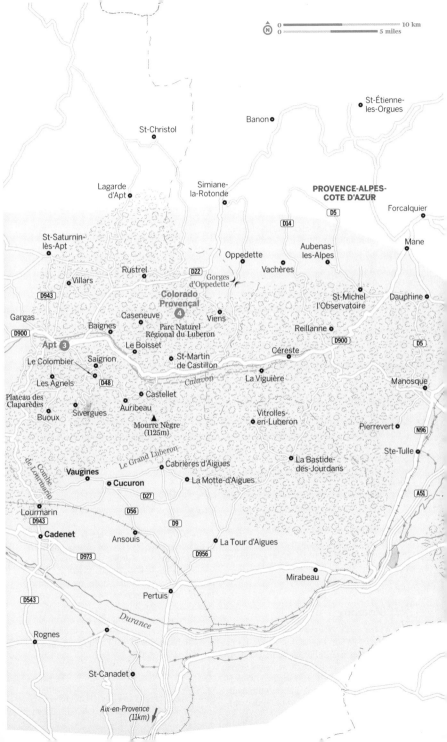

guided tour. Reservations are essential, as are conservative dress and reverential silence.

It's a 1½-hour walk from Gordes on the GR6 trail. The track up to the abbey gets rough and muddy during heavy rain.

Village des Bories   ARCHITECTURE
(🗷 04 90 72 03 48; adult/child €6/4; ⊙ 9am-8pm, shorter hours winter) Beehive-shaped *bories* bespeckle Provence, and at the Village des Bories, 4km southwest of Gordes, an entire village of them can be explored. Constructed of slivered limestone, *bories* were built during the Bronze Age, inhabited by shepherds until 1839, then abandoned until their restoration in the 1970s. Visit early in the morning or just before sunset for the best light. Note that the lower car park is for buses; continue to the hilltop car park to avoid hiking uphill in the blazing heat.

Moulin des Bouillons   MUSEUM
(🗷 04 90 72 22 11; www.moulindesbouillons.com; rte de St-Pantaléon; adult/child €5/3.50; ⊙ 10am-noon & 2-6pm Wed-Mon Apr-Oct) Heading 3.5km south from Gordes along rte de St-Pantaléon (D148), you hit this marvellous rural museum: an olive-oil mill with a 10m-long Gallo-Roman press weighing 7 tonnes – reputedly the world's oldest. The adjoining stained-glass museum showcases beautiful translucent mosaics; a joint ticket costs adult/child €7.50/5.50.

Musée de la Lavande   MUSEUM
(🗷 04 90 76 91 23; www.museedelalavande.com; D2, Coustellet; adult/child €6.80/free; ⊙ 9am-7pm May-Sep, 9am-noon & 2-6pm Oct-Apr) To get to grips with Provence's most prestigious crop, this excellent eco-museum makes an ideal first stop. An audioguide and video (in English) explain the lavender harvest, and giant copper stills reveal extraction methods. Afterwards you can take a guided **tour** of the fields at 1pm and 5pm daily May to September. The on-site boutique is an excellent (if pricey) one-stop shop for top-quality lavender products.

There's also a picnic area in the lavender-festooned garden.

🛏 Sleeping

★ Le Mas de la Beaume   B&B €€
(🗷 04 90 72 02 96; www.labeaume.com; rte de Cavaillon, Gordes; d €130-180; 🛜 🞲) In a visually stunning hilltop locale at the village's edge, this impeccable five-room *maison d'hôte* is like a Provençal postcard come to life, with yellow-washed stone-wall rooms decorat-

ed with bunches of lavender hanging from wood-beamed ceilings. Beds are dressed in high-thread-count linens, and breakfast is delivered to your room.

Auberge de Carcarille   HOTEL €€
(🗷 04 90 72 02 63; www.auberge-carcarille.com; rte d'Apt; d €81-128; 🞲 🛜 🞲 🞲) Old outside, new interior: this country hotel marries the atmosphere of a traditional *bastide familiale* (family house) with spotless, modern rooms. There's a delightful garden to wander, and the restaurant serves superior Provençal food; half-board deals are great value. It's 3km from Gordes at the bottom of the valley.

Mas de la Régalade   B&B €€
(🗷 04 90 76 90 79; www.masregalade-luberon.com; D2, Quartier de la Sénancole; d €130-160; ⊙ mid-Apr–mid-Nov; 🛜 🞲) A stone farmhouse on a grassy plain surrounded by oak woodlands, 3.5km south of Gordes, Mas de la Régalade's four rooms artfully blend mod cons with playful antiques. In the garden, a vintage blue Citroën peeks between scented hedgerows of lavender and rosemary, beyond the big pool. Discounts for longer stays.

Les Balcons du Luberon   B&B €€
(🗷 06 38 20 42 13; www.lesbalconsduluberon.fr; rte de Murs; d €135-165; 🛜 🞲) Uphill from Gordes' centre on the D15, this ravishing four-room B&B makes a wonderful bolthole. It's in an 18th-century stone farmhouse, but the decor is totally 21st century – all designer furniture, funky lights and minimal clutter. There's a gorgeous pool, and owner Étienne Marty (a trained chef) offers a lavish dinner by reservation.

🍴 Eating

La Boulangerie de Mamie Jane   BOULANGERIE €
(🗷 04 90 72 09 34; lunch menus €6.50 or €7.90; ⊙ 6.30am-1pm & 2-6pm Thu-Tue) Those short of time or money in Gordes should follow the locals downhill along rue Baptistin Picca to this pocket-sized boulangerie, in the same family for three generations. Mamie Jane cooks up outstanding bread, pastries, cakes and biscuits (including purple, lavender-perfumed *navettes,* canoe-shaped biscuits), and the baguettes (€4.50) and lunch menus are unbeatable value.

★ Le Mas Tourteron   GASTRONOMIC €€€
(🗷 04 90 72 00 16; www.mastourteron.com; chemin de St-Blaise les Imberts; menu lunch €48, dinner €57; ⊙ dinner 7.30-9.30pm Wed-Sat, lunch 12.30-2pm

THE COLORADO PROVENÇAL

Reds and oranges, scarlets and yellows, purples and crimsons – the fiery colours burned into the earth between Roussillon and Rustrel are astonishing. They're the result of the area's rich mineral deposits, especially hydrated iron oxide, otherwise known as ochre, which has been mined in this part of the Luberon since Roman times. Traditionally used to colour earthenware and paint buildings, around the late 18th century, the extraction process was industrialised, and large mines and quarries sprang up. In 1929, at the peak of the ochre industry, some 40,000 tonnes of ochre was mined around Apt.

There are several ochre-themed sites to visit around Roussillon, but for the full technicolour experience, head for the Colorado Provençal (☑ 04 32 52 09 75; www.colorado-provencal.com; ☉ 9am-dusk), a quarry site where ochre was mined from the 1880s until 1956. With its weird rock formations and rainbow colours, it's like a little piece of the southwest USA plonked down amongst the hills of Provence.

Colour-coded trails lead from the car park, signposted south of Rustrel village, off the D22 to Banon. Parking costs €5 (free November to March), or you can walk down from the village. The site gets blazingly hot in summer: start early, carry water and wear hiking boots and a hat – and don't be surprised if you take some ochre home with you on your clothes (the best idea is to wait till it dries and brush it off).

Sun only Apr-Oct) The welcome is warm at this country house, surrounded by gardens clearly created with perfect lazy lunches alfresco in mind. The stone-walled dining room has a vaguely boho-chic feeling, befitting chef Elisabeth Bourgeois-Baique's stylised cooking. Husband Philippe selects from over 200 wines to pair with her seasonal, inventive menus. Desserts are legendary. It's 3.5km south of Gordes, off the D2.

ⓘ Information

Tourist Office (☑ 04 90 72 02 75; www.gordes-village.com; place du Château; ☉ 9am-noon & 2-6pm Mon-Sat, from 10am Sun) Inside Gordes' medieval chateau, which was enlarged and given its defensive Renaissance towers in 1525.

Roussillon

Red by name, red by nature, that's Roussillon – once the centre of local ochre mining, and still unmistakably marked by its crimson colour (villagers are required to paint their houses according to a prescribed palette of some 40 tints). Today it's home to artists' and ceramicists' workshops, and its charms are no secret: arrive early or late.

The village was the hideout for the playwright Samuel Beckett during WWII, who helped the local Resistance by hiding explosives at his house and occasionally going on recce missions.

Parking (€3 March to November) is 300m outside the village.

◎ Sights & Activities

Conservatoire des Ocres et de la Couleur MUSEUM
(L'Usine d'Ocre Mathieu; ☑ 04 90 05 66 69; www.okhra.com; rte d'Apt; guided tours adult/student €6.50/5; ☉ 10am-7pm Jul & Aug, to 6pm Sep-Jun, closed Mon & Tue Jan & Feb; ♿) This art centre is a great place to see ochre in action. Occupying a disused ochre factory on the D104 east of Roussillon, it explores the mineral's properties through hands-on workshops and guided tours of the factory. The shop upstairs stocks paint pigments and other artists' supplies.

The centre also rents bikes (adult/child €28/22).

★ Sentier des Ocres WALKING
(Ochre Trail; adult/child €2.50/free; ☉ 9.30am-5.30pm; ♿) In Roussillon village, groves of chestnut and pine surround sunset-coloured ochre formations, rising on a clifftop. Two circular trails, 30 or 50 minutes, twist through mini-desert landscapes – it's like stepping into a Georgia O'Keeffe painting. Information panels highlight 26 types of flora to spot, the history of local ochre production and so on. Wear walking shoes and avoid white!

☐ Sleeping

Les Passiflores B&B €
(☑ 04 90 71 43 08; www.passiflores.fr; Les Huguets; d/q incl breakfast €73/120; ☎ ❄) Quiet and friendly, this *chambre d'hôte* is hidden in the hamlet of Les Huguets, 4km south of Roussillon. Spotless rooms are decorated with pretty

flourishes of country-Provençal prints. The four-person suite is excellent value. Outside, the 'pool' is a small filtered pond. *Table d'hôte* (set menu at a fixed price; €28) by reservation, includes wine and coffee.

Clos de la Glycine HOTEL €€

(☑ 04 90 05 60 13; www.luberon-hotel.fr; d €135-190; ✳ 🛜) You're paying a hefty premium for the view at this attractive hotel in the middle of Roussillon – but, boy, what a view! Rooms overlook your choice of ochre cliffs or the Luberon valley, and feel distinctively French, with artfully distressed paintwork and rococo furniture. The restaurant is good too, but breakfast is steep at €14.

Domaine des Finets COTTAGE €€

(☑ 04 90 74 11 92; www.domainedesfinets.fr; per week Jul & Aug €700-920, rest of year €420-650; 🛜 ✸) Four cute cottages, tinted orange like the rest of Roussillon, and surrounded by grassy lawns. They're rustic, and all have self-contained kitchens, washing machines, log-burning stoves and barbecues. We particularly liked 'Les Ocres' with its mezzanine floor.

✗ Eating

Comptoir des Arts BISTRO €€

(☑ 04 90 74 11 92; place du Pasquier; menus €18-28; ☉ lunch noon-2pm, dinner 7.30-10pm) Arrive early (or book ahead) to bag yourself one of the prime outside tables at this village bistro, which serves local specialities such as *aïoli de cabillaud* (cod with garlic mayonnaise) and *daube provençale* (a rich stew flavoured with Provençal herbs).

ℹ Information

Tourist Office (☑ 04 90 05 60 25; www. roussillon-provence.com; place de la Poste; ☉ 9am-noon & 1.30-5.30pm Mon-Sat)

St-Saturnin-lès-Apt & Around

About 9km north of Apt and 10km northeast of Roussillon, St-Saturnin-lès-Apt (population 2479) is refreshingly ungentrified and just beyond the tourist radar. Shops (not boutiques), cafes and bakeries line its cobbled streets. It has marvellous views of the surrounding Vaucluse plateau – climb to the ruins atop the village for knockout views. Or find the photogenic 17th-century windmill, Le Château les Moulins, 1km north, off the D943 towards Sault.

⊙ Sights

Moulin à Huile Jullien FARM

(☑ 04 90 75 56 24; www.moulin-huile-jullien.com; rte d'Apt, St-Saturnin-lès-Apt; ☉ 10am-noon & 3-7pm Jul & Aug, 10am-noon & 2-5.30pm or 6pm rest of year, closed Sun year-round) FREE On the edge of the village, this working olive-oil mill allows you to follow the process from tree to bottle. They also make delicious honey. Tastings and mill tours are free.

Mines de Bruoux HISTORIC SITE

(☑ 04 90 06 22 59; www.minesdebruoux.fr; rte de Croagnes; adult/child €8.10/6.50; ☉ 10am-7pm Jul & Aug, to 6pm Apr-Jun, Sep & Oct) In Gargas, 7km east of Roussillon, this former mine has more than 40km of underground galleries where ochre was once extracted. Around 650m are open to the public, some of which is as much as 15m high. Visits are only by guided tour; you need to reserve ahead.

The caverns sometimes provide a stunning setting for concerts; check the website for schedules.

🛏 Sleeping

Le Saint Hubert HOTEL €

(☑ 04 90 75 42 02; www.hotel-saint-hubert-luberon. com; d €56-62, tr €72) Charm personified, this quintessential village *auberge* (inn) has welcomed travellers since the 18th century and is a gorgeous spot to stay. Rooms are simple but elegant, and the sweeping view of the southern Luberon from valley-facing rooms is breathtaking. Breakfast €8.

Guests reluctant to stray too far can opt for half-board (€116 for two people) – dining on the panoramic terrace is no short straw.

Au Point de Lumière B&B €€

(☑ 04 90 04 83 14; www.upointdelumiere.com; 771 chemin de Perréal; d €100-135; 🛜 ✸) What a find this stylish B&B is. The three rooms all have their own theme – choose from soothing Alizarine, cool Zen or exotic Sienne – and all come with luxurious spoils like Italian showers and private terraces overlooking the garden. There's a lovely pool shaded by trees, and owner Jean-Claude gets breakfast goodies straight from the market every day.

Le Mas Perréal B&B €€

(☑ 04 90 75 46 31; www.masperreal.com; Quartier la Fortune; d €130-140, self-catering studios €100-150; 🛜 ✸) Surrounded by vineyards, lavender fields and cherry orchards, on a vast 7-hectare property outside St-Saturnin-lès-Apt, this farmhouse B&B offers a choice of cosy rooms or self-catering studios, both filled with country antiques and Provençal fabrics. Outside there's a heavenly pool and big garden with mountain views. Elisabeth, a long-time French teacher, offers cooking and French lessons.

Mas de Cink APARTMENT €€
(☑ 06 11 99 80 88; www.lemasdecink.com; Hameau des Blanchards; per 3 nights from €200, per week €450-1650; ✸ 🛜 🛏) Apartments evocatively blend northern contemporary cool with earthy Provençal comfort in this sprawling old farmhouse and barn. All have fully equipped kitchens, and a couple are suitable for larger groups. Private terraces and trellised outdoor dining areas overlook a wild garden, lavender fields and vineyards.

✗ Eating

L'Estrade BISTRO €€
(☑ 04 90 71 15 75; 6 av Victor Hugo; lunch menu €14, mains €14-28; ⊙ noon-2.30pm & 7.30-10.30pm, closed Nov-Mar) Tiny and friendly, this village restaurant is a popular local's tip for solid, fuss-free Provençal cooking. Everything's cooked fresh on the day, so it's worth arriving early to make sure you have the full menu choice.

★ La Table de Pablo MODERN FRENCH €€€
(☑ 04 90 75 45 18; www.latabledepablo.com; Les Petits Cléments, Villars; lunch menus €19 & €25, dinner menus €36 & €57, mains €17-26; ⊙ 12.30-2pm & 7-10pm Mon, Tue, Fri & Sun, 7-10pm Thu & Sat) The incongruous setting in a simple house near Villars is not momentous, but the cuisine and attitude of chef Thomas Gallardo are. From the basil grown on a Bonnieux farm to Forcalquier pigeon, cheese ripened by René Pellégrini, and Luberon wine, everything is locally sourced. Children are welcomed with fruity 'cocktails' and their own gastronomic 'petits bouts' menu (€15).

★ La Coquillade FRENCH €€€
(☑ 04 90 74 71 71; www.coquillade.fr; Le Perrotet, Gargas; menus lunch €38, dinner €72-115; ⊙ sittings 12.30-1.30pm & 7.30-9.30pm mid-Apr–mid-Oct) Overnighting at this luxurious hilltop estate won't suit everyone's budget, but everyone should try to fork out for the great-value Bistrot lunch menu. Michelin-starred and run by renowned chef Christophe Renaud, it'll be one of the most memorable meals you'll have in the Luberon. It's 5km northwest of Apt, signposted off the D90. The hotel (doubles €325–390) itself is a stunner, with luxurious rooms overlooking a sea of vines.

WORTH A TRIP

LAGARDE D'APT

Lagarde d'Apt, 20km northeast of St-Saturnin-lès-Apt, is home to an 80-hectare lavender farm, **Château du Bois** (☑ 04 90 76 91 23; www.lechateaudu-bois.com), where a 2km lavender trail blazes from late June until mid-July, when the sweet-smelling flower is harvested.

Also in Lagarde d'Apt, beneath some of Europe's darkest night-time skies, the **Observatoire Sirene** (☑ 04 90 75 04 17; www.obs-sirene.com; Lagarde d'Apt; adult day/night €10/16, child free; 🅿) reveals astronomical wonders using high-powered telescopes. Reservations are essential for stargazing sessions.

APT

POP 11,500 / ELEV 250M

The Luberon's principal town, Apt is edged on three sides by sharply rising plateaux surrounding a river that runs through town – the gateway to Haute-Provence. Its Saturday-morning market is full of local colour (and produce), but otherwise Apt is mainly a place you pass through to get somewhere else. Nonetheless, it makes a decent base, if only for a night or two.

Apt is known throughout France for its *fruits confits* (candied fruits, sometimes also known as glacé or crystallised fruit). Strictly speaking, they're not sweets: they're actually made with real fruit, in which the water is removed and replaced with a sugar syrup to preserve them. As a result, they still look (and more importantly taste) like pieces of the original fruit. There are several makers around town where you can try and buy straight from the source.

It's also a hub for the 1650-sq-km **Parc Naturel Régional du Luberon** (www.parcduluberon.fr), a regional nature park and an official Unesco Biosphere Reserve, crisscrossed by hiking trails.

◉ Sights

Musée de l'Aventure Industrielle du Pays d'Apt MUSEUM
(Industrial History Museum; ☑ 04 90 74 95 30; 14 place du Postel; adult/child €4/free; ⊙ 10am-noon & 2-6.30pm Mon-Sat, to 5.30pm Tue-Sat Oct-May) Gain an appreciation for Apt's artisanal and agricultural roots at this converted candied-fruit factory. The well-curated museum

GORGES D'OPPEDETTE

The Gorges du Verdon aren't the only canyons to explore in this part of France. Lying 18km east of Rustrel, the Gorges d'Oppedette is a system of gorges gouged out from the limestone over the millennia by the Calavon River. Several marked trails wind though the gorges, lasting from around half an hour to three hours; the tourist office in Apt has route leaflets. It's a gorgeous and quiet area to explore, and the canyons' high walls ensure they remain mercifully cool even on a blazing August day. Pack a picnic and hiking boots.

The small car park is signed off the D201 as you travel north from Viens towards Simiane-la-Rotonde.

interprets the fruit and candying trade, as well as ochre mining and earthenware production from the 18th century.

Ancienne Cathédrale Ste-Anne CHURCH

(rue Ste-Anne; ⊘ 9.30am-12.30pm & 2.30-6pm Mon-Fri, 2.30-6pm Sun) The 11th-century Ancienne Cathédrale Ste-Anne houses the relics of St Anne, and 11th- and 12th-century illuminated manuscripts.

Confiserie Kerry Aptunion FACTORY

(📞04 90 76 31 43; www.lesfleurons-apt.com; D900, Quartier Salignan; ⊘ shop 9am-12.15pm & 1.30-6pm Mon-Sat, no lunch break Jul & Aug) **FREE** Allegedly the largest *fruits confits* maker in the world, this factory produces sweets under the prestigious Les Fleurons d'Apt brand. Free tastings are offered in the shop, and guided tours of the factory allow you to watch the process in action; they run at 2.30pm Monday to Friday in July and August, with an extra tour at 10.30am in August. The rest of the year there's just one weekly tour, usually on Wednesday at 2.30pm – but confirm ahead.

The factory is 2.5km outside Apt.

🛏 Sleeping

Hôtel le Palais HOTEL €

(📞04 90 04 89 32; www.hotel-le-palais.com; 24bis place Gabriel-Péri; s/d/tr/q €45/55/65/80; 🛜🅿) Young, friendly owners lend a real air of dynamism to this veteran cheap-as-chips hotel, right in the heart of town. Rooms are on the poky side, but breakfast is a bargain at €5.

★ Le Couvent B&B €€

(📞04 90 04 55 36; www.loucouvent.com; 36 rue Louis Rousset; d €98-130; 🅿🛜🏊) Hidden behind a wall in the old town, this enormous five-room *maison d'hôte* occupies a 17th-century former convent. Staying here is as much architectural experience as accommodation: soaring ceilings, stonework, grand staircase, plus five palatial rooms (one has a sink made from a baptismal font). There's a sweet garden, and breakfast is served in the old convent refectory.

Hôtel Sainte-Anne HOTEL €€

(📞04 90 74 18 04; www.apt-hotel.fr; 62 place Faubourg-du-Ballet; d €92-123; ❄🅿🛜) Lovely seven-room hotel in a 19th-century dwelling, completely renovated in 2010. Spotless, crisp-at-the-edges rooms mix modern and traditional furnishings, with exceptional beds and big bathtubs (though small toilets). Little extras include homemade jams and breads, made by the charming owner, served as part of the copious breakfast (€10).

🍴 Eating

L'Auberge Espagnole TAPAS €

(http://laubergeespagnole-apt.com; 1 rue de la Juiverie; tapas €4.50-8, lunch menu €13.50) Dominated by an ancient plane tree, the old-town square onto which this colourful tapas bar spills could not be more enchanting – or typically Provençal. Take your pick from 22 Spanish-inspired tapas chalked on the board, and soak up the atmosphere on the square.

Thym, Te Voilà BISTRO €€

(📞04 90 74 28 25; www.thymtevoila.com; 59 place St-Martin; menus lunch €17.50-21.90, dinner €21.90-25.90; ⊘noon-2pm & 7.30-10pm Tue-Sat; 🅿) '*Cuisine du monde*' is what's on offer at this charming little bistro – in other words, a little bit of everything, from a splash of Asian spice to a traditional Hungarian goulash. It's on a lovely square in the old town, with outside tables next to the tinkling fountain in summer.

Au Platane MODERN FRENCH €€

(📞04 90 04 74 36; 25 place Jules Ferry; menus €15-30, mains €20; ⊘noon-2.30pm & 7.30-10pm Tue-Sat; 🅿) Hearty French food, with ever-changing menus that depend on what the chef's picked up at the market. Ask for a terrace table if the weather's warm.

🔒 Shopping

Confiserie Marcel Richaud FOOD

(📞04 90 74 43 50; confiserie-marcel-richaud@ wanadoo.fr; 112 quai de la Liberté; ⊘9am-noon & 2-5pm Tue-Sat) A small sweet shop selling locally made *fruits confits* (candied fruits) and *calissons d'Aix* (marzipan-like sweets). It's been in business for three generations.

ℹ Information

Maison du Parc du Luberon (☎04 90 04 42 00; www.parcduluberon.fr; 60 place Jean Jaurès; ⊙8.30am-noon & 1.30-6pm Mon-Fri, 9am-noon Sat Apr-Sep, shorter hours rest of year) A central information source for the Parc Naturel Régional du Luberon, with maps, walking guides and general info. There's also a small fossil museum.

Tourist Office (☎04 90 74 03 18; www.luberon-apt.fr; 20 av Philippe de Girard; ⊙9.30am-1pm & 2.30-7pm Mon-Sat, 9.30am-12.30pm Sun) Excellent source of information for activities, excursions, bike rides and walks.

ℹ Getting There & Around

BUS

Trans Vaucluse (p231) buses go to the following towns, and charge a flat-rate €2 to most destinations:

Aix-en-Provence (Line 9.1, two hours, one daily) Via Bonnieux, Lourmarin and Lauris.

Avignon (Line 15.1, 1½ hours, every two hours Monday to Saturday, two on Sunday) Travels via the Pont Julien near Bonnieux, Cavaillon and Avignon's TGV station.

Cavaillon (Line 15.2, 45 minutes, one daily) Via Bonnieux, Ménerbes and Oppède; extra buses run during school terms.

Banon (Line 16.2, 1¾ hours, one daily Monday to Saturday) Via Caseneuve and Simiane-la-Rotonde; an extra bus runs on Wednesday and Sunday.

BICYCLE

Rent bikes from Luberon Cycles (p231).

LE GRAND LUBERON

Divided from the hills of the Petit Luberon to the west by a deep river canyon, the Combe de Lourmarin, the scenic hills of the Grand Luberon are made for exploring. Take your time along the winding back roads: the scenery deserves to be savoured.

Buoux

Dominated by the hilltop ruins of Fort de Buoux, the tiny village of Buoux (the 'x' is pronounced) sits across the divide from Bonnieux, 8km south of Apt. The village itself is little more than a collection of a few tumbledown houses, but the fort is worth walking up to for the views – be careful, as

the path is badly worn and crumbling in places. Signs show you the way, but ask anywhere in the village for directions.

🛏 Sleeping & Eating

Auberge des Seguins   HOTEL €€
(☎04 90 74 16 37; www.aubergedesseguins.com; incl half-board dm €45, s €74-82, d €114-134, f €143-247, menu €25; ⊙dinner 7-9.30pm Mon-Fri, lunch 12.30-2.30pm Sat & Sun May-Sep, phone ahead at other times; ⚐⚐) At the bottom of the valley, this rural *auberge* feels like a Provençal summer camp, with two pools (one for kids), a fireside game room and a convivial dining room with long wooden tables. Four stone-walled buildings house simple rooms (no TVs) and a dorm. The restaurant serves fresh, local produce, and room rates include half-board. It's 2.5km below Buoux.

Auberge de la Loube   PROVENÇAL €€
(☎04 90 74 19 58; lunch/dinner menu from €25/33; ⊙by reservation noon-3pm & 7.30-9pm) You won't get a more honest Provençal lunch than at Maurice Leporati's roadside inn, where the feast always starts with wicker trays filled with hors d'oeuvres such as tapenade and anchöiade (olive and anchovy dips), quail's eggs, braised artichokes, aïoli and hummus. The showpiece Sunday lunch is legendary.

Maurice himself is a horse nut – ask nicely and he might show you his collection of antique carriages.

Saignon & Around

Even in a land of heart-stoppingly pretty villages, little Saignon still manages to raise an admiring eyebrow. Perched high on a rocky flank, surrounded by lavender fields and overlooked by the crumbling remains of a medieval castle, its cobbled streets and central square (complete with cascading fountain) are the stuff of which Provençal dreams are made.

A short trail leads up to the castle ruins and the aptly titled Rocher de Bellevue, a fabulous viewpoint overlooking the entire Luberon range, stretching north to Mont Ventoux on a clear day.

Above the village, the D113 climbs to the Distillerie Les Agnels (☎04 90 74 34 60; www.lesagnels.com; rte de Buoux, btwn Buoux & Apt; adult/child €6/free; ⊙10am-7pm Apr-Sep, to 5.30pm Oct-Mar), which uses locally grown lavender, cypress and rosemary in its fragrant products. It also rents three gorgeous self-contained cottages (€1300 to €2000 per week) that share a glorious heated pool covered by a greenhouse roof.

🛏 Sleeping

Chambre avec Vue B&B €€

(☑ 04 90 04 85 01; www.chambreavecvue.com; rue de la Bourgade, Saignon; r €90-110; ☺ closed Dec-Feb) Half posh B&B, half art gallery, this lovingly renovated 16th-century townhouse on the edge of Saignon's cobbled centre is run by art enthusiasts Kamila Regent and Pierre Jaccaud. Practically all the artworks on display are for sale, and the three guest rooms have been renovated in surprisingly cosmopolitan style. The back garden is idyllic, and filled with sculptures.

La Pyramide B&B €€

(☑ 04 90 04 70 00; www.lapyramidesaignon.com; rue du Jas, Saignon; d €79-110, f €135-145) A cute little country B&B, set around a delightful walled garden with its own natural spring. Rooms feel a touch old-fashioned, but they're cosy and clean. There's a €10 supplement in July and August. It's just south of town, on rue du Jas; look out for the turn-off as you drive up on the D48.

✕ Eating

Le Petit Café PROVENÇAL €€

(☑ 04 90 76 64 92; place de l'Horloge, Saignon; 2-/3-course menus €25/29; ☺ 10am-5pm Mar-Oct & Dec) This village cafe near the town clock is great for a bowl of chilled pea soup, crayfish mousse with mint, wraps, and other contemporary lunchtime creations by British chef Andrew Goldsby. Come dusk, backtrack downhill to **La Petite Cave** (☺ 7.30am-9.30pm Tue-Sat Apr-Sep), a romantic, stone-vaulted cellar restaurant by the same chef.

⭐**Le Sanglier Paresseux** MODERN FRENCH €€

(☑ 04 90 75 17 70; www.sanglierparesseux.com; Caseneuve; menus lunch €25, dinner €31-41; ☺ 7.30-10pm Mon, noon-2pm & 7.30-10pm Tue-Sat) There's one reason to make a detour to the hilltop village of Caseneuve, 10km east of Saignon, and that's to eat at this stellar restaurant. Run by Brazilian chef Fabricio Delgaudio, it's fast become one of the Luberon's most talked-about tables. Cuisine is inventive, unfussy, seasonal and the perfect showcase for regional ingredients – reservations are a must.

The view from the sunset terrace is almost worth a visit in its own right.

LE PETIT LUBERON

The westernmost extent of the Luberon massif, the Petit Luberon's craggy hills are interspersed with wooded valleys, vineyards and rural farms.

It's separated from the Grand Luberon by the slash of the Combe de Lourmarin, which cuts north–south through the mountains and is tracked by the D943 between Bonnieux and Lourmarin.

Bonnieux

Settled during the Roman era, Bonnieux is another bewitching hilltop town that still preserves its medieval character. It's intertwined with alleyways, cul-de-sacs and hidden staircases: from place de la Liberté, 86 steps lead to 12th-century **Église Vieille du Haut**. Look out for the alarming crack in one of the walls, caused by an earthquake.

The pleasure here is just to wander – especially if you time your visit for the lively Friday market, which takes over most of the old town's streets.

⊙ Sights & Activities

Musée de la Boulangerie MUSEUM

(☑ 04 90 75 88 34; 12 rue de la République; adult/student/child €3.50/1.50/free; ☺ 10am-12:30pm & 2.30-6pm Wed-Mon Apr-Oct) A museum all about the history of breadmaking might not sound like a Bonnieux must-see, but it's actually an intriguing visit. Located in a 17th-century building that was used as a bakery until 1920, it explores the baker's art both in Bonnieux and further afield, with antique millstones, tools, vintage posters and various other bread-related exhibits.

⭐**Fôret des Cèdres** FOREST

In the scrubby hills south of Bonnieux, a twisty back road slopes up to this wonderful cedar forest, the spreading boughs of which provide welcome relief from Provence's punishing summer heat. Various paths wind through the woods, including a new nature trail that's accessible for wheelchairs. The trip up to the forest is worth the drive by itself: the wraparound views of the Luberon valley and its *villages perchés* (hilltop towns) are out of this world.

The forest is about 6km south of Bonnieux; take the D36 towards Buoux and look out for the signs.

Pont Julien
BRIDGE

Situated 6km north of Bonnieux, near the junction of the D36 and D900, is one of the Luberon's most impressive Roman landmarks. Dating from around 3 BC, the 85m-long Pont Julien was built to allow the region's main Roman road, the Via Domitia, to traverse the Calavon River. Amazingly, the bridge's three graceful tiers were still carrying cars as recently as 2005 – a testament to the ingenuity and skill of its engineers.

Thankfully, it's now off limits to all traffic except bikes and sightseers.

Cave de Bonnieux
WINERY

(☑ 04 90 75 80 03; www.cave-bonnieux.com; La Gare de Bonnieux; ⏰ 2.30-6pm Mon, 9am-noon & 2.30-6pm Tue-Sat) Sample local wines at this superior cellar, 5km from Bonnieux on the D36.

🛏 Sleeping

La Bouquière
B&B €€

(☑ 04 90 75 87 17; www.labouquiere.com; chemin des Gardioles; d €80-90, apt €340) On a side road off the D149, surrounded by orchards and vineyards, this rural hideaway has four country-charming rooms with a mishmash of rustic antiques. All open onto flower-filled gardens and share a kitchen. The three-room apartment is ideal for families. There's a three- or four-night minimum in summer. It's tricky to find; call for directions.

Le Clos du Buis
HOTEL €€

(☑ 04 90 75 88 48; www.leclosdubuis.fr; rue Victor Hugo; d €135-153; ⏰ Mar–mid-Nov; ❈ 🛜 🏊) This elegant stone townhouse in Bonnieux spills onto big terraced gardens, lovely for whiling away the afternoon. The dining room has panoramic views, and there's a self-catering kitchen.

★ Maison Valvert
B&B €€€

(☑ 06 72 22 37 89; www.maisonvalvert.com; rte de Marseille; d €195-220, treehouses €280) Wow – for our money, this could well be the most stylish B&B in the Luberon. On an 18th-century *mas* (farm), lovingly renovated by Belgian owner Cathy, it's straight out of a designer magazine: neutral-toned rooms, natural fabrics, solar-heated pool and fabulous buffet breakfast. For maximum spoils, go for the ultra-romantic treehouse.

🍴 Eating

L'Arôme
FRENCH €€€

(☑ 04 90 75 88 62; 2 rue Lucien Blanc; menus €35-43; ⏰ noon-2pm Fri-Tue, 7-9.30pm Thu-Tue) Lodged

HILL TOWNS OF THE LUBERON BONNIEUX

LUBERON MARKETS

If there's one thing you really have to do in the Luberon, it's visit a local market. Luckily, there's at least one every day of the week, so there's no excuse not to shop. They generally run from 8am to 1pm from April to September; some villages also host summer evening markets. If you only have time to visit one, Apt's bustling Saturday-morning **Grand Marché** is hard to beat for atmosphere.

Monday Cadenet, Cavaillon, Lauris.

Tuesday Apt, Cucuron, Gordes, Lacoste, La Tour d'Aigues, St-Saturnin-lès-Apt.

Wednesday Gargas, Mérindol, Pertuis, Viens, Rustrel (evening market).

Thursday Roussillon, Ménerbes, Saignon, Goult, Céreste.

Friday Bonnieux, Lourmarin, Pertuis, St-Saturnin-lès-Apt (Friday-evening farmers market).

Saturday Apt, Cadenet, Manosque, Oppède, Pertuis, Vaugines.

Sunday Coustellet, Vaugines, Villars.

in a charming vaulted cellar in Bonnieux, L'Arôme is a pricey but prestigious address, run by well-respected chef Jean-Michel Pagès. The menu revolves around gourmet ingredients with impeccable local provenance, dashed with spice and surprises – and the romantic stone-walled setting is a winner.

Le Fournil
MODERN FRENCH €€€

(☑ 04 90 75 83 62; www.lefournil-bonnieux.com; 5 place Carnot; 2-/3-course lunch menus €24/30, dinner menus €40-52, lunch/dinner mains €17/26; ⏰ 12.30-2pm & 7.30-9.30pm Wed-Sun) In the middle of town next to the fountain, 'The Oven' is Bonnieux's top place to eat. There's a choice of settings: the swish interior (carved straight into the hillside) or the lovely terrace on the square. Either way, the menu's the same: rich, delicious Mediterranean dishes, making much of the chef's homemade *jus concentrés* (concentrated sauces).

They also run an ice-cream shop on the same square.

Silencio à la Maison de L'Aiguebrun
BISTRO €€€

(☑ restaurant 06 85 23 22 02; www.maisondelaiguebrun.com; ⏰ 8am-11pm; ❈ 🛜 🏊) Lying 6km southeast of Bonnieux off the D943, this inn once belonged to French film director Agnès

Varda and is now run by her daughter, Rosalie. The rooms are exclusively for members of the 'Silencio', a creative club based in Paris, but you can still visit to have lunch or dinner at the lovely restaurant, with views of the sylvan gardens.

ⓘ Information

Bonnieux Tourist Office (☑ 04 90 75 91 90; www.tourisme-en-luberon.com; 7 place Carnot; ☉ 9.30am-12.30pm & 2-6.30pm Mon-Fri, 2-6.30pm Sat May-Oct, shorter hours rest of year) Covers the entire Petit Luberon.

Lacoste

Situated 6.5km west of Bonnieux, Lacoste has nothing to do with the designer brand – although it does have couturier connections. In 2001 designer Pierre Cardin purchased the 9th-century **Château de Lacoste** (☑ 04 90 75 93 12; www.chateau-la-coste.com), and much of the village, where the Marquis de Sade (1740–1814) retreated in 1771, when his writings became too scandalous for Paris. The château was looted by revolutionaries in 1789, and the 45-room palace remained an eerie ruin until Cardin arrived. He created a 1000-seat theatre and opera stage adjacent, only open during July's month-long **Festival de Lacoste** (www.festivaldelacoste.com).

Daytime visits to the castle are possible, but only by reservation.

Ménerbes

Hilltop Ménerbes is another wonder for wandering, with a maze of cobbled alleyways that afford sudden glimpses over the surrounding plains. It's best known as the former home of British-expat author Peter Mayle, whose books *A Year in Provence* and *Toujours Provence* recount his tales of renovating a farmhouse

---

LUBERON WINES

The Luberon is graced with three main wine appellations: the Côtes du Ventoux, the Côtes du Luberon and the Coteaux de Pierrevert. There is a huge number of wine-growers both large and small – if you're up for some tasting, the best idea is to stop by the nearest tourist office and request a map that shows all the local vineyards, co-ops and cellars. The website **Les Vins Luberon** (www.vins-luberon.fr) also has a comprehensive list of producers.

---

outside the village in the late 1980s. Monsieur Mayle now lives in Lourmarin.

◉ Sights

Musée du Tire-Bouchon   MUSEUM
(☑ 04 90 72 41 58; http://domaine-citadelle.com; adult/child €5/free; ☉ 9am-noon & 2-7pm Apr-Oct, 10am-noon & 2-5pm Mon-Sat Nov-Mar) A shrine to corkscrews, this quirky museum displays over 1000 of them at Domaine de la Citadelle, a winery on the D3 toward Cavaillon, where you can sample Côtes du Luberon.

Maison de la Truffe et du Vin   WINERY
(House of Truffle & Wine; ☑ 04 90 72 38 37; www.vin-truffe-luberon.com; place de l'Horloge; ☉ 10am-noon & 2.30-6pm Apr-Oct, Thu-Sat Nov-Mar) Opposite the town's 12th-century church, this establishment is home to the Brotherhood of Truffles and Wine of the Luberon, and represents 60 local *domaines* (estates producing wine). From April to October, there are free wine-tasting sessions daily, and afterwards you can buy the goods at bargain-basement prices. Winter brings truffle workshops.

🛏 Sleeping

La Bastide du Bois Bréant   HOTEL €€€
(☑ 04 90 05 86 78; www.hotel-bastide-bois-breant. com; 501 chemin du Puits-de-Grandaou, Maubec; d incl breakfast €175-240, 2-/4-person treehouses €170/320; ☉ mid-Mar–Oct; ❋ @ 🛜 ❄) Shaded by 200-year-old oaks, this 2-hectare former truffle plantation midway between Gordes and Ménerbes sprawls seductively behind an iron gate. Inside the early-19th-century *bastide* (country manor) are 12 romantic rooms, decked out in an upmarket country-Provençal style. Outside, hidden between branches, are two treehouses and a wonderfully bucolic and old-fashioned *roulotte* (caravan). Dinner with reservation costs €30.

🍴 Eating

Café du Progrès   CAFE €
(☑ 04 90 72 22 09; place Albert Roure; menus €13-16; ☉ 6am-midnight) Ménerbes' tobacconist-newsagent-bar is the hub for all the village gossip, and a good bet for lunchtime *plats du jour*.

★ **Café Véranda**   MODERN FRENCH €€€
(☑ 04 90 72 33 33; www.cafe-veranda.com; 104 av Marcellin Poncet; mains €21-46, menus €35-76; ☉ noon-3pm & 7-10pm Tue-Sun) This high-class bistro is a surprise in little Ménerbes – the kind of place where you'll need to unbuckle your belt, and your wallet. Dishes are seasonal, ranging from a copious shellfish platter

(€49) to a seven-hour slow-cooked lamb with black-olive pesto. There's a small patio, but the main dining room is the spot for valley views.

Oppède-le-Vieux

Jutting from a craggy hilltop 3km from the modern town of Oppède, Oppède-le-Vieux was abandoned in 1910, when villagers moved down the hill to the valley to cultivate the plains.

From the car parks (€3), a wooded path leads up to the village's snaking, atmospheric alleyways. At the very top of town, the village's ruined castle provides a formidable vantage point over the surrounding valley – although the ruins themselves are off limits while the village raises funds for the castle's restoration.

Several artists and ceramicists have set up their studios here, and sell their wares during the summer. Signs from the car parks also direct you to the Sentier Vigneron, a 1½-hour viticulture trail through olive groves, cherry orchards and vineyards.

For lunch, Le Petit Café (☎04 90 76 74 01; www.petitcafe.fr; place de la Croix; menus €18-25; ⏰8.30am-11.30pm) serves inventive Provençal dishes on the village square.

SOUTH OF THE LUBERON MOUNTAINS

Lourmarin

As you emerge from the deep Combe de Lourmarin through the Luberon massif, the first village you'll strike is Lourmarin. Once a quiet farming town, it's now a chichi place, its streets lined with upmarket homewares shops and boutiques – something that's accelerated since the arrival of celebrated expat author Peter Mayle.

Apart from a walk around town, the main sight of note is the Renaissance Château de Lourmarin (☎04 90 68 15 23; www.chateau-de-lourmarin.com; adult/child €6.50/3; ⏰10am-6.30pm Jul & Aug, 10.30am-12.30pm & 2.30-5.30pm or 6.30pm Sep-Jun) – the first of its kind to be built in Provence. Constructed during the 16th century and later expanded, the castle has had a string of aristocratic owners, and is now owned by the Vibert family. Its rooms are filled with impressive antiques and objets d'art.

Literary pilgrims might also want to peep into the town cemetery, the last resting place of Albert Camus (1913–60), who was living nearby when he was killed in a car accident in 1960, and the French author Henri Bosco (1888–1976).

🛏 Sleeping

La Cordière   B&B €
(☎04 90 68 03 32; www.cordiere.com; rue Albert Camus; d for 3 nights €170-225; 🐾) In Lourmarin's village centre, this character-rich house, built 1582, surrounds a tiny flower-bedecked courtyard, with adjoining summer kitchen for guests. Rooms are filled with atmospheric Provençal antiques and sport spacious bathrooms. Also rents three great-value studios with kitchens. Minimum three-night stay. Breakfast €7.50.

Le Mas de Foncaudette   B&B €€
(☎04 90 08 42 51; www.foncaudette.com; d €98-125, tr €145, q €160; ⏰Apr-Oct; 🐾🏊♿) A friendly base on the edge of Lourmarin, in a colourful 16th-century farmhouse surrounding a fig-shaded central courtyard. Rooms are cosy and feminine: we liked split-level Marius (good for families) and Paneloux, with its Moroccan-inspired decor. Owner Aline Edme is full of local knowledge, and the pool's a beauty. It's signposted off the D27 between Lourmarin and Puyvert.

🍴 Eating

★Café Gaby   CAFE €
(☎04 90 68 38 42; place de l'Ormeau; salads €10-12, omelettes €9-12; ⏰7am-midnight) One of a trio of delightful cafes on place de l'Ormeau, Café Gaby – its royal blue and cream woven bistro chairs winking in the lunchtime sun – is unadulterated Provençal charm. Cuisine is French classic and homemade, climaxing each Friday with a giant *aïoli maison* (veg, boiled potatoes, a boiled egg and shellfish dunked in a pot of garlicky mayonnaise).

Auberge La Fenière   GASTRONOMIC €€€
(☎04 90 68 11 79; www.reinesammut.com; rte de Lourmarin, Cadenet; d from €180, menus €38 & €78; 🐾🏊) It doesn't get more Provençal than this wonderful old stone farmhouse – the exquisite domain of Michelin-starred chef Reine Sammut, who cooks up outstanding multi-course meals using produce from her *potager* (kitchen garden). The wine list is sufficiently fine to justify an overnight stay in one of its 16 beautiful rooms and suites.

Cooking classes start at around €70 for two hours, or €165 with lunch.

ⓘ Information

Lourmarin Tourist Office (☑ 04 90 68 10 77; www.lourmarin.com; place Henri Barthélémy; ☺10am-12.30pm & 3-6pm Mon-Sat) Leads 10am guided walks (adult/child €4/free) dedicated to Albert Camus (Tuesday), Henri Bosco (Wednesday) and exploring the village (Thursday).

Vaugines & Cucuron

From Lourmarin the D56 shadows the GR97 walking trail 5km east to Vaugines, where Claude Berri's Pagnol films *Manon des Sources* and *Jean de Florette* (1986) were partly shot with the village's horse-chestnut tree as a backdrop.

Cucuron, 2km further east, is the starting point for walks up **Mourre Nègre** (1125m), the highest hill in the Luberon range. Maps are available from the tourist office.

If you feel like you've earned a posthike dinner, you're in luck: Cucuron has its own Michelin-starred bistro, **La Petite Maison de Cucuron** (☑ 04 90 68 21 99; www.lapetitemaisondecucuron.com; place de l'Etang; menus €50-70; ☺noon-2pm & 8-10pm Wed-Sun), where chef Eric Sapet creates sumptuous things from produce sourced from local farms. It's quite upmarket (definitely high heels rather than hiking boots), and reservations are essential in season. The restaurant offers cooking classes on Saturday morning for €70.

Ansouis

Little changed in centuries, the part-fortified village of Ansouis has justifiably earned its place amongst France's *plus beaux villages* (most beautiful villages). Ramparts, watchtowers and gateways ring the village's old centre and the medieval **Château d'Ansouis** (☑ 04 90 09 82 70; adult/6-18yr €6/3; ☺ call for hours), which is now privately owned but can be visited on a guided tour.

The village is also home to an oddball museum, the **Musée Extraordinaire** (☑ 04 90 09 82 64; adult/under 16yr €3.50/1.50; ☺2-6pm or 7pm; ♿), founded by Provençal painter and diver Georges Mazoyer, whose passion for the sea shows in the museum's fossil exhibits and oceanic art.

✕ Eating

L'Art Glacier   ICE CREAM €
(☑ 04 90 77 75 72; Les Hautes Terres; ☺vary) Go off the beaten path to find ice cream that's an art. Michel and Sigrid Perrière handcraft mind-boggling varieties of the sweet stuff:

from lavender to sesame to cassis. The ice creamery sits between Ansouis and La Tour d'Aigues on a hilltop off the D9 (look for the signs posted on roundabouts).

★**La Closerie**   FRENCH €€€
(☑ 04 90 09 90 54; www.lacloserieansouis.com; bd des Platanes; menus €29-65; ☺noon-2pm Fri-Tue, 7-10pm Mon, Tue, Fri & Sat) A renowned fine-dining establishment in Ansouis, overseen by chef Olivier and his wife Delphine. The food here is sophisticated but full of flavour and flair – which explains why it's practically impossible to get a table in season, especially for the excellent-value lunch *menu*. It feels surprisingly relaxed for a Michelin-starred place too.

South of Lourmarin

Beyond the southern bank of the languid River Durance, the sunbaked countryside stretches south over vineyards and scrubby hills all the way to Aix-en-Provence.

◉ Sights

Jardin Conservatoire de Plantes Tinctoriales   GARDEN
(☑ 04 90 08 40 48; www.couleur-garance.com; Lauris; adult/child €5/free; ☺ 9am-noon & 2-7pm May-Oct) In the days before synthetic dyes, natural colours obtained from plants, fruit and seeds were the main way of creating tints for clothing, textiles and tapestries. This garden in the village of Lauris contains a collection of such plants, and hosts regular workshops demonstrating how they were used. Guided visits (€8) run on Tuesday and Saturday at 5pm.

Abbaye de Silvacane   CHURCH
(☑ 04 42 50 41 69; www.abbaye-silvacane.com; adult/child €7.50/6; ☺10am-6pm Jun-Sep, 10am-1pm & 2-5pm Oct-Apr) Lying 7km southwest of Cadenet, Abbaye de Silvacane is one of a trio of medieval abbeys built in Provence by Cistercian monks. Constructed between 1175 and 1230, it has all the hallmarks of the Romanesque style, from the unadorned chapel to the peaceful cloister. Today it hosts concerts and art exhibitions.

Observatoire Ornithologique de Mérindol   WILDLIFE RESERVE
(☑ 04 90 71 32 01) This bird reserve on the River Durance is home to some 243 species, including herons and great cormorants. Hides are strategically positioned along the 3km trail (1½ hours), marked with yellow blazes. The site is near the Mérindol-Mallemort dam (signposted 1.5km from the roundabout at the entrance to Mérindol on the D973).

Haute-Provence & the Southern Alps

Best Places to Eat

➡ Auberge le Robur (p262)

➡ Restaurant Le 9 (p249)

➡ La Ferme Girerd-Potin (p260)

➡ La Bastide de Moustiers (p255)

➡ La Ferme Ste-Cécile (p255)

Best Places to Stay

➡ Moonlight Chalet (p263)

➡ Les Méans (p258)

➡ La Bastide de Moustiers (p255)

➡ Gîte de Chasteuil (p255)

➡ Relais d'Elle (p248)

Why Go?

Provence might conjure up images of rolling fields and gentle hills, but west of the Luberon you'll find yourself travelling through altogether more dramatic landscapes. Rising like a tooth-lined jawbone along the border with Italy, just an hour's drive north of Nice, lie the Alps – France's most famous mountain range, a haven for mountaineers, hikers and wildlife-spotters, and home to some of the region's most unforgettable scenery.

Cloaked in snow well into springtime, the mountains of Haute-Provence are divided by six main valleys, connected by some of the highest and most hair-raising road passes anywhere in Europe – an absolute must for road-trippers. At the heart of the area sprawls the huge Parc National du Mercantour, home to a host of rare wildlife, mountain-top villages and pristine natural habitats. Make sure you keep the camera close to hand: there's a picture around every corner.

Driving Distances (km)

	Barcelonnette	Castellane	Digne-les-Bains	Forcalquier
Castellane	75			
Digne-les-Bains	76	45		
Forcalquier	120	83	48	
Moustiers Ste-Marie	125	35	47	51

Haute-Provence & Southern Alps Highlights

① Trace the unforgettable clifftop roads around the **Gorges du Verdon** (p251).

② Ride the **Train des Pignes** (p257) through the mountains from Nice to Digne-les-Bains.

③ Hike through the high mountains around **St-Martin-Vésubie** (p262).

④ Watch semi-wild wolves at the **Alpha wildlife reserve** (p262).

⑤ Conquer Europe's highest road pass, the **Col**

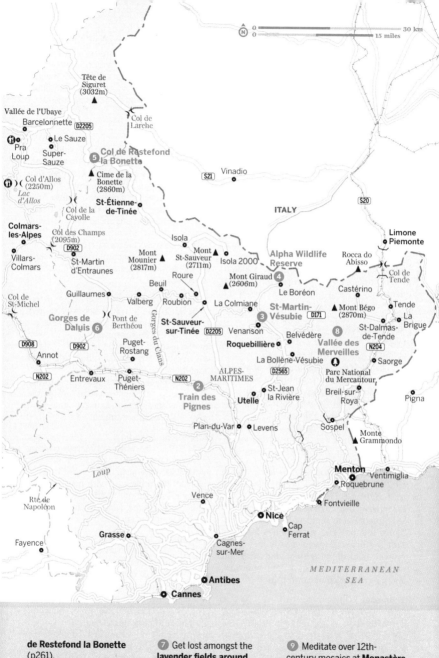

de Restefond la Bonette (p261).

⑥ Motor through the scarlet canyons of the **Gorges de Daluis** (p260).

⑦ Get lost amongst the **lavender fields around Manosque** (p250).

⑧ Admire the work of ancient rock artists in the **Vallée des Merveilles** (p263).

⑨ Meditate over 12th-century mosaics at **Monastère Notre Dame de Ganagobie** (p250).

PAYS DE FORCALQUIER

Beyond mass tourism's radar, Pays de Forcalquier's expansive landscapes comprise wildflower-tinged countryside and isolated hilltop villages. It's the portal to Haute-Provence from the Luberon, and the fastest way in from Marseille too. At its heart lies namesake Forcalquier, famous for its market and absinthe. Saffron grows here.

Forcalquier & Around

The area's only sizeable town, Forcalquier (population 5000) has an upbeat, slightly bohemian vibe – a hangover from the 1960s and '70s, when artists and back-to-the-landers arrived and fostered a now-booming organics (*biologiques*) movement. You'll see the town long before you reach it thanks to the gold-topped 'citadel' that crowns the nearby hilltop.

The town's at its liveliest on Monday morning for the weekly market, one of the area's best.

◉ Sights & Activities

Old Town AREA

To reach the citadel and its little octagonal chapel, it's a 20-minute walk uphill via shady backstreets and winding steps. At the top there's a viewing platform offering panoramic views. On the way back down, keep an eye out for some of the town's impressive **wooden doorways**, dating from the days when Forcalquier was the pre-Revolutionary seat of power for the Comtes de Provence.

★ **Prieuré de Salagon** MONASTERY, GARDEN

(☑ 04 92 75 70 50; www.musee-de-salagon.com; adult/child/family €7/5/20; ⊙ 10am-8pm Jun-Aug, to 7pm May & Sep, to 6pm Oct–mid-Dec & Feb-Apr; 🅿) Situated 4km south of Forcalquier near Mane, this peaceful priory dates from the 13th century. It's worth a visit to wander around its medieval herb gardens, fragrant with native lavender, mint and mugwort, and a show garden of world plants.

Ecomusée l'Olivier MUSEUM

(☑ 04 92 72 66 91; www.ecomusee-olivier.com; adult/child €4/free; ⊙ 10am-6pm Mon-Fri, 1.30-6pm Sat; 🅿) 🅿 If all the olive groves around Forcalquier have inspired curiosity, head 15km southeast to Volx, where this intriguing eco-museum allows you to learn all about the extraction process and the olive tree's importance to Mediterranean culture. There's also a posh shop where you can pick up souvenirs, and taste various olive-oil varieties, as well as an excellent Provençal restaurant, **Les Petites Tables** (☑ 04 86 68 53 14; lespetitestables@gmail.com; lunch mains €10-16; ⊙ noon-3pm Tue-Sat), that's perfect for lunch.

It has sister shops in Gordes, Roussillon, Aix-en-Provence and several other towns.

🛏 Sleeping

★ **Relais d'Elle** B&B €

(☑ 04 92 75 06 87, 06 75 42 33 72; http://relais-delle.com; rte de la Brillane, Niozelles; s/d/tr/q from €56/70/88/110; 🕸🚫🅿) What a stunner of a B&B this is, 8km from Forcalquier in a delightful ivy-covered farmhouse dating from 1802, surrounded by tended gardens, bucolic countryside and a grand pool. The sweet, feminine rooms all have views – we liked Collines for its cosiness and Pierres for its atmosphere. The owners are passionate about horses, and also offer a delicious dinner by reservation.

Grand Hotel HOTEL €

(☑ 04 92 75 00 35; www.grandhotel-forcalquier.com; 10 blvd Latourette, Forcalquier; s/d/tr/f €48/59/67/99; 🕸) If you want to be in town for the market, this hotel is smack bang in the middle of things, a minute downhill from the main square. It's a simple, old-fashioned place – a touch musty, but spruce and friendly. The nicest rooms are at the back; the ones at the front get some road noise. Half-board is available.

Bergerie de Beaudine B&B €

(☑ 04 92 75 01 52; www.gite-labeaudine.com; rte de Limans, Forcalquier; s/d €56/66; 🕸🚫) This genial B&B is colourfully decorated in floral style and has a big yard with pool, outdoor summer kitchen and barbecue. It's 2km from town via the D950 towards Banon. Limited wi-fi. Cash only.

Couvent des Minimes HOTEL €€€

(☑ 04 92 74 77 77; www.couventdesminimes-hotelspa.com; Chemin des Jeux de Maï, Mane; r from €235; 🕸🚫🕸🚫) A real budget-buster, but boutique in every sense of the word. Housed in a converted convent, it pulls out all the luxury stops: beautiful rooms, an indulgent spa and a superb restaurant, all wrapped up in wonderful medieval architecture. Low-season and last-minute deals often bring prices down a notch.

🍴 Eating

There are several brasseries around Forcalquier's main square, place du Bourguet.

L'Entre d'Eux
CAFE €

(23 bd des Martyrs, Forcalquier; dishes €5-10; 8:30am-6pm Mon-Sat, to 3pm Wed;) Small cafe near the main square that serves mixed plates of cheese, charcuterie and other nibbles.

Le Baratin
BISTRO €€

(04 92 77 14 84; 22 blvd Latourette, Forcalquier; mains €10-14; lunch noon-3pm) A popular lunch spot, good for speedy classics like *salade de chèvre* (melted goat's-cheese salad), steak with shallots and burgers served with rough-cut chips.

Restaurant Le 9
PROVENÇAL €€

(04 92 75 03 29; www.le9-forcalquier.fr; av Jean Giono, Forcalquier; menus €17-28; lunch noon-2.30pm, dinner 7.30-10pm Wed-Mon) High in Forcalquier, behind the Citadel with a panoramic terrace, Le 9 (pronounced luh-nuf) is the town's most reliable address for earthy, market-driven cooking, incorporating fresh-from-the-farm ingredients in simple bistro fare, like honey-braised rabbit or grilled lamb with tomato and basil. The best idea is usually just to go for whatever's on the blackboard. Reservations recommended.

Café de Niozelles
PROVENÇAL, ITALIAN €€

(04 92 73 10 17; http://bistrot.niozelles.net; place du Village, Niozelles; set menu €26; lunch 12.30-2.30pm, dinner 7-9pm, closed Thu;) For just-like-maman-made-it French cuisine, it's worth the 5km drive to this unashamedly old-fashioned bistro in Niozelles. You'll need an appetite, and a taste for all the traditional trimmings, like offal, tripe and sheep trotters – but you won't find a more authentic French meal in the Pays de Forcalquier.

Shopping

Distilleries et Domaines de Provence
DRINK

(04 92 75 15 41; www.distilleries-provence.com; 9 av St-Promasse, Forcalquier; 10am-12.30pm & 2-6pm Mon & Wed-Sat Apr-Dec) In business since 1898, this friendly distillery makes its own pastis and absinthe. Look for the sign marked 'Espace Dégustation' and the antique still outside.

Information

Forcalquier Tourist Office (04 92 75 10 02; www.forcalquier.com; 13 place du Bourguet; 9am-noon & 2-6pm Mon-Sat) Info on walks, bike routes, hot-air ballooning and other activities in the Forcalquier area. Useful iPhone app: 'visit 04'.

BISTROT DE PAYS

To help attract diners to the more rural towns and villages of Haute-Provence, **Bistrot de Pays** (www.bistrotdepays. com) is an organisation that champions small restaurants known for serving traditional Provençal cuisine and their commitment to using local produce. Many also host live music and community events. The idea is so successful that the rest of France is adopting it. There are dozens of participating venues scattered around the countryside: you can pick up a free booklet at tourist offices, or consult listings on the website.

Getting There & Around

LER (Lignes Express Régionales; 08 21 20 22 03; www.info-ler.fr) busses connect Forcalquier, Mane and St-Michel l'Observatoire with Apt, Avignon, Digne-les-Bains, Sisteron, Manosque, Aix-en-Provence and Marseille. The tourist office has complete info.

Bachelas Cycles (p231) rents mountain, road, tandem and electric bicycles (€19 to €26 per day).

St-Michel l'Observatoire

Driving through the scrubby back roads around St-Michel l'Observatoire, an unexpected sight appears on the hills ahead: a futuristic dome-shaped observatory, built in 1937 to take advantage of Haute-Provence's wonderfully clear night skies. The village is beautiful in its own right, but it buzzes in summer with amateur astronomers.

Sights & Activities

Observatoire de Haute-Provence
OBSERVATORY

(04 92 70 64 00; www.obs-hp.fr; adult/child €4.50/2.50; guided visits 2-5pm Tue-Thu Jul & Aug, 2.15-4pm Wed Sep-Jun) Tours of St-Michel's observatory include the chance to see its working 193cm central telescope, plus a film about the centre's research. Buy tickets for the 30-minute guided tour from the ticket office in St-Michel's village square; in July and August there's a free shuttle. The observatory is at the end of the D305, 2km north of St-Michel l'Observatoire. Call ahead in the low season.

Centre d'Astronomie
OBSERVATORY

(☑ 04 92 76 69 69; www.centre-astro.fr; Plateau du Moulin à Vent; adult/6-16yr €7.15/5.10; ⊙ by reservation only) It's also possible to visit the nearby astronomy centre by arrangement, where you'll have the chance to make both solar and stellar observations – but you'll need good French to make the most of it.

Simiane la Rotonde

POP 602 / ELEV 630M

Jutting out along the rocky skyline on top of a 630m hilltop, this heart-stoppingly pretty village is celebrated for its unmistakable landmark: the **Rotonde** (www.simiane-la-rotonde.fr; adult/12-18yr/under 12yr €4.50/2.50/free; ⊙ 10.30am-1pm & 2-7pm May-Aug, 1.30-6pm Wed-Sun Mar, Apr & Sep–mid-Nov) after which the town is named.

Forming part of the 12th-century fortified castle built by the Simiane-Agoult family, who were one of the region's most powerful medieval dynasties, it's particularly notable for its magnificent central cupola, graced by a soaring dome, 12 supporting ribs and a forest of decorative columns and intricate stonework. It's a true masterpiece of medieval engineering, and every year provides the unforgettable setting for classical-music festival **Les Riches Heures Musicales de la Rotonde**.

Banon

POP 940 / ELEV 760M

The little village of Banon is famous for its eponymous cheese, *chèvre de Banon* – made from goat's milk, wrapped in a chestnut leaf and tied with raffia string. It's a prized local delicacy, eaten both fresh and cooked. You'll see it for sale at many local markets, including Banon's own on Tuesday morning. The town also hosts its own **cheese festival** in May.

At other times, you can pick it up at the wonderful cheese-and-sausage shop, **La Brindille Melchio** (☑ 04 92 73 23 05; place de la République; ⊙ 8am-7pm daily Jul & Aug, 8am-12.30pm & 2.30-6.30pm Wed-Sun Sep-Jun). The tourist office also keeps a list of local farms you can visit, including the **Fromagerie de Banon** (☑ 04 92 73 25 03; www.fromagerie-banon.fr; rte Carniol; ⊙ 2.30-5.30pm Mon-Fri Apr-Oct), a couple of kilometres south of town on the D201.

VALLÉE DE LA DURANCE

Halfway between the Luberon and the high Alps lies the broad, flat floodplain of the River Durance. Centuries ago, this natural pass was crossed by the Via Domitia, the main road that enabled Roman legionnaries and traders to travel through the south of Gaul. It's now crossed by a more modern equivalent: the A8 motorway.

The area is also famous for its lavender fields, especially around Manosque and the nearby Plateau de Valensole. Many growers offer guided visits and sell products direct: ask in any local tourist office for one of the free *Routes de la Lavande* leaflets.

◉ Sights

Les Mées
ARCHAEOLOGICAL SITE

Travelling north from Forcalquier towards Sisteron, you can't miss the mysterious Rochers des Mées: rows and rows of rocky pinnacles, some as much as 100m high. Legend claims they were once monks, turned to stone for lusting after Saracen women. A loop trail travels through the formations, taking around 3½ hours from end to end.

Monastère Notre Dame de Ganagobie
MONASTERY

(www.ndganagobie.com; Ganagobie; ⊙ 3-5pm Tue-Sun, shop 10.30am-noon & 2.30-6pm Tue-Sun) **FREE** Ganagobie's otherworldly monastery is an essential stop. Founded in the 10th century, it's still home to a working Benedictine community, who produce products including soaps, honey, jam and beer, all for sale in the monastery shop. The chapel (worth a visit for its fabulous 12th-century floor mosaics) is the only area open to the public, but you're free to wander round most of the grounds.

It's located at the end of a winding 4km lane; look out for signs on the D4096 as you travel between Forcalquier and Sisteron. Note that the monastery is closed during times of monastic retreat.

Citadelle de Sisteron
FORT

(www.citadelledesisteron.fr; admission €6.40; ⊙ 9am-6pm Apr-Oct, to 7pm Jul & Aug) For the finest views of the valley, make a beeline for Sisteron's hilltop citadel, perched on a flank of rock high above the town. Built in stages between the 13th and 16th centuries, it was badly damaged by bombardment in August 1944 but has since been meticulously restored.

ROUTE DU TEMPS

The Route du Temps (Road of Time) is a signed route that winds through some of the area's most dramatic valleys, historical sites and rock formations; it starts just north of Sisteron and follows the D3 to St-Geniez, up and over Col de Font-Belle (1304m) to the medieval fortified village of Thoard.

Interpretive panels along the way explain what you're seeing, and if you fancy a closer look, various trails criss-cross their way into the surrounding hills. It's also worth stopping in Thoard for a visit to the **Distillerie du Siron** (☑04 92 34 61 96, 06 25 12 67 17; www.distilleriesiron-lavande.fr; Thoard; ⊙tours by reservation 10am-noon & 2-6pm daily Jul & Aug, by appointment rest of year) **FREE**, a small-scale organic lavender factory run by local maker Marc Malagutti.

In total, it's a journey of around two to three hours, depending on how many stops you make. For further information and a route map (€2), contact the Sisteron tourist office.

🛏 Sleeping & Eating

Mas Saint-Joseph   B&B €
(☑04 92 62 47 54; www.lemassaintjoseph. com; Châteauneuf-Val-St-Donat; s/d/tr/q €60/69/88/107; ⊙Apr-Oct; ☒) This converted farmhouse sits atop a wooded hillside 10km northwest of Peyruis. Wood beams and stone walls make the whitewashed rooms feel extra special. There's a hot tub and shared kitchen facilities. The *table d'hôte* (hosts' dinner) is copious and includes wine; it's a bargain at €17 or €23, depending on the menu you choose.

La Magnanerie   GASTRONOMIC €€
(☑04 92 62 60 11; www.la-magnanerie.net; N85, Aubignosc; menus lunch €22-29, dinner €32-55; ⊙lunch 12.15-1.30pm, dinner 7.15-9.30pm Tue-Sun; @�]) A stylish, if starchy, restaurant-hotel on the road 10km south of Sisteron. Chef Stéphan Paroche is known for his colourful, creative cooking – edible flowers and microherbs adorn his exquisite plates of fine French food. Upstairs rooms (€78–98) are equally playful: some have comic-book murals, others are styled after classic cinematic scenes. Reservations essential.

GORGES DU VERDON

For sheer, jaw-dropping drama, there are few sights in France that can match the epic Gorges du Verdon. The Grand Canyon of Europe slices a 25km swath through Haute-Provence's limestone plateau all the way to the foothills of the Alps. Etched out over millions of years by the Verdon River, the gorges have formed the centrepiece of the Parc Naturel Régional du Verdon since 1997. With their sheer, plunging cliffs – in some places 700m high, twice the height of the Eiffel Tower – the gorges are a haven for birds, including a colony of reintroduced *vautours fauves* (griffon vultures).

From the top of the cliffs, the Verdon River itself seems little more than a silver trickle, but down at gorge level it takes on a different character: it's one of France's best spots for white-water rafting. The canyon floors are only accessible by foot or raft, and it's worth experiencing the gorges from both bottom and top to get a proper sense of their brain-boggling size.

The main gorge begins at Rougon, near the confluence of the Verdon and Jabron Rivers. The most useful jumping-off points are Moustiers Ste-Marie, in the west, and Castellane, in the east.

🏃 Activities

Cycling & Driving

A complete circuit of the Gorges du Verdon from Moustiers Ste-Marie involves 140km of driving, not to mention a relentless series of hairpin turns. There's a cliffside road on either side of the gorges, but passing spots are rare, roads are narrow and rockfalls are possible – so take it slow and enjoy the scenery.

Spring and autumn are ideal times to visit: the roads can be traffic clogged in summer and icy in winter – note that the Route des Crêtes (D952 & D23) is snowbound (closed) from mid-November to mid-March.

The only village en route is La Palud-sur-Verdon (930m), so make sure you've got a full tank of gas before setting out.

Walking & Hiking

Dozens of blazed trails traverse the wild countryside around Castellane and Moustiers. Tourist offices carry the excellent *Canyon du Verdon* (€4.70), detailing 28 walks in English, as well as maps of five principal walks (€2.40).

Note that wild camping anywhere in the gorges is illegal. Don't cross the river, except at bridges, and always stay on marked trails, lest you get trapped when the upstream dam opens, which happens twice weekly. Check water levels and the weather forecast with local tourist offices before embarking.

Outdoor Sports

Castellane is the main water-sports base (April to September, by reservation); its tourist office has lists of lots of local operators. Most charge roughly similar rates: around €35 for two hours, €55 for a half-day and €75 for a full day. Safety kit is provided, but you'll get (very) wet, so dress appropriately.

Lac de Castillon's beaches are popular for swimming and paddle boating, while St-André-les-Alpes, on the lakeshore, is France's leading paragliding centre.

Des Guides pour l'Aventure
OUTDOOR ACTIVITIES

(☑06 85 94 46 61; www.guidesaventure.com; Moustiers Ste-Marie) Offers activities including canyoning (€45 per half-day), rock climbing (€40 for three hours), rafting (€45 for 2½ hours) and 'floating' (€50 for three hours), which is like rafting, except you have a buoyancy aid instead of a boat.

MARKET DAYS

Markets generally run 8am to noon.

Monday Forcalquier.

Tuesday Breil-sur-Roya, Colmars-les-Alpes.

Wednesday Barcelonnette, Castellane, Digne-les-Bains, La Foux d'Allos, La Palud-sur-Verdon, Riez, Sisteron, St-André-les-Alpes, Tende.

Thursday Allemagne-en-Provence, Allos, Les Salles-sur-Verdon, Montagnac, Sospel.

Friday Colmars-les-Alpes, Entrevaux, Moustiers Ste-Marie, Quinson, Seyne-les-Alpes.

Saturday Barcelonnette, Castellane, Digne-les-Bains, Riez, Sisteron, St-André-les-Alpes.

Sunday Bauduen (summer), Castellane, La-Palud-sur-Verdon (summer).

Daily St-Martin-Vésubie.

Aboard Rafting
WATER SPORTS

(☑04 92 83 76 11; www.aboard-rafting.com; 8 place de l'Église, Castellane) White-water rafting, cano-raft, air-boat and canyoning trips. Most activities start at €35 for two hours.

Latitude Challenge
ADVENTURE SPORTS

(☑04 91 09 04 10; www.latitude-challenge.fr; jumps €115) Bungee jumps from Europe's highest bungee site, the 182m Pont de l'Artuby (Artuby Bridge). Also skydiving.

Aérogliss
PARAGLIDING

(☑04 92 89 11 30; www.aerogliss.com; chemin des Iscles, St-André-les-Alpes; intro flights from €75) Offers 'baptism' flights for novice paragliders, as well as catering to more experienced fliers.

Wildlife Watching

Sortie de Découverte des Vautours du Verdon
BIRDWATCHING

(☑04 92 83 61 14; adult/child €10/6; ⊙9.30am & 6pm Tue, Wed & Fri mid-Jun–mid-Sep) Guided tours to watch vultures in the Gorges du Verdon. Book through the tourist office in Castellane.

❶ Information

Castellane Tourist Office (☑04 92 83 61 14; www.castellane.org; rue Nationale; ⊙9am-7.30pm Jul & Aug, shorter hours rest of year) Best source for info on river trips and the eastern side of the Gorges du Verdon.

Moustiers Ste-Marie Tourist Office (☑04 92 74 67 84; www.moustiers.eu; ⊙9.30am-7pm Mon-Fri, 9.30am-12.30pm & 2-7pm Sat & Sun Jul & Aug, shorter hours rest of year; ☎) Excellent service, general info on the Gorges du Verdon and free wi-fi.

❶ Getting Around

BUS

Public transport in the gorges is limited, but there's a useful **shuttle-bus service** (☑04 92 34 22 90; autocars.delaye@orange.fr; ⊙twice daily Jul & Aug, only runs on weekends Apr-Jun & Sep) linking Castellane with Point Sublime, La Palud and La Maline (but not Moustiers).

There's also a daily **LER** (☑08 21 20 22 03; www.info-ler.fr) bus from Marseille to Riez (€16.90), Moustiers (€18.30) and Castellane (€25.80). The single fare from Moustiers to Castellane is €7.10.

TRAIN

The Train des Pignes (p257) travels north of the gorges: the nearest stops are at St-André-les-Alpes, 21km north of Castellane, and Barrême, 25km northwest.

Lacs de Ste-Croix & de Quinson

The largest of the lakes in Parc National Régional du Verdon, Lac de Ste-Croix (southwest of Moustiers Ste-Marie) is a reservoir formed in 1974. It has scads of watercraft – windsurfers, canoes, kayaks – to rent, and pretty Bauduen sits on its southeastern banks.

Lac de Quinson lies at the southernmost foot of the lower Gorges du Verdon. In the village of Quinson, taxidermy-rich Musée de la Préhistoire des Gorges du Verdon (☎04 92 74 09 59; www.museeprehistoire.com; rte de Montmeyan; adult/student/family €7/5/20; ☉10am-8pm Jul & Aug, to 7pm Apr-Jun & Sep, to 6pm Feb, Mar & Oct–mid-Dec, closed mid-Dec–Jan; ▣) explores the gorges' natural history and archaeological treasures. From March to October, it organises monthly expeditions to the Grotte de la Baume Bonne, a prehistoric cave.

Nearby Allemagne-en-Provence is named for Roman goddess of fertility Alemona. Her likeness appears on the village's focal point, the turret-topped 12th- to 16th-century Château d'Allemagne (☎04 92 77 46 78; www.chateau-allemagne-en-provence.com; guided tours adult/child €7/free; ☉tours 4pm & 5pm Tue-Sun Jul–mid-Sep, Sat & Sun only Easter-Jun & mid-Sep–Oct) – straight from a fairy tale.

Moustiers Ste-Marie & Around

POP 710 / ELEV 634M

Dubbed 'Étoile de Provence' (Star of Provence), jewel-box Moustiers Ste-Marie crowns towering limestone cliffs, which mark the beginning of the Alps and the end of Haute-Provence's rolling prairies. A 227m-long chain, bearing a shining gold star, is stretched high above the village – a tradition, legend has it, begun by the Knight of Blacas, who was grateful to have returned safely from the Crusades. Twice a century, the weathered chain snaps, and the star gets replaced, as happened in 1996. In summer it's clear that Moustiers' charms are no secret.

◉ Sights & Activities

Chapelle Notre Dame de Beauvoir   CHURCH
(guided tours adult/child €3/free; ☉24hr) FREE
Lording over the village, beneath Moustiers' star, this 14th-century church clings to a cliff ledge like an eagle's nest. A steep trail climbs beside a waterfall to the chapel, passing 14 stations of the cross en route. On 8 September, Mass at 5am celebrates the nativity of the Virgin Mary, followed by flutes, drums and breakfast on the square.

Musée de la Faïence   MUSEUM
(☎04 92 74 61 64; rue Seigneur de la Clue; adult/student/under 16yr €3/2/free; ☉10am-12.30pm, 2-7pm Jul & Aug, to 6pm mid-Mar–Jun & Sep-Oct, to 5pm Nov & Dec, closed Tue year-round & Jan–mid-Mar) Moustiers' decorative faïence (glazed earthenware) once graced the dining tables of Europe's most aristocratic houses. Today, each of Moustiers' 15 ateliers has its own style, from representational to abstract. Antique masterpieces are housed in this little museum, adjacent to the town hall. Village galleries sell new pieces; working ateliers are down the hill; ask the tourist office to direct you to the best.

⌂ Sleeping

★ Gîte du Petit Ségriès   FARMSTAY €
(☎04 92 74 68 83; www.chambre-hote-verdon.com; d incl breakfast €69-79; ⊛▣) Friendly hosts Sylvie and Noël offer five colourful, airy rooms in their rambling farmhouse, 5km west of Moustiers on the D952 to Riez. Family-style tables d'hôte (€21 with wine) are served at a massive chestnut table, or outside beneath a foliage-covered pergoda in summer. Noël is a mountain-bike guide and runs excellent tours (from €65).

Clos des Iris   HOTEL €
(☎04 92 74 63 46; www.closdesiris.fr; chemin de Quinson; d €74-80, f €108-135; ☉closed Oct-Dec; ⊛) A sweet, simple family hotel, shaded by shutters and pergolas, and surrounded by lovely leafy gardens. There are nine bedrooms, and the owners also run a self-catering cottage down the road.

Domaine du Petit Lac   CAMPGROUND €
(☎04 92 74 67 11; www.lepetitlac.com; rte des Salles en Verdon; camping per 2 people €15.30-22.90; ☉mid-Apr–mid-Oct; ⊛▣⊛▣) Large, activity-oriented campsite on the shores of Lac Ste-Croix; also has wooden chalets and mobile homes.

★ La Ferme Rose   HOTEL €€
(☎04 92 75 75 75; www.lafermerose.com; chemin de Quinson; d €85-157; ⊛⊛) This Italianate terracotta-coloured farmhouse, signposted off the D952 to Ste-Croix de Verdon, is as eclectic and charming as it gets in Provence. Its interior is crammed with quirky collectibles – including a Wurlitzer jukebox, a display case

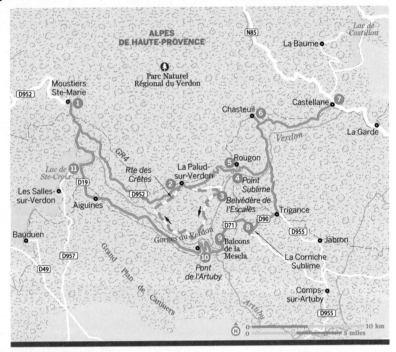

Driving Tour
Gorge Explorer

START MOUSTIERS STE-MARIE
END MOUSTIERS STE-MARIE
LENGTH 140KM; FOUR TO FIVE HOURS

If you're here in summer, be sure to get an early start. The narrow, winding roads through the gorge slow to a crawl during high-season afternoons, especially on weekends.

Set out from ❶**Moustiers Ste-Marie**, via the rte de Castellane (D952). Aim for the ❷**Route des Crêtes**, a 23km-long loop with 14 lookouts along the northern rim with drop-dead vistas of the plunging river gorge. (Note that there are two turn-offs for the Route des Crêtes. To make the entire loop, take the second turn-off, after the hamlet of La Palud-sur-Verdon. If you're tight on time, or if traffic is terrible, take the first turn-off, see a few overlooks, then turn back toward Moustiers. But pay close attention, as the road soon becomes one way in the wrong direction. En route, the most thrilling view is from ❸**Belvédère de l'Escalès** – one of the best places to spot vultures overhead.

After rejoining the D952, the road corkscrews east, past ❹**Point Sublime**, which offers a wide view of serrated rock formations falling away to the river. At Point Sublime, from the D952, the narrow D317 scales 3km north to mountain hamlet ❺**Rougon**. Without stops or traffic, that's about two hours' driving. You could rest in Chasteuil, at cosy ❻**Gîte de Chasteuil**, or forge onward. If considering a river expedition – or if you're just passing through on your way to the Côte d'Azur – aim for ❼**Castellane**. Otherwise, return toward Moustiers Ste-Marie (in two hours) along a different, heart-palpitating route, ❽**La Corniche Sublime** (D955 to D90, D71 and D19). It twists along the southern rim, taking in spectacular landmarks including the ❾**Balcons de la Mescla** (Mescla Terraces) and ❿**Pont de l'Artuby** (Artuby Bridge), Europe's highest bridge. On the return to Moustiers Ste-Marie, you'll pass the emerald-green waters of the ⓫**Lac de Ste-Croix**.

of coffee grinders, and vintage steam irons on the turquoise-tiled staircase. Colourful, airy and uncluttered rooms look out onto unending flowery gardens. Breakfast €11.

✕ Eating

Most of Moustiers' restaurants shut up shop in winter.

Clérissy CRÊPERIE €
(☑ 06 33 34 06 95; www.clerissy.fr; place du Chevalier-de-Blacas; dishes €8-12; ☺ lunch noon-3pm Fri-Tue, dinner 7-10pm Thu-Tue) A good lunch spot in the village, with crispy pizzas, filling crêpes and generous salads.

★ La Grignotière PROVENÇAL €
(☑ 04 92 74 69 12; rte de Ste-Anne; mains €6-15; ☺ 11.30am-10pm May-Sep, to 6pm Feb–mid-May) Hidden away behind the soft pink facade of Moustier's Musée de la Faïence is this utterly gorgeous, blissfully peaceful garden restaurant. Tables sit between olive trees and the colourful, eye-catching decor – including the handmade glassware – is the handiwork of talented, dynamic owner Sandrine. Cuisine is 'picnic chic', meaning lots of creative olive-oil-doused salads, tapenades, quiches and so on.

La Treille Muscate PROVENÇAL €€
(☑ 04 92 74 64 31; www.la-treille-muscate.com; place de l'Église; lunch/dinner menus from €22/31; ☺ lunch noon-2pm Fri-Wed, dinner 7.30-10.30pm Fri-Tue) The top place to eat in the village proper: classic Provençal cooking served with panache, either in the stone-walled dining room or the valley-view terrace. Reservations recommended.

La Ferme Ste-Cécile GASTRONOMIC €€
(☑ 04 92 74 64 18; D952; menus €29-38; ☺ lunch noon-2pm Tue-Sun, dinner 7.30-10pm Tue-Sat) Just outside Moustiers, this wonderful *ferme auberge* (country inn) immerses you in the full Provençal dining experience, from the sun-splashed terrace and locally picked wines right through to the chef's meticulous Mediterranean cuisine. It's about 1.2km from Moustiers; look out for the signs as you drive towards Castellane.

La Bastide de Moustiers GASTRONOMIC €€€
(☑ 04 92 70 47 47; www.bastide-moustiers.com; chemin de Quinson; menus €38-79; ☺ lunch noon-2pm & 7.30-9.30pm daily May-Sep, closed Tue & Wed Oct-Apr; ❋ ⛲) This splurge-worthy Provençal nest, domain of legendary chef Alain Ducasse, is famous for fine cuisine – hence the helicopter pad in the garden – and

provides the chance to dress for dinner, as well as swish bedrooms if you want the full flashy-hotel experience (double from €260). It's 500m down a country lane, signposted off the D952 to Ste-Croix de Verdon.

Castellane & Around

POP 1539 / ELEV 723M

At the opposite end of the gorges, Castellane is a more run-of-the-mill town, teeming with visitors in summer and all but deserted out of season. Its main feature is the amazing Chapelle Notre Dame du Roc, perched high above the town on a 184m-high rock pillar. On 15 August (Assumption Day) pilgrims ascend by torchlight for Mass.

◉ Sights

Musée Sirènes et Fossiles MUSEUM
(☑ 04 92 83 19 23; place Marcel Sauvaire; adult/child €4/3; ☺ 10am-1pm & 3pm-6.30pm daily Apr, Jul & Aug, Wed, Sat & Sun only May, Jun & Sep, closed Oct-Mar; ⓐ) Mermaids and fossils feature at this worthwhile paleontology museum; admission includes access to a nearby 90-minute, 2km family-friendly walk, the Sentier des Siréniens (Col des Lèques), passing beside 40-million-year-old fossilised rock.

Musée de la Résistance MUSEUM
(☑ 04 92 83 78 25; www.resistancecastellane.free.fr; rte de Digne; adult/child €4/2; ☺ by appointment Apr-Oct) Haute-Provence was a hotbed of the Resistance during WWII, and this small museum, 1.5km along the road to Digne, is dedicated to local heroes of the Maquis. Call ahead to arrange a visit.

🛏 Sleeping & Eating

Mas du Verdon B&B €
(☑ 04 92 83 73 20; www.masduverdon.com; Quartier d'Angles; r €55-72; ☺ Apr-Oct) A peaceful farmhouse retreat, hidden away 1km south of town on the Verdon's banks. It's lodged inside an attractive 18th-century farmhouse, and offers four rooms named after herbs and flowers, as well as a self-catering apartment. *Table d'hôte* (€22) dinners are available by reservation from May to September.

Gîte de Chasteuil B&B €
(☑ 04 92 83 72 45; www.gitedechasteuil.com; Hameau de Chasteuil; incl breakfast d €84-89, tr €102; ☺ Mar-Nov) Some 12km west of Castellane, this excellent-value *chambre d'hôte* resides in a former schoolhouse with gorgeous mountain views and is an ideal stop for

HAUTE-PROVENCE & THE SOUTHERN ALPS CASTELLANE & AROUND

hikers along the GR4. Excellent *table d'hôte* (€20/24 with/without advance reservation).

Nouvel Hôtel Restaurant du Commerce HOTEL €€

(☎04 92 83 61 00; www.hotel-du-commerce-verdon.com; place Marcel Sauvaire; d €80-105, tr €100-130, f €110-185; ⊙Apr-Oct; 🛜🎐) By far the best of the hotels on Castellane's main square, with rooms decorated in 'traditional' and 'cosy' styles. Both are smart, with wooden floors and cool colour schemes, although none are hugely spacious. The Provençal restaurant (mains €14 to €22) is excellent; the best tables are in the shady garden.

Auberge du Teillon PROVENÇAL, GASTRONOMIC €€

(☎04 92 83 60 88; www.auberge-teillon.com; D4805/rte Napoléon, La Garde; menus €29-56) Situated 5km east of Castellane on the road to Grasse, this much-loved roadside hotel has a handful of simple rooms (€65–80) up top, but it's the restaurant that's the main draw. Cuisine is 'Provençal classic': the Sunday lunch is a feast to be remembered.

PARC NATIONAL DU MERCANTOUR

Created in 1979, this vast national park – one of 10 in France – covers seven separate alpine valleys and a total area of 685 sq km. Pocked by deep valleys and spiked with jagged peaks, it's a pristine landscape that's rightly celebrated for its flora and fauna, including rare species such as the ibex, the mouflon, the golden eagle and even a few wild grey wolves. At the heart of the park rises the Cime du Gélas, the third-highest mountain in the Alps-Maritimes at 3143m.

Unsurprisingly, it's a haven for outdoor activities: skiing and snowboarding in winter, hiking and biking in summer, and pretty much everything else besides.

Digne-les-Bains

POP 17,680 / ELEV 608M

There's little to merit an extended stop in Digne-les-Bains – it's a useful crossroads when you're travelling between the Luberon and Haute-Provence, but it's short on sights and charm. Originally the town grew up as a hot-spring spa; it's now an important centre for the lavender industry. The city celebrates August's harvest with a five-day festival, the **Corso de la Lavande**.

Although not officially part of the Parc National du Mercantour, the town is a useful gateway to the park.

◉ Sights & Activities

Fondation Alexandra David-Néel MUSEUM

(☎04 92 31 32 38; www.alexandra-david-neel.com; 27 av Maréchal Juin; ⊙2hr tours 10am, 2pm & 3.30pm) FREE Paris-born writer and philosopher Alexandra David-Néel – among France's great historical figures – was the first woman to enter (incognito) into Tibet's temples. Later she settled in Digne. This museum pays homage to both the woman and her fascination with Tibet. A festival, **Journées Tibetaines** (Tibetan Days), happens in August or September.

Musée Gassendi MUSEUM

(☎04 92 31 45 29; www.musee-gassendi.org; place des Récollets; adult/student €4/free; ⊙11am-7pm Apr-Sep, 1.30-5.30pm Oct-Mar, closed Tue) This museum displays compelling contemporary art by Andy Goldsworthy, natural-history exhibits, and works by 16th-century philosopher-scientist Pierre Gassendi.

Refuge d'Art SCULPTURE

(www.refugedart.fr) In the mountains around Digne, British contemporary artist Andy Goldsworthy has created a series of outdoor sculptures along a 150km hiking circuit through awe-inspiring alpine landscapes. Called the Refuge d'Art, the loop passes giant rock hives and cairns that stand like sentinels. You can even sleep inside some of them (by advance reservation). Contact the Digne tourist office for maps and details on guided walks.

Via Ferrata du Rocher de Neuf Heures ROCK CLIMBING

(www.ot-dignelesbains.fr; ⊙6am-8pm high season, 8am-5pm low season) Inspired by the system of fixed ladders and cables that Italian troops used to travel through the Dolomites in WWII, Digne's via ferrata course allows you all the thrill of rock climbing without the need for experience. If you've done it before, you can rent the necessary kit at the tourist office – or arrange a guide if it's your first time.

All you'll need is to be fit, and have a head for heights.

🛏 Sleeping & Eating

Hôtel Villa Gaïa HISTORIC HOTEL €€

(☎04 92 31 21 60; www.hotelvillagaia.fr; 24 rte de Nice; s €55-110, d €72-120, f €110-180; ⊙Apr-Oct)

DON'T MISS

TRAIN DES PIGNES

Zipping between mountains and sea, the narrow-gauge Train des Pignes (Pine Cone Train; www.trainprovence.com; single fare Nice to Digne €23.30) is one of Provence's most picturesque trips. Conceived in 1861 and opened in 1911, the line was originally served by steam locomotives: a vintage train still puffs a few stops around Puget-Théniers on Sunday between spring and autumn.

Rising to 1000m in altitude, the 151km track passes through 50 tunnels and over 16 viaducts and 15 metal bridges along its cliff-hugging journey to Digne-les-Bains, stopping at nearly 50 villages en route. The mountain views on all sides are magnificent.

The entire trip from Nice to Digne-les-Bains takes 3¼ hours (€23.30 one way). There are usually five trains a day; if you don't have time for the whole journey, hop off at Entrevaux, 1½ hours from Nice (€11.80 one way), have a wander around the village, then catch the train back a couple of hours later.

Schedules are available at Chemins de Fer de Provence (04 97 03 80 80; www.trainprovence.com).

Digne's hotels leave a lot to be desired, so it's worth heading 2km west of town to this lovely 19th-century villa, brimful of antiques and architectural élan. It feels like the private mansion it once was, with Italianate gardens, tennis court, library and grand dining room. *Tables d'hôte* by reservation. The gate shuts at 11pm.

Le 28 MEDITERRANEAN €
(04 92 35 23 38; 28 rue de l'Hubac; tapas dishes €3-6; ⏰10am-11pm) Great wine and even better tapas are what's on the menu at this super (if tiny) Franco-Spanish bar. You can buy olive oils, wines, pickled peppers and other goodies to take home too.

Le Chaudron FRENCH €€
(04 92 31 24 87; 40 rue de l'Hubac; mains €9-17.50; menus €23-32; ⏰lunch noon-2.30pm, dinner 7.30-10pm Fri-Tue) Hidden in the old town, this is a reliable bet for Provençal staples – especially fish and meat cooked over a wood fire.

ⓘ Information

Tourist Office (04 92 36 62 62; www.ot-dignelesbains.fr; place du Tampinet; ⏰9am-noon & 2-6pm daily, closed weekends winter)

ⓘ Getting There & Away

BUS

LER operates local buses.
Marseille Line 28; €21.50, two hours, four to six daily Monday to Saturday. Via Volx and Manosque.
Nice Line 31; €22.20, 3½ hours, two daily.
Avignon Line 22; €28.40, 2½ hours, every two hours. Via Forcalquier and Apt.

Barcelonnette Line 34; €12.50, 1½ hours, one daily.

TRAIN
The Train des Pignes serves Nice and stations in between.

Vallée de L'Ubaye

The national park's northern edge and least-visited area, the narrow Ubaye Valley runs east–west beneath snowcapped mountains, delimiting the high Alps from Haute-Provence.

The valley's only town, Barcelonnette (elevation 1135m), has an unexpected Mexican heritage and exceptional, very un-alpine architecture. From the 18th century until WWII, some 5000 residents emigrated to Mexico to seek their fortunes in the silk-and wool-weaving industries; upon their return, they built mansions, one of which houses the town museum. The town hosts an annual Mexican festival in mid-August, complete with mariachis and street parades.

◉ Sights & Activities

Musée de la Vallée MUSEUM
(04 92 81 27 15; 10 av de la Libération, Barcelonnette; adult/10-18yr/under 10yr €4/2/free; ⏰10am-noon & 2.30-6.30pm daily mid-Jul & Aug, 2.30-6pm Wed-Sat rest of year, closed mid-Nov–mid-Dec) This intriguing museum explores the valley's history. Highlights include a fascinating collection of Bronze Age arrowheads, axes, rings and bracelets, various exhibits relating to the adventurous naturalist Émile Chabrand, and some fine pieces

WORTH A TRIP

RÉSERVE GÉOLOGIQUE DE HAUTE-PROVENCE

It's somewhat hard to believe now, but back in the dim and distant past, the Alps actually sat at the bottom of a vast temperate sea. Today, this secret past is etched right into the living rock. Footprints of prehistoric birds, outsized ammonites and ram's-horn spiral shells are among the amazing fossils to be found in the 1900-sq-km Réserve Géologique de Haute-Provence. You'll need a detailed regional map (sold at tourist offices) and your own transport to reach the 18 sites, most of which lie around Barles (north) and Barrême (south). An impressive limestone slab with some 500 ammonites sits 3km north of Digne on the road to Barles.

Another must-see detour is the **Musée Promenade** (☑ 04 92 36 70 70; musee-promenade@hotmail.com; 10 montée Bernard Dellacasagrande; adult/7-14yr €8/5; ⊙ 9am-7pm Jul & Aug, 9am-noon & 2-5.30pm Apr-Jun & Sep-Nov, closed some weekends in low season) in St-Bénoît, 2km north of Digne-les-Bains en route to Barle, where four trails explore the region's geology and natural history. Highlights include a sculpture park, a Japanese garden, a waterfall and the gorgeous Jardin des Papillons (Butterfly Garden), which attracts more than half of France's butterfly species.

of Mexican art brought back by the town's emigrés.

Bureau des Guides
de l'Ubaye
OUTDOOR ACTIVITIES

(☑ 06 86 67 38 73; www.guides-montagne-ubaye. com; rue Manuel, Barcelonnette) Unsurprisingly, the Ubaye is great for outdoor sports – particularly hardcore cycling, thanks to its absurdly high mountain passes. In summer Le Martinet, 15km west of Barcelonnette, is a base for mountain-biking and rafting trips. Practically every activity you can think of, from rafting to paragliding, can be arranged through this Barcelonnette outdoors provider.

Pra Loup
SKIING, BIKING

(☑ 04 92 84 10 04; www.praloup.com) This sprawling ski resort is 8.5km southwest of Barcelonnette, and has two main areas: Pra Loup 1500 (sometimes called Les Molanes) and Pra Loup 1600 (with more infrastructure and nightlife). Together they form the southern Alps' largest snow-sports destination, and in summer the lifts provide transport for mountain bikers and hikers.

🛏 Sleeping

⭐ Les Méans
B&B €€

(☑ 04 92 81 03 91; www.les-means.com; D900, Méolans-Revel; d €109-119, f €139-149; 🐾) 🌾 This ravishing mountain B&B combines the rustic architecture of the 15th-century house with all the trappings of a modern B&B. The rooms are charming: our pick is the Suite Alpages, with its *Heidi*-esque decor and original fireplace. The surroundings are supremely peaceful, with a wood-fired hot tub

and mountains on all sides. Ask owners Babette and Frédéric to show you the house's secret tunnel.

Hôtel Azteca
HOTEL €€

(☑ 04 92 81 46 36; 3 rue François Arnaud, Barcelonnette; s €61-93, d €74-118, tr €94-133; 🐾) A sweet hotel with decor dabbling in the town's Mexican connections, from sunny pictures to papier-maché cats and multicoloured bathroom tiles. For maximum Mexicana, ask for the Chambre Mexicaine. Breakfast is served on a glorious terrace.

Villa Morelia
HISTORIC HOTEL €€€

(☑ 04 92 84 67 78; www.villa-morelia.com; Jausiers; s €120-140, d €150-280, ste €240-350; 🌸🐾🐾) In the hamlet of Jausiers, this is the regal choice: a veritable mini-château, complete with turret, 18th-century furnishings and a gorgeous leafy park. The bedrooms are very elegant: some have rococo detailing and clawfoot baths, others are more modern in style.

🍴 Eating

Le Patio
PIZZERIA €€

(☑ 04 92 81 36 86; www.lepatio-barcelonnette.com; 1 Rue Manuel, Barcelonnette; mains €9-15; ⊙ lunch noon-2pm, dinner 7-10pm) A relaxed, friendly and quite stylish diner overlooking Barcelonnette's handsome main square, place de la Mairie. Pizzas and pastas are the speciality, but it does heartier mountain fare too.

Poivre d'Âne
FRENCH €€

(☑ 04 92 81 48 67; www.le-poivre-ane-barcelonnette. fr; 49 rue Manuel, Barcelonnette; menus €21-31; ⊙ lunch 12.30-2pm, dinner 7.30-9.30pm) On Barcelonnette's main shopping street, this timber-clad *auberge* is the place to stuff yourself silly with mountain sausages, cheesy *tartiflettes* (potatoes, cheese and bacon baked in a casserole) and even cheesier fondues. With its cute shutters, vintage skis and other alpine ephemera, all it really lacks is the lonely goatherd.

❶ Information

Parc National du Mercantour, Barcelonnette Visitors Centre (☑ 04 92 81 21 31; www. mercantour.eu; D900, Barcelonnette; ⊙ 9am-noon & 2-6pm Jul & Aug only) Info on the national park supplied by rangers and clued-up park staff.

Barcelonnette Tourist Office (☑ 04 92 81 04 71; www.barcelonnette.net; place Frédéric Mistral, Barcelonnette; ⊙ 9am-12.30pm & 1.30-7.30pm Jul & Aug, 9am-noon & 2-6pm Mon-Sat Sep-Jun) Ask for info on the Mexican Festival and the Tour de France, which rolls through town most years.

❶ Getting There & Away

Buses to the valley are erratic, especially outside school term times.

Autocars SCAL (☑ 04 92 51 06 05; www.scalamv-voyages.com) Daily bus to Barcelonnette from Gap (€25, four hours) and Digne (€8.60, 90 minutes).

Vallée du Haut Verdon

It's only an hour or so's drive from Digne, but there's something about this valley that feels truly remote; especially the further north you travel, as the villages peter out, the mountains stack up along the horizon and the road draws ever closer to the dizzying Col d'Allos, the high mountain pass that connects this valley with the Vallée de l'Ubaye to the north (unsurprisingly, at 2250m, the pass is usually snowbound between October and May).

In winter there's skiiing around Foux d'Allos (www.valdallos.com), a prettier resort than nearby Pra Loup (p258), where ugly towers lurk just beyond the pass. In summer the whole area becomes a hiker's haven, but in the shoulder months the whole place feels decidedly quiet.

◉ Sights & Activities

Colmars-les-Alpes VILLAGE
With its towers, turrets and ramparts, this medieval village looks like a relic from a Monty Python film set. In the late 14th century, the valleys around Allos and Barcelonnette to the north were given to the Duchy of Savoy, and Colmars became an important border town, which meant it also required fortification. Despite some additions by the military architect Vauban in the 18th century, the village looks largely as it would have during medieval times.

There's a small museum detailing the village's history, but the main attraction is just wandering round its shady cobbled streets. Some sections of the ramparts are open in summer. The square Fort de France and larger Fort de Savoie to the north were Vauban's additions.

Lac d'Allos LAKE
It's worth the trek (and metered traffic) to reach Europe's largest alpine lake, Lac d'Allos (2226m; inaccessible autumn to spring). From Allos, narrow, bumpy D226 climbs 12km to parking; then it's a 40-minute walk. Trail maps are available from the summeronly **Parc National du Mercantour hut** (☑ 06 32 90 80 24; www.mercantour.eu; ⊙ Jul & Aug) at the car park. Sited right beside the lake, the **Refuge du Lac d'Allos** (☑ 04 92 83 00 24; www.refugedulacdallos.com; dm incl breakfast & dinner €41, menu of the day €19.50) is an ideal spot for lunch, and has dorms if you're planning an overnight hike.

Retrouvance HIKING
(www.onf.fr/retrouvance/sommaire/sejours/haut-verdon; 6-day hikes €570) Run by the Office Nationale des Fôrets, this fantastic multiday hike runs through the mountains from Thorame to Lac d'Allos, and includes an official guide as well as overnight accommodation in *gîtes* (self-catering cottages) and farmhouses. Reservations can be made online or through Colmars' tourist office.

⊨ Sleeping & Eating

Le Martagon HOTEL €
(☑ 04 92 83 14 26; www.le-martagon.com; Villars Colmars; mains €14.50-19.50, d €50-72, f €72-113) A smart, modern restaurant-with-rooms in the quiet village of Villars Colmars. The accommodation is basic but comfortable, with small rooms enlivened by splashes of magenta, lime and brown; there are also timber camping pods in the hotel's grassy grounds. The restaurant serves filling mountain fare such as cheesy *tartiflette,* veal cutlet and 'gargantuan' cheeseburgers.

HAUTE-PROVENCE & THE SOUTHERN ALPS VALLÉE DU HAUT VERDON

Hotel Le France   HOTEL €

(☑ 04 92 83 42 93; www.hotel-lefrance-colmars. com; Colmars-les-Alpes; s €47-56, d €58-66, tr €75-87, f €77-90; ☎) Situated right opposite the main gate of Colmars-les-Alpes, this simple, good-value hotel makes a decent base in the valley. It's far from luxurious, but the rooms are reasonable and the restaurant serves generous portions. There are also a couple of small apartments with kitchenettes.

Les Transhumances   B&B, APARTMENT €

(☑ 04 92 83 44 39; www.lestranshumances.fr; Les Espiniers, Colmars-les-Alpes; s/d/tr/q incl breakfast €60/80/95/105, cottages per week €430-520; ☎) ⊘ This quiet 18th-century farm, high above Colmars, has incredible mountain vistas, spotless rooms with wooden accents, and self-catering apartments. Gentle, kind owners. The guest-only *table d'hôte* (€23) includes wine.

★**La Ferme Girerd-Potin**   FRENCH €€

(☑ 04 92 83 04 76; www.chambredhotes-valdallos. com; rte de la Foux; r per person incl breakfast & dinner €50-59; ⊘ by reservation Oct-Apr, Jul & Aug; ♿) On a working 17th-century farm, high above the Verdon, this cosy *ferme auberge* grows all provisions for its thrilling rustic-alpine dinners, served fireside in a candlelit, wood-and-stone dining room. Everything – from vegetables to foie gras, bread to cheese – is homemade. Make reservations 24 hours in advance. The farm is 5km north of Allos.

Upstairs are B&B rooms, some with kitchenette and wood-burning fireplace.

🛍 Shopping

**Maison des Produits de
Pays des Alpes du Verdon**   FOOD

(☑ 04 92 83 58 57; www.maisonproduitspays-alpesduverdon.fr; Beauvezer; ⊘ 9.30am-12.30pm & 2.30-7pm) This attractive co-operative shop is a great place to pick up local souvenirs, from goat's cheeses, jams and honeys to handmade candles and woodcrafts.

❶ Information

Val d'Allos Tourist Office (☑ 04 92 83 02 81; www.valdallos.com; ⊘ 9am-noon & 2-6pm) Covers activities and accommodation around the entire Haut-Verdon.

Colmars-les-Alpes Tourist Office (☑ 04 92 83 41 92; www.colmars-les-alpes.fr; Ancienne Auberge Fleurie; ⊘ 9am-12.30pm & 2-6.30pm Jul & Aug, 9am-noon & 2-5.45pm Sep-Jun, shorter hours Sun) Colmar's tourist office provides comprehensive advice on hiking, mountain biking, rafting and horse riding in the valley.

Vallée du Haut-Var

The Gorges du Verdon get the plaudits, but the Vallée du Haut-Var has its own spectacular twinset of valleys: the crimson Gorges de Daluis and Gorges du Cians, which can be linked in a memorable 82km loop.

It makes a great (if long) day trip from Nice, but be prepared for narrow roads and a lot of driving. The best route is to take the D6202 west, then turn off onto the D902 towards Daluis and the gorges. On the D28, the ski town of Valberg and the small village of Beuil (elevation 1450m) make useful lunch stops, before you return south along the D28 through the Gorges du Cians, then return to Nice.

⦿ Sights & Activities

★**Gorges de Daluis**   CANYON

This stunning network of scarlet gorges looks for all the world like it's been collected from Arizona and plonked down in Haute-Provence. Carved out over the millennia by the Var River, it runs for 6km between Guillaumes and Daluis, twisting high above the river past towering sandstone cliffs, weird rock formations and plunging waterfalls. It's best seen in a northbound direction on the D902/D2202, as tunnels on the southbound lane obscure most of the views.

Along the way, it's worth stopping at viewpoints including the Tête du Femme, a rock formation shaped like a lady's head, and the Cascade d'Amen, an impressive waterfall that tumbles down a sheer cliff into the river far below. Also look out for the Pont de la Mariée, where a local girl supposedly committed suicide to avoid her impending marriage. You can see why she chose this spot: it's dizzyingly high, and a popular location for bungee jumping. Contact Top Jump (☑ 04 93 73 50 29; http://topjump.free.fr; jumps €60; ⊘ 11am-7pm Tue-Sun summer) if you're feeling brave.

Sentier du Point Sublime   VIEWPOINT

This 4km hiking trail starts at the Pont de Berthéou, 8km south of Guillaumes on the D2202. It climbs through oak-and-pine forest and scarlet rock forms to a famous panoramic viewpoint, aptly known as Point Sublime. It's a 90-minute hike there and back, longer in hot weather.

❶ Information

Maison du Parc National du Mercantour
(📞 04 93 02 58 23; varcians@mercantour-parcnational.fr; rue Jean Mineur, Valberg; ⏰ 9am-noon & 2-6pm Thu-Tue, also Wed school holidays) General information on the Mercantour national park.

Valberg Tourist Office (📞 04 93 23 24 25; www.valberg.com; place du Quartier, Valberg; ⏰ 9am-noon & 2-6pm) Valberg's tourist office makes room reservations and organises local activities.

Vallée de la Tinée

This steep, V-shaped valley runs north for 149km all the way from the pretty little town of St-Sauveur-sur-Tinée (elevation 490m) to the Vallée de l'Ubaye. En route, it climbs up and over the Col de Restefond la Bonette, Europe's highest road pass – and invariably the last one to open after the spring thaw (usually in late May but sometimes as late as early June). It's a favourite for road-trippers and motorbikers, and occasionally features on the Tour de France. During winter, the valley can only be accessed from the south.

If you're road-tripping, there are good options for lunch in St-Sauveur-sur-Tinée and the smaller, less-touristed village of St-Dalmas-le-Selvage. At 1100m elevation, the mountain-top village of Roure is also worth a detour thanks to its amazing alpine arboretum – as long as you can handle the hair-raisingly steep, twisty mountain road. From the 1920s until 1961, villagers used a 1850m-long cable to transport items up the mountain; the cable still remains.

◉ Sights

★ **Arboretum Marcel Kroenlein**   GARDEN
(📞 09 77 31 68 33; www.arboretum-roure.org; Roure; suggested donation adult/child €5/free; ⏰ 10am-6pm; 🅿️) This alpine garden is probably the last thing you'd expect in tiny Roure. It's a pet project of Monaco's Prince Rainier, who's covered 15 steep-sided hectares (ranging in altitude from 1200m to 1700m) with mountain trees and flora, interspersed with sculptures by Niçois artists. If you're really lucky, you might even spot an eagle or vulture wheeling over the garden terraces.

🛏 Sleeping & Eating

Ma Vieille École   B&B €
(📞 04 93 03 43 05; www.mavieilleecole.com; D61, Roya; incl breakfast dm €25, half-board per adult/child €45/35; ⏰ May-Sep) Hidden high in the mountains, this family-run *auberge* is great for a traditional lunch, with plates piled with cheese, charcuterie and other goodies. It also has *gîte* rooms if you're looking for somewhere to kip on a mountain walk. From D2205, look for the turn-off 5km south

---

DRIVING IN HAUTE-PROVENCE

It's only an hour north of Nice, but make no mistake: you're in the Alps proper in Haute-Provence. Heavy snowfall means that the highest passes (*cols*) are usually only open between May and September. Access roads have signs indicating whether the pass is 'ouvert' (open) or 'fermé' (closed), or you can check in advance with local tourist offices.

A road map is indispensable: GPS units have a nasty habit of leading you up steep, narrow roads that really aren't designed for cars and frequently don't have guard rails. Also look out for deep gullies along the roadsides – if you run a front wheel into them you'll need a tow truck to get you out. Note that snow tyres are required on many roads during winter.

From west to east, the main passes that close in winter are:

Col d'Allos (2250m) Links the north–south D126/D908 from Allos in the Vallée du Haut Verdon to Barcelonnette in the Vallée de l'Ubaye.

Col de la Cayolle (2326m) Links the Vallée du Haut Var with the Vallée de l'Ubaye along the D2202/D902, running north–south from St-Martin-d'Entraunes to Barcelonnette.

Col de Restefond la Bonette (2802m) Europe's highest mountain pass links the D64 from St-Étienne-de-Tinée in the Vallée de la Tinée to Barcelonnette in the Vallée de l'Ubaye.

Col des Champs (2095m) The east–west D2/D72 road connecting St-Martin-d'Entraunes in the Vallée du Haut Var with Colmars-les-Alpes in the Vallée d'Allos.

of St-Etienne-la-Tinée or 9km north of Isola; Roya lies 6km west of D2205.

Auberge Le Robur GASTRONOMIC €€€
(☑ 04 93 02 03 57; www.aubergelerobur.fr; Roure; d €76, d incl breakfast & dinner €166-186) Perched at 1100m, this village restaurant is a destination in its own right – for not just the food but the views. Young chef Christophe Billau has worked in kitchens in France and overseas, and he brings a playful, pan-global style to his refined food. Upstairs are seven spotless valley-view rooms, making this an ideal one-nighter two hours from Nice.

ℹ Information

Mercantour National Park Office, St-Étienne-de-Tinée (☑ 04 93 02 42 27; quartier de l'Ardon, St-Étienne-de-Tinée; ☺ Jul & Aug)

Vallée de la Vésubie

Dotted with hilltop mountain towns and flanked by craggy peaks, the Vallée de la Vésubie stakes a reputable claim as the prettiest valley in Haute-Provence – it's known as 'La Suisse Niçoise' for a reason. Once the private hunting reserve of King Victor Emmanuel II of Italy, it's now a hub for all manner of outdoor activities: hiking, biking, wildlife watching, paragliding and via ferrata, to name a few.

The main town, **St-Martin-Vésubie** (elevation 1000m) is a central place to base yourself for wider forays around the Mercantour, with plenty of hotels, restaurants and activity providers in the area. Roughly halfway along the valley, this attractive mountain town has preserved much of its medieval character: you can still glimpse vestiges of its original ramparts and one of its town gates on its steep main street, which climbs sharply through the centre of the old town. In the late 19th and early 20th centuries – the heyday of the era of railway tourism in Provence – St-Martin was a popular spot for overnighting, and the facades of a few of the old grand hotels can still be seen around town. It's also a hub for hiking, with 13 marked trails climbing through the surrounding mountains, intersecting with four *Grande Randonnée* (GR) paths.

The hilltop villages of **Belvédère** (820m), 12km south of St-Martin-Vésubie, and **La Colmiane** (1795m), 7km west, are well worth visiting for their wraparound mountain views.

◉ Sights

★**Alpha, Le Parc des Loups** WILDLIFE RESERVE
(☑ 04 93 02 33 69; www.alpha-loup.com; Le Boréon; adult/child €12/10; ☺10am-5pm or 6pm Apr-Oct; ⊞) The grey wolf was hunted to extinction in France by 1930, but in 1992 two 'funny-looking dogs' were spotted near Utelle, presumably having loped across the Italian border. Since then, the animals have made a comeback in the French Alps, and though they're hard to spot in the wild, you'll have a good chance of a sighting at this fascinating wolf reserve, where three packs live in semifreedom.

Several trails wind through the reserve, where you can stop and watch the wolves from specially constructed hides. The park's mountain-top location in Le Boréon is worth a visit in its own right; you can stay overnight at one of the on-site *gîtes* (€350 to €600 in summer) or treehouses (€150 per night).

La Madone de Fenestres CHURCH
At an altitude of 1904m, this impressively situated hilltop church was supposedly founded on the site where a local villager had a vision of the Virgin Mary; twice a year, on 15 August and 8 September, there's a solemn procession to commemorate the event. The statue of Mary inside is thought to have been carved from a Lebanese cedar in the 14th century.

The church is also the starting point for a number of hiking trails, including several that run over the Italian border.

⚐ Activities

Bureau des Guides du Mercantour HIKING
(☑ 04 93 03 31 32; www.guidescapade.com; place du Marché, St-Martin-Vésubie; ☺ Jul & Aug) Experienced hiking guides who run walks, climbs and canyoning excursions, plus expeditions into the Vallée des Merveilles.

Horse&Ventures HORSE RIDING
(☑ 06 22 29 58 86; www.horseandventures.com; Le Boréon; 2hr ride €30, full-day ride €60) English-speaking Denis Longfellow runs horseback trips from Le Boréon as well as longer tuition courses.

⌖ Sleeping & Eating

Le Boréon HOTEL €
(☑ 04 93 03 20 35; www.hotel-boreon.com; d/tr/q from €75/105/135, menus from €35; ☺ closed Nov-Mar; 🕿) Magical mountain views unfurl from this large Swiss-chalet-style hotel

8km north of St-Martin-Vésubie. Ground-floor rooms are cosiest, with pine walls and shared terrace. The restaurant serves alpine specialities.

★ **Moonlight Chalet** BOUTIQUE HOTEL €€
(☑ 06 89 25 36 74; www.moonlightchalet.com; 8 rue Rumplemeyer, St-Martin-Vésubie; r incl break-fast €110-130; ⊠ ⊕) You might have found your perfect mountain getaway: three be-witching lodges and two duplex rooms next to a chattering creek, surrounded by silent mountains and dense forest. They sleep two to four people and feature decorative details inspired by nature – bathtubs made from riv-er rocks, furniture crafted from tree trunks – and one is even built around a fir tree.

The lodges have private kitchens, and the chalet rooms have shared cooking facilities. Electricity is solar powered, but there's no TV or wi-fi – a deliberate choice to ensure you make the most of the bucolic surround-ings. A lovely organic breakfast is included in the rates.

La Bonne Auberge HOTEL €€
(☑ 04 93 03 20 49; www.labonneauberge06.fr; 98 allée du Verdun, St-Martin-Vésubie; s/d/f from €46/59/78; ⊘ Feb–mid-Dec; ⊛ ⊕) A classic, old-fashioned family-run French hotel – in the same hands since 1946. Pine-clad rooms and a traditional restaurant (*menus* €25 to €31) full of mountain knick-knacks (boars' heads, snowshoes, hunting horns) reinforce the alpine vibe. Peek into the bar to see St-Martin's first TV set (c 1960). The best rooms overlook the village's *pétanque* (a variant on the game of bowls) square.

❶ Information

St-Martin-Vésubie Tourist Office (☑ 04 93 03 21 28; www.saintmartinvesubie.fr; pl Félix Faure, St-Martin-Vésubie; ⊘ 8.30am-12.30pm & 2-7pm daily Jul & Aug, 9am-noon & 2-7pm Mon-Sat Sep-Jun; ☎) St-Martin's efficient tourist office organises walks and has lists of local activity providers.

Maison du Parc National du Mercantour (Visi-tor Centre; ☑ 04 93 03 23 15; www.mercantour. eu; rue Serrurier, St-Martin-Vésubie; ⊘ 9am-noon & 2-6pm mid-Jun–mid-Sep) Summer-only office staffed by park rangers.

❶ Getting There & Away

Conseil Général des Alpes-Maritimes (www. cg06.fr) buses (€1) connect Nice with St-Martin-Vésubie (one hour) and La Colmiane (1¼ hours).

OFF THE BEATEN TRACK

VALLÉE DES MERVEILLES

Wedged between the Vésubie and Roya valleys, this narrow, remote canyon (the Valley of Wonders) is famous for its amazing Bronze Age petroglyphs (an-cient pictures carved into rock). In total, the valley contains more than 36,000 prehistoric carvings of figures, symbols and animals, thought to have been etched by members of a Ligurian cult between 1800 and 1500 BC.

Most can only be seen on foot. Trails remain snow covered into late spring; the best time is June to October. Access is restricted without a guide, which you can arrange through the Mercantour National Park visitor centres or the Bureau des Guides du Mercantour in St-Martin-Vésubie.

Access to the valley from the south is on the D171 from the Vallée de la Vésu-bie, or from the west on the D91 from the Vallée de la Roya via Casterino.

Vallée de la Roya

Occupied by Italy during WWII, the Roya only became part of France in 1947. Wedged hard against the Italian border, the valley runs all the way from the coast to Tende, where a tunnel built in 1892 burrows under the mountains into Italy. It's a great day trip from Nice, either by car or aboard the grand-ly titled Train des Merveilles (p264).

St-Dalmas-de-Tende and nearby Casteri-no are the main gateway into the Vallée des Merveilles. From St-Dalmas-de-Tende, the D91 winds 10km west to Lac des Mesches (1390m), where trails lead into the valley (plan on eight hours' hiking, round trip). Al-ternatively, you can cheat and catch a 4WD.

◉ Sights

Monastère de Saorge MONASTERY
(☑ 04 93 04 55 55; http://saorge.monuments-nationaux.fr/en; ⊘ 10am-noon & 2-5pm Wed-Mon) Situated 9km north of Breil-sur-Roya, the dramatic Gorges de Saorge lead to the for-tified village of Saorge (elevation 520m). Perched on sheer cliffs, the village is a maze of tangled streets, with lots of 15th- to 17th-century houses, as well as this Fran-ciscan monastery, notable for its baroque church, decorated with frescoes of St Francis.

Notre Dame des Fontaines CHURCH
(admission €2; ⊙10am-12.30pm & 2-5.30pm May-Oct) Dubbed the Sistine Chapel of the Southern Alps, this church is famous for its wall-to-wall 15th-century frescoes, created by Piedmontese painters Jean Canavesio and Jean Baleison. It's 4km north of La Brigue.

Musée des Merveilles MUSEUM
(⏺04 93 04 32 50; av du 16 Septembre 1947, Tende; ⊙10am-6.30pm May–mid-Oct, to 5pm mid-Oct–Apr, closed Tue Sep-Jun) FREE In Tende, this museum explores the valley's archaeological and historical significance.

Maison du Miel et de l'Abeille MUSEUM
(⏺04 93 04 76 22; place Lieutenant Kalck, Tende; ⊙2-5pm Wed-Fri, 9.30am-12.30pm & 1-5pm weekends Jul & Aug only) This little museum celebrates the craft of local honey-makers. Needless to say, there are plenty of opportunities to taste the goods – this is France, after all.

🏃 Activities

Train des Merveilles TOUR
(return from Nice adult/child €15/7.50; ⊙May-Oct) For fans of the iron horse, this scenic rail ride is a trip not to be missed. It runs north from Nice right through the Vallée de la Roya, passing hilltop villages, dramatic canyons and mountain vistas en route. You even get a commentary (in French) courtesy of the conductor.

From June to September, the train leaves Nice every day at 9.23am, arriving in Tende at 11.24am. It only runs on weekends in May and October. Bookings can be made online or in Nice's main station. The train makes stops in Sospel, Breil-sur-Roya, St-Dalmas-de-Tende and Tende.

Roya Évasion CYCLING, CANYONING
(⏺04 93 04 91 46; www.royaevasion.com; 1 rue Pasteur, Breil-sur-Roya) Breil-sur-Roya is the valley's water-sports base. This experienced outfit organises kayaking, canyoning and rafting on the Roya River, plus hiking and mountain biking. It also conducts English-language rock-art tours to the Merveilles.

4x4 Merveilles ADVENTURE SPORTS
(www.4x4merveilles.com; adult/child €85/50) Local 4WD guides run regular trips to see the rock art of the Vallée des Merveilles. Bookings are made through the tourist office in Tende.

Bike Park Sospel CYCLING
(www.espace-vtt-sospel.com) Local bike enthusiasts have created 150km of trails just out-

side Sospel, but most are designed for experienced riders. Contact the tourist office in Sospel (⏺04 93 04 15 80; www.sospel-tourisme.com; 19 av Jean Medecin; ⊙10am-2.30pm & 1.30-5.30pm Mon-Sat, 10am-12.30pm Sun) for further information.

🛏 Sleeping & Eating

Le Prieuré HOTEL €
(⏺04 93 04 75 70; www.leprieure.org; rue Jean Medecin, St-Dalmas-de-Tende; s €50.50-68, d €58.50-78, tr €69-93.50) It was once a priory, and there's still a whiff of the monastical about this place – in the ecclesiastical architecture and the rather spartan decor. Still, if you can bag a room overlooking the river, you'll be thoroughly blessed. The restaurant (mains €10.50–14 is great too, with intriguing dishes like chestnut gnocchi and *soupe de pierres* (literally 'friar's soup'; meat-and-veg stew).

Chamois d'Or HOTEL €€
(⏺04 93 04 66 66; www.hotelchamoisdor.net; Hameau de Casterino; s €75-90, d €90-135) The Golden Mountain Goat could have come straight from the Swiss Alps, with its chalet-style balconies, timber cladding and brightly coloured shutters. The rooms are plain – wooden floors, wardrobe, not much else – but the restaurant is altogether more generous, especially with regard to mountain dishes like raclette (cheesy potato bake) and spit-roasted meat.

ℹ Information

Tende Tourism & Mercantour National Park Office (⏺04 93 04 73 71; www.tendemerveilles.com; av du 16 Septembre 1947; ⊙9am-noon & 2-5pm Mon-Sat, 9am-noon Sun) Tende's tourist office provides details on guided archaeological walks and 4WD trips to Mont Bégo and the Vallée des Merveilles.

ℹ Getting There & Away

CAR
The tortuous mountain roads around Sospel (especially from the Vésubie) are scenic but not for the faint of heart. From Nice, the fastest route is to take the autoroute to Ventimiglia (across the Italian border), then follow it north back into France towards the Col de Tende (Italian signs read 'Colle di Tenda').

TRAIN
The Train des Merveilles runs from Nice through the valley to Tende.

Understand Provence & the Côte d'Azur

Provence & the Côte d'Azur Today

If you've always dreamt of staking out your own corner of paradise in Provence and the Côte d'Azur, you're certainly not alone. This most celebrated of coastlines is by far and away France's most desirable place to live, and with so much going for it, it's little wonder: the scenery is heart-stopping, the quality of life is second to none, there are *fêtes* (festivals) galore, and the politics? Well, nowhere's perfect...

Best on Film

To Catch a Thief (1956) Cary Grant and Grace Kelly cruise the coast in this Hitchcock thriller.

Et Dieu Créa la Femme (1956) A classic of the French New Wave, with Brigitte Bardot in a bikini.

Le Gendarme de St-Tropez (1964) Knockabout comedy caper, worth watching for the St-Tropez locations.

Jean de Florette & **Manon des Sources** (1986) Dreamy, sun-dappled, and stuffed with gorgeous scenery.

A Good Year (2006) Glossy Hollywood adaptation of Peter Mayle's Provence-set novel.

Best in Print

The Count of Monte Cristo (Alexandre Dumas) Swashbuckling Marseille-set adventure by the author of *The Three Musketeers*.

My Father's Glory (Marcel Pagnol) Tales of rural life by Provence's best-loved writer.

A Year in Provence (Peter Mayle) The book that sent a generation of expats in search of the Provençal good life.

Perfume (Patrick Süskind) Pitch-black tale of the seductiveness of scents, partly set in Grasse.

Tender Is the Night (F Scott Fitzgerald) High life on the Riviera in the jazzy 1920s.

The Southern Dynamo

It might be known for its long lunch breaks and easy-going lifestyle, but Provence and the Côte d'Azur (or PACA, as it's often known) has long been one of France's economic powerhouses. It's the third-largest region in France by population (with around five million inhabitants, or 7.8%), has three of the largest urban areas in France (Aix-Marseille, Nice and Toulon), and comes third in the nation's richest areas by GDP.

Tourism remains by far the region's biggest industry: more than 35 million people visit the PACA area every year, bringing in some €5 billion to the region's coffers – it's estimated that between a quarter and a third of the region's jobs rely in some way on the industry's proceeds. But it's far from the only thing the region does well: agriculture, pharmaceuticals, IT, aeronautics and space engineering all have a big presence in the south, and in total the region accounts for nearly 8% of the nation's annual wealth.

Throw in a cracking cultural sector – epitomised by Marseille, Aix and Avignon's successful stints as European Capitals of Culture in 2013 – and you have a region that continues to punch above its weight in nearly every sphere.

The Cost of Living

Unfortunately economic success has its drawbacks. The region's popularity as a place to live and work means that it also has some of the highest property prices anywhere in France. In 2013 the average price of a house along the Côte d'Azur was nearly double the national average (€320,000 and €430,000 for the Var and Alpes Maritimes *départements* respectively). In 2014 La Leopolda Villa in Villefranche-sur-Mer officially became the third-most-expensive house in the world: it's currently valued at €750 million and is owned by Monaco-based billionaire Lily Safra.

It's an issue that's compounded by a rapidly ageing population (more than a quarter of the region's residents are now senior citizens) and a huge rise in second homes. Though the powers that be are trying to address the problem with innovative development schemes such as the massive Eco Vallée de la Plaine du Var (www.ecovallee-cotedazur.com), the fact remains that for most average workers, the dream of owning their own home anywhere near the Côte d'Azur is fast becoming a fantasy.

Right in Paradise

Over the last 30 years, the region has been one of the main strongholds for the far right. It was here that Jean-Marie Le Pen's Front National scored their first significant victories in the early 1990s, and the party – now run by its founder's daughter, Marine Le Pen – has continued to perform strongly at elections. In 2015 the party took 22% of the final vote in regional elections and won 62 seats, coming second to the conservative UMP party.

The Front National now has elected members in many city councils and *départemental* assemblies across the south, with a particularly strong showing in the Vaucluse. How this will play out at the presidential elections in 2017 is anyone's guess, but with issues such as immigration, terrorism, multiculturalism, low wages and soaring house prices all hot topics in Provence and the Côte d'Azur, one thing's for sure – Marine Le Pen and her party look set to retain a foothold in the south for the foreseeable future.

POPULATION: **4.9 MILLION**

AREA: **31,400 SQ KM**

AVERAGE INCOME: **€17,892**

UNEMPLOYMENT: **11%**

COASTLINE: **115KM**

SUNSHINE: **300 DAYS PER YEAR**

....

if Provence were 100 people

48 would work in Services
34 would work in Public Sector
9 would work in Industry
7 would work in Construction
2 would work in Agriculture

....

urban vs rural

(% of population)

Urban   Rural

....

population per sq km

FRANCE   PROVENCE & CÔTE D'AZUR   CANNES

= 100 people

History

Prehistoric Man

Provence was inhabited from an exceptionally early age: primitive stone tools more than a million years old were found near Roquebrune-Cap-Martin. Neanderthal hunters occupied the Mediterranean coast from about 90,000 BC to 40,000 BC, living in caves such as Grottes de l'Observatoire in Monaco. Modern man arrived with creative flair in 30,000 BC. The ornate wall paintings inside the decorated Grotte Cosquer, near Marseille, date from 20,000 BC, while the outstanding collection of 30,000 petroglyphs decorating Mont Bégo in the Vallée des Merveilles dates back to 1800–1500 BC.

Archaeologists have found that the people living around Châteauneuf-les-Martigues, northwest of Marseille, about 6000 to 4500 years ago were among the first ever to domesticate wild sheep, allowing them to shift from a nomadic to a settled lifestyle.

Greeks to Romans

Massalia (Marseille) was colonised around 600 BC by Greeks from Phocaea in Asia Minor; from the 4th century BC they established more trading posts along the coast at Antipolis (Antibes), Olbia (Hyères), Athenopolis (St-Tropez), Nikaia (Nice), Monoïkos (Monaco) and Glanum (near St-Rémy-de-Provence). They brought olives and grapevines to the region.

While Hellenic civilisation was developing on the coast, the Celts penetrated northern Provence. They mingled with ancient Ligurians to create a Celto-Ligurian stronghold around Entremont; its influence extended as far south as Draguignan.

In 125 BC the Romans helped the Greeks defend Massalia against invading Celto-Ligurians. Their victory marked the start of the Gallo-Roman era and the creation of Provincia Gallia Transalpina, the first Roman *provincia* (province), from which the name Provence is derived.

Top Prehistoric Sights

Grottes de l'Observatoire, Monaco

Vallée des Merveilles

Musée de la Préhistoire des Gorges du Verdon

Village des Bories, near Gordes

Réserve Géologique de Haute-Provence

TIMELINE	c 90,000 BC	600 BC	126–125 BC
	Neanderthal hunters occupy the Mediterranean coast; starting around 30,000 BC Cro-Magnons start decorating their caves.	The Greeks colonise Massalia (now Marseille) and establish trading posts along the coast, bringing olive trees and grapevines to the region.	Romans create Provincia Gallia Transalpina, from which Provence gets its name, and Provence joins the Roman Empire.

The Gallo-Romans

Provincia Gallia Transalpina, later Provincia Narbonensis, embraced all
of southern France from the Alps to the Mediterranean and the Pyrenees.
In 122 BC the Romans destroyed the Ligurian capital of Entremont and
established the Roman stronghold of Aquae Sextiae Salluviorum (Aix-en-
Provence) at its foot. Around 188BC, they began construction of the Via
Domitia, the first Roman road in Gaul, which stretched all the way from
the Alps via the Durance Valley, Apt, Arles, Nîmes, and Narbonne, where
it intersected with the Via Aquitania to the Atlantic Coast.

The construction of the road helped Rome's further conquest of Gaul
by enabling movement of troops and supplies, but it wasn't completely
conquered until Julius Caesar's final victorious campaign from 58BC to
51BC. Massalia, which had retained its independence since the creation of Provincia, was incorporated by Caesar in 49 BC. In 14 BC the
still-rebellious Ligurians were defeated by Augustus Caesar, who celebrated by building a monument at La Turbie in 6 BC. Arelate (Arles)
became the regional capital.

Under the emperor Augustus, vast amphitheatres were built at Arelate, Nemausus (Nîmes), Forum Julii (Fréjus) and Vasio Vocontiorum
(Vaison-la-Romaine). Triumphal arches were raised at Arausio (Orange),
Cabelio (Cavaillon), Carpentorate (Carpentras) and Glanum, and a series
of aqueducts was constructed. The 275m-long Pont du Gard was part of
a 50km-long system of canals built around 19 BC by Agrippa, Augustus'
deputy, to bring water from Uzès to Nîmes.

Christianity – brought to the region, according to Provençal legend,
by Mary Magdalene, Mary Jacob and Mary Salome, who sailed into Stes-
Maries-de-la-Mer in AD 40 – penetrated the region, was adopted by the
Romans and continued to spread over the next few hundred years.

Medieval Provence

After the collapse of the Roman Empire in AD 476, Provence was invaded
by various Germanic tribes. In the early 9th century the Saracens (an
umbrella term adopted locally to describe Muslim invaders such as Turks,
Moors and Arabs) emerged as a warrior force to be reckoned with. Attacks along the Maures coast, Niçois hinterland and more northern Alps
persuaded villagers to take refuge in the hills. Many of Provence's hilltop
villages date from this chaotic period. In AD 974 the Saracen fortress at
La Garde Freinet was defeated by William the Liberator (Guillaume Le
Libérateur), count of Arles, who consequently extended his feudal control
over the entire region, marking the return of peace and unity to Provence,
which became a marquisate. In 1032 it joined the Holy Roman Empire.

The marquisate of Provence was later split in two: the north fell to
the counts of Toulouse from 1125, and the Catalan counts of Barcelona

The French Riviera: A Cultural History by Julian Hale delves into the modern Côte d'Azur's vibrant past with panache and (Champagne) buckets of anecdotes.

HISTORY THE GALLO-ROMANS

Top Roman Sights

Pont du Gard and Les Arènes, Nîmes

Théatre Antique, Orange

Les Arènes and Théatre Antique, Arles

Glanum, St-Rémy-de-Provence

Puymin and La Villasse, Vaison-la-Romaine

AD 400–900	974–1032	1309–77	1481
The Roman Empire collapses and Germanic tribes invade Provence; Franks (hence the name 'France') encourage villagers to move uphill to avert Saracen attacks.	William the Liberator extends his feudal control over Provence, which becomes a marquisate and joins the Holy Roman Empire.	Pope Clément V moves the Holy Seat to Avignon, and nine pontiffs head the Roman Catholic church from there until 1377; 'home' is the Palais des Papes.	King of Naples, Good King René's nephew and successor, Charles III, dies heirless and Provence falls to Louis XI of France.

Ladder of Shadows: Reflecting on Medieval Vestiges in Provence & Languedoc by Gustaf Sobin is a beautiful lyrical narrative on Roman and early Christian relics in southern France.

gained control of the southern part (stretching from the Rhône to the River Durance and from the Alps to the sea). This became the county of Provence (Comté de Provence). Raymond Bérenger V (1209–45) was the first Catalan count to reside permanently in Aix (the capital since 1186). In 1229 he conquered Nice and in 1232 he founded Barcelonnette. After Bérenger's death the county passed to the House of Anjou, under which it enjoyed great prosperity.

The Popes

In 1274 Comtat Venaissin (Carpentras and its Vaucluse hinterland) was ceded to Pope Gregory X in Rome. In 1309 French-born Clément V (r 1305–14) moved the papal headquarters from feud-riven Rome to Avignon. A tour of the papal palace illustrates how resplendent a period this was for the city, which hosted nine pontiffs between 1309 and 1376.

The death of Pope Gregory XI led to the Great Schism (1378–1417), during which rival popes resided at Rome and Avignon and spent most of their energies denouncing and excommunicating each other. Even after the schism was settled and a pope established in Rome, Avignon and the Comtat Venaissin remained under papal rule until 1792.

The arts in Provence flourished under the popes. A university was established in Avignon as early as 1303, followed by a university in Aix a century later. In 1327 Italian poet Petrarch (1304–74) encountered his muse, Laura, in Fontaine-de-Vaucluse. During the reign of Good King René, king of Naples (1434–80), French became the courtly language.

French Provence

In 1481 René's successor, his nephew Charles III, died heirless and Provence was ceded to Louis XI of France. In 1486 the state of Aix ratified Provence's union with France, and the centralist policies of the French kings saw the region's autonomy greatly reduced. Aix Parliament, a French administrative body, was created in 1501.

A period of instability ensued, as a visit to the synagogue in Carpentras testifies: Jews living in French Provence fled to ghettos in Carpentras, Pernes-les-Fontaines, L'Isle-sur-la-Sorgue, Cavaillon or Avignon. All were part of the pontifical enclave of Comtat Venaissin, where papal protection remained assured until 1570.

An early victim of the Reformation that swept Europe in the 1530s and the consequent Wars of Religion (1562–98) was the Luberon. In April 1545 the populations of 11 Waldensian (Vaudois) villages in the Luberon were massacred. Numerous clashes followed between the staunchly Catholic Comtat Venaissin and its Huguenot (Protestant) neighbours to the north around Orange.

In 1580, as in much of Europe, plague devastated the region – a problem that continued to recur over the ensuing decades.

Top Religious Architecture

- Palais des Papes, Avignon
- Chartreuse du Val de Bénédiction, Villeneuve-lès-Avignon
- Abbaye Notre-Dame de Sénanque, Gordes
- Monastère de la Verne, Collobrières
- Abbaye de Thoronet, Lorgues

1530s	1539	1545	1560
The Reformation sweeps through France, prompting the core of Catholicism to be questioned.	French (rather than Provençal) is made the official administrative language of Provence.	People of 11 Luberon villages are massacred under the terms of the Arrêt de Mérindol, a bill condemning anyone of Waldensian faith to death.	Nîmes native Jean Nicot (1530–1600) becomes the first to import tobacco into France from Portugal, hence the word 'nicotine'.

The Edict of Nantes in 1598 (which recognised Protestant control of certain areas, including Lourmarin in the Luberon) brought an uneasy peace to the region – until its revocation by Louis XIV in 1685. Full-scale persecution of Protestants ensued.

In 1720, Marseille was hit by another devastating outbreak of plague. The disease spread from a merchant ship after the city's chief magistrate, owner of the ship's cargo, ignored quarantine measures to ensure his goods made it to the local fair. Half the city's population died.

The close of the century was marked by the French Revolution in 1789: as the National Guard from Marseille marched north to defend the Revolution, a merry tune composed in Strasbourg several months earlier for the war against Prussia – 'Chant de Guerre de l'Armée du Rhin' ('War Song of the Rhine Army') – sprang from their lips. France's stirring national anthem, La Marseillaise, was born.

From France to Italy, & Back

Provence was divided into three *départements* (administrative divisions) in 1790: Var, Bouches du Rhône and the Basse-Alpes. Two years later papal Avignon and Comtat Venaissin were annexed by France, making way for the creation of Vaucluse.

In 1793 the Armée du Midi marched into Nice and declared it French territory. France also captured Monaco, until then a recognised independent state ruled by the Grimaldi family. When Toulon was besieged by the English, it was thanks to the efforts of a dashing young Corsican general named Napoléon Bonaparte (Napoléon I) that France recaptured it.

The Reign of Terror that swept through France between September 1793 and July 1794 saw religious freedoms revoked, churches desecrated and cathedrals turned into 'Temples of Reason'. In the secrecy of their homes, people handcrafted thumbnail-sized biblical figurines, hence the inglorious creation of the *santon*.

In 1814 France lost the territories it had seized in 1793. The County of Nice was ceded to Victor Emmanuel I, King of Sardinia. It remained under Sardinian protectorship until 1860, when an agreement between Napoléon III and the House of Savoy helped drive the Austrians from northern Italy, prompting France to repossess Savoy and the area around Nice. In Monaco the Treaty of Paris restored the rights of the Grimaldi royal family; from 1817 until 1860 the principality also fell under the protection of the Sardinian king.

Meanwhile, the Allied restoration of the House of Bourbon to the French throne at the Congress of Vienna (1814–15), following Napoléon I's abdication and exile to Elba, was rudely interrupted by the return of the emperor. Following his escape from Elba in 1815, Napoléon landed at Golfe-Juan on 1 March with a 1200-strong army. He proceeded northwards, passing

Top History Museums

Musée des Civilisations de l'Europe et de la Méditerranée, Marseille

Musée d'Archéologie Méditerranée, Marseille

Musée Archéologique, Fréjus

Musée Départemental Arles Antique

The route that Napoléon followed from Golfe-Juan to Grenoble over the course of his 1815 comeback has become the legendary Route Napoléon. It follows mostly the tortuous and scenic N85 and is especially popular with bikers. For a full itinerary, check www.route-napoleon.com.

1562–98	1598	1720	1789–94
The Wars of Religion see numerous bloody clashes between French Catholics and Protestants (Huguenots).	Bourbon king Henry IV gives French Protestants freedom of conscience with the Edict of Nantes – to the horror of Catholic Paris and Roman Catholicism stronghold Avignon.	The Great Plague of Marseille eventually leads to the death of more than half the city's population, and the building of Le Mur de la Peste (Plague Wall).	Revolutionaries storm the Bastille, leading to the beheading of Louis XVI and Marie-Antoinette and the Reign of Terror, seeing religious freedoms revoked.

THE SKY-BLUE COAST

The Côte d'Azur (literally 'Azure Coast') gained its name in 1887 from the first guidebook published on the region. *La Côte d'Azur* was the work of Stéphane Liégeard (1830–1925), a lawyer-cum–aspiring poet from Burgundy who lived in Cannes. The guide covered the coast from Menton to Hyères and was an instant hit. Its title, a reflection of the coast's clear blue cloudless skies, became the hottest phrase in town and never disappeared. The Côte d'Azur is known as the French Riviera by most anglophones.

through Cannes, Grasse, Castellane, Digne-les-Bains and Sisteron en route to his triumphal return to Paris on 20 May. Napoléon's glorious 'Hundred Days' back in power ended with the Battle of Waterloo and his return to exile. He died in 1821.

The Belle Époque

The Second Empire (1852–70) brought to the region a revival in all things Provençal, a movement spearheaded by Maillane-born poet Frédéric Mistral. Rapid economic growth was another hallmark: Nice, which had become part of France in 1860, became Europe's fastest-growing city thanks to its booming tourism. The city was particularly popular with the English aristocracy, who followed their queen's example of wintering on the Riviera's shores. European royalty followed soon after. The train line reached Toulon in 1856, followed by Nice in 1864, the same year work started on a coastal road from Nice to Monaco.

In neighbouring Monaco the Grimaldi family gave up its claim over its former territories of Menton and Roquebrune in 1861 in exchange for France's recognition of its status as an independent principality. Four years later Monte Carlo Casino opened and Monaco leapt from being Europe's poorest state to one of its richest.

The Third Republic ushered in the glittering belle époque, with art nouveau architecture, a whole field of artistic 'isms' including impressionism, and advances in science and engineering. Wealthy French, English, American and Russian tourists and tuberculosis sufferers (for whom the only cure was sunlight and sea air) discovered the coast. The intensity and clarity of the region's colours and light appealed to many painters.

Top Belle Époque Sights

Casino de Monte Carlo

Hôtel Negresco, Nice

Musée Masséna, Nice

Excelsior-Regina, Nice

Carlton Intercontinental, Cannes

WWI & the Roaring Twenties

No blood was spilled on southern French soil during WWI. Soldiers were conscripted from the region, however, and the human losses included two out of every 10 Frenchmen between 20 and 45 years of age. With its primarily tourist-based economy, the Côte d'Azur recovered more quickly from the postwar financial crisis than France's more industrial north.

1790–92	1815	1848	1860
Provence is divided into three *départements* (which still exist today); Papal Avignon and Comtat Venaissin are annexed by France and Vaucluse is created.	Exiled Napoléon Bonaparte escapes Elba and journeys in secret over the mountains near Digne-les-Bains and Gap to reclaim his title in Paris – it'll only last 100 days.	In 1848 French revolutionaries adopt the red, white and blue tricolour of Martigues near Marseille as their own. France's national flag is born.	The County of Nice becomes part of French Provence. Meanwhile, European royalty winters in Nice, Europe's fastest-growing city.

The Côte d'Azur sparkled as an avant-garde centre in the 1920s and 1930s, with artists pushing into the new fields of cubism and surrealism, Le Corbusier rewriting the architectural textbook and foreign writers thronging to the liberal coast.

The coast's nightlife gained a reputation for being cutting edge, with everything from jazz clubs to striptease. Rail and road access to the south improved: the railway line between Digne-les-Bains and Nice was completed, and in 1922 the luxurious Train Bleu made its first run from Calais, via Paris, to the coast. The train only had 1st-class carriages and was quickly dubbed the 'train to paradise'.

The roaring twenties hailed the start of the summer season on the Côte d'Azur. Outdoor swimming pools were built, sandy beaches cleared of seaweed, and sunbathing sprang into fashion after a bronzed Coco Chanel appeared on the coast in 1923, draped over the arm of the Duke of Westminster. France lifted its ban on gambling, prompting the first casino to open on the coast in the Palais de la Méditerranée (today a hotel) on Nice's Promenade des Anglais in 1927. With the advent of paid holidays for all French workers in 1936, even more tourists flocked to the region. Second- and 3rd-class seating were added to the Train Bleu.

Greatly affected by the plague of phylloxera in the 1880s, vineyards were replanted but struggled: France was overproducing and WWI soldiers preferred red wine to rosé for their rations. With the introduction of AOC labels in the 1930s, luck finally turned for Provençal wines.

WWII

With the onset of war, the Côte d'Azur's glory days turned grey. On 3 September 1939 France and Britain declared war on Germany. But following the armistice treaty agreed with Hitler on 22 June 1940, southern France fell into the 'free' Vichy France zone, although Menton and the Vallée de La Roya were occupied by Italians. The Côte d'Azur – particularly Nice – immediately became a safe haven from war-torn occupied France; by 1942 some 43,000 Jews had descended on the coast to seek refuge. Monaco remained neutral for the duration of WWII.

On 11 November 1942 Nazi Germany invaded Vichy France. Provence was at war. At Toulon 73 ships, cruisers, destroyers and submarines -- the major part of the French fleet – were scuttled by their crews to prevent the Germans seizing them. Almost immediately, Toulon was overcome by the Germans and Nice was occupied by the Italians. In January 1943 the Marseille quarter of Le Panier was razed, its 40,000 inhabitants being given less than a day's notice to pack up and leave. Those who didn't were sent to Nazi concentration camps. The Resistance movement, particularly strong in Provence, was known in the region as *maquis,* after the Provençal scrub in which people hid.

Two months after D-Day, on 15 August 1944, Allied forces landed on the southern coast at beaches including Le Dramont near St-Raphaël, Cavalaire, Pampelonne and the St-Tropez peninsula. St-Tropez and Provence's hinterland were almost immediately liberated, but it was only

Villa Air-Bel: WWII, Escape & a House in Marseille by Rosemary Sullivan is a compelling book based on the true story of American heiress Varian Fry, who turned a villa in Marseille into a refuge for Nazi-persecuted artists and intellectuals.

1914–18	1920s	1939–45	1946
The human cost of WWI is enormous: of the eight million French men called to arms, 1.3 million are killed and almost one million crippled.	The Côte d'Azur sparkles as Europe's avant-garde centre and the luxurious Train Bleu (Blue Train) makes its first run from Calais to the Mediterranean coast.	Nazi Germany occupies France, establishing a puppet state led by ageing WWI hero General Pétain in Vichy; Provence is liberated two months after D-Day.	The first international film festival opens at Cannes' old casino, and is a smashing success, helping revive postwar life on the coast.

after five days of heavy fighting that Allied troops freed Marseille on 28 August (three days after the liberation of Paris). Toulon was liberated on 26 August, a week after French troops first attacked the port.

Italian-occupied areas in the Vallée de La Roya were only returned to France in 1947.

In his 1982 pamphlet *J'Accuse, The Dark Side of Nice*, Graham Greene denounced the endemic conniv- ance between Nice's ruling elite and the local mafia. The book was banned in France, and Jacques Médecin, Nice's mayor, sued Greene for libel.

Les 30 Glorieuses: France's Golden Decades

The 30-odd years following WWII saw unprecedented growth, creativi- ty and optimism in France, and Provence and the Côte d'Azur were no exception. After a false start, Cannes' 1946 international film festival her- alded the return of party madness. The 1950s and 1960s saw a succession of society events: the fairy-tale marriage of Monaco's prince to Holly- wood film-legend Grace Kelly in 1956; Vadim's filming of *Et Dieu Créa la Femme* (And God Created Woman) with a smouldering Brigitte Bardot in St-Tropez the same year; the creation of the bikini; the advent of topless sunbathing (and consequent nipple-covering with bottle tops to prevent arrest for indecent exposure); and Miles Davis, Ella Fitzgerald and Ray Charles appearing at the 1961 Juan-les-Pins jazz festival.

Rapid industrialisation marked the 1960s. A string of five hydroelectric plants was constructed on the banks of the River Durance and in 1964 Élec- tricité de France (EDF), the French electricity company, dug a canal from Manosque to the Étang de Berre. The following year construction work began on a 100-sq-km petrochemical zone and an industrial port at Fos- sur-Mer, southern Europe's most important. The first metro line opened in Marseille in 1977 and TGV high-speed trains reached the city in 1981.

From the 1970s mainstream tourism started making inroads into Provence's rural heart. Concrete blocks sprang up along the coast and up on the ski slopes. The small flow of foreigners that had trickled into Provence backwaters to buy crumbling old *mas* (Provençal farmhouses) in the late 1970s had become an uncontrollable torrent by the 1980s. By the turn of the new millennium, the region was welcoming nine million tourists annually.

ENTER THE BIKINI

Almost called *atome* (French for atom) rather than bikini after its pinprick size, the scanty little two-piece bathing suit was the 1946 creation of Cannes fashion designer Jacques Heim and automotive engineer Louis Réard. Top-and-bottom swimsuits had existed for centuries, but it was the French duo who plumped for the name bikini – after Bikini, an atoll in the Marshall Islands chosen by the USA in 1946 as a testing ground for atomic bombs.

Once wrapped around the curvaceous rear of 1950s sex-bomb Brigitte Bardot on St-Tropez's Plage de Pampelonne, there was no looking back. The bikini was born.

1947	1956	1981	2002
Vallée de La Roya, in eastern Provence, which had been occupied by the Italians during WWII, is returned to France.	Rainier Louis Henri Maxence Bertrand Grimaldi, Count of Polignac, aka Prince Rainier III of Monaco, weds his fairy-tale prin- cess, Hollywood film legend Grace Kelly.	The superfast TGV makes its first com- mercial journey from Paris to Lyon, breaking all speed records to complete the train journey in two hours instead of six.	The French franc, first minted in 1360, is dumped on the scrap heap of history as the country adopts the euro as its official currency.

NICE TREATY

No pan-European agreement has been more influential on the future map of Europe than the Treaty of Nice, a landmark treaty thrashed out by the then 15 EU member states in late December 2000. Enforced from February 2003, the treaty laid the foundations for EU enlargement starting in 2004, determined the institutions necessary for its smooth running and – not without controversy – established a new system of voting in the Council of Ministers for the 25 EU countries from 1 November 2004.

Corruption, the Mafia & the Front National

Writer Somerset Maugham had famously described Monaco as 'a sunny place for shady people', but over the course of the 1980s and 1990s many increasingly felt that this could apply to the region as a whole. Although it was well-known that the Italian, Russian and Corsican mafias all operated on the coast, their true extent was revealed after a series of corruption scandals, none more dramatic than the assassination of *député* (member of parliament) Yann Piat in 1994: she was shot in her Hyères constituency following her public denunciation of the Riviera mafia.

The same year, former Nice mayor Jacques Médecin, who had run the city from 1966 to 1990, was found guilty of income-tax evasion and misuse of public funds after being extradited from Uruguay where he'd fled. And in 1995 Bernard Tapie, the flamboyant owner of Olympique de Marseille football club, was found guilty of match fixing and sentenced to two years in jail.

Many now think that it was these high-profile corruption cases, combined with economic recession and growing unemployment, that helped fuel the rise of the extreme-right Front National (FN). Led by firebrand Jean-Marie Le Pen, infamous for having described the Holocaust as a 'detail of history', the FN won municipal elections in Toulon, Orange and Marignane in 1995, and Vitrolles in 1997. The party also gained 15.5% of votes in regional elections in 1998 and 14.7% in 2004.

The FN never succeeded in securing the presidency of the Provence-Alpes-Côte d'Azur *région*, but Le Pen's success in the first round of presidential elections in 2002 – he landed 16.86% of votes, with his main support base in the south of France – shocked many people. He eventually lost in the second round, after a massive 80% turnout at the ballot boxes, and 82% of votes in favour of his opponent, Jacques Chirac.

The far right continues to exert a strong pull over the region's political fortunes; now run by Jean-Marie's daughter, Marine Le Pen, FN has recently polled strongly in several important elections – perhaps most notably in 2014, when it came within a whisker of taking control of Avignon.

Top Unusual Museums

Musée Ocean-ographique de Monaco

Musée Jean Cocteau Collection Séverin Wunderman, Menton

Musée International de la Parfumerie, Grasse

Musée de Tire-Bouchon, Ménerbes

Musée de la Boulangerie, Bonnieux

2004	**2005**	**2013**	**2014**
A local diver uncovers the wreckage of the plane of Antoine de Saint-Exupéry, author of *Le Petit Prince*, who plunged to his death in the Mediterranean in July 1944.	After the end of a three-month mourning period for his father, Prince Albert II of Monaco is crowned monarch of the world's second-smallest country.	Marseille and Aix celebrate their tenures as joint Capitals of Culture, with major museum openings and celebratory events.	City authorities in Nice announce bid for the Promenade des Anglais to become a World Heritage Site.

Painters in Provence & the Côte d'Azur

Whether it was the search for a refuge, light or more clement weather, it seems that the painters who settled in Provence came here looking for something – and found a lot more than they'd hoped for.

The Impressionists

Van Gogh

Vincent van Gogh (1853–90) arrived in Arles from Paris in 1888, keen to escape the excesses of the capital. He found inspiration amid the region's landscapes, customs and, above all, the intense quality of light. By the time he left Arles a year later, he'd completed more than 200 oil paintings – including masterpieces such as *Bedroom in Arles* (1888) and *Still Life: Vase with Twelve Sunflowers* (1888).

Throughout his life, van Gogh was wracked with self-doubt and depression, conditions that were compounded by his lack of commercial success – famously, he sold just a single painting during his entire career, and never received any kind of serious critical acclaim. He was prone to fits of manic depression – including the famous incident in December 1888, when he cut off part of his left ear following a spat with Paul Gauguin.

In May 1889, he voluntarily committed himself to an asylum in St-Rémy-de-Provence; despite his illness, he continued to work at a feverish pace, producing many key works including *Starry Night* (1889) and several haunting self-portraits. Van Gogh left St-Rémy in May 1890 to join his brother Theo in Auvers-sur-Oise; he shot himself two months later, aged just 37.

Van Gogh is now acknowledged as one of the 20th-century's greatest painters. Most of his works now reside in international museums, although a few have stayed in Provence – notably at Musée Angladon (p197) in Avignon and Musée Granet (p169) in Aix-en-Provence.

Cézanne

Paul Cézanne (1839–1906) is perhaps the most Provençal of all the impressionists. His work is generally credited with providing a transition from 'traditional' 19th-century art to the radical new art forms of the 20th century, notably cubism.

Cézanne was born in Aix-en-Provence and spent most of his life there, save for a decade in Paris and another ferrying between Provence and the capital. He met writer Émile Zola at school in Aix and the pair remained friends for years – until Zola used Cézanne as the main inspiration for his character Claude Lantet, a failed painter, in his novel *L'Oeuvre* (The Work 1886).

Provence was Cézanne's chief inspiration: the seaside village of L'Estaque, the Bibémus quarries near Aix (said to have inspired his cubist trials by their geometric character) and the family house, Jas de Bouffan, in

Cézanne Sights

Atelier Cézanne, Aix-en-Provence

Le Jas de Bouffan, Aix-en-Provence

Carrières de Bibemus, Aix-en-Provence

L'Estaque

Aix appear in dozens of paintings. But it was the Montagne Ste-Victoire that captivated him the most, its radiance, shape and colours depicted in no fewer than 30 oil paintings and 45 watercolours.

Sadly, Cézanne's admiration for Provence was not mutual: few of Aix's conservative bourgeoisie appreciated Cézanne's departure from the creed of classical painting and there were even calls for him to leave the city.

In 1902, Cézanne moved into a purpose-built studio, Atelier Cézanne, from where he did much of his painting until his death in 1906. The studio has been left untouched and is one of the most poignant insights into his art.

Renoir

In 1892, Pierre-Auguste Renoir (1841–1919), started to develop rheumatoid arthritis. The condition gradually worsened, and in 1907 doctors ordered Renoir to move to the sunny climes of Cagnes-sur-Mer in a bid to alleviate his pains.

In 1909, Renoir bought a farm in Cagnes-sur-Mer called Les Colettes, where he lived until his death. Far from being a retirement home, however, Renoir enjoyed a new lease of life in the south of France and painted vigorously throughout his twilight years. Although he had to adapt his painting technique – he was wheelchair-bound and suffered from ankylosis in his shoulder – many credit his late works with displaying the same joy and radiance that were the hallmark of his earlier (and most famous) works.

Renoir's house at Les Colettes is now the Musée Renoir (p97), where you can see the artist's studios, his gorgeous garden and several of his works. The museum reopened after extensive renovations in 2013.

Matisse Sights

Musée Matisse, Nice

Chapelle du Rosaire, Vence

Cemetery at Monastère de Cimiez, Nice

Matisse

Originally from drab northern France, leading Fauvist exponent Henri Matisse (1869–1954) spent his most creative years lapping up the sunlight and vivacity of the coast in and around Nice.

Matisse travelled to southern France on a number of occasions, including a visit to impressionist Paul Signac in St-Tropez, which inspired one of his most famous works: *Luxe, Calme et Volupté* (Luxury, Calm and Tranquility; 1904). But it was a trip to Nice to cure bronchitis in 1917 that left Matisse smitten – he never really looked back.

Matisse settled in Cimiez, in the hills north of Nice's centre, and it was here that he started experimenting with his *gouaches découpées* (collages of painted paper cut-outs) in the 1940s, after an operation. The famous *Blue Nude* series and *The Snail* epitomise this period.

Matisse's ill health was also a key factor in the creation of his masterpiece, the Chapelle du Rosaire in Vence. The artist had been looked after by a nun during his convalescence and the chapel was his mark of gratitude. Matisse designed everything, from the stained-glass windows

CLASSIC PAINTING

Although Provence and the Côte d'Azur are best known for their relatively modern artistic legacy, the region's reputation as a haven for artists goes back centuries.

In the 14th century Sienese, French and Spanish artists thrived at the papal court in Avignon and created an influential style of mural painting to decorate the palace.

Renaissance painter Louis (Ludovico) Bréa (c 1450–1523), often dubbed the 'Fra Angelico Provençal', is best remembered for his signature burgundy colour known as *rouge bréa*.

Two centuries later, it was the rococo influences in his landscapes and the playful and often licentious scenes of his paintings that made Jean-Honoré Fragonard (1732–1806), a native of Grasse, so popular with French aristocrats.

CONTEMPORARY ART

One look at the portfolio of **Documents d'Artistes** (www.documentsdartistes.org), an association in Marseille that catalogues and diffuses the work of contemporary regional artists around the world, proves that contemporary art is well and truly alive in Provence: be it tracing a line along the surface of the planet, creating sound installations, or producing inflatable or mechanical art, it is all happening here.

There are many galleries where you can admire contemporary art. In Marseille, make a beeline for exhibition space La Friche La Belle de Mai (p151); in Arles, check out the Fondation Vincent Van Gogh (p182); or amble the gallery-lined streets of St-Paul de Vence and Mougins.

to the altar, the structure of the chapel and the robes of the priests. The chapel took four years to complete and was finished in 1951.

Matisse died in Nice in 1954 and is buried in Cimiez' cemetery.

Picasso

Although Pablo Picasso (1881–1973) moved to the Côte d'Azur rather late in life (the Spanish artist was in his midsixties when he moved to Golfe-Juan with his lover Françoise Gilot in 1946), his influence over the region and the region's influence on him were significant.

Antibes & Vallauris

It was following an offer from the curator of Antibes' Château Grimaldi (now the Musée Picasso, p89) that Picasso set up a studio on the 3rd floor of the historic building. Works from this period are characterised by an extraordinary *joie de vivre* and a fascination with Mediterranean mythology.

It was that same year that Picasso visited the nearby potters' village of Vallauris and discovered ceramics. Picasso loved the three-dimensional aspect of the art and experimented endlessly. His method was somewhat unorthodox: he melted clay, used unglazed ceramics and decorated various pieces with relief motifs; he also eschewed traditional floral decorations for a bestiary of his favourite mythological creatures.

Picasso settled in Vallauris in 1948 and although he left in 1955, he carried on working with ceramics until his death. His time in Vallauris wasn't only dedicated to ceramics, however; it was here that Picasso got 'his chapel' (arch-rival Matisse had finished his in 1951). It was the chapel of the town's castle, in which he painted *War and Peace* (1952), the last of his monumental creations dedicated to peace, after *Guernica* (1937) and *Massacre in Korea* (1951).

Vauvenargues & Mougins

In 1959, Picasso bought the Château de Vauvenargues near Aix-en-Provence. The castle slumbered at the foot of the Montagne Ste-Victoire, depicted so often by Cézanne, whom Picasso greatly admired. It was Cézanne's early studies on cubism that had led Picasso and his peers to launch the cubist movement (which seeks to deconstruct the subject into a system of intersecting planes and present various aspects of it simultaneously); Picasso was also an avid collector of Cézanne's works.

In 1961, Picasso moved to Mougins with his second wife Jacqueline Roque. He had many friends in the area, including photographer André Villers, to whom Picasso gave his first camera and who in turn took numerous portraits of the artist.

Picasso died in Mougins in 1973 and is buried in Château de Vauvenargues, which remains the property of his family.

Picasso Sights

Musée Picasso, Antibes

Musée Picasso La Guerre et La Paix, Vallauris

Château de Vauvenargues

Musée de la Photographie André Villers, Mougins

Modern Art

Chagall

Belorussian painter Marc Chagall (1887–1985) moved to Paris from Russia in 1922. He was well-known for his dazzling palette and the biblical messages in his later works (inspired by his Jewish upbringing in Russia and trips to Palestine). Chagall managed to escape to the US during WWII and it was upon his return to France in the early 1950s that he settled in St-Paul de Vence on the Côte d'Azur. Both Matisse and Picasso lived in the area at the time and many artists regularly visited; it was this sense of 'artistic colony' that attracted Chagall.

Though Provence and the Côte d'Azur never featured explicitly in Chagall's works, he was clearly fascinated by the region's light and colour – something that becomes obvious looking at the luminous works on display at the Musée National Marc Chagall (p48) in Nice. Chagall is buried in St-Paul de Vence.

New Realism

Provence and the Côte d'Azur produced a spate of artists at the forefront of modern art in the middle of the 20th century. Most famous perhaps was Nice-born Yves Klein (1928–62), who stood out for his series of daring monochrome paintings, the distinctive blue he used in many of his works (supposedly inspired by the colour of the Mediterranean) and his experiments in paint-application techniques: in his series *Anthropométrie*, paint was 'applied' by women covered from head to toe in paint and writhing naked on the canvas.

Also making a splash in modern-art circles was native Niçois Arman (1928–2005), who became known for his trash-can portraits, made by framing the litter found in the subject's rubbish bin, and Martial Raysse, born in Golfe-Juan in 1936, renowned for pioneering the use of neon in art: his 1964 portrait of *Nissa Bella* (Beautiful Nice) – a flashing blue heart on a human face – is typical.

Klein, Arman and Raysse were among the nine people to found New Realism in 1960. The movement was one of several avant-garde trends of the time and was often perceived as the French interpretation of American pop art. In 1961, another prominent Provençal artist, Marseillais César Baldaccini (1921–1998), known for his crushed cars and scrap metal art, joined the New Realists' rank, as did Niki de Saint Phalle (1930–2002), famous for her huge, colourful papier mâché sculptures.

Nice's Musée d'Art Moderne et d'Art Contemporain has one of the best collections of New Realist artists' works; the building itself is a work of art too.

Hungarian-born Victor Vasarely (1908–97), best-known for his bold, colourful geometrical forms and shifting perspectives, had a summer house in Gordes from 1948. He opened a first museum there in 1970 (which closed in 1996) and a second one, Fondation Vasarely, in Aix-en-Provence in 1976, which you can still visit.

Yves Klein's famous blue became more than a signature colour: it was actually patented. It is now known in art circles as International Klein Blue (or IKB), a deep, bright hue close to ultramarine.

Cinema & the Arts

The artistic pace in this pocket of southern France has always been fast and furious, fuelled by a constant flux of new arrivals who brought with them new ideas, traditions and artistic know-how. From the novels of Fitzgerald to the films of the Nouvelle Vague, this is a region where creativity and inspiration go hand in hand.

Cinema

Provence and cinema have had a thing going on for more than a century: one of the world's first motion pictures, by the Lumière brothers, premiered in La Ciotat (between Marseille and Toulon) in September 1895. The series of two-minute reels, entitled *L'Arrivée d'un Train en Gare de La Ciotat* (The Arrival of a Train at La Ciotat Station), made the audience leap out of their seats as the steam train rocketed forward.

Early Days

French film flourished in the 1920s, Nice being catapulted to stardom by Hollywood director Rex Ingram, who bought the city's Victorine film studios in 1925 and transformed them overnight into the hub of European film-making.

A big name in the 1930s and '40s was Aubagne-born writer and film-maker Marcel Pagnol (1895–1974), whose career kicked off in 1931 with *Marius*, the first part of his Fanny trilogy, portraying prewar Marseille. Pagnol's work was famous for his endearing depiction of Provençal people, and he remains a local icon.

Cannes & St-Tropez

With the Cannes Film Festival taking off after WWII, French cinema started to diversify. Jean Cocteau (1889–1963) eschewed realism with two masterpieces of cinema: *La Belle et la Bête* (Beauty and the Beast; 1945) and *Orphée* (Orpheus; 1950). The director's life and work is explored at the fantastic Musée Jean Cocteau Collection Séverin Wunderman in Menton.

Nouvelle Vague (New Wave) directors made films without big budgets, extravagant sets or big-name stars. Roger Vadim turned St-Tropez into the hot spot to be with his *Et Dieu Créa la Femme* (And God Created Woman; 1956), starring Brigitte Bardot. Jacques Démy's *La Baie des Anges* (The Bay of Angels; 1962) is set in Nice, while François Truffaut filmed part of *La Nuit Américaine* (The American Night; 1972) in the Victorine studios, the Niçois hinterland and the Vallée de la Vésubie.

Cinema buffs should download the CinePaca app. It lists some 50 films shot on locations across Provence and the Côte d'Azur and includes clips of the films in the location and interviews with the actors.

Contemporary Cinema

Provence and the Côte d'Azur continue to inspire and play host to hundreds of films. For a classic vision of sun-dappled Provence, it's hard to beat Claude Berri's dreamy double bill, *Jean de Florette* and *Manon des Sources*, adapted from the classic books by Marcel Pagnol.

More action-packed tales such as *The Transporter* (starring Jason Statham) and the *Taxi* trilogy (by Luc Besson, complete with a home-

MUSIC

Traditional Provençal music is based on polyphonic chants; as a music form, they have gone out of fashion, although they remain part and parcel of traditional celebrations, notably Christmas and Easter.

Where Provence has really made a contribution to the French contemporary music scene is in rap, jazz and world music, with Marseille's multicultural background proving an inspiration to many artists.

The phenomenal hip-hop lyrics of 1991 smash-hit album *de la Planète Mars* (From Planet Mars, Mars being short for Marseille) by rapping legends IAM – France's best-known rap group from Marseille – nudged rap into the mainstream. IAM have since gone on to collaborate with everyone from Beyoncé to film-director Luc Besson.

Since that time, the city's music scene has transcended its rap roots. Cheb Khaled, Cheb Aïssa and Cheb Mami – all from Marseille – have contributed hugely to the development of Algerian raï, encouraging other world-music talents such as Iranian percussionist Bijan Chemiranito, who plays the *zarb* (Persian goblet drum), to thrive.

The Riviera has also fostered a special relationship with jazz music over the years. Nice launched its jazz festival in 1948; Antibes-Juan-les-Pins followed in 1960 after legendary saxophonist Sidney Bechet settled there in the 1950s. Numerous jazz greats have played here since – including Ella Fitzgerald, Miles Davis and Ray Charles, as well as modern artists like Jamie Cullum.

CINEMA & THE ARTS ARCHITECTURE

grown rap soundtrack) were set on the Riviera and in Marseille respectively, while James Bond drops by Monaco in *GoldenEye*. The cult comedy *Bienvenu Chez les Ch'tis* tells the story of a Provençal public servant being relocated – shock horror – to northern France, and was a huge national hit.

The highlight of the calendar is Cannes' famous film festival, when major stars descend on the town to celebrate *la septième art* (the '7th art', as the French call cinema). The year's top film is awarded the Palme d'Or.

Architecture

Antiquity

Although there is plenty of evidence suggesting the region was inhabited several thousand years ago, early populations left little in the way of architecture. It was the Massiliots (Greeks) who, from 600 BC, really started building across Provence; the Romans, however, took it to a whole new level. Their colossal architectural legacy includes amphitheatres, aqueducts, arches, temples and baths.

A distinctive feature to look out for in rural Provence are *bories*, small dome-shaped buildings made of stone and usually used as storehouses and sometimes as dwellings. Their design stretches back into prehistory, but the same essential shape was still being used by local farmers right up to the 20th century. A small village of restored *bories* can be seen near Gordes in the Luberon.

Romanesque to Renaissance

A religious revival in the 11th century ushered in Romanesque architecture, so-called because of the Gallo-Roman architectural elements it adopted. Round arches, heavy walls with few windows, and a lack of ornamentation were characteristics of this style, Provence's most famous examples being the 12th-century abbeys in Sénanque and Le Thoronet.

Gothic architecture swapped roundness and simplicity for ribbed vaults, pointed arches, slender verticals, chapels along the nave and chancel, refined decoration and large stained-glass windows. Provence's

Roman
Splendour

Pont du Gard

Théâtre Antique, Orange

Les Arènes, Nîmes

Trophée des Alpes, La Turbie

Les Arènes, Arles

LE CORBUSIER

It was rather late in life that Swiss-born Charles-Édouard Jeanneret (1887–1965), alias Le Corbusier, turned to the south of France. He first came to visit his friends Eileen Gray, an Irish designer, and Romanian-born architect Jean Badovici in the 1930s. Gray and Badovici had a very modern seaside villa, E-1027, on Cap-Martin, and Le Corbusier was a frequent guest.

However, following a spat with Gray in 1938, Le Corbusier built his own holiday pad, Le Cabanon. It remained his summer cabin until his death in 1965 (he died of a heart attack while swimming).

Le Cabanon is unique because it is a project that Le Corbusier built for himself, but his most revolutionary design is undoubtedly the Marseille concrete apartment block L'Unité d'Habitation. Built between 1947 and 1952 as a low-cost housing project, it comprised 337 apartments arranged inside an elongated block on stilts; deeply controversial at the time, it's been protected as a historical monument since 1986.

Le Corbusier is buried with his wife in section J of Roquebrune-Cap-Martin cemetery.

most important examples of this period are Avignon's Palais des Papes and the Chartreuse du Val de Bénédiction in Villeneuve-lès-Avignon.

The French Renaissance scarcely touched the region – unlike mighty citadel architect Sébastien Le Prestre de Vauban (1633–1707), who notably reshaped Antibes' star-shaped Fort Carré and Île Ste Marguerite's Fort Royal.

Classical to Modern

Classical architecture fused with painting and sculpture from the end of the 16th to late 18th centuries to create stunning Baroque structures with interiors of great subtlety, refinement and elegance: Chapelle de la Miséricorde in Nice and Marseille's Centre de la Vieille Charité are classics.

Neoclassicism came into its own under Napoleon III, the Palais de Justice and Palais Masséna in Nice demonstrating the renewed interest in classical forms that it exhibited. The true showcase of this era, though, is 1878 Monte Carlo Casino, designed by French architect Charles Garnier (1825–98). Elegant Aix-en-Provence's fountains and *hôtels particuliers* (private mansions) date from this period too, as do the intricate wrought-iron campaniles.

The belle époque heralded an eclecticism of decorative stucco friezes, trompe l'œil paintings, glittering wall mosaics, brightly coloured Moorish minarets and Turkish towers. Anything went.

The three decades following WWII were marked, as in much of Europe, by the rise of modernist architecture – concrete blocks and highrise towers – partly as a response to pressing housing needs. Marseille's notorious suburbs, Monaco's forest of skyscrapers and the emblematic pyramidal Marina Baie des Anges in Villeneuve-Loubet all date back to this era. Many now bemoan the flurry of post-war construction, often built for speed and cost rather than aesthetic value.

Urban 20th-century architecture is the focus of Patrimoine XXe, a label protecting 34 urban landmarks in the Provence-Alpes-Côte d'Azur region. Find the full list of landmarks on www.paca.culture.gouv.fr/dossiers/xxeme/menu.html.

Contemporary Architecture

As with every other art form, Provence and the Côte d'Azur have kept innovating in architecture. Mouans-Sartoux's 2004 lime-green Espace de l'Art Concret, designed by Swiss-based architects Annette Gigon and Mike Guyer to complement the village's 16th-century château, has to be the boldest example of late.

Most recent is Rudy Ricciotti's new Musée Jean Cocteau in Menton (he also designed the Pavillon Noir in Aix-en-Provence). The cow-print-like seafront building couldn't contrast more with the old town's Italianate architecture and is an ode to Cocteau's own surrealist style.

Another famous contemporary architect to have left his print on Provence and the Côte d'Azur is British master Sir Norman Foster, who designed Nîmes' steel-and-glass Carré d'Art, the Musée de la Préhistoire des Gorges du Verdon in Quinson and the new five-storey building for Monaco Yacht Club, which opened in the summer of 2014.

Literature

Courtly Love to Prophecies

Lyric poems of courtly love, written by troubadours solely in the Occitan language, dominated medieval Provençal literature.

Provençal life featured in the works of Italian poet Petrarch (1304–74), exiled in 1327 to Avignon, where he met Laura, to whom he dedicated his life's works. Petrarch lived in Fontaine-de-Vaucluse from 1337 to 1353, where he wrote poems and letters about local shepherds, fishermen he met on the banks of the Sorgue and his pioneering ascent up Mont Ventoux.

In 1555 Nostradamus (1503–66), the philosopher and visionary writer from St-Rémy-de-Provence, published (in Latin) his prophetic *Centuries* in Salon de Provence, where he lived until his death (from gout, as he had predicted).

Mistral to Mayle

The 19th century witnessed a revival in Provençal literature, thanks to poet Frédéric Mistral (1830–1914). Mistral set up the literary movement Le Félibrige with six other young Provençal poets in a bid to revive the Provençal dialect and codify its orthography. The result was Provençal dictionary *Lou Trésor dou Félibrige*.

Numerous writers passed through or settled in Provence over the course of the 20th century: Colette (1873–1954) lived in St-Tropez from 1927 until 1938; her novel *La Naissance du Jour* (Break of Day) evokes an unspoilt St-Tropez. F Scott Fitzgerald enjoyed several stays in the interwar years; playwright Samuel Beckett sought refuge in Roussillon during WWII; Lawrence Durrell (1912–90) settled in Somières, near Nîmes; and Graham Greene lived in Antibes for many years and even wrote an incendiary pamphlet about political corruption in the 1980s.

Most famous perhaps is Peter Mayle, whose novels about life as an Englishman in Provence have greatly contributed to the popularity of the region.

Frédéric Mistral remains the only minority-language writer so far to have been awarded the Nobel Prize in Literature (1904) for his work as a Provençal philologist and in recognition of his poetic talent.

Traditional Provençal chants form the root of the powerful percussion-accompanied polyphony by Lo Còr de la Plana (www.myspace.com/locordelaplana), a male choir born in Marseille. Their album, *Tant deman* (2007), is essential listening.

CINEMA & THE ARTS LITERATURE

Provençal Food & Wine

If there's one thing you'll take home with you from your time in France, it's food memories – whether it's feasting on bouillabaisse in Marseille, savouring *pissaladière* (Niçoise pizza) in Nice, trying olive oil in St-Rémy-de-Provence, munching *calissons* (marzipan-like sweets) in Aix or just sipping a shot of pastis while watching a game of *pétanque* (similar to the game of bowls) on the village square.

Sunny Gastronomy

Olive Oil

Olive oil is the keystone of Mediterranean cuisine. It moistens every salad, drizzles croutons and cheeses, fries fish and onions, and generally finds its way into every dish in some form.

There are dozens of varieties, many of which are protected by the Appellation d'Origine Protégée (AOP), a label protecting regional products. There are seven AOPs for olives and olive oil across Provence and the Côte d'Azur: Nyons, Baux-de-Provence, Nice, Aix-en-Provence, Nîmes, Haute-Provence and Provence.

Each oil has a distinctive colour, flavour and texture, which can be attributed to the olive variety but also the pressing techniques and maturing processes used.

Olives are picked from November to February. Table olives are harvested first; olives destined to be pressed come last. Black and green olives are used; on average, it takes 5kg of olives to yield 1L of oil.

Bread & Cheese

Just like everywhere else in France, bread and cheese have pride of place in the Mediterranean diet.

Local cheeses are predominantly *chèvre* (goat's cheese), which can be eaten *frais* (fresh, a mild creamy taste) or enjoyed after they've matured into a tangy, stronger-tasting *demi-sec* (semidry) or *sec* (dry). *Fromage de Banon*, which comes wrapped in chestnut leaves, is a Luberon speciality.

The region's signature bread is picnic favourite *fougasse*, a flat bread stuffed with olives, pancetta or anchovies.

Seafood

Unsurprisingly for a region that takes up much of France's Mediterranean coast, seafood is a huge highlight of Provençal cuisine.

The region's pièce de résistance is bouillabaisse – a copious fish stew, generally served for two. Lots of places claim to offer it, but for the real thing, you'll have to head to one of the renowned seafood restaurants in Marseille or Nice, where the bouillabaisse nearly always needs to be ordered a day in advance to give chefs time to prepare it.

Another fishy speciality is *soupe de poissons* – a rich fish soup, often served with spicy *rouille* (saffron-garlic sauce), grated gruyère cheese and crispy croutons.

Best Places to Taste Olive Oil

Moulin à Huile du Calanquet, St-Rémy-de-Provence

Moulin à Huile Jullien, St-Saturnin-lès-Apt

Écomusée d'Olivier, Volx

Moulin à Huile d'Olive Alziari, Nice

Other typical fishes to look out for on the menu are *St-Pierre* (John dory), *daurade* (sea bream), *rascasse* (scorpion fish), *turbot* (turbot), *galinette* (tub gurnard), *merlan* (whiting), and especially *loup* (sea bass, also known as *bar* or *loup de mer*). The local speciality is to cook it *en croûte de sel* (in a salt crust – the result is surprisingly unsalty).

Shellfish is another delight: *crevettes* (prawns) and *gambas* (king prawns) are plentiful, as are oysters, mussels, *oursin* (sea urchin, a delicacy) and *coquilles St-Jacques* (scallops). They're often served in grand-looking *plateaux de fruits de mer* (seafood platters), which make for a truly decadent meal with a bottle of crisp white wine.

Meat

The meat offering of Provence and the Côte d'Azur is as diverse as its seafood: beef, pork and lamb are staples; rabbit is very popular in stews; and game meat (wild boar and pheasant especially) is a winter favourite.

Preparation follows the seasons: stews in winter, *grillades* (grilled meat) in summer. Favourites include *sauté de lapin aux olives* (rabbit in a tomato sauce with olives) and *daube* (a beef stew from Nice).

A popular-yet-controversial component of Provençal cuisine is foie gras, a food product made from the fattened livers of ducks or geese. In the majority of cases, the production of foie gras involves force-feeding the animals via a feeding tube, often in amounts far exceeding what they would eat voluntarily. Animal welfare groups argue that the process is cruel and inhumane, and the production and import of foie gras is banned in several countries around the world.

Fruit & Vegetables

Vegetables form the backbone of Provençal cooking. Staples like onions, tomatoes, aubergines (eggplant) and courgettes (squash or zucchini) are stewed alongside green peppers, garlic and various aromatic herbs to produce that perennial Provençal stew favourite, ratatouille. Other seasonal wonders include asparagus and artichokes (spring) and courgette flowers (summer).

In summer the tomato is king. There are more than 2500 known varieties in the region and they come in all shapes, sizes and colours. They are outstanding in salads (with chunks of goat's cheese, basil leaves and drizzled with olive oil) or *farcies* (stuffed).

Provence also produces marvellous fruit: sun-ripened strawberries, cantaloupe melons, apricots, peaches, nectarines, plums and cherries all grow in abundance and are a riot of flavour (not to mention colour on the market stands).

Best for Seafood

Le Mazet du Vaccarès, Camargue

Chez Camille, Ramatuelle

La Mère Germaine, Villefranche-sur-Mer

La Cabane aux Coquillages, Stes-Maries-de-la-Mer

Le Rhul, Marseille

PROVENÇAL FOOD & WINE SUNNY GASTRONOMY

BLACK DIAMONDS

Prized by chefs and connoisseurs alike, *la truffe noir* (black truffle, *Tuber melanosporum*) is the most illustrious ingredient of Provençal cuisine. Growing wild on the roots of oak trees, these fungi were traditionally snouted out by pigs but these days are mostly hunted by dogs. It's a lucrative business: depending on their quality, black truffles can fetch as much as €1000 per kilo, so it's no wonder that they're often known in France as *la diamant noir* (black diamond).

Peak truffle season runs from November to March; truffles also grow in summer (when they're known as *truffes d'été*) but fetch lower prices, as they're thought to lack the fine flavour of their winter cousins.

Vegetarians & Vegans

In a country where *viande* (meat) once meant 'food' too, it comes as no surprise that vegetarians and vegans are not catered for well. Here are some tips to help you make the best of Provençal cuisine:

➡ Starters are often vegetarian, so order two or three starters instead of the usual starter and main.

➡ Dishes that can easily be customised include pasta, pizza and salads, all very common across Provence and the Côte d'Azur.

➡ Small restaurants serving just a few daily specials will find it harder to accommodate dietary requirements, so opt for larger establishments instead.

➡ Note that most cheeses in France are made with *lactosérum* (rennet), an enzyme derived from the stomach of a calf or young goat.

Authentic *herbes de Provence* mixes (they are protected by a label) contain 26% rosemary, 26% savory, 26% oregano, 19% thyme and 3% basil. They tend to be used on grilled meat and fish in Provençal cooking.

Condiments & Sauces

Garlic gives Provençal cuisine its kick, and it's a key ingredient in several of the region's dips and condiments.

➡ *Anchoïade* is a strong anchovy paste laced with garlic and olive oil and is delicious served with *bagna cauda* (raw mixed vegetables).

➡ Tapenade is a sharp, black-olive-based dip seasoned with garlic, capers, anchovies and olive oil.

➡ Aïoli, garlic mayonnaise, is an essential component of *aïoli Provençal* – a mountain of vegetables, boiled potatoes, a boiled egg and *coquillages* (small shellfish), all of which are dunked into the pot of aïoli.

➡ *Rouille*, a fiery-pink saffron-flavoured aïoli, is served with *soupe de poisson* (fish soup), bite-sized toasts – and a garlic clove. Rub the garlic over the toast, spread the *rouille* on top, bite it and breathe fire.

PROVENÇAL WINES

With the exception of Châteauneuf-du-Pape and Muscat, Provençal wines might not have the world-famous reputation of some French wine regions, but local vineyards turn out a fantastic range of wines: red, white, rosé.

APPELLATION	BEST FOR	CHARACTERISTICS
Côtes de Provence	rosé, red	rosé is drunk young, reds can be served young or mature, Correns wines are now a leading organic sublabel
Coteaux d'Aix-en-Provence	rosé, red	rosé is dry, aromatic reds
Coteaux-Varois-en-Provence	red, rosé, white	reds must be drunk mature, rosés and whites are ideal summer-meal companions
Côtes du Ventoux & Côtes du Luberon	red	light and fruity
Gigondas	red	pungent fruit and spice aroma, best drunk mature (seven years or older), hence its relatively high price
Bandol	red, rosé	made with the rare *mourvèdre* grape, deep-flavoured reds, well-balanced rosés
Cassis	white	crisp, ideal with seafood
Beaumes de Venise	white	a sweet Muscat wine, drunk as an aperitif or for dessert
Châteauneuf-du-Pape	red, white	strong (minimum alcohol content 12.5%), full bodied, ages beautifully, mineral flavour, can be drunk both young and aged

Sweets & Treats

There is plenty to keep sweet tooths happy. Anise and orange blossoms give *navettes* (canoe-shaped biscuits from Marseille) and *fougassettes* (sweet bread) their distinctive flavours. Almonds are turned into *gâteaux secs aux amandes* (snappy almond biscuits) around Nîmes, and black honey nougat is everywhere.

Nice and Apt excel at *fruits confits* (glazed or crystallised fruits). Even more decadent is St-Tropez' *tarte tropézienne*, a cream-filled sandwich cake christened by Brigitte Bardot. A popular dessert in the Vaucluse is cantaloupe melon doused in Muscat de Beaumes de Venise, a local dessert wine.

Drinks

Pastis: The Milk of Provence

When in Provence, do as the Provençaux do: drink pastis. An aniseed-flavoured, 45%-alcohol drink, pastis was invented in 1932 in Marseille by industrialist Paul Ricard (1909–97).

Amber coloured in the bottle, it turns milky white when mixed with water. It is a classic aperitif but can be drunk any time of day. Bars and cafes serve it straight, allowing you to add the water (five parts water to one part pastis).

A dash of *sirop de menthe* (mint syrup diluted with water) transforms a regular pastis into a *perroquet* (literally 'parrot'). A *tomate* (tomato) is tarted up with one part *grenadine* (pomegranate syrup) and the sweet *Mauresque* is dressed with *orgeat* (a sweet orange and almond syrup).

Leading pastis brands are Pastis 51 and Ricard, both owned by the Ricard empire. Taste them at Marseille's La Maison du Pastis.

Top Local Food Shops

Au Baiser du Mitron, Menton

Fromagerie Ceneri, Cannes

Joël Durand, St-Rémy-de-Provence

Brindille Melchio, Banon

WHERE TO TRY/BUY IT	AREA
Maison des Vins Côtes de Provence, Les Arcs-sur-Argens; Vignerons de Correns, Correns; Château Ste-Roseline, Les Arcs-sur-Argens	Haut-Var
Domaine de la Brillane, Aix-en-Provence	Aix-en-Provence
La Maison des Vins des Coteaux Varois en Provence, La Celle; Château de Miraval, Correns	Haut-Var
Maison de la Truffe et du Vin, Ménerbes; Cave de Bonnieux, Bonnieux; Domaine Faverot, Maubec	Luberon
Caveau de Gigondas, Gigondas	Dentelles de Montmirail
Maison des Vins, Bandol; Domaine de Terrebrune, Ollioules	Bandol
Le Chai Cassidain, Cassis	Cassis
Balma Venitia, Beaumes-de-Venise	Dentelles de Montmirail
Caves du Verger des Papes, Châteauneuf-du-Pape; Domaine de la Solitude, Châteauneuf-du-Pape	Châteauneuf-du-Pape

THE 13 DESSERTS OF CHRISTMAS

December in Provence sees families rush home after Mass on Christmas Eve for *Caleno vo Careno*, a traditional feast of 13 desserts – symbolising Jesus and the 12 apostles – eating at least one bite of each to avoid bad luck in the coming year. Among the culinary delights are *pompe à huile* (leavened cake baked in olive oil and flavoured with orange blossom), sweet black and white nougats (made from honey and almonds), dried figs, almonds, walnuts, raisins, pears, apples, oranges or mandarins, dates, quince jam or paste and *calissons d'Aix* (marzipan-like sweets).

Essential pastis etiquette:

➡ Never order 'a pastis' at the bar – ask for it by brand such as Ricard, Janot or Casanis.

➡ If you find it too strong, add sugar.

➡ Bars in Marseille serve pastis in four glass sizes: a *momie* or *mominette* (dinky shot glass), a *bock* (double-height shot glass), a *tube* (tall, thin juice glass) and a *ballon* (like a brandy balloon).

Best Wine Shops

Cave de la Tour, Nice

La Part des Anges, Marseille

Cave du Félibrige, Aix-en-Provence

Aperitifs & Digestifs

The region is home to a rainbow of spirits and liqueurs, traditionally drunk as a pre- or postdinner treat. Aperitifs tend to be served on the rocks, whilst *digestifs* are served neat in shot-sized glasses.

Liqueur de Châtaignes A chestnut liqueur added to wine for a *kir.*
RinQuinQuin A peach-flavoured aperitif.
Vin d'oranges amères A bitter orange-flavoured aperitif.
Vin de noix A walnut-flavoured aperitif.
Farigoule A thyme-flavoured *digestif.*
Verveine A verbena-flavoured *digestif.*
Amandine An almond-flavoured *digestif.*

Survival Guide

Directory A–Z

Accommodation

For information on accommodation in Provence & the Côte d'Azur, see p29.

Customs Regulations

Goods imported and exported within the EU incur no additional taxes, provided duty has already been paid somewhere within the EU and the goods are for personal consumption. Duty-free shopping is only available if you are leaving the EU. For full details, see www.douane.gouv.fr.

Coming from non-EU countries, the following duty-free adult allowances apply:

➡ 200 cigarettes

➡ 50 cigars

➡ 1L of spirits

➡ 2L of wine

SLEEPING PRICE RANGES

The following price ranges apply to a standard double room with private bathroom, breakfast not included.

€ less than €90

€€ €90–190

€€€ more than €190

Climate

Nice

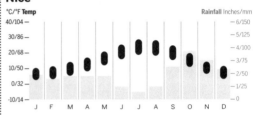

➡ 50mL of perfume

➡ 250mL of eau de toilette

Discount Cards

Many museums and monuments sell *billets jumelés* (combination tickets). Some cities have museum passes. Seniors over 60 or 65 are entitled to discounts on public transport, museums and cinemas. Train discounts are available.

French Riviera Pass (www.frenchrivierapass.com; 1-/2-/3-day pass €26/38/56) Admission to all Nice's paying attractions, plus many nearby.

Snowball Pass (www.snowballpass.com) Skiing discounts.

Electricity

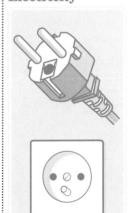

230V/50Hz

BOOK YOUR STAY ONLINE

For more accommodation reviews by Lonely Planet authors, check out http://lonelyplanet.com/hotels/. You'll find independent reviews, as well as recommendations on the best places to stay. Best of all, you can book online.

Embassies & Consulates

All embassies are in Paris, but several countries have consulates in Marseille or Nice.

Australian Embassy (☑01 40 59 33 00; www.france. embassy.gov.au; 4 rue Jean Rey, 15e; MBir Hakeim)

Canadian Embassy (☑01 44 43 29 00; www.amb-canada. fr; 35 av Montaigne, 8e; MFranklin D Roosevelt)

Dutch Consulate (☑04 91 25 66 64; www.amb-pays-bas. fr; 146 rue Paradis, Marseille)

Dutch Consulate (☑04 93 87 52 94; www.amb-pays-bas. fr; 14 rue Rossini, Nice)

German Consulate (☑04 91 16 75 20; www.marseille. diplo.de; 338 av du Prado, Marseille)

Irish Consulate (☑93 15 70 45; www.dfa.ie; av des Citronniers, Monaco)

New Zealand Embassy (☑01 45 01 43 43; www. nzembassy.com/france; 7ter rue Léonard de Vinci, 16e; MVictor Hugo)

UK Consulate (☑04 91 15 72 10; www.gov.uk/government/ world/organisations/british-embassy-paris/office/british-consulate-marseille; 24 av du Prado, Marseille)

US Consulate (☑04 91 54 92 00; http://marseille. usconsulate.gov; place Varian Fry, Marseille)

US Consulate (☑04 93 88 89 55; http://marseille. usconsulate.gov; 7 av Gustave V, Nice)

Food

For information on food in Provence & the Côte d'Azur, see p31 and p284.

Gay & Lesbian Travellers

France is liberal about LGB-TIQ matters, but, as always, rural Provence tends to be more conservative than its big cities. Aix-en-Provence, Nice and Cannes have gay bars, while Marseille has the region's biggest gay community and hosts the late-June **Lesbian & Gay Parade** (www.lgpmarseille.fr).

Centre Évolutif Lilith (CEL; ☑06 99 55 06 02; http:// celmrs.free.fr; 93 La Canebière) Lesbian socialising, activism.

Gay Provence (☑04 91 84 08 96; www.gay-provence.org) Hotel listings.

Gay Map Marseille (www. gaymapmarseille.com) Entertainment in Aix and Marseille.

Health

Before You Go

➡ Carry medications in original, clearly labelled containers in carry-on luggage.

➡ Dental care in France is good; get a predeparture check-up to minimise risk.

➡ No vaccinations required for France, but the World Health Organization recommends travellers be vaccinated against diphtheria, tetanus, measles, mumps, rubella and polio, regardless of destination.

➡ French tap water is safe to drink, but water from fountains reading 'eau non potable' is not.

Availability & Cost of Healthcare

➡ For emergencies, dial ☑15 for ambulance (SAMU) or urgent house call. Or find the nearest hôpital (hospital) or salles des urgence (emergency rooms). Doctors' offices are cabinets médicals.

➡ For medical referrals and minor illnesses, pharmacists dispense advice and sell medications: look for green neon crosses.

➡ Doctor visits cost about €25.

➡ Emergency contraception is available by prescription. Condoms (préservatifs) are commonly available.

Insurance

Medical Insurance

EU citizens and those from Switzerland, Iceland, Norway and Liechtenstein are covered for emergencies by the European Health Insurance Card (EHIC), but not for nonemergencies or repatriation. Every family member needs a card. Seek care from state providers (conventionnés); private healthcare is not covered. Pay directly and keep receipts for reimbursement.

If you're not from Europe you need to determine whether your country has reciprocity with France for

EATING PRICE RANGES

The following prices refer to two-course menus – appetiser and main, or main and dessert.

€ less than €20

€€ €20–40

€€€ more than €40

PRACTICALITIES

Weights & Measures France uses the metric system. To convert kilometres to miles, multiply by 0.6; miles to kilometres, multiply by 1.6.

Electricity Plugs have two round pins; electrical current is 220V/50Hz AC.

Radio Regional news and chat airs in English on Monte Carlo–based Riviera Radio (www.rivieraradio.mc).

Newspapers French-language regional newspapers are *Nice Matin* (www.nicematin.fr) and *La Provence* (www.laprovence.com). English-language regional newspapers are the *Riviera Reporter* (www.riviera-reporter.com) and *Riviera Times* (www.rivieratimes.com).

TV French TV networks broadcast a second audio program in the program's original language, often English: fiddle with your remote.

free medical care. If you need health insurance, strongly consider a policy that covers worst-case scenarios, including emergency medical evacuation. Determine in advance if your insurance pays directly for overseas expenditures or reimburses you later (it's probably the latter). Keep all documentation.

Travel Insurance

We recommend travel insurance covering theft, loss and medical problems. Some policies exclude dangerous activities, including diving, motorcycling and mountaineering. Read the fine print.

Worldwide travel insurance is available at www.lonelyplanet.com/travel-insurance. You can buy, extend and claim online, even if you're already on the road.

Purchasing airline tickets with a credit card may provide *limited* travel-accident insurance. Ask your credit-card company.

Internet Access

➡ Wi-fi (pronounced wee-fee) is offered by many hotels, cafes and some tourist offices. If you need the password, ask for *le code*.

➡ Wi-fi is also available in many public spaces;

check coverage at www.journaldunet.com/wifi.

➡ 3G is widely available in urban areas, but check roaming rates with your provider before you switch it on.

➡ Internet cafes provide access for €4 to €6 per hour but are becoming rare.

Language Courses

The government site www.diplomatie.gouv.fr (under 'Francophony') and www.europa-pages.com/france list language schools.

The **Centre Méditerranéen d'Études Françaises** (☑ 04 93 78 21 59; www.centremed.monte-carlo.mc; chemin des Oliviers, Cap d'Ail) is a Côte d'Azur language school, operating since 1952.

Legal Matters

➡ French police have wide powers of search and seizure, and may demand identification at any time, regardless of 'probable cause'.

➡ Foreigners must be able to prove immigration status (eg passport, visa, residency permit).

➡ Verbally (or physically) abusing police officers carries hefty fines, even imprisonment.

➡ You may refuse to sign a police statement, and you have the right to request a copy.

➡ Those arrested are innocent until proven guilty but may be held until trial. The website www.service-public.fr details rights.

➡ French police are ultra-strict with security. Never leave baggage unattended at airports or stations: suspicious objects may be destroyed.

➡ French law makes no distinction between 'hard' and 'soft' drugs.

➡ The penalty for personal use of *stupéfiants* (including cannabis) can be a one-year jail sentence and a €3750 fine but may be lessened to a stern talking-to or compulsory rehab.

➡ Public drunkenness (*ivresse*) is punishable by a €150 fine. It's illegal to drive with a blood-alcohol concentration (BAC) over 0.05%. Police conduct random breathalyser tests.

➡ Smoking is illegal in public interiors, including restaurants and bars.

Maps

Driving, cycling and hiking maps are widely available at *maisons de la presse* (newsagencies), *papeteries* (stationery shops), tourist offices, bookshops and petrol stations. Quality maps cost about €7 or €8. The website http://fr.mappy.com has online maps and a journey planner, including tolls and petrol costs.

Free street *plans* (maps) distributed by tourist offices range from superb to useless.

FFRP (www.ffrandonnee.fr) Topographic hiking maps.

Institut Géographique National (IGN; www.ign.fr)

France's definitive map publishers, great for hiking and cycling.

Michelin (sales www.michelin-boutique.com) Brilliant atlases and driving maps.

Money

The euro (€) is the only legal tender in France and Monaco. To track rates and find local exchange bureaux, see http://travelmoney. moneysavingexpert.com.

ATMs

ATMs (*distributeurs automatiques de billets* or *points d'argent*) are the easiest means of obtaining cash, but banks charge foreign-transaction fees (usually 2% to 3%), plus a per-use ATM charge. Check with your bank. Cirrus and Maestro networks are common.

Credit & Debit Cards

Credit and debit cards are widely accepted, although some restaurants and B&Bs may only accept cash.

North American cards with magnetic stripes don't work on (certain) autoroutes or at unattended 24-hour petrol stations – which can leave you in a sticky situation if you have no alternative method of payment.

➡ Nearly everywhere requires a card with a

chip and PIN. Notify your bank/card provider before departure to avoid a block on your account.

➡ Visa (Carte Bleue – or CB – in France) and Master-Card (Access or Eurocard) are common. American Express is less so, but Amex offices provide exchange and travel services.

➡ Credit cards generally incur a more favourable exchange rate than debit cards, but it depends entirely on your bank/credit-card provider.

➡ Most credit cards charge a foreign-transaction fee (generally around 2.5%), but again it depends on the provider. Some credit cards charge a 0% fee for overseas use.

➡ Consider getting a prepaid currency card, which you can load with currency before departure. You won't incur a foreign-transaction fee, and if it's lost you just cancel the card and order a replacement. Most importantly, you don't lose the funds.

Money Changers

➡ Banks usually charge stiff €3 to €5 fees per foreign-currency transaction – if they change money at all.

➡ *Bureaux de change* (exchange bureaux) are

faster and easier, are open longer and usually have better rates.

➡ Some post offices exchange travellers cheques and banknotes but charge a €5 commission for cash; most won't take US$100 bills.

Travellers Cheques

Secure and fee free, but not widely accepted. Must be converted at exchange bureaux, and rates aren't always favourable.

Opening Hours

French business hours are regulated by a number of laws, including the 35-hour working week. We generally list high-season hours.

➡ Most businesses close over lunch, usually between noon and 2pm.

➡ French law requires that most businesses close on Sunday, with the exception of grocery stores, *boulangeries* (bakeries), florists and tourist businesses.

➡ Restaurants usually close at least one or two days a week.

➡ Most museums are closed on Monday or Tuesday.

➡ In rural Provence, most businesses open only Pâques à la Toussaint (Easter to All Saints' Day, 1 November).

Public Holidays

French Public Holidays

The following *jours fériés* (public holidays) are observed in France:

New Year's Day (Jour de l'An) 1 January

Easter Sunday & Monday (Pâques & lundi de Pâques) Late March/April

May Day (Fête du Travail) 1 May

TIPPING

By law, restaurants and cafes are *service compris* (15% service included), thus there's no need to leave a *pourboire* (tip). If you're satisfied with the service, it's customary to leave a euro or two on the table.

Bars Round to nearest euro

Hotel housekeepers €1 to €1.50 per day

Porters €1 to €1.50 per bag

Restaurants Generally 2% to 5%; 10% if exceptional

Taxis 10% to 15%

Toilet attendants €0.20 to €0.50

Tour guides €1 to €2 per person

Victoire 1945 8 May – celebrates the Allied victory that ended WWII

Ascension Thursday (L'Ascension) May – the 40th day after Easter

Pentecost/Whit Sunday & Whit Monday (Pentecôte & lundi de Pentecôte) mid-May to mid-June – celebrated seventh Sunday after Easter

Bastille Day/National Day (Fête Nationale) 14 July

Assumption Day (L'Assomption) 15 August

All Saints' Day (La Toussaint) 1 November

Remembrance Day (L'onze Novembre) 11 November – marks WWI armistice

Christmas (Noël) 25 December

Monégasque Public Holidays

Monaco shares the same holidays, except 8 May, 14 July and 11 November. Additionally:

Feast of Ste-Dévote 27 January – Monaco's saint's day

Corpus Christi June – three weeks after Ascension

National Day (Fête Nationale) 19 November

Immaculate Conception 8 December

Safe Travel

France is a safe destination. Petty theft and burglary are the main problems, but assault is rare.

France's hunting season runs September to February. Warning signs on trees and fences read *'chasseurs'* or *'chasse gardée'.* Wear bright colours when hiking.

Beaches & Rivers

Watch for pale-purple jellyfish on beaches.

Major rivers are connected to hydroelectric stations and flood suddenly when dams open. Ask tourist offices about *l'ouverture des barrages,* (opening dams) commonplace in summer.

Swimming is prohibited in reservoirs with unstable banks (eg Lac de Ste-Croix, southwest of Gorges du Verdon; Lac de Castillon; and Lac de Chaudanne, northeast of the gorges). Sailing, windsurfing and canoeing are restricted to flagged areas.

Extreme Weather

Thunderstorms – sometimes violent and dangerous – are common August and September. Check weather (*la météo*) before embarking on hikes. Carry pocket rain gear and extra layers to prevent hypothermia. Year-round, mistral winds can be maddening.

Forest Fires

In fire emergency, dial 🕿18. Forest fires are common July and August, and spread incredibly fast. July to mid-September, high-risk trails close. Never walk in closed zones.

Forests are criss-crossed by fire roads. Signposted DFCI (Défense de la Forêt Contre l'Incendie; forest-fire defence team) tracks are closed to motorists but open to walkers.

Campfires are forbidden. Barbecues are forbidden in many areas in July and August.

Theft

Theft from luggage, pockets, cars, trains and launderettes is widespread, particularly along the Côte d'Azur. Beware pickpockets in crowded tourist areas.

➡ Keep close watch on bags, especially in markets, at train and bus stations, at outdoor cafes, on beaches and during overnight train rides (lock your compartment door).

➡ Break-ins to unattended vehicles are a big problem – leave nothing of value inside.

➡ If travelling on trains, don't leave laptops, tablets and smartphones on display if you go to the toilet or fall asleep. Try not to stare at your smartphone in train stations; conceal it when not using it.

➡ If you're worried, lock your passport in your safe, or ask at reception to use the hotel's safe if your room doesn't have one.

➡ Bring photocopies of important documents such as passports, driving licences and travel-insurance policies; they're much easier to replace if you have copies.

➡ Carry your passport number (or a photocopy) and your driver's licence for ID.

STANDARD HOURS

Banks 9am to noon and 2pm to 5pm Monday to Friday or Tuesday to Saturday

Bars 7pm to 1am Monday to Saturday

Cafes 7am or 8am to 10pm or 11pm Monday to Saturday

Clubs 10pm to 3am, 4am or 5am Thursday to Saturday

Post offices 8.30am or 9am to 5pm or 6pm Monday to Friday, 8am to noon Saturday

Restaurants Lunch noon to 2.30pm, dinner 7pm to 11pm

Shops 9am or 10am to 6.30pm or 7pm Monday or Tuesday to Saturday

Supermarkets 8.30am to 7pm Monday to Saturday, 8.30am to 12.30pm Sunday

➤ When swimming, don't leave valuables unattended – you might have to take turns. On the Prado beaches in Marseille, consider placing valuables in one of the free (staffed) lockers.

➤ Aggressive theft from cars stopped at red lights is an occasional problem in Marseille, Nice and larger cities; keep doors locked and windows up when idling.

➤ Common cons: thief finds a gold ring in your path, or lays a newspaper on your restaurant table, or approaches to ask if you speak English. Ignore children with clipboards, especially those playing deaf.

Telephone

Mobile Phones

➤ French mobile-phone numbers begin with 06 or 07.

➤ France uses GSM 900/1800, compatible with Europe and Australia but incompatible with North American GSM 1900 or the Japanese system, unless you have a tri-band or quad-band phone.

➤ France's main carriers are **Bouygues** (www.bouyguestelecom.fr), **Orange** (www.orange.fr) and **SFR** (www.sfr.com).

➤ For European travellers, roaming charges have recently come down thanks to EU regulation, but it's still likely to be more expensive than back home. You'll probably receive a text message detailing rates when you first switch on your phone. SMS texting is always cheaper than making a call.

➤ Some providers offer call and data packages that cover travel in other European countries; check before you leave.

➤ For non-European travellers, it may be cheaper to buy a French SIM card or a French pay-as-you-go handset than to use your own

phone. If so, buy when you land in Paris, where more salespeople speak English than in Provence.

Dialing Codes

➤ **Calling France (or Monaco) from home** Dial your country's international-access code, then 33 for France (or 377 for Monaco), then the 10-digit number, without the initial zero.

➤ **Calling abroad from France** Dial ♪00 for international access, then the country code (1 for US, 44 UK, 16 Australia), then the area code and local number, minus any initial zeros.

➤ **Hotel calls** Very expensive and unregulated, usually €0.30 per minute locally.

Phonecards & Pay Phones

For instructions on using public phones, push the button engraved with dual flags.

Public phones accept two kinds of *télécartes* (phonecards): *cartes à la puce* (magnetic-chip cards) issued by Orange for €8 or €15; and *cartes à code* (cards with free access number and prepaid scratch-off code). Find cards at post offices, *tabacs* (tabacconists) and newsagents.

Phonecards with codes have cheaper rates than Orange.

Useful Numbers & Codes

Emergency numbers Free from pay phones.

International access code ♪00

France country code ♪33

Monaco country code ♪377

Directory enquiries ♪12 or ♪11 87 12 (€1, plus €0.23 per minute). Not all operators speak English. For help in English with all Orange services, see http://www.orange.com/en/home or call 09 69 36 39 00.

International directory enquiries ♪11 87 00

Time

France uses the 24-hour military clock (eg 20.00 is 8pm) and Central European Time, one hour ahead of GMT/UTC. During daylight saving (last Sunday in March to last Sunday in October), France is two hours ahead of GMT/UTC.

Toilets

➤ Public toilets are signposted *toilettes* or WC. In towns, look for public toilets near the town hall, port, public squares or parking areas.

➤ Mechanical, coin-operated toilets are free or €0.20. (Never dodge in after the previous user or you'll be doused with disinfectant!) If you exceed 15 minutes, the door automatically opens. Green means *libre* (available); red *occupé* (busy).

➤ A few older cafes and petrol stations still have hole-in-the-floor Turkish-style toilets. Provided you hover, they're hygienic, but stand clear when flushing!

➤ The French are used to unisex facilities.

Tourist Information

Almost every city, town and village has an *office de tourisme* (tourist office, occasionally still known as a *syndicat d'initiative* in some areas). They're usually well run and can provide loads of information on accommodation, activities and places to visit. In larger towns and cities, most offices have English-speaking staff.

Travellers with Disabilities

France is slowly improving access for travellers with disabilities (*visiteurs handicapés*), but inevitably there are problems – narrow streets, cobbles, a lack of curb ramps and a lack of elevators in old hotels, to name a few.

➡ Check carefully whether your hotel or B&B has an elevator and is fully accessible – steps and small bathrooms are all common pitfalls.

➡ Most parking areas have dedicated sections for drivers with disabilities (bring your parking placard).

➡ Some beaches are wheelchair accessible – flagged *handiplages* on city maps – in Cannes, Marseille, Nice, Hyères, Ste-Maxime and Monaco.

➡ Michelin's *Guide Rouge* and **Gîtes de France** (www. gites-de-france-paca.com) flag wheelchair access in their listings.

➡ Most SNCF trains are wheelchair accessible; major train stations will have staff who can assist you as you get on board.

➡ Detailed information is available on the SNCF Accessibilité website (www. accessibilite.sncf.com).

Visas

For up-to-date information on visa requirements see www.diplomatie.gouv.fr.

➡ EU nationals and citizens of Iceland, Norway and Switzerland need only passport or national identity card to enter France and work. However, nationals of the 12 countries that joined the EU in 2004 and 2007 are subject to residency and work limitations.

➡ Citizens of Australia, Canada, Israel, Hong Kong, Japan, Malaysia, New Zealand, Singapore, the USA and many Latin American countries need no tourist visa for stays shorter than 90 days.

➡ Others must apply for a Schengen visa, allowing unlimited travel throughout 26 European countries for a 90-day period. Apply at the consulate of the country that's your first port of entry or that will be your principal destination. Among other particulars, you must provide proof of travel and repatriation insurance, and prove you have sufficient money to support yourself.

➡ Tourist visas *cannot* be extended, except in emergencies (such as medical problems). Leave before your visa expires and reapply from outside France.

Transport

GETTING THERE & AWAY

Entering the Country

With the exception of travellers coming from the UK, the Channel Islands and Andorra, there are no checkpoints between European countries. Arriving in France from any non-EU countries, you'll need to show a valid passport (and visa, if applicable) to clear customs.

Flights, tours and rail tickets can be booked online at lonelyplanet.com/booking.

Air

Airports & Airlines

Air France (www.airfrance.com) is the main national carrier, and provides the most links between French cities – although it's often cheaper and faster to catch a TGV (high-speed train). Budget airlines (including easyJet, Flybe, City-jet and Ryanair) serve various European destinations.

Provence has two major airports: Marseille-Provence and Nice-Côte d'Azur. The much smaller regional airports in Avignon, Nîmes and Toulon offer seasonal flights.

Avignon-Provence (AVN; ☑04 90 81 51 51; www.avignon.aeroport.fr; Caumont) Eight kilometres southeast of Avignon. Currently served by budget carriers Flybe (Southampton and Birmingham); Cityjet (London City) and VLM (Liège).

Marseille-Provence (MRS; ☑04 42 14 14 14; www.marseille.aeroport.fr) Twenty-five kilometres northeast of Marseille. Year-round flights around France, Europe, North Africa, the Middle East and Canada.

Nice-Côte d'Azur (☑08 20 42 33 33; www.nice.aeroport.fr; ☎) Six kilometres west of Nice. Year-round flights to most European cities, plus North Africa, the Middle East, New York and Quebec.

Nîmes (FNI; ☑04 66 70 49 49; www.nimes-aeroport.fr) Fifteen kilometres south of Nîmes. Served by Ryanair, with current flights to London Luton, Liverpool, Brussels and Fez (in Morocco).

Toulon-Hyères (TLN; ☑08 25 01 83 87; www.toulon-hyeres.aeroport.fr; ☎) Twenty-five kilometres east of Toulon. Daily flights to Paris, as well as seasonal routes to Rotterdam, Bournemouth, Brussels and London.

Land

Bicycle

European Bike Express (☑in UK 01430-422 111; www.bike-express.co.uk) Transports cyclists and bikes from the UK to destinations across France.

Bus

Eurolines (☑08 92 89 90 91; www.eurolines.com) operates Europe's largest international bus network, with routes between major cities, including Nice, Marseille and Avignon, and the rest of Europe.

Buses operate daily in summer, several times a week in winter; advance tickets required. The **Eurolines**

CLIMATE CHANGE & TRAVEL

Every form of transport that relies on carbon-based fuel generates CO_2, the main cause of human-induced climate change. Modern travel is dependent on aeroplanes, which might use less fuel per kilometre per person than most cars but travel much greater distances. The altitude at which aircraft emit gases (including CO_2) and particles also contributes to their climate change impact. Many websites offer 'carbon calculators' that allow people to estimate the carbon emissions generated by their journey and, for those who wish to do so, to offset the impact of the greenhouse gases emitted with contributions to portfolios of climate-friendly initiatives throughout the world. Lonely Planet offsets the carbon footprint of all staff and author travel.

TRANSPORT LAND

Pass (www.eurolines.com/en/eurolines-pass; 15-/30-day high-season adult pass €375/490, under 26yr €315/405) allows unlimited travel between 51 cities.

From within France – and often from other nearby countries such as Spain and Italy – it's easiest to reach Provence by train.

Car & Motorcycle

From Paris, consider riding the high-speed TGV to Avignon or Marseille, then picking up a rental car; this shaves four hours off travel time to Provence and dodges tolls.

To bring your own vehicle, you'll need the registration papers, proof of third-party (liability) insurance and a valid driving licence. Vehicles entering France must display a sticker identifying country of registration.

Between the UK and France, high-speed Auto-Trains by **Eurotunnel** (☑France 08 10 63 03 04, UK 08 443 35 35 35; www.eurotunnel.com) shuttle through the Channel Tunnel between Folkestone and Coquelles (35 minutes, up to four hourly, 24 hours). Note: LPG and CNG tanks are not permitted, and campers and caravans must take ferries.

See p301 for full road rules.

Train

Rail Europe (☑in Canada 1 800 361 7245, in the UK 0844 848 5848, in the USA 1 800 622 8600; www.raileurope.com) offers online booking and general advice on European rail travel.

The **Man in Seat 61** (www.seat61.com) is another great resource, with timetables and insider tips.

FROM THE REST OF FRANCE

France's pride and joy is the state-owned **SNCF** (Société Nationale des Chemins de Fer Français; www.voyages-sncf.com), which runs the country's entire rail network.

The SNCF's flagship train service is the high-speed, formidably punctual **TGV** (Train à Grande Vitesse; www.tgv.com), which is capable of carrying you all the way from Paris to the Côte d'Azur in under four hours. The route runs from Paris' Gare du Nord via destinations including Orange, Avignon, Aix-en-Provence and Marseille (unfortunately, a second proposed route to Nice has been shelved). Note that the TGV stations are several kilometres from the town centre but are linked by trains or shuttle buses.

➠ You can choose to travel in 1st or 2nd class; 1st has bigger seats, better food and free wi-fi.

➠ Booking online in advance is always cheaper than buying on the day, especially for intercity services. Travelling off-peak gets a considerable discount.

➠ You can also buy tickets direct from mainline train stations, or SNCF ticket centres (boutiques).

➠ As a rough guide, a single 2nd-class fare from Paris to Marseille starts at around €89.50 and the trip takes just under 3½ hours.

➠ An important note if you buy online with a foreign credit card: SNCF automated ticket machines often have trouble recognising overseas cards, so you will probably have to collect your tickets from the ticket office instead (just show them your reservation receipt or reservation number).

WITH CAR

SNCF **AutoTrains** (☑in UK 0844 848 4066; http://auto-train.uk.voyages-sncf.com/en) take the discomfort out of cross-France travel, allowing you to drop off your car at the AutoTrain station at Paris Bercy, and let the train driver do the rest of the work. Cars are loaded one hour before departure, and unloaded 30 minutes after arrival at your station of choice. (Avignon,

Marseille, Nice, Fréjus and Toulon are all options.) As a price guide, a one-way fare to the south starts at £107; at the time of writing, bookings were taken only by telephone. Note that you have to arrange your own travel separately.

WITH BICYCLE

On certain trains (flagged with bike symbols on timetables), bikes are allowed in luggage vans without being packed; usually you don't need to reserve space, but it's worth asking when you book, as space is not always available on peak-time trains. On TGVs, bike space must be reserved in advance. See the multilingual SNCF brochure *Guide Train & Vélo* (free), available at stations, or www.velo.sncf.com.

The useful **Bagages à domicile** (☑00 33 892 35 35 35; http://bagages.voyages-sncf.com/) luggage service transports bicycles door to door in France, for €80, delivering within 48 hours, excluding Saturday afternoon, Sunday and holidays.

FROM UK

The **Eurostar** (www.eurostar.com) whisks you between London and Paris in 2¼ hours, with onward trains across the rest of France. Eurostar's new integrated service to the south of France runs direct from London to Lyon (four hours, 41 minutes), Avignon (five hours, 49 minutes) and Marseille (6½ hours). All trains travel via Lille, where you are required to leave the train briefly for security and immigration checks. Standard single fares start at £99.

For other destinations in the south (including Aix-en-Provence), you can catch the Eurostar to Paris, and then catch a high-speed TGV – although it's worth noting that this requires a schlep on the metro across Paris from the Gare du Nord to the Gare du Lyon, which can be a real pain if you have lots of luggage.

FROM ITALY & SPAIN

Nice is the major rail hub along the busy Barcelona–Rome line.

➡ **Nice–Rome** Around €85, nine hours

➡ **Nice–Barcelona** Around €130, 10 hours

➡ **Nice–Milan** Around €72, five hours

Sea

Ferries cross from Nice, Marseille and Toulon to Corsica (France), Sardinia (Italy) and North Africa. Vehicles allowed; reservations essential.

From the Rest of France

Ferries from Corsica to Provençal ports are operated by the following companies.

Corsica Ferries (☑04 95 32 95 95; www.corsicaferries.com) Year-round; Nice and Toulon to Ajaccio, Bastia, Calvi and Île Rousse.

La Méridionale (☑08 10 20 13 20; www.lameridionale.fr) SNCM subsidiary; year-round between Marseille and Ajaccio, Bastia and Propriano.

SNCM (☑08 91 70 18 01; www.sncm.fr; 61 bd des Dames; M Joliette) Regular ferries from Nice and Marseille to Corsica and Sardinia, plus long-distance routes to Algeria and Tunisia.

From Italy

SNCM runs multiple car ferries weekly, from Marseille to Sardinia (Sardaigne, in French). Sailing time 17 hours. High-season, one-way passage, including tax, costs around €100/120 for an armchair/cabin berth. Discounts for passengers under 25 and over 60. Transporting cars costs an extra €110.

Tickets and information are available in Provence from SNCM offices.

From UK & Ireland

There are no direct ferries to Provence, but year-round ferries connect the UK with French ports including Calais, Roscoff, Cherbourg, Dunkerque and St-Malo. Dover to Calais is shortest. There are lots of companies, including big players **Brittany Ferries** (☑08 25 82 88 28; www.brittany-ferries.co.uk) and **P&O Ferries** (www.poferries.com).

Check out online booking agencies such as **Ferry Savers** (☑In the UK 371 8021; www.ferrysavers.co.uk) for cheap fares; phone bookings incur fees.

GETTING AROUND

Bicycle

Provence, particularly the Luberon, is great for cycling, with quiet back roads and a number of dedicated bike paths – although it's worth considering summer temperatures when planning your expedition.

By law, bicycles must have two functioning brakes, bell, red reflector on back, yellow reflectors on pedals. After sunset, and when visibility is poor, cyclists must be equipped with a white light in front and red light in rear. Cyclists must ride single file when being overtaken by vehicles or other cyclists. Cycling off-road in national parks is forbidden.

Useful resource: **Fédération Française de Cyclisme** (☑01 49 35 69 00; www.ffc.fr).

Most towns have bike-rental outlets; the daily cost is €18 to €25.

Boat

Ferries connect the mainland with offshore islands, notably to/from St-Tropez and St-Raphaël, Port Grimaud and Ste-Maxime in warmer months (generally April to October).

Canal boating is a popular pastime in France. The Canal du Midi – France's most popular – stretches 240km east from Toulouse towards the Camargue and the Canal du Rhône. West of Toulouse, the Canal du Midi connects with the Garonne River,

INTERPRETING SCHEDULES

Transport schedules use abbreviations. The most common:

tlj (tous les jours) daily

sauf except

lun Monday

mar Tuesday

mer Wednesday

jeu Thursday

ven Friday

sam Saturday

dim Sunday

jours fériés (jf) holidays

---

leading west to the Atlantic Ocean. Anyone over 18 can pilot a houseboat or barge, but first-timers must undergo brief training to obtain a temporary pleasure-craft permit (*carte de plaisance*). The speed limit is 6km/h in canals, 10km/h on rivers.

Prices range from €450 to over €3000 per week. A few online rental agencies:

➡ **Canal Boat Holidays** (www.canalboatholidays.com)

➡ **H2olidays** (Barging in France; www.barginginfrance.com)

➡ **Le Boat** (☑in France 04 68 94 42 80, in the UK 0844 463 3594; www.leboat.net)

➡ **Rive de France** (☑04 67 37 14 60; www.rive-de-france.tm.fr)

Bus

Services and routes are extremely limited in rural areas, where buses primarily transport school children. Bus transport is useful only if you have no car, and trains don't go where you want, but you may get stuck until the next day. Tourist offices always have schedules.

Autocars (regional buses) are operated by multiple companies, which have offices at *gares routières* (bus stations) in larger towns.

PRIORITÉ À DROITE

The key road rule that catches foreign drivers out in France is *priorité à droite*. This means that, unless otherwise indicated, any car entering at an intersection (eg via a slip road onto a motorway) has the right of way. Drivers may shoot out from intersections directly in front of you: approach with caution!

Sometimes intersections are marked *vous n'avez pas la priorité* (you do not have right of way) or *cédez le passage* (yield); follow the rules accordingly.

Priorité à droite is suspended on priority roads, which are marked by a yellow diamond with a white border; it's reinstated when you see a black bar through the yellow diamond.

Car & Motorcycle

Your own vehicle is essential for exploring Provence's smaller towns, many inaccessible by public transport.

Autumn to spring, driving is easy along the Côte d'Azur, but *not* in July and August, when intense traffic chokes all roads and it takes hours to go a few kilometres. For English-language traffic reports, tune to 107.7MHz FM, which updates every 30 minutes in summer.

There are four types of intercity roads, each with alphanumeric designation:

Autoroutes (eg A8) High-speed multilane highways with *péages* (tolls)

Routes Nationales (N, RN) National highways

Routes Départementales (D) County roads

Routes Communales (C, V) Tertiary routes

Autoroutes are always fastest (summer traffic notwithstanding), but they're expensive due to *péages* – Marseille to Nice costs €13.20 in tolls, Paris to Nice €75.

Pay close attention at toll booths: 'CB' (Carte Bleue) indicates credit-card lanes; yellow arrows are exclusively for prepaid drivers; green arrows are for cash. If you choose the wrong lane, you'll have to back up – nearly impossible in summer.

For traffic information, see www.autoroutes.fr.

Calculate toll and fuel costs at www.viamichelin. com and www.mappy.fr.

Fuel & Spare Parts

Essence (petrol or gasoline), also called *carburant* (fuel), costs roughly €1.65 a litre, €1.40 a litre for diesel. Autoroute service areas (*aires*) are priciest but open 24 hours; hypermarkets cheapest.

➡ Unleaded (*sans plomb*) pump handles are usually green; diesel (*diesel, gazoil or gazole*) pumps are yellow or black.

➡ Many service stations close Saturday afternoon and Sunday, and in small towns during lunch.

➡ Some petrol pumps dispense fuel after hours, but *only* with chip-and-pin credit cards.

➡ North American credit cards (with magnetic stripe instead of chip and PIN) do *not* work at 24-hour pumps. To purchase fuel at night with magnetic-stripe cards, take the autoroute.

➡ When travelling in mountain regions, keep the tank full.

➡ If your car is *en panne* (broken down), you'll need services for your particular *marque* (make). Peugeot, Renault and Citroën garages are common, but you may have trouble in remote areas finding mechanics to service foreign cars.

Hire

All the major car-hire firms (including Hertz, Avis, Europcar, Budget and Sixt) have a presence at airports, TGV stations and major town centres. Smaller French firms like ADA and DLM sometimes offer cheaper rates.

Most companies require drivers to be at least 21, to have had a driving licence for at least a year, and to pay with an international credit card. Drivers under 25 usually pay a surcharge.

Online comparison services such as **Auto Europe** (☑in the US 1 888 223 5555, from France 800 223 55555; www.autoeurope.com), **Holiday Autos** (☑0871 472 5229; www. holidayautos.co.uk) and **Moneymaxim** (www.moneymaxim. co.uk) offer good discounts, especially for longer hire periods, but make sure you check very carefully what's included in the package – especially insurance, breakdown cover, tax, unlimited mileage (*kilométrage limité* or *illimité*) and, most importantly, the excess.

Extra points:

➡ Automatic transmissions are very rare: reserve well ahead.

➡ French rental cars have distinctive licence plates, making them a target for thieves. Don't leave any valuables inside.

➡ Remember to check whether the car takes *gazole* (diesel) or *sans-plomb* (unleaded), and whether it was supplied with a full or empty tank when you picked it up.

➡ Rental cars should come with registration papers (usually in the glove compartment), but double-check before you drive off.

MAJOR HIRE FIRMS

ADA (☑08 25 16 91 69; www. ada.fr)

Avis (☑08 20 05 05 05; www. avis.com)

Budget (☑08 25 00 35 64; www.budget.com)

Easycar (☎in France 08 26 10 73 23, in the UK 08710 500 444; www.easycar.com)

Europcar (☎08 25 35 83 58; www.europcar.com)

Hertz (☎08 25 09 13 13; www.hertz.com)

Enterprise Rent-a-Car (☎08 25 16 12 12; www. enterprise.fr)

Purchase-Repurchase Plans

If you live outside the EU and will be in France (or Europe) from one to six months (up to a year, if studying), by far the cheapest option is to 'purchase' a brand-new car, then 'sell' it back – called *achat-rachat*. You only pay for the time it's in your possession, but the 'temporary transit' (TT) paperwork makes the car legally yours – and it's exempt from huge taxes. Such cars carry red licence plates, instantly identifying drivers as foreigners.

Eligibility is restricted to non-EU residents (EU citizens are eligible only if they reside outside the EU); minimum age is 18 (sometimes 21). You must order at minimum six weeks ahead and prepay your balance before the factory builds your car – and you get to pick the model. Diesel (*gasoil*) vehicles are more expensive up front, but you pay less for fuel. All plans include unlimited kilometres, 24-hour towing and breakdown service, and comprehensive insurance with zero deductible/excess.

Companies offering *achat-rachat* are **Citroën** (www.eurocartt.com, www. citroendriveeurope.com, www. citroentt.com), **Peugeot** (www.peugeot-openeurope. com) and **Renault** (www. renault-eurodrive.com).

Insurance

Car-hire companies provide mandatory third-party liability insurance, but other important insurances cost extra, including collision-damage waiver (CDW, *assurance tous risques*), which covers the cost of the vehicle in the event of accident or theft.

Most hire agreements come with a hefty excess (known as the *franchise* or *déductible*, and usually between €750 and €1500, depending on the size of the vehicle. This is the maximum sum for which you will be liable if you have an accident or bring the car back damaged.

All car-hire firms will offer you the chance to reduce this excess to zero, but it is nearly always very expensive – often adding between €5 and €20 extra to the daily hire rate. It's up to you whether you take it out, but it's worth remembering that even a minor scrape will often incur a hefty bill.

An alternative is to take out separate excess insurance – if you damage the car, you pay the agreed excess when you return the vehicle, and then claim the sum back from your insurance provider (take photos and keep hold of all relevant documents such as accident reports, damage sheets and so on). It's more complicated but works out much, much cheaper than the rental firms. Some credit-card providers also cover CDW if you pay using their card; check their terms before you travel.

If you don't have a zero-excess contract, most rental firms will preload a sum onto your credit card to cover the excess when you pick up the vehicle. Make sure you have enough available credit on your card to cover this amount.

Parking

Provence's ancient villages and cities can be hellish on drivers, with narrow streets, confusing one-way systems and limited parking. Many hotels have no garages: guests drop off bags, then either claim a resident's parking permit from the hotel (if available at all) and find street parking or hunt down a garage. Ask when reserving.

In city centres, look for 'P' signs to locate parking (often underground); expect to pay about €2.50/20 per hour/day.

Road Rules

Enforcement of French traffic laws (see www.securite-routiere.gouv.fr) has been stepped up considerably. Speed cameras are common and hard to spot (they're the small grey boxes you'll see by the roadside). Sometimes the presence of a speed camera is indicated by signs (reading *Contrôles Radar Fréquents*) – but not always.

Mobile radar traps, unmarked police vehicles and roadside drug tests are also commonplace. If you see a flash, you've probably been caught. If you're driving a rental car, tickets are usually charged to your credit card, often with a hefty administration charge. If you're driving your own vehicle, you might receive a ticket in the mail, or you might not – minor infractions may not be worth the trouble for police to pursue, but there are no hard and fast rules.

Fines for many infractions are given on the spot; serious violations can lead to confiscation of licence and vehicle. If you have an accident, you will be drug tested.

Key points:

➡ Blood-alcohol limit is 0.05% (0.5g per litre of blood) – roughly the equivalent of two glasses of wine for a 75kg adult. Stick to one glass to be on the safe side.

➡ All passengers must wear seat belts.

SPEED LIMITS

Populated areas 50km/h

Undivided N and D highways 90km/h (80km/h if raining)

Non-autoroute divided highways 110km/h (100km/h if raining)

Autoroutes 130km/h (110km/h if raining, 60km/h if icy)

➡ Children less than 10kg must travel in backward-facing child seats; children up to 36kg must travel in child seats in the vehicle's rear seat.

➡ UK and Irish vehicles must fit headlight reflectors to avoid dazzling oncoming traffic.

➡ Only hands-free, speaker-phone mobiles are allowed – no handsets, no texting.

➡ US and Canadian drivers, note: turning right at a red light is illegal.

➡ All vehicles in France must carry a high-visibility safety vest (stored inside the vehicle, not the trunk) and a reflective warning triangle. The recent law mandating a single-use breathalyser kit has effectively been shelved; in theory you are still supposed to carry one, but you can't be fined for not doing so.

➡ Drivers of two-wheeled motorised vehicles (except electric bicycles) must wear helmets. No special licence is required for motorbikes under 50cc.

➡ Some roads in Haute-Provence require the use of snow chains in winter.

➡ In forested areas, fire roads signposted DFCI (Défense de la Forêt Contre l'Incendie) are strictly off limits to private vehicles.

Taxi

Find taxi ranks at train and bus stations, or telephone for radio taxis. Fares are metered, with minimum fare €6; rates are roughly €1.60 per kilometre for one-way journeys.

Train

SNCF's regional train network is served by TER (Trains Express Régionales) trains; bookings and timetables are handled by the SNCF. A popular journey is the narrow-gauge **Train des Pignes** (Pine Cone Train; www.train-

STAMP YOUR TICKET!

You must time-stamp your ticket in a *composteur* (free-standing yellow post at the entrance to train platforms) immediately before boarding, or you'll incur a hefty fine. Smartphones displaying barcode boarding passes are exempt.

provence.com; single fare Nice to Digne €23.30), which links Nice with Digne-les-Bains.

Reservations are not mandatory on most regional trains, but advance purchase is a good idea in summer.

SNCF Fares

Train fares vary widely according to demand and your chosen times and dates of travel. Generally the further in advance you book, the cheaper the fare.

The new **Ouigo** (www.ouigo.com) service allows cut-price travel on certain TGVs (including some to Aix-en-Provence and Avignon). Tickets must be purchased from three weeks to four hours prior to departure; tickets are sent by email and must be printed out, or downloaded via the Ouigo app (Android and iPhone). You're allowed one piece of cabin luggage and one piece of hand luggage and a pushchair; you can buy extra bags for €5 in advance, or a hefty €20 on the day of travel.

➡ Booking via the **SNCF** (www.voyages-sncf.com) website is the easiest way to compare fares. A 1st-class fare costs 20% to 30% more than a 2nd-class one.

➡ The cheapest fares are Prem's, which are non-changeable and non-refundable. Flexible tickets always cost more.

➡ Children under four travel free, or €9 to anywhere if they need seats. Ages four to 11 travel half-price.

➡ Travellers aged 12 to 25 and those aged over 60 receive discounts.

➡ *Bons plans* are last-minute tickets advertised on the SNCF website (http://www.voyages-sncf.com/bons-plans/derniere-minute/).

Rail Passes & Discounts

Guaranteed discounts of 25% (last-minute booking) to 60% (advance bookings for low-volume 'blue periods') are available with several cards:

Carte Jeune (€50) For travellers aged 12 to 27.

Carte Enfant+ (€75) For one to four adults travelling with a child aged four to 11.

Carte Week-end (€75) For travellers aged 26 to 59, booking return journeys of at least 200km that include weekend-only travel, or a Saturday night away.

Carte Sénior+ (€56) For travellers over 60.

Two regional passes are available, valid July through September.

Pass Bermuda (https://www.ter.sncf.com/paca/offres/cartes-et-abonnements/pass-bermuda; 1 adult €6, 2 adults €10) is a one-day pass for weekends and holidays, with unlimited 2nd-class travel between Marseille and Miramas. It can't be used on TGVs.

Pass Isabelle (https://www.ter.sncf.com/paca/offres/cartes-et-abonnements/pass-isabelle-famille; family of 4 €35) is a one-day family pass covering two adults and two children under 16. It permits unlimited travel along the coast between Fréjus and Ventimiglia, inland between Nice and Tende, and Cannes to Grasse.

Language

Standard French is taught and spoken throughout France. The heavy southern accent is an important part of regional identity in Provence, but you'll have no trouble being understood anywhere if you stick to standard French, which we've also used in the phrases in this chapter.

The sounds used in spoken French can almost all be found in English. There are a couple of exceptions: nasal vowels (represented in our pronunciation guides by o or u followed by an almost inaudible nasal consonant sound m, n or ng), the 'funny' u (ew in our guides) and the deep-in-the-throat r. Bearing these few points in mind and reading our pronunciation guides below as if they were English, you'll be understood just fine.

BASICS

French has two words for 'you' – use the polite form *vous* unless you're talking to close friends or children in which case you'd use the informal *tu*. You can also use *tu* when a person invites you to use *tu*.

All nouns in French are either masculine or feminine, and so are the adjectives, articles *le/la* (the) and *un/une* (a), and possessives *mon/ma* (my), *ton/ta* (your) and *son/sa* (his, her) that go with the nouns. In this chapter we have included masculine and femine forms where necessary, separated by a slash and indicated with 'm/f'.

Hello.	*Bonjour.*	bon·zhoor
Goodbye.	*Au revoir.*	o·rer·vwa
Excuse me.	*Excusez-moi.*	ek·skew·zay·mwa

WANT MORE?

For in-depth language information and handy phrases, check out Lonely Planet's *French Phrasebook*. You'll find it at **shop.lonelyplanet.com**, or you can buy Lonely Planet's Fast Talk app at the Apple App Store.

Sorry.	*Pardon.*	par·don
Yes.	*Oui.*	wee
No.	*Non.*	non
Please.	*S'il vous plaît.*	seel voo play
Thank you.	*Merci.*	mair·see
You're welcome.	*De rien.*	der ree·en

How are you?
Comment allez-vous? ko·mon ta·lay·voo

Fine, and you?
Bien, merci. Et vous? byun mair·see ay voo

You're welcome.
De rien. der ree·en

My name is ...
Je m'appelle ... zher ma·pel ...

What's your name?
Comment vous appelez-vous? ko·mon voo·za·play voo

Do you speak English?
Parlez-vous anglais? par·lay·voo ong·glay

I don't understand.
Je ne comprends pas. zher ner kom·pron pa

ACCOMMODATION

Do you have any rooms available?
Est-ce que vous avez des chambres libres? es·ker voo za·vay day shom·brer lee·brer

How much is it per night/person?
Quel est le prix par nuit/personne? kel ay ler pree par nwee/per·son

Is breakfast included?
Est-ce que le petit déjeuner est inclus? es·ker ler per·tee day·zher·nay ayt en·klew

campsite	*camping*	kom·peeng
dorm	*dortoir*	dor·twar
guest house	*pension*	pon·syon
hotel	*hôtel*	o·tel
youth hostel	*auberge de jeunesse*	o·berzh der zher·nes

PROVENÇAL

Despite the bilingual signs that visitors see when they enter most towns and villages, the region's mother tongue – Provençal – is scarcely heard on the street or in the home. Just a handful of older people in rural Provence (Prouvènço) keep alive the rich lyrics and poetic language of their ancestors.

Provençal (prouvençau in Provençal) is a dialect of the langue d'oc (Occitan), the traditional language of southern France. Its grammar is closer to Catalan (spoken in Spain) than to French. In the grand age of courtly love – the period between the 12th and 14th centuries – Provençal was the literary language of France and northern Spain and was even used as far afield as Italy. Medieval troubadours and poets created melodies and elegant poems, and Provençal blossomed.

The 19th century witnessed a revival of Provençal after its rapid displacement by the langue d'oïl, the language of northern France which originated from the vernacular Latin spoken by the Gallo-Romans and gave birth to modern French (francés in Provençal). The revival of Provençal was spearheaded by Frédéric Mistral (1830–1914), a poet from Vaucluse, whose works in Provençal won him the 1904 Nobel Prize for Literature.

a ... room	une chambre ...	ewn shom·brer ...
single	à un lit	a un lee
double	avec un grand lit	a·vek un gron lee
twin	avec des lits jumeaux	a·vek day lee zhew·mo
with (a)...	avec ...	a·vek ...
air-con	climatiseur	klee·ma·tee·zer
bathroom	une salle de bains	ewn sal der bun
window	fenêtre	fer·nay·trer

DIRECTIONS

Where's ...?
Où est ...?   oo ay ...

What's the address?
Quelle est l'adresse?   kel ay la·dres

Could you write the address, please?
Est-ce que vous pourriez   es·ker voo poo·ryay
écrire l'adresse,   ay·kreer la·dres
s'il vous plaît?   seel voo play

Can you show me (on the map)?
Pouvez-vous m'indiquer   poo·vay·voo mun·dee·kay
(sur la carte)?   (sewr la kart)

at the corner	au coin	o kwun
at the traffic lights	aux feux	o fer
behind	derrière	dair·ryair
in front of	devant	der·von
far (from)	loin (de)	lwun (der)
left	gauche	gosh
near (to)	près (de)	pray (der)
next to	à côté de	a ko·tay der
opposite	en face de	on fas der

right	droite	drwat
straight ahead	tout droit	too drwa

EATING & DRINKING

What would you recommend?
Qu'est-ce que vous   kes·ker voo
conseillez?   kon·say·yay

What's in that dish?
Quels sont les   kel son lay
ingrédients?   zun·gray·dyon

I'm a vegetarian.
Je suis végétarien/   zher swee vay·zhay·ta·ryun/
végétarienne.   vay·zhay·ta·ryen (m/f)

I don't eat ...
Je ne mange pas ...   zher ner monzh pa ...

Cheers!
Santé!   son·tay

That was delicious.
C'était délicieux!   say·tay day·lee·syer

Please bring the bill.
Apportez-moi   a·por·tay·mwa
l'addition,   la·dee·syon
s'il vous plaît.   seel voo play

I'd like to reserve a table for ...	Je voudrais réserver une table pour ...	zher voo·dray ray·zair·vay ewn ta·bler poor ...
(eight) o'clock	(vingt) heures	(vungt) er
(two) people	(deux) personnes	(der) pair·son

Key Words

appetiser	entrée	on·tray
bottle	bouteille	boo·tay
breakfast	petit déjeuner	per·tee day·zher·nay

children's menu	menu pour enfants	mer·new poor on·fon
cold	froid	frwa
delicatessen	traiteur	tray·ter
dinner	dîner	dee·nay
dish	plat	pla
food	nourriture	noo·ree·tewr
fork	fourchette	foor·shet
glass	verre	vair
grocery store	épicerie	ay·pees·ree
highchair	chaise haute	shay zot
hot	chaud	sho
knife	couteau	koo·to
local speciality	spécialité locale	spay·sya·lee·tay lo·kal
lunch	déjeuner	day·zher·nay
main course	plat principal	pla prun·see·pal
market	marché	mar·shay
menu (in English)	carte (en anglais)	kart (on ong·glay)
plate	assiette	a·syet
spoon	cuillère	kwee·yair
wine list	carte des vins	kart day vun
with/without	avec/sans	a·vek/son

LANGUAGE MEAT & FISH

Meat & Fish

beef	bœuf	berf
chicken	poulet	poo·lay
crab	crabe	krab
lamb	agneau	a·nyo
oyster	huître	wee·trer
pork	porc	por
snail	escargot	es·kar·go
squid	calmar	kal·mar
turkey	dinde	dund
veal	veau	vo

Fruit & Vegetables

apple	pomme	pom
apricot	abricot	ab·ree·ko
asparagus	asperge	a·spairzh
beans	haricots	a·ree·ko
beetroot	betterave	be·trav
cabbage	chou	shoo
cherry	cerise	ser·reez
corn	maïs	ma·ees
cucumber	concombre	kong·kom·brer
grape	raisin	ray·zun

lemon	citron	see·tron
lettuce	laitue	lay·tew
mushroom	champignon	shom·pee·nyon
peach	pêche	pesh
peas	petit pois	per·tee pwa
(red/green) pepper	poivron (rouge/vert)	pwa·vron (roozh/vair)
pineapple	ananas	a·na·nas
plum	prune	prewn
potato	pomme de terre	pom der tair
prune	pruneau	prew·no
pumpkin	citrouille	see·troo·yer
shallot	échalote	eh·sha·lot
spinach	épinards	eh·pee·nar
strawberry	fraise	frez
tomato	tomate	to·mat
vegetable	légume	lay·gewm

Other

bread	pain	pun
butter	beurre	ber
cheese	fromage	fro·mazh
egg	œuf	erf
honey	miel	myel
jam	confiture	kon·fee·tewr
lentils	lentilles	lon·tee·yer
pasta/noodles	pâtes	pat
pepper	poivre	pwa·vrer
rice	riz	ree
salt	sel	sel
sugar	sucre	sew·krer
vinegar	vinaigre	vee·nay·grer

Drinks

beer	bière	bee·yair
coffee	café	ka·fay
(orange) juice	jus (d'orange)	zhew (do·ronzh)
milk	lait	lay
tea	thé	tay

Question Words

How?	Comment?	ko·mon
What?	Quoi?	kwa
When?	Quand?	kon
Where?	Où?	oo
Who?	Qui?	kee
Why?	Pourquoi?	poor·kwa

(mineral) water	*eau (minérale)*	o (mee·nay·ral)
(red) wine	*vin (rouge)*	vun (roozh)
(white) wine	*vin (blanc)*	vun (blong)

EMERGENCIES

Help!
Au secours!　o skoor

I'm lost.
Je suis perdu/perdue.　zhe swee·pair·dew (m/f)

Leave me alone!
Fichez-moi la paix!　fee·shay·mwa la pay

There's been an accident.
Il y a eu un accident.　eel ya ew un ak·see·don

Call a doctor.
Appelez un médecin.　a·play un mayd·sun

Call the police.
Appelez la police.　a·play la po·lees

I'm ill.
Je suis malade.　zher swee ma·lad

It hurts here.
J'ai une douleur ici.　zhay ewn doo·ler ee·see

I'm allergic to ...
Je suis allergique ...　zher swee za·lair·zheek ...

SHOPPING & SERVICES

I'd like to buy ...
Je voudrais acheter ...　zher voo·dray ash·tay ...

May I look at it?
Est-ce que je peux le voir?　es·ker zher per ler vwar

I'm just looking.
Je regarde.　zher rer·gard

I don't like it.
Cela ne me plaît pas.　ser·la ner mer play pa

How much is it?
C'est combien?　say kom·byun

It's too expensive.
C'est trop cher.　say tro shair

Can you lower the price?
Vous pouvez baisser le prix?　voo poo·vay bay·say ler pree

Signs

Entrée	Entrance
Femmes	Women
Fermé	Closed
Hommes	Men
Interdit	Prohibited
Ouvert	Open
Renseignements	Information
Sortie	Exit
Toilettes/WC	Toilets

There's a mistake in the bill.
Il y a une erreur dans la note.　eel ya ewn ay·rer don la not

ATM	*guichet automatique de banque*	gee·shay o·to·ma·teek der bonk
credit card	*carte de crédit*	kart der kray·dee
internet cafe	*cybercafé*	see·bair·ka·fay
post office	*bureau de poste*	bew·ro der post
tourist office	*office de tourisme*	o·fees der too·rees·mer

TIME & DATES

What time is it?
Quelle heure est-il?　kel er ay til

It's (eight) o'clock.
Il est (huit) heures.　il ay (weet) er

It's half past (10).
Il est (dix) heures et demie.　il ay (deez) er ay day·mee

morning	*matin*	ma·tun
afternoon	*après-midi*	a·pray·mee·dee
evening	*soir*	swar
yesterday	*hier*	yair
today	*aujourd'hui*	o·zhoor·dwee
tomorrow	*demain*	der·mun
Monday	*lundi*	lun·dee
Tuesday	*mardi*	mar·dee
Wednesday	*mercredi*	mair·krer·dee
Thursday	*jeudi*	zher·dee
Friday	*vendredi*	von·drer·dee
Saturday	*samedi*	sam·dee
Sunday	*dimanche*	dee·monsh
January	*janvier*	zhon·vyay
February	*février*	fayv·ryay
March	*mars*	mars
April	*avril*	a·vreel
May	*mai*	may
June	*juin*	zhwun
July	*juillet*	zhwee·yay
August	*août*	oot
September	*septembre*	sep·tom·brer
October	*octobre*	ok·to·brer
November	*novembre*	no·vom·brer
December	*décembre*	day·som·brer

TRANSPORT

Public Transport

boat	bateau	ba·to
bus	bus	bews
plane	avion	a·vyon
train	train	trun

I want to go to ...
Je voudrais aller à ... zher voo·dray a·lay a ...

Does it stop at (Amboise)?
Est-ce qu'il s'arrête à es·kil sa·ret a
(Amboise)? (om·bwaz)

At what time does it leave/arrive?
À quelle heure est-ce a kel er es
qu'il part/arrive? kil par/a·reev

Can you tell me when we get to ...?
Pouvez-vous me poo·vay·voo mer
dire quand deer kon
nous arrivons à ...? noo za·ree·von a ...

I want to get off here.
Je veux descendre zher ver day·son·drer
ici. ee·see

first	premier	prer·myay
last	dernier	dair·nyay
next	prochain	pro·shun
a ... ticket	un billet ...	un bee·yay ...
1st-class	de première classe	der prem·yair klas
2nd-class	de deuxième classe	der der·zyem las
one-way	simple	sum·pler
return	aller et retour	a·lay ay rer·toor

aisle seat	côté couloir	ko·tay kool·war
delayed	en retard	on rer·tar
cancelled	annulé	a·new·lay
platform	quai	kay
ticket office	guichet	gee·shay
timetable	horaire	o·rair
train station	gare	gar
window seat	côté fenêtre	ko·tay fe·ne·trer

Driving & Cycling

I'd like to hire a ...	Je voudrais louer ...	zher voo·dray loo·way ...
4WD	un quatre-quatre	un kat·kat
car	une voiture	ewn vwa·tewr

Numbers

1	un	un
2	deux	der
3	trois	trwa
4	quatre	ka·trer
5	cinq	sungk
6	six	sees
7	sept	set
8	huit	weet
9	neuf	nerf
10	dix	dees
20	vingt	vung
30	trente	tront
40	quarante	ka·ront
50	cinquante	sung·kont
60	soixante	swa·sont
70	soixante-dix	swa·son·dees
80	quatre-vingts	ka·trer·vung
90	quatre-vingt-dix	ka·trer·vung·dees
100	cent	son
1000	mille	meel

bicycle	un vélo	un vay·lo
motorcycle	une moto	ewn mo·to

child seat	siège-enfant	syezh·on·fon
diesel	diesel	dyay·zel
helmet	casque	kask
mechanic	mécanicien	may·ka·nee·syun
petrol/gas	essence	ay·sons
service station	station-service	sta·syon·ser·vees

Is this the road to ...?
C'est la route pour ...? say la root poor ...

(How long) Can I park here?
(Combien de temps) (kom·byun der tom)
Est-ce que je peux es·ker zher per
stationner ici? sta·syo·nay ee·see

The car/motorbike has broken down (at ...).
La voiture/moto est la vwa·tewr/mo·to ay
tombée en panne (à ...). tom·bay on pan (a ...)

I have a flat tyre.
Mon pneu est à plat. mom pner ay ta pla

I've run out of petrol.
Je suis en panne zher swee zon pan
d'essence. day·sons

I've lost my car keys.
J'ai perdu les clés de zhay per·dew lay klay der
ma voiture. ma vwa·tewr

GLOSSARY

Word gender is indicated as (m) masculine or (f) feminine; (pl) indicates plural.

abbaye (f) – abbey
AOP – Appellation d'Origine Protégée (formerly Appellation d'Origine Contrôlée [AOC], still commonly used in France); wines and olive oils that have met stringent government regulations governing where, how and under what conditions the grapes or olives are grown and the wines and olive oils are fermented and bottled
arrondissement (m) – one of several districts into which large cities, such as Marseille, are split
atelier (m) – artisan's workshop
auberge (f) – inn
autoroute (f) – motorway or highway

baie (f) – bay
bastide (f) – country house
billetterie (f) – ticket office or counter
borie (f) – primitive beehive-shaped dwelling, built from dry limestone around 3500 BC
boulangerie (f) – bread shop or bakery

calanque (f) – rocky inlet
carnet (m) – a book of five or 10 bus, tram or metro tickets sold at a reduced rate
cave (f) – wine or cheese cellar
centre (de) hospitalier (m) – hospital
chambre d'hôte (f) – B&B accommodation, usually in a private home
charcuterie (f) – pork butcher's shop and delicatessen; also cold meat
château (m) – castle or stately home
chèvre (m) – goat; also goat's-milk cheese
col (m) – mountain pass
conseil général (m) – general council

corniche (f) – coastal or cliff road
corrida (f) – bullfight
cour (f) – courtyard
course Camarguaise (f) – Camargue-style bullfight

dégustation (f) – the fine art of tasting wine, cheese, olive oil or seafood
département (m) – administrative area (department)
DFCI – Défense de la Forêt Contre l'Incendie; fire road (public access forbidden)
digue (f) – dike
domaine (m) – an estate producing wines

église (f) – church
épicerie (f) – grocery shop
étang (m) – lagoon, pond or lake

faïence (f) – earthenware
féria (f) – bullfighting festival
ferme auberge (f) – family-run inn attached to a farm or *château*; farmhouse restaurant
fête (f) – party or festival
formule (f) – fixed main course plus starter or dessert
fromagerie (f) – cheese shop

galets (m) – large smooth stones covering Châteauneuf du Pape vineyards
gardian (m) – Camargue horseman or cattle-herding cowboy
gare (f) – train station
gare maritime (m) – ferry terminal
gare routière (m) – bus station
garrigue (f) – ground cover of aromatic scrub; see also *maquis*
gitan (m) – Roma Gitano person, gypsy
golfe (m) – gulf
grotte (f) – cave
halles (f pl) – covered market; central food market
hôtel de ville (m) – town hall
hôtel particulier (m) – private mansion

jardin (botanique) (m) – (botanic) garden

mairie (f) – town hall
manade (f) – bull farm
maquis (m) – aromatic Provençal scrub; name given to the French Resistance movement; see also *garrigue*
marché (m) – market
mas (m) – Provençal farmhouse
menu (m) – meal at a fixed price with two or more courses
mistral (m) – incessant north wind
monastère (m) – monastery
Monégasque – native of Monaco
moulin à huile (m) – oil mill
musée (m) – museum

navette (f) – shuttle bus, train or boat
Niçois – native of Nice

office du tourisme, office de tourisme (m) – tourist office (run by a unit of local government)
ONF – Office National des Forêts; National Forests Office

parc national (m) – national park
parc naturel régional (m) – regional nature park
pétanque (f) – a Provençal game of boules, similar to lawn bowls
pic (m) – mountain peak
place (f) – square
plage (f) – beach
plan (m) – city map
plat du jour (m) – dish of the day
pont (m) – bridge
porte (f) – gate or door; old-town entrance
préfecture (f) – main town of a *département*
presqu'île (f) – peninsula
prieuré (m) – priory

quai (m) – quay or railway platform

LANGUAGE GLOSSARY

quartier (m) – quarter or district

rade (f) – gulf or harbour

région (m) – administrative region

rond-point (m) – roundabout

salin (m) – salt marsh

santon (m) – traditional Provençal figurine

sentier (m) – trail, footpath

sentier littoral (m) – coastal path

SNCF – Société Nationale des Chemins de Fer Français; state-owned railway company

SNCM – Société Nationale Maritime Corse-Méditerranée; state-owned ferry company linking Corsica and mainland France

stade (m) – stadium

tabac (m) – tobacconist (also sells newspapers, bus tickets etc)

TGV – Train à Grande Vitesse; high-speed train

théâtre antique (m) – Roman theatre

vendange (f) – grape harvest

vieille ville (f) – old town

vieux port (m) – old port

vigneron (m) – winegrower

Behind the Scenes

SEND US YOUR FEEDBACK

We love to hear from travellers – your comments keep us on our toes and help make our books better. Our well-travelled team reads every word on what you loved or loathed about this book. Although we cannot reply individually to your submissions, we always guarantee that your feedback goes straight to the appropriate authors, in time for the next edition. Each person who sends us information is thanked in the next edition – the most useful submissions are rewarded with a selection of digital PDF chapters.

Visit **lonelyplanet.com/contact** to submit your updates and suggestions or to ask for help. Our award-winning website also features inspirational travel stories, news and discussions.

Note: we may edit, reproduce and incorporate your comments in Lonely Planet products such as guidebooks, websites and digital products, so let us know if you don't want your comments reproduced or your name acknowledged. For a copy of our privacy policy visit lonelyplanet.com/privacy.

OUR READERS

Many thanks to the travellers who used the last edition and wrote to us with helpful hints, useful advice and interesting anecdotes: Isabelle Anderson, Reiter Angela, Dominique Boin, Urshla & Nelson Duarte, Veronica Graham, Jean Luc Le Formal, Keith Lofstrom, Cary Marie-Laurence, David Nicol, Chantal Palmer, Andy Wilson.

AUTHOR THANKS

Alexis Averbuck

Boundless thanks to Amy, Rod, Lola and Romy for making Marseille always feel like home to me. Life on the road wouldn't be nearly so wonderful without the kindness of strangers, so many thanks to the countless individuals who eased my trip and shared their tips. Then, to my trusty copilot, Ryan Ver Berkmoes: what a peachy treat to share springtime in Provence. And finally, thanks to Kate, Nicola and Olly for being such a super team.

Oliver Berry

Thanks to all the people who provided special help while I was out on the road: Jean-Marie and Yvette Duchamp, Gabriel Boucher, Marcel Allard, Alexandre Berri, Theo Girard and Susie and Gracie Berry. Biggest thanks as always go to fellow authors Nicola Williams and Alexis Averbuck for all their help, contributions and sage advice, and to editor Kate Morgan for giving me the opportunity to revisit one of my favourite corners of France.

Nicola Williams

Having written the 1st edition of this book in 1998, it was with immense joy that I retraced my footsteps for this 8th edition – this time with three intrepid children in tow. Un grand merci Niko, Mischa et Kaya (und Christa!). Otherwise, sincere thanks to Eva Fournial (Mougins), Alain Corroyer (Nice), Richard Auray (Courmes) and Clare Bouvier (Antibes) for insider tips and recommendations. At home, thanks to husband Matthias Lüfkens for his joie de vivre, love of travel and gracious tolerance of a temperamental workaholic wife.

ACKNOWLEDGEMENTS

Climate map data adapted from Peel MC, Finlayson BL & McMahon TA (2007) 'Updated World Map of the Köppen-Geiger Climate Classification', *Hydrology and Earth System Sciences*, 11, 1633–44.

Illustrations pp64–5, pp146–7 by Javier Zarracina. Cover photograph: Provençal village, Konstanttin/Shutterstock.

THIS BOOK

This 8th edition of Lonely Planet's *Provence & the Côte d'Azur* guidebook was researched and written by Alexis Averbuck, Oliver Berry and Nicola Williams. The previous edition was written by Emilie Filou, Alexis Averbuck and John A Vlahides.

This guidebook was produced by the following:

Destination Editor
Kate Morgan

Product Editors Briohny Hooper, Kathryn Rowan

Senior Cartographer
Valentina Kremenchutskaya

Book Designer
Jessica Rose

Assisting Editors Sarah Bailey, Elizabeth Jones, Charlotte Orr, Simon Williamson

Assisting Cartographers
Mark Griffiths, Corey Hutchison, Alison Lyall

Cover Researcher
Campbell McKenzie

Thanks to Sasha Baskett, Claire Murphy, Karyn Noble, Martine Power, Samantha Russell-Tulip, James Smart, Lauren Wellicome, Tony Wheeler

Index

Map Pages **000**
Photo Pages **000**

Map Legend

Sights
- Beach
- Bird Sanctuary
- Buddhist
- Castle/Palace
- Christian
- Confucian
- Hindu
- Islamic
- Jain
- Jewish
- Monument
- Museum/Gallery/Historic Building
- Ruin
- Shinto
- Sikh
- Taoist
- Winery/Vineyard
- Zoo/Wildlife Sanctuary
- Other Sight

Activities, Courses & Tours
- Bodysurfing
- Diving
- Canoeing/Kayaking
- Course/Tour
- Sento Hot Baths/Onsen
- Skiing
- Snorkelling
- Surfing
- Swimming/Pool
- Walking
- Windsurfing
- Other Activity

Sleeping
- Sleeping
- Camping

Eating
- Eating

Drinking & Nightlife
- Drinking & Nightlife
- Cafe

Entertainment
- Entertainment

Shopping
- Shopping

Information
- Bank
- Embassy/Consulate
- Hospital/Medical
- Internet
- Police
- Post Office
- Telephone
- Toilet
- Tourist Information
- Other Information

Geographic
- Beach
- Gate
- Hut/Shelter
- Lighthouse
- Lookout
- Mountain/Volcano
- Oasis
- Park
- Pass
- Picnic Area
- Waterfall

Population
- Capital (National)
- Capital (State/Province)
- City/Large Town
- Town/Village

Transport
- Airport
- Border crossing
- Bus
- Cable car/Funicular
- Cycling
- Ferry
- Metro station
- Monorail
- Parking
- Petrol station
- S-Bahn/S-train/Subway station
- Taxi
- T-bane/Tunnelbana station
- Train station/Railway
- Tram
- Tube station
- U-Bahn/Underground station
- Other Transport

Note: Not all symbols displayed above appear on the maps in this book

Routes
- Tollway
- Freeway
- Primary
- Secondary
- Tertiary
- Lane
- Unsealed road
- Road under construction
- Plaza/Mall
- Steps
- Tunnel
- Pedestrian overpass
- Walking Tour
- Walking Tour detour
- Path/Walking Trail

Boundaries
- International
- State/Province
- Disputed
- Regional/Suburb
- Marine Park
- Cliff
- Wall

Hydrography
- River, Creek
- Intermittent River
- Canal
- Water
- Dry/Salt/Intermittent Lake
- Reef

Areas
- Airport/Runway
- Beach/Desert
- Cemetery (Christian)
- Cemetery (Other)
- Glacier
- Mudflat
- Park/Forest
- Sight (Building)
- Sportsground
- Swamp/Mangrove

OUR STORY

A beat-up old car, a few dollars in the pocket and a sense of adventure. In 1972 that's all Tony and Maureen Wheeler needed for the trip of a lifetime – across Europe and Asia overland to Australia. It took several months, and at the end – broke but inspired – they sat at their kitchen table writing and stapling together their first travel guide, *Across Asia on the Cheap*. Within a week they'd sold 1500 copies. Lonely Planet was born.

Today, Lonely Planet has offices in Franklin, London, Melbourne, Oakland, Beijing and Delhi, with more than 600 staff and writers. We share Tony's belief that 'a great guidebook should do three things: inform, educate and amuse'.

OUR WRITERS

Alexis Averbuck

St-Tropez to Toulon, Marseille to Aix-en-Provence, Arles & the Camargue, Avignon & Around Alexis Averbuck first came to Provence when she was four and now visits every chance she gets. Whether careening through hilltop villages in the Haut-Var, exploring art and antiquities in Arles, or browsing markets in the Dordogne (she also contributes to the *France* book), she immerses herself in all things French. A travel writer for two decades, Alexis has lived in Antarctica for a year, crossed the Pacific by sailboat and is also a painter – see her work at www.alexisaverbuck.com.

Read more about Alexis at: https://auth.lonelyplanet.com/profiles/alexisaverbuck

Oliver Berry

Plan Your Trip, Hill Towns of the Luberon, Haute-Provence & the Southern Alps, Understand Provence & the Côte d'Azur, Survival Guide Oliver Berry is a travel writer and photographer based in Cornwall. He has worked on many guidebooks for Lonely Planet, including several editions of the bestselling *France* guide. He first travelled to Provence on a family holiday aged two, and has been travelling back at every possible opportunity ever since. For this book he covered the Hill Towns of the Luberon and the mountains of Haute-Provence, covered 3582km, got lost six times and ate an awful lot of olives and fruit confits. His latest work is published at www.oliverberry.com.

Read more about Oliver at: https://auth.lonelyplanet.com/profiles/oliverberry

Nicola Williams

Cannes & Around; Nice, Monaco & Menton British writer Nicola Williams has lived in France and written about it for more than a decade. From her hillside house on the southern shore of Lake Geneva, it's an easy hop to France's hot south where she has spent endless years revelling in its extraordinary art, architecture, cuisine and landscape. In 1998 she wrote the 1st edition of *Provence & the Côte d'Azur* and worked on several subsequent editions. Her travels these days are frequently in the company of her three trilingual children. Find Nicola on Twitter at @Tripalong.

Read more about Nicola at: https://auth.lonelyplanet.com/profiles/NicolaWilliams

Published by Lonely Planet Publications Pty Ltd
ABN 36 005 607 983
8th edition – Jan 2016
ISBN 978 1 74321 566 1
© Lonely Planet 2016   Photographs © as indicated 2016
10 9 8 7 6 5 4 3 2 1
Printed in China

Although the authors and Lonely Planet have taken all reasonable care in preparing this book, we make no warranty about the accuracy or completeness of its content and, to the maximum extent possible, disclaim all liability arising from its use.

All rights reserved. No part of this publication may be copied, stored in a retrieval system, or transmitted in any form by any means, electronic, mechanical, recording or otherwise, except brief extracts for the purpose of review, and no part of this publication may be sold or hired, without the written permission of the publisher. Lonely Planet and the Lonely Planet logo are trademarks of Lonely Planet and are registered in the US Patent and Trademark Office and in other countries. Lonely Planet does not allow its name or logo to be appropriated by commercial establishments, such as retailers, restaurants or hotels. Please let us know of any misuses: lonelyplanet.com/ip.